White-Collar Crime

Third Edition

While 2020 was like no other year we have seen, somehow it was a year that I have grown even closer to my family—Kathleen, Chloe, Charles, and Claire. During the journey, they understood the long days spent on my full-time job in the day time and working on this new edition in the evening hours. Kathleen—my wife of 25 years by the time this is published—reminded me that true love is not simply an idea, but if you are lucky, it can be a reality. Chloe's hard work ethic instilled great pride in me and provided me occasional jolts that kept me moving forward. Charles's pensiveness, patience, and empathy grounded me during those times when calmer moments were needed. Claire, who is intellectually disabled and unable to speak, provided me daily reminders about what really matters in life. Because she is not able to talk or communicate, I occasionally imagine what she sees when she looks at me. Is it a criminologist? An author? A professor? A vice provost? Absolutely not. I hope she sees someone who loves her, her sister, her brother, and her mother more than anything. Because that's what I see when I look at myself.

—bkp

White-Collar Crime

A Systems Approach

Third Edition

Brian K. Payne

Old Dominion University

Los Angeles | London | New Delhi
Singapore | Washington DC | Melbourne

FOR INFORMATION:

SAGE Publications, Inc.
2455 Teller Road
Thousand Oaks, California 91320
E-mail: order@sagepub.com

SAGE Publications Ltd.
1 Oliver's Yard
55 City Road
London EC1Y 1SP
United Kingdom

SAGE Publications India Pvt. Ltd.
B 1/I 1 Mohan Cooperative Industrial Area
Mathura Road, New Delhi 110 044
India

SAGE Publications Asia-Pacific Pte. Ltd.
18 Cross Street #10-10/11/12
China Square Central
Singapore 048423

Acquisitions Editor: Jessica Miller
Editorial Assistant: Sarah Wilson
Production Editor: Gagan Mahindra
Copy Editor: Michelle Ponce
Typesetter: C&M Digitals (P) Ltd.
Indexer: Integra
Cover Designer: Candice Harman
Marketing Manager: Victoria Velasquez

Printed in the United States of America

Library of Congress Cataloging-in-Publication Data

Names: Payne, Brian K., author.

Title: White-collar crime : a systems approach / Brian K. Payne, Old Dominion University, USA.

Description: Third edition. | Thousand Oaks, California : SAGE Publishing, [2022] | Includes bibliographical references and index.

Identifiers: LCCN 2021011527 | ISBN 9781071833902 (paperback) | ISBN 9781071848722 (epub) | ISBN 9781071833926 (epub) | ISBN 9781071848715 (pdf)

Subjects: LCSH: White collar crimes.

Classification: LCC HV6768 .P396 2022 | DDC 364.16/8—dc23
LC record available at https://lccn.loc.gov/2021011527

This book is printed on acid-free paper.

21 22 23 24 25 10 9 8 7 6 5 4 3 2 1

BRIEF CONTENTS

DETAILED CONTENTS

PREFACE

Most would agree that the year 2020 was unlike any we have experienced. A pandemic, escalating racial tensions following police brutality against Black Americans, and a highly contested election will most certainly keep authors of history books busy in the years to come. The election itself was fascinating in that it was very much shaped by concepts related to white-collar crime. On the one hand, then-President Donald Trump alleged concerns about widespread voter fraud both before and after the presidential election. On the other hand, his efforts to overturn the election through lawsuits and other political maneuvers were seen by his opponents as harming the democratic fabric of our society. Though few used the phrase *white-collar crime* to describe the alleged voter fraud or the efforts to overturn the election, these instances do, in fact, embody the kinds of behaviors white-collar crime researchers characterize as within the concept's domain.

Compared to other subjects in the social sciences, relatively few white-collar crime texts are available for use in criminal justice, criminology, and sociology courses. Those that are available have done a great job introducing students to the topic. One thing I found missing among available texts, however, was a book that approached the topic as a crime problem, a criminal justice problem, and a social problem. In effect, my intent has been to create a work that examines the many facets of white-collar crime by focusing on different crimes committed during the course of work as well as the various systems that are given the task of responding to white-collar misconduct.

In addition, I have addressed white-collar crime by balancing consensus and conflict perspectives. The need to objectively understand white-collar offending and the most appropriate response to white-collar offending is central to my approach in this text. All too often, white-collar crimes and white-collar criminals are vilified with little thought given to the intricacies surrounding the event or the system's response to the event. This vilification limits our understanding of the topic.

To demonstrate why it is important to address white-collar crime objectively, consider a book we can call *Introduction to Criminal Justice* as an example. If the author presented crime and criminals as inherently evil, readers would not be given an accurate picture of criminal justice (or crime, for that matter). The same can be said of a white-collar crime book—if authors discuss white-collar crime or white-collar criminals as inherently evil, an inaccurate foundation from which readers can understand the criminal justice response to white-collar crime is created.

Of course, I am not saying that white-collar crime is not bad or that white-collar criminals do not harm society. Instead, I am suggesting that we need to go beyond these emotions and perceptions in order to fully understand white-collar crime. Indeed, throughout *White-Collar Crime: A Systems Approach*, readers will learn about the various consequences stemming from white-collar misconduct. Readers will also be exposed to the different systems involved in both perpetrating and responding to white-collar crime.

This book summarizes each relevant topic and creates a foundation from which readers will be able to understand various issues related to white-collar crime. The book is intended as either a stand-alone or a supplemental book for undergraduate and graduate classes focusing on white-collar crime.

The book will be of value to criminal justice, criminology, and sociology courses focusing on white-collar crime. Criminal justice and criminological topics related to white-collar crime are integrated throughout the text. Because many white-collar crime texts fail to address either criminal justice or criminological themes, integrating these topics together should make the text more appealing to a wider audience.

This book is divided into 15 chapters that represent the topics covered in most white-collar crime courses. They include the following:

- Introduction and Overview of White-Collar Crime

- Understanding White-Collar Crime

- Crime in Sales-Related Occupations

- Crime in the Health Care System

- Crime in Systems of Social Control

- Crime in the Political System

- Crime in the Educational System

- Crime in the Economic System

- Crime in the Cyber System

- Crime by the Corporate System

- Environmental Crime

- Explaining White-Collar Crime

- Policing White-Collar Crime

- Judicial Proceedings and White-Collar Crime

- The Corrections Subsystem and White-Collar Crime

Several features have been included to make the book more user friendly for students and professors. These features include these elements:

1. Each chapter concludes with a bulleted summary statement.

2. A list of 5 to 10 critical thinking questions is included after the summary statements.

3. Each chapter includes between two and four photographs that are appropriate to the topic.

4. A list of key terms is included at the end of each chapter and defined in the glossary.

5. Recent examples, particularly those that are interesting to college students, are integrated throughout the work.

6. Each chapter includes a feature called "White-Collar Crime in the News." These features include recent press releases describing white-collar crime cases "plucked from the media."

7. Each chapter includes a feature called "Streaming White-Collar Crime." These features describe television shows, movies, and documentaries related to topics addressed in each chapter.

It is my hope that this text will help readers to fully appreciate and understand white-collar crime and the justice system's response to this misconduct.

WHAT'S NEW IN THE THIRD EDITION

- The title of the book was changed to better emphasize the systems approach driving the discussion. As the amount of research included in the book grew, it was clear that labeling the book with the subtitle "The Essentials" was no longer appropriate.

- A chapter on crime in the political system was added. Recent debates about the connections between crime and politics warranted the development of a specific focus on this topic.

- Material about mortgage fraud from the previous edition's chapter on crime in the housing system was moved to the "Crimes in the Economic System" chapter.

- New research and cases are included throughout. This included more than 450 new references. Some of the new research added builds on prior studies, while other additions provide new directions for white-collar crime research.

- New photos were added throughout the text.

- New figures and tables were added throughout the text where appropriate.

- Box features called "Streaming White-Collar Crime" were added to each chapter. These boxes highlight television shows, movies, and documentaries related to white-collar crime and include questions students should consider as they expand their understanding about the topic.

- Original data on corporate crime prosecutions are used to provide students up-to-date information on prosecutions of corporate offenses.

- Information on how to access 15 original data sets on various types of white-collar crime is included.

- Updated statistics and data on white-collar crime trends have been added.

- Topics new to the third edition include the following:
  - The legalization of marijuana and white-collar crime
  - Telemedicine fraud
  - Police brutality as a form of white-collar crime
  - The Volkswagen emissions scandal
  - The Wells Fargo deceptive sales case
  - The Fyre Festival fraud and the focus on college-age victims
  - The Mueller investigation, impeachment, and crimes connected to Donald Trump
  - The Operation Varsity Blues investigation involving the efforts of rich parents to get their children fraudulently admitted to elite colleges.
  - Efforts of the United States to uncover conflicts of interest between U.S. professors and China.
  - The impact of technology on crimes in the economic system

- o Larry Nassar and Jerry Sandusky sex abuse scandals and the response of their respective higher education institutions
- o White-collar cybercrime
- o The EPA as a part of the political machine
- o Joe the Tiger King and white-collar crime
- o An expanded focus on biosocial, gender, and life-course explanations for white-collar crime
- o White-collar criminals and reintegration

ACKNOWLEDGMENTS

FOR THE FIRST EDITION

This work would not have been completed without the guidance, direction, and support of many different individuals. I am indebted to Craig Hemmens (Boise State University) for calling me one Thursday afternoon and asking if I would be interested in authoring the work. Also, SAGE Executive Editor Jerry Westby had a way of making it seem like deadlines really meant something, and his excitement about this project helped me to move along. I very much appreciate the efforts of Jerry's development editors, Erim Sarbuland and Leah Mori, in helping to move the project along as smoothly as possible. In addition, I am indebted to production editors Karen Wiley and Libby Larson, and to Patrice Sutton for her detailed skills as a copy editor. Thanks also to Erica Deluca for her careful attention given to marketing this work. As well, the rest of the SAGE team has been a pleasure to work with.

I am also indebted to a small army of graduate assistants who helped with different parts of the project. Tatum Asante, Andrea Barber, Erin Marsh, Susannah Tapp, and Johnnie Cain spent countless hours locating references for me. Danielle Gentile and Katie Taber created the glossary and performed numerous other tasks that I often assigned at the last minute. A white-collar crime professor could not ask for a better group of graduate assistants!

Several friends and colleagues also helped in different ways. Randy Gainey and Ruth Triplett (both at Old Dominion University) read different parts of the book and provided valuable feedback. Leah Daigle (Georgia State University) was an invaluable sounding board for those moments when I felt like whining about workload. It was particularly enjoyable to write the book at the same time that Randy and Leah were working on their own separate projects for SAGE. Just as I would not want to be stranded in the desert by myself, it was refreshing to have friends plowing through this sort of project at the same time.

FOR THE SECOND EDITION

Obviously, a second edition never comes to fruition without a successful first edition. I would be remiss, then, not to repeat my appreciation to everyone (described above) who helped get this first edition to the finish line. For the second edition, I again relied on many individuals for help and support. Susannah Tapp (Georgia State University) updated tables, figures, and statistics throughout the book and updated the new reference list. Lora Hadzhidimova (Old Dominion University) helped locate many of the new studies included in this edition. The SAGE team (led by Jerry Westby) continued to offer a level of support and professionalism that I seriously doubt others could match. I am especially grateful to David Felts for guiding this book through production and Elizabeth Swearngin for her copy-editing skills.

I also very much appreciate the feedback that students and professors have provided about the first edition. I have listened to their feedback and shaped this edition in a way that makes the work even more responsive to the world we now live in. My appreciation is also extended to the cadre of white-collar crime researchers who continue to bring scholarly attention to this problem. I hope that we can bring other scholars into this fold (new scholars and seasoned scholars alike) so that this problem receives the attention it deserves. All of the researchers whose work is cited in this edition deserve a note of personal gratitude for helping me to better understand white-collar crime. As well, some suggest that the criminal justice system does very little to respond to this behavior. While we most certainly need a stronger response to these crimes, I am certain that there are many criminal justice officials who do, in fact, respond appropriately and aggressively to the misdeeds committed by white-collar professionals. A special thanks to those working in this understaffed and underresourced area.

FOR THE THIRD EDITION

In addition to thanking those who helped to make the first and second editions, I am indebted to a number of individuals who helped with *White-Collar Crime: A Systems Approach*. The willingness of Jessica Miller (SAGE Acquisitions Editor) to initially consider a new edition and then support and encourage the work is most appreciated. While it is hard to remember the specific moment when I started working with Jessica several years ago, it has been a pleasure and honor to work with her as we progress through our careers. Sarah Wilson (Senior Editorial Assistant at SAGE) kept me on task, provided invaluable editorial feedback, and made sure that deadlines were met and new ideas were incorporated. Gagan Mahindra's leadership of the production team and Michelle Ponce's copy editing also warrant praise. I also appreciate the members of the SAGE team that I've never actually met or talked with—from the designers to the sales and marketing teams and beyond. So many at SAGE are committed to the success of their authors. It is difficult to find the right words to say how much it means to be a part of such a respected professional community. The best I can come up with is this—thank you!

Speaking of professional communities, the white-collar crime scholars who have helped to generate understanding about white-collar crime throughout the years continue to be held in high regard in my mind. From the white-collar crime pioneers to the modern leaders in the field to newer scholars, I find great wisdom in your work and feel significant pride to be a part of your network. I have learned from each of you and hope that I—like you—can help to provide scientific insight that will help us to better understand and respond to white-collar offending.

FOR THE REVIEWERS

I cannot say enough about the invaluable feedback provided by reviewers throughout this process. The final product looks nothing like the original proposal. The feedback from the reviewers helped me to shape a book that best meets the needs of the discipline. I am grateful to the following reviewers for their input on different editions of this text:

Cindy A. Boyles, University of Tennessee at Martin

George Burrus, Southern Illinois University Carbondale

William Calathes, New Jersey City University

John Casten, Old Dominion University

William Cleveland, Sam Houston State University

Heith Copes, University of Alabama at Birmingham

Dean Dabney, Georgia State University

Lisa Eargle, Francis Marion University

Gary Feinberg, St. Thomas University

Robert Handy, Arizona State University

Patrick Hegarty, Stonehill College

Roy Janisch, Pittsburg State University

Bob Jeffery, Sheffield Hallam University

Shayne Jones, University of South Florida

Kent Kerly, University of Alabama at Birmingham

Jiletta Kubena, Sam Houston State University

Paul Leighton, Eastern Michigan University

Tom O'Connor, Austin Peay University

Nicole Leeper Piquero, Florida State University

Michael S. Proctor, Texas A&M University–San Antonio

Jerome Randall, University of Central Florida

Dawn Rothe, Old Dominion University

Christopher Salvatore, Montclair State University

Andrea Schoepfer, California State University, San Bernardino

Zahra Shekarkhar, Fayetteville State University

Rashi Shukla, University of Central Oklahoma

Christopher Warburton, John Jay College

Bruce Zucker, California State University, Northridge.

ABOUT THE AUTHOR

Brian K. Payne is vice provost for academic affairs and professor of sociology and criminal justice at Old Dominion University. He also serves as the director of the Coastal Virginia Center for Cyber Innovation, a regional node of the Commonwealth Cyber Initiative. His research interests include family violence and criminal justice, elder abuse, electronic monitoring, and white-collar crime. He has published seven books, including *Introduction to Criminal Justice: A Balanced Approach* (with Will Oliver and Nancy Marion, 2019), *Incarcerating White-Collar Offenders: The Prison Experience and Beyond* (2003), and, with R. Gainey, *Family Violence and Criminal Justice* (3rd ed., 2009). Payne is the former president of the Academy of Criminal Justice Sciences and the Southern Criminal Justice Association.

INTRODUCTION AND OVERVIEW OF WHITE-COLLAR CRIME

A Systems Perspective

The summer of 2020 was one for the history books. A global pandemic ruptured our economy, political turmoil paralyzed lawmaking in the United States, racial tensions escalated in the aftermath of police brutality incidents protested across the world, and an impeached president blamed the news and the democratic party for the state of the country. At the same time, President Donald J. Trump was warning the American public that if Joe Biden were to become president, crime would soar in the United States. Many certainly recognized that the president's claims were political rhetoric designed to encourage his base to continue to support him while trying to scare undecided voters into supporting him. Some even pointed to the irony of the president's comments—after all, crime was increasing by as much as 26% in some urban communities on the president's watch (Lopez, 2020). While this debate about crime unfolded, with the exception of a few criminologists, most were paying very little attention to white-collar crimes because of the extensive political focus on behaviors that have historically been called traditional crimes or street crimes. In other words, most individuals were ignoring those offenses that potentially have the most widespread effect on individuals, communities, and the economy.

Indeed, we could pick any week from that unprecedented summer and highlight a number of criminal offenses that caused harm but which are not typically considered in our discussions about crime. On June 19th, for example, a Virginia doctor, who once temporarily lost his license for overprescribing drugs, was sentenced to 10 years in prison after an undercover investigation found that the doctor was once again violating the public trust by overprescribing opioids (USDOJ, 2020, June 19). Unfortunately, this time a patient died as a result of the doctor's actions. The following week, the owner of a third-party payment processing company was sentenced to 70 months in prison for stealing millions of dollars from more than 375,000 victims (USDOJ, 2020, June 24); two pharmacy companies agreed to pay $345 million in corporate fines for violation of the Foreign Corrupt Practices Act (USDOJ, 2020, June 25); and a Russian national was sentenced to nine years in prison for operating websites that sold stolen credit card information of cardholders who were subsequently charged for more than $20 million in fraudulent purchases (USDOJ, 2020, June 26).

Three similarities exist across each of these examples: (1) In terms of time, they were committed during the course of work; (2) in terms of location, they occurred in a work setting; (3) in terms of offender role, the offender served as a worker. At the most general level, one might be tempted to refer to these behaviors as workplace offenses. On another level, one could argue that each of these examples helps us understand what is meant by the concept of white-collar crime.

Edwin Sutherland first introduced the concept of *white-collar crime* in 1939 during a presentation to the American Sociological Association. A decade later, in his now classic book, *White Collar Crime*, he defined the concept as "crime committed by a person of respectability and high social status in the course of his occupation" (Sutherland, 1949, p. 9). Sutherland was calling attention to the fact that criminal acts were committed by individuals from all social and economic classes. He used the phrase *white-collar* to emphasize the occupational status assigned to individuals.

In Chapter 2, more attention will be given to how white-collar crime is conceptualized. As a brief introduction to the concept, three factors are typically used to distinguish white-collar crimes from other crimes. First, white-collar crimes are committed during the course of one's job. Second, the offender's occupational role plays a central feature in the perpetration of the crime. Third, the offender's occupation is viewed as a legitimate occupation by society (e.g., a drug dealer's occupation is illegitimate, but a pharmacist's occupation is legitimate).

Perhaps an example can help to clarify what is meant by crime committed as a part of one's employment. Believe it or not, some professors have committed crimes. Consider a case in which a psychology professor was charged with scientific fraud for hiring actors to pretend that they had participated in his research study. The actors were interviewed by investigators, but they did not realize that the interviews were official because the professor had told them the interviews were part of a mock trial he was conducting for his research study (Office of New York State Attorney General, 2010). This would be a white-collar crime—the offender's employment role was central to the act. Alternatively, consider cases where a tenured psychology professor plead no contest to taking photos up his colleague's skirt (Friedman, 2019) and a former journalism professor was arrested and charged with drug offenses and burglary (Sokol, 2020). The latter two cases would not typically be considered white-collar crimes because the offender's employment role was not central to the commission of the act.

Distinguishing between white-collar crime and traditional crimes is not meant to suggest that one form of crime is worse than the other. Instead, the intent is to note that different forms of crime exist and that full understandings of crime, explanations of crime, and responses to crime will not occur unless the differences between these forms of crime are understood.

WHY STUDY WHITE-COLLAR CRIME?

Seven reasons support the need to study white-collar crime. First, and perhaps foremost, white-collar crime is a serious problem in our society. Estimates provided by the Federal Bureau of Investigation (FBI) routinely suggest that far more is lost to white-collar crimes than to traditional property crimes, such as larceny, robbery, and burglary. Beyond these economic costs, and as will be shown later in this text, white-collar offenses have the potential to cause serious physical and emotional damage to victims.

Second, it is important to recognize that, unlike some offense types, white-collar offenses affect everyone. While a specific street offense might have just one or two victims, white-collar offenses tend to have a large number of victims, and on a certain level, some white-collar offenses are so traumatic that they actually may influence all members of society. For instance, Bernie Madoff 's Ponzi scheme duped thousands of individuals and organizations out of billions of dollars. It was not just these individuals, however, who were victims. Members of society who then felt distrust for financial institutions and their employees were also affected by Madoff's behavior. Members of society may also experience what one social scientist calls "demoralization costs" (Coffee, 1980). In this context, demoralization means that individuals have less faith in societal values, and this reduction in faith may actually create a situation where individuals justify their own future misdeeds based on the illicit behaviors of those white-collar and corporate organizations we have been socialized to trust.

A third reason it is important to study white-collar offending is that by studying white-collar offending we can learn more about all types of crime. Just as medical researchers might learn more about all forms of diseases by studying one form of disease, so the study of white-collar crime allows criminologists, students, members of the public, and policy makers greater insight into all variations of criminal behavior and types of criminal offenders.

Fourth, it is important to study white-collar crime so that effective prevention and intervention systems and policies can be developed. It cannot be assumed that prevention and intervention policies and strategies developed for, and used for, traditional forms of crime are appropriate for responding to offenses committed during the course of one's occupation. The underlying dynamics of different forms of white-collar crime need to be understood so that response strategies and policies based on those dynamics can be developed.

Fifth, and as will be discussed in more detail later in this chapter, studying white-collar crime provides important information about potential careers related to white-collar crime. This is not meant to suggest that you can learn how to be a white-collar criminal by studying white-collar crime; rather, a number of occupations exist that are designed to help the criminal and civil justice systems respond to white-collar crimes. These occupations typically require college degrees, and many are more lucrative than traditional criminal justice occupations. To actually enter one of those careers, one would need a keen understanding of white-collar crime. Thus, we study white-collar crime in order to develop the critical thinking skills and base of awareness needed to understand white-collar crime.

Sixth, compared to research on traditional crime, there simply is not enough research being done on white-collar offending. Common reasons cited for this lack of research on the topic have to do with the lack of funding to support white-collar crime studies and the lack of suitable publication outlets for white-collar crime studies. Fortunately, recent changes have begun to address these problems. Regarding funding, the National Institute of Justice (NIJ) has begun to solicit proposals for research on white-collar crime, with specific topics of interest identified. Table 1.1 shows an overview of the 2019 request for proposals and the projects funded that year. Three proposals were collectively awarded $2.4 million, which pales in comparison to the total amount of research funding provided for traditional crimes by NIJ that same year ($213 million). Still, the availability of funding should help to increase white-collar crime studies.

Regarding the lack of suitable publication outlets, white-collar crime scholars Greg Barak and Anne Alvesalo-Kussi recently created the very first scholarly journal focused on white-collar crime. Published by SAGE in association with the American Society of Criminology's Division on White-Collar and Corporate Crime, the *Journal of White-Collar and Corporate Crime* "is aimed at uncovering the interrelations of theoretical and empirical investigation of the crimes of powerfully organized people and institutions while advancing the knowledge of white-collar and corporate crime as well as the practices of social intervention and policy

TABLE 1.1 ■ NIJ Funded Projects from Research and Evaluation on White-Collar Crime: Health Care and Elder Fraud, FY 2019		
Language From Request for Proposals	NIJ is seeking applications for funding research and evaluation projects that will improve our knowledge on how to identify, prevent, and reduce white-collar crime in the United States. There are many types of offenses that may be classified as white-collar crime. This solicitation focuses on three types of white-collar crime: health care fraud, cyber-crime against individuals, and elder fraud. NIJ will support scientifically rigorous research and evaluation projects that will advance our understanding of white-collar crime and effective approaches for identifying, preventing, investigating and prosecuting white-collar crime related to health care fraud, cybercrime against individuals, and elder fraud and financial exploitation. This solicitation supports the U.S. Department of Justice's strategic goals associated with enhancing national security and promoting the rule of law, integrity and good government.	
Project Title	**Funding Info.**	**Published Research Summary**
Using Physician Behavioral Big Data for High Precision Fraud Prediction and Detections	$842,768 University of Maryland, College Park	Using existing data from a variety of public sources, this project will involve constructing a database to identify physician behavioral factors (illegal behavior, patient complaints and malpractice, disciplinary actions, conspicuous consumption, and life stressors) that predict engagement in health care fraud. Data sources include federal databases on fraud, as well as state and local court records, state medical records, and online review websites. The project will use retrospective matched design that includes a sample of physicians assigned to one of two groups: those who have and have not been excluded from participation in federal health care programs, such as Medicare, due to fraud, from 2015–2019.
Prevention of Financial Abuse Among Elders Affected by Cognitive Decline: A Randomized Controlled Trial in Three Rural Communities	$595,961 Michigan State University	This randomized controlled trial (RCT) will test the efficacy, effectiveness and cost benefit of a financial abuse prevention model for elders living in rural Michigan (MI) who experience cognitive declines. The intervention targets elders, their caregivers, and service professionals providing psychosocial education, case management, and local Financial Abuse Specialist Teams (FAST) to raise awareness, build competence, and provide coaching and consultation to safeguard against and intervene in financial abuse. The researchers have partnered with local aging service agencies in Battle Creek, Manistee, and Marquette. The agencies serve 11 rural counties in the surrounding areas. A total of 106 older adults, 78 family caregivers and 70 service professionals will be enrolled and randomly assigned to intervention groups or control groups across the three sites. Qualitative data collected from community financial abuse prevention caseworkers and participants in the intervention groups will be analyzed to determine program efficacy
Mass Marketing Elder Fraud Intervention	$988,159 Research Triangle Institute	This study will be conducted in collaboration with the U.S. Postal Inspection Service (USPIS), the law enforcement arm of the U.S. Postal Service. The project will involve secondary analysis of USPIS investigatory data; a randomized controlled trial (RCT) to test the efficacy of several variations on a USPIS-mailed intervention for preventing the revictimization of older adults; and a follow-up survey to a subsample of RCT participants. Using 20 years of USPIS investigative data collected from US fraud victims, the researchers will link addresses across three data files, each containing more than 1 million victim records, to gather information about the incidence, frequency, and patterns of repeat victimization. The researchers will also test the use of a mailed intervention in preventing mass marketing fraud revictimization.

Source: Compiled from https://nij.ojp.gov/funding/opportunities/nij-2019-15383

change" (SAGE, n.d.). The journal's launch in 2020 offered, for the first time, an outlet for crime scholars focused solely on white-collar crime. The importance of having a scholarly journal devoted to a specific topic cannot be understated. Besides providing the topic scientific legitimacy, the outlet also provides scholars and students a central publication where they can find recent and high-quality additions to white-collar crime literature.

The seventh and final reason to study white-collar crime is that the research findings will provide additional insight into a particular culture and various subcultures. On the one hand, the study of white-collar crime provides an insider's view of the American workforce and the cultural underpinnings that are the foundation of values driving the activities of the workforce. On the other hand, the study of white-collar crime provides all of us additional insight into specific occupational subcultures with which we have some degree of familiarity—whether accurate or inaccurate.

Many individuals assume that a trip to the auto mechanic has the potential to result in unnecessary repairs and outrageous bills. Few, however, assume that trips to the doctor or pharmacist might result in similar outcomes. As will be shown later in this text, however, white-collar crime research shows that misconduct occurs in all occupations. By understanding misconduct in these occupations, we better understand the occupational subcultures where the misconduct occurs.

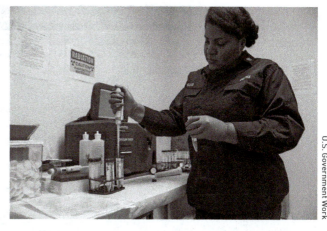

PHOTO 1.1 Many careers exist that target white-collar offending. In this photo, an FDA official examines a dietary supplement to determine if the product is unsafe.

U.S. Government Work

RESEARCHING WHITE-COLLAR CRIME

Several different research strategies are used to study white-collar crime and white-collar criminals. For the most part, these research strategies are similar to those used to study other social problems. The way that these strategies apply to white-collar crime, however, is somewhat different from how they might be applied to research studies of other topics. Strategies that can be used to research white-collar crime include but are not limited to the following:

- Surveys
- Archival research
- Field research
- Experiments
- Case studies

Survey Research and White-Collar Crime

Surveys are perhaps among the more common research strategies used to study white-collar crime. Survey methods include on-site administration surveys, face-to-face interviews, telephone interviews, and mail surveys. Strengths and weaknesses exist for each of these strategies (see Table 1.2). The aim of surveys is to gather information from a group of individuals and use that information to paint a picture of the topic under consideration.

TABLE 1.2 ■ Strengths and Weaknesses of Different Survey Methods		
Survey Method	**Strengths**	**Weaknesses**
On-site administration	• Surveys occur in one setting • Large sample is possible • Does not take long to gather • Convenient	• Difficult to give surveys on site to both offenders and victims • No database of white-collar offenders • Educational differences make it hard to use the same surveys for everyone • Hard for some to recall incidents • Gaining entrance and trust of victims hard
Face-to-face interviews	• Can watch respondent's reactions • Probing is an option • Rapport is easier to develop	• More time consuming • More expensive • Difficulty in finding participants and place to conduct interviews • Trust and rapport are important • Must gain access and permission of businesses
Telephone interviews	• Most comprehensive studies have been conducted using telephone interviews. • Respondents seem more open to answering questions over the phone.	• Excludes people without home phones • Many do not answer the phone
Mail surveys	• Less costly • Able to survey a large number of respondents	• May not fully understand the questions • No opportunity to develop rapport • Takes time to develop a comprehensive list of residents • Certain subjects are excluded from mailing list

Source: Adapted from Payne, Brian K. (2005) *Crime and elder abuse: An integrated perspective.* 2nd ed. Springfield, IL: Charles C Thomas.

Groups who are surveyed in white-collar crime research studies include criminal justice officials, members of the public, victims of white-collar crime, and white-collar offenders. Each of these groups has the potential to provide important information about various issues related to white-collar crime.

Surveys of criminal justice officials in the white-collar crime literature tend to focus on the strategies used to identify and respond to white-collar offenses, the kinds of offenses encountered by the officials, and the barriers that must be overcome to successfully respond to the cases. One author interviewed probation officers to determine how white-collar offenders were supervised by community corrections officials (Mason, 2007). Another author team surveyed 240 judges to generate understanding about judicial sentencing behaviors (Bennett, Levinson, & Hioki, 2017). As will be shown later, the research helped shed some light on the dynamics of sentencing policies within a systems framework.

White-collar crime researchers have also surveyed members of the public to assess attitudes about, and experiences with, white-collar crime. Such research is useful for at least five reasons. First, determining what members of the public think about white-collar crime provides a baseline that helps to paint a picture about a culture at a given moment of time. For example, if surveys of the public show that the public is tolerant of white-collar offending, this would tell us something about the culture at that moment in time. Second, focusing on citizens' attitudes about white-collar crime provides an indication of the likelihood that individuals might engage in white-collar criminal activity. Third, surveying members of the public potentially allows researchers access to a larger group of white-collar offenders than they might otherwise get, particularly in self-report studies. Fourth, and in a similar way, surveys of members of the public could provide researchers access to a large group of **white-collar crime victims**. A survey of 400 residents of Tennessee, for example, found that 227 (58%) reported being victimized by fraud in the prior five years (Mason & Benson, 1996). Fifth, surveys of the public could provide policy makers with information they can use to develop policies and laws designed to prevent white-collar crime.

Researchers have also surveyed white-collar crime victims to increase our understanding about the victimization experiences of this group. In this context, victims could be (1) individuals, (2) businesses and nongovernmental institutions, or (3) "government as a buyer, giver, and protector-gatekeeper" (Edelhertz, 1983, p. 117). One of the issues that arise in such studies is the ability to identify a sample of white-collar crime victims. An early study on appliance "repairman" fraud used a sample of 88 victims of one offender, "Frank Hanks" (not his real name) (Vaughan & Carlo, 1975). Victims were identified through press reports, prosecutors' files, and public files. Incidentally, the researchers identified 133 victims who had complained about the repairman to various consumer agencies. Through this survey, the researchers were able to identify complaint patterns, provide insight into the victims' interactions with Hanks, and delineate the experience of victimization. The authors also drew attention to the plight of victims trying to formally resolve the cases. They noted that "pursuing justice became more expensive than being a victim and they [often] dropped the matter" (Vaughan & Carlo, 1975, p. 158).

Another issue that arises in surveys of white-collar crime victims is that victims may be reluctant to discuss their experiences. Survey respondents may not trust researchers who ask about fraud victimization, perhaps partly because they are on guard about having been scammed in the first place (Mason & Benson, 1996), or they may be embarrassed to talk about their victimization (Jansen & Leukfeldt, 2018). Despite these issues, the need to study white-collar crime victims continues because they have been ignored historically in victimization studies and the victims' movement (Moore & Mills, 1990). One recent avenue of white-collar crime victimization research has explored whether white-collar crime victims should be eligible to participate in victim compensation programs, which have typically focused primarily on victims of street crimes (Galvin, Loughran, Simpson, & Cohen, 2018).

Surveys of white-collar offenders are equally difficult to conduct. Sutherland (1941) recognized this as a barrier in white-collar crime research shortly after introducing the concept. White-collar offenders simply do not want to participate in research studies. As noted above, general self-report surveys of members of the public might help to develop samples of white-collar offenders. Other times, researchers have surveyed members of specific occupational groups. Criminologist Dean Dabney, for example, interviewed nurses (1995) and pharmacists (2001) to shed light on the types of crimes occurring in those fields. After he built up rapport over time, participants in his study were willing to open up about crimes in their occupations, particularly crimes committed by their coworkers. More recently, a research team interviewed 17 convicted white-collar offenders to better understand the impact that the conviction had

PHOTO 1.2 Interviews can provide important insight into white-collar criminal behavior. While white-collar professionals might be open to doing interviews, it is very difficult to convince white-collar offenders to be interviewed.

on the offenders (Button, Shepherd, & Blackbourn, 2018). Pointing out that interviewing white-collar offenders "pose[s] significant access challenges to the researcher," this research team developed their sample by including those who had been out of the justice system for a number of years, which possibly reduced any stigma effects that may have kept subjects from participating.

Other researchers have confronted barriers in their efforts to interview convicted white-collar offenders. This group of offenders experiences a significant amount of stigma, and that stigma may keep them from wanting to talk about their experiences with researchers. In an effort to get offender contributions to a story she was writing, one journalist tried contacting 30 different convicted white-collar offenders who had been released from prison. She described their resistance to talking with her the following way: "Understandably, most of them told me to get lost. They had done their time and that part of their life was a closed chapter. They had made new lives and did not want to remind anyone of their pasts" (Loane, 2000).

Alluding to difficulties of finding white-collar criminals willing to be interviewed and the fact that criminologists tend to spend more of their time studying street crime, one criminologist began an article with this simple observation: "Criminology gazes down" (Oleson, 2018, p. 45). He partly attributes this gazing down to the ease of studying traditional criminals in comparison to white-collar offenders, but he also draws attention to research dynamics in these studies. While researchers have a higher class status and economic advantage over subjects in street crime studies (which some presumably use to assert power in interviews), they have no educational or class power when interviewing white-collar offenders.

Across each of these survey types, a number of problems potentially call into question the validity and reliability of white-collar crime surveys. First, as one research team has noted, the field of criminology has not yet developed "comprehensive measures . . . that tap into the concepts of white-collar and street crime" (Holtfreter, Van Slyke, Bratton, & Gertz, 2008, p. 57). The lack of comprehensive measures makes it difficult to compare results across studies and generalize findings to various occupational settings. Second, difficulties developing representative samples are inherent within white-collar crime studies. It is particularly difficult to develop a random sample of white-collar crime victims or offenders. Third, questions about white-collar crime on surveys are potentially influenced by other items on the survey, meaning the findings might actually reflect methodological influences as opposed to actual patterns. Fourth, the scarcity of certain types of white-collar crime surveys (like those focusing on offenders) has made it even more difficult to develop and conduct these sorts of studies—if more researchers were able to do these surveys, then others would learn how to follow in their path. Despite these potential problems, surveys are useful tools for empirically assessing various issues related to white-collar offending.

Archival Research and White-Collar Crime

Archival research is also relatively common in the white-collar crime literature. In this context, archival research refers to studies that use some form of record (or archive) as a database in the study (Berg, 2009). Archives commonly used in white-collar crime studies include official case records, presentence reports, media reports, and case descriptions of specific white-collar offenses.

Case records are official records that are housed in an agency that has formal social control duties. One problem that arises with using case records is locating a sample that would include the types of offenders that criminologists would label as white-collar offenders (Wheeler, Weisburd, & Bode, 1988). Still, with a concerted effort, researchers have been able to use case records to develop databases from which a great deal of valuable information about white-collar crime will flow. Matt Greife, for example, used court records and other publicly available information to create a database providing information about 169 environmental crime cases. His efforts showed that environmental crime court records could be analyzed through a quantitative framework (Greife & Maume, 2020a) and that certain companies experience negative collateral sanctions after being fined for environmental offending (Greife & Maume, 2020b). Note that there is absolutely no other way Greife could have found these findings other than by reviewing case records.

Researchers have also used presentence reports to study different topics related to white-collar crime. **Presentence reports** are developed by probation officers and include a wealth of information about offenders, their life histories, their criminal careers, and the sentences they received. In one of the most cited white-collar crime studies, criminologist Stanton Wheeler and his colleagues (Wheeler, Weisburd, Waring, & Bode, 1988) used the presentence reports of convicted white-collar offenders from seven federal judicial circuits to gain insight into the dynamics of offenders, offenses, and sentencing practices. The authors focused on eight offenses: securities fraud, antitrust violations, bribery, tax offenses, bank embezzlement, post and wire fraud, false claims and statements, and credit and lending institution fraud. Their research provided ground-breaking information about how white-collar offenders compared to traditional offenders, as well as information about the way offenders are sentenced in federal court. The findings are discussed in more detail in later chapters of this text. This ground-breaking study was replicated roughly three decades later by Galvin and Simpson (2019). Focusing on the same offenses committed by a group of more than 16,000 federally convicted offenders, the authors of the more recent study found that offenders pleading guilty to white-collar crime did not receive "discounts" in terms of their sentence lengths.

Researchers have also used **media reports** to study white-collar crime. Using news articles, press reports, and television depictions of white-collar crimes helps researchers (a) demonstrate what kind of information members of the public are likely to receive about white-collar crime and (b) uncover possible patterns guiding white-collar offenses that may not be studied through other means. With regard to studies focusing on what information the public receives about white-collar offenders, criminologist Michael Levi (2006) focused on how financial white-collar crimes were reported in various media outlets. His results suggested that these offenses were portrayed as "infotainment" rather than serious crimes, suggesting that the cases were sensationalized to provide somewhat inaccurate portrayals of the offenses. Another researcher who used newspaper articles to study the portrayal of white-collar crime found that the cases tended to be reported in business or law sections rather than the crime sections of newspapers, suggesting that the behaviors are not real crimes (Stephenson-Burton, 1995).

With regard to the use of press reports to describe patterns surrounding specific forms of white-collar crimes, a series of studies by Philip Stinson have explored various dynamics associated with police sexual misconduct (Stinson, Brewer, Mathna, Liederbach, & Englebrecht, 2015), family violence by police officers (Stinson & Leiderbach, 2013), crimes by female police officers (Stinson, Todak, & Dodge, 2015), arrests in police corruption cases (Stinson, Liederbach, Lab, & Brewer, 2016), and police crime and violence in general (Stinson, 2009, 2020). In using media reports, Stinson was able to access a larger number of police misconduct cases than he would have been able to access through other methods. His findings provide useful fodder for those interested in generating awareness about police misconduct.

Another archive that may be of use to white-collar crime researchers involves case descriptions of specific white-collar offenses that may be provided by some agencies. In some states, for example, the state bar association publishes misdeeds committed by attorneys. Researchers have used these case descriptions to examine how lawyers are sanctioned in Alabama (Payne & Stevens, 1999) and Virginia (Payne, Time, & Raper, 2005). Some national agencies provide reports of white-collar crimes committed by occupations they are charged with regulating. The National Association of Medicaid Fraud Control Units, for instance, describes cases prosecuted by Medicaid Fraud Control Units in a publication titled *Medicaid Fraud Reports.* This publication has served as a database for studies on crimes by doctors (Payne, 1995), crimes in nursing homes (Payne & Cikovic, 1995), crimes in the home health care field (Payne & Gray, 2001), and theft by employees (Payne & Strasser, 2012).

As digital publishing has grown, the information that is made available has also changed. The U.S. Health and Human Services Office of Inspector General now provides updated information on specific health care fraud and abuse cases addressed by federal and state officials in annual reports published on the agency's website. The information can be culled for a number of different types of studies. Table 1.3 provides a summary of the kinds of information that would be available from the agency.

TABLE 1.3 ■ Types of Information About Health Care Crimes Provided Online	
Crime Type	**Case Information Example**
Patient Abuse	Attorney General Ashley Moody today announced the arrest of an individual who allegedly abused a mentally disabled adult. Following an investigation by the Attorney General's Medicaid Fraud Control Unit, the Orange County Sheriff's Office today arrested ++++++ on one count of aggravated abuse of a mentally disabled person. The investigation found that +++++, a former employee at the LaMirada group home in Winter Springs, maliciously punished a mentally disabled adult under +++++'s care. (November 19, 2019, Florida case).
Prescription Fraud	Two women pleaded guilty yesterday for their respective roles in helping run a "pill mill," which led to the fraudulent dispensing of thousands of prescription opioid pills. According to court documents and statements made in court,++++++, 41, of Haymarket, was the office manager, and +++++++, 29, of Leesburg, was a medical assistant at an addiction/pain treatment clinic and an OB/GYN practice ("The Medical Practices"), which both operated in the same location in Northern Virginia. (March 23)
Durable Medical Equipment Fraud	Florida man who operated a durable medical equipment company has been charged for his alleged participation in a Medicare kickback and telemedicine fraud scheme.++++++++++++, 48, of Belleair Beach, Fla., the operator of Wilmington Island Medical Inc., which does business as WI Medical Inc., a Georgia company, is accused of conspiring to pay kickbacks for "leads." (May 13. 2020)
Home Health Fraud	From 2015 to 2018, ++++++ certified patients for home health services without any knowledge of their medical condition or homebound status. +++++++++ paid ++++++ approximately $6,200 in exchange for signing these fraudulent Medicare home health certifications and plans of care. +++++ also fraudulently signed a fellow physician's name on these certifications and plans of care without that physician's authorization, permission or knowledge. (May 14, 2020)
Medical Transportation Fraud	+++++++ age 30, was sentenced today to 18 months in prison, to be followed by 3 years of supervised release, and ordered to pay $50,000 in restitution, for committing fraud and paying bribes in connection with Medicaid-funded transportation. From 2015 through May 2018, +++++ worked for and helped operate Ti Taxi Inc. ("Ti Taxi"), and worked for other Medicaid-funded transportation companies, all based in Essex County, New York. (April 17, 2020)
Telemedicine Fraud	A Georgia woman who operated a telemedicine network through two companies has been charged for her alleged participation in an ever-growing healthcare and telemedicine fraud scheme. ++++++, the operator of Royal Physician Network, LLC and Envision It Perfect, LLC, both Georgia companies, is accused of conspiring to pay medical providers, like physicians and nurse practitioners, in exchange for obtaining orders for durable medical equipment (DME) that would then be sold to DME providers and, ultimately, billed to Medicare.

Source: Compiled from https://oig.hhs.gov/fraud/enforcement/criminal/index.asp

With each of these types of archival research, researchers often develop a coding scheme and use that scheme much as they would use a survey instrument. Instead of interviewing an individual, the researcher "asks" the archive a set of questions. Several advantages exist with the use of case records for white-collar crime research (see Payne, 2005). For example, such strategies provide white-collar crime researchers access to a large group of subjects that they would not be able to otherwise access. It would have been impossible, for example, for Stinson to locate and interview more than 1,700 police officers who had been arrested for misconduct. Another benefit is that these strategies enable white-collar crime researchers to explore changes over long periods of time, particularly if the researchers have access to case records that cover an extended period of time. A third benefit is that the research subject, in this case the white-collar offender or victim described in the case record, will not react to being studied simply because there are no interactions between the researcher and the subject.

Finally, the widespread availability of archival data provides criminologists numerous opportunities for white-collar crime students. Table 1.4 highlights 15 such data archives.

TABLE 1.4 ■ White-Collar Crime Data Sources	
Crime Type	**Website Where Data Can Be Accessed**
Crimes Against Consumers	https://www.ftc.gov/enforcement/data-visualizations
Health Care Crimes	https://oig.hhs.gov/fraud/enforcement/
Nursing Home Violations	https://projects.propublica.org/nursing-homes/
Drug Diversion Cases Against Doctors	https://www.deadiversion.usdoj.gov/crim_admin_actions/index.html https://apps2.deadiversion.usdoj.gov/CasesAgainstDoctors/spring/main?execution=e1s1
Police Brutality	https://github.com/themarshallproject/doj14141#the-department-of-justices-14141-civil-rights-investigations
Judicial Misconduct Cases	https://cjp.ca.gov/
Education Investigations	https://www2.ed.gov/about/offices/list/oig/newsroom.html
Research Misconduct Cases	https://ori.hhs.gov/content/case_summary
SEC Investigations	https://www.sec.gov/litigation/litreleases.shtml
Cybercrimes	https://www.justice.gov/criminal-ccips/ccips-press-releases-2020
Data Breaches	https://privacyrights.org/data-breaches
Corporate Violations	https://www.goodjobsfirst.org/violation-tracker
Corporate Crime Prosecution Registry	http://lib.law.virginia.edu/Garrett/corporate-prosecution-registry/browse/browse.html
Environmental Crime	https://www.epa.gov/enforcement/environmental-crimes-case-bulletin
Unsafe Products	https://www.cpsc.gov/Data

As with any research strategy, a number of limitations arise when researchers use archives to study white-collar crime. The saying, "you get what you get," comes to mind. The case files are inflexible, and white-collar crime researchers will not be able to probe as they would with interview strategies. Also, the way that records are coded or saved over time may change, which will create problems when researchers try to study white-collar crimes over longer periods of time. In addition, there is no central repository for most types of white-collar crime (Reinhart, 2019). The absence of a central database makes it that much more difficult to find available data. Perhaps the most significant problem that arises is that these cases typically represent only those that have come to the attention of the authorities. In effect, unreported white-collar crimes would not be included in most types of archival research. Common reasons that victims will not report white-collar crimes include (a) a belief that there is not enough evidence; (b) the offense is not seen as that serious; (c) concerns that reporting would be futile; (d) concerns that reporting the victimization could be costly, particularly for businesses that are victims of white-collar crimes; (e) shame; (f) businesses may want to handle it on their own; and (g) realization that it may take more time than it seems worth taking to respond to the case (Crofts, 2003). If nobody reports the white-collar crime, it will not be a part of an official record.

Indeed, Sutherland (1940) recognized decades ago that official statistics (and records) typically exclude many white-collar crimes.

Field Research

Field research involves strategies where researchers enter a particular setting and gather data through their observations in those settings (Berg, 2009). In some instances, researchers will share their identity as a researcher with those in the setting, while in other instances, researchers may choose to be anonymous. These strategies can be quite time consuming and are conducted much less frequently than other white-collar crime studies, but they have the potential to offer valuable information about behavior in the workplace. For example, Stannard (1973) entered a nursing home as a janitor and worked there for several months. While the staff knew that he was a researcher, they seemed to forget this over time, and their actions included various types of misconduct (ranging from minor offenses to more serious ones that could have resulted in one resident's death).

In many white-collar crime studies, field research methods are combined with other research strategies. As an illustration, Croall (1989) conducted court observations as part of a broader study focusing on crimes against consumers. She observed 50 cases and used the time she spent doing those observations to develop rapport with the justice officials involved in handling the cases. Over time, the officials later granted Croall access to their case files. Had she not "put in her time," so to speak, she probably would have been denied access to the case files. Recognizing the lack of similar types of studies, some white-collar crime criminologists have called for more field-based qualitative research to better understand the processes and mechanisms leading to criminal behavior and how underlying cultural and technological variables shape white-collar misconduct (Jordanoska & Schoultz, 2020).

Experiments

Experiments are studies where researchers examine how the presence of one variable (the causal or independent variable) produces an outcome (the effect or dependent variable). The classic experimental design entails using two groups—an experimental group and a control group. Subjects are randomly selected and assigned to one of the groups. Members of the **experimental group** receive the independent variable (or the treatment), and members of the control group do not. The researcher conducts observations before and after the independent variable is introduced to the experimental group to determine whether the presence of the independent variable produced observable or significant changes.

Consider a situation where we are interested in whether a certain treatment program would be useful for reintegrating white-collar offenders into the community. The researcher would develop a measurement for assessing white-collar offenders' reintegration values. As well, a sample of white-collar offenders would be randomly assigned to two groups—an experimental group and a control group. The researcher would ask members of both groups to complete the reintegration values survey. Then the experimental group would be exposed to the treatment program, and the control group would receive traditional responses. At some point after the treatment has been completed, the researcher would ask members of both groups to complete a similar (or even the same) reintegration values survey. Any differences between the two groups of offenders could then potentially be attributed to the treatment (or independent variable) received by the experimental group.

An experiment in the Netherlands compared the way that car mechanics sell goods to consumers (students) in different scenarios. The experiment found that mechanics frequently provided more services than were necessary, presumably because "experts often face strong incentives for providing 'safe solutions'" (Beck, Kerschbamer, Qiu, & Sutter, 2014). This study demonstrates that experiments can, in fact, be done on topics related to white-collar crime. Of course, the use of students as consumers limited the generalizability of the findings.

Because of difficulties in recruiting white-collar individuals to participate in these studies, very few white-collar crime studies have actually used a classic experimental design. Some, however, have used what are called **quasi-experimental designs**. Quasi-experiments are studies that mimic experimental designs but lack certain elements of the classic experimental design. One author team, for example, compared two similar businesses (health care offices) to determine whether an "ethical work climate" contributed to employee theft (Weber, Kurke, & Pentico, 2003). The two organizations included one in which an internal audit revealed that workers were stealing and one in which an audit did not reveal theft. The authors surveyed workers from both businesses and found that an ethical work climate appeared to influence theft. In this case, the authors did not randomly select the comparison groups, and they did not manipulate the independent variable (ethical work climate). Still, their design mimicked what would be found in an experimental design.

While some criminologists have used quasi-experiments to study white-collar crime issues, the use of experiments in the broader body of white-collar crime research remains rare. This may change in the future, however, as experimental research is becoming much more common in criminology and criminal justice. In 1998, for example, a group of criminologists created the Academy of Experimental Criminology (AEC) to recognize those criminologists who conduct experimental research. Part of AEC's current mission is to support the *Journal of Experimental Criminology*, which was created in 2005 as an outlet for promoting experimental research on crime and criminal justice issues. According to the journal's website, the *Journal of Experimental Criminology* "focuses on high quality experimental and quasi-experimental research in the development of evidence based crime and justice policy. The journal is committed to the advancement of the science of systematic reviews and experimental methods in criminology and criminal justice" (http://www.springer.com/social+sciences/criminology/journal/11292, "About This Journal"). Incidentally, the founding editor of the journal (David Weisburd) has a long history of conducting prominent white-collar crime research studies.

Case Studies

Case studies entail researchers selecting a particular crime, criminal, event, or other phenomena and studying features surrounding the causes and consequences of those phenomena. Typically, the sample size is "one" in case studies. Researchers might use a variety of other research strategies (such as field research, archival research, and interviews) in conducting their case studies. Case studies are relatively frequent in the white-collar crime literature. An early case study was conducted by Frank Cullen and his colleagues (Cullen, Maakestad, & Cavender, 1987), who focused on what is now known as the *Ford Pinto Case*. In the mid- to late 1970s,

Ford Motor Company had come under intense scrutiny over a series of high-profile crashes. Eventually, prosecutor Michael Cosentino filed criminal charges against Ford Motor Company after three teenage girls—Judy, Lin, and Donna Ulrich—driving a Ford Pinto, were killed in an August 1978 collision. The authors chronicled the situational and structural factors that led to Cosentino's decision to pursue criminal penalties against the large automaker. While the details of this case will be described in more detail later, as Cullen and his coauthors note, this case "signified the social and legal changes that had placed corporations under attack and made them vulnerable to criminal intervention in an unprecedented way" (p. 147).

Different criminologists and social scientists have also studied the role of white-collar and corporate crime in the U.S. savings and loan crisis, which occurred in the 1980s and 1990s. Perhaps the most comprehensive case study of this crisis was conducted by criminologists Kitty Calavita, Henry Pontell, and Robert Tillmann (1997). The research team, through a grant funded by the National Institute of Justice, explored those criminogenic factors contributing to the collapse of the savings and loan institutions in the late 1980s and 1990s. The authors relied on public records, congressional testimony, media reports, and interviews with key informants to demonstrate how white-collar offending contributed to a significant proportion of the bank failures. While Calavita and her colleagues focused on the crisis from a national perspective, other researchers used a more specific case study approach to consider specific instances where a bank failed. One author team, for example, conducted a case study on the Columbia Savings and Loan Association of Beverly Hills (Glasberg & Skidmore, 1998b). Using congressional testimony, interviews, and media reports, their research drew attention to the way that structural changes in the economic policies (deregulation and federal deposit insurance policies) promoted individual greed.

Case studies are especially useful for corporate crime studies, which were historically published as news reports by muckrakers (Dodge, 2020). Other criminologists have added that white-collar crime case studies are most effective when they contextualize the impact of organizational, social, and cultural factors on decision making in the specific white-collar crime being studied (Griffin & Spillane, 2016). A case study on one organization, for example, might yield different results than a case study elsewhere because of cultural differences in those organizations. Tying organizational frames, social context, and cultural perspectives into case studies arguably helps to delineate the precise mechanism at force in shaping white-collar and corporate behaviors (Griffin & Spillane, 2016). Consider, for example, if one were to do a case study on the 2010 BP oil spill (discussed later in this text). To fully understand the oil spill, researchers must consider the organizational dynamics promoting behavior at BP as well as the broader cultural and social factors that influenced the behavior of the company and the justice system in its response to the disaster.

Case studies are advantageous in that they allow criminologists an insider's view of specific white-collar and corporate crimes. As well, these studies have provided a great deal of insight into the dynamics, causes, and consequences of various types of white-collar crimes. In many ways, because case studies use multiple strategies to gather data, the potential strengths of those strategies (e.g., nonreactivity for archival research, etc.) exist with case studies. At the same time, though, the same disadvantages that arise with these other strategies also manifest themselves in case studies. In addition, it is important to note that case studies can take an enormous amount of time to complete.

STUDYING WHITE-COLLAR CRIME FROM A SCIENTIFIC PERSPECTIVE

Almost everyone has heard about crimes committed by individuals in the workplace or by white-collar offenders. In recent times, a great deal of media attention has focused on infamous white-collar offenders, such as Bernie Madoff, Martha Stewart, and Ken Lay. The reality is, however, that these media depictions—while providing a glimpse into the lives and experiences of a select few high profile white-collar offenders—provide a superficial, and somewhat confusing, introduction to white-collar crime. To fully understand white-collar crime, it is best to approach the topic from a scientific perspective.

Studying white-collar crime from a scientific perspective requires that students understand how the principles of science relate to white-collar crime. In 1970, Robert Bierstedt described how various principles of science were related to the study of human behavior. Fitzgerald and Cox (1994) used these same principles to demonstrate how social research methods adhered to traditional principles of science. Taking this a step further, one can use these principles as a framework for understanding why, and how, the principles of science relate to the study of white-collar crime. The principles include these qualities:

- Objectivity

- Parsimony

- Determinism

- Skepticism

- Relativism

Objectivity and White-Collar Crime

Objectivity as a principle of science suggests that researchers must be value free in doing their research. The importance of objectivity is tied to the research findings. Researchers who allow their values to influence the research process will be more apt to have findings that are value laden rather than objective. Researchers who violate this principle may create significant damage to the scientific endeavor.

With regard to white-collar crime, the challenge is to approach the behaviors and the offenders objectively. In many cases, white-collar offenders are vilified and portrayed as evil actors who have done great harm to society. While the harm they create is clearly significant, demonizing white-collar offenders and white-collar offenses runs the risk of (a) ignoring actual causes of white-collar crime, (b) relying on ineffective intervention strategies, (c) failing to develop appropriate prevention strategies, and (d) making it virtually impossible for convicted white-collar offenders to reintegrate into society.

Consider that many individuals attribute the causes of white-collar crime to greed on the part of the offender. Intuitively, it makes sense that individuals who already seem to be making a good living are greedy if they commit crime in order to further their economic interests. However, as Benson and Moore (1992) note, "self-reports from white-collar offenders suggest that they often are motivated not so much by greed as by a desire to merely hang on to what they already had" (p. 267). Inadequately identifying the causes of behavior will make it more difficult to respond appropriately to these cases.

Furthermore, in promoting understanding about the criminal justice system's response to white-collar offenders, it cannot be automatically assumed that the justice system is doing a bad job or treating these offenders more leniently than other offenders. An objective approach requires an open mind in assessing the ties between white-collar crime and the criminal justice system. As will be seen later, for example, several studies show that convicted white-collar offenders are more likely than other convicted offenders to be sentenced to jail, albeit for shorter periods of time (Payne, 2003b). The lack of an objective approach might force some to automatically assume that white-collar offenders are treated more leniently than conventional offenders. This is problematic because a lack of objectivity may create faulty assumptions about the criminal justice system's handling of white-collar crime cases, which in turn could reduce the actual deterrent power of the efforts of criminal justice practices.

On another level, some criminologists have argued that a lack of objectivity among criminologists has resulted in some researchers overextending the concept of white-collar crime. According to V. Ruggiero (2007),

> given the increasing variety of white-collar criminal offenses being committed, and the avalanche of crime committed by states and other powerful actors, scholars are faced with a fuzzy analytical framework, with the result that some may be tempted to describe as crime everything they, understandably, find disturbing. . . . The word nasty is not synonymous with criminal, and the concept of crime may be useless if it is indiscriminately applied to anything objectionable by whoever uses the term. (p. 174)

In terms of objectivity and the study of white-collar crime, researchers should not define white-collar crimes simply as those things that are "nasty" or as behaviors that offend them. Instead, white-collar crime must be objectively defined, measured, researched, and explained.

Parsimony and White-Collar Crime

The principle of **parsimony** suggests that researchers and scientists keep their levels of explanation as simple as possible. For explanations and theories to be of use to scientists, practitioners, and the public, it is imperative that the explanations be reduced to as few variables as possible and explained in simple terms. In explaining white-collar crime, for instance, explanations must be described as simply as possible. One issue that arises, however, is that many white-collar crimes are, in fact, very complex in nature and design. As will be shown later in this text, this complexity often creates obstacles for criminal justice officials responding to these cases.

While many types of white-collar crimes may be complex and it may be difficult to explain the causes of these offenses in simple terms, this does not mean that the offenses cannot be understood through relatively simple explanations. Consider fraud by physicians, misconduct by lawyers, or misdeeds by stockbrokers. One does not need to be a doctor, attorney, or financial advisor to understand the nature of these offenses, ways to respond to these offenses, or the underlying dynamics contributing to these behaviors. By understanding relatively simple descriptions of these behaviors, readers will be able to recognize parallels between the offenses and will develop a foundation from which they can begin to expand their understanding of white-collar crime.

Determinism and White-Collar Crime

Determinism means that behavior is caused or influenced by preceding events or factors. With regard to crimes in the workplace, a great deal of research has focused on trying to explain (or "determine") why these offenses occur. Understanding the causes of white-collar crime is important because such information would help in developing both prevention and intervention strategies. In terms of prevention, if researchers are able to isolate certain factors that seem to contribute to white-collar misconduct, then policy makers and practitioners can use that information to develop policies and implement practices that would reduce the amount of crime in the workplace. Consider a study on student cheating that finds that the cheating is the result of the nature of the assignments given. With this information, professors could redo the assignment so that cheating is more difficult and less likely.

Understanding the causes of white-collar crime also helps to develop appropriate intervention strategies. If, for example, a study shows that certain types of white-collar offenses are caused by a lack of formal oversight, then strategies could be developed that provide for such oversight. One study, for example, found that patient abuse in nursing homes was at least partially attributed to the fact that workers were often alone with nursing home residents

(Payne & Cikovic, 1995). To address this, the authors recommended that workers be required to work in teams with more vulnerable patients and video cameras be added where feasible.

To some, the principle of determinism is in contrast to the idea of free will, or rational decision making. However, it is not necessary, at least in this context, to separate the two phenomena. Whether individuals support deterministic ideals or free-will ideals, with white-collar offenses it seems safe to suggest that understanding why these offenses occur is informative and useful. For those adhering to deterministic ideals, explaining the source of workplace misconduct helps to develop appropriate response systems. For those adhering to free-will ideals, the same can be said: Figuring out what makes individuals "choose" to commit white-collar offenses means that strategies can be developed that would influence the offender's decision making. In other words, choices are caused by, and can be controlled by, external factors. Put another way, by understanding *why* individuals commit crime in the workplace, officials are in a better position to know *how* to respond to those crimes.

Skepticism and White-Collar Crime

Skepticism simply means that social scientists must question and requestion their findings. We must never accept our conclusions as facts! Applying this notion to the study of white-collar crime is fairly straightforward and simple. On the one hand, it is imperative that we continue to question past research on white-collar crime in an effort to develop and conduct future white-collar crime studies. On the other hand, in following this principle, some may find it difficult to think differently about the occupations covered in this book. Put simply, crime and deviance occur in all occupations.

Sociologist Emile Durkheim noted that deviance occurs in all cultures and subcultures. He used the example of a "society of saints" to illustrate this point. Even a group of nuns or priests would have someone committing deviant behavior. So, as readers, when we think of any occupation, we must question and requestion how and why crime is committed in that occupation. We cannot assume that because the occupation is "trustworthy" that crime does not occur in that occupation. Doing so would provide an inaccurate and incomplete picture of white-collar crime.

Relativism and White-Collar Crime

Relativism means that all things are related. If all things are related, then, this principle implies that changes in one area will lead to changes in other areas. A simple example helps to highlight this principle. Think of a time when you are driving your car, listening to your favorite Lady Gaga, Eminem, or Taylor Swift song with the music turned up loudly, and you suddenly smell something that makes you think that your engine is failing. What's the first thing you do? For many of us, the first thing we do is turn the music down so we smell better. Think about that—we do not smell with our ears; we smell with our noses. But we turn the music down because it helps us to smell. Changes in one area (smelling) lead to changes in other areas (hearing).

White-collar crime is related to the ideal of relativism in three ways: (1) how white-collar crime is defined, (2) the nature of white-collar crime, and (3) how the criminal justice system responds to white-collar crime. First, the notion of *white-collar* is a relative concept in and of itself. What makes someone a white-collar worker? Is it the clothes worn to work? Are your professors "white-collar" workers? Do they all wear "white collars" to work? Are you a white-collar worker? Will you ever be a white-collar worker? In using the concept of white-collar to describe these offense types, Sutherland was highlighting the importance of status. However, the very concept of status is relative in nature. What is high status to one individual might actually be low status to another person. What one group defines as a white-collar occupation may be different from what another group defines as white-collar. A basic understanding of white-collar crime requires an appreciation for the relative nature of status and occupations.

Second, the principle of relativism highlights the need to recognize how changes in society have resulted in changes in white-collar offending. Throughout history, as society changed and workplace structures changed, the nature of, and types of, workplace offenses changed. Describing this pattern from a historical review of the 1800s, one author team commented:

> During this time period, large scale changes within the business environment brought new opportunities for acts of workplace taking, particularly those associated with "respectable" echelons of staff hierarchies. Such acts were labeled as illegitimate and criminalized. . . . The representation of fraud and embezzlement as activities that were criminal was bolstered through a reconceptualization of the nature of property rights and, in particular, the relationship between staff and the property worked with. (Locker & Godfrey, 2006, p. 977)

In effect, changes in the occupational arena create new opportunities for, and strategies for, white-collar crime. In our modern society, note that globalization has created worldwide opportunities for white-collar offending (Johnstone, 1999). As an example of the way that changes in society result in changes in misbehavior that may hit home with some students, "studies by the Center for Academic Integrity show a decline in traditional peeking over someone's shoulder cheating, but a steady increase in Internet plagiarism" (Zernike, 2003). Changes in society resulted in changes in the way some students cheat.

Third, the notion of relativism relates to white-collar crime in considering how the criminal justice system responds to white-collar crimes and the interactions between the criminal justice system and other societal systems. John Van Gigch's (1978) **applied general systems theory** helps to illustrate this point. Van Gigch noted that society is made up of a number of different types of systems and that these systems operate independently, and in conjunction with, other systems (see Figure 1.1). At a minimum, systems that are related to white-collar crime include those shown in Figure 1.1.

At the most basic level, the **political system** is involved in defining laws and regulations relating to all forms of crime, including white-collar crimes. Three levels of the political system include local, state, and federal systems of government. Each of these levels plays a role in defining various white-collar offenses, detecting offenders, adjudicating cases, and punishing offenders. On a separate level, one chapter of this book will focus on crimes committed in the political system. Note also that the political system plays a central role in developing and implementing policies designed to prevent and respond to white-collar crime. Throughout this text, significant attention is given to the interplay among white-collar crime policies, the occurrence of white-collar crimes, and the actions of various systems assigned the tasks of preventing and responding to white-collar crime.

The **educational system** relates to white-collar crime inasmuch as white-collar careers typically come out of this system. From preschool through higher education, one can see that the educational system prepares individuals for their future careers and lives. Some research has focused on how the educational system might promote certain forms of white-collar offending, with students potentially learning why committing crimes is part of their training (Keenan, Brown, Pontell, & Geis, 1985). At the same time, the educational system provides opportunities to increase understanding about white-collar crime through college coursework and advanced training for criminal justice professionals. As with the political system, white-collar crimes occur in the educational system.

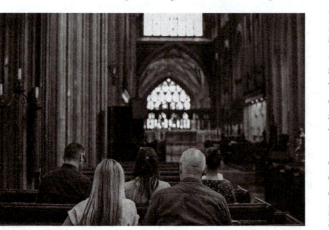

Unsplash, Stefan Kunze.

PHOTO 1.3 Crime occurs in all societal systems, even the religious system. You will read more about offenses in colleges and universities in Chapter 7.

FIGURE 1.1 ■ The Systems Perspective

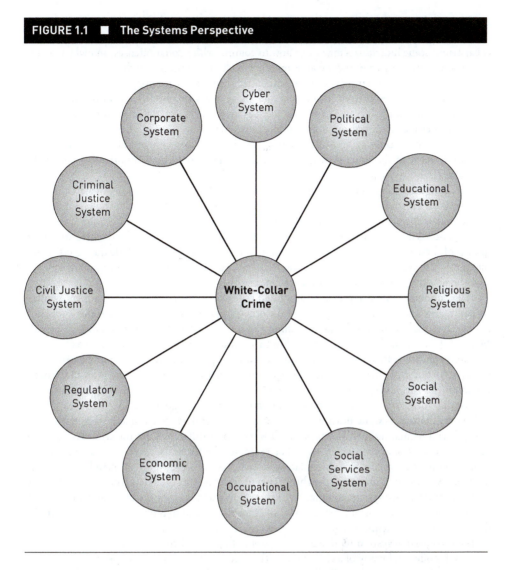

The **religious system** relates to white-collar crime (and other crimes) in that this system has been seen as providing institutions that have the potential to prevent misconduct. Many studies have focused on the ties between religion and crime, and while few have focused on how religion relates to white-collar crime, the underlying assumption is that religion has the potential to prevent these behaviors or, at least, provide a setting where definitions of appropriate and inappropriate misconduct can be developed. Interestingly, white-collar crime pioneer Edwin Sutherland's father "was a religious fundamentalist who believed in strict adherence to the Baptist faith" (Martin, Mutchnick, & Austin, 1990, p. 140). While Sutherland eventually parted ways with his father's church, it has been noted that "a prominent and overt expression of his moralistic side appears in *White Collar Crime* (1949) where Sutherland calls for something other than a strict legal definition of acceptable behavior" (Martin et al., 1990, p. 141). As an aside, just as crime is found in the political and educational systems, so do white-collar offenses occur in the religious system.

The **technological or cyber system** has evolved greatly over the past few decades. This system is related to white-collar crime in at least two distinct ways. First, and as was noted earlier, changes in the technological system have led to changes in the way that some white-collar offenders commit their crimes. Second, the technological system has provided additional tools that government officials can use in their pursuit of identifying and responding to white-collar crimes.

The **social system** represents a setting where individuals have various needs fulfilled and learn how to do certain things, as well as reasons for doing those behaviors. In terms of white-collar crime, some individuals may learn how to commit white-collar offenses, and why to commit those offenses, as part of the social systems in which they exist. Research, for example, shows that nurses learn from their peers how to rationalize their workplace misdeeds (Dabney, 1995).

The **social services system** includes numerous agencies involved in providing services to members of the public. In some cases, the services they provide might be in direct response to white-collar crime victimization. For example, individuals who lose their life savings to fraudulent investors may need to seek assistance from the social service system to deal with their victimization. As with the other systems, white-collar crimes could be committed by workers in the social services system.

The **occupational system** is, for the purposes of this discussion, that system where the bulk of professions are found. This system is composed of other systems, which at the broadest level can be characterized as lower-class and upper-class occupational systems. Within the lower-class and upper-class occupational systems, specific subsystems exist. White-collar offenses are found in each of these subsystems. As outlined in this text, these subsystems include the legal system, the health care system, the higher education system, the religious system, the technological system, the housing system, the insurance system, and the economic system.

The **economic system** represents the system that drives our economy. This system is influenced by, and has an influence on, each of the other types of systems. In recent times, problems in the economic system have had far-reaching and serious effects on countries across the world. Many of the white-collar crimes discussed in this text originate in the economic system.

The **corporate system** includes the businesses and corporations that carry out business activity as part of our capitalist system. These corporations strive to make profits and grow in strength and numbers. Various types of white-collar crimes have been uncovered in the corporate system. As well, the corporate system is sometimes given the power to regulate itself.

The **regulatory system** describes those local, state, and federal agencies that have been charged with regulating various businesses. This system is different from the criminal and civil justice systems in many different ways. For example, the formal source of rules comes from administrative regulations in the regulatory system. As well, the rights of offenders, corporations, and victims are different in the three types of systems (e.g., offenders have one set of rights in the criminal justice system, another set of rights in the civil justice system, and another set of rights in the regulatory system). Procedures and guidelines used to process the cases also vary in the three types of systems.

The **civil justice system** represents that system of justice where individuals (plaintiffs) seek recourse for offenses by way of a civil lawsuit. The accused (defendant) could be an individual or a company. In cases of white-collar crime, for example, it is common for lawsuits to be filed by victims in order to recover their losses. Note that the victim, in many cases, may actually be an individual, company, or governmental agency.

The **criminal justice system** is that system of justice where violations of the criminal law are handled. The criminal law is the branch of law dealing with crimes against the state. Like each of these systems, our criminal justice system is composed of various subsystems: the police, courts, and corrections. On one level, the criminal justice system operates independently from other agencies when white-collar offenses are investigated, prosecuted, and sentenced. On another level, it is imperative to note that the system's responses to white-collar crimes, and behaviors of actors in the criminal justice system, are influenced by changes in other societal systems. Changes in the technological system (brought about by advances in the educational system) led to the development of the Internet. The Internet, in turn, created new ways for criminals to offend. These new strategies, then, meant that the criminal justice system had to alter its practices. As society changes, criminal justice and other systems of formal control are forced to change how they respond to white-collar offenses (Edelhertz, 1983). As one author put it several years ago, "an emerging area of difficulty is the challenge of devising powers of investigation that are responsive to the needs of enforcement in a modern corporate society" (Fisse, 1991, p. 7). Two decades later, this same challenge remains "an emerging area of difficulty."

Because broader societal changes have created different types of careers, work settings, employees, employers, and industries, new varieties of white-collar crime potentially requiring new strategies for addressing them have surfaced (Hochstetler & Mackey, 2016). For example, the evolution of white-collar cybercrime, discussed in Chapter 9 represents an offense variety that has changed dramatically in recent years. A full understanding of white-collar crime requires an understanding of (a) the changing nature of crime occurring in various systems; (b) how the criminal justice, civil justice, and regulatory systems respond to white-collar crimes; and (c) how interactions between the systems influence criminal behavior as well as response systems. To promote broad insight into white-collar crime, this text relies on the systems perspective to guide the discussion about white-collar crime. In doing so, it argues that students (a part of the educational system) have a significant role in white-collar crime.

THE STUDENT ROLE IN WHITE-COLLAR CRIME

Some readers may have given very little thought to their role in white-collar crime. In reading this text, students are encouraged to think about how white-collar crime relates to their lives—their past, their present, and their future. In effect, students have at least 10 potential roles in white-collar crime. These roles include (1) past victims, (2) past offenders, (3) current victims, (4) current offenders, (5) future victims, (6) future offenders, (7) future crime fighters, (8) future policy makers, (9) current research subjects, and (10) future white-collar crime researchers.

First, most students have been victimized by white-collar crimes in the past, though many likely may not have realized they were victimized at the time. From being overcharged for services to being a victim of corporate misconduct, students—like the rest of society—are not immune from victimization by white-collar or corporate offenders. Consider, for example, how landlords have been accused of taking advantage of college students. As an illustration, here is how one student described landlords providing housing in her community:

> They have very little regard for the safety and health of their tenants. For example, most buildings were painted many years go with lead paint (which can be expected from buildings from the 1800 to 1900's), which poses a serious health risk to tenants. The floors in these buildings appear to be in their original condition, as they bend and bow when someone jumps or even just stands on them. The exterior of many of these rented out buildings are in rough shape with visibly old siding and chipping paint. (Geisler, 2020).

Second, some students may have actually been past offenders, particularly if broader definitions of occupational offending are used. These definitions will be addressed in Chapter 2. For now, several questions could be asked to determine whether students have broken the rules in their past jobs: Did they take breaks for too long? Did they give away company food or merchandise? Did they skip work and lie to their boss about the reason? One of the exercises I use in my white-collar crime classes is to have students write about occupational offenses they have committed in past jobs. Very few of my students ever had a problem identifying past misdeeds. Some even described actions that would have resulted in felony convictions had they been caught for their transgressions! One student proudly boasted how stealing stereos from his place of business was helping to pay his tuition, and another shared a rather innovative (albeit criminal) way he made extra money working in a hotel. More details on the latter example are provided in Chapter 3.

Third, students may also be current victims of white-collar crime. In Chapter 7, we will look at the way colleges and universities sometimes break rules in recruiting students and providing financial aid. (Some have even argued that ineffective instruction by college professors victimizes students, but that can be saved for another text.) Students might also be victims of white-collar and corporate misconduct in their roles as consumers of various goods and services that extend beyond the college boundaries. Or, they may be targets of cybercrime. See this chapter's White-Collar Crime in the News for a recent press release showing how video conferences similar to those used in online teaching could be hacked.

Fourth, some students can also be seen as current occupational offenders if they are violating the rules of their jobs or the rules set by their educational institution. This will be discussed in more detail in Chapter 7. At this point, it is sufficient to suggest that college students can be seen as "pre-white-collar" professionals. In this context, then, some misdeeds that college students commit could technically be seen as versions of white-collar offending.

WHITE-COLLAR CRIME IN THE NEWS
ZOOM AND CYBERCRIME

The following is a press release from April 17, 2020 from the Eastern District of Pennsylvania.

PHILADELPHIA—United States Attorney William M. McSwain warned the community today about the potential for hackers to invade and disrupt videoconference meetings that are taking place as Americans use video-teleconferencing (VTC) platforms to conduct online meetings during the coronavirus pandemic.

"In the weeks following the coronavirus outbreak, videoconferencing platforms have become a part of daily living, used in a variety of ways—from conducting online classes, to hosting extended family gatherings, to holding large corporate meetings," said U.S. Attorney McSwain. "Unfortunately, we have also seen an uptick in video hacking, where cyber actors hijack VTC meetings and cause a variety of harms, from showing inappropriate images to making death threats. Hackers beware: this behavior is not funny in any way and will not be tolerated."

As individuals continue to engage in online learning and social and business meetings during the pandemic, law enforcement recommends exercising due diligence and caution and encourages users to take the following steps to mitigate videoconferencing threats:

- **Do not make the meetings or classrooms public**. Videoconferencing platforms have options under "settings" to make meetings private by requiring participants to enter a meeting password, follow a link to a meeting, or wait in a virtual "waiting room." These are all features that allow the host to limit public access and control admission of guests.

- **Do not share a meeting link publicly**. Do not use publicly accessible social media platforms to share your meeting link with participants. Provide the link directly to specific people.

- **Manage screen-sharing options**. Most VTC platforms have screen-sharing capability so that participants can see a host's presentations, a feature often used in online classroom settings. Change the screen-sharing setting to "Host-Only" so that participants cannot share their screens.

- **Download updates.** Ensure that users are using the updated version of remote access/meeting applications, as many VTC platforms have built in additional security measures in their latest updates.

- **Familiarize yourself with the VTC platform's capability to remove intruders and lock meetings.** Most VTC platforms have ways for hosts to remove participants and prevent them from re-joining and to lock meetings once all participants have joined. Consult with your employer's IT professionals for more information about these features.

Reprinted from US Department of Justice.

Source: https://www.justice.gov/usao-edpa/pr/united-states-attorney-mcswain-fbi-warn-potential-videoconferencing-hacking-during

Fifth, all college students will be future victims of white-collar and corporate misconduct at least on some level. There is no reason to expect that these offenses will end. Because the consequences of white-collar offenses are so far reaching, none of us will be completely immune from future misdeeds—though we may not always know when we have been victimized.

Sixth, some college students may have the role of future white-collar offenders. Note that most white-collar offenders have at least some college education. While most readers of this text will not (it is hoped) go on to careers of white-collar offending, the fact remains that some college graduates eventually graduate into these criminal careers.

Seventh, some college students will also have a future role as white-collar crime fighters or white-collar criminal defense lawyers. At first blush, a career battling white-collar offenders may not seem as exhilarating as other law enforcement careers. However, nothing could be further from the truth. A major focus of this text will be on how the criminal justice system and criminal justice professionals respond to white-collar offenses. In addressing the mechanics of the response to these offenses, it is hoped that readers will see just how important, and exciting, these careers are. From going undercover in a doctor's office to sifting through complex computer programs, the search for misconduct and clues of wrongdoing can far outweigh more mundane or routine criminal justice practices.

Eighth, some college students will go on to employment positions where they will play a role in developing and implementing various crime policies. As future policy makers, college students will be better prepared to develop policies addressing white-collar crime if they have a full understanding of the dynamics of white-collar crime, the causes of the behavior, and the most effective response systems. Without an understanding of these issues, future (and current) policy makers run the risk of relying on crime prevention policies and strategies that might work for traditional forms of crime but not necessarily for white-collar crimes. A recent study found that less than 7% of all studies published in 15 top criminal justice journals between 2001 and 2010 were focused on white-collar crime (McGurrin, Jarrell, Jahn, & Cochrane, 2013). The discipline is counting on you to change this!

Ninth, some college students will also assume the role of research subjects. It is particularly useful to study students as white-collar crime subjects because, presumably, many will be entering white-collar careers after graduating (Watt, 2012). Many researchers have used college student samples to generate understanding about white-collar offending. One researcher used a sample of college students to learn about the kinds of crimes committed in fast-food restaurants (O'Connor, 1991). Another research team surveyed students to learn about digital piracy and illegal downloading (Higgins, Fell, & Wilson, 2006). The same research team surveyed college students to test the ability of criminological theories to explain different forms of occupational misconduct. Another study of 784 undergraduate students found that the way items are sequenced in questionnaires influences attitudes about white-collar crime (Evans & Scott, 1984). The simple fact of the matter is that criminology and criminal justice scholars have a great deal to learn from students, just as students have a great deal to learn from their professors! Indeed, many of the studies cited in this book will come from studies involving college students on some level.

Tenth, as you read about the studies discussed in this text, one thing to bear in mind is that the authors of these studies and articles were students themselves in the not-so-distant

©iStockphoto.com/Vasyl Dolmatov

PHOTO 1.4 While many careers exist to respond to white-collar crime, most of those careers require employees to have a college degree. It is equally important that college students have an understanding of white-collar crime so they are better able to enter those careers.

past (well, maybe the more distant past for some of us). Edwin Sutherland, once a college student at Grand Island College, went on to create the study of white-collar crime. His students, his students' students, and their students have created a field of study that has significantly evolved over the past 80 years. Thus, the tenth role that students have in white-collar crime is that the discipline of criminology and criminal justice is counting on some of you to take the torch and become future white-collar crime researchers. This text provides a foundation for understanding white-collar crime. It is hoped that this foundation will spark your interest so that you will want to learn more about this important criminological issue and one day go on to help generate future empirical and scientific awareness about white-collar crime.

PLAN FOR THE BOOK

This text uses the systems perspective as a guide for understanding white-collar crime. Each chapter provides readers an introduction to topics related to white-collar crime. The text is divided into the following chapters:

2. Understanding White-Collar Crime: Definitions, Extent, and Consequences

3. Crime in Sales-Related Occupations: A Systems Perspective

4. Crime in the Health Care System

5. Crime in Systems of Social Control: White-Collar Crime in Criminal Justice, Military, and Religious Systems

6. Crime in the Political System

7. Crime in the Educational System

8. Crime in the Economic System

9. Crime in the Cyber System

10. Crime by the Corporate System

11. Environmental Crime

12. Explaining White-Collar Crime

13. Policing White-Collar Crime

14. Judicial Proceedings and White-Collar Crime

15. The Corrections Subsystem and White-Collar Crime

Throughout each chapter, both criminological and criminal justice themes are covered. White-collar crime has been addressed with little or no attention given to white-collar criminal justice. Pulling together criminological and theoretically driven issues with criminal justice-oriented discussions will help to provide a full picture of white-collar crime and the responses to white-collar crime.

Summary

- According to Edwin Sutherland, white-collar crime is "crime committed by a person of respectability and high social status in the course of his occupation" (1949, p. 9). The distinguishing features of white-collar crime are that the crime was committed (a) during work, (b) when the offender was in the role of worker, and (c) as part of the employment duties of the offender.

- We study white-collar crime (a) because it is an enormous problem, (b) because it affects everyone, (c) to learn more about all forms of crime, (d) to develop prevention and intervention systems, (e) to learn about careers, and (f) to learn about subcultures.

- Survey research with white-collar offenders tends to include surveys of offenders, victims, criminal justice officials, and members of the public.

- Archival research on white-collar offenders includes reviews of case records, presentence reports, media reports, and case descriptions of specific white-collar offenses.

- Field research involves situations where researchers enter a particular setting to study phenomena. While relatively rare in the white-collar crime literature, these studies provide direct insight into issues related to the behaviors of offenders, criminal justice officials, and other members of society.

- Experiments involve studies where researchers assess the influence of a particular variable on an experimental group (which receives the "treatment" or the variable) and a control group (which does not receive the treatment or the variable). It is expected that white-collar crime experiments will increase in the future as experimental criminology grows as a research strategy.

- Case studies entail researchers selecting a particular crime, criminal, event, or other phenomenon and studying features surrounding the causes and consequences of those phenomena.

- It is important that those studying white-collar crime be objective in conducting research on the topic. As well, readers are encouraged to keep an open mind about the topic to help as they critically assess issues related to white-collar crime and the study of the topic.

- Researchers are encouraged to keep their explanations as simple as possible. For white-collar crime researchers, this means that one does not need to understand everything about a career in order to understand issues related to crime in that career.

- The aim of many white-collar crime studies is to explain why white-collar crime occurs. Determinism suggests that behavior can be explained. Explaining why white-collar crimes occur enables development of appropriate prevention and intervention remedies.

- Skepticism as a principle of science means that scientists question and requestion everything. For students of white-collar crime, this means that we must question and requestion all of our assumptions about various careers and recognize that crime occurs in all careers.

- Relativism means that all things are related. From a systems perspective, this means that all societal systems are influenced by and have an influence on white-collar crime. Those systems considered in this chapter included the (1) political-governmental system, (2) educational system, (3) religious system, (4) technological system, (5) social system, (6) social services system, (7) occupational systems, (8) economic system, (9) corporate systems, (10) regulatory system, (11) civil justice system, and (12) criminal justice system.

- Students have at least 10 potential roles in white-collar crime. These roles include (1) past victims, (2) past offenders, (3) current victims, (4) current offenders, (5) future victims, (6) future offenders, (7) future crime fighters, (8) future policy makers (9) current research subjects, and (10) future white-collar crime researchers.

Key Terms

Applied general systems theory 18	Experimental group 12	Regulatory system 20
Archival research 8	Experiments 12	Relativism 17
Case records 8	Field research 12	Religious system 19
Case studies 13	Media reports 9	Skepticism 17
Civil justice system 20	Objectivity 15	Social services system 20
Corporate system 20	Occupational system 20	Social system 20
Criminal justice system 20	Parsimony 16	Technological System 19
Determinism 16	Political system 18	White-collar crime victims 7
Economic system 20	Presentence reports 9	
Educational system 18	Quasi-experimental designs 13	

Discussion Questions

1. The following items are examples of misdeeds committed by celebrities. Read each of them, and classify them according to whether the acts are white-collar crimes, traditional crimes, or, to borrow Ruggiero's concept, just "nasty."

   a. In 2008, former boy-band manager Lou Pearlman (former manager of 'N Sync and Backstreet Boys) was convicted of defrauding more than $300 million from investors as part of a Ponzi scheme.

   b. In June 2020, rapper Trick Daddy was arrested on drunk driving and drug charges.

   c. Cardi B threw her shoe at Nicki Minaj at the 2018 New York Fashion Week, and a fight broke out.

   d. "Real Housewife" Teresa Giudice was sentenced to prison after she and her husband were convicted of bankruptcy and mortgage fraud.

   e. Kanye West interrupted the MTV music awards in 2009 while Taylor Swift was giving an acceptance speech.

   f. In January 2009, Dane Cook's manager, Darrly J. McCauley, was charged with embezzling $10 million from Cook. McCauley is Cook's half-brother.

   g. Actor Zac Efron told a reporter that he had stolen costumes from movie sets after filming ended. He said, "I think I stole some of the stuff. Always, on the last day, they try and get it out of your trailer really quick. Always steal some of your wardrobe. You never know what you're going to need" (Hasegawa, 2010).

   h. Actor Bill Cosby was convicted in 2018 of sexually assaulting numerous women by using a sedative and taking advantage of them.

i. Suge Knight was convicted and sentenced to prison in 2018 after running over a man with his truck and killing him.

j. Martha Stewart was convicted of perjury in 2004 after it was found that she lied to investigators about some of her stock purchases.

2. Why does it matter how you classify these behaviors?

3. How are the behaviors you labeled *white-collar crime* different from those you labeled as *traditional crimes*?

4. Why do we study white-collar crime?

5. What is your current role in white-collar crime? What will your future role in white-collar crime be?

UNDERSTANDING WHITE-COLLAR CRIME

Definitions, Extent, and Consequences

As noted in Chapter 1, Edwin Sutherland created the concept of white-collar crime more than eight decades ago to draw attention to the fact that crimes are committed by individuals in all social classes. Fast forward 80 years, and it is safe to say that May 2020 was a busy month in the world of white-collar crime. Paul Manafort and Michael Cohen, both previous confidants of President Donald Trump, made headlines for their imprisonments for convictions relating to, but not fully implicating, Trump. Cohen was approved for temporary release due to Covid-19 concerns in prisons, but he was subsequently denied early release right around the same time he received a letter from a Trump attorney warning him not to pen a "tell-all" book about Cohen's relationship with Trump. Just days later, the Department of Justice dropped perjury charges against Lieutenant General Michael Flynn. The decision was applauded by President Trump but decried by others including former prosecutors and criminal justice leaders from the right and left. While these national headlines were appearing on the news scrolls of CNN, MSNBC, and Fox News, other white-collar offenses were making local and state headlines. Consider the following examples quoted from their sources:

> A Fultondale doctor has pleaded guilty to prescribing controlled substances without a legitimate medical purpose. (Grantin, 2020)

> [The professor] was charged with one count of Wire Fraud. The complaint charges that +++ had close ties with the Chinese government and Chinese companies, and failed to disclose those ties when required to do so in order to receive grant money from NASA. These materially false representations to NASA and the University of Arkansas resulted in numerous wires to be sent and received that facilitated +++'s scheme to defraud. (U.S. Department of Justice, 2020, May 11)

> A former San Francisco Building Commission president has been charged in federal court with bank fraud for allegedly diverting to his personal bank account $478,000 that clients of his engineering company intended to be paid to the city. (Associated Press, 2020, May 12)

> The operators of a business coaching scheme will pay at least $1.2 million to settle Federal Trade Commission charges that they targeted people who were trying to start new businesses online and used deception to sell them bogus marketing products and services. (Federal Trade Commission, 2020, May 13)

In reviewing these examples, five questions come to mind. First, is each of these cases a white-collar crime? Second, how often do these kinds of crimes occur? Third, what are the consequences of these crimes? Fourth, how serious do you think these crimes are? Finally, who are the offenders in these cases? While the questions are simple in nature, the answers to these questions are not necessarily quite so simple. As will be seen in this chapter, one of the greatest difficulties in understanding white-collar crime has centered on an ongoing debate about how to define white-collar crime. After discussing various ways that white-collar crime can be defined, attention will be given to the extent of white-collar crime, the consequences of this illicit behavior, public attitudes about white-collar crime, and patterns describing the characteristics of white-collar offenders.

WHITE-COLLAR CRIME: AN EVOLVING CONCEPT

While Edwin Sutherland is the pioneer of the study of white-collar crime, the development of the field and the introduction of the concept of white-collar crime did not occur in a vacuum. Indeed, prior academic work and societal changes influenced Sutherland's scholarship, and his scholarship, in turn, has had an enormous influence on criminology and criminal justice. Tracing the source of the concept of white-collar crime and describing its subsequent variations help demonstrate the importance of conceptualizing various forms of white-collar misconduct.

Sutherland was not the first social scientist to write about crimes by those in the upper class. In his 1934 *Criminology* text, Sutherland used the term *white-collar criminaloid* in reference to the **"criminaloid concept"** initially used by E. A. Ross (1907) in *Sin and Society*. Focusing on businessmen who engaged in harmful acts under the mask of respectability, Ross further wrote that the criminaloid is "society's most dangerous foe, more redoubtable by far than the plain criminal, because he sports the livery of virtue and operates on a titanic scale" (p. 48). Building on these ideas, Sutherland called attention to the fact that crimes were not committed only by members of the lower class. As noted in the introduction, Sutherland (1949) defined

white-collar crime as "crime committed by a person of respectability and high social status in the course of his occupation" (p. 9).

Sutherland's appeal to social scientists to expand their focus to include crimes by upper-class offenders was both applauded and criticized. On the one hand, Sutherland was lauded for expanding the focus of the social sciences. On the other hand, the way that Sutherland defined and studied white-collar crime was widely criticized by a host of social scientists and legal experts. Much of the criticism centered on five concerns that scholars had about Sutherland's use of the white-collar crime concept. These concerns included (1) conceptual ambiguity, (2) empirical ambiguity, (3) methodological ambiguity, (4) legal ambiguity, and (5) policy ambiguity.

In terms of **conceptual ambiguity**, critics have noted that white-collar crime was vaguely and loosely defined by Sutherland (Robin, 1974). Robin further argued that the vagueness surrounding the definition fostered ambiguous use of the term and vague interpretations by scholars and practitioners alike. Focusing on the link between scholarship and practice, one author suggested that the concept was "totally inadequate" to characterize the kinds of behavior that are at the root of the phenomenon (Edelhertz, 1983). Further describing the reactions to this conceptual ambiguity, white-collar crime scholar David Friedrichs (2002) wrote, "perhaps no other area of criminological theory has been more plagued by conceptual confusion than that of white-collar crime" (p. 243).

One result of this conceptual ambiguity—which continues today—is that two individuals could draw different conclusions about whether specific behaviors are, in fact, white-collar crime. Consider as an example Sweet Dixie Chicken, a restaurant that made national news in 2017 when the world learned that the establishment was reportedly serving a $4.00 Popeye's chicken dinner at $13.00 a meal instead of serving a meal prepared by Sweet Dixie. The apparent overpriced chicken (or false advertising?) came to light when a Yelp reviewer reported seeing an employee from Sweet Dixie bring boxes of Popeye's chicken into the restaurant. After being asked about the source of the chicken, the owner did not deny it. In fact, she defended using Popeye's chicken, saying that it was no different than getting any type of food from a supplier. She further explained that she didn't name the chicken on the menu because she thought that would be a potential copyright violation.

After the news surfaced, the Internet came to life. Labeling the incident #Popeyesgate, critics levied accusations against Sweet Dixie. One Youtuber said, "Clearly Illegal. Classic case of deception" ("SoCal Restaurant Proudly Serves Popeye's Chicken as Their Own," 2017). Another Youtuber was more forgiving writing, "Tell me where it is. I hate standing in line at Popeye's" ("Restaurant Admits to Serving Popeye's Chicken as Its Own," 2017). In this case, different people came to different conclusions about the same behavior. The same can be said of white-collar crime—different individuals reach different conclusions about what constitutes criminal behavior. Incidentally, it was reported the Sweet Dixie was closing down in 2019 (Rosner, 2019). It doesn't appear that the #Popeyesgate led to their closure, however. In fact, when Popeye's announced its brand new chicken sandwich, as part of its marketing the company asked Sweet Dixie to sell its sandwiches for two days in advance of the introduction of the new Popeye's item. The owner of Sweet Dixie was understandably surprised by the gesture, saying "To be honest, I thought they were calling to sue me" (Mettler, 2019). So, some would define Sweet Dixie's use of Popeye's chicken as wrong, while others would say it was a good business practice. The same sort of conceptual ambiguity plagues Suthlerland's white-collar crime definition.

Criticism about Sutherland's work also focused on the **empirical ambiguity** surrounding the concept. In effect, some argued that the concept only minimally reflected reality. For example, one author said that Sutherland's definition underestimated the influence of poverty on other forms of crime (Mannheim, 1949). Another author argued that by focusing on the offender (in terms of status) and the location (the workplace) rather than the offense, the concept did not accurately reflect the behaviors that needed to be addressed (Edelhertz, 1983). Edelhertz went as far as to suggest that this vague empirical conceptualization created barriers with practitioners and resulted in a lack of research on white-collar crime between the 1950s and 1970s. Shapiro (1990) also recognized the problems that the conceptualization of white-collar crime created for future researchers. She wrote,

> The concept has done its own cognitive mischief. It . . . is founded on a spurious correlation that causes sociologists to misunderstand the structural impetus for these offenses, the problems the offenses create for systems of social control, and the sources and consequences of class bias in the legal system. (p. 346)

Describing the tendency to treat lower-class workers as white-collar offenders has been described as "improper and misleading" (Dobovsek & Slak, 2015, p. 310). In a similar way, some believe that criminologists have oversimplified or trivialized the definition of white-collar crime to the extent that more serious crimes of the powerful are downplayed if not ignored (Pontell, 2016).

The consequences of this empirical ambiguity are such that findings from white-collar crime studies sometimes call into question the nature of white-collar offenders. One study of white-collar offenders convicted in seven federal districts between 1976 and 1978, for example, found that most offenses described as white-collar were actually "committed by those who fall in the middle classes of our society" (Weisburd, Chayet, & Waring, 1990, p. 353).

PHOTO 2.1 Music producer Phil Spector was sentenced to prison after being convicted of murder in the death of Lana Clarkson. Although he was a white-collar professional, because he committed a crime that was unrelated to his work, he would not be considered a white-collar criminal.

Sutherland was also criticized for methodological ambiguity. He defined white-collar crime as behaviors committed by members of the upper class, but his research focused on all sorts of offenses, including workplace theft, fraud by mechanics, deception by shoe salespersons, and crimes by corporations (see Robin, 1974). One might say that Sutherland committed a "bait and switch" in defining one type of crime but actually researching another variety.

A fourth criticism of Sutherland's white-collar crime scholarship can be coined "legal ambiguity." Some legal scholars contended that the concept was too sociological at the expense of legal definitions of white-collar offending (Tappan, 1947). To some, white-collar crimes should be narrowly defined to include those behaviors that are criminally illegal. Some even take it a step further and suggest that white-collar criminals are those individuals convicted of white-collar crimes (suggesting that if one were not caught for a white-collar crime one actually committed, then one would not be a white-collar criminal). Sutherland, and others, have countered this argument by suggesting that conviction is irrelevant in determining whether behaviors constitute white-collar crimes (Geis, 1978). Still, the criticism that the term is too general persists.

A final criticism of the white-collar crime concept is related to the policy ambiguity surrounding the concept. In particular, some have argued that the vagueness of the definition and its purely academic focus created a disconnect between those developing policies and practices responding to white-collar crime and those studying white-collar crime (Edelhertz, 1983). Over the past decade or so, criminologists have become more vocal about the need for evidence-based practices to guide criminal justice policies and activities. In terms of white-collar crime, an issue that has been cited is that unclear definitions about white-collar crime make it extremely difficult for policy makers and practitioners to use criminological information to guide policy development and criminal justice practices. In effect, how can criminologists call for evidence-based practices for certain types of crime when they have not adequately provided the evidence needed to develop subsequent practices?

Sutherland was aware of the concerns about the concept potentially being vague. He noted that his point was not precision but to note how white-collar crime is "identical in its general characteristics with other crime rather than different from it" (Sutherland, 1941, p. 112). He wrote,

> The purpose of the concept of white-collar crime is to call attention to a
> vast area of criminal behavior which is generally overlooked as criminal behavior,
> which is seldom brought within the score of the theories of criminal behavior, and
> which, when included, call for modifications in the usual theories of criminal
> behavior. (p. 112)

Thus, Sutherland conceded that the concept was vague in nature, but it was necessarily vague in order to promote further discussion about the concept.

Sutherland was successful in promoting further discussion about the phenomenon, though the topic received very little attention in the 1950s and 1960s. This began to change in the early 1970s when criminologists Marshall Clinard and Richard Quinney published *Criminal Behavior Systems*. Building on Sutherland's work, Clinard and Quinney (1973) argued that white-collar crime can be divided into two types: corporate crime and occupational crime. They focused their definition of **corporate crime** on illegal behaviors that are committed by employees of a corporation to benefit the corporation, company, or business. In contrast, they described **occupational crime** as law violations committed at work with the aim of benefiting the employee-offender. By distinguishing between crimes by corporations and crimes against corporations, Clinard and Quinney took an important step in addressing some of the ambiguity surrounding the white-collar crime concept. Indeed, corporate crime and occupational crime are viewed as "the two principal or 'pure' forms of white-collar crime" (Friedrichs, 2002, p. 245).

After Clinard and Quinney's (1973) work, white-collar crime research by criminologists escalated in the 1970s and 1980s. Much of this research focused on ways to conceptualize and define the phenomenon in ways that addressed the criticisms surrounding Sutherland's definition. Table 2.1 shows eight different concepts and definitions that criminologists have used to describe these behaviors. Just as Sutherland's definition was criticized, each of the concepts provided in Table 2.1 is imperfect. Still, they illustrate the impact that Sutherland's white-collar crime scholarship has had on criminology and criminal justice.

A definition of white-collar crime acceptable to all groups is yet to be developed. This is troublesome for at least six reasons. First, the lack of a sound definition of white-collar crime has hindered detection efforts. Second, without a concrete definition of white-collar crime, the most effective responses to the problem cannot be gauged. Third, varying definitions among researchers have made it difficult to draw comparisons between different white-collar crime studies. Fourth, vague conceptualizations have made it more difficult to identify the causes of the behavior. Fifth, varied definitions of white-collar crime have made it difficult to determine with great accuracy the true extent of white-collar crime. More specifically, how the concept is defined will determine whether it is counted/measured in various estimates (Wall-Parker, 2020). Sixth, as Melissa Rorie (2020) notes, definitions impact research methodologies, which impact findings, which impact conclusions and implications, with the end result being the lack of a common body of knowledge about white-collar crime.

Highlighting these themes, former American Society of Criminology president Sally Simpson (2019) delivered the 2018 Sutherland Address at the association's annual meeting. In her lecture on corporate crime, she noted "the subject matter is amorphous" (p. 201). The ambiguity, she said, made it hard to understand the systemic response to the behavior and to identify evidence-based recommendations that could help in responding to these crimes. More recently, David Friedrichs (2019) made the important observation that white-collar crime is best seen as

TABLE 2.1 ■ Evolution of the White-Collar Crime Concept		
Concept	**Definition**	**Reference**
Criminaloid	The immunity enjoyed by the perpetrator of new sins has brought into being a class for which we may coin the term *criminaloid*. . . . Often, indeed, they are guilty in the eyes of the law; but since they are not culpable in the eyes of the public and in their own eyes, their spiritual attitude is not that of the criminal. The lawmaker may make their misdeeds crimes, but, so long as morality stands stock-still in the old tracks, they escape both punishment and ignominy.	E. A. Ross (1907, p. 48)
White-collar crime	Crime committed by a person of respectability and high social status in the course of his occupation.	Sutherland (1949, p. 9)
Corporate crime	Offenses committed by corporate officials for their corporation and the offenses of the corporation itself.	Clinard and Yeager (1980, p. 189)
Occupational crime	Offenses committed by individuals in the course of their occupations and the offenses of employees against their employers.	Clinard and Yeager (1980, p. 189).
Organizational deviance	Actions contrary to norms maintained by others outside the organization . . . [but] supported by the internal operating norms of the organization.	Ermann and Lundman (1978, p. 7)
Elite deviance	Acts committed by persons from the highest strata of society . . . some of the acts are crimes . . . may be criminal or noncriminal in nature.	Simon (2006, p. 12)
Organizational crime	Illegal acts of omission or commission of an individual or a group of individuals in a formal organization in accordance with the operative goals of the organization, which have serious physical or economic impact on employees, consumers, or the general public.	Schrager and Short, (1978, p. 408)
Occupational crime	Any act punishable by law that is committed through opportunity created in the course of an occupation that is legitimate.	Green (1990)

"an umbrella term—a broad term encompassing a wide range of activities" (p. 17). He further advised that "we should give up the illusion that white-collar crime can—or even should—have a single meaning or definition" (p. 22). Another white-collar crime expert, Mary Dodge (2016), offers a similar perspective and suggests that the debate about white-collar crime definitions takes away from the amount of time and attention given to other important topics in the field. While definitions vary, there is agreement among the definitions around one core theme: White-collar offenders are different from street offenders (Benson,Van Slyke, & Cullen, 2016).

MODERN CONCEPTUALIZATIONS OF WHITE-COLLAR CRIME

Today, criminologists and social scientists offer various ways to define white-collar crime (see Table 2.1). These variations tend to overlap with one another and include the varieties shown in Figure 2.1.

Defining *white-collar crime as moral or ethical violations* follows ideals inherent within principles of what is known as natural law. **Natural law** focuses on behaviors or activities that are defined as wrong because they violate the ethical principles of a particular culture, subculture, or group. The immoral nature of the activities is seen as the foundation for defining certain

FIGURE 2.1 ■ Defining White-Collar Crime

types of white-collar activities as criminal. Some individuals, for example, define any business activities that destroy animal life or plant life as immoral and unethical. To those individuals, the behaviors of individuals and businesses participating in those activities would be defined as white-collar crimes.

Some prefer to define *white-collar crime as* **violations of criminal law**. From this framework, white-collar crimes are criminally illegal behaviors committed by upper-class individuals during the course of their occupation. From a systems perspective, those working in the criminal justice system would likely define white-collar crime as criminally illegal behaviors. Crime, in this context, is defined as "an intentional act or omission committed in violation of the criminal law without defense or justification and sanctioned by the state as a felony or misdemeanor" (Tappan, 1960, p. 10). Applying a criminal-law definition to white-collar crime, white-collar crimes are those criminally illegal acts committed during the course of one's job. Here are a few examples:

- An accountant embezzles funds from his employer.

- Two nurses steal drugs from their workplace and sell them to addicts.

- A financial investor steals investors' money.

- A prosecutor accepts a bribe to drop criminal charges.

- Two investors share inside information that allows them to redirect their stock purchases.

- A disgruntled employee destroys the computer records of a firm upon her resignation.

These acts are instances where the criminal law has been violated during the course of employment. Accordingly, members of the criminal justice system could be called on to address those misdeeds.

Certainly, some rule breaking during the course of employment does not rise to the level of criminal behavior, but it may violate civil laws. Consequently, some may define *white-collar crime as* **violations of civil law**. Consider cases of corporate wrongdoing against consumers. In those situations, it is rare that the criminal law would be used to respond to the offending corporation. More often, cases are brought into the civil justice system. When the *Exxon Valdez* ran aground in Prince William Sound, Alaska and caused untold damage to the environment, for example, the case was brought into the civil justice system. Eventually, it was learned that the cause of the crash could be attributed to the ship's overworked crew. To date, Exxon has paid $2 billion in cleanup efforts and another $1 billion in fines. Ongoing legal battles are focusing on whether Exxon should pay even more in damages.

Individuals have also defined *white-collar crime as* **violations of regulatory law**. Some workplace misdeeds might not violate criminal or civil laws but may violate a particular occupation's regulatory laws. Most occupations and businesses have standards, procedures, and regulations that are designed to administratively guide and direct workplace activities. The nursing home industry provides a good example. The government has developed a set of standards that nursing home administrators are expected to follow in providing care to nursing home residents. At different times during the year, government officials inspect nursing homes to see if they are abiding by the regulations. In most instances, some form of wrongdoing is uncovered. These instances of wrongdoing, however, are not violations of criminal law or civil law; rather, they are violations of regulatory law. Hence, some authors focus on white-collar crimes as violations of regulatory law.

Sometimes, behaviors performed as part of an occupational routine might be wrong but not necessarily illegal by criminal, civil, or regulatory definitions. As a result, some prefer to follow definitions of *white-collar crime* as **workplace deviance**. This is a broader way to define white-collar crime, and such an approach would include all of those workplace acts that violate the norms or standards of the workplace, regardless of whether they are formally defined as illegal or not. Violations of criminal, civil, and regulatory laws would be included, as would those violations that are set by the workplace itself. Beyond those formal violations of the law, consider the following situations as examples of workplace deviance:

- Professors cancel class simply because they don't feel like going to class.

- A worker takes a 30-minute break when she was only supposed to take a 15-minute break.

- A worker calls his boss and says he is too sick to come to work when in fact he is not actually sick (but he uses that "fake sick voice" as part of his ploy).

- A wedding photographer gets drunk at a client's wedding, takes horrible pictures, and hits on the groom.

- An author uses silly examples to try to get his point across.

In each of these cases, no laws have necessarily been broken; however, one could argue that workplace or occupational norms may have been violated.

Somewhat related, one can also define *white-collar crime* as **definitions socially constructed by businesses**. What this means is that a particular company or business might define behaviors that it believes to be improper. What is wrong in one company might not necessarily be wrong in another company. Some businesses might have formal dress codes while others might have casual Fridays. Some companies might tolerate workers taking small quantities of the goods it produces home each night, while other companies might define that behavior as inappropriate and criminal. The expectations for workplace behavior, then, are defined by the workplace. These expectations can change over time. Highlighting broader policy changes, one author team observed that "in some cases, legal definitions have changed, turning 'crime' into 'not crime,' officially legitimizing once-prohibited forms of profiteering" (Headworth & Hagan, 2016, p. 278).

Incidentally, some experts have suggested that expectations be defined in such a way as to accept at least minor forms of wrongdoing (see Mars, 1983, for a description of the rewards individuals perceive from workplace misconduct). The basis for this suggestion is that individuals are more satisfied with their jobs if they are able to break the rules of their job at least every now and then. As a simple example, where would you rather work: (1) in a workplace that lets you get away with longer breaks every now and then or (2) in a workplace where you are docked double pay for every minute you take over the allotted break?

In some cases, workplace behaviors might not be illegal or deviant, but they might actually create forms of harm for various individuals. As a result, some prefer to define *white-collar crime* as **social harm**. Those defining white-collar crime from this perspective are more concerned with the harm done by occupational activities than whether behavior is defined either formally or informally as illegal or deviant. According to one author, "by concentrating on what is defined as illegal or criminal, a more serious threat to society is left out" (Passas, 2005, p. 771). Galbraith (2005, p. 731) offers the following examples: "The common practices of tobacco companies, hog farmers, gun makers and merchants are legal. But this is only because of the political nature of the perpetrators; in a democracy free of their money and influence, they would be crimes." Additional examples of white-collar crimes that are examples of this social harm perspective have been noted by Passas (2005), who highlighted the following "crimes" that occur without lawbreaking occurring: cross-border malpractices, asymmetrical environmental regulations, corrupt practices, child labor in impoverished communities, and pharmaceutical practices such as those allowing testing of drugs in third world countries. Passas emphasized that lawbreaking does not occur when these actions are performed but argues the actions are, in fact, criminal.

Another way to define these behaviors is to consider *white-collar crimes* as **research definitions**. When researchers study and gather data about white-collar crime, they must operationalize or define white-collar crime in a way that allows them to reliably and validly measure the behavior. As an example, in 2005, the National White-Collar Crime Center conducted its second national survey on white-collar crime. The results of this survey will be discussed later. For now, the way that the researchers defined white-collar crime illustrates what is meant by research-generated white-collar crime definitions. The researchers defined white-collar crime as "illegal or unethical acts that violate fiduciary responsibility or public trust for personal or organizational gain" (Kane & Wall, 2006, p. 1). Using this definition as their foundation, the researchers were able to conduct a study that measured the characteristics of white-collar crime, its consequences, and contributing factors. Note that had they chosen a different definition, their results might have been different. The way that we define phenomena will influence the observations we make about those phenomena.

Another way to define these behaviors is to consider *white-collar crime* as *official* **government definitions**. Government agencies and employees of those agencies will have definitions of white-collar crime that may or may not parallel the way others define white-collar crime. The Federal Bureau of Investigation (FBI), for example, has used an offense-based perspective to define white-collar crime as part of its Uniform Crime Reporting Program. The FBI defines white-collar crime as

> those illegal acts which are characterized by deceit, concealment, or violation of trust and which are not dependent upon the application or threat of physical force or violence. Individuals and organizations commit these acts to obtain money, property, or services to avoid payment or loss of money or services; or to secure personal or business advantage. (U.S. Department of Justice, 1989, p. 3, as cited in Barnett, n.d.)

In following this definition, the FBI tends to take a broader definition of white-collar crime than many white-collar crime scholars and researchers do. *Identity theft* offers a case in point. The FBI includes identity theft as a white-collar crime type. Some academics, however, believe that such a classification is inappropriate. One research team conducted interviews with 59 convicted identity thieves and found that offenses and offenders did not meet the traditional characteristics of white-collar crimes or white-collar offenders. Many offenders were unemployed and working independently, meaning their offenses were not committed as part of a legitimate occupation or in the course of their occupation (Copes & Vieraitis, 2009).

Another way to define white-collar crime is to focus on *white-collar crime* as **violations of trust** that occur during the course of legitimate employment. To some authors, offenders use their positions of trust to promote the misconduct (Reiss & Biderman, 1980). Criminologist Susan Shapiro (1990) has argued for the need to view white-collar crime as abuses of trust, and she suggests that researchers should focus on the *act* rather than the *actor*. She wrote,

> Offenders clothed in very different wardrobes lie, steal, falsify, fabricate, exaggerate, omit, deceive, dissemble, shirk, embezzle, misappropriate, self-deal, and engage in corruption or incompliance by misusing their positions of trust. It turns out most of them are not upper class. (p. 358)

In effect, Shapiro was calling for a broader definition of white-collar crime that was not limited to the collars of the offenders' shirts.

Others have also called for broader conceptualizations that are not limited to wardrobes or occupational statuses. Following Clinard and Quinney's 1973 conceptualization, some have suggested that these behaviors classified as *white-collar crimes* should be classified as occupational crimes. One author defines occupational crimes as "violations that occur during the course of occupational activity and are related to employment" (Robin, 1974). Robin (1974) argued vehemently for the broader conceptualization of white-collar crime. He noted that various forms of lower-class workplace offenses "are more similar to white-collar crime methodologically than behaviorally," suggesting that many occupational offenders tend to use the same methods to commit their transgressions. He further stated that the failure of scholars to broadly conceive white-collar crime "results in underestimating the amount of crime, distorts relative frequencies of the typology of crimes, produces a biased profile of the personal and social characteristics of the violators, and thus affects our theory of criminality" (p. 261).

Criminologist Gary Green (1990) has been a strong advocate of focusing on occupational crime rather than a limited conceptualization of white-collar crime. He defined occupational crime as "any act punishable by law which is committed through opportunity created in the course of an occupation that is legal" (p. 13). Green described four varieties of occupational crime: (1) organizational occupational crimes, which include crimes by corporations; (2) state authority occupational crimes, which include crimes by governments; (3) professional occupational crimes, which include those crimes by individuals in upper-class jobs; and (4) individual occupational crimes, which include those crimes committed by individuals in lower-class jobs. The strength of his conceptualization is that it expands white-collar crime to consider all forms of misdeeds committed by employees and businesses during the course of employment.

Using each of the above definitions as a framework, white-collar crime can also be defined as *violations occurring in occupational systems*. This text uses such a framework to provide a broad systems perspective about white-collar crime. White-collar crime can therefore be defined as "any violation of criminal, civil, or regulatory laws—or deviant, harmful, or unethical actions—committed during the course of employment in various occupational systems." This definition allows us to consider numerous types of workplace misconduct and the interactions between these behaviors and broader systems involved in preventing and responding to white-collar crimes. As will be shown in the following paragraphs, the extent of these crimes is enormous.

EXTENT OF WHITE-COLLAR CRIME

Determining the extent of white-collar crime is no simple task. Two factors make it particularly difficult to accurately determine how often white-collar crimes occur. First, many white-collar crimes are not reported to formal response agencies. One study found that just one third of white-collar crime victims notify the authorities about their victimization (Kane & Wall, 2006). When individuals are victims of white-collar crimes, they may not report the victimization because of shame, concerns that reporting will be futile, or a general denial that the victimization was actually criminal. When businesses or companies are victims, they may refrain from reporting out of concern about the negative publicity that comes along with "being duped" by an employee. If victims are not willing to report their victimization, their victimization experiences will not be included in official statistics. The bottom line is that a lack of data has made it hard to determine the extent of white-collar crime (Simpson, 2013).

A second factor that makes it difficult to determine the extent of white-collar crime has to do with the conceptual ambiguity surrounding the concept (and discussed above). Depending on how one defines white-collar crime, one would find different estimates about the extent of white-collar crime. The federal government and other government agencies offer different definitions of white-collar crime than many scholars and researchers might use. The result is that white-collar crime researchers typically caution against relying on official statistics or **victimization surveys** to determine the extent of white-collar crime victimization. Despite this caution, the three main ways that we learn about the extent of white-collar crime are from official statistics provided by government agencies, victimization surveys, and research studies focusing on specific types of white-collar crime.

With regard to official statistics and white-collar crime, the FBI's Uniform Crime Reports (UCR) and National Incident Based Reporting System (NIBRS) provide at least a starting point from which we can begin to question how often certain forms of white-collar crime occur. These data reflect crimes known to the police. The UCRs include eight Part I (or index) offenses (homicide, robbery, rape, aggravated assault, motor vehicle theft, larceny, arson, and burglary) and 29 Part II offenses, which are typically defined as *less serious* crimes. With regard to white-collar crime, Part II offenses have been regarded as possible white-collar crimes. Figures 2.2a, 2.2b, and 2.2c show the trends in arrests for three Part II offenses that are often considered white-collar offenses. A few patterns are worth highlighting. For example, arrests for each offense type have been declining over the past decade, with arrests for fraud and forgery/counterfeiting dropping more and over a longer period of time. Also, compared to 1980 arrests, there were fewer fraud and forgery/counterfeiting arrests in 2018 but a higher number of embezzlement arrests.

A word of caution is needed in reviewing these estimates. Not all criminologists agree that these offenses are appropriate indicators of white-collar crimes. Many of these offenses may have occurred outside the scope of employment. Also, because the UCR program does not capture information about offender status, it is not possible to classify the crimes according to the occupational systems where the offenses occurred.

Limitations in the UCR program prompted the federal government to expand its efforts in reporting crime data through the NIBRS. NIBRS data provide more contextual information surrounding the crimes reported to the police. For example, this reporting system provides information about where the crime occurred, the victim-offender relationship, victim characteristics, and so on. While more contextual information is provided from NIBRS data, the same limitations that plague the UCR data with regard to the measurement of white-collar crime surface: (1) Not everyone would agree these are white-collar crimes, (2) the database was created for law enforcement and not for researchers, (3) many cases are reported to regulatory agencies rather than law enforcement, (4) some white-collar crime victims are unaware of their victimization, and (5) shame may keep some victims from reporting their victimization (Barnett, n.d.). Also, the NIBRS data are not as "user friendly" as UCR data at this point.

The phrase "official data" is often used to characterized data reported by government officials. Experts seem to agree that "official" data greatly underestimates the extent of white-collar crime (Simpson, 2019; Soltes, 2019). Organizations' internal data often show much higher numbers of violations, though those numbers only include offenses coming to the attention of the business (Soltes, 2019). Soltes cites examples where internal data show certain types of offenses occurring 64 times more often than they are reported in federal data. As Sally Simpson (2019) tells us, "getting reliable and valid rates of corporate law-breaking is still especially difficult—more difficult than it should be (p. 195).

Simpson and Yeager (2015) proposed a data series that would publish information about white-collar crimes handled by various federal agencies. The primary purpose of such a series would be to assist in policy development and research on the topic. The types of data included in the series should include information about criminal and civil offenses, offenders, and case outcomes from those agencies addressing the cases. After piloting their ideas through a grant from the National Institute of Justice, the authors recommended developing a working group that would be assigned the task of creating the processes needed for a white-collar crime database, developing a memorandum of understanding between those agencies currently holding the data on the offenses, and initiating an incremental approach to develop the database. Such an approach is needed because relying on official government data currently produces a limited view of white-collar crime. Said one author, "Reproducing FBI property crime rates from the 1990s to the present without noting the Savings and Loan looting, Enron era scams and the latest episode of barely contained looting is tantamount to propaganda" (Leighton, 2013, p. 45).

Victimization surveys offer an opportunity to overcome some of these problems. These surveys sample residents and estimate the extent of victimization from the survey findings. Unfortunately, national surveys focusing specifically on white-collar crime are rare. The 2010 National

FIGURE 2.2A, 2.2B, AND 2.2C ■ Arrest Trends for Three White-Collar Offenses, 1980–2018

A.

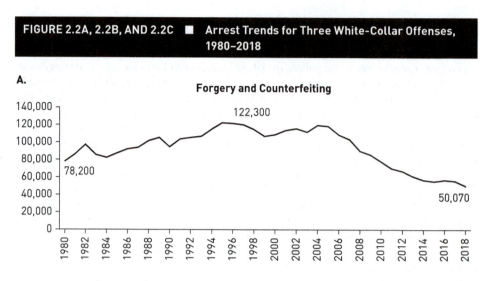

Forgery and Counterfeiting

B.

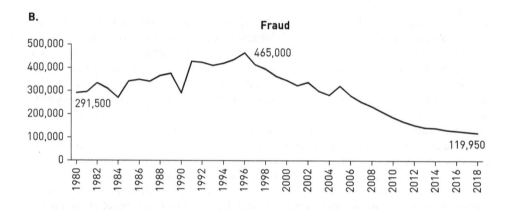

Fraud

C.

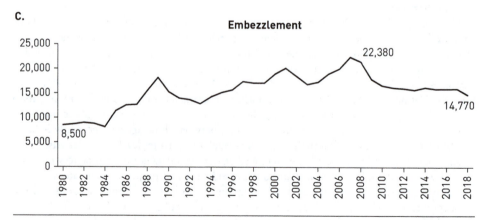

Embezzlement

Source: OJJDP Statistical Briefing Book. (2019, October). *Trends in the number of arrests by age group for embezzlement, fraud, and forgery.* Retrieved from https://www.ojjdp.gov/ojstatbb/crime/ucr_trend.asp?table_in=1

White-Collar Crime Center (NW3C) victimization survey is the most recent, and most comprehensive, white-collar crime victimization survey available. The results of this survey, a collection of phone interviews with a random sample of 2,503 adults in the United States, show that 24% of households and 17% of individuals reported being victims of white-collar crime in the prior year (Huff, Desilets, & Kane, 2010). Researchers have also used specific studies to gauge the extent of various forms of white-collar crime. One author, for example, cites a study by the Government Accountability Office that found fraud in "every single case" of the savings and loan institutions included in the study (Galbraith, 2005). Another study found that one in 30 employees (out of 2.1 million employ-

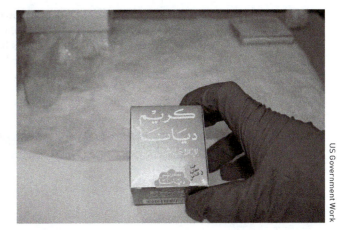

PHOTO 2.2 The FDA monitors dietary supplements in an effort to limit the distribution of unsafe or ineffective products. Here an FDA scientist is showing products seized after being illegally imported into the United States. Millions of victims report purchasing ineffective weight loss products.

ees) was caught stealing from his or her employer in 2007 ("Record Number of Shoplifters," 2008). A Federal Trade Commission (FTC) survey of 3,638 adults in the United States found that consumer fraud was rampant (Anderson, 2013). Based on the survey findings, Anderson (2013) estimates that "an estimated 10.8 percent of U.S. adults—25.6 million people—were victims of one or more of the frauds included in the 2011 FTC Consumer Fraud Survey" (p. ES-1). The most popular form of victimization that year was purchasing fraudulent weight loss products. It was estimated that 5 million individuals experienced this victimization. Anderson further estimated that nearly 38 million cases of consumer fraud occurred in 2011.

Figure 2.3 shows the extent of the types of fraud reported to the Federal Trade Commission (FTC) between 2001 and 2019. As shown in the figure, fraud reports increased nearly tenfold between 2001 and 2019 (from 325,519 to 3.2 million). Three possible explanations exist for this increase: (1) fraud occurred more, (2) fraud was reported more, or (3) fraud occurred more and was reported more. The third explanation is the most plausible.

Figure 2.4 shows the top ten types of fraud reported to the FTC in 2019. The most common reported complaints included imposter scams, telephone and mobile services complaints, and

FIGURE 2.3 ■ Reports of Fraud Made to FTC, 2001–2019

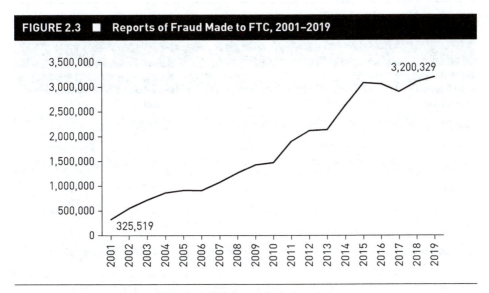

Source: Consumer Sentinel Network Data Book 2019, Federal Trade Commission

online shopping issues. Data from the FTC shows a relation between victim age and amount of money lost to fraud (see Table 2.2). Essentially, while younger people reported losing money more often in frauds, the median loss from fraud increases as individuals grow older. The data are easily located and reviewed on the FTC's website. In fact, the agency has added dashboards that allow consumers to explore a variety of patterns related to the complaints received. This chapter's White-Collar Crime in the News provides insight into how to access and use the information provided by the agency.

FIGURE 2.4   ■   Top Ten Types of Fraud Reported to FTC, 2019

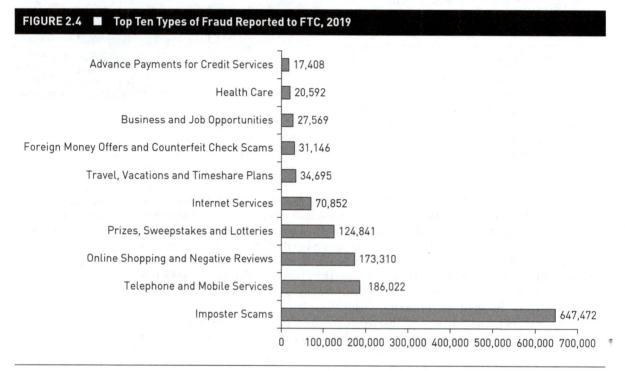

Source: Consumer Sentinel Network Data Book 2019, Federal Trade Commission

TABLE 2.2   ■   Reported Frauds and Losses by Age, 2019

Age Range	# of Reports	%	Total $ Lost	Median $ Loss
Under 20	23,862	3%	$14M	$
20-29	110,411	13%	$124M	$448
30-39	137,780	16%	$168M	$379
40-49	125,849	15%	$178M	$410
50-59	141,525	16%	$186M	$500
60-69	169,282	20%	$223M	$600
70-79	103,595	12%	$150M	$800
80 and Over	45,995	5%	$72M	$1,600

Percentages are based on the total number of 2019 fraud reports in which consumers provided their age: 858,299. Of the 1,697,943 total fraud reports in 2019, 51% included consumer age information.

Source: Consumer Sentinel Network Data Book 2019, Federal Trade Commission. https://www.ftc.gov/enforcement/data-visualizations

WHITE-COLLAR CRIME IN THE NEWS
FTC DASHBOARDS

The following is a press release from the Federal Trade Commission from April 15, 2020.

The Federal Trade Commission announced the launch of two new interactive dashboards detailing consumer reports about international fraud and scams.

One of the new interactive dashboards provides data on cross-border complaints submitted by consumers to econsumer.gov, a site created in 2001 by members of the International Consumer Protection and Enforcement Network (ICPEN) to gather and share consumer complaints about international scams. The dashboard is updated quarterly, and includes information on the top consumer complaints, total reported losses, the top locations for fraud, and the top locations for consumer victims.

In 2019, consumers reported losing a total of $151.3 million to international scams, based on the 40,432 reports they submitted to econsumer.gov. Complaints related to online shopping topped the list of consumer complaints, and included reports about misrepresented products, merchandise that didn't arrive, and refund issues. Other top complaint categories reported to econsumer.gov included government imposter scams, business imposter scams, travel and vacation fraud, and romance scams. Consumers from the United States, France, India, Australia, United Kingdom, and Canada filed the most complaints, while companies located in the United States, China, United Kingdom, India, Hong Kong, and Canada were the subjects of the largest number of consumer complaints.

The second set of dashboards details data on international reports submitted to the FTC's Consumer Sentinel Network. These dashboards present reports from econsumer.gov and other data contributors. The international reports dashboard includes data about complaints filed by foreign consumers against U.S.-based companies, reports submitted by U.S. consumers against foreign companies, and data by geographic region.

In 2019, consumer reports received by the Consumer Sentinel Network showed consumers lost a total of $276.5 million to foreign scams, based on the 91,560 reports against companies located outside the United States. Online shopping was the top complaint category about non-U.S. companies, followed by tech support scams, romance scams, advance fee loans/credit arrangers, and prizes/sweepstakes/lotteries. For non-U.S. companies, Canada was the subject of the largest number of consumer complaints, followed by China, India, United Kingdom, and Germany.

ICPEN is an international network of consumer protection authorities that aims to protect consumers' economic interests around the world by sharing information about cross-border issues and encouraging global cooperation among law enforcement agencies. The dashboard was announced as part of ICPEN's program of work under the current ICPEN Presidency, held by the Colombian Superintendency for Industry and Commerce.

Source: https://www.ftc.gov/news-events/press-releases/2020/04/ftc-icpen-launch-new-online-tools-sharing-data-about

---

While our risk of being victimized by white-collar crime increases as we grow older, it should not be assumed that younger people are not targeted or victimized by fraudulent behavior. The Fyre Festival fraud provides an example of a scheme that primarily targeted younger people. Billy McFarland, mastermind behind the Fyre Festival, raised $26 million from investors and concert-goers to hold the "Fyre Festival" in 2017 in the Bahamas (U.S. Department of Justice, 2018, October 11). McFarland charged concert goers thousands for what was supposed to be a once-in-a-lifetime experience. Most of the concert-goers were younger individuals who were attracted to loud music, crowds, and partying. When they arrived in the Bahamas, they got such an experience but not in the way they were hoping. McFarland was not able to actually organize the festival. He apparently had overestimated the amount of work that would be required to pull off the festival. Festival-goers were asked to sleep in makeshift tents, eat underwhelming meals, and spend their days hanging out without the entertainment they were promised. It may sound like was not that bad, but consider the following scene described by one of the attendees:

> The first thing we see is people running for tents and fighting over tents. . . . People spent $10,000 to go to this thing. How could they not have anything set up? This is not what I signed up for. (American Greed, 2019).

Some guests reportedly paid up to $250,000 per ticket (Noto, 2018).

CONSEQUENCES OF WHITE-COLLAR CRIME

Crime, by its very nature, has consequences for individuals and communities. White-collar crime, in particular, has a set of consequences that may be significantly different from the kinds of consequences that arise from street crimes. In particular, the consequences can be characterized as (1) individual economic losses, (2) societal economic losses, (3) emotional consequences, (4) physical harm, and (5) "positive" consequences.

Individual economic losses refers to the losses that individual victims or businesses experience due to white-collar crimes. One way that criminologists have captured these losses is to compare them to losses experienced by victims of conventional crimes. The insurance specialist Hiscox conducts periodic surveys on embezzlement patterns. The company's 2018 survey found that the average embezzlement loss was $357,650 (Hiscox, 2018).

By comparison, consider the following:

- The average street or highway robbery entails losses of $1,739.

- The average gas station robbery entails losses of $1,028.

- The average convenience store robbery entails losses of $961 (Federal Bureau of Investigation, 2018).

It is important to note that a small group of offenders can create large dollar losses. One study found that 27 white-collar offenders were responsible for a combined dollar loss of $2,494,309 (Crofts, 2003). Each offender stole an average of $95,935. Other studies have also found large dollar losses as a central feature of white-collar crimes (Wheeler, Weisburd, & Bode, 1988). In fact, Sutherland (1949) argued that white-collar crimes cost several times more than street crimes in terms of financial losses. While his estimate may be a little dated, the fact remains that a white-collar crime will likely cause larger dollar losses to victims than a street crime would. Consider, for example, a Medicare fraud scheme that stole more than $1 billion dollars from the U.S. government (Federal Bureau of Investigation, 2019). Two dozen offenders collectively stole between $17 and $22 million a week from Medicare in the scheme.

Societal economic losses refers to the total amount of losses incurred by society from white-collar crime. An effort by Mark Cohen (2016) to combine all types of white-collar crime costs uncovered in prior studies resulted in an estimate suggesting that white-collar crime losses exceed $1.6 trillion a year. That's trillion, not billion! These costs are potentially increased when considering the secondary societal economic costs such as business failures and recovery costs. In terms of business failures, one estimate suggests that one third to one half of business failures are attributed to employee theft (National White Collar Crime Center, 2009). With regard to recovery costs, taxpayers pay billions of dollars to support the efforts of the criminal, civil, and regulatory justice systems. As an illustration of how these costs can quickly add up, one white-collar criminal involved in a $7 million Ponzi scheme eventually lost everything and was unable to afford his own attorney. In this case, the federal public defender's office was assigned the task of representing the accused (Henning, 2010). Attorney costs in white-collar crime cases are believed to be particularly exorbitant.

Emotional consequences are also experienced by victims of white-collar crime and by all members of society exposed to this misconduct. These emotional consequences include stress from victimization, violation of trust, and damage to public morale. With regard to stress, any experience of victimization is stressful, but the experience of white-collar crime victimization is believed to be particularly stressful. Much of the stress stems from the violation of trust that comes along with white-collar crimes. Indeed, these consequences can include serious negative psychological repercussions for victims (Croall, 2016).

According to Sutherland (1941), the violation of trust can be defined as the "most general" characteristic of white-collar crime. Victims of a street robbery didn't trust the stranger who robbed them in the first place. Victims of a white-collar crime, in addition to the other losses incurred from the victimization, have their trust violated by the offender. There is reason to believe that the level of trust may be tied to the specific level of trust given to different types of white-collar offenders (e.g., we trust doctors and pharmacists at a certain level but auto mechanics on another level).

Researchers have used various strategies to consider how these trust violations manifest in white-collar crimes. Spalek (2001) interviewed 25 individuals who lost some of their pension funds to a fraudulent scheme by Robert Maxwell. She focused on the degree to which victimization bred distrust. She found that many of the victims already distrusted their offender before the victimization came to light. The victims said that they felt forced or coerced into trusting the offender as part of his investment scheme. In terms of trust, they placed their trust in outside agencies to protect them from the offender. The following comments from Spalek's (2001) participants highlight this pattern:

- I've always mistrusted Maxwell. But I felt that because pensioners were, to a large extent, the province of the state . . . that there was very little Maxwell could do to make off with the money.

- I suppose at the time I actually thought that the law would actually safeguard against anything that was mine so I wasn't too worried about it, although I thought that Maxwell would do his best to get his hands on the money.

With regard to public alienation, violations of trust potentially do damage to the economy and social relationships. According to Frankel (2006), "with few exceptions, trust is essential to economic prosperity" (p. 49). If individuals do not trust financial institutions, they are not likely to invest their funds in the economy. Sutherland (1941) recognized this relationship between trust, the economy, and social relationships. He wrote,

The financial loss from white-collar crime, great as it is, is less important than the damage to social relations. White-collar crime violates trust and therefore creates distrust; this lowers social morale and produces disorganization. Many white-collar crimes attack the fundamental principles of the American institutions. Ordinary crimes, on the other hand, produce little effect on social institutions or social organization. (p. 13)

Building on Sutherland's ideas, Moore and Mills (1990) described the following consequences of white-collar crime:

- Diminished faith in a free economy and in business leaders

- Erosion of public morality

- Loss of confidence in political institutions, processes, and leaders (p. 414)

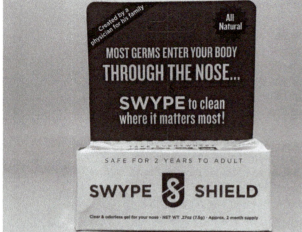

PHOTO 2.3 The FDA issued a warning about using the nasal gel Swype Shield to protect against COVID-19. The warning said that the "product is promoted with unapproved claims to prevent, treat, mitigate, or cure COVID-19." The FDA included a link to a detailed letter it had sent Swype Shield about the agency's concerns with the product.

Criminologist Michael Lynch (2013) provided an impassioned plea for recognizing these serious consequences. He wrote the following:

> Societies do not collapse because of the behavior of street offenders, but rather in many cases because the power elite and the capitalist system of exploitation in which they are enmeshed, lead us in the wrong direction. The financial crimes of the power elite and the inability of other segments of the power elite to control those crimes presents a serious example of how it becomes possible for the power elite to undermine the very basis of social organization, and, indeed, even undermine the social organization on which their system depends. (p. 58)

Physical harm may also result from white-collar crime victimization. In the words of one author, "white-collar crime can easily lead to violent results" (Verstein, 2014, n.p.). Sometimes, physical harm may be a direct result of the white-collar offense. For example, cases of physical or sexual patient abuse will result in physical harm for victims. Or, using unsafe products could cause physical injuries. Other times, experiencing financial harm can lead to physical problems. The loss of one's entire retirement savings, for example, has been found to contribute to health problems for white-collar crime victims (Payne, 2005).

Death or serious physical injury is also a possible consequence of white-collar crimes. In one case, for instance, seven people died after a doctor "used lemon juice instead of antiseptic on patients' operation wounds" (Ninemsn Staff, 2010). In another case, Reinaldo Silvestre was running a medical clinic in Miami Beach when it was discovered that he was practicing without a license, using animal tranquilizers as sedatives for humans, and performing botched surgeries. In a widely publicized case, a male body builder was given female C-cup breast implants—he had requested pectoral implants to make his chest look bigger ("Fugitive Phony Doctor Nabbed," 2004).

It is possible to more generally highlight the physical harm stemming from white-collar crime. Consider the following estimates:

- In 2019, 13.4 million individuals in the United States were injured by consumer products (National Safety Council, 2020).

- Across the world, "occupational exposure to asbestos causes an estimated 107,000 deaths each year" (Takahashi, Landrigan, & Ramazzini, 2016).

- Causing approximately 440,000 nationwide deaths each year, medical errors were cited as the third most common type of death in the United States in 2016 (Stahel, VanderHeiden, & Kim, 2017).

- Estimates from the World Health Organization suggest that ambient air pollution was a contributing factors in 7.6% of all deaths across the world in 2016 (World Health Organization, n.d.).

- Consumer advocate Ralph Nader (2013) cites estimates suggesting that 60,000 Americans die each year from unsafe working conditions.

In line with the objective approach presented in Chapter 1, it is important to stress that not all consequences of white-collar crime are necessarily bad. Sociologist Emile Durkheim has highlighted four functions of crime that illustrate how crime in some ways has positive influences on individuals and communities (see Martin et al., 2009). These four functions can also be applied to white-collar crime. They include warning light syndrome, boundary maintenance, social change, and community integration.

The **warning light syndrome** refers to the fact that outbreaks of white-collar crime could potentially send a message to individuals, businesses, or communities that something is wrong in a particular workplace system. If an outbreak of employee theft occurs in a hospital, for example, then the administrators would be warned that they need to address those aspects of the occupational routines that allowed the misconduct to occur.

In terms of **boundary maintenance**, it is plausible to suggest that individuals learn the rules of the workplace when some individuals are caught breaking those rules. In effect, they learn the boundaries of appropriate and acceptable behaviors by seeing some individuals step over those boundaries. Some even recommend that white-collar offenders, when caught, be arrested at times when the vast majority of workers would be able to see the arrests (Payne & Gray, 2001). What this is suggesting is a strategy for promoting boundary maintenance.

With regard to **social change**, our society has changed significantly because of white-collar misdeeds. Some people have talked about how survivors of violent crime actually become stronger because of their experience with violence. Following this same line of thinking, those who survive white-collar crime victimization might actually become stronger. As well, when cultures and societies survive corporate victimization, they too may actually grow stronger.

Community integration is a fourth function of white-collar crime. In particular, groups of individuals who otherwise would not have become acquainted with one another may come together in their response to white-collar crime. When there is a crime outbreak in a neighborhood, those neighbors come together to share their experiences and make their neighborhood stronger (Martin et al., 2009). A crime outbreak in a business could have the same result. Coworkers who never talked with one another might suddenly become lunch buddies simply because they want to get together to talk about the crimes that occurred in their workplace. As well, at the societal level, new groups have been formed to prevent and respond to white-collar crime.

Consider the NW3C. Formed in 1992, the center includes professionals, academics, and researchers interested in addressing white-collar crime on different levels. The NW3C's mission is "to provide training, investigative support, and research to agencies and entities involved in the prevention, investigation, and prosecution of economic and high tech crime" (National White Collar Crime Center, 2009). Without the problem of white-collar crime, this center would never have been created and its members would never have been brought together (or integrated as a community).

Other possible positive consequences of white-collar crime can be cited. For example, some criminologists have noted that occasional forms of deviance might be enjoyable or pleasurable to commit. The 2010 Conan O'Brien–Jay Leno debacle comes to mind. It was announced in January 2010 that O'Brien was to be replaced by Leno after he had been promised a long-term contract to host *The Tonight Show*. In the last several episodes of his National Broadcasting Company (NBC) show, O'Brien spent much of his show trashing his bosses at NBC. He even had skits suggesting that he was blowing NBC's money on pointless props for his show. The studio and home audiences raved about these skits. Who wouldn't want to go on national television every now and then and blow their company's money while trashing their bosses? (For the record, the thought never entered my mind.) In a similar way, some cases of workplace deviance might have the positive benefit of making the worker a more satisfied worker (see Mars, 1983). Authors have talked about "the joy of violence" (Kerbs & Jolley, 2007). In some ways, there might also be "the joy of white-collar deviance."

For some students, the numerous careers available to respond to white-collar crime might also be seen as a positive. Most large businesses have loss prevention and security specialists who deal with workplace misconduct. Whenever I teach my criminal justice classes, I always ask my students if they would make crime go away if they could. Seldom do any students indicate that they would make crime disappear. In their minds, if they made crime disappear, they'd have to change their majors! So, in some ways, white-collar crime helps keep some criminal justice officials employed. A few of these careers can be particularly lucrative—one defense attorney was paid $50,000 simply for providing counsel to a white-collar worker who had to testify in a grand jury proceeding (Nelson, 2010).

Still another function of white-collar crime is that it can be a form of entertainment. Several movies, novels, and television shows revolve around the concept. But entertainment by itself may have little value if viewers aren't learning from what they are watching or reading. To show how students can both be entertained by white-collar crime shows, and learn at the same time, each of the remaining chapters includes a feature called "Streaming White-Collar Crime" that describes a series or dealing with white-collar crime.

STREAMING WHITE-COLLAR CRIME *Dirty Money*

Plot	What You Can Learn	Discussion Questions
A Netflix documentary directed by critically acclaimed filmmakers, each episode addresses specific corporate behaviors profiting the powerful and harming the powerless. Episodes focus on alleged fraudulent activities at Wells Fargo, exposure to harmful chemicals, the fraudulent tactics of payday lenders, the harmful practices of the pharmaceutical giant Valeant, and more. People with first-hand experience provide personal insight into each topic, and experts provide empirical and scientific insight.	Powerful companies and individuals are able to use their power to become more powerful. Individuals experience long-term harm from the harmful behaviors of corporations and businesses. The international nature of these behaviors presents specific dilemmas for victims and justice officials.	Can you identify other examples when a company was able to use its power to become more powerful? What is it about power that makes companies want more power? How might you have been harmed by similar offenses?

Of course, this brief overview of the "functions of white-collar crime" should not be interpreted as an endorsement of white-collar criminal behavior. In fact, the seriousness of many white-collar crimes means that the offenses cannot be taken lightly. The question that arises is whether members of the public view the offenses seriously.

PUBLIC ATTITUDES TOWARD WHITE-COLLAR CRIME

A large body of criminological research has focused on public attitudes about crime and different crime policies. Unfortunately, of the hundreds of criminological studies focusing on attitudes about crime, only a handful have focused on what the public thinks about white-collar crime.

Yet, research on white-collar crime attitudes is important for empirical, cultural, and policy-driven reasons (Piquero, Carmichael, & Piquero, 2008). In terms of empirical reasons, because so few studies have considered what the public thinks about white-collar crime, research on this topic will shed some light on how members of the public actually perceive this offense type. As well, such research will provide interesting and important insight into a particular culture or subculture. Perhaps most important, such research provides policy makers information they can use to implement prevention, response, and sentencing strategies.

In one of the first studies on public attitudes toward white-collar crime, Cullen and his colleagues (Cullen, Clark, Mathers, & Cullen, 1983) surveyed a sample of 240 adults and assessed various perceptions of this behavior. The researchers found that the sample (1) supported criminal sanctions for white-collar offenders, (2) viewed white-collar crimes as having greater moral and economic costs than street crimes, and (3) did not define the offenses as violent. In a separate study, Cullen, Link, and Polanzi (1982) found that perceptions of the seriousness of white-collar crime increased more than any other offense type in the 1970s and that physically harmful offenses were viewed as the most serious forms of white-collar crime (see Cullen et al., 1982).

Other studies have shown similar results. A study of 268 students found that perceptions of the seriousness of white-collar crime have increased over time and that these perceptions were tied to wrongfulness and harmfulness (Rosenmerkel, 2001). The NW3C national victimization survey also included items assessing perceptions of seriousness. The researchers found that the sample of 1,605 adults viewed (1) white-collar crime as serious as conventional crime, (2) physically harmful white-collar offenses as more serious than other white-collar crimes, (3) organizational offenses as more serious than individual offenses, and (4) offenses by higher-status offenders as more serious than offenses by lower-status offenders (Kane & Wall, 2006).

Subsequent research builds on these findings. A telephone survey of 402 residents of the United States focused on perceptions about white-collar crime and the punishment of white-collar offenders (Holtfreter, Van Slyke, Bratton, & Gertz, 2008). The authors found that one third of the respondents said that white-collar offenders should be punished more severely than street criminals. They also found that two thirds of the respondents believed that the government should "devote equal or more resources towards white-collar crime control" (Holtfreter, Van Slyke, Bratton, & Gertz, 2008, p. 56).

Around the same time, telephone interviews with 1,169 respondents found that the majority of respondents defined white-collar crime equally serious as, if not more serious than, street crime (Piquero, Carmichael et al., 2008). They also found that the presence of a college education impacted perceptions of seriousness. Those with a college education were more likely to define street crime and white-collar crime as equally serious. Another study using the same data set found that respondents believed that street criminals were more likely than other white-collar offenders to be caught and to receive stiffer sentences (Schoepfer, Carmichael, & Piquero, 2007). Respondents also believed that robbery and fraud should be treated similarly. Another way to suggest this is that the respondents believed that robbers and occupational offenders committing fraud should be handled the same way. A more recent study found that respondents perceived Ponzi schemes and embezzlement as more serious than street crimes, such as burglary and prostitution (Dodge, Bosick, & Van Antwerp, 2013). Describing these findings, the authors suggested that the "general public might be willing to support devoting greater resources to fighting white-collar crime" (Dodge, Bosick, & Van Antwerp, 2013, p. 412).

A more recent study on public opinion about white-collar crime found that survey respondents (n=408) have misconceptions about white-collar crime (Michel, Cochran, & Heide, 2016). The study found that less than 10% of respondents were actually informed or very informed about white-collar crime, though the respondents thought they knew more than they actually knew about it. According to the research team, the respondents tended to be "superficially informed" about white-collar crime subject matter. Based on objective measures assessing knowledge about white-collar crime, 75% of the sample was not well informed about the topic, while subjective measures suggested that just 12.5% of the sample was not well informed. A study using the same

PHOTO 2.4 After his dispute with NBC when the coveted 11:30 time slot was taken away from him, Conan O'Brien mocked his employer, joking about ways he could waste the company's money.

sample explored the respondents' perceptions of white-collar crime in comparison to violent street crime and found that less punitive sanctions were recommended for white-collar crimes, leading the author to conclude that "violent street offenses still seem to elicit a more pronounced societal response" (Michel, 2016, p. 137).

Making sense of the public's unwillingness to incarcerate white-collar offenders, Cullen and his coauthors (Cullen, Chouhy, & Jonson, 2020) note that such findings might actually stem from methodological issues related to how punitiveness is measured. They note that a simple survey item fails to capture the wide range of factors that might actually shape punishment attitudes. When more details about white-collar crime are added to survey items, it is plausible that attitudes about incarceration will shift. Here is how they described this likelihood:

> The Cullen et al. (1985, p. 21) survey contained this item: "Fixing prices of a consumer product like gasoline." Only 35.6% favored a prison term. But what if the price-fixing item had been described in this way? "For a three-year-period, executives from three major oil companies met secretly once a month to make sure that gasoline prices were 50 cents higher per gallon. This price-fixing scheme earned each of their companies $500 million in illegal profits. What sentence do you believe that the executives who engaged in this conspiracy should receive?" Because the degree of culpability would be clear and the economic impact revealed as enormous, it is likely that a high percentage of the public would endorse a prison term. (Cullen et al., 2020, p. 220)

It is believed that the media play a strong role in shaping our attitudes about white-collar crime. More so than in the past, social media is likely beginning to play an important role in generating understanding about white-collar offending and all types of crime for that matter. White-collar crime scholar Ellen Podgor has discussed how some of the past "highlights" from white-collar crime research and incidents might have been tweeted about if Twitter had existed several decades earlier. Table 2.3 provides a synopsis of Podgor's "tweets."

CHARACTERISTICS OF WHITE-COLLAR OFFENDERS

Because white-collar offenses are viewed as equally serious as street crimes, there may be a tendency among some to view white-collar criminals as similar to street criminals (Payne, 2003b). Such an assumption, however, is misguided and represents an inaccurate portrait of "the white-collar criminal." As well, focusing narrowly on white-collar offenders may result in individuals failing to recognize the interactions between the offenders' background characteristics and their offensive behaviors (Wheeler et al., 1988).

Criminologists have devoted significant attention to describing the characteristics of various types of white-collar offenders. Comparing records of street offenders and white-collar offenders, Benson and Moore (1992) concluded: "Those who commit even run-of-the-mill garden variety white-collar offenses can, as a group, be clearly distinguished from those who commit ordinary street offenses" (p. 252). In one of the most comprehensive white-collar crime studies, Wheeler and his colleagues (1988) found that white-collar offenders were more likely than

TABLE 2.3 ■ Tweeting About Significant White-Collar Crimes Over Time

Incident	What Happened	Podgor's Tweet
Sutherland's definition	In the 1940s, critics complained that the definition was too sociological.	"Focus on the offense—not the offender" (p. 542).
New York Central and Hudson River Railroad Company v. U.S.	Supreme Court case from 1909 that found that corporations could be held criminally liable for misdeeds.	Defense attorneys might tweet, "At last (sigh) paying clients" (p. 538).
Bernie Madoff's Ponzi Scheme	Bernie Madoff plead guilty in 2009 to orchestrating the largest and most brazen Ponzi scheme in U.S. history, stealing billions of dollars.	"Bernie Madoff did what!!!" (p. 548)
Lengthy prison sentences given to prominent offenders	Following the development of sentencing guidelines, in 2005 WorldCom CEO Bernard Ebbers was sentenced to 25 years in prison, and Enron CEO Jeffrey Skilling was sentenced to 24 years following their convictions.	"Ebbers to Skilling—must be tough being runner up" (p. 556).
Martha Stewart's case	Martha wore a poncho during her incarceration and served the end of her sentence on electronic monitoring with house arrest in 2005.	"Nice Poncho and Bracelet, Martha" (p. 554).

Source: Adapted from Podgor, E. (2011). 100 years of white-collar crime in Twitter. *The Review of Litigation*, *30*(3), 535–58.

conventional offenders to (1) have a college education, (2) be white males, (3) be older, (4) have a job, (5) commit fewer offenses, and (6) start their criminal careers later in life. Focusing on the interactions between offender characteristics and offense characteristics, the same research demonstrated that white-collar crime was more likely than street crime to involve the following:

- National or international scope
- Involve a large number of victims
- Have organizations as victims
- Follow demonstrated patterns
- Be committed for more than a year
- Be committed in groups

Pulling together prior research on the characteristics of white-collar offenders, Klenowski and Dodson (2016) point out the white-collar offenders tend to be middle-aged; white; late entrants to the criminal lifestyle; from middle-class backgrounds; college educated (some); married; and connected to their families, religious groups, and communities. These are the predominant characteristics; not all white-collar offenders are married, and females engage in the behavior as well. In addition, evidence points to the possibility that more minorities are becoming involved in white-collar crime (Benson & Chio, 2020).

More recent research shows race differences across white-collar crime types. Focusing on the same offenses and locations used in the earlier Wheeler study, Benson and Chio (2020) examined convictions in 2015 and found that white people made up more than half of convicted offenders for bank embezzlement, lending and credit fraud, mail/wire fraud, and SEC crimes. Conversely, they made up less than half of those convicted for antitrust, bribery, and false claims offenses. Asians made up the majority of antitrust offenders (because of the government's decision to focus on a large case involving a Japanese auto manufacturer), and Black Americans and Hispanics appeared to be overrepresented in bribery and false claims cases. Though more white people are convicted of white-collar crimes than persons of color are, more persons of color were convicted of white-collar offenses in 2015 than in 1988. Describing these racial patterns, Benson and Chio concluded, "Since the 1970s, [white-collar crime] has somehow been democratized and is now available to a broader mass of people from different racial and ethnic backgrounds" (p. 102). The authors also found that offenses tended to be committed by men, except for bank embezzlement (of which 64% of the offenders were women). In addition, the authors found a higher percentage of women convicted of bribery and securities violations in 2015 in comparison to the earlier study. Specifically, the authors found that female offenders "comprise 17.9 and 9.2% of the offenders (respectively) of offenders in 2015 versus the 1970s, where they made up less than 5% of bribery cases and less than 3% of securities offenses" (p. 102).

Recognizing the differences between white-collar crime and white-collar offenders and between street crimes and street offenders is significant for theoretical and policy reasons. In terms of theory, as will be demonstrated later in this text, if one of the criminological theories can explain both types of crimes, then that theory would be seen as having strong explanatory power. In terms of policy, it is important to recognize that different criminal justice strategies may be needed for the two types of offenses and that street offenders and white-collar offenders may respond differently to the criminal justice process.

Consider efforts to prevent crime. Strategies for preventing street crimes might focus on community building and poverty reduction; preventing white-collar crime is much "more complex" (Johnstone, 1999, p. 116). The impact of convictions and incarceration is also different between street offenders and white-collar offenders (Payne, 2003b). While such events may actually allow street offenders to gain "peer group status," the white-collar offender would not experience the same increase in status as the result of a conviction (Johnstone, 1999; Payne, 2003b). At the most basic level, recognizing the differences between street offenders and white-collar offenders helps to promote more useful prevention and intervention strategies. On a more complex level, recognizing these differences fosters a more objective and accurate understanding of the dynamics, causes, and consequences of the two types of behavior.

Summary

- Sutherland (1949) defined white-collar crime as "crime committed by a person of respectability and high social status in the course of his occupation" (p. 9).

- Criticism of the concept centered on (1) conceptual ambiguity, (2) empirical ambiguity, (3) methodological ambiguity, (4) legal ambiguity, and (5) policy ambiguity.

- Corporate crime and occupational crime are viewed as "the two principal or 'pure' forms of white-collar crime" (Friedrichs, 2002, p. 245).

- Criminologists and social scientists offer various ways to define white-collar crime. These variations tend to overlap with one another and include the following: (1) white-collar crime as moral or ethical violations, (2) white-collar crime as social harm, (3) white-collar crime as violations of criminal law, (4) white-collar crime as violations of civil law, (5) white-collar crime as violations of regulatory laws, (6) white-collar crime as workplace deviance, (7) white-collar crime as definitions socially constructed by businesses, (8) white-collar crime as research definitions, (9) white-collar crime as official government definitions, (10) white-collar crime as violations of trust, (11) white-collar crime as occupational crimes, and (12) white-collar crime as violations occurring in occupational systems.

- Determining the extent of white-collar crime is no simple task. Two factors make it particularly difficult to accurately determine how often white-collar crimes occur: unreported crimes and conceptual ambiguity.

- With regard to official statistics and white-collar crime, the FBI's UCR and NIBRS provide at least a starting point from which we can begin to question how often certain forms of white-collar crime occur.

- The consequences of white-collar crime can be characterized as (1) individual economic losses, (2) societal economic losses, (3) emotional consequences, (4) physical harm, and (5) "positive" consequences.

- Research on white-collar crime attitudes, however, is important for empirical, cultural, and policy-driven reasons (Piquero, Carmichael et al., 2008).

- Because white-collar offenses are viewed as equally serious as street crimes, there may be a tendency among some to view white-collar criminals as similar to street criminals (Payne, 2003b). Such an assumption is misguided and represents an inaccurate portrait of "the white-collar criminal."

- Wheeler and his colleagues (1988) found that white-collar offenders were more likely than conventional offenders to (1) have a college education, (2) be white males, (3) be older, (4) have a job, (5) commit fewer offenses, and (6) start their criminal careers later in life.

Key Terms

Discussion Questions

1. Review the four white-collar crimes described in the list at the beginning of this chapter. Answer the following questions for each offense description:

    a. Is it a white-collar crime?

    b. How often do these crimes occur?

    c. What would the consequences of this crime be?

    d. How serious do you think this crime is?

    e. Who is the offender in each case?

    f. How does that offender differ from street offenders?

2. Why does it matter how we define white-collar crime?

3. How serious is white-collar crime in comparison to street crime?

4. Find three news reports about white-collar offenses, and identify three negative consequences and three positive outcomes from the offenses.

5. How is the Fyre Festival case a type of white-collar crime?

CRIME IN SALES-RELATED OCCUPATIONS

A Systems Perspective

Baby's Burgers and Shakes is a well-known restaurant in State College, Pennsylvania, frequented by college students, their families, and faculty and staff working at Penn State University. Unfortunately, like many other businesses, the restaurant fell victim to employee theft. The investigation revealed that a manager had stolen thousands from the small business. In fact, the owner told a reporter that their losses were so significant that they were about one month away from closing the business when they realized why they were losing so much money (Pallotto, 2019). The manager eventually plead guilty and was sentenced to house arrest and probation. The owner wrote the following in his victim impact statement given to the judge:

> Tassie's deception decision not only greatly impacted our finances over these many years, it also impacted the lives of the many loyal Baby's employees. We obviously have been unable to increase the income of the wait staff, cooks, shift supervisors or assistant managers. Unfortunately under Tassie's leadership we never realized a net profit even while the gross sales rose to nearly one million dollars per year. Her decision to run us into the red each month seriously limited our ability to offer competitive wages to our present employees, or hire new ones at the competitive market rate. During her tenure she used every opportunity to manipulate our efforts to find out why we were falling farther and farther behind. (Center County Gazette, 2019).

Baby's Burgers is one of many businesses existing to serve customers. It's not alone in its efforts, nor is it alone in experiencing victimization in one fashion or another. In fact, as will be shown in this chapter, businesses (and their employees), can either be victims of employee theft, or they can victimize their employees or consumers. Consider the following excerpts quoted verbatim from government press releases and news articles:

> The defendant used violence and other coercive means to compel the victim to work for more than 100 hours a week for no pay at a restaurant managed by the defendant in Conway, South Carolina. The defendant subjected the victim to physical and emotional abuse whenever the victim made a mistake or failed to work fast enough. The defendant beat the victim with a belt, fists, and pots and pans. On one occasion, he dipped metal tongs into hot grease and burned the victim's neck. (U.S. Department of Justice, 2019, November 6)

> A Fred Meyer loss prevention manager, who stole nearly $230,000 from self-checkout machines at one of the chain's Northeast Portland stores, was sentenced last week to four years in prison. . . . Video taken from a camera positioned above the checkout machines shows [the loss prevention manager] wearing a baseball cap. She uses a key to open a door to the machine, then can be seen using a clipboard to partially conceal cash that she removes and slips into the bottom of a cart next to her. (Green, 2019)

> A now fired employee of Florida medical marijuana giant Trulieve was arrested when it was discovered she stole pot from the company's Midway processing facility and was selling it illegally. (Etters, 2020)

> A contractor convicted of scamming 19 New Jersey homeowners following Superstorm Sandy has been sentenced to three years in state prison, authorities announced. (Auciello, 2020)

> Alpharetta police have charged a hotel worker they say stole a guest's heirloom. Now, police are warning others to protect their valuables when they stay in a hotel. (Petchenik, 2020)

As with all white-collar crimes, these offenses have four things in common: (1) They occurred during the course of the offender's work; (2) the offender was engaged in the role of a worker; (3) the offenses occurred in a workplace setting; and (4) on one level or another, each of these offenses involved occupations where employees were selling goods or services. Hundreds of different types of sales-oriented occupations exist. In this chapter, I will introduce students to the nature of crime in these sales-oriented occupations. I will focus on the following crimes and systems: employee theft in the retail system, crime in the entertainment services systems, fraud in the sales and service systems, and crime in the insurance system.

These systems were selected because they capture the kinds of occupational systems of which students likely already have some awareness and a degree of interest. Some of these areas are possibly fields where students have already worked, others are fields they may one day work in, and others are service occupations that students have encountered or will encounter in the future. It is important to stress that other sales-oriented occupations, while not covered here, are not immune from crime.

EMPLOYEE THEFT IN THE RETAIL SYSTEM

The **retail system** is the setting where consumers purchase various types of products. As shown in recent times, the success of our economic system is tied to the success of the retail system.

When individuals buy more in the retail system, our economic system is stronger. While consumers drive the success of the retail system, employees steer the direction of the retail system. The key to success for retail stores lies in having employees able to perform assigned tasks. One problem that retail outlets face is employee theft, a problem that has been called "a poorly defined concept" (Kennedy, 2016, p. 411).

Experts use the concept of *shrinkage* to refer to the theft of goods in the retail industry. Estimates from the 2020 National Retail Security Survey indicated that $61.7 billion was lost to theft in 2019. While the 2020 survey did not provide data on how much of the theft was by employees, a prior estimate suggested that just over one third of retail theft was attributed to employee/internal theft (K. G. Allen, 2015). Another estimate suggests that employee theft costs businesses more than $50 billion a year, with these thefts occurring for two years before being detected and small businesses being particularly at risk (Vaitlin, 2019).

Typically, when addressing employee theft, focus is given to the financial losses, but there can also be emotional consequences. A rather innovative study exploring the emotional consequences of employee theft was conducted by Kennedy and Benson (2016). Interviewing 22 business owners, the researchers found that the victims of employee theft experienced a wide range of emotional consequences centering around feelings of trust violations. The researchers noted that employee theft produces both financial and emotional losses as both a property and personal offense and that a strong connection between the offender and victim "exacerbate the emotional damage caused by the theft" (p. 269). The financial and personal losses from employee theft might explain why a third of business bankruptcies are attributed to employee theft (Vaitlin, 2019).

Theft is believed to increase the amount Americans spend shopping by $403 per household (Fisher, 2015). According to the National Federation of Independent Businesses, "An employee is 15 times more likely than a non-employee to steal from an employer" (J. Anderson, 2015). Employee theft did increase, though, at the end of the 2000s. In line with the idea that changes in one system lead to changes in other systems, some have attributed this increase to the economic changes, such that changes in the economic system resulted in changes in the extent of employee theft in retail settings ("Record Number of Shoplifters," 2008; Rosenbaum, 2009). Explaining this increase in employee theft, loss prevention expert Richard Hollinger has suggested that more workers being alone in stores (because so many workers have been fired or laid off) means that workers will have more opportunities to steal (Goodchild, 2008).

It is difficult to determine with any degree of precision how often employees steal in retail settings. Surveys in these settings would probably underestimate the extent of employee theft (Oliphant & Oliphant, 2001). One study found that 1 in 30 employees (out of 2.1 million) was caught stealing from an employer in 2008 ("Record Number of Shoplifters," 2008). A survey of 92 college students found that 92% reported committing "time theft" (taking longer breaks than allowed, not working when they are supposed to, etc.; Ruankaew, 2019). One third of the students reported stealing property at work, and one fourth engaged in pilferage (repeated theft of small items of limited value such as Post-it notes, staples, etc.). Regardless of the number of employees who steal and the fact that most employees in retail settings do not steal, Daniel Butler, the former vice president of the National Retail Federation, notes, "a habitual internal thief can cost a lot of dollars" (Pratt, 2001, p. 37).

Several different varieties of employee theft in retail settings occur. The following are some examples:

- **Overcharging:** Employees charge customers more than they should have.

- **Shortchanging:** Employees do not give customers all of their change and pocket the difference.

- **Coupon stuffing:** Employees steal coupons and use them later.

- **Credits for nonexistent returns:** Employees give credit for returns to collaborators.

- **Theft of production supplies and raw materials:** Employees steal items used to produce goods in retail settings.

- **Embezzlement:** Employees steal money from an account to which they have access.

- **Overordering supplies:** Employees order more supplies than are needed and keep the supplies that were not needed.

- **Theft of credit card information:** Employees steal customers' credit card information.

- **Theft of goods:** Employees steal the items the retail setting is trying to sell.

- **Theft of money from the cash register:** Employees take money out of the register.

- **Sweetheart deals:** Employees give friends and family members unauthorized discounts (Albright, 2007; Belser, 2008; Mishra & Prasad, 2006).

Explaining why these offenses occur is no simple task. Some have attributed certain types of employee theft to organized crime on the notion that organized crime families have conspired with employees to develop widespread and lucrative employee theft schemes (Albright, 2007). Others have focused on individual motivations among employees and have highlighted the employees' perceived needs, drug problems, and sense of entitlement as causes of employee theft (Leap, 2007). Still others contend that some instances of employee theft (such as stealing from the cash register) are not planned events but impulsive ones that offenders commit when the opportunity presents itself (Anderson, 2007). Some have suggested that retail settings with more turnover will have more employee theft (Belser, 2008). Still others have noted that organizational culture contributes to employee theft (Leap, 2007). Much more attention will be given to explaining all forms of white-collar crime in a later chapter in this text. For now, it is sufficient to suggest that these offenses are caused by multiple factors.

Because so many different factors potentially contribute to employee theft in the retail system, it should not be surprising that many different types of prevention strategies have been cited as ways to limit the extent of employee theft. These prevention strategies include (a) importation strategies, (b) internal strategies, (c) technological strategies, (d) organizational culture strategies, and (e) awareness strategies. **Importation strategies** are those strategies that aim to import only the best types of employees, who are less likely to engage in employee theft. Strategies would include background checks, drug tests, employee screening instruments, and credit checks (Friedman, 2009).

Internal strategies include policies and practices performed within the retail setting in an effort to prevent employee theft. Random inspections, audits, developing rules that guide returns, and developing internal control policies are examples (Mishra & Prasad, 2006). Random inspections include checking cash registers, employee lockers, and other locations for evidence of wrongdoing. Audits are strategies in which supervisors review cash distribution patterns of employees. Rules guiding returns focus on ways to limit the possibility that employees misuse return policies. Internal control policies refer to a "set of policies and procedures that provide reasonable assurance that an organization's assets and information are protected" (Mishra & Prasad, 2006, p. 819). Some companies employ security specialists whose sole purpose is to protect the assets and workers.

©iStockphoto.com/recep-bg

PHOTO 3.1 Overcharging is one type of employee theft. Consumers may not realize they have been overcharged unless they look closely at their receipts on a regular basis.

Technological strategies entail the use of various forms of technology to prevent employee theft in retail settings. The use of video cameras, for example, can be preventive in nature, assuming employees know that they are being "watched." If the cameras don't prevent an employee from stealing, the video will provide direct evidence of the employee "in action" (Holtz, 2009). With color and digital cameras now available, the pictures provided by the videos are even clearer, and security officials can store the video longer than they were able to in the past (Pratt, 2001). Closed-circuit television, in particular, has been hailed as the most effective deterrent in retail settings (Anderson, 2007).

Organizational culture strategies aim to promote a sense of organizational culture that would inhibit theft. Most business and management experts agree that the way bosses treat their employees will influence the workers' behavior (Kresevich, 2007). The task at hand is for supervisors and managers to promote an organizational culture that values honesty and loyalty. One expert advises, "From the start, employees should know company values and feel a part of a team committed to eliminating theft" (Mullen, 1999, p. 12). Along this line, Kent Davies (2003) recommends that supervisors (a) get advice from experts about security incidents, (b) build loyalty between the employee and the employer, (c) establish a trusting relationship between workers, and (d) eliminate temptations. Echoing these themes, Mazur (2001) calls for the building of a "strong integrity program" as a strategy for preventing retail theft. Such a program would entail four elements. First, managers would be held accountable for employees' behavior and provided incentives as part of this accountability. Second, managers would ensure that all employees be aware of the rules of conduct in the retail setting. Third, an effort would be made to give employees a "sense of authority." Fourth, managers would provide employees an outlet for reporting misconduct (Mazur, 2001). Anonymous reporting systems have been found to be particularly useful in detecting wrongdoing (Holtfreter, 2005).

Awareness strategies focus on increasing awareness among employees about various issues related to employee theft. In particular, it is recommended that employees be told about or exposed to the following:

- Anonymous tip lines

- New hire orientation

- Formal codes of conduct

- Bulletin board posters related to theft prevention

- Periodic lectures on theft and the consequences of theft

- Loss prevention compensation programs (Korolishin, 2003)

A loss prevention compensation program would provide employees monetary rewards for reporting and substantiating employee theft by their coworkers. One chief executive of a hiring agency advises that the best way to prevent employee theft is in the hiring process through efforts such as rigorous reviews of employee backgrounds, looking for signs of dishonesty, taking time during orientation to talk about loss prevention, and promoting a culture of integrity (Vaitlin, 2019). Others have noted that the tone of ethical leadership set by business leaders sends a message to employees to avoid unethical behavior (Harris & He, 2019).

The National Retail Security Survey (NRSS) is an annual survey of 69 large national retail outlets focusing on trends in retail theft. Among other items, respondents are asked about the types of loss prevention awareness strategies they use in their stores. Figure 3.1 shows the types of strategies reported in the 2018, 2019, and 2020 survey. Two patterns shown in the figure are worth highlighting. First, discussing loss prevention and codes of conduct during hiring were reported most often. Second, use of most strategies increased each year. This suggests that businesses were increasing their loss prevention efforts across the board.

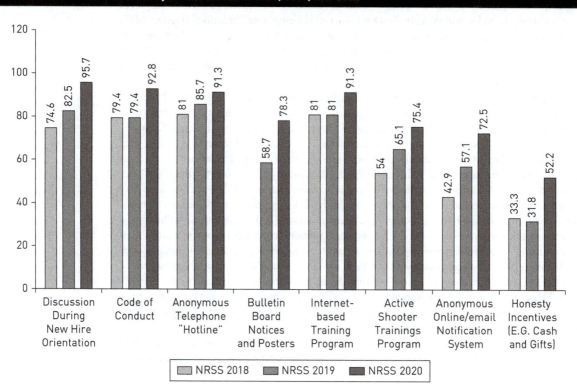

FIGURE 3.1 ■ Percentage of Businesses Using Different Loss Prevention Awareness Strategies in NRSS Annual Survey for Fiscal Years 2018, 2019, and 2020

Source: National Retail Foundation. (2020). *National Retail Security Survey.* Available online at https://nrf.com/research/national-retail-security-survey-2020

The NRSS also asks employers about their official responses to employees who stole from their company. Figure 3.2 shows the median numbers of apprehensions, prosecutions, civil demands, and terminations of employees caught stealing. A few patterns are worth noting. First, the average number of apprehensions increased between 2018 and 2019 but is still considerably lower than the 2014–2015 timeframe. Second, the large difference between average and median reflects the fact that a few retail outlets had very large numbers of official actions, which skewed the average. Third, when reviewing the median (which shows the middle point of all of the responses from the companies), it is clear that a larger number of retail outlets have been catching, terminating, prosecuting, and issuing civil demands to dishonest employees since 2015.

CRIME IN THE ENTERTAINMENT SERVICES SYSTEM

While the retail system encompasses the setting where retail goods are sold to consumers, the **entertainment services system** describes settings where consumers consume or purchase various forms of services designed at least partially for entertainment or pleasure. Many different occupations exist in the entertainment services system. For purposes of simplicity, in this text, attention will be given to just two types of industries in this system: the restaurant industry and the hotel industry.

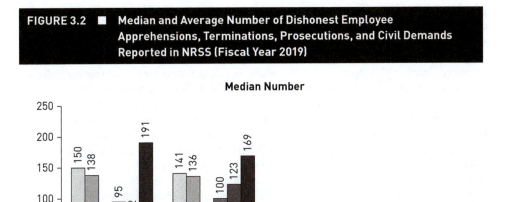

FIGURE 3.2 ■ Median and Average Number of Dishonest Employee Apprehensions, Terminations, Prosecutions, and Civil Demands Reported in NRSS (Fiscal Year 2019)

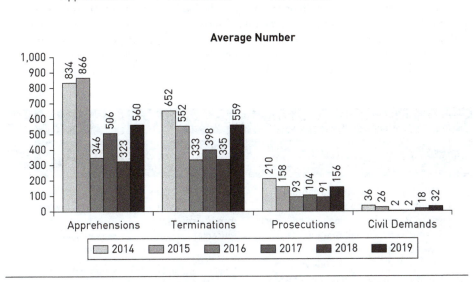

Source: National Retail Foundation. (2020). *National Retail Security Survey.* Available online at https://nrf.com/research/national-retail-security-survey-2020

Crime in the Restaurant Industry

In considering crimes in the restaurant industry, two broad categories of crime can be highlighted: crimes by the restaurant against consumers and crimes by workers against the restaurant. In her review of crimes by businesses, Hazel Croall (1989) identified four types of crimes committed by restaurants against consumers: (1) adulterating food, (2) failing to keep the restaurant as clean as required by standards, (3) using false advertising to describe goods and prices, and (4) selling food at a smaller amount than advertised (short weighting). Restaurants appeared to be overrepresented in "hygiene" offenses in her study. Croall studied 118 businesses and uncovered 37 hygiene offenses; restaurants accounted for 29 of the 37 offenses. Croall also calls attention to the consequences of short-weighting or short-measuring products. She writes, "Fiddles, including the sale of short-measure drinks, are so institutionalized that they represent part of an 'informal reward structure'" (p. 160). As Croall notes, while one person being ripped off over a drink may not be significant, when one adds up the number of short-measures, the total sum can be especially significant. Other specific labels for thefts in restaurants including "wagon wheel" (transferring costs to another receipt and removing cash paid by the restaurant customer), "comping" (keeping money by coding the sale as a comp meal), and voiding (deleting the sale altogether and pocketing the money) (Chan, Chen, Pierce, & Snow, 2020).

Using a theft security algorithm placed on restaurants' point of sale systems, Chan et. al. (2020) explored the behavior of 83,153 servers across 1,049 restaurants. Their research showed that an average of at least half of the servers in each restaurant appeared to commit at least one theft. They found that 1% of the servers were believed to steal 50 or more times, and 1.8% stole at least $400 or more. The authors uncovered evidence of peer influence with high-theft workers appearing to encourage theft in others, and new employees seeming to be especially vulnerable to peer effects. This chapter's Streaming White-Collar Crime highlights the prevalence of these behaviors in certain types of bars.

Some experts include "food fraud" as a type of crime that might be committed in restaurants, though these offenses could be committed anywhere in the food supply chain. One author team offers the following definition of this type of crime: "illegal, fraudulent behaviors that are dishonestly concealed within and behind lawful market acts and processes by legitimate occupational actors for some form of profit or advantage in the food system" (Lord, Spencer, Albanese, & Elizondo, 2017, p. 486). Varieties of food fraud include health certificate violations, serving food after the expiration date, mislabeling products, and illegally importing food products. Factors promoting food fraud include food supply, demand for the food products, regulatory policies and behaviors, and competition for different foods (Lord et al., 2017).

STREAMING WHITE-COLLAR CRIME *Bar Rescue*		
Plot	**What You Can Learn**	**Discussion Questions**
Jon Taffer is an entrepreneur, restaurant consultant, and loud-mouthed television show host. Bar Rescue chronicles his efforts to save rundown bars and restaurants from their eventual demise. Each episode follows the same formula—Jon privately visits a bar that has been selected for one of his renovations. His film crew captures a wide range of shocking practices—from serving harmful food, to employees ripping off customers, to employees ripping off the bar in various ways. Jon then meets the owner and workers, shuts down the establishment, and spends five days renovating and remaking the business. The episode ends with the unveiling of the new bar with seemingly bright futures ahead for the bars rescued by Taffer. Incidentally, Taffer has said that in his first partnership, he lost $600,000 to the actions of an unscrupulous business partner. From white-collar crime victim to television star, Taffer was able to recover from that experience.	Some restaurants have sold unsafe products in their pursuit of profits. If you own a restaurant and don't supervise your staff, they will steal from you. As will be shown later in the chapter, businesses design their physical spaces in order to limit opportunities for workplace offending.	If you opened a restaurant, what would you do to limit the likelihood of theft? When you visit a restaurant, what might make you worry about whether the food is safe? What can consumers do to protect themselves against offending by restaurant workers?

In terms of crimes by workers against the restaurant, patterns similar to those of employee theft in retail settings are found. Surveys of 103 restaurant employees found that their most common offenses included eating the restaurant's food without paying for it, giving food or beverages away, selling food at a lower price than it was supposed to be sold for, and taking items for personal use (Ghiselli & Ismail, 1998). In this same study, three fourths of respondents admitted committing some type of employee deviance.

A combination of factors is believed to foster theft by workers in restaurants. Restaurants tend to hire younger workers, and younger people in general have been found to be more prone toward deviance than older people. The low wages paid to workers

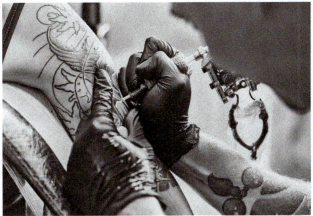

PHOTO 3.2 Who knew having a tattoo was related to white-collar crime?

may create settings where workers feel they are underpaid and underappreciated. The nature of the work is part-time, meaning that workers will be less invested in their employer. Also, the erratic hours of restaurant work may contribute to various opportunities for misconduct (Ghiselli & Ismail, 1998). Some researchers have suggested that theft may be part of a dynamic process resulting from mistreatment of the workers by bosses or customers. Interestingly, one experiment found that workers get better tips if they are mistreated but continue to offer good services (Jin, Kim, & DiPietro, 2020).

A team of researchers recently explored whether tattoos are related to workplace deviance. Surveying 518 restaurant workers, with nearly half of the workers having tattoos, the researchers found that having a tattoo was not related to committing workplace deviance, but that there was a correlation between deviance and the number of tattoos workers had. The more tattoos individuals had, the more likely they were to commit workplace deviance. There was an even stronger correlation between those with darker tattoos and workplace crimes. The authors note that tattoos don't cause crime, but perhaps bosses and coworkers treat tattooed staff differently and this differential treatment may result in workplace deviance. Despite this warning to interpret the findings with caution, the authors conclude, "there is some truth to the deviant tattoo stereotype" (Tews & Stafford, 2019).

To address all crimes in restaurants, Ghiselli and Ismail (1998) cite the following policies as strategies for reducing theft in restaurants: (1) inventory control, (2) controlled exits so managers know when workers are leaving, (3) inspections of employees' belongings, (4) video cameras, (5) locks on goods and items, and (6) restricted access to the cash register. Note that there is no reference to avoiding tattoos as a strategy to limiting the offenses. The recommendations focused on exits, video cameras, restricted access, and the physical layouts of restaurants. More specifically, it is reasonable to note that restaurant owners design their physical spaces in order to reduce opportunities for theft. As a simple example, think about where cash registers are located (e.g., in clear view of consumers rather than in a hidden room).

Crime in the Hotel Industry

White-collar crime also occurs in the hotel industry. Crime types include theft of hotel food, theft of items owned by the hotel, and theft of hotel guests' items. These crimes are particularly difficult to detect (Bloomquist, 2006). When offenders are caught, it is usually because they did something that made the case truly easy to solve. Consider, for example, a case in which two security guards were arrested for stealing three cellular phones and two wallets from a hotel room. They were caught because they used one of the cell phones (Nammour, 2009). In another case, a hotel employee stole $32,000 from hotel guests by placing additional charges on guests'

PHOTO 3.3 A study by Ghiselli and Ismail (1998) found that three fourths of restaurant employees reported committing some variety of employee deviance. Consumers would rarely notice these violations.

credit cards, and when guests disputed the charges, the worker shed those correspondences from the credit card company (Hytrek, 2019). Certainly, some of the crimes committed in the hotel industry might be committed by hotel guests. However, there is reason to believe that most hotel crimes are committed by workers. One early estimate suggested that 90% of all crimes committed in hotels were due to employee theft (Worcester, 1998). According to Worcester, employee theft in hotels is believed to be particularly problematic during summer months when temporary employees are hired.

Few studies have focused specifically on white-collar crimes in the hotel industry. Nonetheless, anecdotal evidence suggests that these crimes are somewhat pervasive. Recall that I mentioned that I have students enrolled in my white-collar crime classes write about crimes they committed on their jobs. One of my students worked in a hotel and described his typical workday as beginning when his manager told him the going rates for that evening. The manager would say something like, "The rate tonight is $90.00 a night. If customers ask for the rate, tell them it is $100.00 a night. If they don't like the rate, tell them you will lower it to $90.00 to get them to stay." The student then shared that he would tell customers that the rate was $120 a night. If customers paid that rate in cash, he would pocket $30 each night and tell his boss that the customer paid $90.00. If the customer said the price was too high, he would offer to reduce it a little and still keep the difference if it was higher than $90.00. Just to be clear, this was not a student at my current university. One can't help but wonder, though, where this student is now working. One hopes he's not working anywhere that we will be vacationing!

One study seeking to explain crime in hotels surveyed 29 undergraduate interns working in the industry and found that feelings of adrenaline and low wages appeared to be the most common motivations for theft (Goh & Kong, 2018). "Getting back at the hotel" was another motivation, with respondents reporting that their coworkers would steal alcohol and wine because they felt their bosses were depriving them of their tips. The researchers found that peers, managers, hotel security, and hotel guests impacted employees' decisions to steal. For each group, different connections to theft surfaced, including: (1) when around peers who were committing crimes, workers were more likely to do so; (2) if managers approved of the behavior, workers were more likely to engage in that behavior; (3) if workers believed guests could misbehave, workers believed they should be able to do as well; and (4) if security ignored misconduct, workers believed the conduct was okay. Another author notes that separation from other workers facilitates offenses such as "using the same cloths to clean toilets and drinking glasses in a hotel room to reduce time" (Lugosi, 2019).

FRAUD IN THE SALES/SERVICE SYSTEM

Whereas the entertainment services system sells goods and services that are designed to provide some form of entertainment to consumers, the **sales/service system** entails businesses that sell basic goods and services to consumers. These "basic" goods and services are those that most individuals need in order to function in their communities. The home and the automobile are two examples of basic goods many individuals need in order to carry out their daily routines. When considering fraud in this system, one can draw attention to automotive repair/sales fraud and home repair fraud. While few studies have empirically demonstrated how often these types of fraud occur, they are believed to be particularly pervasive.

Home Repair Fraud

Home repair fraud occurs when contractors and repair persons rip off individuals for various types of repairs. One police department cites the following offenses as the most common types of home repair fraud: roof repair, asphalt paving or driveway sealing fraud, house painting fraud, termite and pest control fraud, and tree pruning and landscaping fraud (St. Louis Police Department, 2006). In most of these cases, the fraud begins as part of a door-to-door scam initiated by the offender. Experts believe that the door-to-door scams target older persons more often, partly because they are more likely to be home during the day (Coffey, 2000) and partly because they are seen as more vulnerable (Davila, Marquart, & Mullings, 2005).

Scammers are able to profit significantly from their offenses. Estimates suggest, for example, that those involved in driveway paving scams make $10,000 a day from their schemes. Typically, they underestimate the repair costs and then try to charge more once they are done (Sambides, 2009).

To be sure, while some of the frauds result from aggressive door-to-door targeting by offenders, others occur as a result of consumers seeking repairs. Consumers are particularly vulnerable to repair frauds when considering the underlying dynamics of repair seeking. When individuals seek repairs, they are already admitting to the repairer—at least indirectly—that they do not know how to fix the item themselves. If the contractor commits fraud, the consumer may not even know it. Even when consumers are aware of the fraud, they are often unsure whom they should report the offense to (Vaughan & Carlo, 1975).

The consequences of home repair fraud can be particularly problematic. If items are not fixed appropriately, further damage to the home can result. Additional expenses will be incurred by homeowners seeking to repair their homes. Such an experience can cause significant stress to those dealing with the fraud. Family relationships can also be negatively influenced for those living in homes in need of repair as a result of contractor fraud (Burnstein, 2008a, 2008b). Perhaps recognizing the seriousness of these consequences, one police officer made the following comments to a reporter: "Some of the contractors that we arrest, I think of them as worse than armed robbers. At least when it's an armed robbery, you know you're being robbed" (Lee, 2009).

This chapter's White-Collar Crime in the News shows just how costly home repair fraud offenses can be.

WHITE-COLLAR CRIME IN THE NEWS
HOME REPAIR FRAUD CASE

The following is a press release from the Middle District of North Carolina from May 1, 2020.

Greensboro, N.C.—Matthew G.T. Martin, United States Attorney for the Middle District of North Carolina, announced today that two individuals have been charged with conspiracy to defraud in a home repair scheme.

On April 30, 2020, ++++++ and ++++, both of Chapel Hill, North Carolina, were charged in a criminal Complaint with conspiracy to commit wire fraud, that is, to devise a scheme and artifice to defraud and to obtain money and property by means of materially false and fraudulent pretenses, representations and promises.

"The allegations in the Complaint lay bare a depraved scheme: two individuals working in concert to take money from elderly and vulnerable people," said U.S. Attorney Martin. "The defendants allegedly presented themselves as helpers and the victims trusted them, only to be left poorer, and still in need of repairs to the place where they should feel most secure—their homes. We should honor our elders, not deceive and

(Continued)

(Continued)

defraud them. We applaud the law enforcement agencies whose diligent work and collaboration resulted in these charges."

The Complaint alleges that from on or about September 2015 to and including April 2020, +++++++ and +++++++ approached elderly, retired individuals at their private residences in Durham, Orange, and Chatham Counties, offering home improvement services using the business names "J&J Home Improvement" and "JH Home Improvements, Inc." +++++++—who never had a state general contractor's license—would offer to perform home improvement projects and these elderly individuals would, in turn, pay him prior to the completion of any construction work via personal checks, credit cards, or withdrawals from investment accounts. +++++++ would often direct that these individuals leave the "to" line of the check blank (which would later be completed in the name of +++++++), or issue the check directly to +++++++ who, in turn, deposited the checks into personal accounts in her name or that of her business, [business name]. +++++++ would then withdraw the money in cash and/or issue a cashier's check made out to +++++++. +++++++ and +++++++ would also take the checks to the elderly individual's bank or their bank and cash the checks without depositing the funds into their bank accounts.

+++++++ would develop personal relationships with these elderly individuals, calling them "Momma" and "Poppa," and encourage them to solicit their neighbors to engage his services in home improvement projects for their residences, as well. +++++++ also solicited loans from some of the elderly individuals for whom he had already contracted to perform home improvement projects, separate and apart from those projects.

However, +++++++ would not complete the contracted home improvement projects, nor would he repay any loans in full. When the contracting individual, a concerned relative of that person, or a local law enforcement officer confronted +++++++ about the payments, +++++++ and +++++++ would respond in the following ways: a) +++++++ would promise to send workers to complete the project but never fully complete the project; b) +++++++ or +++++++ would return a small percentage of the monies paid for the project; and/or c) +++++++ or +++++++ would write a personal check to the contracting individual that would be returned by the issuing bank as lacking sufficient funds.

Review of records from bank accounts known to be controlled by +++++++ and/or +++++++ for the time period spanning February 2016 through November 2019 indicates that, as a result of the above-described scheme to defraud, +++++++ and +++++++ obtained a total of approximately $2,200,000 from more than fifty victims.

Reprinted from U.S. Department of Justice

Allegations of home repair fraud appear to increase after natural disasters, likely because many homeowners are in need of labor to fix their damaged homes. In the wake of Hurricane Katrina, authorities investigated more than 400 cases of contractor fraud. Said one official, "There's not enough skilled labor out there, and it's causing chaos" (Konigsmark, 2006, p. 3A). News of similar incidents have routinely surfaced after other disasters. In the aftermath of Hurricane Harvey in 2017, a contractor was sentenced to 10 years in prison after admitting to stealing $180,000 from 26 victims ("Hurricane Harvey Contractor," 2020). After 2018's Hurricane Michael, three men preyed on Floridians and stole more than $319,000 from homeowners who paid for repair services never provided ("Three Men Plead Guilty," 2020). These incidents are so frequent that Florida has now developed a Disaster Fraud Action Strike team to prevent and respond to disaster frauds. The teams are called into action before and after hurricanes and asked to "work to educate and inform the public on signs of post-storm fraud and ensure contractors are following Florida workers' compensation law while conducting repairs" ("Florida Oks emergency adjusters," 2020).

Along with new educational efforts, in the wake of home repair fraud scandals, many states have passed criminal laws specifically targeting home repair fraud. The advantage of criminal laws (and policies) directed toward home repair fraud is that officials have clear guidance on how these cases should be processed. Whereas these wrongs would have been handled as civil wrongdoings in the past, if they were handled at all, the criminal laws create additional formal policies that can be used to respond to this group of offenders.

In addition to formal policies to respond to home repair fraud, experts urge homeowners to use various prevention strategies to try to avoid fraud in the first place. Common suggestions for preventing home repair fraud include the following practices: obtaining references, relying on local businesses, verifying licensure, obtaining multiple estimates, and using written contracts (Riggs, 2007).

Auto Repair/Sales Fraud

At the broadest level, one can distinguish between auto repair fraud and auto sales fraud. In the early 1990s, auto repair rip-offs were "the most frequently reported consumer complaint" (Munroe, 1992, p. C3). An early estimate suggested that "consumers lose $20 billion annually on faulty auto repairs" (Brown, 1995, p. 21). Automotive industry insiders counter that "faulty" repairs are not the same as "fraudulent" repairs. Recall the discussion in Chapter 1 about white-collar crime being defined differently by various groups. To those in the automotive repair industry, faulty repairs would not be a white-collar crime. To those following a broader approach to defining white-collar crime, such repairs can be conceptualized as white-collar crime.

Auto repair fraud includes *billing for services not provided, unnecessary repairs, airbag fraud, and insurance fraud*. **Billing for services not provided** occurs when auto mechanics bill consumers (or insurance companies) for services not provided. Consider a study by the California Department of Consumer Affairs/Bureau of Automotive Repair (BAR) that found "42% of collision repair work done in California to be fraudulent" (Sramcik, 2004, p. 16). In this study, the Bureau inspected 1,315 vehicles that received collision repairs and found that on 551 of the vehicles, "parts or labor listed on the invoice . . . were not actually supplied or performed" (Thrall, 2003, p. 6). Industry insiders critiqued the BAR study for being methodologically flawed and for using vague definitions of fraud, which included billing mistakes (Grady, 2003). Again, the importance of how one defines white-collar crime surfaces. Critics also suggested that the BAR study was politically driven as a strategy to suggest that the Bureau's existence was justified in a time of tough budgets in order to protect consumers from fraud (Thrall, 2003).

Unnecessary auto repairs occur when mechanics perform mechanical services that are not necessary and bill the consumer for those services. Such practices are believed to be well planned by those who perform them. These actions are particularly difficult for consumers to detect. Said one assistant attorney general to a reporter, "Most consumers are not knowledgeable enough about auto repairs to know if their cars have been subjected to unneeded repairs" (Munroe, 1992, p. C3). Presumably, an automotive repair shop will advertise cheap specials as a way to get consumers into the shop and then convince consumers that they need certain repairs. One owner of 22 repair shops agreed to pay $1.8 million in fines in response to allegations that he engaged in this type of scam (Olivarez-Giles, 2010, p. 7).

Airbag fraud occurs when mechanics fraudulently repair airbags. In general, two types of airbag fraud exist (Adams & Guyette, 2009). The first type involves outright fraud in which mechanics clearly intend not to fix the airbag appropriately. Adams and Guyette (2009) provide the example of situations where "old rags or foam are shoved into dashboard cavities" (p. 56). The second type of airbag fraud is inaccurate repair. This entails situations in which mechanics simply fail to repair the airbag correctly. Unfortunately, these fraudulent or inept repairs may not be noticed until an accident occurs.

Auto insurance fraud occurs when mechanics dupe the insurance company into paying for unnecessary or nonexistent repairs. Types of auto insurance fraud include enhancing damages, substituting parts, and creating damage. Enhancing damages involves situations where mechanics cause further damage to a damaged car in order to collect more from the insurance company.

Substituting parts includes situations where mechanics put used parts in the repaired car but bill the insurance company for new parts (Seibel, 2009). Creating damage occurs when mechanics work with car owners to damage a car so that the owner can file a claim with the insurance company (Bertrand, 2003). This would include stripping and vandalizing cars so that they will be paid to repair the damage they created.

One strategy that has been shown to be effective in limiting auto insurance fraud involves the use of direct repair programs and aftermarket auto parts (Cole, Maroney, McCullough, & Powell, 2015). Presumably, when auto repair shops are working directly with the insurer, the opportunity and motivation for fraud decreases. Also, using after-market auto parts (or used parts) is much cheaper than using new parts.

In some cases, professionals may collaborate with a wide range of individuals to perpetrate their fraudulent acts. Some health care businesses have been labeled as "auto insurance treatment mills" in reference to the overrepresentation of certain health care businesses in auto insurance claims (Schram, 2013, p. 33). Lawyers are frequently blamed for being ambulance chasers, but it turns out that some ambulances may consistently be going to the same health care facility!

Very few academic studies have focused on auto repair fraud. In one of the first studies done on the subject, Paul Jesilow and his colleagues (Jesilow, Geis, & O'Brien, 1985) conducted a field experiment in which they sought battery testing services from 313 auto shops in California. The researchers found that honesty was related to the size of the shop, with smaller shops exhibiting more honesty than larger shops. How workers were paid (commission vs. hourly rate) was not related to honesty. Commissioned workers tended to be just as honest as hourly workers.

Building on this study, the authors (Jesilow, Geis, & O'Brien, 1986) studied a publicity campaign to see if publicity and awareness would influence mechanics' honesty. The public awareness campaign included letters from a formal regulatory agency, a major lawsuit, and press announcements. After the campaign, the research assistants revisited the shops for battery testing. They found that honesty rates were similar among the shops exposed to the public awareness campaigns and the shops that were not exposed to the campaign. In other words, the campaign had no effect.

Automotive sales fraud is another type of fraud in the automotive industry. Varieties of auto sales fraud include turning odometers back, selling unsafe cars, and selling stolen cars (Smith, 1997). Odometer fraud, also known as clocking (see Croall, 1989), is sometimes part of a broader scheme. In those situations, mechanics work in collaboration with dealers in an effort to maximize a particular car sale. One estimate suggested that 452,000 cases of odometer fraud occur each year in the United States, costing consumers more than a billion dollars annually (National Highway Traffic Safety Administration [NHTSA], 2002).

In addition to these types of auto repair fraud, one author team also identifies overtreatment, overcharging, and undertreatment (Beck, Kerschbamer, Qui, & Sutter, 2013). **Overtreatment** refers to instances when mechanics do more work than is needed, either to rip the customer off or because they want to make sure the customer is safe. **Overcharging** refers to instances when mechanics do the repairs but charge for more expensive repairs. **Undertreatment** involves doing shoddy or ineffective work on the automobile. A recent automobile repair field experiment using undercover researchers found that "under and overtreatment are widespread and that reputation via a repeat business mechanism does not improve outcomes significantly" (Schneider, 2012, p. 406).

Fraud in the Marijuana Sales Industry

Colorado and Washington were the first two states to make the recreational use of marijuana legal in 2012. One result of marijuana legalization was a windfall in tax revenue. By 2019, Colorado was receiving more than a billion dollars a year in marijuana tax revenue (Rosenbaum, 2019). As of July 2020, 11 states and the District of Columbia had legalized recreational marijuana use, and several other states were considering following suit. In addition, 33 states have legalized marijuana for medical use so long as the drug is prescribed by a physician. Ironically, by legalizing marijuana, a new variety of white-collar crime surfaced: legalized marijuana crimes. Generally speaking, two types of "legalized marijuana crimes" exist: crimes by marijuana business owners and crimes against marijuana businesses.

Regarding crimes by marijuana business owners, it is important to recognize that marijuana business owners must follow a vast array of federal and state laws governing their business (Ward, Thompson, Iannacchione, & Evans, 2019). The state marijuana laws govern how the drug can be sold and transported, where it can be used, and how the drug can be determined to be safe (Klieger et al., 2017). The violation of these laws would be forms of white-collar crime. At least eight types of work-related misdeeds can be committed by marijuana business owners:

1. Unlicensed establishments

2. Marketing offenses

3. False advertising

4. Distribution of harmful products

5. Underage sales

6. Unlawful distribution of medical marijuana

7. Quantity violations

8. Federal law violations

Unlicensed establishments are businesses selling marijuana without the appropriate licenses and approvals. These establishments are a concern to authorities for several reasons. Selling product that may be harmful or dangerous is the most obvious problem. The ability to evade regulatory fees and taxes is also problematic (Riggins, 2020). Less obvious is the fact that the physical structure of the dispensary may be unsafe. As one author notes, unlicensed establishments might lack fire safety equipment or other items resulting in "potentially dangerous work environments and safety hazards" (Riggins, 2020).

Marketing offenses includes the violation of rules and regulations designed to make sure that marijuana businesses market their product in a safe and fair manner. States have developed guidelines regulating how marijuana can be marketed. Washington State, for instance, stipulates that all advertising must include these warnings:

a. "This product has intoxicating effects and may be habit forming."

b. "Marijuana can impair concentration, coordination, and judgment. Do not operate a vehicle or machinery under the influence of this drug."

c. "There may be health risks associated with consumption of this product."

d. "For use only by adults twenty-one and older. Keep out of the reach of children." (Washington State Liquor Control Board, n.d.)

Washington also bans advertising near locations children frequent, on public transit, and on public property. In addition, advertising that promotes overconsumption, misrepresentations, medical benefits, or use by children is prohibited.

A research team reviewed the websites of 97 marijuana dispensaries to determine whether the businesses used marketing strategies that encouraged misuse (Cavazos-Rehg et al., 2019). They found that two thirds made questionable claims about the medical efficacy of their products, and less than half warned consumers about possible side effects. In addition, three fourths of the websites didn't have an age verification gate to weed young people out (pun intended!). Some "medical marijuana" sites even promoted marijuana as a recreational drug that can help users get high.

False advertising involves the misrepresentation of marijuana product. The general crime of false advertising will be discussed in Chapter 10. At this point, two varieties of false advertising in the marijuana industry can be highlighted. The first includes instances when businesses substitute an expensive product with an inferior product and sell that product at the higher price. The second includes situations where marijuana businesses misrepresent the effects of marijuana. A study on medical marijuana dispensaries found that "a large proportion of dispensaries make unsupported claims regarding the effectiveness of cannabis as a treatment for [opioid use disorder], including that cannabis should replace FDA-approved MOUDs [methadone, buprenorphine, naltrexone]" (Shover et al., 2020). The authors cite research showing that opioid addicts who do not use these approved MOUDs in their treatment "more than double their risk of mortality." In a sense, then, false advertising in these cases may be a matter of life and death.

Distribution of harmful products refers to situations where dispensaries distribute product that has not been approved by the FDA and that may be potentially harmful to consumers. As an example, a Canadian medical marijuana producer sold marijuana containing five harmful pesticides, including one that kills mildew and another that was an insecticide (Robertson, 2017). Customers who used the marijuana experienced a wide range of serious illnesses. It's believed that producers ignored quality control regulations in efforts to produce medical marijuana and increase their profits (Robertson, 2017).

Underage sales include instances when marijuana businesses market or sell their product to children. One author team audited the retail environment of 163 California marijuana dispensaries near 333 public schools. The researchers found few violations on the outside of the dispensaries, but a wide range of age-related violations on the inside. In fact, at least three-fourths of the dispensaries "had at least on instance of child-appealing products, packages, paraphernalia, or advertisements (Cao et al., 2020, p. 72). The authors note that vague laws make it hard for owners to follow the law and regulators to enforce the law.

Unlawful distribution of medical marijuana refers to medical marijuana dispensaries distributing medical marijuana to individuals who do not have prescriptions. Some states have developed regulatory bodies that specifically focus on how medical marijuana is being distributed. While those units focus on regulations, law enforcement agencies may proactively seek out instances when medical marijuana dispensaries are committing crimes. In a recent case in Oklahoma, for example, an undercover officer visited the "Herbs-N-Legends" three times and purchased marijuana without a medical marijuana card (Rael, 2019).

Quantity violations involve marijuana dispensaries selling customers more marijuana in a given time period than they are allowed to sell. States have regulations dictating how much marijuana product a business can sell to a customer on a given day. The term *looping* is used to describe those situations when customers return to a dispensary to buy additional product even though they have met their daily limit. Three owners of Sweet Leaf dispensaries in Colorado were sentenced to a year in prison after pleading guilty to overselling marijuana to customers (Kennedy, 2019). Their criminal case was the first such case in Colorado and possibly the first of its kind in the country (Tabachnik, 2019).

Federal law violations include instances where marijuana businesses are charged with crimes covered by federal jurisdiction. In some ways, all marijuana businesses are breaking federal law simply by their existence. Federal legislation stipulates that marijuana is a Schedule 1 offense, which means that the federal government sees the drug as harmful and of no medical value. Based on this classification, federal law prohibits the possession, use, and distribution of marijuana. The discrepancy between federal and state laws creates the need for a balancing act among marijuana businesses. The balancing act has been described in this way:

Cannabis businessmen currently operate in a gray area of the not-quite-legal, where their ability to conduct business requires conformity to complex state regulatory regimes while also attempting to remain outside of existing federal enforcement guidelines for activities that are still a clear, formal violation of federal criminal law (Yablan, 2019, p. 339).

To date, few federal prosecutions against businesses abiding by state marijuana laws have occurred, but they have happened. For example, a Michigan medical marijuana dispensary owner was convicted on federal charges of illegally distributing marijuana and "maintaining drug-involved premises" (Agar, 2020). He was not able to use the fact that Michigan had legalized marijuana as part of his defense. Having previously faced state charges that were dropped, the owner defended his business on the grounds that he thought it was legal. Federal authorities did not accept that defense, perhaps because the dispensary existed for years before the state made marijuana legal. They also cited federal law. Sentencing the owner to more than 15 years in prison, the federal judge said, "The fact is, marijuana is a Schedule 1 controlled substance" (Agar, 2020).

Crimes committed by employees against marijuana dispensaries include theft of product and theft of cash. Cannabis security experts estimate that 90% of theft in the marijuana sales industry stems from employees stealing money or product (Schroyer, 2015; Yagielo, 2019). Many dispensaries accept only cash, which makes it easier for employees to take (Yagielo, 2019). In addition, selling the product at a discount to friends would be a form of theft from the business owner. One security official told a reporter about a case where an employee cost the marijuana dispensary $20,000 a month by giving out unauthorized discounts to his friends (Schroyer, 2015). Strategies that have been suggested to reduce employee theft in marijuana businesses include using electronic access doors to products and money, conducting daily inventory audits, and hiring full-time employees (who would have more commitment to the business than part-time employees would) (Schroyer, 2015).

Few studies have empirically examined the dynamics of these offenses or how businesses and the justice system respond to them. What is clear, however, is that marijuana business owners are concerned about employees stealing from them. In fact, there are now businesses that exist solely to provide security to marijuana businesses. One website (https://indicaonline.com) has identified the top five cannabis security businesses. The top five businesses identified include (1) Cannaguard Security, (2) Canna Security America, (3) MPS Security Services, (4) Operational Security Solutions, and (5) Senseon Secure Services (Lynn, 2020). Touting Senseon in the ranking, Lynn (2020) notes the following about the company's locks: "Eliminating the need for keys will prevent them from falling into the wrong hands and reduce theft from customers or staffers."

Some companies even specialize in providing dogs to marijuana dispensaries in need of cannabis security. While the dogs might be used to protect from burglaries or other offenses against the business by nonemployees, some dispensaries use dogs to try and keep employees from taking marijuana out of the dispensary (Carrera, 2018). One security official told a reporter that he had his marijuana dog, Nero, search all employees whenever they left the establishment—whether for a break or at the end of the shift. "He stopped some theft," the security official quipped to the reporter (Carrera, 2018). One company selling marijuana security dogs with narcotics training sets the starting price for the dogs at $35,500 (Paladin Security, n.d.).

©iStockphoto.com/gradyreese

PHOTO 3.4 Recreational use of marijuana has been legalized in 11 states as of July 2020. Ironically, the legalization of a formerly illegal drug has created a new category of white-collar crime—legalized marijuana crimes.

CRIME IN THE INSURANCE SYSTEM

The insurance system includes the wide range of agencies and institutions responsible for providing insurance to consumers. Many different types of insurance exist, including home-owners insurance, rental insurance, auto insurance, property insurance, and more. The topic is rarely studied for two reasons: (1) It is hard to understand, and (2) people don't typically know when they have been victimized by insurance crimes (Ericson & Doyle, 2006). Of the research that has been done, much has focused on crimes by consumers against insurance companies, including overstating losses, arson for profit, bogus insurance claims, and understating property value to get lower insurance rates (Litton, 1998). Crimes by consumers, however, encompass just one portion of the types of crimes committed in the insurance system. As with other occupa-tions, a wide range of offenses are committed by those working in the insurance system. In the following paragraphs, attention is given to the types of crimes in this system, the consequences of insurance crimes, and the patterns surrounding these offenses.

Types of Insurance Crimes by Professionals

Four different categories of insurance crimes by workers in the insurance system exist: (1) crimes by agents against the insurance company, (2) investment-focused crimes, (3) theft crimes against consumers, and (4) sales-directed crimes against consumers. With regard to crimes by agents against the insurance company, some agents or brokers engage in activities that ultimately defraud the insurance company. Examples include lying about a potential client's income and unauthorized entity fraud (lying about assets). By lying about these items to the company, the agent is able to provide benefits to the consumer and thereby get the consumer to purchase the insurance.

Investment-focused crimes occur when insurance agents commit crimes that are designed to get consumers to invest in various insurance products. These include viatical settlement fraud, promissory note fraud, and annuities fraud. **Viatical settlement fraud** occurs when agents conceal information on viatical settlement policies, which allow individuals to invest in other people's life insurance policies (meaning they collect money when the other person dies). Fraud occurs when agents lie about the income, health of the insured individual, or other matters the investors should know about (Brasner, 2010; Federal Bureau of Investigation [FBI], 2010a).

Promissory note fraud refers to situations where agents get clients to invest in promissory notes that ultimately are scams. A promissory note is basically an IOU. Consumers are told that if they invest in a particular business, then after a certain amount of time, they will get their entire investment back plus interest. While promissory notes are legitimate investment strate-gies, here is how investment strategy fraud schemes work:

> A life insurance agent . . . calls with an intriguing investment opportunity. A company is looking to expand its business and needs to raise capital. But instead of borrowing money from a traditional lender such as a bank, it is offering investors an opportunity to purchase "promissory notes," typically with a maturity of nine months and an annual interest rate between 12 percent and 18 percent. Investors are sometimes told the promissory notes, which are like IOUs, are "guaranteed" by a bond from an offshore bonding company. Investors lose money either because fake promissory notes that look authentic are issued on behalf of fraudulent companies, or the crooks abscond with people's money before the notes mature. (Singletary, 2000, p. H01)

In some cases, insurance agents are not aware that they are selling fraudulent promissory notes because they too have fallen for the scam. In other cases, they are knowing conspirators who profit from the crimes. A series of investigations in the late 1990s found 800 incidents of promis-sory note fraud costing investors $500 million (Knox, 2000).

Annuities fraud occurs when insurance agents misrepresent the types of returns that their clients would get from investing in annuities. Annuities are "insurance contracts that offer a guaranteed series of payments over time" (Jenkins, 2008). Insurance agents get a 3% to 8% commission for selling annuities, giving them incentive to get clients to invest in annuities (Haiken, 2011). However, annuities can sometimes be quite risky investments, and agents have been known to persuade investors, particularly older individuals, to take their investments out of safe investment portfolios and place them in annuities that could eventually result in the investors' losing their savings. One victim described his experiences with annuities fraud in this way:

> The first scam started when the agent showed up and did not tell us he was from Salt Lake City, Utah. . . . His sales pitch convinced me I could use the immediate monthly income from an annuity, it was not disclosed he was selling "life insurance" or that Mr. Smiley was actually an insurance salesman. I was misled into thinking I was investing into a . . . mutual fund program. The instructions he gave me about the contract details such as "single life contract," "no guarantee," "no beneficiary," "no joint annuitant," and "no IRA disclosure statement was presented," these details were all misleading and coordinated in favor of [the insurance company]. Now I understand, the more I was defrauded, the bigger the commission for the insurance agent, they are trained to deceive. I have now ultimately lost the entire $57,779.00 IRA savings and I have nothing for my years of work and no retirement nest egg. (Adam, 2008)

Theft crimes against consumers occur when agents steal directly from insurance clients. Examples include broker embezzlement, forgery, and falsifying account information (FBI, 2010a). In broker embezzlement cases, agents steal funds from a client's account that the agents have access to. In forgery cases, agents sign clients' names on documents and forms and benefit financially from the deception. **Falsifying account information** refers to instances when agents or brokers change account information without the client's knowledge. In these crimes, no actual sale, or even effort to make a sale, occurs, and agents are not trying to get clients to invest in anything—they are simply stealing from consumers.

Sales-directed crimes against consumers occur when agents or brokers steal from consumers by using fraudulent sales tactics. Premium diversion theft is the most common form of sales-directed insurance crime (FBI, 2010a). In these situations, brokers or agents persuade clients to purchase insurance, but they never actually forward the payment from the client to the insurance company; instead, they pocket the payment. This means that clients don't actually have insurance when they think they do.

Other forms of sales-directed insurance crimes are more institutionalized in the insurance sales process. For instance, **churning** refers to situations where agents and brokers introduce new products and services simply to get policyholders to change their policies so the agents and brokers can collect commissions (Ericson & Doyle, 2006). Such practices are often called "good business" among officials in the insurance agency; the practice certainly is distinguished from cases of direct theft, which are not institutionalized as part of sales strategies. Other sales-directed insurance crimes include the following:

- **Stacking:** persuading persons to buy more policies than are needed

- **Rolling over:** persuading customers to cancel an old policy and replace it with a more expensive "better" policy

- **Misrepresentation:** deliberately misinforming the customer about the coverage of the insurance policy

- **Switching:** where the sales person switches the consumer's policy so that the coverage and the premiums are different from what the victim was told

- **Sliding:** when agents include insurance coverage that was not requested by customers (Payne, 2005)

Beyond the deception that is tied to these offenses, consumers and the rest of society experience a number of different consequences from crimes committed in the insurance system.

Consequences of Insurance Crimes

Estimates suggest that insurance fraud collectively "raises the yearly cost of premiums by $300 for the average household" (FBI, 2009). For individuals victimized by these offenses, the consequences of insurance crimes can be particularly devastating. Consider cases of premium diversion thefts—where individuals pay for insurance they don't actually receive. One woman didn't realize she didn't have insurance until after an automobile accident. Her garage called and told her that the insurance company had no policy in her name. She had thought for more than two years that she had insurance. The investigation revealed that the agent did the same thing with 80 other clients. In another scheme, an agent who sold fake policies "left dozens of customers without coverage during hurricane seasons [in Florida] in 2003, 2004, and 2005 during which eight hurricanes struck the neighborhood" ("Insurance Agent Accused," 2007, p. 1).

Many of the insurance crimes target elderly persons, making the consequences of lost income particularly significant. One Florida insurance agent defrauded 60 victims, but only 37 of them participated in the trial. Many of the others "died before the trial took place" (Varian, 2000, p. 1). The agent had asked them "to invest in expansions of his insurance business or for short-term loans to book entertainers from the former Lawrence Welk program." In another case, 75-year-old Martha Cunningham "owned a $417,000 home in Prince George's County and held $61,000 in annuities before she met Edward Hanson [an insurance agent]. . . . Today the widow is essentially broke and inundated with debt" (Wiggins, 2009, p. B02). Hanson stole everything the elderly woman owned. The breadth of these schemes is but one pattern surrounding insurance crimes.

Insurance Crime Patterns

In addressing the dynamics of crimes in the insurance system, industry insiders either attribute the offenses to rotten apple explanations or engage in victim blaming (Ericson & Doyle, 2006). The rotten apple explanations suggest that a few rogue agents and brokers commit the vast majority of insurance crimes, while the victim blaming explanations suggest that failures on the part of victims (and greed) make them potential targets for the few rogue insurance employees that exist. Ericson and Doyle point out that these explanations are shortsighted and argue that insurance crimes are institutionalized in the industry by the practices and strategies encouraged among insurance employees. Aspects of the insurance industry that they discuss as evidence for the way that these crimes are institutionalized in the insurance system include the following:

- The complex products sold by insurance companies

- The construction of risk as calculable

- The commission structure

- A revolving door of agents

- Mixed messages about an aggressive sales culture

- Limited regulation of market misconduct

A related pattern that surfaces is that these are offenses that seem to occur in various cultures. What this suggests is that the insurance market and practices at the core of this industry might promote fraud. The phrase "opportunistic fraud" has been used to describe those times when fraudulent insurance providers use a disaster or other misfortune to commit their offenses (Pao, Tzeng, & Wang, 2014). As will be discussed later, sometimes white-collar crimes are rationalized by offenders as "sharp business practices." This is particularly the case in insurance crime cases. One former life insurance agent is quoted as saying, "you have to understand, everything is crooked" (Ericson & Doyle, 2006, p. 993). Ericson and Doyle (2006) provide an example that describes how "deceptive sales are rife and institutionalized in the life insurance industry" and point to the scare tactics used by agents and brokers that are euphemistically called "backing the hearse up to the door" by insurance insiders. Good business practices or crime? You can decide for yourself.

Summary

- This chapter gave attention to the crimes occurring in the following systems: (1) the retail system, (2) the entertainment services system, (3) the sales/service system, and (4) the insurance system.

- Several varieties of employee theft occur in retail settings. Here are some examples: overcharging, shortchanging, coupon stuffing, credits for nonexistent returns, theft of production supplies and raw materials, embezzlement, overordering supplies, theft of credit card information, theft of goods, theft of money from the cash register, and sweetheart deals.

- Employee theft prevention strategies include (a) importation strategies, (b) internal strategies, (c) technological strategies, (d) organizational culture strategies, and (e) awareness strategies.

- In considering crimes in the restaurant industry, two broad categories can be highlighted: crimes by the restaurant against consumers and crimes by workers against the restaurant.

- The most common types of home repair fraud are believed to be roof repair, asphalt paving or driveway sealing fraud, house painting fraud, termite and pest control fraud, and tree pruning and landscaping fraud.

- Auto repair fraud includes billing for services not provided, unnecessary repairs, airbag fraud, and insurance fraud.

- Types of crimes committed in the legal marijuana industry include unlicensed establishments, marketing offenses, harmful products, underage sales, unlawful distribution of medical marijuana, quantity violations, and federal law violations.

- Insurance crimes are rarely studied for two reasons: (1) They are hard to understand, and (2) people don't typically know when they have been victimized by insurance crimes (Ericson & Doyle, 2006).

- Four different categories of crimes by workers in the insurance system exist: (1) crimes by agents against the insurance company, (2) investment-focused crimes, (3) theft crimes against consumers, and (4) sales-directed crimes against consumers.

- Estimates suggest that insurance fraud collectively "raises the yearly cost of premiums by $300 for the average household" (FBI, 2009).

- For individuals victimized by insurance crimes, the consequences can be particularly devastating.

- Industry insiders either attribute the insurance offenses to rotten apple explanations or engage in victim blaming (Ericson & Doyle, 2006).

- Ericson and Doyle (2006) point out that insurance crimes are institutionalized in the industry by the practices and strategies encouraged among insurance employees.

Key Terms

Discussion Questions

1. What types of employee theft do you think are most serious? Why?

2. Should employees always be fired if they are caught engaging in crime in a restaurant? Explain.

3. How are home repair frauds and auto repair frauds similar to one another?

4. Why do you think insurance crimes occur?

5. Do you think you have ever been overcharged by an auto mechanic? If so, why do you think the offense occurred?

6. Do you know anyone who has committed retail theft? Why do you think that person committed the offense?

7. How can marijuana sales be considered a white-collar crime?

8. Compare and contrast crime in the legal marijuana industry with the illegal drug industry.

CRIME IN THE HEALTH CARE SYSTEM

Eighteen-year old Florida resident Malachi Love-Robinson was arrested in February 2016 and subsequently convicted for practicing medicine without a license. The wanna-be doctor, who nicknamed himself "Dr. Love," was caught after providing services to an undercover law enforcement officer. The case made national news after the teenager was arrested, and the media attention continued throughout the case. Love-Robinson's case was featured on *Inside Edition* and *Good Morning America*, among others. After being arrested, the teen proclaimed his innocence. Why wouldn't people believe he was a doctor? He had an impressive looking website, a lab coat, medical supplies, an actual doctor's office, and had made more than $35,000 from his patients. While Love-Robinson's arrest stemmed from an investigation into a medical office he opened in January 2016, he had actually been cited by Florida health officials for similar actions in October 2015 (Chan, 2016). He was convicted and served 20 months of a 3-and-a-half-year sentence. In a 2018 prison interview with *Inside Edition*, he confessed, "I 100 percent regret what I have done," adding that he still hopes to one day be a doctor ("21-year-old Jailed for Posing as a Doctor," 2018).

A few years later in 2021, a doctor plead guilty to medical fraud and an assortment of charges related to his health care practice. At the crux of his misdeeds was his practice of reusing medical equipment that was supposed to be used just once. For example, staff used rectal pressure sensors on patients getting rehab to strengthen their pelvic muscles; though the sensors are designed to only be used once, the doctor ordered staff to reuse the same sensors on multiple patients. The doctor also reused disposable catheters in a diagnostic study he was conducting. In addition to admitting that he was reusing disposable medical supplies, he also plead guilty to billing Medicare for more expensive services than he actually provided (Krafcik, 2020). This doctor is not alone. While it is generally agreed that most health care professionals are honest, a handful of them engage in deviant, criminal, or harmful behavior. Here are a few examples quoted from their original sources:

A physician working in the emergency room of the University of Vermont Medical Center was arrested on multiple counts of voyeurism on Friday evening. Burlington Police said Dr. +++++++++ concealed a recording device in a secure staff bathroom, a "KNOWYOURNANNY" camera, that was found by the hospital's security staff. (Abrami, 2020)

According to court documents and as previously announced, +++++, who owned and operated a series of durable medical equipment companies, oversaw a multi-year scheme resulting in nearly $10 million in claims billed to Medicare. Working with a number of others, ++++++ operated a network that paid kickbacks to obtain patient information, specifically that of Medicare patients. Through a third-party biller, +++++ would then bill Medicare Part B and Part C plans for medically unnecessary medical equipment and orthotics, including a variety of back and knee braces that were not ordered as medically necessary by a physician. (USDOJ, 2019, May 3)

[The dentist] was convicted on 46 felony and misdemeanor counts in Anchorage Superior Court on Friday by Judge Michael Wolverton, who called the evidence presented by the state during a five-week bench trial "overwhelming.". . . A lawsuit filed by the state in 2017 charged ++++ with "unlawful dental acts," saying his patient care did not meet professional standards. ++++++ . . . "performed a dental extraction procedure on a sedated patient while riding a hoverboard," filmed the procedure and then sent it to several people. (Andone, 2020)

++++++, a pharmacist and former vice president of PCA, and +++++++, a pharmacy technician, were charged in late April with conspiring to commit healthcare fraud by submitting bogus claims for prescribed drugs to the federal Tricare program for thousands of military service members and veterans who didn't need them. The former PCA employees are accused of mixing ingredients to create expensive pain creams to treat the scars of military personnel with questionable prescriptions who were not charged any co-payments for the drugs. (Weaver, 2020)

As this brief synopsis shows, health care employees from a range of health care occupations have been accused of wrongdoing. To shed some light on white-collar crime among these employees, in this chapter, attention is given to crimes committed by offenders working in the health care system. Five points about the health care system help to create a foundation from which insight about health care crimes will evolve:

- Most offenders in the health care system have specific training related to their occupations, and some have advanced degrees.

- Individuals seek services from those in the health care system when they are in need of some form of medical care. This may create vulnerability for those seeking services.

- The health care system interacts with other systems. For example, changes in the educational and technological systems influence the type of health care provided. These broader changes also impact the types of crimes committed in the health care system.

- For the most part, citizens place a great deal of trust in health care providers, with significant respect given to upper-class members of both groups.

- The health care profession tends to self-regulate itself in an effort to promote appropriate conduct.

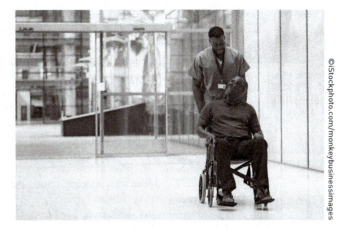

PHOTO 4.1 Crimes occur in all professions, even in health care. Bear in mind, though, that most health care professionals are honest.

©iStockphoto.com/monkeybusinessimages

When we go to see our doctors, dentists, pharmacists, or other health care providers, most of us likely give little thought to the possibility that these professionals would engage in criminal actions. In fact, most of us likely assume that our health care providers would never even consider breaking their ethical code or the criminal law. For the most part, we are correct in this assumption because most health care providers do not commit occupational crimes. Some, however, do.

FRAUD BY DOCTORS

As Paul Jesilow and his colleagues (Jesilow, Pontell, & Geis, 1985) note, few criminal justice and criminology textbooks give a great deal of attention to crimes by doctors, "probably because of the respect, power, and trust that the profession engenders" (p. 151). Even Sutherland implied that doctors were unlikely to engage in white-collar crime, and as a result, Sutherland gave "only scant attention to doctors [and] maintained that physicians were probably more honest than other professionals" (Wilson, Lincoln, Chappell, & Fraser, 1986, p. 129).

The level of trust that individuals place in doctors cannot be overstated. Illustrating the trust that we have in the profession, one author team quoted a Federal Bureau of Investigation (FBI) agent who said to them, "What other stranger would you go in and take your clothes off in front of? It's that kind of trust." (Pontell, Jesilow, & Geis, 1984, p. 406). While readers might be able to think of at least one other profession where "clients" remove all of their clothes in front of strangers, that other profession is an illegal profession in most places in the United States (except parts of Nevada). The medical profession is a legal profession that is plagued by illegal acts.

The most pervasive form of fraud committed by doctors entails the commission of Medicare and Medicaid fraud and abuse. Both medical programs were created in the mid-1960s. **Medicare** was created as a federal program to serve elderly citizens, while **Medicaid** operates at the state level to serve the poor. When Medicare and Medicaid were first created, there was no concern about fraud; instead, the concern was whether doctors would actually participate in the programs because Medicare and Medicaid faced opposition from the American Medical Association. (Pontell et al., 1984).

In time, doctors increasingly participated in the insurance programs, and by the mid-1970s, authorities recognized that fraud was pervasive in Medicare and Medicaid. This pervasiveness continues today. It was estimated that between 3% and 10% of health care spending is lost to fraud. This means that in the United States between 68 and 226 billion dollars is lost to fraud each year (National Health Care Anti-Fraud Association [NHCAA], 2010). The NHCAA (2010) points out that the lower limit of these estimates is still "more than the gross domestic product of 120 different countries including Iceland, Ecuador, and Kenya." A decade later, with annual health care spending exceeding $3.6 trillion, it is estimated that the U.S. may be losing upward of $300 billion a year to fraud in the health care system (National Health Care Anti-Fraud Association, 2020).

Several varieties of misconduct are committed by doctors. At the broadest level, legal experts make a distinction between fraud and abuse. **Fraud** refers to intentionally criminal behaviors by physicians, whereas abuse focuses on unintentional misuse of program funds. If a doctor intentionally steals from Medicaid, this would be fraud. Alternatively, if a doctor accidentally overuses Medicaid services, this would be abuse. Note that authorities will respond to abuse cases as well in an effort to recoup lost funds. The distinction is significant because it predicts the types of justice systems that are likely to respond to the cases. In fraud cases, the criminal justice system will be involved, and criminal penalties, such as incarceration, probation, and fines, will be applied. In abuse cases, the civil justice system or other regulatory systems will respond, and penalties will be monetary in nature.

Within these broader categories, several specific forms of fraud and abuse exist (FBI, 2010a; Payne, 1995; Pontell, Jesilow, & Geis, 1982). **Phantom treatment** occurs when providers bill Medicare, Medicaid, or other insurance agencies for services they never actually provided. This is also known as fee-for-service reimbursement. **Substitute providers** occur when the medical services were performed by an employee who was not authorized to perform the services. **Upcoding** (or upgrading) refers to situations where providers bill for services that are more expensive than the services that were actually provided. The **provision of unnecessary services** occurs when health care providers perform and bill for tests or procedures that were not needed (just as auto mechanics might perform unnecessary repairs to our cars). **Misrepresenting services** occurs when providers describe the service differently on medical forms in an effort to gain payment for the services (e.g., elective surgeries might be defined as medically necessary). **Falsifying records** occurs when providers change medical forms in an effort to be reimbursed by the insurance provider. **Overcharging patients** refers to situations where providers charge patients more than regulations permit. **Unbundling** refers to instances when the provider bills separately for tests and procedures that are supposed to be billed as one procedure (imagine that you ordered a package meal and the restaurant tried to bill you for each type of food separately). **Pingponging** occurs when patients are unnecessarily referred to other providers and "bounced around" various medical providers. **Ganging** refers to situations where providers bill for multiple family members, though they treated only one of them. **Kickbacks** occur when providers direct patients to other providers in exchange for a pecuniary response for the other provider. **Co-pay waivers** occur when providers waive the patient's co-pay but still bill the insurance company. **Medical snowballing** occurs when providers bill for several related services, though only one service was provided.

Several studies have considered different aspects of fraud by physicians. One consistent finding from early studies on the topic is that psychiatrists and psychologists are accused of fraud more often than other providers (Geis, Jesilow, Pontell, & O'Brien, 1985; Payne, 1995). Current national data show that this pattern continues today. Figure 4.1 shows the types of providers in fraud cases handled by fraud control units and open at the end of the fiscal year for 2019. It is striking that so many of the cases involved psychiatrists and psychologists—as compared to the number of psychiatrists and psychologists in the medical profession. In 2019, psychiatrists made up 3.5% of physicians but 11% of those accused of fraud, suggesting they are more than three times more likely to be accused of fraud than other health care professionals.

FIGURE 4.1 ■ Types of Physicians in Open Fraud and Abuse Cases at the end of Fiscal Year 2019 and in 2019

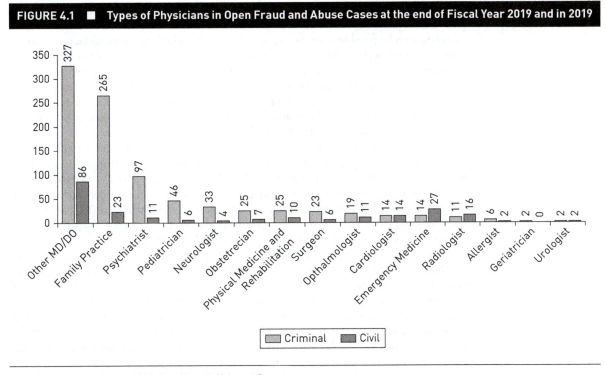

Source: Medicaid Fraud Control Unit Fiscal Year 2019 Annual Report

Before assuming that their overrepresentation stems from levels of honesty, it is important to consider the nature of billing practices for psychiatrists and psychologists as compared to other health care professionals (Geis et al., 1985). Briefly, mental health professionals often bill for time, whereas other professionals bill for more complicated medical procedures. For investigators, it is much easier to prove "time violations" than "treatment violations." Investigators can ask patients how long they spent with their provider and compare the patient's statement with the providers' bill submitted to the insurance company. If investigators ask about the treatment they received from physicians, it is unlikely that the patient would be able to identify the services with the same degree of precision.

It is important to realize that other health care professionals also bill for time rather than services. Estimates suggest that one in five anesthesiologists, for instance, round up their time in five-minute increments (Coustasse, Frame, & Mukherjee, 2018). This may not seem like a lot, but the cumulative results of these rounding practices across all anesthesiologists would be in the millions.

Other patterns characterizing health care fraud have also been identified in prior research. For example, research shows that when females are accused of health care fraud, they tend to be accused along with other providers more than male offenders are (Payne, 1995). It is plausible that females are prosecuted along with more powerful providers in an effort to get female providers to testify against their colleagues, or in some cases, their bosses.

Another pattern surrounding health care fraud is related to the systems approach—changes in the broader system have influenced the distribution and characteristics of health care fraud (Payne, 2005). For example, just as the nature of health care changes, so too does the nature of health care fraud. As the technological system changed, opportunities for health care fraud changed. As the number of doctors changed in the 1970s and 1980s (a period in which the number of doctors increased by 66%), allegations of fraud and convictions for health care fraud also increased (Bucy, 1989). In fact, "convictions of health care providers increased almost 234% between 1979 and 1986" (Bucy, 1989, p. 870).

Explanations for fraud have focused on structural explanations, socialization factors, cultural factors, and enforcement dynamics. In terms of structural explanations, some have argued that the structure of the Medicare and Medicaid systems is believed to "invite fraud and abuse" (Pontell et al., 1982, p.119). Low reimbursement rates, complex red tape, and bureaucratic confusion make participation in the programs difficult for health care providers. To get paid the same amount that they get paid for treating patients with private insurance, some physicians and other health care providers have fraudulently billed Medicare and Medicaid.

Socialization explanations focus on how medical students perceive Medicaid and Medicare. In general, research shows that students have less than favorable attitudes toward the programs (Byars & Payne, 2000; Keenan, Brown, Pontell, & Geis, 1985). Surveys of 144 medical students found that the students supported tougher penalties for fraudulent providers, but they also believed that structural changes in Medicare and Medicaid were warranted (Keenan, Brown, Pontell, & Geis, 1985). In effect, there is a possibility that medical students are learning to perceive the insurance programs negatively during their medical training.

Cultural factors explore how health care fraud occurs in various cultures. Across the globe, it has been estimated that "any health care organization will lose between 3 and 10 percent to fraud and abuse" (Brooks, Button, & Gee, 2012). The amount lost is tied to specific features of the health care system. In Sweden, for example, the country shifted its health care system toward privatization. According to Jesilow (2012), the move "will likely increase fraud" (p. 32). His suggestion is traced to the fee-for-service payment system that, in his view, incentivizes fraud. In essence, cultures with public health care would, theoretically, have less fraud than those that have payment systems encouraging fraud.

Enforcement explanations suggest that the pervasiveness of fraud is attributed to the historical lack of criminal justice enforcement activities against health care providers. This changed in the 1990s when state and federal enforcement efforts in this area increased. Legislative changes were also enacted. For example, the **Health Insurance Portability Act of 1996** was passed to make health care fraud a federal offense, with penalties ranging from 10 years to life (if the fraud leads to a death). Even with these stiffer penalties, responding to health care fraud is difficult to say the least. Many of the typical problems plaguing white-collar crime investigations surface; these will be discussed in Chapter 13. The types of witness problems that surface in health care fraud cases are likely unique to this variety of white-collar crime. The following are some of the witness problems that make it harder to enforce health care laws:

- Patients don't understand billing processes.

- The patients are sick and aren't able to review bills.

- The value placed on life encourages health care fraud at any cost.

- Patients aren't as concerned about insurance fraud given that a third-party is paying for the services (Sullivan & Hull, 2019).

In considering the prevalence of health care fraud, attention should be drawn to the fact that not all health care fraud cases are committed by those working in the medical field. Some offenders might be patients or increasingly organized crime units. Organized crime fraud actually includes large-scale frauds where offenders create phantom clinics and processes that may lack any type of health care delivery services whatsoever (Meyers, 2017). It is believed that the structure of health care provides opportunities for widespread fraud by organized crime entities. Consider, for example, the fake Covid-19 testing sites and medical treatments that surfaced during the coronavirus pandemic. A research brief from the United Nations Office on Drugs and Crime (2020) published just three months into the pandemic drew attention to the point that "high demand coupled with low supply in key sectors opens way for organized crime groups" (p. 1). The high demand for health care to treat and test for Covid-19, combined with the limited availability of health care and testing, created opportunities for organized crime to flourish during the pandemic.

Unnecessary Surgery

The phrase unnecessary surgery refers to surgical procedures performed on patients that are medically unnecessary. It is difficult to gauge the true extent of the problem. A *USA Today* study found that "tens of thousands" of unnecessary surgeries are committed each year, and that "unnecessary surgeries might account for 10% to 20% of all operations in some specialties, including a wide range of cardiac procedures—not only stents, but also angioplasty and pacemaker implants—as well as many spinal surgeries" (Eisler & Hansen, 2013). Describing the overuse of screening methods and treatments for prostate cancer, Otis Brawley (2009), chief medical officer for the American Cancer Society, commented, "Every treatment looks good, when *more than* 90% of men getting it *do not* need it" (p. 1295).

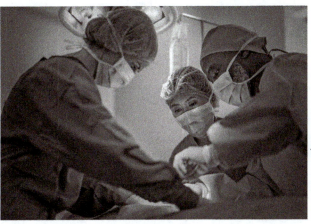

PHOTO 4.2 Unnecessary surgeries are one type of white-collar offense in the health care field. The vast majority of these cases go undetected.

At least six overlapping reasons help explain the pervasiveness of unnecessary surgeries. First, differing opinions among medical providers will likely result in some providers recommending surgery and other providers recommending a different course of action. Medicine is not an exact science, and those providing unnecessary services would likely justify the services on various medical grounds.

Second, the stigma of various forms of disease is such that patients are willing to expose themselves to procedures in order to battle and overcome the disease. Consider prostate cancer. While Brawley (2009) notes that many prostate cancer treatments are not needed, he recognizes that the very concept of cancer creates fear in individuals who have long assumed that all forms of cancers must be eradicated to live a full life. Most of us would never assume that we can live with cancer or that it would go away on its own. Brawley suggests that we are misinformed in that sense.

Third, the degree of trust that individuals have for their health care providers is such that patients tend to assume that procedures ordered by doctors are necessary. Assuming otherwise opens us up to the risk of the consequences of whatever ailment we are battling. The adage "better safe than sorry" comes to mind. In general, we trust our doctors and will follow their surgical and procedural advice as a matter of protecting ourselves from harm. The irony is that unnecessary procedures may create harm.

Fourth, while we are socialized to trust our health care providers, we have at the same time been socialized not to trust insurance companies. Regularly, we hear of situations where insurance companies deny coverage on the grounds that procedures are not needed. The typical reaction is to assume that the medical provider's recommendation is correct and any suggestion otherwise, particularly those offered by representatives of the insurance industry, are cast aside.

Fifth, and somewhat related to the above explanations, one can draw attention to what can be coined the "medicalized socialization" that we experience in our lives. In effect, we are socialized to turn to the health care system to fix our illnesses, diseases, and ailments. Although more attention has recently been given to preventing diseases in the first place, as consumers, we have an expectation that our health care needs will be met by health care providers. In effect, we have long played a passive role in receiving health care rather than administering our own health care. As a result, we pass our health care decisions off to our providers.

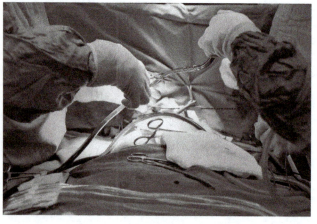

©iStockphoto.com/baranozdemir

PHOTO 4.3 Health care providers hold the lives of their patients in their hands. It is generally agreed that most are ethical and law abiding. Those who are not create serious consequences for their victims.

Finally, one can point to conflict explanations to address the persistence of unnecessary surgeries. Conflict explanations point to the economic gains of health care for those with power. Consider that the United States spends 53% more on health care per person than other countries spend (Anderson, Hussey, Frogner, & Waters, 2005). Anderson and his coauthors (2005) argue that it is not overuse that is causing these high expenditures but high prices in the first place. From a conflict perspective, those with power control the pricing of health care. Moreover, by pricing surgeries and procedures at a high price, an even stronger incentive may exist to commit unnecessary surgeries. It's one thing to perform an unnecessary wart removal, which would be a low-cost surgery; it's quite another to perform unnecessary coronary bypass, which was cited as the most common unnecessary surgery in the United States in 2005 (Black, 2005). It's not clear if bypass surgeries are still the most common, but recent research led by Stanford scientists (e.g., the International Study of Comparative Health Effectiveness With Medical and Invasive Approaches) continues to call into question the necessity of a large number of heart procedures. The results from the study, highlighted in the *Washington Post,* "suggest that invasive procedures, stents and bypass surgery, should be used more sparingly in patients with stable heart disease and the decision to use them should be less rushed" (Johnson, 2019). As another example, consider that women in the United States have four times more hysterectomies than women in Sweden (Parker, 2009). According to Black (2005), "the only people who seem to really benefit from these unnecessary medical procedures are the medical professionals who stand to make exorbitant amounts of money from performing them."

Many severe consequences may arise from unnecessary surgeries. A case described by Jesilow and his colleagues (1985) suggests that unnecessary surgeries are analogous to assaults. They cite a case where an ophthalmologist performed several unnecessary eye surgeries that left patients with either impaired vision or blindness. The doctor performed the procedures simply so he could bill Medicaid for them. Also, note that unnecessary surgeries and other types of health care fraud deprive people in lower socioeconomic groups of the health care they need (Pontell et al., 1982; Sullivan & Hull, 2019). By spending government funds on unnecessary health care procedures, those funds are diverted from those individuals who actually need the health care. Another irony is that when practitioners dole out health care procedures to people who don't need them, those who do need the health care services are deprived of them.

Other consequences also surface. For example, the element of time is relevant. Think about how long a visit to the doctor takes. Individuals need to leave work, drive to the office or clinic, wait in the waiting room, get moved back to the exam room only to wait some more, and then undergo the procedure or surgery. Then, they are sent to the pharmacist where they will have to spend more time to complete that particular transaction. In the end, if the procedure or surgery was unnecessary, all of this time was wasted (Payne & Berg, 1997). Another consequence of an unnecessary surgery or procedure is that it may cause mental anguish or stress for people. That the surgeries or procedures are unnecessary but still happen suggests that providers may be mentally bullying patients into getting these procedures.

Surgical errors are a related problem. It is important to note that there are different degrees of surgery errors. Some are less serious and perhaps mistakes but not crimes. Others are quite serious and can cause serious damage and potentially death. In one case, for example, a doctor was sentenced to life in prison after a series of botched surgeries including one that paralyzed a patient, with a review showing "implants placed in muscle instead of in bone, a screw drilled into [the patient's] spinal cavity, and a nerve root that had been amputated" (Ballor, 2017).

Medication Errors

Medication errors occur when health care providers deliver or prescribe the wrong medications to patients. These errors can be harmful in two ways: (1) The patient is given a drug he or she does not need, and this drug could cause harm; or (2) the patient could experience harm from not getting the drug that is actually needed. Cox (2010) notes that doctors have long said, "Do not let your friends and family schedule hospital visits in July." The basis for this "warning" is the increase in medication errors that seem to occur each July. Cox describes a study by sociologists David Phillips and Gwendolyn Parker that addressed why this spike in errors seems to occur.

Phillips and Parker, sociologists from the University of San Diego, examined 244,388 deaths occurring from medication errors between 1979 and 2006. They found that deaths at a high number of teaching hospitals increased by 10% in July each year. This finding supported previous speculation that the "July effect" could be attributed to the fact that new doctors and residents begin practicing in July. Thus, their lack of experience is believed to contribute to medication errors.

Phillips shared an interesting exchange with another reporter: "One physician—not knowing I was studying this issue—referred to the issue and said to me: 'It's possible, you should probably avoid going in [being hospitalized] during July'" (Raloff, 2010).

General Offending by Doctors

A number of other types of misconduct are committed by malfeasant doctors during the course of their occupational routines. These other types can be characterized as general offending by doctors. The nonprofit group, Public Citizen, collects data on physicians involved in misconduct and has published a report and database called **Questionable Doctors**. The report includes information about doctors, their violations, and sanctions given to doctors (Lim, 2002). According to Public Citizen, the types of physician misconduct are wide ranging. From most serious to least serious, the general types of offending by doctors include the following:

- Conviction of a crime

- Practicing without a license or issuing and writing prescriptions without a license

- Losing hospital privileges

- Failing to comply with an order from a medical board

- Deceiving a medical board

- Providing substandard or incompetent care

- Sexually abusing a patient

- Drug or alcohol abuse

- Overprescribing drugs

- Practicing medicine with a mental illness that inhibits service delivery

- Committing insurance fraud

- Falsifying patient records

- Overcharging

- Professional misconduct (e.g., unprofessional behavior)
- Failure to comply with a professional rule (e.g., child abuse reporting) (Lim, 2002, pp. 154–155)

Lim (2002) used the Questionable Doctors database to review the types of violations and crimes committed by women doctors in California between 1990 and 1994. Of the 425 violations she reviewed, just 30 were committed by female physicians. Most frequently, female physicians were sanctioned for being convicted of a crime, providing substandard care, and failing to comply with a professional rule. Lim noted that the violations committed by women doctors were usually "self-inflicted" (p. 163).

TELEMEDICINE FRAUD

Telehealth or **telemedicine** refers to the provision of health services through the telephone, computer, or other telephonic or digital mediums. While some may think that telemedicine is new, it has actually been around in different forms for some time. In fact, more than 25 years ago, a doctor from the Mayo clinic said that telemedicine was in a stage of "giddy adolescence." If that's the case, telemedicine today is in adulthood. With growth in technology, patients all over the world can now access health care with methods not available just a few decades ago. At the same time, just like other types of health care, telemedicine is not immune from health care fraud and abuse. Like other types of health care fraud, the structure of the telehealth process provides increased opportunities for fraud and abuse.

Telehealth industry fraud is affected by telemedicine structure in six ways:

1. ***The nature of telemedicine services makes certain types of fraud easier to commit.*** Because no physical office or in-person appointment is needed, offenders simply need to access the technology and do not have to physically access the office or written records. Telehealth fraud offenders would also have no physical contact with the patients. In effect, some types of telemedicine fraud might be conceptualized as varieties of cybercrime (discussed more in Chapter 9). One of the largest health care fraud cases investigated by the FBI, for example, involved a 1.2 billion (yes, billion) dollar scheme involving five telemedicine companies conspiring with durable medical equipment companies to fraudulently distribute unnecessary medical equipment to elderly and disabled patients contacted only by phone, if they even contacted patients at all. Highlighting the seriousness of this scheme, the attorney general announcing the investigation said, "These defendants—who range from corporate executives to medical professionals—allegedly participated in an expansive and sophisticated fraud to exploit telemedicine technology meant for patients otherwise unable to access health car," (U.S. Department of Justice, 2019).

2. ***Technology allows for easier collection of evidence.*** While telemedicine fraud might be easier to commit, technological advances have made it easier to detect or gather evidence about a telehealth fraud. Because telehealth connections are done digitally, it is easy to track how much time providers are spending with patients. Recall that psychiatrists are overrepresented in fraud allegations, primarily because they bill for time. With telehealth, investigators and auditors can determine whether excessive billing or billing irregularities are occurring by comparing bills to digital records. The electronic evidence provides clear and indisputable evidence about how much time was spent in the provision of health care.

3. ***Some types of telehealth fraud might be easier to rationalize or excuse.*** Since the field is still relatively new with complex regulations, practitioners may blame the maze of confusing and changing rules for their errors. Analogous to the way that drivers might blame new traffic laws when they are stopped by the police, legal experts routinely highlight how difficult it is to understand telehealth law (Kadzielski & Kim, 2014). Said one health lawyer,

> Licensing laws and unclear liability rules result in formidable barriers to the expanded use of telemedicine. At the same time, these laws fail to provide sufficient patient protection. Unduly restrictive licensing laws create onerous burdens on health care providers while failing to protect the people for whose benefit they were supposedly enacted. Similarly, unclear liability rules expose both providers and consumers to the possibility of catastrophic losses (Daly, 2000, p. 75).

Two decades after Daly drew attention to the unclear laws, legal scholars continue to point to the ambiguity surrounding telemedicine laws (Mazur, Helak, Van Demark, & Stauffer, 2020).

4. ***More regulations mean more opportunities to break the rules.*** Simply, if there are no rules, there are no crimes. When there are more rules, there are more crimes. As one author notes, "The bottom line is that there is wide variation from state to state in telehealth rules and regulations. [Practitioners] working in several states (in person or via telemedicine) could be at risk for legal action from regulatory authorities such as the Board of Nursing if they do not have the appropriate licenses, certifications, and training or experience within the scope of practice in each state required to practice" (Balestra, 2018, p. 34).

5. ***The types of fraud perpetrated in telemedicine are connected to the structure of the telehealth industry.*** Simply put, one wouldn't expect procedures such as unnecessary surgeries or patient abuse to be committed in the telehealth sector. After all, there is no physical contact between the provider and the patient. Other varieties of fraud, however, are more likely. For example, allegations of illegal kickback schemes, upcoding, and billing for services never provided appear to be reported more often in cases described in the media.

6. ***The need for secure telehealth practices is paramount.*** In fact, health care providers who fail to provide secure cyber technology for the delivery of telehealth practices could be held liable if their patients' health data is breached. As a result, several businesses have developed solely to help telehealth providers secure their clients' health information. The existence of these businesses is justified by data showing the high percentage of identity theft cases connected to medical data. A 2009 estimate from the Federal Trade Commission (FTC) showed that 3% of identity theft cases could be traced to medical data (Terry, 2009). Asked by a reporter whether telemedicine was more susceptible to identity theft than traditional medicine, a security respondent said, "That would be a big fat yes. It's almost like the perfect crime as far as identity theft and telemedicine security medical identity theft is concerned. The long-distance nature of this type of treatment fuels the anonymity of it all" (Terry, 2009). Data support the expert's prediction. By 2017, estimates from Experian suggested that 27% of all data breaches were related medical data (O'Connor, 2017).

Some have argued that concerns about fraud in telemedicine are exaggerated and that telemedicine "should decrease the potential for fraud and abuse" (Bashshur, 1995). However, the claims that telemedicine decreases fraud mostly predate the technological revolution. Today's technology is much different than the technology of the mid-1990s, and these technological shifts would potentially make telemedicine fraud, as a form of cybercrime, much easier

(Holt, 2018). Additionally, recall that there was little concern about fraud in Medicaid and Medicare when those programs were initially created. That lack of concern potentially contributed to the widespread growth of fraud in the health care programs.

Experts point to regulatory changes as a primary tool to limit telemedicine fraud. The loose regulations in the industry have been cited as a potential source of "virtual abuse" in telemedicine (Zhang, 2016). Tightening up those regulations, then, could help to limit misconduct in telemedicine. Crafting rules to clarify how telemedicine can be used across state borders is also a possible solution (Bashshur, Doarn, Frenk, Kvedar, & Woolliscroft, 2020). With technological changes occurring so rapidly—much more rapidly than policy changes—technology has outpaced law and policy in the health care arena. This chapter's *White-Collar Crime in the News* shows just how enormous these schemes can be.

WHITE-COLLAR CRIME IN THE NEWS
TELEMEDICINE COMPANY OWNER CHARGED IN $60 MILLION FRAUD SCHEME

The following is a press release from the Southern District of Georgia from April 23, 2020.

SAVANNAH, GA: A Georgia woman who operated a telemedicine network through two companies has been charged for her alleged participation in an ever-growing healthcare and telemedicine fraud scheme.

++++++++, the operator of ++++++++ and ++++++++, both Georgia companies, is accused of conspiring to pay medical providers, like physicians and nurse practitioners, in exchange for obtaining orders for durable medical equipment (DME) that would then be sold to DME providers and, ultimately, billed to Medicare. The financial total for orders facilitated through this scheme is alleged to be in excess of $60 million for thousands of patient orders. Medicare beneficiaries were located in the Southern District of Georgia and elsewhere. The defendant was charged by way of an Information, filed in the U.S. District Court for the Southern District of Georgia.

"Our prosecutors and law enforcement partners will continue to use all available resources to dismantle networks engaging in unlawful schemes that place profit over legitimate medical treatment," said U.S. Attorney Bobby L. Christine. This prosecution, arising out of the related "Operation Brace Yourself" and "Operation Double Helix," together with those previously announced, involve the largest fraud operation in the history of the Southern District of Georgia. Previously charged in this string of cases include eight physicians, two nurse practitioners, two operators of different telemedicine companies, two brokers of patient data, and several owners of durable medical equipment companies. The

Medicare and Medicaid beneficiaries whose identities were used as part of the scheme are located throughout the country, including throughout the Southern District of Georgia.

The combined $470 million in fraud charged in the Southern District of Georgia is part of nationwide operations by the Department of Justice that thus far has included allegations involving billions of fraudulent claims for genetic testing, orthotic braces, pain creams, and other items.

"This $60-million fraud scheme is one small piece of a much larger operation that has put tremendous strain on our federally-subsidized healthcare programs," said Chris Hacker, Special Agent in Charge of FBI Atlanta. "We will always protect our tax paying citizens, who are all victims of greedy providers, especially those who need government assistance for their health care needs."

"Let this criminal charge be a warning to anyone who feels the need to fraudulently enrich themselves at the expense of our nation's Medicare beneficiaries," said Derrick L. Jackson, Special Agent in Charge at the U.S. Department of Health and Human Services, Office of Inspector General in Atlanta. "HHS/OIG, along with our partners, vows to continue the fight against such fraudulent schemes."

"Cases of this magnitude can only be tackled using a strategy that recognizes that the most effective way to fight these large criminal networks is by combining the strengths, resources, and expertise of our federal agencies," said Resident Agent in Charge Glen M. Kessler of the U.S. Secret Service. "Our nation's healthcare system cannot tolerate kickbacks to physicians and pharmacies while criminals line their pockets with taxpayer-funded healthcare dollars."

Indictments or criminal informations contain only charges; defendants are presumed innocent unless and until proven guilty.

This investigation is ongoing. As telemedicine becomes an increasing part of our healthcare system, vigilance in ensuring that fraud and kickbacks do not usurp the legitimate practice of medicine by electronic means is more important than ever.

Reprinted from US Department of Justice

Source: https://www.justice.gov/usao-sdga/pr/telemedicine-company-owner-charged-60-million-fraud-scheme

FRAUD BY PHARMACISTS

Doctors are not the only upper-class members of the health care profession to engage in fraudulent activities. Pharmacists have also been implicated in numerous frauds and abuses against the insurance system. Interestingly, pharmacists have long been rated among the top most trusted professions on trust surveys of the public. That some of them commit fraud is not a reason to lower the profession's trust ratings, but one must be careful not to assume that all pharmacists are playing by the rules that guide their occupational activities.

Because pharmacists have long been viewed as so trustworthy, few criminologists have focused on deviant action in this profession. One researcher, Dean Dabney, conducted several studies examining illicit drug use by pharmacists. Interviewing dozens of pharmacists, Dabney's research suggests that proximity to drugs that are readily available and belief that they know enough about the drugs to self-medicate contribute to their decisions to use and subsequently abuse drugs.

In one of his pharmacist studies, Payne and Dabney (1997) (that's me, by the way) examined 292 cases of **prescription fraud** prosecuted by fraud control units across the United States. Our research uncovered eight types of fraud among the prosecuted cases. **Generic drug substitution** involved cases where the pharmacist gave the consumer a generic drug but billed the insurance company for a more expensive drug (imagine if you bought a box of your favorite cereal made by one of the top cereal makers and generic cereal was in the box, but the box was branded with the more expensive cereal). **Short counting** occurs when pharmacists dispense fewer pills than prescribed, but they bill the insurance company as if they had dispensed all of the pills (do you count the pills to make sure you got them all?). Like fraud by doctors, **double billing** occurs when pharmacists bill more than two parties for the same prescription. **Billing for nonexistent prescriptions** occurs when pharmacists bill for prescriptions that never actually existed. Forgery occurs when pharmacists forge the signature of the doctor or the consumer or forge the name of a more expensive drug on the prescription. **Mislabeling of drugs** occurs when pharmacists label drugs incorrectly in an effort to hide the fact that the pharmacist did not provide the prescribed drug to the patient. **Delivery of a controlled substance** is more of a legal term and a reference to instances when the pharmacist wrongfully, perhaps without a prescription, provides controlled substances to consumers. Finally, **illegally buying prescriptions** involves situations where pharmacists buy prescriptions from patients and then bill the insurance company without filling the prescription.

This last variety of prescription fraud typically involves schemes whereby pharmacists work with drug addicts to carry out the offense. The pharmacist instructs the addict to go to different doctors and get prescriptions filled. The addict is instructed to fake an illness (one that the pharmacist suggests) so that the doctor writes an expensive prescription for the addict. The addict gives the pharmacist the prescription. The pharmacist gives the addict some drugs (usually something addictive like painkillers); then, the pharmacist bills the insurance agency for the prescription that was never actually filled. As will be shown in the policing chapter, to respond to these cases, undercover law enforcement officers sometimes pose as drug addicts to establish a case against the pharmacist.

Past research has demonstrated difficulty convicting pharmacists. Excluding those schemes where pharmacists illegally buy prescriptions, a common defense used by pharmacists is that they must have misread the doctor's handwriting. If you have ever tried to read a prescription, you will likely be inclined to accept this claim. After all, the handwriting of doctors does, in fact, seem to be very difficult to read. However, pharmacists are trained to read their shorthand, and if they are unable to read it, regulations stipulate that they are supposed to call the doctor's office for clarification.

My research with Dabney identified six patterns of prescription fraud by pharmacists. First, offenders tended to be male. Second, the cases rarely resulted in incarceration, except for egregious cases. Third, in some cases, assistants were convicted, presumably in an effort to sustain a conviction against the pharmacist. Fourth, the vast majority of convictions were obtained through guilty pleas, with 95% of the convicted pharmacists entering guilty pleas. Fifth, the cases of misconduct were hard to detect, with forgery being the hardest to detect. Finally, when cases were identified, convicted pharmacists tended to have committed several cases of misconduct. Consider the following case:

> [Defendant] submitted false claims for 9,042 prescriptions for 43 patients whose physician never issued the prescriptions and for patients who never received the prescriptions. On some occasions, it is alleged that [the defendant] billed for as many as 37 fraudulent prescriptions for a single patient on the same day. . . . [The defendant] was paid a total of $220,588 to which he was not entitled by the Medicaid program for these fraudulent claims. (National Association of Medicaid Fraud Control Units, 1991, p. 18)

Certainly, the case demonstrates how some instances of prescription fraud can be particularly egregious.

DRUG USE BY PHARMACISTS

Illicit drug use by pharmacists is another area of concern in the pharmacy industry. Estimates suggest that up to 65% of practicing pharmacists have engaged in "some form of illicit drug use at least once during their career" and approximately one fifth "used drugs regularly enough that they experienced negative life outcomes" (Dabney & Hollinger, 2002, p. 182). It appears that, compared to other professionals, pharmacists have higher rates of substance abuse problems.

To determine how pharmacists initiated their drug use, Dabney and Hollinger (2002) interviewed 50 drug-addicted pharmacists who were in recovery. They identified two distinct pathways to drug use among addicted pharmacists. Twenty-three of the pharmacists followed a **"recreational path"** to their addiction. These pharmacists began by using illegal street drugs, and then, after entering pharmacy training, they expanded their drug use to include prescription drugs. Experimentation and social acceptability themes (by fellow pharmacy students) were common patterns found in the pharmacists' recreational drug use.

The second type of pharmacist addict was labeled **"therapeutic self-medicators"** by Dabney and Hollinger (2002). These pharmacists had little exposure to recreational drug use in their pre-employment lives. Their involvement in drug use typically "focused on specific therapeutic goals" (p. 196) and was often the result of health problems (such as insomnia, arthritis, etc.) or trauma (from car accidents, broken bones, or other traumatic incidents). The authors suggested that in the early stages of use, these pharmacists appeared to be "model pharmacists." They defined their drug use in noble terms, suggesting, for example, that they did not want to miss work as a result of their ailment and the drug use allowed them to go to work and help consumers who needed their own prescriptions filled. Eventually, these pharmacists began to create illnesses in order to convince themselves that they needed more drugs. Calling these pharmacists "drug-thirsty pharmacists," the research team quoted one pharmacist who said, "I had a symptom for everything I took" (p. 199).

Elsewhere, the same research team focused on how opportunity, awareness about drugs, and technical knowledge interacted to promote drug use by pharmacists (Dabney & Hollinger, 1999). They wrote, "In the absence of proper appreciation of the risks of substance abuse, [technical knowledge and opportunity] can delude pharmacists into believing that they are immune to prescription drug use" (Dabney & Hollinger, 1999, p. 77). The authors characterized 40 of the 50 pharmacists as *poly-drug* users, meaning that the pharmacists used more than one type of drug. Thirty of the pharmacists were referred to as "garbage heads," alluding to a drug treatment term that describes those who use whatever drug they can get their hands on. The authors also highlighted the process of "titrating," where pharmacists used "their pharmaceutical knowledge to manage their personal drug use, enhancing or neutralizing specific drug effects by ingesting counteractive drugs" (Dabney & Hollinger, 1999, p. 90).

Dabney and Hollinger (1999) described the "paradox of familiarity" that characterized pharmacists' drug using patterns. Pharmacists were exposed to positive aspects of the substances through aggressive marketing campaigns by pharmaceutical representatives, and their routine exposure to prescription drugs was such that drugs were defined as positive substances designed to help consumers. As the authors wrote, "they believed that these drugs could only improve lives; and therefore, they dismissed or minimized the dangers. Self-medication became a viable and attractive form of medicating every problem" (p. 95). In other words, pharmacists believed they knew enough about drugs that they would not succumb to the dangers of drug use.

Note that drug use by pharmacists is not in and of itself a white-collar crime. One of two conditions must be present for the substance abusing behavior to be considered a white-collar crime. First, if drugs are stolen from the workplace in order to feed the pharmacist's habit, then a white-collar crime has been committed. Second, if the pharmacist is under the influence of illicit substances while at work, one can argue that a white-collar crime has occurred. It is also important to point out that other health care professionals may also abuse drugs (Foli, Reddick, Zhang, & Edwards 2019; Lowry, 2018). Many health care professionals have access to drugs, familiarity with the effects of the drugs, opportunities to conceal their drug use, feelings of invincibility over drugs, and stressful work situations. These dynamics increase the risk of drug abuse by health care providers. This chapter's Streaming White-Collar Crime provides insight on one television show capturing these themes.

STREAMING WHITE-COLLAR CRIME *Nurse Jackie*

Plot	What You Can Learn	Discussion Questions
Jackie is a seasoned nurse who cares deeply about her patients. As a nurse, she is skilled, capable, and committed to helping her patients however she can. A capable mentor and colleague, she has one weakness—she's a drug addict. The show chronicles her addictions, including white-collar crimes such as drug theft and performing health care while under the influence. Efforts by the hospital to control drug theft are a reminder that offenders will find ways to overcome security strategies. Through it all, Jackie is portrayed more as a flawed character who succumbs to addiction rather than a criminal who is putting her patients and herself at risk.	Drug addiction is a real problem among health care professionals. Working in the health care system is incredibly stressful. Health care institutions implement a wide range of activities to prevent drug theft.	How can drug use be classified as a white-collar crime? Why does it matter if we consider medical drug crimes white-collar crimes rather than street crimes? Should medical professionals who abuse drugs be punished differently than traditional drug offenders?

SEXUAL ABUSE

In this context, **sexual abuse** refers to situations where health care providers (doctors, dentists, psychologists, psychiatrists, etc.) engage in sexual relationships with their patients. The belief that doctors shouldn't have sexual relationships with patients has been described as "one of the most universally agreed upon ethical principles in medicine" (Abudagga, Carome, & Wolfe, 2019, p. 1330). Despite this widespread agreement, four types of health care provider-patient sexual relationships exist: (1) power and prestige relationships, (2) mental health controlling relationships, (3) drug-induced relationships, and (4) sexual assault.

First, in terms of power and prestige relationships, patients may become enamored of their health care providers. This can lead them to open themselves up to relationships with their providers based on the prestige and power that the providers have over the patients. Such relationships run counter to the provider's ethical codes and can do a great deal of emotional harm to patients.

Second, mental health controlling relationships occur in situations where individuals have sexual relationships with mental health providers (psychiatrist, psychologist, counselor, etc.). It is impossible to know how often these relationships occur, but note that those who seek mental health counseling are in vulnerable states. Surveys of adult incest survivors found that the 30 survivors sought professional therapy from 113 different professionals. Seven of those 30 survivors had a sexual relationship with their helping professional (Armsworth, 1989). Research suggests that psychiatrists are overrepresented in accusations of sexual misconduct with patients (Morrison & Morrison, 2001). Factors that contribute to this include the following dynamics:

- Working in isolation

- An increased amount of direct contact with patients

- Longer appointments

- More personal discussions with patients

- Vulnerability of patients (Morrison & Morrison, 2001)

Third, drug-induced relationships occur when health care providers get their patients addicted to drugs so they can have sex with the patients in exchange for access to drugs. These actions are clearly illegal on several different levels. In addition, besides feeding a chemical addiction and harming the victim physically, the health care provider is harming the victim emotionally. In one recent case, a doctor had his license suspended after it was alleged that the he had provided a "pain-killer addicted woman drugs in exchange for sex" (Pulkkinen, 2010). In another case, it was alleged that Dr. Michael Rusling, a doctor in Britain, "threatened to withhold drugs from a depressed patient if she refused to have sexual intercourse with him" ("Doctor 'Threatened to Withhold,'" 2009). Three patients said they had sexual relationships with Rusling, with one of them having sex with him at her home so often that one of her neighbors thought she had a serious health condition.

Fourth, sexual assault occurs when the provider sexually abuses (e.g., rapes) a patient during the course of providing care. Dentist Mark Anderson, for example, was convicted of "feeling up" women as part of their dental treatment. In all, 27 women claimed that Anderson groped their breasts during dental examinations. Anderson defended his actions on the grounds that he was providing medical therapy in an effort to treat temporo-mandibular joint disorder, better known as TMJ ("Accused Dentist," 2007). The dentist was eventually convicted and sentenced to six years in prison.

It is important to note that offenders may commit sexual abuse and particularly sexual harassment against their colleagues. A survey of 141 emergency medicine faculty, including 51 female faculty, found that female doctors experienced gender-based discrimination at the hands of patients, doctors, and nursing staff (Lu et al., 2020). More than half of the female doctors reported experiencing "unwanted sexual behavior in their careers," with unwanted advances and sexual remarks being the most common" (Lu et al., 2020).

While sexual abuse by physicians against patients is a serious concern, equally concerning and most certainly more prevalent is sexual harassment between medical professionals. After publishing a study showing a high prevalence of sexual harassment among physicians, a medical researcher wrote a follow-up article summarizing the reaction to her study after the article was published (Jagsi, 2018). The researcher shared several stories about victims who had reached out to her to discuss their own experiences with sexual harassment in the health care field. She also provided a glimpse into how prevailing attitudes might support, if not promote, the behavior. Consider the following example:

> But standing up to harassment is clearly hard. In one case, a talented physician researcher had engaged in a witnessed act of unwanted sexual contact with a trainee. Yet two department chairs in his field independently told me they were trying to recruit the transgressor, who was considered a hot prospect, even as sexual misconduct proceedings were under way at his home institution. "It was just a mistake; we need to forgive and forget," said one. "I have both sons and daughters, so I can see both sides," said the other. Both worried about fallout if the behavior were to recur, but neither wanted to forgo the opportunity to steal away a super-star. These discussions high-lighted how easy it can be to turn a blind eye to offenses by luminaries like Harvey Weinstein and Kevin Spacey. (Jagsi, 2018, 210).

One author team has described three dilemmas that arise in responding to these cases. First, for a wide variety of reasons, victims are often unwilling to report these cases to the authorities. Second, organizations, hospitals, and medical groups may circumvent and ignore reporting requirements if they become aware of abuse. Third, as with other types of violations by doctors, medical boards may be lax in how they respond to these crimes (Abudagga et al., 2019). An additional dilemma is that finding information about these cases to protect against future victimization is complicated with allegations hidden from future patients and researchers alike (Brockman, 2018).

Available data show that 9.5 out of 10,000 physicians in the United States faced disciplinary actions for sexual misconduct between 2003 and 2013 (Abudagga et al., 2019). Studying these allegations, Abudagga and colleagues (Abudagga, Wolfe, Carome, & Oshel, 2016) identified the following patterns:

- Offenders were more likely to be between 40 and 59 years old, with fewer younger physicians participating in sexual misconduct (in comparison to the total percentage of younger physicians).

- Among 167 sexual misconduct malpractice reports, victims tended to be younger (between 20 and 39) and female (87%).

- The vast majority of malpractice cases were classified as "emotional injury only" (82%).

The classification "emotional injury only" should not minimize the injuries the offenders caused. In some cases, in fact, emotional injuries outlast physical injuries.

ELDER ABUSE BY HEALTH CARE WORKERS

Elder abuse can be defined as "any criminal, physical, or emotional harm or unethical taking advantage that negatively affects the physical, financial, or general well-being of an elderly person" (Payne, Berg, & Byars, 1999, p. 81). In terms of crimes by workers in the health care field, the following types of elder abuse are relevant: (1) elder physical abuse, (2) elder financial abuse, (3) elder neglect, (4) elder sexual abuse, and (5) failure to report crimes.

In this context, **elder physical abuse** entails instances where workers hit, slap, kick, or otherwise physically harm an older person for whom they are being paid to provide care. **Pacification** (or overmedicating) and restraining are also included as forms of elder physical abuse. In one of the earliest studies on physical patient abuse, Pillemer and Moore (1990) conducted phone interviews with 577 nurses' aides and nurses working in nursing homes in Massachusetts. In all, more than a third of the workers said they had seen instances where a resident was abused in the previous year, and one tenth of the respondents indicated they had been abusive themselves in the prior year. In another study, researchers suggested that 8 out of 10 nurses and aides saw elder abuse cases in the prior year (Crumb & Jennings, 1998).

Payne and Cikovic (1995) examined 488 cases of patient abuse prosecuted by Medicaid Fraud Control Units across the United States. They found that the offenses typically occurred in isolation, and aides seemed to be overrepresented in allegations of abuse. They also found that the victim-offender relationship followed gender patterns: Males were more likely to abuse males, and females were more likely to abuse females. More recently, a study of 801 cases of patient abuse identified three types of offenders: (1) stressed offenders who committed the offense as a result of a stressful interaction with the patient, (2) serial abusers who committed multiple offenses at work, and (3) pathological tormentors who committed heinous offenses designed to humiliate or control victims (Payne & Gainey, 2006).

Elder financial abuse is a second type of elder abuse committed by care providers. The National Center on Elder Abuse offers the following definition of elder financial abuse:

> Financial or material exploitation is defined as the illegal or improper use of an elder's funds, property, or assets. Examples include, but are not limited to, cashing an elderly person's checks without authorization or permission; forging an older person's signature; misusing or stealing an older person's money or possessions; coercing or deceiving an older person into signing any document (e.g., contracts or will); and the improper use of conservatorship, guardianship, or power of attorney. (National Center on Elder Abuse, 2008)

Researchers have suggested that elder financial abuse can be distinguished from elder physical abuse in the following ways: Financial abuse occurs more often, it has different causes, different response systems are used to address the crimes, and it has different consequences from other forms of elder abuse (Payne & Strasser, 2012).

In one of the largest studies on theft in nursing homes, criminologists Diane Harris and Michael Benson (1999) surveyed 1,116 nursing home employees and 517 family members of nursing home residents. Their results showed that one fifth of the workers suspected that their colleagues had stolen something from residents, and one fifth of the family members believed that a staff member had stolen something from their relative.

In another study, Harris and Benson (1996) interviewed employees, relatives, and nursing home residents to gain insight into the patterns surrounding theft in nursing homes. They found that the items stolen most often tended to be items of value that could be easily concealed, such as jewelry and money. They also found that theft increased around the holidays and that new workers and dissatisfied workers were more apt to engage in theft. Other research suggests that theft in nursing homes is related to aggressive behaviors by nursing home residents—workers who experienced abuse at the hands of residents were suggested to be more likely to steal from residents (Van Wyk, Benson, & Harris, 2000). Harris and Benson (1999) argue that theft is even less socially acceptable than physical patient abuse on the grounds that the behaviors are intentional and not simply a reaction to a stressful working situation.

In another study, Payne and Strasser (2012) compared cases of elder physical abuse ($n = 314$) and elder financial abuse ($n = 242$) provided in the *Medicaid Fraud Reports* (described in the Chapter 1). Financial abusers were more likely to be directors or employees in another category, while physical abusers tended to be aides. The authors also found that "physical abusers were more likely to be sentenced to jail than financial abusers were, but financial abusers were more likely to be sentenced to prison" (n.p.). A comparison of sentence lengths indicated that financial abusers received longer probation sentences, shorter prison sanctions, and higher fines than physical abusers did.

The authors identified four patterns that characterized the financial exploitation cases: (1) Victims often had serious health issues, (2) multiple victims were frequently targeted by specific offenders, (3) offenses occurred on multiple occasions, and (4) a lack of witnesses made it difficult to investigate the cases.

Elder neglect is a third type of elder abuse. Elder neglect occurs when workers fail to provide the appropriate level of care required by the patient. Experts distinguish between active (intentional) and passive (unintentional) neglect. In cases of active neglect, offenders know the type of care that an individual requires—they simply choose not to provide that care. In cases of passive neglect, offenders are not aware of the most appropriate care—their neglect stems from ignorance. In terms of workplace offenses, neglect is more likely to be active than passive in nature. Workers typically know the type of care the patient needs. In some situations, workplace demands may foster neglect inasmuch as administrators expect workers to provide care to a higher number of patients than is actually possible.

Elder sexual abuse is another variety of elder abuse. One expert cites three types of elder sexual abuse: (1) hands-on offenses where the offender inappropriately touches victims, (2) hands-off offenses such as voyeurism and exhibitionism, and (3) harmful genital practices where genital contact is made between the offender and the victim (Ramsey-Klawsnik, 1999). Sexual abuse is believed to be particularly common against disabled residents of long-term care institutions.

A study of 126 elder sexual abuse cases and 314 elder physical abuse cases committed as part of the offender's workplace activities and prosecuted by criminal justice officials found that elder sexual abuse cases were more likely to involve (1) male offenders, (2) cognitively impaired victims, and (3) instances without witnesses (Payne, 2010). Payne (2010) highlighted the element of control involved in elder sexual abuse cases.

An expose by CNN reporters Ellis and Hicken (2017) showed how one nurse's assistant sexually abused six nursing home residents in three different nursing homes. The investigation found that "more than 1,000 nursing homes [had] been cited for mishandling suspected cases of sex abuse." The study showed that 10% of the homes were cited multiple times.

Sexual abuse cases in nursing homes may also target younger victims who live in the long-term-care facility. Consider a case where a 36-year-old nurse was arrested after a 29-year-old comatose woman in his care gave birth (Hanna & Allen, 2019). No one in the health care facility knew the woman was pregnant until she gave birth. Because she was obviously unable to consent, it was clear that sexual assault had occurred. An investigation revealed that the nurse's DNA matched that of the baby's. The health care facility was understandably apologetic. In the 911 call seeking help for the pregnancy, the caller admitted, "we had no idea she was pregnant" (Hanna & Allen, 2019).

A final type of elder abuse by workers in the health care field is the **failure to report** suspected cases of elder abuse. The vast majority of states have laws stipulating that certain types of workers are mandated to report elder abuse cases to the authorities if they suspect an elder abuse incident has occurred. These laws are known as mandatory reporting laws. Several criticisms surround the use of mandatory reporting laws. These criticisms include the following:

- A lack of empirical basis supporting the need for the laws

- Questions about the effectiveness of the laws

- Concerns that the laws are based on ageist assumptions

- Concerns about patient–health care worker confidentiality

- The likelihood that revictimization will occur from reporting

- A belief that discretion results in inconsistent reporting (Payne, 2013)

In a study focusing on mandatory reporting laws, three patterns were found. First, mandatory reporting violations tend to involve multiple collaborators who work together to cover up a case of elder abuse. Second, mandatory reporting violators come from a wider range of health care occupations than is found in other types of elder abuse. Third, fines were commonly used as a sentencing tool in these cases (Payne, 2013). Based on these patterns, my research suggests policy implications that center on broadening investigations to capture multiple offenders and increasing awareness about the laws.

Health care administrators use a number of different practices and follow various policies in an effort to prevent elder abuse in the workplace. Surveys of 76 nursing home directors identified four broad types of measures commonly used to prevent crimes against nursing home residents (Payne & Burke-Fletcher, 2005). First, facility-based measures are those strategies that directors choose to implement that are driven by facility policies, such as background checks, drug tests, and safety committees. Second, educational strategies focus on increasing awareness among workers and residents about strategies for preventing abuse. Third, community outreach efforts entail strategies where crime prevention officials from outside the nursing home are called on to provide information and resources to protect residents. Finally, building security strategies includes measures that are designed to make the actual physical structure safer (e.g., locked doors, security alarms, and video cameras). The results of this survey showed that the conceptual ambiguity surrounding elder abuse laws made it more difficult to prevent elder abuse. Also, the results showed that the lack of clear and consistent elder abuse response policies created an obstacle to identifying and responding to cases of elder abuse occurring in nursing homes.

Figure 4.2 shows the types of health care professionals convicted of patient abuse between 2015 and 2019. Notice that nurse's assistants were convicted most often for patient abuse. This should not be interpreted to mean that this group is more likely to commit these offenses; there are more nurse's assistants than other types of medical professionals, and they spend more time with patients than other providers do. Therefore, it is not surprising that they are convicted more often. Also notice that in 2019 there was an increase in the number of nurse/physician assistants and other providers convicted of patient abuse. The reason for this increase is not clear. Paying attention to future numbers will help to determine whether this increase is a trend or an anomaly.

FIGURE 4.2 ■ Medicaid Fraud Control Unit Patient Abuse Convictions, FY 2015–2019

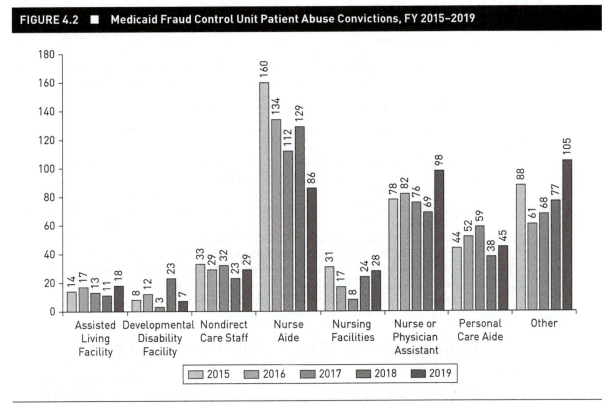

Source: Medicaid Fraud Control Unit Fiscal Year 2019 Annual Report.

HOME HEALTH CARE FRAUD

Home health care entails the provision of health care services at home. In recent years, there has been an increase in the use of home health care due to demographic changes, changes in patient preferences, technological advancements, legislative changes, and cost containment strategies (Payne, 2003a). Along with these changes, there has been evidence of an increase of crimes committed by home health care workers. In *Crime in the Home Health Care Field* (Payne, 2003a), I describe the way that the following crimes occur in the home health industry: (a) murder, (b) physical abuse, (c) sexual abuse, (d) neglect, (e) drug-related offenses, (f) emotional abuse, (g) theft from patients, and (h) theft from Medicare and/or Medicaid.

I argue that fraud against the Medicare and Medicaid systems is particularly pervasive. I describe eight different types of fraud that home health care workers have committed:

1. Providing unnecessary services to clients and billing the system for those services

2. Billing the system for services that were not provided to the client

3. Overcharging either the system or client for services

4. Forging signatures on medical documents

5. Negative charting (changing the clients' medical records so clients seem sicker than they are, thereby convincing the insurance provider to pay for services that may not have been necessary)

6. Having unlicensed (or substitute) workers provide medical care and billing the insurance company as if the services were provided by a licensed professional

7. Double billing the client and one or more insurance companies

8. Providing kickbacks to other service providers in exchange for client referrals

Reviewing hundreds of home health care fraud cases, I identified three patterns that were common in the cases. First, I noted that many of the cases involved offenders who had past criminal histories. Second, the offenses were described as occurring over time. Whereas a robbery occurs in one moment in time, fraudulent acts may be more spread out over time. Third, I called attention to the fact that many home health care frauds were committed in groups, and the groups sometimes included workers and clients conspiring together to defraud the system. Based on these patterns, the following three policy implications were suggested: (1) the need for background checks in hiring home health care workers, (2) the need to conduct lengthy investigations to substantiate cases, and (3) the practice of investigating multiple offenders simultaneously in an effort to build a case against a specific offender (Payne, 2003a).

DURABLE MEDICAL EQUIPMENT FRAUD

Another variety of fraud in the health care system can be coined durable medical equipment fraud. In this context, durable medical equipment fraud refers to criminal behaviors that involve the rental or sale of health equipment. Durable medical equipment includes items such as prosthetics, orthotics, wheelchairs, oxygen equipment, walkers, and other items that are supposed to be used over the long term. In the Medicaid system alone, it is estimated that a billion dollars a year is spent on this equipment (Policastro & Payne, 2013). Two aspects of the industry—(1) the types of services provided and (2) the types of employees involved—distinguish this field from other health care fields. In terms of types of services, the durable medical equipment industry sells items rather than providing a specific form of health care. The employees would not necessarily be licensed health care professionals but act more as salespersons (Policastro & Payne, 2013).

As with other health care fields, initially there was little concern about fraud in the durable medical equipment field when the industry first began to provide equipment to Medicaid recipients. As in other health care occupations, however, fraud does occur in this field. Below are two recent examples of fraud in this industry:

- Attorney General Abbott announced on November 10 that ****, *****, and **** were indicted by a state grand jury for engaging in organized criminal activity. ****** owners of Steadfast Healthcare, allegedly billed for power wheelchairs and provided scooters, billed for dead clients, and billed for power wheelchairs that were not prescribed by physicians. The identified overpayment is approximately $266,000. (National Association of Medicaid Fraud Control Units, 2014, p. 3)

- Attorney General Abbott announced on December 17 that *****, owner and operator of Unity Medical Equipment & Supply was indicted by a state grand jury for theft. ***** allegedly billed Medicaid for incontinence supplies, namely adult diapers, not provided to recipients or recipients received a different product or diapers in quantities less than billed Medicaid. (National Association of Medicaid Fraud Control Units, 2014, p. 4)

In one of the few studies on fraud in the durable medical field, Policastro and Payne (2013) examined the characteristics, causes, and patterns surrounding durable medical equipment fraud against Medicaid. Among other things, their study of 258 equipment fraud cases revealed the following:

- Roughly six in ten cases involved male offenders.

- Owners were implicated in three fourths of the cases.

- False claims were the most common offense.

- In nearly two thirds of the cases, offenders committed their offense along with another offender.

- Wheelchairs and incontinence supplies were the types of equipment most often involved in fraudulent cases.

- When sanctions were given, fines were given in 90% of the cases.

- For every offender involved in an incident, the odds of incarceration increased 1.3 times.

One aspect of their findings is that the types of fraud committed in the durable medical field were different from those fraudulent acts committed in other health care fields. Using past research as a guide, the authors attribute the differences to the structural organization of various occupations rather than class status. In effect, it's not class that predicts offending but rather the types of opportunities that may surface based on the way that various fields are organized and structured.

Another point worth stressing is that although these offense types have been discussed separately according to the health care occupation, in many cases, offenders collaborate with various types of professionals. Doctors, nurses, aides, pharmacists, and other professionals—depending on the nature of the offense type—might in fact commit crimes together.

Related to durable medical equipment fraud, other types of health care products have also been used to defraud consumers and the government. During the coronavirus pandemic, for example, bogus claims of prevention medicine skyrocketed. These scams worked a couple of different ways. In some cases, scammers targeted consumers and tried to sell them fake medicine that yielded no results for the consumers. In other cases, scammers tried to get investors to buy into companies purporting to sell coronavirus cures. Not surprisingly, one of the first arrests for coronavirus frauds occurred on March 25th, just days after the nationwide shutdown and related orders began to roll out (USDOJ, 2020, March 25).

MEDICAL MALPRACTICE

Medical malpractice refers to situations where health care providers "accidentally" injure patients while delivering health care. These cases are almost never be treated as crimes. As a result, they do not enter the criminal justice system. Strategies for recourse for victims of medical malpractice include (1) filing a lawsuit against the health care provider and (2) filing an insurance claim with the provider's insurance company.

With regard to filing an insurance claim with the provider's insurance company, it may be useful to compare medical malpractice with automobile "accidents." If driver A runs into driver B and is clearly responsible for an accident, then driver B's insurance company will file a claim with driver A's insurance company. In the end, driver A's insurance company will be responsible for paying the claim. In medical malpractice insurance cases, a similar process is followed: The "accident" victim or his or her representative files a claim with the provider's insurance company. Here is an overview of how medical malpractice claims work:

A medical malpractice insurance claim arises when a person (the claimant) alleges that negligent medical treatment resulted in an injury. The treatment may have been provided by a physician, surgeon, or other health care professional or an organization, such as a hospital, clinic, or nursing home.

In a typical medical malpractice claim, the person claiming an injury or a related family member retains an attorney to file a claim with the medical provider's insurance carrier requesting compensation for the injury. After a claim is filed, the insurance carrier may settle, negotiate with the claimant over the amount of compensation, or refuse to compensate the claimant. If the parties do not come to an agreement, the claimant's attorney may file a lawsuit in the appropriate court or abandon the claim.

> Some states require review of medical malpractice claims before a panel of experts prior to a lawsuit, while other states mandate arbitration or alternative dispute resolution as a means of resolving medical malpractice claims. The filing of a lawsuit may produce several outcomes. These include the settlement of the case prior to or during trial, a trial decision in favor of the claimant or the defendant, or the dismissal of the case by the court. Claims may also be abandoned or withdrawn after a lawsuit (Cohen & Hughes, 2007).

A review of 43,000 medical malpractice insurance claims in seven states between 2000 and 2004 found that "most medical malpractice claims were closed without any compensation provided to those claiming a medical injury" (Cohen & Hughes, 2007, p. 1). Payouts were higher for those who suffered "lifelong major or grave permanent injuries" and lower in cases with temporary or emotional injuries. Other patterns found in the medical malpractice insurance claims included the following:

- Claims were typically filed 15 to 18 months after the injuries.

- It generally took about two to two and a half years to close the claims.

- In some states, less than 10% of the claims resulted in payouts. In other states, payouts were given in about a third of the cases.

- When injuries occurred, they were more likely to occur in hospitals.

- Females were claimants in 54% to 56% of the cases.

- Approximately 95% of the claims were settled without going to trial.

- The amount of payouts to claimants increased as the case progressed through the justice system.

- Medical malpractice insurance payouts increased from 1990 to 2004.

Figure 4.3 shows medical malpractice payments and adverse action reports filed against physicians between 1991 and 2019. Adverse action reports are defined in the National Practitioner Data Bank as "(1) an action taken against a practitioner's clinical privileges or medical staff membership in a health care organization, (2) a licensure disciplinary action, (3) a Medicare/Medicaid Exclusion action, or (4) any other adjudicated action." Interestingly, adverse action reports increased dramatically over the two decades. At the same time, medical malpractice cases resulting in payments dropped. This could be because the adverse action reports are deterring more egregious behavior that would result in malpractice suits; it is also possible that the adverse action reports are making it harder for patients to file medical malpractice cases. Additional research is needed to make sense of these trends.

FIGURE 4.3 ■ Trends in Medical Malpractice and Adverse Action Reports

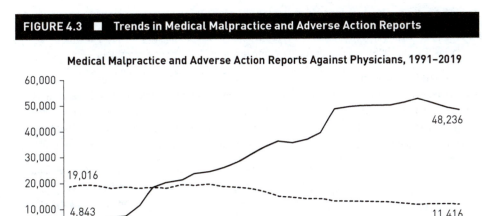

Medical Malpractice and Adverse Action Reports Against Physicians, 1991–2019

Source: National Practitioner Databank

Summary

- In general, categories of crimes committed by health care providers include fraud by doctors, fraud by pharmacists, drug use, unnecessary surgery, medication errors, sexual abuse, elder abuse, home health care fraud, and medical malpractice.

- Sutherland implied that doctors were unlikely to engage in white-collar crime, and as a result, Sutherland gave "only scant attention to doctors [and] maintained that physicians were probably more honest than other professionals" (Wilson et al., 1986).

- The most pervasive form of fraud committed by doctors entails the commission of Medicare and Medicaid fraud and abuse.

- *Fraud* refers to intentionally criminal behaviors by physicians, whereas *abuse* focuses on unintentional misuse of program funds.

- Several specific forms of fraud and abuse exist, including phantom treatment, substitute providers, upcoding, provision of unnecessary services, misrepresenting services, falsifying records, overcharging patients, unbundling, pingponging, ganging, kickbacks, co-pay waivers, and medical snowballing.

- Briefly, mental health professionals often bill for time, whereas other professionals bill for more complicated medical procedures. For investigators, it is much easier to prove "time violations" than "treatment violations."

- Research shows that when females are accused of health care fraud, they tend to be accused along with other providers more than male offenders are (Payne, 1995).

- Explanations for fraud have focused on structural explanations, socialization factors, and enforcement dynamics.

- It is estimated that 7.5 million unnecessary surgeries and medical procedures occur annually, and 12,000 Americans are killed each year from these unnecessary surgeries (Black, 2005).

- At least six overlapping reasons help explain the pervasiveness of unnecessary surgeries: differing opinions, stigma, trust of health care, lack of trust of insurance companies, medicalized socialization, and conflict explanations.

- Many severe consequences may arise from unnecessary surgeries.

- Medication errors occur when health care providers deliver or prescribe the wrong medications to patients.

- Public Citizen has identified 15 varieties of misconduct by physicians. The group believes that variations in sanctions for violations across states can be attributed to differences in the way state medical boards sanction offenders.

- Telemedicine fraud is becoming more common given the rapid pace of the technological revolution.

- Eight types of prescription fraud are generic drug substitution, overbilling, double billing, billing for nonexistent prescriptions, short counting, mislabeling, delivery of a controlled substance, and illegally buying prescriptions.

- The following types of elder abuse can be seen as white-collar crimes: (1) elder physical abuse, (2) elder financial abuse, (3) elder neglect, (4) elder sexual abuse, and (5) failure to report crimes.

- Types of home health care fraud include providing unnecessary services, billing the system for services that were not provided to the client, overcharging, forgery, negative charting, substitute workers, double billing, and kickbacks.

- Durable medical equipment fraud involves the fraudulent sale or rental of medical supplies, such as wheelchairs, walkers, scooters, and so on.

- Medical malpractice refers to situations where health care providers perform negligent care and/or injure patients. Patients can seek recourse by filing medical malpractice insurance claims against the provider's insurance company or by filing a lawsuit against the provider.

Key Terms

Billing for nonexistent prescriptions 89
Co-pay waivers 80
Delivery of a controlled substance 89
Double billing 89
Elder abuse 94
Elder financial abuse 94
Elder neglect 95
Elder physical abuse 94
Elder sexual abuse 95
Failure to report 96
Falsifying records 80
Fraud 80
Ganging 80
Generic drug substitution 89

Health Insurance Portability Act of 1996 82
Home health care 97
Illegally buying prescriptions 89
Kickbacks 80
Medicaid 79
Medical malpractice 99
Medical snowballing 80
Medicare 79
Medication errors 85
Mislabeling of drugs 89
Misrepresenting services 00
Overcharging patients 80
Pacification 94
Phantom treatment 80

Pingponging 80
Prescription fraud 89
Provision of unnecessary services 80
Questionable Doctors 85
Recreational path 90
Sexual abuse 92
Short counting 89
Substitute providers 80
Telemedicine 86
Therapeutic self-medicators 90
Unbundling 80
Upcoding 80

Discussion Questions

1. What's worse—retail theft or health care fraud? Explain.

2. What can be done to limit crimes by health care professionals?

3. What are the consequences of health care fraud?

4. What are the similarities between misconduct by pharmacists and crimes by doctors? What about the differences?

5. Why do unnecessary surgeries occur? Do you know anyone who has had a potentially unnecessary surgery? What can be done to prevent them?

6. Do you expect telemedicine fraud to increase in the future? Explain.

7. How is drug use a white-collar crime? What can be done to prevent drug use by health care providers?

CRIME IN SYSTEMS OF SOCIAL CONTROL

White-Collar Crime in Criminal Justice, Military, and Religious Systems

It sounds like a bad joke—a police officer, lawyer, judge, correctional officer, military officer, and priest walk into a bar together. What do you think they could discuss that they have in common? Several answers come to mind. For example, they could talk about the fact that they each are public servants. Their occupations exist to serve members of the public. They could also talk about the fact that their salaries are not the highest one would find among various occupations. Or they could talk about their colleagues who have been caught committing white-collar crimes. After all, no profession is immune from white-collar misconduct. As well, they could talk about the main thing their professions have in common across all of their professions: They each work in *systems of social control*. In other words, each of their employers are either formally or informally charged with controlling human behavior.

As examples of the crimes committed by professionals in these systems of social control, consider the following examples quoted from their original sources:

- Evidence at trial established that Garbacz, while employed as a priest with the Catholic Diocese in Rapid City, devised a scheme to steal monies collected from parishioners at various church services by secretly entering the areas in three parish churches where such monies were stored. He took steps such as entering the church buildings late in the evening, removing and replacing special, tamper-proof bank bags, making multiple same-day deposits totaling tens of thousands of dollars of stolen money in ATMs well after midnight, and laundering such stolen money through a variety of banks, investment firms, and credit card companies. (Internal Revenue Service, 2020).

- A retired 30-year veteran of the Philadelphia Police Department, was sentenced today to serve 40 months in prison, followed by two years' supervised release, and to pay a $15,000 fine. ++++++ was also ordered to forfeit $653,319.10 in proceeds from his crimes. . . . The charges arose from ++++++'s orchestration of a seven-year bribery scheme during which he paid a Philadelphia Police detective for special access to law enforcement databases in order to build up ++++++' lucrative towing business. (U.S. Department of Justice, 2019, April 9b).

- [The judge] was accused of pressuring young male defendants into activities of a sexual nature in exchange for lighter sentences. ++++++ agreed to permanently depart the bench in 2016 after the commission leveled ethics charges against him that detailed years of abuse of his office. For example, +++++++ gave male defendants credit for community service by photographing them from behind as they bent over to pick up trash. At the time, Sachar called it "the worst case of judicial misconduct in Arkansas history." (Moritz, 2020).

- In February 2019, ++++++ and +++++ were beaten by Elmore Correctional Facility Sgt. ++++++, who faces up to 20 years in prison after he pleaded guilty to assaulting the pair . . . ++++++ and +++++++ filed a lawsuit this month against ++++++ and other prison employees stating they violated the men's constitutional rights and conspired to conceal the violations, according to the media outlet. ++++++ lost consciousness, defecated on himself and was later hospitalized with a concussion, the lawsuit said. ++++++ suffered a broken wrist, and multiple contusions, the suit added (Associated Press, 2020, April 30).

One irony arises when considering crimes by officials in social control systems: Their occupations exist in order to reduce or prevent wrongful behaviors, but in some cases, those given the duty to stop misconduct actually engage in misconduct themselves.

CRIME IN THE CRIMINAL JUSTICE SYSTEM

Entrusted to enforce the law, criminal justice officials have duties that are not given to any other occupational group. Unfortunately, as with other professions, crime occurs in the criminal justice professions. The types of white-collar crime occurring in the criminal justice system include the following:

- Police corruption

- Police brutality

- Attorney misconduct

- Judicial misconduct

- Prosecutorial misconduct

- Correctional officer misconduct

Police Corruption

Police corruption occurs when police officers violate the trust they have been given and abuse their law enforcement authority (Punch, 2009). Different typologies have been presented to characterize the numerous types of police corruption known to occur. One of the clearest (and earliest) typologies was set forth by Barker and Roebuck (1973), who identified the following types of police corruption:

Corruption of authority (e.g., using the law enforcement role to gain favors such as gratuities)

Kickbacks (e.g., sending victims or offenders to certain service providers—such as tow truck drivers—in exchange for a fee from the service provider)

Opportunistic theft (e.g., stealing from crime scenes when the opportunity arises)

Shakedowns (e.g., taking or soliciting bribes from offenders in exchange for not enforcing the law)

Protection of illegal activities (e.g., protecting gangs, organized crime units, or others in exchange for payment)

Fixing cases (e.g., fixing traffic tickets or changing testimony)

Direct criminal activities (e.g., engaging in crime while on the job)

Internal payoffs (e.g., engaging in schemes where other criminal justice officials are paid off for their illicit participation in the scheme)

Criminologist Phil Stinson (2015) offered another useful typology captured under the heading of "police deviance." His conceptualization focuses on all types of deviance by police officers—including those committed on the job and off the job. The categories of deviance identified by Stinson include (1) drug-related police crimes, (2) profit-motivated police crimes, (3) violence-related police crimes, (4) alcohol-related offenses (such as being drunk in public or driving under the influence), and (5) sex-related deviance. This final category includes harassment, intimidation, and sexual misconduct. Tromadore (2016) offers the following definition of **police sexual misconduct**:

Sexual misconduct by law enforcement is defined as any behavior by an officer that takes advantage of the officer's position in law enforcement (whether on-duty or off-duty) to misuse authority and power in order to commit a sexual act, manipulate sexual favors, initiate sexual contact with another person, or respond to a perceived sexually motivated cue (from a subtle suggestion to an overt action) from another person. Targets of officer-involved sexual misconduct will most likely be vulnerable and marginalized populations, such as women of color, and transgender and gender non-conforming people. But any person can be victimized. Police sexual misconduct also includes any communication or behavior by an officer that would likely be construed as lewd, lascivious, inappropriate, or conduct unbecoming an officer in violation of general principles of acceptable behavior common to law enforcement. (p. 181)

Examples of sexual misconduct exist on a continuum, ranging from situations where no contact occurs between the officer and the citizen to situations where forced contact occurs. Surveys of 40 police officers by Maher (2003) showed evidence of police behaviors dictated by sexual interests. Officers reported routinely stopping motorists to "check out" those that they found attractive. A study of 501 cases of police sexual violence found that many of the offenders committed multiple acts of sexual violence (McGurrin & Kappeler, 2002). The authors suggested that the badge and gun were substitutes for physical force, particularly in situations where police officers solicited sexual favors in exchange for police decisions that would benefit the victim. Another author highlighted that this kind of misconduct was fostered by the following conditions of the law enforcement profession: power dynamics, authority, unsupervised jobs, male/patriarchal field, and working with vulnerable victims (Heil, 2019).

The consequences of police corruption can be far reaching. As Hunter (1999) notes, "one incident of police misbehavior in a distant locality can have adverse effects on police community relationships in police agencies across the country" (p. 156). For departments where corruption occurs, the corruption diminishes police effectiveness, creates demoralization in the department, and creates barriers between the department and the community (Hunter, 1999). These consequences are likely some of the reasons that the judicial system responds quite seriously to instances of misconduct when those cases enter the judicial system. A question that arises is why so many of the police brutality cases making national attention fail to make it into the judicial system in the first place. Part of the answer lies in the way that local officials define, interpret, and respond to these cases. This chapter's White-Collar Crime in the News shows how seriously judicial officials viewed corruption in one case.

WHITE-COLLAR CRIME IN THE NEWS
OFFICER PLEADS GUILTY TO CORRUPTION

The following is a press release from the Eastern District of Michigan from February 13, 2020.

Former Detroit Police Officer Michael Mosley, age 48, pleaded guilty today before the Honorable George Caram Steeh to bribery for taking $15,000 in cash bribes from a drug trafficker, announced U.S. Attorney Matthew Schneider.

Joining Schneider in the announcement was Steven M. D'Antuono, Special Agent in Charge of the Detroit Field Office of the Federal Bureau of Investigation.

Officer Mosley is a nineteen-year veteran of the Detroit Police Department. As stated during Mosley's guilty plea, in April 2019, Mosley was a member of the Police Department's Major Violators Unit. On April 3, 2019, Detroit police officers, including Officer Mosley, searched a drug trafficker's house pursuant to a search warrant. The search uncovered two kilograms of heroin, one kilogram of cocaine, and six firearms. The drug trafficker confessed to owning the three kilograms of drugs to Officer Mosley, and the trafficker signed a confession. After the April 3 search, Officer Mosley remained in contact with the drug trafficker in an effort to secure the trafficker's cooperation concerning other criminal activity.

Subsequently, the drug trafficker offered Officer Mosley a cash bribe of $15,000 in exchange for not pursuing criminal charges based on the three kilogram drug seizure. Officer Mosley agreed to the deal. On May 2, 2019, Officer Mosley collected $10,000 in cash that the drug dealer left for Mosley in the backyard of an abandoned house in Detroit. On May 23, 2019, Officer Mosley accepted another $5,000 in cash left for him by the drug trafficker at the abandoned house. In exchange, Officer Mosley gave the drug trafficker the original copy of his confession.

In addition to pleading guilty to one count of bribery, Mosley will be forfeiting the $15,000 he took in bribes.

U.S. Attorney Matthew Schneider commended the outstanding work of the FBI in conducting this criminal investigation of a corrupt police officer.

"It's rare that a police officer commits a crime, but in this case Officer Mosley betrayed his oath as a police officer, and he betrayed the citizens of Detroit and the vast majority of his fellow officers who seek to protect and serve with integrity," stated United States Attorney Matthew Schneider. "This prosecution demonstrates that we will not tolerate public officials who abuse their authority and seek to use their power to line their own pockets."

"The citizens of Detroit deserve better from their public servants. Wrongdoing by police officers undermines the public's trust and confidence in law enforcement officers who are sworn to defend and uphold the law," said Special Agent in Charge D'Antuono. "The men and women of the Detroit Police Department are dedicated to serving this community and misconduct by one of its officers is not a reflection of the entire force. However, the FBI will do everything in its power to bring corrupt police officers to justice and to restore faith in the integrity of law enforcement throughout the city."

Reprinted from U.S. Department of Justice.

Source: https://www.justice.gov/usao-edmi/pr/former-detroit-police-officer-pleads-guilty-taking-15000-cash-bribes-drug-trafficker

Police corruption cuts across all countries. Even countries that have low rates of other forms of workplace offending have some police corruption. Describing this phenomenon in Australia, one author team wrote, "There will always be at least a small group of corrupt police officers, even though Australians are culturally averse to corruption" (Lauchs, Keast, & Yousefpour, 2011, p. 110).

Various perspectives have been offered in an effort to explain police corruption. The phrase "bad apples" has frequently been used to suggest that corruption is limited to a few rogue officers in a department. More recently, it has been suggested that the phrase "bad orchards" would more aptly describe how the broader police culture and dynamics of policing contribute to police misconduct (Punch, 2009). Others have suggested that overreaching cultural and community factors are potential causes of police misconduct (Kane, 2002).

Some researchers have explored social psychological factors that might contribute to corruption. The phrase **noble cause corruption** describes situations where officers engage in corruption in order to assure what they see as justice (Cooper, 2012). In these situations, "getting the bad guys off the street to protect the innocent" (Cooper, 2012, p. 171) is viewed as the noble cause. Cooper (2012) asserts that some officers experience role conflict in these cases. Officers who are more protector-oriented are believed to experience more role conflict than those who focus more on community policing.

In an effort to identify the individual officer characteristics that contribute to police misconduct, one study compared all 1,543 police officers dismissed from the New York Police Department between 1975 and 1996 with a sample of police recruits who had never been disciplined. This study found that those who were dismissed for misconduct were more likely to have past arrests, traffic violations, and problems with previous jobs. Those who had college degrees were less likely to be dismissed (Fyfe & Kane, 2005).

Others have attributed police misconduct to a lack of policies to prevent misconduct, faulty control mechanisms, and a lack of appropriate training (Kinnaird, 2007). **Organizational justice** explanations consider the way that organizational features might lead to corruption. Research shows that police supervisors' attitudes about corruption will influence how officers in their chain of command view corruption. Not surprisingly, those who have lax attitudes toward corruption will be more prone to employ officers who hold less serious views about corruption (Lee, Lim, Moore, & Kim, 2013).

A survey of 208 police managers found that for some types of police misconduct, the police manager would not be likely to report the behavior (Vito, Wolfe, Higgins, & Walsh, 2011). Out of 109 sergeants surveyed, nearly 86% reported that they would not report officers working off duty in a security business. Just under half indicated that they would not report instances when officers receive free meals. Middle managers offered similar results, though they were slightly more likely to indicate they would report misconduct (Vito et al., 2011). One author team concludes, "Police departments themselves play an important role in shaping the patterns and timing of officer misconduct" (White & Kane, 2013, p. 1301).

Another recent study also found that perceptions of organizational justice in a police department are tied to misconduct (Wolfe & Piquero, 2011). Officers perceiving their department as adhering to ideals of organizational justice tend to engage in a lower amount of misconduct. Based on this, the researchers suggest that treating officers in a fair and transparent way will increase the likelihood that officers will do the same in their interactions with citizens. Strategies suggested for demonstrating fairness included the following:

- Ensuring that promotions are distributed and awarded fairly

- Communicating clearly about the purpose of discipline

- Conducting internal investigations in a fair manner

- Reviewing policies to make sure they are consistent with ideals of fairness

- Demonstrating that police leaders value the contributions of officers (Wolfe & Piquero, 2011)

Other suggestions for preventing police misconduct have centered on addressing these potential causal factors. One author stresses that police agencies must have policies that clearly define police misconduct so officers are aware of the rules and sanctions (Martinelli, 2007). Other strategies that have been suggested include screening backgrounds (White & Kane, 2013), promoting external accountability (Barker, 2002), improving police supervision strategies (Hunter, 1999; Martinelli, 2007), focusing on early warning signs (Walker & Alpert, 2002), and promoting ethics (Hunter, 1999).

PHOTO 5.1 George Floyd's killing by Derek Chauvin sparked outrage across the United States. Unlike prior protests, the summer 2020 protests spread rapidly across the country and the world.

Police Brutality

Police brutality is the misuse of force on the part of law enforcement officers. The legal authority to use force has been identified as the primary factor distinguishing law enforcement officers from private citizens. The authority vested in police officers as government officials affords them the right to use force in those situations where force is deemed to be legally appropriate. Not only do police officers have the legal right to use force in certain situations, we also expect them to use force to protect us. When use of force crosses the line into excessive and unnecessary force, it becomes police brutality.

Police brutality is not a new phenomenon, but the country was given a wake-up call about the systemic problem in the summer of 2020. The wake-up call started on the last Monday of May 2020 when Minnesota police officer Derek Chauvin killed George Floyd, an unarmed Black man, after Chauvin pressed his knee into Floyd's neck for more than eight minutes. At no point did Floyd act violently or in any way that suggested the need for what amounted to deadly force. Bystanders filmed the incident, providing the world a front-row view to excessive force in action. In the video, Floyd can be heard saying "I can't breathe." Three other officers stood by and did nothing to intervene; they were fired, as was Chauvin who was also charged with third degree murder for Floyd's death. A subsequent review showed that Chauvin had more than a dozen complaints filed against him over his career and, despite these complaints, he was never disciplined.

Floyd was killed on a Monday. By Friday, protests against police brutality had erupted across the United States. Though most protests were peaceful, there were instances of riots, looting, vandalism, and destruction of police cars and businesses at some protests. Other protests saw police officers kneeling beside protestors as sign of solidarity and understanding. Less than two weeks after George Floyd was killed, an unarmed Black man named Rayshard Brooks was shot and killed by a police officer in a Wendy's parking lot in Atlanta. Officers were arresting Brooks for a DUI charge when Brooks began to struggle with them before taking one of their stun guns and running away. Officer Garrett Rolf pursued him on foot, at which point Brooks attempted to fire the stun gun at Rolf. Officer Rolf fired three rounds at Brooks, hitting him twice from behind. Atlanta Mayor Keisha Lance Bottoms fired Rolf within a day, and just five days later, Fulton County District Attorney Paul Howard charged the officer with felony murder.

These incidents are nothing new. Figure 5.1 summarizes police brutality cases gaining national attention. The fact that this violence was spread over three decades points to the pervasiveness of police violence over time. Figure 5.2 shows police killings of unarmed citizens by race between 2013 and 2019. Some individuals minimize police violence against minorities by pointing out that police officers kill more white people than Black people. However, such comments fail to recognize that minorities are overrepresented as victims in police killings. Between 2013 and 2019, about one third of all police killings were against Black people even though Black people only make up 13.5% of the U.S. population.

FIGURE 5.1 ■ Police Brutality Timeline

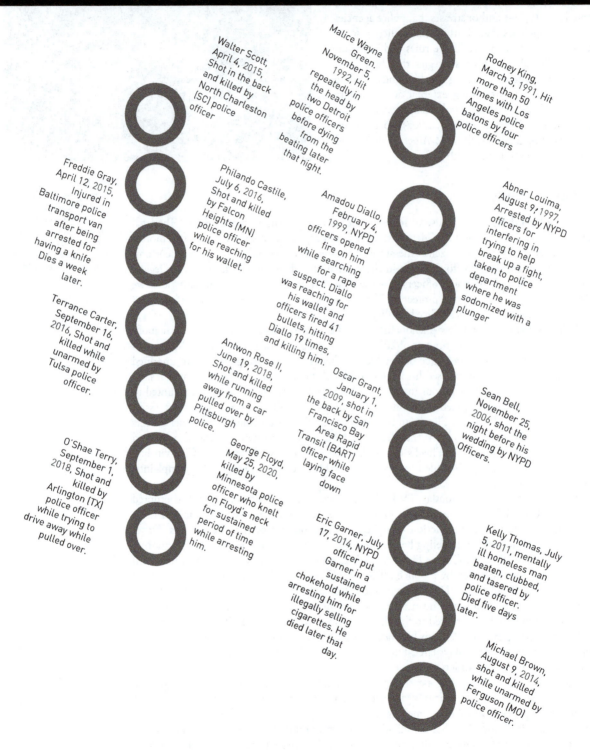

Walter Scott, April 4, 2015, Shot in the back and killed by North Charleston (SC) police officer

Malice Wayne Green. November 5, 1992, Hit repeatedly in the head by two Detroit police officers before dying from the beating later that night.

Rodney King, March 3, 1991, Hit more than 50 times with Los Angeles police batons by four police officers

Freddie Gray, April 12, 2015, Injured in Baltimore police transport van after being arrested for having a knife Dies a week later.

Philando Castile, July 6, 2016, Shot and killed by Falcon Heights (MN) police officer while reaching for his wallet.

Amadou Diallo, February 4, 1999, NYPD officers opened fire on him while searching for a rape suspect. Diallo was reaching for his wallet and officers fired 41 bullets, hitting Diallo 19 times, and killing him.

Abner Louima, August 9, 1997, Arrested by NYPD officers for interfering in trying to help break up a fight, taken to police department where he was sodomized with a plunger

Terrance Carter, September 16, 2016, Shot and killed while unarmed by Tulsa police officer.

Antwon Rose II, June 19, 2018, Shot and killed while running away from a car pulled over by Pittsburgh police

Oscar Grant, January 1, 2009, shot in the back by San Francisco Bay Area Rapid Transit (BART) officer while laying face down

Sean Bell, November 25, 2006, shot the night before his wedding by NYPD Officers.

O'Shae Terry, September 1, 2018, Shot and killed by Arlington (TX) police officer while trying to drive away while pulled over.

George Floyd, May 25, 2020, killed by Minnesota police officer who knelt on Floyd's neck for sustained period of time while arresting him.

Eric Garner, July 17, 2014, NYPD officer put Garner in a sustained chokehold while arresting him for illegally selling cigarettes. He died later that day.

Kelly Thomas, July 5, 2011, mentally ill homeless man beaten, clubbed, and tasered by police officer. Died five days later.

Michael Brown, August 9, 2014, shot and killed while unarmed by Ferguson (MO) police officer.

Source: Adapted from: CNN.com, (2021).

FIGURE 5.2 ■ Police Killings of Unarmed Citizens by Race of Victim

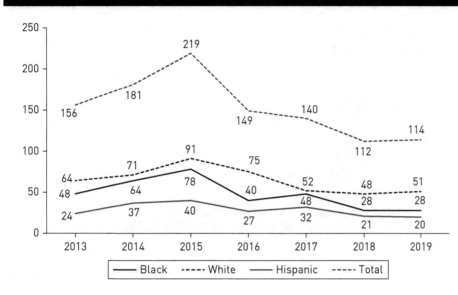

Source: Compiled from Police Scorecard

https://mappingpoliceviolence.org/nationaltrends

Reporters, researchers, and advocates for racial justice and police reform have brought more attention to the problem of police misconduct in recent years. For example, *USA Today* created a "Decertified Police Officer Database" sharing information about 30,000 police officers who were banned from policing in 44 states across the United States (Kelly & Nichols, 2019). The research team examined 85,000 police officers in all who had been accused of more than 200,000 cases of police misconduct. Among other findings from their review, they found that 22,924 of the complaints were for excessive force, 3,145 were for rape allegations, and 2,227 were for evidence tampering or perjury. The researchers also found that 2,500 of the officers had been investigated at least 10 times and that 20 of the officers had 100 or more allegations against them (Kelly & Nichols, 2019).

Researchers and advocates Samuel Sinyangwe, DeRay McKesson, and Johnetta Elzie created the Mapping Police Violence database and website to help shed light on different patterns in police killings. The data (which were used in Figure 5.2) are comprehensive, user-friendly, and helpful for seeing patterns in police killings across time. Among other things, those using the data can review geographic patterns, temporal trends, racial differences, and cause-of-death dynamics. The team also created a Police Scorecard as part of its Campaign Zero project. The Police Scorecard rates California police departments by considering the number of misconduct allegations, proportion of misdemeanor arrests, and police killings. Departments are given a grade (A-F). The message is clear: Departments receive more favorable ratings when they have fewer misconduct allegations and killings by police officers.

In Chicago, advocates and researchers from the Invisible Institute joined forces to create the Citizen's Police Data Project, which compiles data from the Chicago Police Department and the Civilian Office of Police Accountability to allow members of the public to identify patterns in police misconduct. On the data website, the researchers noted that "officers with at least ten complaints against them generate 64% of all complaints" (https://invisible.institute/police-data). The database includes detailed information on officers accused of misconduct and even places the officers into percentiles based on the number of

FIGURE 5.3 ■ Top 12 Complaints about Chicago Police Officers, 1988–2019

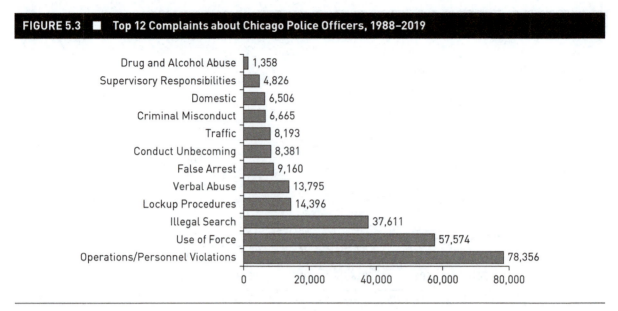

Complaint	Count
Drug and Alcohol Abuse	1,358
Supervisory Responsibilities	4,826
Domestic	6,506
Criminal Misconduct	6,665
Traffic	8,193
Conduct Unbecoming	8,381
False Arrest	9,160
Verbal Abuse	13,795
Lockup Procedures	14,396
Illegal Search	37,611
Use of Force	57,574
Operations/Personnel Violations	78,356

Source: Citizens Police Data Project.

(1) citizen allegations, (2) officer allegations, and (3) use of force allegations. Access to available reports is included as is information about the officers' units, salaries, work history, and other variables that may be of interest. The Citizens Police Data Project includes data on nearly 250,000 complaints against police officers in Chicago between 1988 and 2019. Figure 5.3 shows the 12 most common complaints in this database. Of all the complaints, just 7% resulted in disciplinary action (Citizens Police Data Project, 2020). The largest number of complaints, operations/personnel violations, includes instances when officers are accused of failing to provide service, providing inadequate service, neglect of duty, insubordination, and other personnel rule violations.

More recently identified strategies to reduce police brutality include federal consent decrees, sunshine laws, and personal liability for officers. In this context, **federal consent decrees** are judicially approved legal agreements requiring local police departments to implement reforms in order to improve law enforcement operations. Donnelly and Salvatore (2019) reviewed 40 federal consent decrees requiring police agencies to engage in various reform measures. The general types of reform measures focused on community relations, personnel actions, bias elimination, technology assistance, use of force, training, and other policy changes. Within these general categories, federal agencies stipulated specific reforms. For example, community relations reform includes civilian review programs and complaint systems, expansion of community policing, and increasing interactions with community members. Use of force recommendations were those most commonly found in the decrees. The most common recommendations included the development of general guidelines for use of force, regulating specific types of force, reviewing and reporting on the use of force, and the creation of guidelines for de-escalation.

Sunshine laws embrace transparency and call for publicizing public information. In terms of police misconduct, some have called for making police disciplinary records public for those found guilty of misconduct. Twelve states have laws making police disciplinary records public and 15 have records available in limited situations (Bies, 2017). Police unions typically oppose such measures on the grounds that personnel records warrant privacy. The power of these unions over the policy-making process has been highlighted as one of the reasons that sunshine laws are not more widely used (Bies, 2017).

Personal liability measures have also been identified as strategies to combat police misconduct. One example of these measures is the reduction or elimination of immunity protections that shield police officers from being held personally accountable (e.g., sued) for their behaviors. In the aftermath of the police brutality cases in summer 2020, experts and advocates alike stepped up calls to eliminate qualified immunity regulations protecting officers from lawsuits. Another example is pension forfeiture laws stipulating that police officers lose their retirement pensions if they are criminally convicted (Johnsen & Marcus, 2017). Thirty-one states have versions of these laws, with some of those only applying to specific crimes. Research shows that states with these laws have an average of 10 fewer use of force incidents per 100 officers than states without the laws (Johnsen & Marcus, 2017). Also in line with the way that pensions impact behavior, the authors also found that officers with more years put toward retirement are less likely to be convicted of misconduct.

While most will agree that police misconduct is wrong, some question whether police brutality is actually a form of white-collar crime; since it appears to be individual violence, it might seem that police brutality is more akin to traditional violent crimes. However, identifying police brutality as a white-collar crime is appropriate for four overlapping reasons. First, police violence is harmful behavior committed in the course of the offender's employment. Second, the level of trust we give to the police means that violations of that trust are more similar to white-collar crime than traditional crimes. Third, while police misconduct hurts all of us, like many other white-collar crimes, they disproportionately impact disadvantaged and minority communities. Finally, police violence and police corruption cases occur within our government system and highlight the overlap between crime in the streets and crime in our political system. This chapter's Streaming White-Collar Crime describes an older television series that still receives rave reviews.

STREAMING WHITE-COLLAR CRIME   *The Wire:* **The Fine Line Between Drug Crimes and White-Collar Crime by Public Officials**

Plot	What You Can Learn	Discussion Questions
Created by David Simon, a former police reporter for the *Baltimore Sun*, *The Wire* depicts the lives of those involved in the war on drugs in inner-city Baltimore. Transgressions of police officers and politicians are woven into the narrative, with some engaging in relatively minor misdeeds and others clearly crossing the line to the point that one can't help but realize that there is often no difference between those we call "good guys" and those we call "bad guys." Winning multiple awards and lasting five seasons, several criminologists have shown how the show can help us both teach and learn about the realities of crime and justice in the United States (Burke, 2010; Guastaferro, 2013; Taylor & Eidson, 2012).	As shown in this chapter, law enforcement officers don't always listen to their supervisors. Crime is inherently political. You will read more about this in the next chapter. As you will read in the theory chapter, distrust in law enforcement breeds criminal behavior.	How can crimes by police officers negatively impact the community? In what ways do the actions of political leaders and police administrators foster criminal behavior? What can community members do to draw attention to harmful actions of the police?

Attorney Misconduct

It is likely that many readers, criminal justice majors in particular, have at one point considered a career as an attorney. After all, the media—in television, movies, and books—have glorified the careers of attorneys. From *Perry Mason* to *L.A. Law* to *Law & Order*, attorneys enter our homes on a regular basis through our televisions. While criminal justice majors might tend to have favorable attitudes toward attorneys, members of the public tend to view attorneys in a less favorable light. One author notes that lawyers are viewed as "simply a plague on society" (Hazard, 1991, p. 1240). Instances of famous attorneys getting into trouble hit the media with great regularity. Consider a few of the more prominent cases:

- Celebrated attorney F. Lee Bailey was sent to jail in 1996 for keeping money from his client that was supposed to be turned over to the court. He spent six months in jail.

- Michael Cohen, who served as President Trump's personal attorney for a number of years, plead guilty to perjury, campaign violations, and tax evasion in 2018.

- In 2019, Donald Watkins and his son were convicted and sentenced to prison for stealing more than $10 million from clients in an investment scam.

- In February 2020, Michael Avenatti, who represented Stormy Daniels in her case against President Trump, was convicted for allegedly extorting Nike after offering to provide a training program to the company in exchange for not bringing the company's misdeeds to light. Apparently, it was an offer Nike was able to refuse as they alerted the authorities about the misdeeds.

The amount of attention these types of cases garner from the media likely contributes to the negative perceptions individuals hold toward attorneys. This negative view of attorneys, then, potentially contributes to formal complaints about attorney conduct (or misconduct). Over the past several decades, the number of accusations against attorneys has increased to the point that a heightened concern about being accused of misconduct has arisen (Payne & Stevens, 1999). The reason for their concern is that complaints to a state bar association have the potential to result in drastic consequences to an attorney's career.

States have different expectations and definitions for what is viewed to be appropriate conduct for attorneys. In Alabama, for example, the state bar identifies the following behaviors as warranting discipline toward attorneys:

- Failing to respond to charges brought forth by the state bar

- Violating disciplinary rules

- Neglecting a legal matter

- Felony conviction

- Misdemeanor conviction

- Keeping a client's money that should have been returned

- Keeping a client's money after failing to provide services

- Keeping fraudulently obtained money

- False statements to authorities

- False statements to clients

- Misuse of the client's funds

- Failure to provide competent representation

- Disciplined for a violation in another state

- Failure to comply with an order from a disciplinary authority

- Excessive, unfair, or unclear fees

- Failure to meet legal education requirements

- Financial conflict of interest with a client

- Behavior unbecoming a court official (Payne & Stevens, 1999, pp. 42–43)

In the few studies that have been done on attorney misconduct, the focus tends to be on types of sanctions levied against attorneys. Morgan (1995) identified three reasons that such research is important, both for society and the field of criminal justice. First, understanding how and why attorneys are sanctioned helps clarify "what the substantive law really is" (p. 343). Second, such research helps formulate degrees of misconduct by understanding how severity of sanction is tied to misconduct type. Third, such research helps dispel misguided beliefs that "professional standards are largely unenforced and unenforceable" (p. 343). In fact, research shows that offenders are routinely disciplined, and this discipline may result in loss of prestige, destruction of self-worth, embarrassment, social and professional ostracism, loss of professional affiliation, and strain in personal relationships.

If attorneys violate criminal or civil laws, they can be subjected to penalties stemming from those bodies of law (e.g., incarceration, probation, fines, restitution, etc.). Research shows that allegations of misconduct against solo, inexperienced attorneys are more likely to be prosecuted, particularly during economic recessions (Arnold & Hagan, 1992). This relationship is attributed to (a) the powerlessness of solo professionals and (b) conceptions about the legal profession that suggest that inexperienced attorneys are more likely to engage in deviance, which then results in more surveillance of these attorneys. As an analogy, if law enforcement targets particular neighborhoods prone to crime, they will arrest more offenders from those neighborhoods. If controlling authorities target inexperienced attorneys more, they will catch more inexperienced attorneys engaging in misconduct.

Various sanctions can be given to attorneys by their professional associations. Such sanctions usually include warning letters, private reprimands, public reprimands, suspensions, and disbarment. With the exception of the private reprimands, all of the sanctions are public knowledge, and many states identify sanctioned attorneys on the state bar website. Figure 5.4 shows the way attorneys were disciplined in 2017 across the United States. These disciplinary patterns show that states use public sanctions and private sanctions with similar frequency. Note that simply participating in the disciplinary complaint process can be an informal sanction for attorneys accused of misconduct. At the same time, it is important to recognize that these disciplinary proceedings typically do little to actually help the individual harmed by the attorney's wrongdoing (Kreag, 2019).

Researchers have also considered factors that contribute to sanctioning decision making. Authors have examined how attorneys are sanctioned in Alabama (Payne & Stevens, 1999) and Virginia (Payne, Time, & Raper, 2005). The Alabama study found gender patterns: Female attorneys were more likely to be publicly reprimanded, and they were slightly more likely to be accused of failing to provide competent representation. One third of female attorneys were accused of this, as compared to one fifth of male attorneys.

These patterns can be at least partially understood through an application of the systems approach or patriarchal theory. Broader societal changes resulted in more females in the legal field in the 1980s. Because female attorneys, in general, have fewer years of experience than male attorneys, the lack of experience may contribute to the accusation of failing to provide competent representation. Indeed, research shows that years of experience are tied to allegations

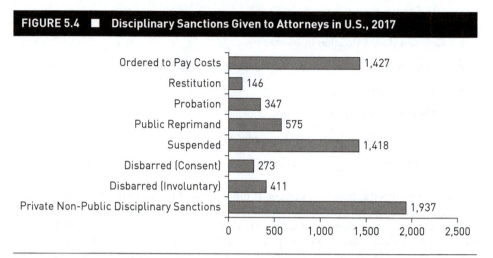

FIGURE 5.4 ■ Disciplinary Sanctions Given to Attorneys in U.S., 2017

Source: American Bar Association (2019). Standing Committee on Professional Regulation Center for Professional Responsibility 2017 Survey on Lawyer Discipline Systems (S.O.L.D.). Available online at https://www.americanbar.org/content/dam/aba/administrative/professional_responsibility/2017sold-results.pdf.

of misconduct. Conversely, it could be that a male-dominated profession uses its sanctioning body to control females. Such a possibility is in line with patriarchal theory.

On the surface, these differences point to the varied response systems between states. Also, the difference in the way misconduct is defined between states is in line with a social construction definition of white-collar misconduct, or attorney misconduct, in this case. Though these differences exist, the bottom line is that all states define appropriate behavior for attorneys, and all states have formal structures for responding to and controlling attorney misconduct. A similar pattern is evident with regard to judicial misconduct.

Judicial Misconduct

Just as lawyers are depicted in certain ways in television shows and movies, judges are a regular part of the "cast of characters" portrayed in crime-related media. These portrayals often show cantankerous judges controlling their courtrooms by humiliating attorneys and other courtroom participants. Such a portrayal is not an accurate depiction of judicial conduct. In fact, in many situations if judges actually behaved the way they are portrayed on television shows and in the media, they would face disciplinary behaviors for conduct unbecoming a judge. Consider the following description of the popular *Judge Judy* show:

Visually, Judge Judy's courtroom looks very much like one might imagine a New York State courtroom to appear if they had never actually been inside one. . . . However, there is one very significant difference between what is seen in Judge Judy's courtroom and what occurs in a real courtroom: the behavior of the judge. Judges have several checks on how they do their job. . . . In addition to laws that prescribe how the judiciary will function, the personal reputation of judges is a major incentive to do their job in an appropriate manner. . . . Because the behavior of a syndic-court judge has Nielsen ratings as a standard, they are allowed to engage in acts that would generally not be appropriate in court. The more "straight-talking" that a judge appears, which often means being as mean as possible to unlikable litigants, the better ratings he or she receives. (Kimball, 2005, p. 150)

The Model Code of Judicial Conduct outlines various rules that prescribe appropriate behavior by judges. The rules cover judicial behavior throughout the entire justice process, which means that misconduct can occur at different phases of judicial proceedings. During jury deliberations, for example, two kinds of misconduct are known to occur: (1) pressuring the jury for a verdict and (2) communicating with jurors in private. Instances where misconduct occurs during jury deliberation may result in an appeal, but appellate courts will not automatically overturn the jury's decision. The cases of judicial error are reviewed on a case-bycase basis (Gershman, 1999).

Similar to the way that states define attorney misconduct differently, states offer different typologies for judicial misconduct. Kentucky, for example, identifies three general types of judicial misconduct: (1) improper influence, (2) improper courtroom decorum, and (3) improper illegal activities on or off the bench (Judicial Conduct Commission, 2011). Within each of these general categories, specific types of misconduct are identified. In California, a more exhaustive list of types of judicial misconduct is provided by the state's judicial commission. The acts identified as misconduct in California include the following:

PHOTO 5.2 Judges have an incredible amount of power in the courtroom. Most judges do not abuse that power. A few, however, do.

- Abuse of contempt/sanctions

- Administrative malfeasance, improper comments, treatment of colleagues

- Alcohol or drug related criminal conduct

- Bias or appearance of bias toward particular groups

- Bias or appearance of bias but not toward particular groups

- Comment on pending case

- Decisional delay

- Demeanor or decorum

- Disqualification, disclosure, or post-disqualification conduct

- Ex parte communications

- Failure to cooperate with regulatory authority

- Failure to ensure rights

- Gifts, loans, favors, or ticket fixing

- Improper business, financial, or fiduciary activities

- Improper political activities

- Inability to perform judicial duties

- Miscellaneous off-bench conduct

- Misuse of court resources

- Nonperformance of judicial functions, attendance, or sleeping

- Nonsubstance abuse criminal conviction

- Off-bench abuse of authority

- On-bench abuse of authority

- Pre-bench misconduct

- Sexual harassment or inappropriate comments

- Substance abuse (State of California Commission on Judicial Performance, 2010)

There can be a wide range of seriousness in judicial misconduct cases. Consider the following three cases reported in Kansas:

- After a public hearing, a judge who [used] judicial letterhead to conduct personal business, was publicly ordered to cease and desist from using official letterhead to conduct personal business as it could lend the prestige of judicial office to advance the judge's personal interest.

- A judge, who [made] inappropriate comments about a defendant during a hearing, was cautioned to be diligent about future word choices and the importance of considering public perception.

- A judge, who [denied] a defendant the right to be heard within 21 days of the filing of a petition under K.S.A. 60-31a05, was publicly ordered to cease and desist from failing to comply with the law and denying litigants the right to be heard. (Commission on Judicial Qualifications, 2019).

Just as allegations of attorney misconduct increased in the past few decades, allegations of judicial misconduct increased significantly in the early 1990s (Coyle, 1995). Part of this increase was likely caused by the development of formal commissions in different states that provided citizens with a mechanism they could use to file judicial complaints. In California, voters approved Proposition 190 around this same time. Proposition 190 created the Commission on Judicial Performance and authorized the commission to review judicial misconduct cases and impose sanctions, which would be reviewed by the state Supreme Court.

The way the complaint process is designed in California mirrors the complaint process followed in other states. Anyone can file a written complaint to the commission. If the complaint describes an allegation of misconduct, the judge is asked to provide information in response to the allegation. Members of the commission will interview witnesses and review court transcripts and case files. The judge will be given 20 days to respond to the complaint. After the information has been reviewed, the commission meets to review cases. On average, the commission meets every seven weeks or so (State of California Commission on Judicial Performance, 2010). Figure 5.5 shows how these cases flow through the misconduct review process.

It is estimated that 90% of complaints filed against judges are dismissed (Gray, 2004). Many of the complaints are dismissed because the allegations do not rise to levels of misconduct outlined in judicial regulations. By the very nature of their jobs, judges will, at the end of the day, make decisions that disappoint or even anger several of the individuals participating in the judicial process. The result is that a number of egregious allegations are made. It is also important to note that a difference exists between "making a mistake" and committing judicial misconduct. Said Gray (2004), "It is not unethical to be imperfect, and it would be unfair to sanction a judge for not being infallible while making hundreds of decisions under pressure" (p. 1247). Somewhat related is that if a judge makes an error, then that error will not automatically result in the judicial decision being overturned. Instead, the case would be reviewed, and the relevance of the mistake would be considered in determining whether the case should be overturned. It is important to stress that judicial misconduct commissions cannot overturn judicial decisions made in courts of law. Only appellate courts have the authority to reverse judicial decisions.

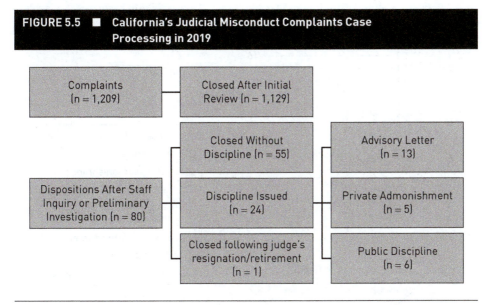

FIGURE 5.5 ■ California's Judicial Misconduct Complaints Case Processing in 2019

Source: State of California Commission on Judicial Performance. (2020). *2019 annual report.* Available online https://cjp.ca.gov/wp-content/uploads/sites/40/2020/04/2019_Annual_Report.pdf

States set their own guidelines for how they sanction judicial misconduct, though they follow somewhat similar parameters. In California, strategies include the following:

- A confidential advisory letter that informs the judge that his or her behavior violated rules of conduct

- A private admonishment rebuking the judge after the judicial commission substantiated the claim

- A public admonishment with details made available online, to the media, and to the judge

- A public **censure**, which is similar to public admonishments, but viewed as a more serious response

- Removing the judge from the bench

Figure 5.6 shows how California resolved their judicial misconduct resolutions between 2010 and 2019. As shown in the figure, the vast majority of cases are closed after an initial review. When sanctions were administered, advisory letters were the most common response. Just one California judge was removed from the bench due to misconduct over the timeframe.

Legal scholars point to specific things that defense attorneys can do to either prevent or respond to judicial misconduct. For instance, Cicchini (2019) advises that defense attorneys who are concerned about a judge's ability to treat their client in a fair manner do any of the following:

- Request that a new judge be substituted into the case.

- File for a motion of recusal if the judge shows signs of unfair treatment.

- File a motion in limine, which is "a pretrial motion seeking an advanced ruling on the admission of evidence or some other issue likely to arise at trial" (p. 1304).

- Write a one-page trial brief for the judge describing the defense attorney's concerns.

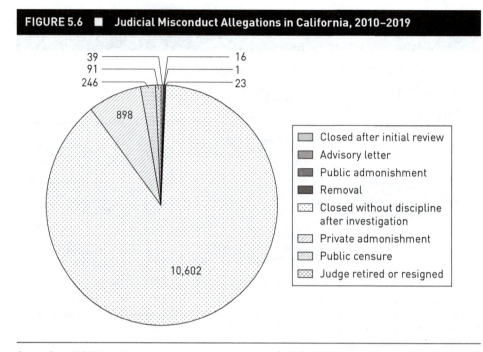

FIGURE 5.6 ■ Judicial Misconduct Allegations in California, 2010–2019

Legend:
- Closed after initial review
- Advisory letter
- Public admonishment
- Removal
- Closed without discipline after investigation
- Private admonishment
- Public censure
- Judge retired or resigned

Values shown: 39, 16, 91, 1, 246, 23, 898, 10,602

Source: State of California Commission on Judicial Performance. (2020). *2019 annual report.* Available online https://cjp.ca.gov/wp-content/uploads/sites/40/2020/04/2019_Annual_Report.pdf

Each of these measures allows defense attorneys to put their concerns on the official record and also helps them to raise concerns later in the case. Responses after the misconduct occurs include raising objections, requesting a remedy from the judge, mentioning concerns in closing arguments, appealing the case, and reporting the judge to the state bar (Cicchini, 2019).

An entire chapter of this text will discuss why white-collar misconduct occurs. In terms of judicial misconduct, some have argued that a combination of three factors contributes to misdeeds by judges. These factors include (1) office authority, (2) heavy case loads, and (3) interactions with others in the judicial process (Coyle, 1995). Briefly, judges have a great deal of power, but they are expected to express that power under the demands of large caseloads, and their interactions with others in the judicial network may provide opportunities for misconduct. One group they interact with is prosecutors—a group that also is not immune from misconduct.

Prosecutorial Misconduct

The prosecutor position has been described as "the most powerful position in the criminal justice system" (Schoenfeld, 2005, p. 250). In addition to deciding whether charges should be filed against individuals, prosecutors have a strong voice in deciding what sanction should be given to defendants. While the judge ultimately assigns the sanction, it is the prosecutor who decides what types of charges to file against defendants, and these charges will help determine the sentence given by the judge. For instance, it is the prosecutor who decides whether a defendant should be tried for capital murder—a crime that may ultimately result in the death penalty.

Criminologist Jocelyn Pollock (2004) has identified several different types of prosecutorial misconduct. First, instances where prosecutors have improper communications with defendants (e.g., without their attorney present if one was requested, personal communications) are examples of misconduct. Second, if prosecutors have ex parte communications (without the other party present) with the judge, then the prosecutor has developed an unfair advantage over the defense. Third, if prosecutors fail to disclose evidence, which they are required to do by law, then misconduct has occurred. Fourth, if a prosecutor knows that a witness has provided false testimony and fails to correct the testimony, the prosecutor has committed misconduct just as the perjurer did.

Legal expert Alschuler (1972) discussed a different set of prosecutorial misconduct examples. Examples of misconduct he discussed include the following:

- Commenting on the defendant's lack of testimony

- Asserting facts that are not supported by the evidence

- Expressing personal beliefs about the defendant's guilt

- Verbal abuse of the defense attorney

- Verbal or mental abuse of the defendant

More recently, Cramm (2009) discussed additional forms of prosecutorial misconduct, including (a) "withholding, destroying, or changing evidence"; (b) "failing to preserve evidence"; (c) "making prejudicial comments about the defendant during opening or closing remarks"; (d) "coercing guilty pleas from defendants"; (e) "intimidating defense witnesses"; and (f) "obstructing defense attorney access to prosecution witnesses."

Although it is difficult to identify precisely how often prosecutorial misconduct occurs, estimates suggest that these behaviors are particularly common. One author notes that prosecutorial misconduct is "a factor in 42 percent of DNA exonerations" according to Barry Scheck and Peter Neufeld's Innocence Project (Roberts, 2007). Another estimate suggests that one fifth of all death penalty reversals stem from prosecutorial misconduct (Perlin, 2016).

A joint effort of the University of California – Irvine Center for Science and Society, University of Michigan Law School, and Michigan State law school is the National Registry of Exonerations. This registry tracks exonerations and provides detailed descriptions of all known exonerations since 1989. The team produces an annual report each year detailing specific exonerations and highlighting trends and patterns in the exonerations. Figure 5.7 shows the contributing factors in exonerations that occurred in 2018 and 2019. The 2019 annual report revealed 143 exonerations with 93 of those attributed to official misconduct (National Registry of Exonerations, 2020).

A number of direct and indirect negative consequences arise from prosecutorial misconduct. Beyond limiting the defendant's right to a fair trial, influencing the jury, and creating public resentment (Alschuler, 1972), prosecutorial misconduct has the potential to breed crime. If the most powerful representatives of the justice system break the rules, others might use the "official misbehavior" to justify their own transgressions. Also, and perhaps more significant, prosecutorial misconduct has the potential to wrongfully sentence individuals to life in prison or, even worse, death. Schoenfeld (2005) cites a *Chicago Tribune* study that found "since 1963, 381 people have had their convictions for homicide overturned because of prosecutorial misconduct. Sixty-seven of those defendants were sentenced to death" (p. 266).

Students should not think that they are insulated from cases of prosecutorial misconduct. Consider the case of the Duke Lacrosse players accused of raping Crystal Gail Magnum. Overzealous in his efforts to prosecute the students from the moment the allegations surfaced, former prosecutor Mike Nifong was initially praised by advocates, university faculty, and feminists because he was demonstrating a willingness to prosecute seemingly elite students accused of raping an African American woman. His zeal for the case did not dissipate, even after evidence surfaced that seemed to refute the woman's claim. Eventually, the case was dismissed.

A state bar examination of Nifong's actions in the case found that he had (a) refused to hear exculpatory evidence, (b) made false statements to the media to "[heighten] public condemnation

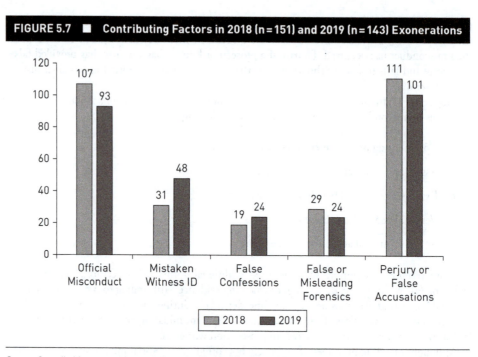

FIGURE 5.7 ■ Contributing Factors in 2018 (n = 151) and 2019 (n = 143) Exonerations

Source: Compiled from annual reports from the National Registry of Exonerations.

of the accused," (c) failed to provide evidence to the defendants, (d) failed to provide the results of tests to the defendants, and (e) denied knowing about the results of a rape kit exam that potentially exonerated the defendants. Nifong was disbarred but not before sending some rather interesting letters to the state bar. In one letter, for instance, Nifong claimed that the license he was surrendering to the state bar was damaged because his puppy had chewed on it. According to News and Observer, the falsely accused students incurred legal expenses in excess of $3 million in their efforts to respond to Nifong's misconduct.

Conviction integrity units exist in some prosecutor's offices as official units to review prosecutor's cases and ensure the case integrity. In 2017, 33 such units existed across the nation. Two years later, 59 conviction integrity units were operating across the United States (National Registry of Exonerations, 2020). In 2019, the units were responsible for 55 exonerations. In addition to helping exonerate offenders, they are believed to help address prosecutor's cognitive biases that might inadvertently result in misconduct (Bloch, 2019). The units frequently collaborate with professional exonerators, which include nonprofit innocence organizations that provide pro bono (free) support to inmates believed to be innocent. Between 1989 and 2019, professional exonerators contributed to the exonerations of 610 cases (National Registry of Exonerations, 2020).

Remedies to prosecutorial misconduct include retrials, disciplinary proceedings, expensive and time-consuming independent investigation, civil lawsuits (which are rarely successful), and criminal prosecutions (which are even rarer in occurrence) (Kreag, 2019). Kreag critiques these remedies on the grounds that they do very little to actually reduce or limit the harm from the misconduct. This is especially problematic if a criminal case proceeds in spite of the bad behavior from the prosecutor.

Legal scholars point to specific things that defense attorneys can do to either prevent or respond to prosecutorial misconduct. Some scholars have said that better prepared defense attorneys can limit prosecutorial misconduct. According to Vars (2017), "good defense counsel at trial is the most potent weapon against prosecutorial misconduct" (p. 460). Cicchini (2018) advises that defense attorneys file pretrial motions about what the prosecutor can say in closing arguments where it is believed that misconduct is "rampant" (p. 887).

Not surprisingly, there appears to be great disagreement in the legal field about the pervasiveness of prosecutorial misconduct, and some vehemently disagree with the characterization of the problem as "rampant." One legal scholar argues that "prosecutorial misconduct occurs with admirable infrequency . . . empirical data do not substantiate the vitriol with which [prosecutors] are attacked" (Harker, 2018). Harker (2018) notes that many of the perceptions about prosecutorial behavior are based on "dated case citations" and broad definitions of misconduct that characterize normal prosecutorial decisions (i.e., plea bargaining, selective prosecution, and overcharging) as misconduct. At the other extreme, there are those who are willing to accept prosecutorial misbehavior because, as Perlin (2016) writes, "there are still some who adhere to the magical thinking that authentically innocent people cannot be convicted" (p. 1543).

Correctional Officer Misconduct

Much more research has focused on police corruption, judicial misconduct, and attorney misconduct than on corruption by correctional officers. One of the first studies done on corruption by correctional officers was a doctoral dissertation by Bernard McCarthy (1981). McCarthy's dissertation was a case study of misconduct in one state's prison system. He classified the offenses into theft (from inmates, from the institution, and from civilians), trafficking (bringing contraband into the prison), abuse of authority, and embezzlement (from prison accounts, nonprison accounts, and so on). Various patterns were tied to misconduct in the prison system. First, the degree of discretion given to low-level workers in an isolated work environment appeared to promote the opportunity for corruption. Second, the nature of the prison as an institution was such that inmate demand for contraband was high. Third, low morale (with workers' individual goals being different from the collective goals of the criminal justice system) was viewed as a predictor of correctional misconduct.

As with the law enforcement profession, sexual misconduct has been cited as a variety of misconduct occurring in the corrections profession. The Bureau of Justice Statistics uses the following definitions of correctional officer sexual misconduct:

Staff-on-inmate sexual victimization includes sexual misconduct or sexual harassment perpetrated against an inmate by staff. Staff includes an employee, volunteer, contractor, official visitor, or other agency representative. Family, friends, and other visitors are excluded.

Staff sexual misconduct includes any consensual or nonconsensual behavior or act of a sexual nature directed toward an inmate by staff, including romantic relationships. Such acts include

- intentional touching, either directly or through the clothing, of the genitalia, anus, groin, breast, inner thigh, or buttocks that is unrelated to official duties or that is with the intent to abuse, arouse, or gratify sexual desire;
- completed, attempted, threatened, or requested sexual acts; and
- occurrences of indecent exposure, invasion of privacy, or staff voyeurism for reasons unrelated to official duties or for sexual gratification.

Staff sexual harassment includes repeated verbal comments or gestures of a sexual nature to an inmate by staff. Such statements include

- demeaning references to an inmate's gender, or sexually suggestive or derogatory comments about their body or clothing; and
- repeated profane or obscene language or gestures. (Bureau of Justice Statistics, n.d.)

In line with this definition, varieties of sexual misconduct in the corrections field have been categorized as sexual contact offenses, sexual assault, and sexual gratification between officer and supervisee (Smith & Yarussi, 2007). Another author team classifies sexual misconduct by corrections officials into the following four categories: (1) verbal harassment, (2) improper visual surveillance, (3) improper touching, and (4) consensual sex (Burton, Erdman, Hamilton, & Muse, 1999). It is believed that "consensual relations" are the most common forms of sexual misconduct between correctional officers and inmates, with rape believed to be infrequent (Layman, McCampbell, & Moss, 2000). The phrase "consensual relations," though, is problematic. The underlying assumption of correctional sex misconduct laws is that inmates are not able to consent because (1) unequal power exists between the parties, (2) staff may be exploiting the troubled pasts of inmates by developing sexual relationships, and (3) inmates could manipulate staff by threatening to expose the sexual relationship to authorities (Heil, 2019).

All states criminalize any type of sexual contact between correctional staff and inmates, but just 19 states indicate that defendants can't use inmate consent as a defense to prosecution (Kowalski, Mei, Turner, Stohr, & Hemmens, 2020). This suggests that in other states—while relations may be prohibited by policy—corrections staff might be able to use inmate consent as a defense against sexual misconduct or harassment charges. State laws governing correction officer sexual misconduct also vary on the following factors:

- When the laws were passed
- Recommended sanctions
- Terminology used to characterize sexual relations
- How power, consent, and coercion are defined
- Types of legal defenses permitted
- Training regulations
- Reporting requirements (Kowalski et al., 2020)

In 2015, 24,661 allegations of sexual assault were reported in corrections institutions; 585 of those allegations involved attacks by corrections staff against inmates (Heil, 2019). Figure 5.8 shows the number of sexual assault allegations made by inmates against correctional staff between 2012 and 2015. The vast majority of allegations are unfounded, though a sizable number of them are unsubstantiated, meaning officials can't determine for certain if the allegations are true. Sexual assault was substantiated in more than 2,200 cases.

The consequences of sexual misconduct for inmate sexual assault victims are likely no different from the consequences that other sexual assault victims experience. It is important to note, however, that sexual misconduct by corrections officials will lead to consequences that also impact the correctional system. Potential consequences of correctional sexual misconduct include the following:

- Jeopardizing staff safety if inmates react against nonoffending staff members
- The risk of legal action for staff members, supervisors, and the agency
- Health risks for inmates and staff exposed to sexually transmitted diseases
- Family problems for offenders, victims, and staff responding to the allegations
- Negative perceptions of the corrections department among community members
- Reduced trust between inmates and staff (Smith & Yarussi, 2007)

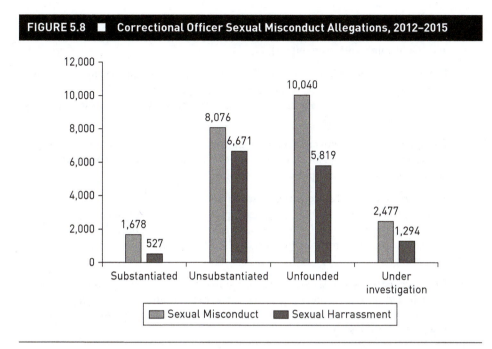

FIGURE 5.8 ■ **Correctional Officer Sexual Misconduct Allegations, 2012–2015**

Source: Rantala, R. (2018). *Sexual victimization reported by adult correctional authorities, 2012–2015.* Retrieved from https://www.bjs.gov/content/pub/pdf/svraca1215.pdf

Concern about an increase in sexual misconduct by community corrections officers led the National Institute of Corrections to develop a 36-hour training program to assist officials in their efforts to prevent and intervene in cases of sexual misconduct. The training focused on defining misconduct, policy development, legal issues, ethical issues, investigatory strategies, and other related topics (Buell & McCampbell, 2003). General strategies that have been suggested for preventing sexual misconduct include (a) developing clear policies that are enforced as needed, (b) improving the quality of workers, (c) enhancing supervisory practices, (d) implementing various social control mechanisms, and (e) providing ethics training to officers and staff (Souryal, 2009).

PHOTO 5.3 White-collar crimes occur in prisons, too.

CRIME IN THE MILITARY SYSTEM

As a system of social control, the military system includes several branches of the military that are charged with various duties related to wartime efforts and the promotion of peace. Clifford Bryant (1979) used the phrase "khaki-collar crime" for situations where individuals in the military break rules guiding their workplace activities. According to Bryant, "khaki-collar crime" occurs in five contexts:

- **Intra-occupational crimes** are crimes committed against the American military system. These crimes include property crimes (e.g., theft of military property, misuse of property, and destruction of property), crimes against persons (e.g., cruelty to subordinates and assaults against superiors), and crimes against performance (e.g., mutiny, faking illness, and conduct unbecoming an officer).

- **Extra-occupational crimes** are committed against the American civilian social system. These crimes include property crimes (e.g., theft, forgery, and vandalism), personal crimes (e.g., rape, robbery, assault, and murder), and performance crimes (e.g., fighting and disturbing the peace).

- **Foreign friendly civilian crimes** are committed against citizens of another country. The same types of crimes found under extra-occupational crimes but committed against foreigners are examples.

- **Enemy civilian social system crimes** are crimes against residents of countries in which the U.S. military is fighting. Examples of such crimes include property crimes (e.g., looting and pillaging), personal crimes (e.g., committing atrocities and massacres), and performance crimes (e.g., colluding with citizens to harm the U.S. military).

- **Inter-occupational crimes** are crimes committed against the enemy military system. These include property crimes (e.g., misappropriation of captured supplies), personal crimes (e.g., torture and mistreatment of prisoners of war), and performance crimes (e.g., helping the enemy).

Bryant notes that the source of law for military crimes, and the application of laws, is different from what would be found with other white-collar crimes. Depending on where the crime was committed and which crime was committed, sources of law in khaki-collar crime cases include the U.S. *Uniform Code of Military Justice*, international treaties, the *Law of Land Warfare*, and the laws of the government of the country where the crime was committed.

It is safe to suggest that the military has more rules than other occupations guiding workplace behavior. Consider the following examples:

©iStockphoto.com/MTMCOINS

PHOTO 5.4 Bryant uses the phrase "khaki-collar crime" to describe white-collar crimes by individuals in the military.

- If my colleagues in my department (that I chair) don't do as I ask them to do, it will make me sad. If members of the military do not do as their bosses tell them, they can be charged with insubordination.

- If I get tired of my job as department chair and quit going to work, I will be fired. If a member of the military leaves his or her military assignment, this will be called desertion.

- If my colleagues try to overthrow my department and run me off as chair, again, I will be sad. If members of the military try to overtake their commanding officer, mutiny is occurring.

- If I fake being sick and try to get out of going to a meeting, this will be a minor form of occupational deviance. If members of the military feign illness to get out of their assignments, this will be called malingering and can be met with a court martial.

- If I quit my job and go work for another university, I will miss my current colleagues tremendously. If members of the military leave and go work for another military, this will be called foreign enlistment.

- Up until recently, if a gay or lesbian soldier told people about his or her sexual orientation, he or she could have been disciplined by the military (Bryant, 1979).

In addition to facing different types of rules and regulations, members of the military will also face different justice processes for breaking those roles. Generally speaking, depending on the seriousness of the allegation, their rule violations will be addressed through one of four types of processes: nonjudicial punishments, summary court martials, special court martials, and general court martials. Table 5.1 provides a comparison of these processes. A few themes are important to highlight. First, the right to counsel varies across the types of court martial; offenders are not afforded the right to counsel in less serious cases processed through nonjudicial punishments and summary court martials. Second, less serious cases are decided either by the commanding officer or a commission officer, while more serious cases are decided by military judges. Third, as cases become more serious, so to do the types of possible sanctions.

TABLE 5.1 ■ Types of Nonjudicial Punishments and Court Martials				
	Nonjudicial Punishment	**Summary Court Martial**	**Special Court Martial**	**General Court Martial**
Purpose	Discipline minor offenses committed by enlisted service members or officers	Adjudicate noncapital offenses committed by enlisted servicemembers; Not a criminal forum, so a guilty finding is not a criminal conviction	Adjudicate any noncapital and some capital offenses committed by enlisted servicemembers or officers	Adjudicate any offenses committed by enlisted servicemembers or officers, including capital offenses
Right to Counsel	None, but the accused is generally entitled to be accompanied by a spokesperson. The accused may demand a court-martial in lieu of nonjudicial punishment (unless serving on a vessel).	None, but the accused must consent to the proceedings and will generally be allowed to have civilian counsel represent the accused if funded by the accused and if the counsel's appearance will not delay proceedings.	The accused is entitled to an appointed military attorney, a military counsel of the accused's own selection (if reasonably available), or may hire civilian counsel.	The accused is entitled to an appointed military attorney, a military counsel of the accused's own selection (if reasonably available), or may hire civilian counsel.

(Continued)

TABLE 5.1 ■ (Continued)				
	Nonjudicial Punishment	**Summary Court Martial**	**Special Court Martial**	**General Court Martial**
Decided By	Commanding officer (or, for the Coast Guard, officers-in-charge)	One commissioned officer	One military judge and four members on a panel, or one military judge sitting alone, if (1) the accused requests a military judge sitting alone, or (2) the case is referred to a military judge sitting alone (which decreases maximum possible punishment). (If case is referred to military judge sitting alone, and parties consent, military judge may designate a military magistrate to preside.) If a panel, at least three fourths of the members must agree on a guilty verdict.	One military judge and eight members on a panel, or, by request of the accused, one military judge sitting alone. Panels require 12 members for all capital cases and eight members for all noncapital cases in a panel; at least three fourths of the members must agree on a guilty verdict; capital verdicts must be unanimous.
Maximum Possible Punishments	Depending on the grade of the commander imposing the punishment and of the member being punished, maximum punishments range widely, for example: Officer: Reprimand, restrictions with or without suspension from duties for up to 30 days; arrest in quarters for up to 30 days, forfeiture of one half month's pay for two months, etc. Enlisted: Reprimand, correctional custody or forfeiture of pay for up to 30 days; reduction in grade; extra duties for up to 14 days; etc.	Confinement for up to 30 days; hard labor without confinement for up to 45 days; forfeiture of two thirds of pay for 1 month; reduction to a lower pay grade	If referred to a court-martial consisting of military judge and panel: Confinement for up to 1 year; hard labor without confinement for up to three months; forfeiture of two thirds of pay for up to one year; reduction to a lower pay grade; bad conduct discharge. If referred to a court-martial consisting of military judge alone: Confinement for up to six months; hard labor without confinement for up to three months; forfeiture of two thirds of pay for up to six months; reduction to a lower pay grade	Any punishment within the limits prescribed by the *Manual for Courts-Martial* for the offenses of which the accused is found guilty, including the death penalty for certain offenses

Source: Reprinted from U.S. GAO (2019). Available online at https://www.gao.gov/assets/700/699380.pdf

Available evidence suggests the discipline and judicial responses vary across military branches (see Figure 5.9). Generally speaking, a higher percentage of members of the Army and Marine Corps faced discipline than those from the Navy, Air Force, and Coast Guard between 2013 and 2017. In fact, nearly one in five members of the Army faced some type of discipline during that time period.

FIGURE 5.9 ■ Types of Discipline and Judicial Processes Used Across Military Branches, Discipline in the Armed Forces, FY 2013–2017

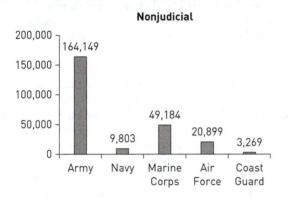

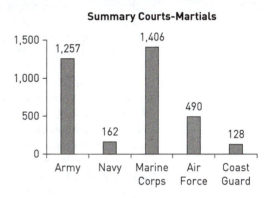

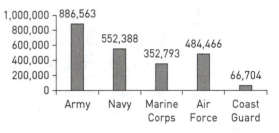

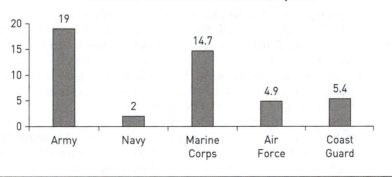

Source: US GAO (2019). Available online at https://www.gao.gov/assets/700/699380.pdf

One recent controversy regarding crimes in the military centers on the use of private contractors, such as Xie, Dyncorp International, and Triple Canopy, to provide military security functions. Regulations stipulate that private contractors should use only defensive types of violence; however, evidence points to several horrific situations where private military contractors initiated violence (Welch, 2009). The case of Blackwater (since renamed Xie), a security firm created in 1997 by a former Navy Seal, is particularly illustrative. By all accounts, Blackwater has been overrepresented in allegations of offensive force by private military contractors. Welch (2009) wrote that Blackwater has a "shooting rate" two times higher than similar private military security businesses. He added that the

company has gained a reputation as one that flaunts a quick-draw image, thereby enticing its guards to take excessively violent actions. Some suggest that its aggressive posture in guarding diplomats reflects the wishes of its principle client, the State Department's Bureau of Diplomatic Security. (p. 356)

Another recent controversy had to do with the way members of the military treat prisoners of war. The tortures occurring at Abu Ghraib made international headlines when photos surfaced showing military officials sexually degrading prisoners. Hamm (2007) noted that three explanations had been offered to explain abuses at Abu Ghraib. First, the government promoted a bad apples explanation, suggesting that just a few bad members of the military were involved in the abusive activities. Second, some suggested that Zimbardo's *automatic brutality* theory applied (suggesting that all individuals have the capacity to torture if they are placed in a situation where it is possible). Third, historian Alfred McCoy argued that the practices had a long history in the Central Intelligence Agency. Hamm concluded that McCoy's theory made the most sense. He said that evidence suggests "that the torturing of detainees at Abu Ghraib followed directly from decisions made by top government officials, from President George W. Bush on down" (p. 259). Hamm stated that the Bush administration "took off the gloves in prisoner interrogation" (p. 259).

CRIME BY OFFICIALS IN THE RELIGIOUS SYSTEM

In the past, many individuals probably gave little thought to the possibility that crime occurs in the religious system. However, like other occupational settings, churches and religious institutions are not immune from misconduct. To provide a general introduction to crimes in the religious system, attention can be given to financial offenses in the religious system, deception in the religious system, and the Catholic Church sexual abuse scandal.

Financial Offenses in the Religious System

One type of white-collar crime occurring in the religious system involves financial offenses, where church leaders embezzle funds from church proceeds. Such acts are relatively simple to commit because church funds are easy to target, and there is often little oversight of the church's bank accounts (Smietana, 2005). One pastor, for example, who was accused of stealing more than a million dollars from his church over a 10-year time frame, alleged that he had the authority to use the church funds as he saw fit because he was the "pastor and overseer" of the church ("Ex-Pastor Testifies in Embezzlement Trial," 2010).

One of the most famous instances of embezzlement by a religious leader involves the case of Rev. Jim Bakker, a former televangelist who cohosted the TV show *The PTL Club* with his wife Tammy Faye. Bakker's television show, which had an acronym standing for "praise the Lord," brought in millions of dollars. Eventually, Bakker and his wife created their own network and organization called the PTL Television Network. In 1989, Bakker was convicted of stealing $3.7 million from the PTL organization. At his sentencing hearing, prosecutor Jerry Miller focused on the vulnerable groups that had given money to Bakker's organization so Bakker could divert funds to support his lavish lifestyle. The judge, nicknamed "Maximum Bob" in reference to the long sentences he had given offenders, sentenced Bakker to 45 years in prison, with parole eligibility after 10 years (Harris, 1989). An appeals court ruled that a new sentencing hearing should be held, and Bakker was subsequently sentenced to eight years and paroled in 1994. He is now the host of the *Jim Bakker Show*, which appears on various networks. He avoided the negative limelight until Spring of 2020, when fraud allegations surfaced about products Bakker was promoting. Specifically, Bakker was sued by the Missouri Attorney General for selling a product he promoted on his television show as a cure for the coronavirus and other illnesses (Briquelet, 2020). The televangelist—at the age of 80—vowed to fight those charges.

Financial offenses by church leaders are often stumbled on only by accident. In one case, for example, it was not until a pastor left his church and "collections went up dramatically" that officials had any suspicion of wrongdoing. The subsequent investigations revealed that the pastor had stolen about $1 million from his church over a five-year time frame (Smietana, 2005). Other times, offenses are uncovered as a result of routine audits (O'Sullivan, 2011). Regardless of how the financial offenses are detected, their consequences can be devastating to the church that was victimized. Said one pastor about these consequences, "It's not about the money so much. It's about the trust" (Smietana, 2005).

Deception in the Religious System

Religious system deception refers to situations in which church leaders lie to their congregants in an effort to promote an appearance of "holier than thou." Lying in and of itself is not illegal. However, the violation of trust that arises in these situations warrants that these cases be classified as white-collar crime. Consider, for instance, the case of Jimmy Swaggart, who was banned from preaching for three months by national leaders of the Assemblies of God Church after he confessed to liaisons with a prostitute. Ironically, Swaggart was implicated by a pastor he had exposed for adultery two years before (Kaufman, 1988). In a more recent case, in the fall of 2006, Rev. Ted Haggard's affairs with a former male escort came to light. At the time, Haggard was the president of the National Association of Evangelicals and the founding pastor of the Colorado Springs-based New Life Church—a megachurch with 14,000 members. After his adultery became public, he resigned from his presidential position, and the board of his church dismissed him from pastoral duties (Banerjee & Goodstein, 2006). Haggard and his wife now travel around the United States, appearing in different churches to talk about forgiveness (Jacobson, 2009).

Catholic Church Sexual Abuse Scandal

Historically, the Catholic Church has been viewed as a safe haven where individuals can retreat for protection. Over the past 15 years, however, the image of the Catholic Church became more and more tarnished as cases of child sexual abuse by priests began to be reported in the media with increasing frequency. After a while, it was clear that the number of allegations was not indicative of a few events but of a problem that appeared to be structurally situated within the Catholic Church. To address the sexual abuse scandal, the U.S. Catholic bishops approved the Charter for the Protection of Children and Young People. Among other things, the Charter developed a National Review Board that was charged with commissioning a study on sexual abuse in the Catholic Church. All dioceses were required to participate in the study. The board hired John Jay College of Criminal Justice of the City University of New York to conduct the study. The resulting study provided the most comprehensive picture of the issue of sexual abuse in the Catholic Church (U.S. Conference of Catholic Bishops, 2004).

Using a variety of research methodologies, including interviews, reviews of case files, mail surveys, and so on, the John Jay study found that 4% of active priests "between 1950 and 2002 had allegations of abuse" (p. 4), and 10,677 individuals accused priests of sexually abusing them as children. The John Jay study also estimated that the Catholic Church had already spent $650 million in settlements and on treatment programs for priests.

Researchers have used the John Jay data to examine similarities between sexual abuse in the Catholic Church and victimization or offending patterns among other offender groups. For example, Alex Piquero and his colleagues (Piquero, Piquero, Terry, Youstin, & Nobles, 2008) used the John Jay data to examine the criminal careers of the clerics and compare their careers to the careers of traditional criminals. The research team found similarities and differences between the two types of offenders. In terms of similarities, both clerics and traditional career criminals exhibited relatively similar rates of prevalence and recidivism. Differences between the two groups were attributed to "a function of the unique position in which the clerics find themselves" (Piquero et al., 2008, p. 596). Their age of criminal onset, for example, is older, likely because they enter their careers at a later age. The researchers also found higher rates of recidivism among married clerics. Marriage typically reduces the likelihood of reoffending, but this did not appear to be the cases among the clerics assessed in the John Jay data.

Michael White and Karen Terry (2008) used the John Jay data to apply the rotten apples explanation to the sex abuse scandal. In doing so, they demonstrated that this explanation does not provide an adequate explanation for the cases of child sexual abuse perpetrated by the clerics. The authors draw out parallels between the police profession and the clergy (e.g., both are unique subcultures that are isolated, where individual members have a significant amount of authority and little oversight) to bring attention to the subcultural factors that may have contributed to the existence of sexual abuse in the Catholic Church. The authors also addressed police deviance prevention strategies that could have been used to limit the abuse. These included (a) careful selection of personnel and training, (b) supervision and accountability, (c) guidelines, (d) internal affairs units, (e) early warning systems, (f) changing the subculture, (g) criminal cases, (h) civil liability, and (i) citizen oversight. The authors conclude that "church leaders would be well advised to follow the lead of professional police departments who institute rigorous internal and external accountability controls" (p. 676).

Other researchers have focused on the Catholic Church scandal, collecting original data. Many of these other studies have examined the consequences of the child sexual abuse for individuals, parishes, the Catholic Church, and society. Research shows that, like other child sexual assault victims, those assaulted by priests are more likely than those who never experienced any sexual abuse to experience social isolation and require extensive therapy (Isely, Isely, Freiburger, & McMackin, 2008). Some researchers have identified consequences that may be unique to victims of clergy. Surveys of 1,810 Catholics found that those who had been abused by priests were more distrustful of religion than those who were sexually abused by someone other than a priest. All sexual assault victims were more likely to experience various forms of "spiritual damage" (Rossetti, 1995). Other studies have found no difference between those abused by priests and victims abused by someone else (Shea, 2008). The long-term consequences are particularly salient for both groups.

A different research team examined 326 child sex abuse cases involved the Protestant church (Denney, Kerley, & Gross, 2018). The authors found that 80% of the cases were "contact" offenses involving some type of physical contact initiated by the offender. Noncontact offenses included sexual harassment, possession of child pornography, and stalking. Nearly 40% of the cases occurred on church grounds, and nearly a third occurred in the offenders' homes. Just 1% involved female offenders, and three fourths of the offenders were white.

While some will say that sexual abuse occurs in all religions, data suggest that the Catholic church is overrepresented. As an example, just five days after victims were permitted to file Child Victim Lawsuits against churches, 105 lawsuits were filed in Western New York, and 98% of those lawsuits identified the Catholic Diocese as the defendant (Herbeck, 2019). Similar legislation opening the door for lawsuits is expected to lead to an even higher number of legal actions by victims. Between 2007 and 2019, 15 states enacted laws removing the statute of limitations for sexual abuse. A review by the *Associated Press* estimates that the removal of the statutes of limitations will open the door to 5,000 new cases that could cost the Catholic church upward of 4 billion dollars (Associated Press, 2019).

Criminal charges against Catholic priests continue to be filed. In one of the larger cases, a Pennsylvania grand jury focusing on 57 of the state's 67 counties spent two years reviewing church documents and interviewing witnesses. The grand jury report, released in 2018, identified more than 200 suspected priests accused of victimizing more than 1,000 children. The scathing grand jury investigation alleged that the church files were written in ways to hide or mask abuse. Examples cited by the grand jury included the following allegations:

- Phrases like "boundary issues" are used instead of "sexual misconduct or rape" in the church files.

- The churches don't really investigate the cases, or they use professors to do investigations.

- The church allows priests to be diagnosed by its own psychologists who use self-reports from the priests.

- When priests are removed, parishioners are not told why.

- Priests continue to get housing while being abusive.

- Priests are transferred instead of removed.

- Police are not called with cases treated as personnel issues rather than crimes.

In spite of these alarming findings, the Catholic church has been increasingly transparent about its efforts to respond to its sexual abuse problem. For more than 15 years, the church has published data and updates in its Annual Report on the Implementation of the Charter for the Protection of Children and Young People. Findings from the 2019 annual report are shown in Figures 5.10 to 5.13. Four patterns shown in these figures are worth highlighting:

- The church has paid more than a billion dollars in responding to the sexual abuse scandal between 2016 and 2019, with $367 million paid in 2019.

- Settlement costs represent the majority of costs paid by the church.

- The number of new credible allegations increased dramatically in recent years, particularly in 2019.

- The vast majority of new credible allegations began or occurred prior to the 1990s, with less than 10% beginning or occurring since the nineties.

The impact of the scandal on the Catholic Church cannot be overstated. Beyond the economic toll that has come along with paying for settlements and treatment programs, raising funds was likely more difficult for their church leaders during these times. Also, the child sexual abuse scandal received widespread coverage in the press, far more coverage than other forms of child sexual abuse have received (Cheit & Davis, 2010). There are no simple answers to what can be done to help victims or the Catholic Church recover.

FIGURE 5.10 ■ New Credible Allegations of Abuse in the Catholic Church, 2014–2019

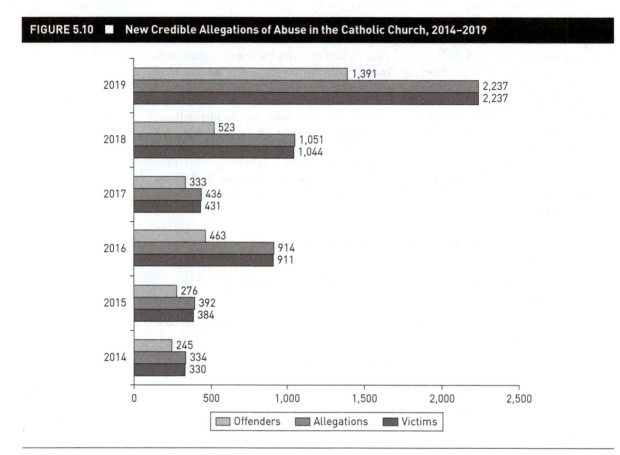

Source: 2019 Report on the Implementation of the Charter for the Protection of Children and Young People. Available online at https://www.usccb
.org/offices/child-and-youth-protection/audits

FIGURE 5.11 ■ Costs Related to FY 2019 Child Sex Abuse Allegations

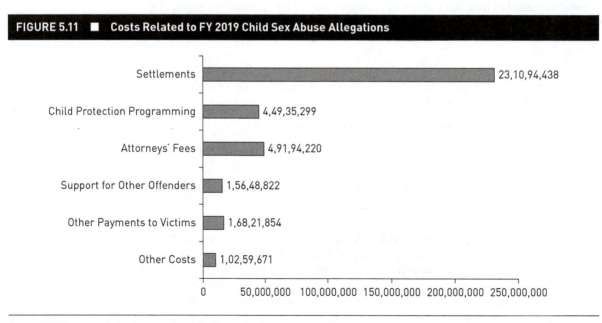

Source: 2019 Report on the Implementation of the Charter for the Protection of Children and Young People. Available online at https://www.usccb
.org/offices/child-and-youth-protection/audits.

FIGURE 5.12 ■ Total Costs of Sexual Abuse to Catholic Church

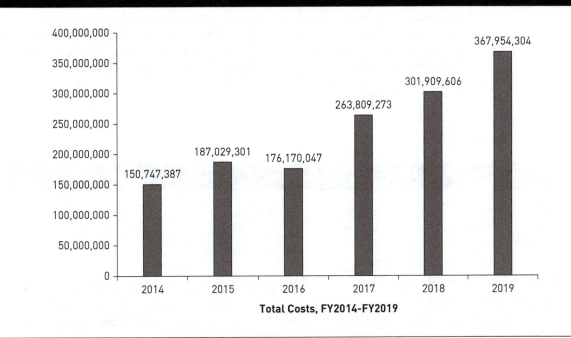

Total Costs, FY2014–FY2019

Source: 2019 Report on the Implementation of the Charter for the Protection of Children and Young People. Available online at https://www.usccb .org/offices/child-and-youth-protection/audits

FIGURE 5.13 ■ Year Alleged Offenses Occurred or Began Cumulatively for 2004–2019 (percentage)

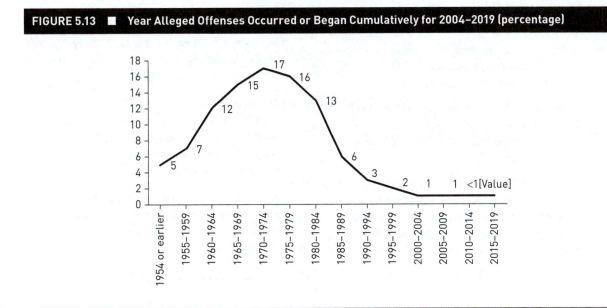

Source: 2019 Report on the Implementation of the Charter for the Protection of Children and Young People. Available online at https://www.usccb .org/offices/child-and-youth-protection/audits.

Some will question whether sexual abuse by priests is actually a form of white-collar crime. After all, the offense of child sexual abuse seems more like a violent street crime than a white-collar crime. A. R. Piquero and his colleagues (2008) do an outstanding job making an argument that these offenses can be characterized as white-collar crimes. The offenses are committed (a) by a trusted professional, (b) who is respected by members of society, (c) during the course of work. Also, recall Rosoff's (1989) concept of status liability: By the very nature of their status, when priests "fall from grace," the response from the public will be far more severe than that associated with other offenders.

Summary

- Varieties of police misconduct include corruption of authority, kickbacks, opportunistic theft, shakedowns, protection of illegal activities, fixing cases, direct criminal activities, internal payoffs (Barker & Roebucks, 1973), and sexual misconduct.

- McCarthy (1981) identified four varieties of corruption in corrections: embezzlement (stealing from the institution), drug smuggling into the institution, coercion, and transporting contraband into the prison system.

- The public's negative view of attorneys likely contributes to formal complaints about attorney conduct (or misconduct).

- States have different expectations and definitions for what is viewed to be appropriate conduct for attorneys.

- Of the few studies that have been done on attorney misconduct, the focus tends to be on types of sanctions levied against attorneys.

- If attorneys violate the criminal or civil laws, they can be subjected to penalties stemming from those bodies of law (e.g., incarceration, probation, fines, restitution).

- A variety of different sanctions can be given to attorneys by their professional associations. Most commonly, these sanctions include warning letters, private reprimands, public reprimands, suspensions, and disbarment.

- Just as lawyers are depicted in certain ways on television shows and movies, judges are also a regular part of the "cast of characters" portrayed in crime-related media.

- Kentucky identifies three general types of judicial misconduct: (1) improper influence, (2) improper courtroom decorum, and (3) improper illegal activities on or off the bench.

- Allegations of judicial misconduct increased significantly in the early 1990s (Coyle, 1995).

- It is estimated that 90% of complaints filed against judges are dismissed (Gray, 2004).

- Some have argued that a combination of three factors contributes to misdeeds by judges. These factors include (1) office authority, (2) heavy caseloads, and (3) interactions with others in the judicial process (Coyle, 1995).

- Criminologist Jocelyn Pollock (2004) has identified five different types of prosecutorial misconduct. Legal expert Alschuler (1972) discussed a different set of prosecutorial misconduct examples.

- While it is difficult to identify precisely how often prosecutorial misconduct occurs, estimates suggest that these behaviors are particularly common.

- A number of direct and indirect negative consequences arise from prosecutorial misconduct.

- Clifford Bryant (1979) used the phrase" khaki-collar crime" to describe situations where individuals in the military break rules guiding their workplace activities.

- The phrase "state-corporate crime" draws attention to the fact that government agencies are employers (or "corporations"), and these agencies and their employees sometimes commit various types of misconduct—either independently or in conjunction with other corporations.

- Religious system deception refers to situations in which church leaders lie to their congregants in an effort to promote an appearance of "holier than thou."

- Historically, the Catholic Church has been viewed as a safe haven where individuals can retreat for protection.

- Over the past 15 years, however, the image of the Catholic Church became more and more tarnished as cases of child sexual abuse by priests began to be reported in the media with increasing frequency.

- Researchers have used the John Jay data to examine similarities between sexual abuse in the Catholic Church and victimization or offending patterns among other offender groups.

- Michael White and Karen Terry (2008) used the John Jay data to apply the rotten apples explanation to the sex abuse scandal.

- Other researchers have focused on the Catholic Church scandal, collecting original data. Many of these other studies have examined the consequences of the child sexual abuse for individuals, parishes, the Catholic Church, and society.

- A different research team examined 326 child sex abuse cases involving the Protestant church and found that 80% of the cases were "contact" offenses involving some type of physical contact initiated by the offender.

- While some will say that sexual abuse occurs in all religions, data suggest that the Catholic Church is overrepresented.

- The Catholic church has been increasingly transparent about its efforts to respond to its sexual abuse problem.

- Some will question whether sexual abuse by priests is actually a form of white-collar crime.

Key Terms

Censure 119
Enemy civilian social system crimes 126
Extra-occupational crimes 126
Federal consent decrees 112
Foreign friendly civilian crimes 126
Inter-occupational crimes 126

Intra-occupational crimes 125
Noble cause corruption 108
Organizational justice 108
Personal liability 113
Police brutality 109
Police corruption 106
Police sexual misconduct 106

Religious system deception 131
Staff-on-inmate sexual victimization 123
Staff sexual harassment 123
Staff sexual misconduct 123
Sunshine laws 112

Discussion Questions

1. Is police brutality a white-collar crime? Explain.

2. All white-collar crimes involve violations of trust. Review the crimes discussed in this chapter, and rank them from the highest trust violation to the lowest trust violation.

3. Compare and contrast the terms *white-collar crime* and *khaki-collar crime*.

4. Should police officers lose their jobs if they commit workplace misconduct? Explain.

5. Why do you think judges commit white-collar crime?

6. Explain how a college education might reduce corruption in the criminal justice system.

7. How is police deviance different from judicial misconduct?

CRIME IN THE
POLITICAL SYSTEM

The movie *Election* tells the story of Tracy Flick, a high school senior who aspires to be class president, and civic teacher Jim McCallister, who has great resentment for the overachieving senior. The thought of Flick (played by Reese Witherspoon) as student body president horrifies McCallister (played by Matthew Broderick), so he recruits the popular but not very smart Paul Metzler (played by Chris Klein) to run against Flick. Much of the movie centers on the campaigns run by the two candidates. In charge of counting the ballots, McCallister sees that Flick won the election by just one vote. Frustrated with the results, McCallister throws two of the ballots in the trash can and announces Metzler as the winner. Flick is stunned! Soon after, McCallister's misdeeds are uncovered, and his storied career as a teacher comes to an end. Twenty years after being released, the movie is still as funny as it ever was.

Bringing us back to reality, real election crimes and other offenses in the political system are no laughing matter. Consider the following examples quoted from their original sources:

- According to the evidence presented at trial, from May 2010 to February 2014, [former U.S. Representative Stephen E. Stockman] and his co-defendants solicited approximately $1.25 million in donations from charitable organizations and the individuals who ran those organizations based on false pretenses, then used a series of sham nonprofit organizations and dozens of bank accounts to launder the money before it was used for a variety of personal and campaign expenses (USDOJ, Public Integrity Section, 2019, p. 13).

- According to the evidence presented at trial, [Jonathan] Woods served as an Arkansas State Senator from 2013 to 2017. Between approximately 2013 and 2015, Woods used his official position as a senator to appropriate and direct state government money, known as General Improvement Funds (GIF), to two non-profit entities by, among other things, directly authorizing GIF disbursements to the non-profits and advising other Arkansas legislators, including former State Representative Micah Neal, to do the same. Specifically, Woods and Neal authorized and directed the Northwest Arkansas Economic Development District, which was responsible for disbursing GIF money, to award a total of approximately $600,000 in GIF money to the two non-profit entities. (USDOJ, Public Integrity Section, 2019, p. 17).

- In 2012, [Kenneth] Smukler engaged in a conspiracy to make a concealed payment of $90,000 to Congressional candidate and former Philadelphia Municipal Judge Jimmie Moore to get Judge Moore to drop out of the primary election race. Smukler, who worked for another candidate, orchestrated the payment of the money through his own companies, a shell company of Judge Moore's campaign manager, Carolyn Cavaness, and another campaign consultant, D.A. Jones. Judge Moore, Cavaness, and Jones all have pleaded guilty separately. (USDOJ, 2018, December 3).

- According to [Harold Russell] Taub's guilty plea, in late 2016, Taub began soliciting donations to an organization he called Keeping America in Republican Control (KAIRC), which he represented to be a legitimate political committee organized in accordance with federal law to support Republican candidates at the state and federal level. In March 2018, Taub began soliciting donations to another purported political action committee, Keeping Ohio in Republican Control (KOIRC), with the stated purpose of supporting Republican candidates in Ohio. Taub collected a total of approximately $1,630,439 in contributions to KAIRC and KOIRC, but never registered either entity with the FEC or made required reports to the FEC, as required by FECA. (USDOJ, 2019, July 24).

Various crimes occur in the political system. Unlike professionals working in some of the other systems, professionals in the political system routinely confront suspicion and distrust from citizens. This distrust stems at least partly from several high-profile political and government scandals that have occurred over the years.

Indeed, it seems every decade has been marked by national political scandals. In the 1970s, Watergate served as an introduction to political corruption on the grandest scale. In June 1972, burglars connected to the Committee to Re-elect the President broke into the Democratic National Committee's offices in the Watergate Office Complex. After the investigation began, President Nixon insisted that he knew nothing about the burglary. During the course of the investigation, recordings were uncovered showing that the president participated in covering up the break-in. The investigation also revealed other abuses, including warrantless wiretaps to listen in on the conversations of reporters. Watergate has been described as "the touchstone, the definitive point of reference for subsequent political scandals in the United States" (Schudson, 2004, p. 1231). Another author noted that while political corruption was

PHOTO 6.1 Richard Nixon resigned from the presidency after being impeached for his role in Watergate. He was later pardoned by President Gerald Ford, allowing him to escape any criminal charges.

not new at the time, efforts to control corruption through public law enforcement efforts can be traced to the 1970s in the aftermath of Watergate (Mass, 1986).

Following Watergate, the next major national political scandal was Abscam. In the late 1970s and early 1980s, Abscam was an FBI investigation in which undercover agents used the fictional identity of Abdul Enterprises, Ltd. to offer bribes to various officials. The bribes were offered in exchange for help making it easier for two sheiks "to emigrate to the U.S." (Gershman, 1982, p. 1572). At least a handful of congressmen immediately accepted bribes. A few offered assistance after being groomed by undercover agents. The same "scam" was repeated in Philadelphia where local officials agreed to the bribe. Once the case became public, media attention uncovered wide-ranging instances of corruption. Gershman (1982) wrote,

> Seen as public theatre, Abscam cast the three branches of government in a morality play whose plot called for the portrayal of disguised heroes and hidden villains, intricate charades with racial overtones, and lavish scenery against invitations to corruption set the characters in motion. (p. 1565)

The **Iran-Contra affair** was the next major national political scandal. In the mid-1980s, political officials authorized the sale of weapons to Iran, despite the presence of an arms embargo, as part of a secret effort to trade arms for hostages. Proceeds from the weapons sales were then sent to the Contras in Nicaragua even though Congress had prohibited Contra funding. While evidence suggested that Reagan was involved in the cover-up, he escaped negative fallout from the scandal, prompting one reporter to call the Iran-Contra affair "the cover up that worked" (Brinkley, 1994) in comparison to the Watergate scandal.

The 1990s and 2000s saw a series of ongoing political scandals. From the Clintons being tied up in allegations of real estate fraud in Whitewater, to President Clinton's sexual contact with Monica Lewinsky, to President George W. Bush's failure to uncover weapons of mass destruction in Iraq, it seemed that at any given moment in time, a political scandal was brewing over these two decades. Under Barack Obama's administration, the major scandal involved allegations that the deaths of four Americans in the 2012 **Benghazi attacks** could be attributed to decisions made by the state department. During Trump's term, the Trump administration was mired in controversies including whether Trump interfered in investigations, held back approved aid to Ukraine in exchange for dirt on Joe Biden, reduced funding to the postal office to impact mail-in voting, politicized the coronavirus epidemic, or misused his pardon powers to reward his supporters. Other controversies, including accusations of discriminatory treatment of housing tenants, mistreatment of women, numerous lawsuits, and unpaid bills began even before President Donald J. Trump was sworn in as president. His inauguration was most certainly memorable and a sign of how his administration would proceed. In fact, President George W. Bush made the following comment to former presidential candidate and Senator Hillary Clinton after Trump's inauguration speech: "That was some weird shit."

ELECTION LAW VIOLATIONS

Election law violations or **voter fraud** involves situations where political officials violate rules guiding the way that elections are supposed to be conducted. Election fraud laws exist in order to guard against crimes such as voter registration fraud, vote counting fraud, and balloting fraud (Aycock & Hutton, 2010). Additional varieties include distributing false information at election polls, conspiring to vote illegally, paying for voter registrations, accepting payment for registering to vote, voting multiple times, and faking citizenship to vote (Williamson, Amann, Athans, Bansal, & Zahedi, 2019) Election fraud generally involves situations where individuals try to corrupt "the process by which ballots are obtained, marked, or tabulated; the process by which election results are canvassed or certified; or the process by which voters are registered" (Donsanto & Simmons, 2007, p. 25). Schemes are characterized as either public or private, depending on who initiated the fraud. The Federal Election Commission can levy civil fines against those who violate provisions of the Federal Election Campaign Act. Criminal prosecutions would be initiated by the U.S. Department of Justice (Aycock & Hutton, 2010).

The extent of voter fraud is particularly hard to assess. Despite the lack of data showing a problem, the Trump administration has maintained that voter fraud is out of control. These claims began after the 2016 election when Trump claimed that voting fraud was the reason he lost the popular vote. Liberally describing the results of a few studies, Trump suggested that millions of individuals may vote illegally in the United States. One of the studies he cited was an article in *Electoral Studies* by Richman, Chattha, and Earnest (2014). The Richman study focused on a subsample of noncitizen voters from a national election survey and extrapolated that survey to statewide and national elections. Based on that extrapolation, the researchers suggested that "non-citizen votes likely gave senate democrats the pivotal 60th vote needed to overcome filibusters in order to pass health care reform and other Obama administration priorities in the 111th Congress" (p. 146). The study was critiqued by scholars suggesting that the small sample size of the subsample should not be extrapolated to statewide or national elections. Despite the criticisms of the study, Trump and his representatives widely touted this and similar studies as evidence that many votes were illegally cast in the 2016 election. Similar claims were made after the 2020 election when Trump lost the election by more than six million votes.

Once the debate about voter fraud seemed to dissipate, Trump began to talk about how prevalent fraud was in mail-in voting. Just a few months before the 2020 election, shortly after Trump expressed concern about mail-in voting, the postmaster general announced cost-cutting changes to the U.S. Postal Service that would most certainly have hindered the mail-in voting process scheduled to occur in the November election. An outcry from the House of Representatives and others resulted in some backtracking and a promise to hold off on any major post office changes until after the election. Interestingly, in an interview with CNN host Jake Tapper, Trump's chief of staff Mark Meadows was told by the host that there is no evidence of fraud in mail-in voting. Meadows stunned Tapper with his response, "There's no evidence that there's not either. That's the definition of fraud, Jake" (CNN.com, 2020). Just to be clear, if your white-collar crime professor asks you to define fraud, do not define it as the lack of evidence that there is fraud. You'll thank me later for that piece of advice!

Although President Trump and others have claimed widespread fraud exists in the election process, most experts believe that election fraud is incredibly rare. News21, a project funded by the Carnegie Corporation of New York and the John S. and James I. Knight Foundation, has developed a database of all election fraud cases reported between 2000 and 2012. The database includes 2,068 allegations of election fraud, which would average about 170 cases a year. Figure 6.1 shows how often various types of election fraud surfaced. Just 56 cases of noncitizen voting were identified. Assuming an average of five noncitizens vote each year, this would mean that just five out of 250 million votes cast in 2018 were from noncitizens.

More recent estimates also call into question the idea that widespread voter fraud exists. For example, a national study of the 2016 election found 30 incidents of possible noncitizen voting among 23.5 million votes in the jurisdiction studied (Famighetti, Keith, & Pérez, 2017). This translates to 0.0001% of the votes cast. Like prior research, this study cast doubt on claims that noncitizen voting is rampant. Election experts Amber McReynolds and Charles Stewart III (2020)

©iStockphoto.com/LPETTET

PHOTO 6.2 There is little reliable empirical evidence that voter fraud is rampant.

FIGURE 6.1 ■ Types of Voting Fraud, 2000–2012

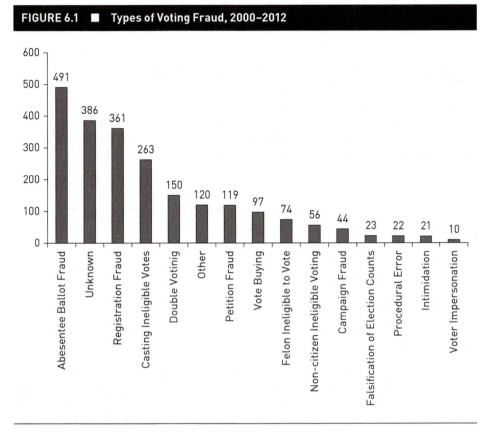

Source: News21 Creative Commons Attribution 3.0 United States License

explored nationwide data on mail-in ballot voting and estimated that over 20 years fraudulent mail-in votes accounted for 0.00006% of all the votes cast.

Voter identification laws have been adopted to curb election offenses. Under some of these laws, voters must prove that they are able to vote by showing a license or other official identification card. Texas has the strictest voter ID laws; they accept gun permits, but not university identification cards, as accepted forms of identification (Lusk, 2017). Some have argued that the laws discriminate against minorities by causing voter suppression. Voter suppression claims were empirically verified in a study finding wider racial voting participation gaps in states with stricter voter ID laws (Hajnal, Lajevardi, & Nielson, 2017). The researchers found that strict laws could suppress primary turnouts by 9% to 12.5% across racial groups. The authors concluded that "voter ID laws skew democracy toward those on the right" (p. 363).

Trump's claims about voter fraud grew after he lost the election to President-Elect Joe Biden. Trump and his legal team alleged widespread fraud and suggested that Trump's loss was due to fraudulent voting in five states Trump had won in the 2016 election: Georgia, Pennsylvania,

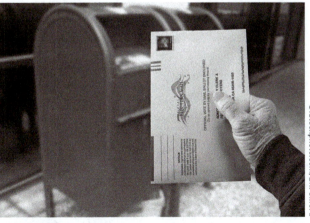

PHOTO 6.3 Weeks before the 2020 presidential election, President Trump initiated discussion about whether voting by mail is a legitimate voting strategy. Days later, he and first lady Melania Trump mailed in their ballots.

©iStockphoto.com/Bill Oxford

Michigan, Wisconsin, and Arizona. His legal team filed more than 40 lawsuits within three weeks after election. Most of the lawsuits were quickly dismissed, withdrawn, or settled.

CAMPAIGN FINANCE VIOLATIONS

Campaign finance laws place restrictions on the way political campaigns are financed, with specific attention given to contributions and expenditures. Expenditures are limited only if candidates "elect to participate in a public funding program" (Aycock & Hutton, 2010, p. 358). These laws prohibit the following types of contributions to political campaigns:

- Excessive contributions

- Corporate and union contributions and coordinated expenditures

- Contributions from government contractors

- Donations from foreign nationals

- Disguised contributions through conduits

- Cash contributions

- Contributions raised through fraud (Federal Prosecution of Election Offenses Manual) (Pilger, 2017).

In general, campaign finance laws are designed to control who can contribute to political campaigns, how much can be contributed, and how campaigns can use those contributions (Williamson et al., 2019; see Figure 6.2). The laws govern all financial transactions connected to elections and include communications and payment for those communications, an area that falls under a branch of law called "electioneering communications" (Pilger, 2017, p. 4). Those opposing the laws cite First Amendment issues and that the laws violate the right to free speech,

FIGURE 6.2   ■   Campaign Finance Laws

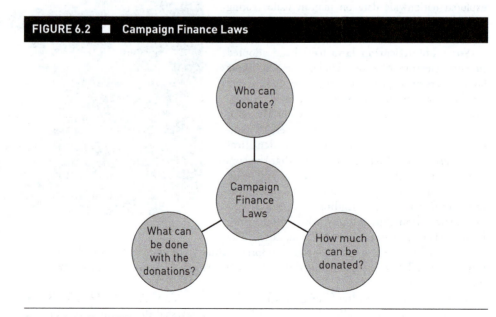

Source: Adapted from Williamson et al. (2019).

with contributions seen as a form of free speech. Historically, the Supreme Court has ruled that preventing corruption or its appearance is more important than any deprivation of speech rights (Williamson et al., 2020).

In 2010, the Supreme Court shifted course in Citizens United v. Federal Elections Commission and held that banning political speech of independent expenditure-only organizations was a violation of the First Amendment. In the words of the Court, "independent expenditures do not lead to, or create the appearance of, quid pro quo corruption." The ruling opened the door for political action committees (PACs) to spend more on political campaigns, particularly in advertisements. The *Citizens United* decision became a campaign issue in the 2016 and 2020 elections when democratic candidates called for a constitutional amendment to overturn the court's decision (Williamson et al., 2019).

Those wanting stricter campaign finance laws often point to the need to control corporate spending in elections. To combat the influence of corporations on elections, one author has called for a "disclose or abstain" model that would require corporations to either publicly disclose their political spending or not donate to political campaigns (Siebecker, 2017). Believing that such a process would make corporate leaders more accountable and less likely to engage in corrupt behavior, Siebecker (2017) notes, "there can be no trust without transparency" (p. 2764).

Not everyone sees transparency as a panacea to stopping corruption. Pointing to the transparent nature of political donations in the United Kingdom, one legal scholar has questioned whether transparency will, in fact, promote trust and reduce corruption (Rowbottom, 2016). As Rowbottom (2016) points out, "transparency is often seen to be the antidote to corruption" (p. 407). The problem that arises with transparency, he argues, is "it is up for the public to decide whether a particular donation was corrupt" (p. 410). So, instead of promoting trust, transparency might actually create distrust while simultaneously providing so much information that it is harder to actually detect corruption when it does occur.

Campaign financing cases sometimes involve high-ranking government officials. Tom DeLay, former house majority leader, was convicted in November 2010 for violations of Texas campaign finance laws after he funneled corporate donations made to the Republican National Committee to candidates in Texas. Texas law prohibits corporate contributions to candidates. In February 2011, DeLay's attorneys appealed the case on the grounds that the Texas law was unconstitutional (Epstein, 2011). An appellate court overturned the conviction in September 2013. A year later, in September 2014, the Texas Court of Criminal Appeals affirmed the lower appellate court's decision, effectively dismissing the conviction.

Campaign finance laws also stipulate that contributions cannot be used for personal use. In 2011, former vice presidential candidate and North Carolina Senator John Edwards was indicted after a grand jury investigation. The investigation found that his campaign used funds to pay Rielle Hunter, a woman with whom he was having an affair, for work she did for his campaign. In particular, she produced three videos for the campaign at a cost of $250,000. Prosecutors alleged that the funds were actually a payment to get Hunter to keep quiet about her affair with the former senator (Smith, 2011). After a mistrial and acquittal on one count, charges were eventually dropped against the former political heavyweight. His political career, however, appears to be over.

POLITICAL CORRUPTION

Corruption has been described as an "evolving concept" (Ouziel, 2018, p. 209). Drawing attention to difficulties defining the concept, Jay Albanese and his colleagues (Albanese, Artello, & Nguyen, 2019) begin one article with the statement, "corruption and obscenity pose similar problems. You know them when you see them, but defining them with clarity is not easy" (p. 2). Scholars note that there is agreement about certain forms of corruption such as "quid pro quo" behaviors where influencers use their power in exchange for some favor (Ouziel, 2018). As Ouziel (2018) notes, less agreement exists about whether more subtle behaviors—such as exerting influence to persuade or negotiate decisions—are corrupt.

An example should help demonstrate this ambiguity. Just before Memorial Day weekend in 2020, dock company owner Tad Dowker posted on Facebook about an interaction he had with Michigan Governor Gretchen Whitmer's husband, Marc Mallory. The post stated that Mallory had asked Dowker if his status as the governor's husband would allow him to get his boat in the water before others. Dowker told the Facebook community that such a status "would put [Mallory] in the back of the line!" The exchange gained national attention, and Whitmer had to explain that her husband was just trying to make a joke (and one she didn't find funny, either!). Still, the uproar was intense, with the chair of the Michigan Republican Party quipping, "The only joke here is that Governor Whitmer doesn't seem to understand how serious it is for a family member to misuse your office" (Egan, 2020).

The question that arises is whether this behavior is, in fact, corruption. The answer would likely depend on who is being asked. Whitmer supporters might call this a "bad joke," and her opponents might define the husband's behavior as egregious. Alternatively, if Mallory told Dowker that Dowker would get money from the state if the dock owner gave him preferential boating access, all would agree that the behavior is corrupt.

Consider how another case shows how corruption, from a criminal law perspective, is grounded in legal definitions. Not long ago, a journalist in Alabama wrote a story about a sheriff who had used $750,000 from his jail's unspent food fund to buy a new house. Alabama law, traced to the depression era, stipulated that sheriffs could use unspent funds from their jail's food account as long as they were willing to contribute their own money if there was shortage in the food account. The food account funds—which come from federal, state, and local services—are intended to cover the costs of feeding inmates. If sheriffs are able to feed inmates appropriately within those means, the law permitted sheriffs to use the excess funds for personal use. The sheriff told the reporter, "In regards to feeding of inmates, we utilize a registered dietitian to ensure adequate meals are provided daily. . . . As you should be aware, Alabama law is clear as to my personal financial responsibilities in the feeding of inmates. Regardless of one's opinion of this statute, until the legislature acts otherwise, the Sheriff must follow the current law" (Sheets, 2018). Not long after the news report, Alabama changed the law and made it illegal to keep the funds, and the sheriff was voted out of office. The following year, another Alabama sheriff was indicted for similar offenses. In that case, the sheriff fraudulently obtained food from his church so he could feed inmates with the church food and save costs from the inmate food fund (Robinson, 2019). So, prior to the new law, the behavior may have been seen as corrupt but legal. After the law, the behavior was treated as corrupt and illegal.

Capturing the ambiguities surrounding corruption, David Friedrichs (2019) offers are straightforward definition: "a form of government crime with a primarily financial character" (p. 243). Corruption provides the impetus for a wide range of financial crimes including **political extortion**, bribery, and **illegal gratuities**. Collectively, these behaviors refer to situations where political officials use their political power to shape outcomes of various processes including lawmaking, awarding of contracts, policy development, and so on. Bribery refers to instances when public officials seek some sort of political favor in exchange for decisions made by the public official; extortion entails charging individuals for services they should have received anyway (Albanese et al., 2019). The line between bribery and illegal gratuities has to do with intent. In bribery cases, authorities must prove that the official intended to provide political favors in exchange for some item, good, or service. In illegal gratuity cases, the official simply received something that they were not supposed to receive (Jarcho & Schecter, 2012).

Figure 6.3 shows the number of public corruption convictions prosecuted by U.S. attorneys from 1999 to 2018. Three patterns shown in the figure are worth illuminating. First, those convicted of public corruption come from one of four categories: federal employees, state employees, public employees, and private citizens. Second, each year federal officials are the group most often convicted of public corruption, which is a pattern that was found in a study of nearly 57,000 federal public corruption convictions between 2015 and 2019 (Albanese et al., 2019). This is interesting given that there are more than six times as many local and state government employees as there are federal government employees (Jessie & Tarleton, 2014). Third, the overall number of public corruption convictions has fluctuated overtime, though the total number of convictions has dropped each year since 2012. Possible explanations for this drop include changing law enforcement priorities among the federal government, better behavior among public officials, improved hiring/appointment processes in government agencies, new difficulties getting convictions, and the likelihood that behaviors are becoming harder to detect (see Albanese et al., 2019).

Available evidence suggests that federal convictions represent the vast majority of corruption cases. Research shows that between 1986 and 2014, 94% of all corruption convictions were at the federal level (Cordis & Milyo, 2016). Several distinct advantages make it preferable to prosecute these crimes at the federal level rather than through state or local processes. These advantages include the following:

- The secretive nature of grand jury proceedings ensures that suspects (most of whom are in the public eye) don't unnecessarily have their reputations damaged.

- Federal jury trials pull from a broader swath of the public, meaning that the jurors will be less likely to know the defendant.

- Federal authorities have more resources than state or local agencies.

- Federal officials are not connected to state or local interests (Pilger, 2017).

Less serious public corruption cases are handled informally outside of the justice process (Albanese & Artello, 2019). For those public corruption cases that do enter the justice system, officials learn about them in one of several ways:

- Whistleblowers/informants alert the authorities about the behavior.

- Investigative journalists uncover the misconduct and report about it in the news.

- Criminal justice officials conducting adjacent investigations learn about the public corruption.

- Routine record reviews and audits show evidence of public crimes.

- A private citizen who was bribed or extorted contacts the authorities (Artello & Albanese, 2020).

It is believed that whistleblowers and informants are involved in public corruption cases more than other types of crimes (Artello & Albanese, 2020).

Reviewing 313 public corruption convictions over three years, Albanese and Artello (2019) created a typology identifying eight categories of public corruption. The categories include the following:

1. **Receiving a public bribe**—taking something in exchange for public action

2. **Soliciting a bribe**—asking for something in exchange for public action

3. **Extortion**—obtaining items or property by threatening public action or inaction

4. **Contract fraud**—receiving contract payments fraudulently

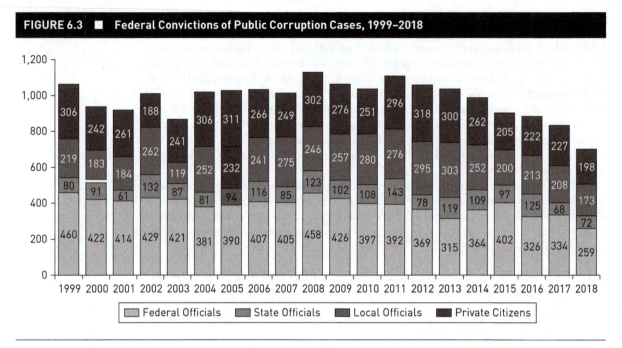

FIGURE 6.3 ■ Federal Convictions of Public Corruption Cases, 1999–2018

Source: https://www.justice.gov/criminal-pin/file/1346061/download

5. **Embezzlement**—abusing access to funds

6. **Official misconduct**—performing unauthorized acts for personal benefit

7. **Obstruction of justice**—compromising legal procedures

8. **Violation of regulatory laws**—breaking legal or administrative rules (p. 6)

Like other white-collar crimes, these categories of public corruption are typically committed in groups. Consider Operation Bid Rig, a political corruption investigation case led by the FBI. One sting in this investigation resulted in the arrests of 44 suspects, including three mayors, a city council president, two state legislators, and five rabbis. In this sting, hundreds of hours of audio and video recordings were collected. In one of the recordings, a newly elected mayor, Peter Cammarano from Hoboken, New Jersey, bragged that he would have won his election even if he had been indicted because he had votes of certain groups "locked down" (Richburg, 2009). The newly minted mayor had been mayor for less than a month when he was arrested. He allegedly took a bribe of $25,000 in exchange for his support of a building project (McShane, 2009). This chapter's White-Collar Crime in the News shows just how costly these crimes can be.

Various sources of public corruption have been identified. Some researchers note that corruption is tied to bureaucratic forces, political forces, and historical/cultural factors (Dincer & Johnston, 2016; Meier & Holbrook, 1992). An early study found that political corruption is lower in political systems that have "closely contested elections and high voter turnouts" (Meier & Holbrook, 1992, p. 151). Finding that an increase in political corruptions results in higher voter turnout in gubernatorial elections, a more recent study calls into question the premise that corruption reduces voter turnout (Escalares, Calcagno, & Shughart, 2012). At the same time, experts note that voter suppression (which is potentially a form of public corruption) may result

WHITE-COLLAR CRIME IN THE NEWS

FORMER ARKANSAS STATE SENATOR SENTENCED TO 220 MONTHS IN FEDERAL PRISON FOR WIRE FRAUD, MAIL FRAUD AND MONEY

The following is a press release from the Western District of Arkansas from September 6, 2018.

Fayetteville, Arkansas—Former Arkansas State Senator Johnathan Woods was sentenced today to 220 months in prison for organizing and leading a bribery scheme in which state funds were directed to non-profit entities in exchange for kickbacks, many of which were funneled through a consultant's business, announced U.S. Attorney Duane "DAK" Kees for the Western District of Arkansas, Assistant Attorney General Brian A. Benczkowski of the Justice Department's Criminal Division, FBI Special Agent in Charge Diane Upchurch and IRS Special Agent in Charge Tamera Cantu.

On May 3 2018, a jury found Jonathan E. Woods, 41, of Springdale, Arkansas, guilty of 15 counts, including conspiracy, honest services wire and mail fraud, and money laundering. In addition to his prison sentence, U.S. District Judge Timothy L. Brooks of the Western District of Arkansas sentenced Woods to serve three years of supervised release and ordered Woods to pay $1,621,500.00 in restitution.

"Jonathan Woods abused his position as an Arkansas State Senator and betrayed the public trust by taking bribes and kickbacks," said Assistant Attorney General Benczkowski. "This conviction demonstrates the commitment of the Department of Justice and our federal partners to investigate and prosecute public officials who misuse their authority to benefit themselves at the expense of the citizens they pledged to serve."

"Jonathan Woods violated the public's trust and misused his authority for the purpose of lining his own pockets," said Special Agent in Charge Diane Upchurch with the Little Rock FBI Field Office, "We are proud of the commitment of our partners at the United States Attorney's Office of the Western Division, the IRS, and the Criminal Division's Public Integrity Section."

According to the evidence presented at trial, Woods served as an Arkansas State Senator from 2013 to 2017. Between approximately 2013 and approximately 2015, Woods used his official position as a senator to appropriate and direct government money, known as General Improvement Funds (GIF), to two non-profit entities by, among other things, directly authorizing GIF disbursements and advising other Arkansas legislators—including former State Representative Micah Neal, 43, of Springdale, Arkansas—to contribute GIF to the non-profits. Specifically, Woods and Neal authorized and directed the Northwest Arkansas Economic Development District, which was responsible for disbursing the GIF, to award a total of approximately $600,000 in GIF money to the two non-profit entities. The evidence further showed that Woods and Neal received bribes from officials at both non-profits, including Oren Paris III, 50, of Springdale, Arkansas, who was the president of a college. Woods initially facilitated $200,000 of GIF money to the college and later, together with Neal, directed another $200,000 to the college, all in exchange for kickbacks. To pay and conceal the kickbacks to Woods and Neal, Paris paid a portion of the GIF to a consulting company controlled by Randell G. Shelton Jr., 39, of Alma, Arkansas. Shelton then kept a portion of the money and paid the other portion to Woods and Neal. Paris also bribed Woods by hiring Woods's friend to an administrative position at the college.

Reprinted from U.S. Department of Justice.

in lower turnout (Anderson, 2018; Wang & Wang, 2012). Perhaps the safest conclusion to make is the connection between corruption and voter turnout is impacted by type of corruption and election dynamics.

Public corruption may also stem from the way that political behavior is defined and conceptualized by policy makers and the public. Ouziel (2018) notes that when questionable behaviors are seen as acceptable (or when acceptable behaviors are seen as questionable), it is harder to actually regulate them. Is it corrupt, for example, when politicians redistrict in order to strengthen their party's interests? Or, is it simply "good" politics? On the other hand, the word *corruption* and its variants are tossed around with seemingly little thought to the precise definition of corruption, with allegations of corruption made when individuals simply don't agree with decisions or behaviors made by others. Think of times when politicians from one party claim members of the other party are corrupt. The effect of the general use of the word *corruption* is simple: It undermines or obfuscates the true harm of corruption.

Evidence suggests there are statewide differences in federal convictions for public corruption. Figure 6.4 shows public corruption conviction rates per 100,000 residents between 2008 and 2019. Montana, Louisiana, and South Dakota have the highest rates while Oregon and Utah have the lowest. In addition, public corruption has been tied to factors such as a country's stage of development (Batabyal & Chowdhury, 2015), how government workers are paid (Mendez, 2014), fiscal decentralization (Goel & Nelson, 2011), and access to information (Candeub, 2013; Ionescu, 2013a, 2013b). One common thread is woven through these factors: technology. Technology is related to a country's stage of development, level of bureaucracy, the ability to decentralize fiscal matters, efforts to promote voter turnout, strategies to strengthen campaigns and create more closely contested elections, and access to information.

FIGURE 6.4 ■ Rates of Corruption between 2008 and 2019 (per 100,000)

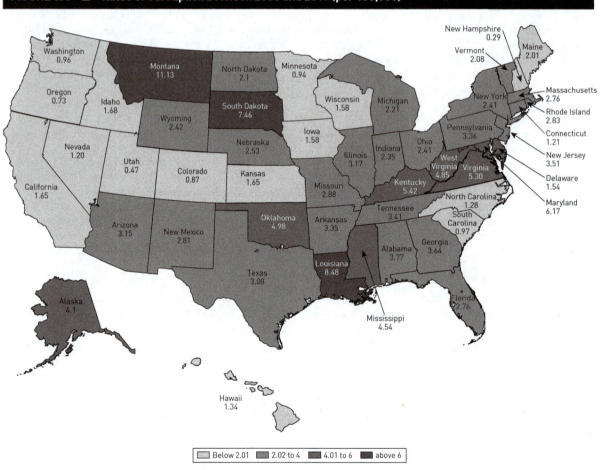

Source: https://www.justice.gov/criminal-pin/file/1346061/download

Few researchers have explored how technology is related to public corruption, though the theoretical foundation for a relationship between the two can be found in the literature. Technological advances such as those that gave rise to the Internet and social media may either prevent political corruption or increase its likelihood. Research shows, for example, that Internet diffusion, which would give more people access to information, reduces political corruption (Kanyam, Kostandini, & Ferreira, 2017). In a similar way, social media—which gives individuals immediate access to a wide range of news and information—has been seen as a tool that may keep political officials form engaging in wrongdoing (Inuwa, Kath, & Ononiwu, 2019) Such findings have led one author to conclude that "access to the internet leads to significant decreases in corruption" (Ionescu, 2013b).

The consequences of such political corruption can be significant. In particular, people lose faith in their government as a result of public corruption. Some experts contend that corruption results in the "lowering of trust in the law and the rule of law, education and consequently the quality of life" (Sumah, 2018, n.p.). Others have noted that corruption reduces public and private investments, lowers a country's gross domestic product (GDP), and promotes inequality (Enste & Heldman, 2018). As well, political scandals have made it more difficult for honest politicians to lead and govern. Government officials must spend at least part of the time (that could be spent governing) warding off ethics attacks from their opponents. Interestingly, acts of corruption do not always result in candidates being voted out of office. In fact, one study recently concluded that "electoral punishment of corruption is rather mild" (DeVries & Solaz, 2017, p. 391). Seemingly, individuals will vote for corrupt individuals if they believe that the elected official's victory will benefit them in some way.

STREAMING WHITE-COLLAR CRIME *House of Cards*: This Is What Gives Politicians a Bad Name		
Plot	**What You Can Learn**	**Discussion Questions**
Frank Underwood is a diabolical politician. The series begins with Underwood serving as the House Majority Whip from South Carolina. He and his wife, Claire, have their eyes set on the White House; they will do anything they can do to get there. As the Underwoods break the trust of their confidantes and the public, the drama focuses on how public opinion can be manipulated and decisions influenced by nefarious behavior. While it is hoped that the plot doesn't accurately reflect political behavior (surely presidents don't actually throw people into the path of a train barreling toward its stop), the storyline likely reflects the manipulative thinking strategies used by corrupt politicians.	Lobbyists have a great deal of sway over political decisions. People who make the rules will sometimes break the rules.	Would you vote for someone who has been accused of corruption? Explain. Is it wrong to try and manipulate public opinion? What if the manipulation is done for the greater good?

APOLITICAL WHITE-COLLAR CRIME

Apolitical white-collar crime refers to situations where politicians get into trouble for doing things that are outside of the scope of politics but are violations of the public trust. In 2009, former South Carolina Governor Mark Sanford came under fire after he told his staff that he was "hiking on the Appalachian Trail" when, in fact, he was in Argentina having an affair with Argentine journalist Maria Belén Chapur. Sanford's wife later divorced him, and his ability to govern in South Carolina took a significant hit. Once a presidential hopeful, Sanford was subsequently censured by his state government for misusing travel funds to support his "hiking." Sanford was able to resuscitate his political career, however. In 2013, he was elected as a South Carolina representative to the U.S. House of Representatives.

The violations of trust in apolitical white-collar crimes often seem out of character for the politicians caught in the scandals. In May 2010, U.S. Representative Mark Souder resigned from office "after admitting to an affair with a female staffer" ("Congressman Resigns Over Affair," 2010). One news outlet found that Souder had actually filmed a public service video with the staffer he had an affair with. The topic of the video was abstinence.

Anthony Weiner's various sexual escapades caught the attention of the national media and eventually led to his downfall. A prominent Democratic congressman from New York, Weiner was forced to resign in 2011 after he was caught sexting with numerous women. The case gained national attention because Weiner's wife was a close confidante of Hillary Clinton. A few years later, he ran for mayor of New York in an effort to regain his political identity and notoriety. During the candidacy, it was revealed that he had continued to send sexually graphic messages to women even though he had lost his previous political position due to the behavior. In September 2016, it was announced the Weiner was being investigated for sending sexual messages to a 15-year-old girl. He eventually plead guilty to obscenity violations and served 18 months in prison (Gold, 2019).

A well-publicized case of apolitical white-collar offending involved Larry Craig, a former U.S. Republican senator. In September 2007, Craig was caught in an undercover sex sting and accused of trying to initiate sex in an airport bathroom with an undercover officer. He tapped his foot in a bathroom stall in a way that signaled his interest in "sharing some time" with the man in the next stall. Craig pleaded guilty, though he later tried to recant his guilty plea. That he was caught in such a scandal was somewhat ironic given his history of voting for legislation restricting the rights of homosexuals. One fellow Republican senator, John Ensign from Nevada, called Craig's actions embarrassing. Less than two years later, Ensign admitted to having an "affair with a former campaign staffer who is married to one of the lawmaker's former legislative aides" (Kane & Cillizza, 2009, p. A01).

STATE-CORPORATE CRIME

The phrase **state-corporate crime** draws attention to the fact that governmental agencies are employers (or "corporations") and that these agencies and their employees sometimes commit various types of misconduct—either independently or in conjunction with other corporations. The concept of state-corporate crime was first introduced by Ronald Kramer in a series of presentations he made at the Southern Sociological Association, the Edwin Sutherland Conference on White-Collar Crime, and the Society for the Study of Social Problems (Kramer, Michalowski, & Kauzlarich, 2002, p. 263). Kramer notes that the term came from a "spontaneous comment" he made at a restaurant while discussing his research with colleagues. Although Kramer developed the concept, he credits Richard Quinney's work for the concept's "intellectual origins."

Quinney's early work drew attention to the need to categorize white-collar crime into corporate crime and occupational crime, and another body of his research focused on the sociology of law, with an emphasis on the way that the powerful shape the law to protect their interests.

Combining Quinney's white-collar crime research with his sociology of law research lends credence to Kramer's call for a focus on "state-corporate crime." At the genesis of the concept is recognition that corporation have great power over the laws, roles, policies, and regulations that guide corporate behavior (Leon & Ken, 2019). This power combined with the power of policy makers who develop the laws, rules, policies, and regulations provides the opportunity to commit state corporate crime. The concept of state-corporate crime is useful in (a) demonstrating how the consequences of behaviors are tied to interrelationships between social institutions and (b) highlighting the power of formal (e.g., political and economic) institutions to harm members of society (Kramer et al., 2002).

In considering state-corporate crime, scholars note that it is virtually impossible to dissect the symbiotic relationship between the "state" and corporations (Rothe & Medley, 2020). Failing to recognize the overlap makes it difficult to understand how state and corporate power reproduce power dynamics while simultaneously keeping individuals powerless and maintaining the status quo. The powerless, it is believed, purchase corporate products (cell phones, clothes, etc.) and gain satisfaction from those products without realizing how state and corporate interactions foster the consumers' purchases. One author describes these interactions as a "mutually beneficial relationships between state institutions and corporations" (Bernat & Whyte, 2020, p. 127). Criminologist Dawn Rothe points out the following:

> State-corporate crime cannot be divorced from our own everyday lives and our
> choices. After all, we, knowingly or blindly, give our consent to the continuation of
> these harms and crimes through our own consumption that cannot be escaped under
> the capitalistic/neoliberalism order. Simply, we are trapped in a corrosive consumer
> culture where corporate and state-corporate crimes have become the "normal abnormal."
> (Rothe, 2020, p. 10)

In some cases, the symbiotic relationship between private and public entities makes the potential for harm or wrongdoing unnoticeable. As an illustration, Leon and Ken (2019) conducted a case study on the Partnership for a Healthier America (PHA). PHA got public and private entities, including major food corporations, to work together to promote healthier eating; PHA also named Michelle Obama as their honorary chair and garnered widespread acclaim for their efforts. Delving into the activities of PHA, Leon and Ken questioned why no studies were done by PHA to evaluate its success. They also note that PHA's focus on easier access to healthier options actually resulted in "easier to find and buy" products that are made by the same companies producing unhealthy foods. In addition, by targeting the diets of children, organizations are able to work with the government to market their products. The PHA/government partnership, then, becomes a marketing ploy for organizations as much as a health tool. In Leon and Ken's view, the power of the corporations, along with relationships they develop with policy makers, allow corporations to "construct high-profile claims that are technically accurate but deceptive, [and] the end result is public–private collusion in (a) actively misleading the public and (b) perpetuating harms that result from inaction in an important public policy arena" (Leon and Ken, 2019, pp. 405–406).

Scholars also use the phrase **state crime** to describe situations where governments or their representatives commit crime on behalf of the government. Again, bear in mind that a government can be seen as a corporation. International law is seen as the "foundation for defining state crime as this includes standards such as human rights, social and economic harms, as well as the judicable offenses" (Rothe, 2009, p. 51). From this perspective, state crime has been defined as

> any action that violates international public law and/or a state's own domestic law when
> these actions are committed by individual actors acting on behalf of, or in the name
> of the state, even when such acts are motivated by their own personal, economical,
> political, and ideological interests. (Mullins & Rothe, 2007, p. 137)

Not surprisingly, it is extremely unlikely that formal governmental institutions will self-police or impose sanctions on themselves for the commission of state crimes. As a result, efforts to control state crime often stem from the actions of advocates, including individuals and organizations, seeking to expose the wrongdoing of particular government officials. According to Ross and Rothe (2009), those who expose state crime offenders run the risk of experiencing the following responses from the state:

1. **Censure**: Officials may withdraw support or withhold information.

2. **Scapegoating**: Officials may blame lower-level employees for the misconduct.

3. **Retaliation**: Officials may target the advocates exposing the wrongdoing.

4. **Defiance or resistance:** Officials may block any efforts toward change.

5. **Plausible deniability**: Officials may conceal actions to make behavior seem appropriate.

6. **Relying on self-righteousness**: Officials may minimize allegations.

7. **Redirection/misdirection**: Officials may feign interest but change the subject.

8. **Fear mongering**: Officials may create fear to "overshadow" real issues.

State crime scholars have addressed a number of different topics, including President Reagan's war on Nicaragua (Rothe, 2009); the state of Senegal's role in the sinking of a ferry, killing more than 1,800 citizens (Rothe, Muzzatti, & Mullins, 2006); the violent deaths of more than 400,000 civilians in the Darfur region of Sudan (Mullins & Rothe, 2007); the torture of prisoners in Abu Ghraib (Rothe & Ross, 2008), environmental harms attributed to the actions or inactions of the policy makers (Heydon, 2019); the government's role in increasing student loan debt (Carlson, 2020); and misuse of data by governments surveilling citizens (Kasm & Alexander, 2018).

Although research on state crime has grown significantly over the last two decades, in general, criminological attention to the concept is seemingly rare (Rothe, 2020). Critical criminologists Dawn Rothe and Jeffrey Ross (2008) reviewed leading criminology texts to determine how much attention was given to state crime. They found that authors typically provided only a description of incidents by government officials when discussing crimes by state officials, thereby "failing to provide the contextual, theoretical, and historical factors associated with this subject" (p. 744). The authors attribute this lack of attention to "the perceived potential of the market" (p. 750). Despite this lack of attention, state crime experts have come a long way in advancing understanding about this phenomenon, and it is entirely likely that an entire field of study will develop in the next several decades, just as the field of study focusing on white-collar crime has grown since the 1940s (Rothe & Friedrichs, 2006).

PRESIDENT DONALD TRUMP AND CRIME IN THE POLITICAL SYSTEM

During his tenure as president, Donald Trump has brought attention to misconduct in the political system. In *Unprecedented: A Simple Guide to the Crimes of the Trump Campaign and Presidency*, Sara Azari details the wide range of criminal allegations levied against Trump during his presidency. There are so many allegations that Azari—a white-collar crime defense attorney—concludes that "the Trump campaign and presidency have most definitely been an exercise in normalizing extraordinary behaviors" (Azari, 2020, p. iv). At the same time, some of Trump's supporters see this behavior and these allegations and believe that the "deep state" is expressing dissatisfaction with Trump and that democrats are conducting a witch hunt. Campaign staff even held a "Witch Hunt Halloween Party" to poke fun at the efforts to investigate the allegations against Trump (Heller, 2019). Whether people support or oppose Trump, five aspects of his presidency warrant consideration in this chapter:

- A personal history of crime allegations

- The Mueller investigation

- The impeachment of Donald Trump

- Political firings and pardons

- Trump's connections with white-collar criminals

PHOTO 6.4 Some of Trump's supporters have claimed that investigations into the Trump presidency are part of a witch hunt and that the election was stolen, with supporters storming the Capital building on January 6, 2021 when the election results were being certified by Congress.

A Personal History of Crime Allegations

It is well accepted that politicians face significant mudslinging and accusations when running for office. It would be more surprising if candidates were *not* accused of bringing some sort of harm to people. Although allegations of wrongdoing surface in all political campaigns, Trump has faced more misconduct accusations than any other president in modern history Many of these allegations were for behaviors that could be conceptualized as white-collar crime. While it is not possible to review all of those allegations here, seven themes shed some light on the accusations Trump faced either while running for president or after becoming president. These accusation themes include the following:

- Housing discrimination

- Mistreatment of workers

- Sexual assault

- Hiring undocumented workers

- Bank and tax fraud

- Trump University

- Civil lawsuits

Housing Discrimination

Housing discrimination charges against Trump and his father first surfaced in 1972. Ironically, these accusations came to light under the Nixon administration (a president who faced numerous charges of corruption himself). Nixon's Department of Justice sued Trump and his father for violations of the Fair Housing Act and alleged that the Trumps

> failed and neglected to exercise their affirmative and nondelegable duty under the Fair Housing Act to assure compliance by their coordinates, with the result that equal housing opportunity has been denied to substantial numbers of persons and that defendant's subordinates have failed to carry out their obligations under the act. (*United States v. Fred C. Trump, Donald Trump, and Trump Management, Inc.*, June 10, 1975)

The allegations suggested that the Trump company would make it harder, if not impossible, for African Americans to rent apartments in certain buildings owned by the Trumps. Though never admitting guilt, Trump Management Inc. eventually agreed to settle the charges with stipulations that the company executives and staff engage in training programs, change the way they advertise vacancies, target a select amount of their advertisements to minority communities, and implement an affirmative employment program. The case was one of the earliest provoking racist claims against Trump. A series of similar allegations followed over the next several decades. When asked during his campaign and presidency to respond to accusations of racial discrimination, Trump asserts that he is not racist. In fact, in 2016 he proclaimed to be "the least racist person you've ever met."

Mistreatment of Workers

Trump has been accused on numerous occasions of mistreating workers over the years. Some of his businesses were accused of not paying private contractors. So many accusations about failure to pay for services surfaced that it almost seem to be normalized within Trump's businesses. A *USA Today* review identified more than 60 lawsuits filed against Trump and his companies by workers alleging they were never paid or underpaid for their services. Those suing Trump included

> A dishwasher in Florida. A glass company in New Jersey. A carpet company. A plumber. Painters. Forty-eight waiters. Dozens of bartenders and other hourly workers at his resorts and clubs, coast to coast. Real estate brokers who sold his properties. And, ironically, several law firms that once represented him in these suits and others. (Reilly, 2016)

In a presidential debate, Trump admitted to not paying workers occasionally and justified those decisions on business judgements grounded in his belief that the work didn't meet his standards.

Sexual Assault

Accusations of sexual assault have also been brought against Trump. Most of the accusations surfaced after the release of an *Inside Edition* recording from 2016. Not aware that his microphone was still live following an earlier interview with *Inside Edition*, Trump can be heard in the recording making inappropriate comments about women to Billy Bush. In the recording, Trump boasts about his sexual history and his view of women. The comment that got the most backlash was,

> I'm automatically attracted to beautiful—I just start kissing them. It's like a magnet. Just kiss. I don't even wait. When you're a star, they let you do it. You can do anything. Grab 'em by the pussy. You can do anything.

The recording was leaked just weeks before the 2016 presidential election. The Trump campaign responded by inviting four women to the audience of the presidential debate taking place a few days after the recording's release. Those women were Juanita Broaddrick, Paula Jones, Kathy Shelton, and Kathleen Willey, each of whom had accused former President Bill Clinton of sexual misconduct. Including complaints made prior to the recording's release, by election day, 19 women came forward accusing Trump of sexual misconduct. Trump has denied all of the allegations.

Hiring Undocumented Workers

Trump's companies have been accused of hiring undocumented workers. In an exposé, reporters from the *Washington Post* interviewed 43 "immigrants without legal status" who had worked or were working at eight different Trump properties. The reporting team notes that by employing workers without legal status, the Trump Organization has an advantage over its competitors, particularly at a time when the economy is strong and the labor market tight. . . . Undocumented employees are less likely to risk changing jobs and less likely to complain if treated poorly. (Partlow & Fahrenthold, 2019)

While outwardly opposing the presence of undocumented persons in the United States, Trump continued to employ undocumented workers. Regarding this irony, one journalist suggested, "It's almost as though the president wants the political benefit of treating undocumented immigrants as subhuman menaces while simultaneously receiving the economic benefit of being able to hire people who he can pay less money and not provide health insurance" (Levin, 2019).

Bank and Tax Fraud

Trump has also faced bank and tax fraud allegations. These allegations are likely fostered in part because of Trump's unwillingness to share his income tax records (which ignored a tradition followed by every modern president). In October 2019, evidence supporting the allegations was published in a report by *ProPublica* suggesting that Trump's businesses lied about their profits when they wanted to borrow money; the report also suggested that Trump's businesses lied about their income when they wanted to avoid taxes (Vogell, 2019). Based on documents obtained by *ProPublica*, Vogell quoted one expert who interpreted data inconsistencies in the documents as "versions" of fraud. Less than a year later, in August 2020, Manhattan District Attorney Cyrus Vance filed court documents suggesting that his office "had been investigating President Trump and his company for possible bank and insurance fraud" (Rashbaum & Weiser, 2020). A few months later, the *New York Times* published a series of articles after it received some of Trump's previously undisclosed tax returns. Among other things, the *New York Times* reported that Trump paid just $750 in federal income taxes in 2017 (Buettner, Craig, & McEntire, 2017). Ongoing business losses and questionable tax write-offs fueled allegations of tax fraud that continued to be investigated by Vance as Trump's presidency concluded.

Trump University

Trump has faced white-collar crime allegations in relation to **Trump University**, a real estate program that promised participants more than the program delivered. Instructors, allegedly handpicked by Trump, participated in Trump University promotions that promised access to content specifically created by those instructors. Students paid thousands of dollars for the program, later reporting that they felt scammed by the course offerings which were nothing more than "a multilevel marketing scheme" (Nelson, 2016). One of the early issues with Trump University surfaced in 2005 when the state education department threatened action against the business for branding itself as a university despite it not being licensed as or functioning like a university. The "university" was eventually renamed "Trump Institute." By 2010, more than 150 Trump University and Trump Institute students had filed complaints in 22 states, indicating they had been ripped off (Feiden, 2010). It was later discovered that the instructors were not handpicked by Trump, the content was not developed by the instructors, and the "university" was indeed not a university. In 2013, New York Attorney General Eric Schneiderman filed a civil lawsuit against Trump, alleging that the company had "used deceptive and unlawful practices" to get more than 5,000 people across the United States to pay for real estate programs. Two additional class action lawsuits were filed by students from other states. The lawsuits continued into the presidential campaign, and Trump vowed not to settle them. Days after winning the presidential election, it was announced that Trump agreed to pay $25 million to settle the lawsuits.

awsuits

ımp has been involved in numerous lawsuits over his business career. A review by *USA* *y* reporters found that Trump was a litigant in more than 3,500 lawsuits across the three ades preceding his 2016 election (Penzenstadler & Page, 2016). Let's do the math on that: 500 divided by 30 years is 116 lawsuits per year. That's approximately one lawsuit filed for every three days! It is important to note that Trump was not being sued in all the cases. Trump or his businesses were suing someone in 1,900 of the cases; he or his businesses were being sued in 1,450 of the cases; and 150 of the cases were bankruptcies or other types of cases. Many of the cases where Trump or his businesses served as plaintiffs involved gamblers being sued because they didn't pay the casino money they owed the business (n=1,600). The *USA Today* reporters note Trump's record in those cases with a public resolution: Trump won 451 of the cases, had roughly 500 of them dismissed, and lost 38. The outcomes of hundreds of the cases are not publicly known (Penzenstadler & Page, 2016).

The way we define white-collar crime affects how we label the allegations against Trump. If we followed a strict legal interpretation of white-collar crime suggesting that white-collar crime behaviors include those resulting in a criminal conviction from work-related misconduct, then it would be inaccurate to label the allegations discussed here against Trump as white-collar crime. Alternatively, if we define white-collar crime as work-related misconduct that harms society or other individuals, then it would be accurate to call at least some of these allegations white-collar crimes.

The Mueller Investigation

During the 2016 presidential campaign, the Department of Justice received information that Russians were interfering in the election. Justice officials initiated an investigation, secured wiretaps, and reviewed available evidence to determine whether Russia was, in fact, trying to influence the outcome of the presidential election. Hillary Clinton referenced these concerns, suggesting that Russia preferred a Trump presidency over a Clinton presidency for a variety of reasons. Trump dismissed Clinton's comments, making the following quip about Clinton's e-mails in a press conference, "Russia, if you're listening I hope you are able to find the 30,000 e-mails that are missing." After Trump won the election, officials began to call for a more in-depth investigation into the role Russia had played, and questions swirled around whether the Trump campaign had colluded with Russia.

On March 20, 2017, FBI Director James Comey confirmed that a federal investigation was underway. On May 9, 2017, Comey was fired as head of the FBI. Two weeks later, Attorney General Jeff Sessions removed himself from his role in the Russia inquiry because of a conflict of interest (he had participated in the Trump campaign). The following day, Deputy Attorney General Rod Rosenstein named Robert Mueller (who had previously led the FBI) as Special Counsel to investigate the allegations of Russian collusion. Trump blamed Sessions for the Special Counsel appointment and later fired him from his post as attorney general. Most experts believe that had Comey not been fired, a Special Counsel would never have been appointed. The specific charge Rosenstein gave to Mueller was to investigate

(1) any links and/or coordination between the Russian government and individuals associated with the campaign of President Donald Trump;

(2) any matters that arose or may arise directly from the investigation; and

(3) any other matters within the scope of 28 C.F.R. § 600.4(a).

Figure 6.5 shows a timeline of the two-year-long **Mueller investigation**. By the end of the investigation, 34 individuals and three Russian companies had been charged with federal offenses.

Twenty-five of the individuals charged were Russian intelligence officers and nationals, and at least six Americans charged had connections to Trump. Trump and his family members were not charged. In the end, Trump stated that the investigation showed "no collusion" in the election and "no obstruction" by him or his administration in the investigation. A closer look at the final Mueller report, however, casts some doubt on whether Trump was completely vindicated. In particular, the report offers this summary about whether obstruction occurred:

> If we had confidence after a thorough investigation of the facts that the President clearly did not commit obstruction of justice, we would so state. Based on the facts and the applicable legal standards, however, we are unable to reach that judgment. The evidence we obtained about the President's actions and intent presents difficult issues that prevent us from conclusively determining that no criminal conduct occurred. Accordingly, while this report does not conclude that the President committed a crime, it also does not exonerate him. (USDOJ, 2019, March)

Regarding the allegations of collusion, the Mueller investigation looked into a meeting that Donald Trump Jr., Paul Manafort, and Jared Kushner had with a Russian lawyer who had sent Trump Jr. an e-mail claiming to have dirt about the Clinton campaign. The investigation findings are clear:

- Trump Jr. received an email stating that the "Crown prosecutor of Russia . . . offered to provide the Trump Campaign with some official documents and information that would incriminate Hillary and her dealings with Russia" as "part of Russia and its government's support for Mr. Trump."

- Trump Jr. immediately responded "if it's what you say I love it."

- Trump Jr. scheduled the meeting with the Russian lawyer.

- Trump Jr., Manafort, and Kushner met with the Russian lawyer. (USDOJ, 2019, March)

On the surface, it may seem like this is a clear case of collusion. However, the Federal Election Campaign Act states that in order for campaign-related violations to be illegal, they must be conducted "knowingly and intentionally." Because it was nearly impossible to determine whether any of the parties knew they were breaking the law or intended to break the law, Mueller did not pursue collusion charges. Here is how this was described in the Mueller report:

> Accordingly, taking into account the high burden to establish a culpable mental state in a campaign-finance prosecution and the difficulty in establishing the required valuation, the Office decided not to pursue criminal campaign-finance charges against Trump Jr. or other campaign officials for the events culminating in the June 9 meeting. (USDOJ, 2019, March)

While this investigation was going on, the Senate Intelligence Committee conducted its own investigation into the Russian interference in the 2016 elections. Chaired by Marco Rubio (Rep.) and Mark Warner (Dem.), in August 2020, the bipartisan committee released a 966-page report that detailed the committee's investigation. The committee report indicated that it was not conducting a criminal investigation, but that it did make criminal referrals if it believed that participants lied during their testimony to the committee. The names of those who received criminal referrals were redacted from the report. Citing unnamed officials as sources, news outlets reported that some of those who received criminal referrals included Donald Trump Jr. and Jared Kushner (Trump's son-in-law).

FIGURE 6.5 ■ Mueller Timeline

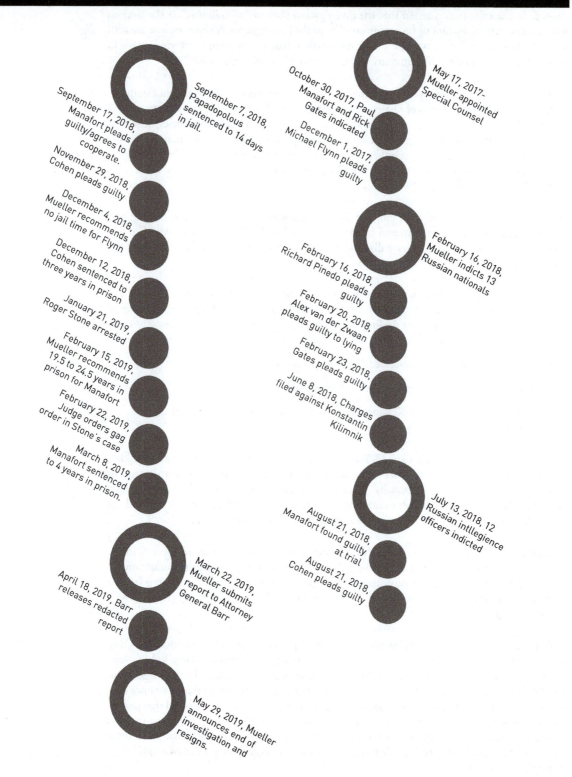

September 17, 2018, Manafort pleads guilty/agrees to cooperate.

September 7, 2018, Papadopolous sentenced to 14 days in jail.

November 29, 2018, Cohen pleads guilty

December 4, 2018, Mueller recommends no jail time for Flynn

December 12, 2018, Cohen sentenced to three years in prison

January 21, 2019, Roger Stone arrested

February 15, 2019, Mueller recommends 19.5 to 24.5 years in prison for Manafort

February 22, 2019, Judge orders gag order in Stone's case

March 8, 2019, Manafort sentenced to 4 years in prison.

April 18, 2019, Barr releases redacted report

March 22, 2019, Mueller submits report to Attorney General Barr

May 29, 2019, Mueller announces end of investigation and resigns.

October 30, 2017, Paul Manafort and Rick Gates indicted

December 1, 2017, Michael Flynn pleads guilty

May 17, 2017- Mueller appointed Special Counsel

February 16, 2018, Richard Pinedo pleads guilty

February 20, 2018, Alex van der Zwaan pleads guilty to lying

February 23, 2018, Gates pleads guilty

June 8, 2018, Charges filed against Konstantin Kilimnik

February 16, 2018, Mueller indicts 13 Russian nationals

August 21, 2018, Manafort found guilty at trial

August 21, 2018, Cohen pleads guilty

July 13, 2018, 12 Russian intllegience officers indicted

Source: Adapted from https://www.axios.com/mueller-russia-investigation-timeline-indictments-70433acd-9ef7-424d-aa01-b962ae5c9647.html

The Impeachment of Donald Trump

Three U.S. presidents have been impeached: Andrew Johnson (1868), Bill Clinton (1998), and Donald Trump (2019). Just one has been impeached twice—Donald Trump. Because of his history of allegations and his lack of political experience, many predicted before Trump took office that he would be impeached. Figure 6.6 shows the timeline for Trump's first impeachment. Calls for his impeachment began shortly after Comey's firing in 2017 and continued in 2018. In January 2019, shortly after being sworn in as a new member of the House of Representatives, Congresswoman Rashida Tlaib gained nationwide attention for telling her supporters, "We're going to impeach the motherfucker." House majority leader Nancy Pelosi kept the calls for impeachment at bay, perhaps because she recognized that an impeachment process deemed to be unfair by the public would negatively harm the Democratic party in subsequent elections (Naylor, 2020).

On August 12, 2019, a whistleblower from the intelligence community told Michael Atkinson, the Inspector General of the Intelligence Community, about concerns he had about a phone call between President Trump and Ukrainian President Volodymyr Zelensky. It was alleged that Trump threatened to withhold congressionally approved aid to Ukraine unless Ukraine announced they were conducting an investigation into Joe Biden's son, Hunter Biden, who had been appointed to the board of a Ukrainian natural gas company during the Obama/Biden term and was being paid $50,000 a month for the board appointment. Because Atkinson found the complaint credible, he notified Congress about the whistleblower's concerns. After the information became public, Trump tried to keep the notes about the call private. He later agreed to turn over the notes from the call to Congress (Savage, 2020).

On September 24, 2019, House Leader Pelosi announced the impeachment inquiry. Requisite proceedings and hearings happened over the next three months. On December 18, 2019, the House voted primarily along party lines to impeach President Trump on two articles of impeachment. Those articles included an abuse of power article and an obstruction of congress article. The abuse of power article impeached Trump for telling the Ukrainian president that the United States would withhold aid unless Ukraine announced an investigation into Hunter Biden's board appointment. This article also stated that Trump had asked the Ukraine president to promote the false theory that it was Ukraine who interfered in the 2016 election, not Russia. The obstruction of congress article stated that Trump had directed White House officials to ignore requests from the congressional committees investigating the president during the impeachment process.

After some negotiating with the U.S. Senate about how the impeachment trial would be conducted, the House of Representatives delivered the impeachment articles to the Senate on January 5, 2020. The Senate trial began on January 23rd with House managers providing their opening statement. The trial was over less than two weeks later. Trump was acquitted on the two articles with just one Republican in the Senate—Mitt Romney—voting to convict, and no Democratic senators voting to acquit. Incidentally, Romney's vote to acquit is the first time in history that a senator has voted to convict a president of the senator's party.

Exactly one year and one day after the House delivered its impeachment articles to the Senate in 2020, and after losing the 2020 election, President Trump delivered a wide ranging call-to-action to his supporters in one of his typical long speeches. Continuing the claims that the election was stolen, he urged his supporters to stop Congress from certifying the election. At the end of his speech, he said "We fight like hell, and if you don't fight like hell, you're not going to have a country anymore. . . . So we are going to walk down Pennsylvania Avenue—I love Pennsylvania Avenue—and we are going to the Capitol" (Petras, Loehrke, Padilla, Zarracina, & Borreson, 2021). Trump's supporters did just that, and when they got to the Capitol, they staged an insurrection that resulted in five deaths. A week later, after being charged with inciting an insurrection, Trump became the first president to ever be impeached twice. Similar to his first impeachment, the Senate acquitted Trump of the charges. Unlike his first impeachment, 17 Republicans (10 in the House and seven in the Senate) voted to impeach the disgraced leader.

FIGURE 6.6 ■ Impeachment Timeline

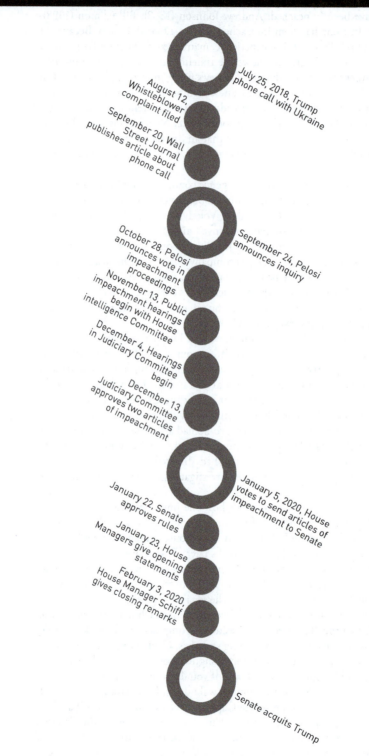

July 25, 2018, Trump phone call with Ukraine

August 12, Whistleblower complaint filed

September 20, Wall Street Journal publishes article about phone call

September 24, Pelosi announces inquiry

October 28, Pelosi announces vote in impeachment proceedings

November 13, Public impeachment hearings begin with House intelligence Committee

December 4, Hearings in Judiciary Committee begin

December 13, Judiciary Committee approves two articles of impeachment

January 5, 2020, House votes to send articles of impeachment to Senate

January 22, Senate approves rules

January 23, House Managers give opening statements

February 3, 2020, House Manager Schiff gives closing remarks

Senate acquits Trump

Source: Adapted from Naylor, 2020 and Janowski, 2020

Political Pardons and Firings

A look at the pardon numbers and commutations suggests that Trump used his power to pardon offenders or grant sentence commutations relatively infrequently, at least in comparison to his predecessors. Data from the Pew Research Center show that as of November 27, 2020, Trump had pardoned or commuted the sentences of just 44 individuals. In contrast, Obama, Bush, and Clinton had pardoned 212, 189, and 386 individuals respectively. These numbers don't include the 1,700+ drug offenders whose sentences were commuted by Obama.

Controversies arise when considering who President Trump fired and pardoned during his presidency. While all presidents have the legal authority to pardon offenders or commute sentences, some have alleged that Trump played favorites with offenders with whom he had some sort of connection. One author team characterizes Trump's pardons and commutations, and how the relate to his predecessors', in the following way:

> Of the 34 people who received pardons or commutations (or both) from President Trump [through July 2020], 29 of them were self-serving. Other presidents have of course issued what can be seen as self-serving pardons: George H. W. Bush's pardon of Defense Secretary Caspar Weinberger; Bill Clinton's pardon of his brother Roger and of Susan McDougal, among others; and George W. Bush's commutation of Scooter Libby's sentence. But no president in American history comes close to matching Trump's systematically self-serving use of the pardon power. (Goldsmith & Gluck, 2020)

Mother Jones reporter Becky Dernbach shared a list of Trump's commutations and controversial pardons (Dernbach, 2020). Most of the offenders making the list were people who had been convicted of white-collar crimes. Here are eight of the offenders along with their crime and their connection to Trump:

- Rod Blagojevich was convicted for trying to sell the senate seat vacated by Barack Obama after he was elected president. Blagojevich was a contestant on *Celebrity Apprentice*, Trump's reality show that some say launched Trump into his political career.

- Bernard Kerik, a former police commissioner for the city of New York, was convicted of various crimes including tax evasion and perjury. Kerik is a frequent guest on *Fox News*, the television channel Trump favors, and a close ally to Trump's one-time personal attorney Rudy Giuliani.

- Michael Milken has been the poster child for white-collar crime after his convictions for security fraud and insider trading in the 1990s. He was pardoned after several supporters—including the president's son-in-law, Jared Kushner, and Giuliani— convinced Trump to issue a pardon.

- Construction business owner Paul Pogue was convicted of tax evasion in 2010. He gave $200,000 to a political action committee supporting Trump.

- Conservative pundit Dinesh D'Souza was convicted for illegal campaign contributions. He spent much of his career spreading Obama conspiracy theories.

- Media mogul Conrad Black was convicted after stealing more than $60 million from investors. The former business leader wrote numerous op-eds applauding Trump's presidency prior to being pardoned.

- Former San Francisco 49ers owner Eddie DeBartolo, Jr. was convicted for not telling authorities that a governor tried to bribe him. Debartolo supported the Trump campaign and hosted a pre-inauguration party for the administration.

- Roger Stone, a close confidant of Trump, was convicted for lying to Congress, witness tampering, and obstruction in the Russia investigation. Trump commuted his sentence shortly before Stone was scheduled to go to prison (Dernbach, 2020).

Trump has also gained some notoriety for his political firings. In his first year as president, the turnover rate among "A-team" cabinet officials in Trump's administration was 35%. This compares to rates of 9% (Obama) and 6% (Bush) for his two previous predecessors (Tenpas, 2020). The turnover rate did not slow down in subsequent years. From chiefs of staff (John Kelley and Reince Preibus), to attorneys general (Jeff Sessions and interim Sally Yates), to national security advisors (John Bolton and Henry McMaster), to defense secretaries (Mike Esper), Trump fired people more quickly as president than he did on Apprentice, the reality show from which his line "You're fired" became known in popular culture. Trump's political firings are certainly within presidential authority since those positions serve the president. Because they have a role in investigating corruption, the firings that particularly raised the eyebrows of Trump critics were a series of inspector general dismissals in 2020.

Inspector general positions are given the duty of investigating allegations of wrongdoing within governmental units. In 2019, Intelligence Community Inspector General Michael Atkinson began an investigation based on whistleblower complaints about Trump's call with Ukraine's president. On April 3, 2020, a year after acting on the whistleblower complaints, Trump fired Atkinson. After firing him, Trump said, "He did a horrible job, absolutely terrible . . . he took a fake report and brought it to Congress with an emergency. Ok? Not a big Trump fan, that I can tell you" (Savage, 2020).

Less than a week after firing Atkinson, Trump removed acting Inspector General Glenn Fine from his post, effectively disqualifying Fine from overseeing how $2.2 trillion in coronavirus relief funds would be spent (Savage & Baker, 2020). Democrats were quick to question the unexpected firing. Republicans countered that Trump didn't violate any laws or policies in firing Fine. Trump explained his decision in this way:

> We have a lot of IGs in from the Obama era. . . . And as you know, it's a presidential decision. And I left them, largely. I mean, changed some, but I left them. . . . But when we have, you know, reports of bias and when we have different things coming in. I don't know Fine. I don't think I ever met Fine. (Nakashima, 2020)

Fine returned to his previous position as principal deputy inspector general but resigned from that position the following month.

On the evening of May 15, 2020, incidentally a Friday, Secretary of State Mike Pompeo fired State Department Inspector General Steve Linick. When pressed about why Pompeo fired the inspector general, the official response was that Linick made unauthorized disclosures of classified information to the news. A closer review by journalists questioned whether the real reasons for Linick's firing stemmed from any of the following:

- Linick was investigating Pompeo's role in a Saudi Arabian Arms deal.

- Linick had also been investigating Pompeo's use of federal employees for personal errands and allegations of misuse of funds.

- Linick led a report exploring alleged harassment at the State Department against those who were not Trump loyalists (Blake, 2020; Vinograd, 2020).

In August 2020, Stephen Ackard, who was hired as acting inspector general as a result of Linick's vacated position, retired from the role, vacating it once again.

Much of the suspicion critics had about these firings centers around the powerful duties assigned to inspectors general. Citing the Inspector General Act of 1978, one OIG office clarifies the authority of inspectors general by listing their powers and responsibilities:

- Determine which audits, investigations, inspections, and reviews are necessary, and issue reports recommending corrective actions without improper interference from agency heads

- Receive full access to all records and materials available to the agency

- Issue administrative subpoenas to nonfederal entities

- Exercise law enforcement authority

- Receive employee and other complaints

- Refer criminal and civil matters to the United States Attorney General

- Hire employees, experts, and consultants, and procure necessary equipment and services

- Obtain assistance from other agencies, including federal, state, and local governments (OIG, 2020).

The Inspector General Act of 1978 more fully details the duties of inspectors general. Included in the legislation is language describing how inspectors general can be removed from their positions. Specifically, the act stipulates the following:

> An Inspector General may be removed from office by the President. If an Inspector General is removed from office or is transferred to another position or location within an establishment, the President shall communicate in writing the reasons for any such removal or transfer to both Houses of Congress, not later than 30 days before the removal or transfer. (OIG, 2020)

Clearly, presidents have the legal authority to remove inspectors general from their positions. The reason opponents of Trump expressed shock at three inspectors general being fired in less than two months had to do with how unexpected the firings were. Supporters of Trump pointed to President Barack Obama's decision to remove Gerald Walpin, a George W. Bush appointee who was serving as inspector general for the Corporation for National Community Service (Coleman, 2020). Obama fired Walpin after the inspector general criticized a grant awarded to a nonprofit being run by Obama supporter and future Sacramento Mayor Kevin Johnson. Walpin found that funds from the grant had been misspent and recommended that Johnson not be given future taxpayer support (Re, 2020). Had the federal government followed through on this recommendation, the city of Sacramento would have lost a significant amount of funding and support. Addressing questions suggesting that the firing was politically motivated, members of Obama's administration cited vague concerns about Walpin's mental health as the justification for his firing.

In the aftermath of Trump's inspector general terminations, Trump supporters were quick to bring up the Walpin firing when asked about the ethical concerns that arise when an inspector general is fired while investigating a supporter. They also asked why Obama didn't get criticized for his inspector general firings. In reality, Obama was criticized by Democrats and Republicans alike for the Walpin case (Re, 2020).

TRUMP'S CONNECTIONS WITH WHITE-COLLAR CRIMINALS

Trump has multiple connections to white-collar criminals. As of November 2020—three years and 10 months into his presidency—15 people connected with Trump were indicted or convicted for white-collar offenses (Kim, 2020). Table 6.1 shows these contacts and the allegations against them, as well as tweets and other responses from Trump in an effort to distance himself from the offenders or to accuse authorities of conducting a baseless investigation.

TABLE 6.1 ■ Trump Associates Indicted or Convicted of Crimes, 2017–2020				
Name/Role	**Connection to Trump**	**Allegations**	**Trump Response**	**Outcome**
Michael Cohen, former personal attorney to Trump	Cohen came to national prominence with reports that he brokered a hush agreement with porn star Stormy Daniels to keep her from talking about her dalliance with Trump.	Cohen was accused of a litany of offenses ranging from perjury to campaign law violations.	"If anyone is looking for a good lawyer, I would strongly suggest that you don't retain the services of Michael Cohen!" (tweet from August 22, 2018)	Cohen plead guilty to tax crimes, making false statements to a financial institution, excessive campaign contributions, and unlawful corporate contributions (Breuninger, 2020). He received a three-year prison sentence. He was released early due to Covid-19 safety concerns.
Chris Collins, U.S. Rep., NY	Collins was the first congressperson to express support for President Trump's candidacy while Trump was running for president in 2016. His support was believed by many to open the door to other Republicans endorsing Trump.	After a long investigation, Collins was accused of sharing inside information about a failed drug trial with his son, who used that information to sell his shares in the drug company and avoid losing more than a half million dollars.	"Two long running, Obama era, investigations of two very popular Republican Congressmen were brought to a well publicized charge, just ahead of the Mid-Terms, by the Jeff Sessions Justice Department. Two easy wins now in doubt because there is not enough time. Good job Jeff . . ." (tweet from September 3, 2018; see entry for Duncan Hunter)	After resigning from Congress, Collins plead guilty to security crimes and was sentenced to 26 months in prison. Collins recognized his dramatic fall from grace, telling the court, "now I stand here today as a disgraced former member of Congress" (Kelly & Jones, 2020).

Name/Role	Connection to Trump	Allegations	Trump Response	Outcome
Rick Gates, political consultant	Gates served as a deputy campaign manager on Trump's 2016 presidential campaign, reporting initially to Paul Manafort and later to Kellyanne Conway.	Gates worked with Paul Manafort on various ventures over the years. The two were accused of laundering millions of dollars they had made working as unregistered agents for Ukraine; they were also accused of lobbying for Ukraine but failing to notify the United States about their roles as lobbyists (Sisak, 2019).	"Sorry, but this is years ago, before Paul Manafort was part of the Trump campaign. But why aren't Crooked Hillary & the Dems the focus????? . . . Also, there is NO COLLUSION." (tweet from October 30, 2017)	Gates participated fully in the Mueller investigation, sharing very specific details about Trump, Manafort, and Stone. After pleading guilty to lying to investigators and conspiracy, he was sentenced to 45 days in jail and three years' probation (Polantz, 2019).
Michael Flynn, lieutenant general (ret.)	A once well-respected military leader, General Flynn was a member of Trump's presidential campaign in 2016 and later appointed Trump's national security advisor.	Flynn was accused of communicating with Russians before Trump was sworn in as president.	"What happened to General Michael Flynn, a war hero, should never be allowed to happen to a citizen of the United States again." (tweet from April 30, 2020])	Flynn initially denied the accusations but later admitted he had lied to the FBI (Obeidallah, 2020). Flynn plead guilty on two different occasions to perjury charges. Before Flynn's sentencing, Trump announced he would be open to pardoning his former national security adviser. Prior to sentencing, DOJ Director William Barr recommended dropping the charges against Flynn. Trump eventually pardoned Flynn.
Duncan Hunter, former U.S. Rep., California	Hunter was an early supporter of President Trump's candidacy.	Hunter and his wife were accused of misusing campaign funds for personal use, including dentist visits and vacations.	"Two long running, Obama era, investigations of two very popular Republican Congressmen were brought to a well publicized charge,	After claiming that the charges were "purely politically motivated," Hunter plead guilty (Jarrett & Reston, 2018). He was sentenced to 11 months in prison.

(Continued)

TABLE 6.1 ■ (Continued)

Name/Role	Connection to Trump	Allegations	Trump Response	Outcome
			just ahead of the Mid-Terms, by the Jeff Sessions Justice Department. Two easy wins now in doubt because there is not enough time. Good job Jeff . . . " (tweet from September 3, 2018; see entry for Chris Collins)	
Paul Manafort, political consultant	Manafort was the chair of Trump's campaign in the summer of 2016. He is credited by some for saving the Trump campaign.	Manafort and Rick Gates were accused of laundering millions of dollars they had made working as unregistered agents for Ukraine; they were also accused of lobbying for Ukraine, but failing to notify the United States. about their role as lobbyists (Sisak, 2019). Manafort subsequently faced charges for mortgage fraud in New York state.	(On Manafort's alleged lying to investigators): "The Phony Witch Hunt continues, but Mueller and his gang of Angry Dems are only looking at one side, not the other . . . Wait until it comes out how horribly & viciously they are treating people, ruining lives for them refusing to lie. Mueller is a conflicted prosecutor gone rogue." (tweet from November 27, 2018)	Initially offering to cooperate in the Mueller investigation and signing a plea agreement, Manafort raised the ire of prosecutors who found him less than helpful. He was convicted and sentenced to 7.5 years in prison, which included 47 months for his financial crimes and 43 months for obstruction. The mortgage fraud charges in New York were dropped.
George Papadopoulos, foreign policy advisor	Papadopoulos served as Trump's foreign policy advisor during the 2016 presidential campaign.	In an investigation about his connections to Russia, Papadopoulos was accused of lying to the FBI. According to the indictment, he "impeded the FBI's ongoing investigation into the existence of any links or coordination	(After Papadopoulos plead guilty): "Few people knew the young, low level volunteer named George, who has already proven to be a liar." (tweet from October 31, 2017)	The Mueller team scheduled a meeting to discuss collaborating on the broader investigation, but Papadopolous was determined untrustworthy because of his openness to talking with the media. After admitting his regret

Name/Role	Connection to Trump	Allegations	Trump Response	Outcome
		between individuals associated with the Campaign and the Russian government's efforts to interfere with the 2016 presidential election."		at sentencing, he pleaded guilty and was sentenced to 14 days in jail (Dilanian, 2018).
Roger Stone, political consultant	An early supporter of Trump's 2016 candidacy, Stone had close personal connections to Trump.	Stone was accused of working with the Trump campaign to get Hilary Clinton's stolen e-mails from Wikileaks founder Julian Assange.	"This is a horrible and very unfair situation. The real crimes were on the other side, as nothing happens to them. Cannot allow this miscarriage of justice!" (tweet from February 10, 2020)	Stone went to trial and was convicted on all seven charges he faced. He was sentenced to 40 months in prison in February 2020. Filing two appeals, he delayed the start of his incarceration. Trump commuted the prison sentence, making it so Stone never spent a day in prison.
Steve Bannon, campaign advisor, White House chief strategist	Bannon played a central role as a campaign advisor in the 2016 election of President Trump and worked for him as White House chief strategist for a short time after he was elected.	Bannon was accused of being a part of a scheme crowdfunding effort called Rebuild the Wall, which purportedly raised $17 million in its first week. The indictment alleged that Bannon used some of the funds for personal expenses.	"I disagreed with doing this very small (tiny) section of wall, in a tricky area, by a private group which raised money by ads. It was only done to make me look bad, and perhaps it now doesn't even work. Should have been built like rest of Wall, 500 plus miles." (tweet from July 12, 2020	The indictment was announced on August 20, 2020. Trump pardoned Bannon of the charges prior to leaving office.

Possible explanations for a president having a high number of personal contacts convicted of white-collar crimes in such a short time period include bad vetting by the administration, a history of crime connections, and aggressive prosecutions by prosecutors in various jurisdictions (Kim, 2020). Historian Paul Gottfredson gives some weight to the effect of aggressive prosecutions: "I don't think Trump is a particularly virtuous individual—I just don't see him as worse than some of his predecessors" (Kim, 2020).

Summary

- Unlike professionals working in some other systems, professionals in the political system routinely confront suspicion and distrust from citizens.

- Types of crime in the political system include election law violations, campaign finance violations, political corruption related to extortion and bribery, apolitical white-collar crime, crimes in the military, and state-corporate crime.

- Election law violations refer to situations in which political officials violate rules guiding the way that elections are supposed to be conducted.

- Campaign finance laws place restrictions on the way political campaigns are financed, with specific attention given to contributions and expenditures.

- Apolitical white-collar crime refers to situations in which politicians get into trouble for doing things that are outside of scope of politics but are violations of the public trust.

- State-corporate crime receives less attention from criminologists than other types of crime.

- Trump's personal history of crime allegations, the Mueller investigation, the impeachment, political firings and pardons, and his connections with white-collar criminals all relate to white-collar crime.

- The Mueller investigation explored allegations that the Trump campaign colluded with Russia in the 2016 election; while the investigation did not result in collusion charges against the president, it did not exonerate him either.

- Donald Trump was impeached by the House of Representatives for threatening to withhold aid to Ukraine unless the country's president announced an investigation into Hunter Biden

- Trump was impeached in January 2021 on charges that he incited an insurrection. The Senate acquitted him on those charges.

- Political firings as well as pardons and commutations of several white-collar offenders by Trump resulted in allegations of favoritism by opponents.

- Trump has personal or business connections with more than a dozen convicted white-collar offenders.

Key Terms

Discussion Questions

1. How are white-collar crimes committed in the political system similar to and different from white-collar crimes in other systems discussed so far?

2. Should politicians who have been convicted of political crimes be permitted to run for office again? What if they were convicted of crimes unrelated to politics?

3. Review the list of individuals affiliated with Trump who have been accused of white-collar crimes. Do these crimes reflect on President Trump? Explain.

4. Why do you think public corruption convictions have decreased in recent years?

5. Why do individuals in the political system engage in various types of misconduct?

6. Find four cases of political misconduct described in the media. Identify three patterns in those cases that were discussed in this chapter.

CRIME IN THE EDUCATIONAL SYSTEM

It was noted previously that crime and misconduct occur in all professions. To be perfectly blunt, criminal justice professors are not immune from allegations of misconduct. In 2003, a prominent criminologist and professor was accused of manufacturing data about how guns make people safer from crime (Kennedy, 2003). The accusations involved a very public spar between the professor and another researcher who questioned the validity of the professor's research. In 2014, a professor of sociology and criminal justice resigned from his job after reportedly e-mailing a student, "will you blow me for an A?" (Collman, 2014). In 2019, a prominent criminologist and professor was accused of fabricating research findings by one of his former doctoral students who had gone on to become a well-regarded criminologist in his own right (Bartlett, 2019; Pickett, 2020). The accusations rattled the field because of the accused's prominence in the field and because several of the articles with alleged fabricated research included top criminologists from the field as coauthors, including the editor of the top journal in the field. While the accusations resulted in the retraction of six published manuscripts, a review panel did not find the researcher guilty of misconduct. Rather, it was determined that researcher errors led to the inaccurate data.

It's not just criminal justice professors accused of misconduct. Consider the following recent examples quoted from their original sources:

- In January 2015, **********, an associate professor at Colorado State University, sent his administration an offer letter he'd received from another university. To entice ********** to stay, Colorado State raised his base pay by $5,000, a university spokeswoman said. Using offer letters from other institutions as leverage in salary negotiations is common practice at colleges and universities. There was just one problem with **********s case: The offer letter was fake (Zahneis, 2018).

PHOTO 7.1 We learn early on as students to respect and grant power to our teachers. This socialization translates into our respecting and giving power to professors. Some professors, unfortunately, abuse this power.

©iStockphoto.com/kali9

- U.S. Attorney Geoffrey S. Berman said: "*****, a college professor and author, went from writing the book on crime—literally writing a book on drug trafficking and organized crime—to committing crimes. Professor ***** admitted today to laundering money for corrupt foreign nationals—the proceeds of bribery and corruption, stolen from the citizens of Venezuela. Bagley now faces the possibility of a long tenure in prison' (USDOJ, 2020, June 1).

- ***** pleaded guilty to a one-count information charging him with "Federal Program Fraud." From 2006 to August 2019, +++++ was a tenured professor at West Virginia University in the physics department, specializing in molecular reactions used in coal conversion technologies. In July 2017, +++++ entered into a contract of employment with the People's Republic of China through its "Global Experts 1000 Talents Plan." China's Thousand Talents Plan is one of the most prominent Chinese Talent recruit plans that are designed to attract, recruit, and cultivate high-level scientific talent in furtherance of China's scientific development, economic prosperity and national security. (USDOJ, 2020, March 10).

- ORI found that Respondent engaged in research misconduct by intentionally, knowingly, and/or recklessly falsifying and/or fabricating data by altering, reusing, and relabeling same source Western blot images, microscopy fields, and data of viral titers and mouse immune response from non-correlated experiments to represent the results of different viral strains in the following seven (7) published papers and two (2) grant applications submitted to NIAID, NIH (Office of Research Integrity, n.d.).

In this chapter, attention is given to crimes committed in the educational system. Students fulfill one of three roles in these cases: (1) they are witnesses, (2) they are victims, or (3) they are offenders. In one case, for example, a graduate student testified that he never met his professor's wife, even though the professor was billing a grant agency for the wife who was purportedly supervising the laboratory team the student was a part of (Hall, 2015). In another case, a professor was convicted after, among other things, he falsely told students they had to return parts of their stipends to him (Wells, 2014). The majority of the discussion in this chapter will focus on crimes by professors and researchers working in the educational system. After discussing how professionals have committed misconduct in this system, attention will be given to the way that students have committed workplace crimes in the educational system.

CRIMES BY PROFESSIONALS IN THE EDUCATIONAL SYSTEM

It's probably not something we go around bragging about, but as professors, we work in an occupation that is not immune from white-collar crime. Not only do we study white-collar crime, but we are also a part of an occupational subculture that experiences various forms of white-collar crime. Four types of misconduct that appear to be among the more common types of academic misconduct include the following:

- Research misconduct by professors

- Ghostwriting

- Pecuniary-oriented offenses

- Sexual harassment

After discussing these varieties of crimes in higher education, attention will be given to crimes by students as types of occupational crimes.

Research Misconduct by Professors

Research misconduct refers to a range of behaviors that center on researchers (many of whom are faculty members) engaging in various forms of wrongdoing during the course of their research. These forms of wrongdoing include, but are not limited to, fabricating data, masking findings, plagiarism, and treating research subjects unethically.

Concern about research misconduct is a relatively modern phenomenon. As one expert points out, this doesn't mean that the problem is new; it's the focus on the problem that is new. As Faria (2018) writes, "It is not possible to state that RM was non-existent, but nor can it be assumed that there is more of it now than there was before. In fact, data on its frequency over time are rare. It would be wiser to state that problematization of RM, as well as regulation and detection efforts, seems much more present today than before." (p. 41).

In the United States, efforts to recognize and manage research misconduct are typically led by the funding agencies providing financial support for the research. The Office of Research Integrity (ORI), part of the Office of Public Health and Sciences within the U.S. Department of Health and Human Services, oversees research supported by the Public Health Services (PHS). The mission of ORI focuses on

> (1) oversight of institutional handling of research misconduct allegations involving research, research training, or related research activities support by the PHS;
> (2) education in the responsible conduct of research; (3) prevention of research misconduct, and (4) compliance with the PHS Policies on Research Misconduct.
> (Office of Research Integrity, 2010)

The increased federal oversight and efforts to respond to research misconduct have not gone unnoticed. Some researchers have tried to explain why the federal government has become so intense in its efforts to weed out research misconduct. Hackett (1993) identified several factors that contributed to the increased oversight. First, the federal government has been investing more and more money in scientific endeavors, and science has become more visible to members of society as a result of this increased funding. Second, science is viewed as a "resource for power," and those who control science would potentially become more powerful through that control. Third, to some, science is like a religion, and enforcement efforts toward misconduct are defined as ways to protect the "religion" of science. Fourth, Hackett noted that opposition to the "intellectual elite" may have contributed to political officials' decisions to increase efforts toward controlling research misconduct. Finally, science has become increasingly important to universities, businesses, and the government. The growing importance of science potentially increased the need of the government to expand its ability to control science.

As with other forms of white-collar crime, it is difficult to estimate how often research misconduct occurs. It may, however, be even more difficult to estimate for the simple reason that few researchers have actually empirically assessed research misconduct. Experts have noted that research misconduct is "real and persistent" (Herman, Sunshine, Fisher, Zwolenik, & Herz, 1994). Anecdotally, the former editor of the *British Medical Journal* indicated that he "dealt with about 20 cases [of research misconduct] a year" Smith, 2006, p. 232).

One of the more infamous cases of research misconduct involved Ward Churchill, a professor of ethnic studies at the University of Colorado at Boulder. Prior to the allegations of misconduct, Churchill had come under fire for making disparaging comments about the victims of the 9/11 attacks. His notoriety grew, and greater attention was given to his work, and accusations surfaced surrounding the authenticity of some of Churchill's writings. An investigation followed, and the university's investigative committee found that Churchill engaged in "serious research misconduct" (University of Colorado Investigative Committee Report, 2006, p. 31). In July 2007, the university's regents fired Churchill. He appealed the decision, and, though a jury found in his favor—awarding him one dollar—the judge overturned the verdict and upheld the university's actions.

One of the charges against Churchill was that he plagiarized some of his writings. Interestingly, researchers have suggested that plagiarism by professors is more likely to occur in the humanities and social sciences than in the hard sciences due to the nature of the disciplines. In particular, the level of creativity required in the humanities and social sciences is higher, and the need for creativity may create situations where professors are more apt to borrow someone else's creativity (Fox, 1994). In the hard sciences, where several authors typically appear on published manuscripts, loose authorship—where some authors are included on the manuscript who should not be—is believed to be more problematic.

Today, plagiarism is often uncovered when computer-based text searching tools are used to search for it (Huckabee, 2009). Plagiarism is discovered in at least four other ways:

- Researchers accidentally stumble upon it.

- Reviewers identify it during the peer review process.

- A disgruntled colleague or subordinate searches for it and finds it.

- The plagiarized author finds it.

Figure 7.1a shows the number of research misconduct accusations made to the National Science Foundation; Figure 7.1b shows the number of cases substantiated by the agency between 2011 and 2019. Both figures only include those cases where the misconduct was alleged in research projects funded by the National Science Foundation (NSF). Three patterns are significant. First, the number of accusations and substantiated cases is relatively low. Second, perhaps because it's easier to detect, more plagiarism cases are reported than other types of cases. Third, the number of plagiarism cases dropped since 2015.

Other varieties of research misconduct exist that do not receive as much attention. Consider image manipulation as an example. Image manipulation refers to "undocumented alterations to research images" (Jordan, 2014, p. 441). It is also known as "photo-fiction." It is believed that researchers do this in order to paint a picture that does not necessarily exist.

FIGURE 7.1A ■ **Research Misconduct Allegations in National Science Foundation Proposals (2011-2019)**

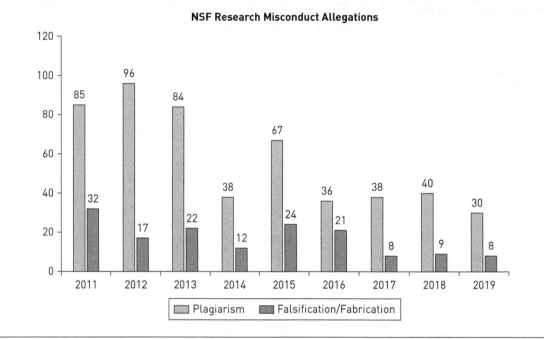

NSF Research Misconduct Allegations

Source: National Science Foundation (2020)

FIGURE 7.1B ■ **Findings of Research Misconduct in NSF Projects (2011-2019)**

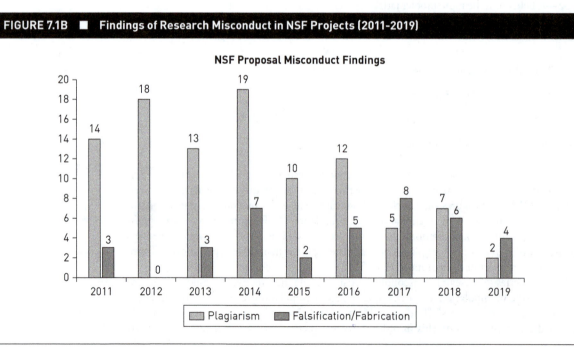

NSF Proposal Misconduct Findings

Source: National Science Foundation (2020)

This picture, then, is misleading and inaccurate in terms of the image's portrayal of the phenomena being studied. Jordan (2014) recommends that images be treated as research data and held to strict ethical standards.

Research misconduct has severe consequences on several different levels. These include (1) consequences for the individual faculty member, (2) financial consequences for the college or university, (3) morale consequences for the college or university, (4) image consequences for science, (5) consequences for members of society, and (6) consequences for various cultures. In terms of individual consequences, when research misconduct is exposed, the status of the offender takes a significant hit. While some may be able to overcome allegations—the president of the Southern Illinois University system was accused of plagiarizing both his master's thesis and 1984 dissertation in 2007, but he remained as president for several years after he told the board of trustees that his faculty committees never told him he had to use quotation marks—others are not able to overcome allegations. For example, the former president of University of Texas–Pan American resigned after it was alleged that she had plagiarized parts of her dissertation 35 years ago (Montell, 2009).

Colleges and universities will also suffer financial consequences from research misconduct. On one level, federal funding agencies may withhold funding if it is determined that the college or university was complacent in its efforts to limit research misconduct. Such a loss could amount to millions of dollars for the higher education institution. In one recent case, the University of Illinois-Chicago was ordered to repay the National Institute of Mental Health on grounds that the university did not provide adequate oversight of a child psychiatrist engaged in a wide range of research misconduct (Cohen, 2019). In another case, Duke University settled a lawsuit with the federal government after rampant fraud by one of the university's researchers was exposed. The lawsuit cost the university $112.5 million (Osei, 2019).

Higher education institutions will also experience morale consequences from the negative exposure that comes with the allegations of research misconduct. Instances where professors are caught engaging in research misconduct and fraud are sure to make the news. Consider the following headlines from several different news sources:

- Former Emory Professor Pleads Guilty to not Reporting Income From China on Tax Returns (Burns, 2020).

- UCLA Professor Faces 219 Years in Prison for Conspiring to Send U.S. Missile Chips to China (Shalby, 2019).

- Top Harvard Professor Arrested, Charged With Lying About Income to Feds (Richer, 2020).

- Ex-SCSU Professor Convicted, Sentenced to Jail Time (Times Staff Report, 2017).

- Arkansas Professor Arrested for Wire Fraud, Accused of Having Ties With Chinese Government (5News Web Staff, 2020).

- A Case for Indiana Jones: Oxford Professor Arrested for Allegedly Selling Stolen Goods and Other Art World Headlines (Dodd, 2020)

- University of Minnesota Law Professor Sentenced in $4 million Fraud Case (Verges, 2020)

- Purdue Prof, Wife Plead Guilty in $1.3M Scheme, Pocketing Federal Research Money (Bangert, 2019).

- University of Kansas Researcher Indicted for Fraud for Failing to Disclose Conflict of Interest With Chinese University (USDOJ, 2019, Aug 31).

- Researcher at University Arrested for Wire Fraud and Making False Statements About Affiliation With a Chinese University (USDOJ, 2020, February 27).

Two interesting patterns appear in these headlines. First, the headlines rarely identify the professor's name. Second, and on the other hand, note that all but one of the headlines lists the name of the college or university where the misconduct occurred. In many ways, research misconduct may damage the higher-education institution's image as much as it damages the actual professor who engaged in the misconduct.

Colleges and universities experience significant time losses in responding to cases of research misconduct. Investigations can take a great deal of time and resources. For example, a University of Washington investigation took seven years to conclude that an assistant professor should be fired. The investigation concluded that the researcher "had falsified seven figures and tables in two research papers" (Doughman, 2010). Time that administrators and faculty could have spent in productive activities had to be directed toward addressing misconduct by the assistant professor.

Research misconduct also has consequences for the image of science. In particular, these sorts of activities ultimately paint the scientific enterprise in a negative light. Consider the case of one anesthesiologist who fabricated his findings in 21 studies. Consequently, "the reliability of dozens more articles he wrote is uncertain, and the common practice supported by his studies—of giving patients aspirin-like drugs and neuropathic pain medicines after surgery instead of narcotics is now questioned" (Harris, 2009).

In a similar way, research misconduct has ramifications for members of society who are exposed to new practices and policies as a result of research. While a goal of research is to provide information that can be used to improve the human condition, if new practices and policies are based on data obtained through flawed research, then individuals exposed to those new practices and policies are put at risk. Giving patients aspirin instead of narcotics after surgery, for example, may have been a risk for patients.

Two patterns are common in research misconduct cases—one that is common in other white-collar crime cases and one that is not. First, as in other white-collar crime cases, many of those who commit research misconduct commit various forms of misconduct on multiple occasions. If researchers engage in one type of misconduct, like fudging data—it is likely that they have engaged in others, like fudging accounting data on funded research (see Schmidt, 2003). A second pattern in these cases—and one that distinguishes it from many other white-collar crimes—is that in most cases, the offenders acted alone. This is part of the process of committing research misconduct. Whereas certain types of health care fraud, for example, might require multiple participants to carry out the fraud, for research misconduct, a rogue professor aiming to achieve a certain end is able to accomplish this task without the help of others. Working alone insulates the professor from detection and allows the academic to continue to use his or her research to gain power and prestige (Walker & Holtfreter, 2015).

Some have pointed to the pressure to publish and get grants as being the source of research misconduct (Faria, 2018). Fox (1994) notes that economic incentives may play more of a role and points out that "the economic stakes of science have heightened" (p. 307). Top professors—with strong research portfolios—can earn hundreds of thousands of dollars in annual salary from their college or university, and some will earn far more providing consulting services. While most of these scientists conduct their research legitimately, it is plausible that those who commit misconduct are doing so, at least partly, for economic reasons.

Another possible reason that faculty engage in these activities is that their mentors did not supervise them appropriately (Brainard, 2008). Brainard cites a study that found that in three fourths of misconduct cases, the supervisors did not give the supervisees appropriate training in reviewing lab results. Recall the university president who indicated that his allegations of plagiarism could be explained by the fact that his faculty committees never told him he was supposed to put quotation marks around quotes.

Because of the potential role that mentors have in contributing to misconduct, some have argued that mentors should play an active role in training their students in how to conduct research appropriately. One author team suggests that mentors should train students how to (a) review source data, (b) understand research standards, and (c) deal with stressful work situations (Wright, Titus, & Cornelison, 2008). In a similar way, mentors should teach their students how to protect the rights of their research subjects, the consequences of research misconduct, and the importance of research integrity. Another author called for a "[shift] to an exploration of the moral issues involved in conducting research" (Gordon, 2014, p. 89).

Typically, accusations of misconduct begin with information from someone involved in the research on at least some level. Rarely are local or state criminal investigations undertaken against researchers, and federal investigations are conducted only when direct evidence of wrongdoing exists. In a rather controversial move, Virginia Attorney General Ken Cuccinnelli launched an investigation into the work of meteorology researcher Michael Mann (McNeill, 2010; Walker, 2010). The case is controversial for at least four reasons:

PHOTO 7.2 White-collar crimes occur in laboratories when scientists fabricate data or violate rules guiding their profession. This scientist, like most scientists, did not break any workplace rules. The few who do, however, create enormous problems for the field of science.

@iStockphoto.com/sanjeri

- The attorney general issued a subpoena for data from the University of Virginia, where Mann *used to* work.

- It is alleged by some that the attorney general was using the case to gain "cool points" from the political Right for "going after" a researcher whose findings showed support for the evidence of global warming.

- State agencies don't typically address these types of issues.

- The professor had already been cleared of misconduct by a Penn State University review panel (McNeill, 2010; Walker, 2010).

It is worth noting that the criminal justice system only sees the most serious research misconduct cases. Most cases are handled either informally or through regulatory or administrative processes. As an illustration of a more serious case, in 2015, an 18-day jury trial resulted in convictions for two researchers found guilty of various types of fraud and records falsification. The researchers, a married couple, were found guilty of misrepresenting their facilities, costs, and letters of support, among other things. They were ordered to pay $10.5 million in restitution. The husband and wife received prison sentences of 15 and 13 years, respectively (National Science Foundation, 2019a).

Sanctions for all types of misconduct in the educational arena will be discussed in later sections. One particular sanction that may be given specifically for research misconduct is retraction of a published research article. *Retraction* means that the journal publisher has "removed" the article from the scientific literature. Of course, the article still remains in print, but the "retraction" label is meant to suggest that the article should not be viewed as a scientific contribution. Journal articles can be retracted for error or fraud. A recent study found that one fourth of retracted articles were due to fraud, while most were retracted because of error (Steen, 2011).

Steen (2010) studied the dynamics of retracted papers due to fraud. The study found that the majority of first authors worked in the United States. Additional findings Steen uncovered from the review of 788 retracted articles included the following:

- Papers retracted for fraud targeted journals with higher impact factors.

- Fraudulent papers were more likely to be written by a repeat offender (e.g., an author who had prior retractions).

- In the United States, more papers were retracted due to fraud than for error in comparison to other countries.

More recent data focusing on retractions of plagiarized articles from all disciplines shows that authors from China and India had the most retractions between 2010 and 2019 (see Figure 7.2). In fact, Chinese authors had more than twice as many articles retracted due to plagiarism between 2010 and 2019 than authors from the United States did. At the same time, other countries such as Germany, Canada, France, and Pakistan had plagiarized articles retracted less frequently than U.S. authors did.

FIGURE 7.2 ■ Countries With 30 or More Articles Retracted Due to Plagiarism, 2010–2019

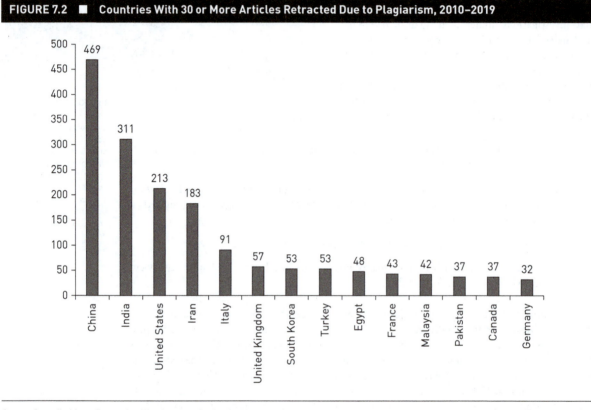

Source: Compiled from Retraction Watch: retractiondatabase.org

Historically, social scientists (criminologists in particular) have paid very little attention to research misconduct. One of the first criminological examinations of research misconduct was a comprehensive study reviewing cases of misconduct reported to federal agencies by Ben-Yehuda and Oliver (2017). The authors point to the interesting balance the scientific community wants to maintain. Specifically, scientists have the capacity to detect and respond to misconduct, but they don't want to detect too much of it because such findings would call into question the veracity of a wide swath of research. At the same time, as Reinhart (2019) noted in reviewing Ben-Yehuda and Oliver's book, focusing on research misconduct helps to understand science more generally—how knowledge is developed, the underlying processes promoting the spread of knowledge, and so on. In Reinhart's words, "Incriminating scientific work routinely raises issues not just of what constitutes the factual truth in a specific case but of what the general standards for scientific truth claims should be" (p. 1599). In other words, studying research misconduct makes science stronger.

Ghostwriting

Ghostwriting refers to situations in which professors or researchers have their work written by someone else, but the professor's name appears on the work. Typically, "papers are produced by companies or other parties whose names do not appear as authors" (Lederman, 2009). Situations where university professors allow their names to be put on papers written by ghost authors hired by pharmaceutical companies have been described as "distressingly common in top medical journals" (Basken, 2009). In some cases, the real author's name appears on the article along with a top scientist who did not actually contribute to the article. In these cases, the top scientists can be labeled "honorary" authors, though in print it appears that they were actually contributing authors.

A study of ghostwriting and honorary authorship published in the *Journal of the American Medical Association* found the following rates of ghost authorship and use of honorary authors among six top medical journals in articles published in 2008: 26% of the articles had honorary authors, 8% had ghostwriters, and 2% had both honorary and ghostwriters (Wislar, Flanagin, Fontanarosa, & Dangelis, 2010). This means that more than one third of the articles published in the top medical journals listed authors who actually should not have been listed!

Research shows that ghostwriting occurs more in research articles than in reviews and editorials (Wislar et al., 2010). In an effort to limit the extent of ghostwriting, many journals now ask authors to sign a form indicating that they are the only authors of the manuscript and that all of the authors listed did, in fact, contribute to the manuscript. Penalties imposed by journals on ghostwriters might include a ban on submitting future articles, retraction of article, and/or notifying the author's institution (Stern & Lemmens, 2011). For the record, the author of this book is no ghost, and he certainly isn't an honorary author.

PECUNIARY-ORIENTED OFFENSES

In this context, **pecuniary-based offenses** include misbehaviors that are committed by professors for the economic gain that comes along with the commission of the offenses. Four varieties of pecuniary-oriented offenses exist, as follows:

- Embezzlement

- Textbook fraud

- Double billing

- Engaging in unapproved outside work

Embezzlement

Faculty embezzlement occurs when faculty members or college and university staff members steal funds from an account to which they have access. Consider a case where a faculty member was accused of embezzling "$185,000 in grant money on strippers, sports bars and iTunes" (Silverman & Almasy, 2020). In another case, a professor was using NSF funds to pay a media company for services delivered to the grant-funded project as well as services given to a company owned by the professor's wife (National Science Foundation, 2019b).

Not all cases of embezzlement by college professors necessarily result in large dollar losses. One scholar, a former professor of anthropology at John Jay College, was accused of stealing $5,000 in grant funds to fund personal trips, purchase heroin, and buy ABBA CDs, an allegation that one author called "the most heinous accusation—a crime against humanity" (Morris, 1999). Incidentally, the charges against him were eventually dropped but not before he lost his job.

Textbook Fraud

Textbook fraud, in this context, refers to instances where faculty sell the complimentary textbooks they receive from publishers to book dealers who resell the books. Some faculty may see nothing wrong with these activities. As a new faculty member, I recall my then-dean's take on this issue. He explained that our college at the time viewed it as unethical and inappropriate to sell textbooks that we had requested from publishers; however, it was legitimate in his view to resell textbooks that we did not actually request from the publisher but received as part of an unsolicited marketing campaign. Not surprisingly, research shows that faculty members view it as more ethical to sell unsolicited books than to sell solicited books (Robie, Kidwell, & King, 2003). To prevent these behaviors, many colleges and universities have express, written policies forbidding the selling of complimentary textbooks under any circumstances. Some of these policies even state that book dealers are not permitted on campus.

More than 20 years ago, it was estimated that publishers lost $60 million a year to these activities (Sipes, 1988). The practice appears to remain widespread and likely costs publishers far more today. A survey of 236 faculty from 13 community colleges and universities found that 30% of the sample had resold complimentary books in the prior year, and they made $80 per sale on average (Robie et al., 2003).

To address this, some publishers stamp the word "complimentary" or "not for resale" on many of the textbooks' pages, others put the professor's name on the book, and some even tell professors that if they do not plan on using the book, they can return it to the publisher, which will make a donation to charity for each returned complimentary book received (Hamermesh, 2009).

For the record, if faculty try to sell their complimentary copies of this book to book dealers, an invisible ink will explode all over both the faculty member and the book dealer.

Double Billing

Faculty double billing occurs when professors bill more than one source for the same effort of work or reimbursement. Examples of double billing include (a) instances where professors bill two sources for the same travel reimbursements and (b) instances where faculty bill multiple universities for the same instructional effort. In one case involving double billing for travel reimbursements, one professor resigned after being placed on unpaid leave after being allegedly caught double billing travel expenses for $150,000. What makes his case particularly interesting is that he was—at the time—the head of Yale's International Institute for Corporate Governance (Sherman, 2005). Sherman (2005) quotes the *Wall Street Journal* as describing the professor as "a strong advocate of prompt disclosure of financial misdeeds."

Engaging in Unapproved Outside Work

Faculty working full time for a college or university also commit workplace offenses by engaging in outside work that is not approved by the institutions. Four overlapping types of conflicts arise with unapproved outside work: (1) research-based conflicts of interest, (2) teaching and service-based conflicts of interest, (3) time-based conflicts of interest, and (4) national conflicts of interest. With regard to research-based conflicts of interest, colleges and universities have policies restricting outside work to ensure that the institution's research agenda does not seem to be influenced by specific companies. For example, medical schools would not want their research to appear to be partial to certain pharmaceutical companies. As a result, these schools limit the amount of consulting and outside work that professors can do with such companies.

In terms of teaching and service-based conflicts of interest that arise from unapproved outside work, when full-time faculty are hired by colleges and universities, the institution in effect "owns" that person's efforts for the duration of the contract. Institutions gain notoriety when certain professors are on their payrolls. Also, having the best professors at a college or university allows institutions to promote their educational mission by suggesting that students will be exposed to some of the greatest minds in higher education. By forbidding outside work, administrators are able to maintain their competitive edge and keep professors from working for their competitors.

In terms of time conflict and unapproved outside work, the expectation is that full-time faculty will work 40 hours a week in performing teaching, research, and service activities. The reality is that most faculty likely work in excess of 55 hours a week on these activities. A handful, however, may actually work fewer hours in teaching, conducting research, and engaging in service activities.

Those who have unapproved outside jobs, for example, might be unable to meet the hourly obligations of a full-time job in higher education. Rarely would these behaviors be treated as illegal criminally, but professors could face formal or informal repercussions from their supervisors or university administrators for these behaviors. If your white-collar crime professor, for instance, routinely canceled class because of outside work (or other unapproved reasons, for that matter), your professor could be subject to a range of potential disciplinary actions. In some instances, canceling even one class could be problematic, and I suspect that readers are grossly disappointed when their professor cancels a class. Typically, colleges and universities will permit occasional cancellations as long as students are given an assignment that corresponds to the topic that students would have covered in class and the topic at hand.

The phrase "time theft," which has been used to describe when workers don't use their time appropriately, also applies to higher education (Butt, Tatlah, Rehman, & Azam, 2019). A research team from Pakistan observed the teaching of ten professors and found that the professors engaged in "time theft" nearly half the time, with the sample teaching only 53% of the time when the class was scheduled. Most often classes either started late or got out early. Sometimes they were canceled entirely (Butt et al., 2019). In the United States, researchers have included "absent" faculty as an item on the Teacher Misbehavior Scale (Kearney, Plax, Hays, & Ivey 1991). Research using the scale shows that course cancellations are a common type of instructor misbehavior identified by students (Kearney et al., 1991; Goodboy and Myers, 2015), though the behavior seemed to less common than in the Pakistan study. A survey of 233 U.S. students, for example, identified 1,783 instances of "teacher misbehavior," with 65 incidents of tardiness and 31 instances of poor "time management" identified by the sample (Goodboy and Myers, 2015). The same study identified time management problems as the eighth most frequent type of misbehavior among a list of 33 types of misbehavior.

The advent of online classes poses different issues in that classes would never be canceled. Most faculty who teach online actually spend more time engaging with their students than faculty spend in traditional courses. For full-time faculty, issues arise when faculty fail to correspond with students and instruct them in ways that are necessary in order to teach students adequately about the topic (in this case, white-collar crime). Again, faculty won't be criminally prosecuted for failing to meet the time demands of the class. Imagine if they were, and if they were actually sent to jail for abusing class time. The following conversation might occur in jail:

Street offender to professor: *Why are you in the pokey?*

Professor to street offender: *I canceled a few too many of my classes.*

Street offender to professor: *You know you're going to get beat up in here, right?*

National conflicts of interest are a related, albeit more serious, variety of unapproved work. These conflicts refer to instances when faculty and researchers in the United States violate laws and policies by sharing confidential or proprietary data with other countries. Currently, colleges and universities are facing intense scrutiny from federal authorities regarding their faculty members' connections to China. The Department of Justice has warned institutions of China's efforts to lure away and recruit faculty who would either knowingly or unknowingly give China trade secrets. These secrets would place the United States at risk for losing intellectual property profits from scientific advancements. These concerns have led the FBI to initiate proactive investigations searching for either conflicts of interest or outright espionage among college faculty. The investigations have supported the FBI's suspicions.

In one of the most attention-grabbing cases, a Harvard scientist was arrested for lying to the U.S. Department of Defense about his ties to China, including lying about a contract he signed with one of China's universities. The scientist, who had been a principal investigator on more than $18 million in grants funded by the U.S. government, was reportedly being paid $50,000 a month, in addition to an annual living expense of $150,000, from the Chinese university (Chappell, 2020).

It's not by accident that U.S.-based scholars end up sharing information with the Chinese government. China has 200 plans to recruit entrepreneurial and scientific talent that could help the country expand its intellectual property base, which translates directly to profits for the country. The most prominent plan is the Thousand Talents Plan, which targets U.S. scientists "who focus on or have access to cutting edge research and technology" (Permanent Subcommittee on Investigations, 2019). Faculty would essentially be receiving two paychecks for the same work: One would come from the United States, and one would come from China.

A few cases announced by the U.S. Department of Justice provide further insight into these conflicts. In one case, while on parental leave for a newborn child, a professor spent roughly three months working in China and being paid by the Chinese Academy of Science. He was being paid in full, at the same time, by his U.S. university (USDOJ, 2020, March 10). Other Department of Justice cases include the following:

- A professor was convicted of failing to pay taxes on $500,000 in income he made from Chinese universities while simultaneously working at a U.S. university (U.S. Department of Justice, 2020, May 11b).

- A professor was arrested after failing to report ties to a Chinese university in an application for funding from a U.S. federal agency (U.S. Department of Justice, 2020, May 11a).

- After receiving NASA funding, an engineering professor was arrested for not revealing that he had ties to China (U.S. Department of Justice, 2020, February 27).

A review by the U.S. Senate was critical of the FBI's initial response to China's efforts to recruit researchers and professors from the United States (Permanent Subcommittee on Investigations, 2019). The Senate believed the FBI was slow in initially responding to the China threat after learning about the recruitment plans. Another criticism was that federal law enforcement agencies did not create a coordinated effort to respond to the threat posed by China. The Senate also criticized the FBI for its decision to disband the agency's National Security Higher Education Board. In addressing the criticisms and the federal response, the Senate included specific descriptions of cases. Three patterns in these cases are noteworthy. First, unlike other forms of research misconduct, these cases often have a group component. Second, the conflicts seem to be motivated by a desire for profit. Third, the cases tend to involve faculty and researchers from select STEM-H (Science, Technology, Engineering, Math, and Health) disciplines. (China doesn't appear to be recruiting criminologists in their efforts!)

SEXUAL HARASSMENT

Sexual harassment refers to a range of behaviors where employees perform sexually inappropriate actions against their colleagues or students. Legal definitions of sexual harassment suggest that sexual harassment is "any unwelcome or unwanted sexual attention [that affects] an individual's job, raise, or promotion" (Andsager, Bailey, & Nagy, 1997, p. 33). Fitzgerald (1990) identified four categories of sexual harassment:

- **Gender harassment:** sexist remarks and behavior

- **Seductive behavior:** inappropriate sexual advances

- **Sexual bribery:** offering rewards for sex

- **Sexual coercion:** threatening punishment to get sex

For purposes of this book, sexual harassment offenses committed by college professors include (a) sexualized comments, (b) sexualized behaviors, (c) academic incest, (d) sexual relationships with students taking their classes, (e) grades for sex, and (f) rape.

With regard to **sexualized comments**, harassment occurs when professors make comments to students that are of a sexual nature. One criminal justice professor, for example, told a researcher that one of her former professors would "make comments about my breasts" (Stanko, 1992, p. 334). Note that simply using foul language is not in and of itself sexual harassment. Typically, the language would need to be of a sexual nature to be considered harassment. I recall one of my sociology professors who began the semester asking the class if anyone minded if he used the "f-word." He didn't use the phrase *f-word* when he asked—he actually said the word. And this really was the very first thing he said to our class that semester. Then, he even wrote the four letters making up the word in huge letters on the chalkboard (this was back when professors used the chalkboard to communicate course notes). The professor explained that by itself, the word is just a word. Depending on the context in which the word is used, the word will have different meanings, consequences, and ramifications. We knew that we would not be taking notes that day—other than writing one word in our notebook.

Sexualized behaviors go beyond comments and include actual activities of a sexual nature committed by the offending party. This could include staring, touching, groping, hugging, and a range of other behaviors. In some cases, such behavior may be unintentional, while in others it may be intentional.

Academic sexual relationships refers to consensual "student faculty relationships in which both participants are from the same department but not necessarily in a student-teacher relationship" (Skinner et al., 1995, p. 139). Surveys of 583 university students and 229 community college students by Skinner and her research team found that students tend to define such relationships as ethically inappropriate. Surveys of 986 students uncovered gender patterns regarding stereotypes about sexual harassment (Hippensteele, Adams, & Chesney, 1992). Perhaps not surprisingly, males were found to have more stereotypical attitudes. They were more likely than females to agree with statements such as, "it is only natural for a man to make sexual advances to a woman he finds attractive."

Sexual contact with students refers to instances where the professor has some form of direct contact of a sexual nature with students in his or her classes or under his or her supervision. Questions are sure to arise about whether sexual relationships are consensual or not between students and faculty. The types of policies that colleges have to address student-faculty relationships exist on a continuum. On one end of the continuum, some colleges and universities have either no policy or permissive policies that allow such relationships so long as they are consensual. At the other end of the continuum, other colleges and universities have more restrictive policies, with some even forbidding consensual relationships altogether. Not only do the policies exist on a continuum, but perceptions of harassment also exist on a continuum. Consider the following comments from a university dean:

A couple of weeks ago, a troubled member of staff came to see me for a confidential meeting. He had started a relationship with an undergraduate and thought he'd better confess. "She's a third year," he blurted, hoping this might mitigate the offense. "Oh, well, that certainly helps," I mused . . . wondering where I filed the number of the university attorney.

"Is she in your course?" [I asked]. She wasn't. She wasn't even in his department. I breathed a sigh of relief. At least he wasn't teaching her. (Feldman, 2009, p. 29)

Another type of sexual harassment in college settings involves professors awarding **grades for sex**. Euphemistically called "an A for a lay" (Fearn, 2008, p. 30), these situations use the power of grading in order to solicit sexual favors from students. Some experts contend that exchanging grades for sex "is accepted without question or noticeable comment by most members of the university community" (Reilly, Lott, & Gallogly, 1986, p. 341).

Recall from the introduction that different cultures define workplace misconduct in varying ways. Cross-cultural definitions of sexual harassment demonstrate this pattern. As an illustration of the cultural variations in defining sexual harassment, note that other countries—such as Britain—are more accepting of faculty-student romantic relationships (Fearn, 2008). Part of their openness to these relationships is based on the differences in the way that colleges function in Britain, as compared to the United States. In Britain, students tend to be slightly older, and faculty begin teaching at a younger age—making the age difference between faculty member and student less pronounced. Also, in the United States, the system of grading creates more power than what is found in grading systems used in Britain (Fearn, 2008). To put this in perspective, Fearn (2008) cites a British study that found that one fifth of "academics reported having sexual relations with a student".

Fearn is quick to note that an increasing trend in Britain is to be less tolerant of these sorts of relationships. Describing this trend firsthand, one British professor commented on her experiences as a student:

I have been chased around offices, leapt on in a lift, groped under . . . tables and been the recipient of unpleasantly explicit anonymous notes, and I do not think I am any different from any other woman of my generation. . . . I welcome the fact that today young women are sufficiently empowered to know that they have a right to complain about it. (Bassnett, 2006, p. 54)

Sexual harassment occurs in all academic disciplines, including criminal justice. A survey of 65 criminologists found that 59% of them experienced some form of sexual harassment during graduate school (Stanko, 1992). One third of the respondents said they were harassed in their field research by criminal justice professionals or by the subjects they were studying. The criminal justice professors described a range of harassment experiences, including the following:

- An ongoing problem occurred when I was a graduate assistant and actually ended up with the professor trying to kiss me. Most of the time, though, he simply managed to direct the conversation . . . to sex.

- My research professor would make comments about my physical attractiveness and invite me to dinner. I declined.

- Faculty told me as a graduate student that my demeanor was not feminine enough.

- At the interview for the RA position which led to my main fellowship in grad school, he grabbed me out of the blue and started kissing me. I did not know what to do, so I pulled away and continued as if nothing happened. He kissed me several more times, my response was the same. . . . On several occasions, he pulled up my shirt and fondled my breast. I started wearing fondle-proof clothes. (Stanko, 1992, p. 334)

The consequences of sexual harassment can be quite devastating for students—both in the short term and the long term. In the short term, being exposed to harassing experiences will make it more difficult for students to learn, which will affect their grades, mental health, and attachment to school. Students might change majors, transfer, or even drop out of college. Each of these decisions will have long-term consequences for victims of sexual harassment. As well, the experience of sexual harassment may impact the victim's own personal relationships with loved ones.

Describing her experience of being sexually harassed by her counseling professor, one former student wrote the following:

> My anxiety was of such concern that I began seeing a therapist. She helped me understand that I had certain personality traits that had made me a likely target for Professor X. I had always idealized teachers and had done so particularly with him. I had trusted him implicitly during a busy, stressful time. . . . My experience of being sexually harassed by my counseling professor has changed my life forever. I know that although the trauma has lessened considerably, it will never disappear. (Anonymous, 1991, p. 506)

As noted above, students who are harassed by their professors tend not to report their victimization to anyone. In fact, as compared to university employees, students are more likely to ignore the behavior, whereas employees are more likely to tell their supervisor or file a complaint (Kelley & Parsons, 2000). One study identified the following as reasons that students, in this case medical students, chose not to report their harassment experience: (a) loyalty to the "team," (b) seen as not serious enough, (c) reporting defined as a weakness, (d) reporting defined as futile, and (e) concern about repercussions on future evaluations (Wear, Aultman, & Borges, 2007).

Of course, colleges are not the only workplace where sexual harassment occurs. The topic was discussed in the context of colleges and universities because, as students, readers will likely better understand the topic by seeing it through the lens of students. What is going on in colleges and universities simply reflects activities that occur in other systems. Unfortunately, what this means is that you won't escape the risk of sexual harassment when you graduate from college. Instead, when you enter your careers, you will be confronted with the potential for different types of sexual harassment.

SEXUAL ABUSE

Sexual abuse refers to nonconsensual sexual contact that offenders have with victims. Sexual abuse cases occur in all systems—the justice system, religious system, health care system, political system, and so on. While some case dynamics are consistent across all sexual abuse cases (such as the unequal power dynamics and trauma), other dynamics in sexual abuse cases are often influenced by the system in which the abuse occurs. To fully understand these dynamics, it is helpful to review two prominent cases: the Penn State Jerry Sandusky case and the Michigan State Larry Nassar case.

Jerry Sandusky was an assistant football coach to Penn State's legendary coach Joe Paterno. Most people probably never heard of Sandusky until November 2011 when it was announced that he was being indicted on more than 50 counts of sexually abusing minors at Penn State. When specific details became public, allegations began to surface that officials at Penn State had failed to protect the young victims. After retiring from his coaching position, Sandusky was permitted to continue to work at Penn State football camps and to use the football facilities. An investigation revealed that at one point, officials were told that Sandusky was seen molesting a boy in the shower. The officials later denied that they were told about the incident and those specific terms and said they were told that Sandusky engaged in horseplay. Regardless of what they were told, they chose to handle the case internally. The officials told Sandusky not to return to campus; they did not alert the authorities about the report. Some believe this allowed him to continue to sexually abuse other victims.

In terms of white-collar crime, the behavior of the officials who had a duty to protect those visiting the campus is relevant. The negative publicity poured down on Penn State soon after the indictment was announced. The Board of Trustees fired Paterno and university President Graham Spanier. Paterno never had the chance to defend himself, dying weeks after Sandusky's indictment.

Reviewing the grand jury reports and other records, *CNN* editorial researchers provided a detailed timeline of the Penn State scandal. The following is a summary:

- March 2, 2002: Graduate assistant Mike McQueary stops by Joe Paterno's home and tells the Hall of Fame coach that the night before, he saw retired assistant coach Jerry Sandusky engaging in inappropriate behavior with a ten-year-old boy in the shower. The next day, Paterno tells athletic director Tim Curly. McQueary is subsequently asked to meet with Curly and senior vice president for finance and business Gary Schultz to share what he saw. The graduate assistant reportedly tells the officials that he saw the retired coach having anal sex with the boy. The officials later deny being told about the allegations.

- 2008: A mother contacts authorities and reports that Sandusky engaged in inappropriate behavior with her son. An investigation ensues. After telling Penn State officials he was being investigated, Sandusky is told not to return to campus. The subsequent investigation uncovers the 2002 allegations and focuses in on the fact that the officials never alerted authorities about the reports of inappropriate behavior. They did, however, tell Penn State President Graham Spanier about the allegations.

- November 4, 2011: The grand jury report is released after a thorough grand jury investigation. Sandusky is indicted on sexual abuse charges, and Curly and Schultz are arraigned and resign from their positions. The downfall of the Penn State officials is swift. Coach Paterno and President Spanier are fired within a week. Several years later, Curly and Schultz plead guilty to child endangerment and are sentenced to short jail terms. Spanier refuses to plead guilty and is convicted of child endangerment at trial. After being sentenced to jail, he appeals his conviction. The day before his jail term is to begin, a judge overturns the trial conviction on the basis that the law Spanier was convicted on didn't actually exist in 2001. Sandusky is convicted of sexually abusing 10 boys and is sentenced to 30-60 years in prison, which is effectively a life sentence (Penn State Scandal, Fast Facts, 2020, May 13).

It's been estimated that the scandal cost the university more than $250 million in settlements with victims, fines from the government, and penalties imposed by the NCAA (Associated Press, 2017, January 9). Much more significant, obviously, is the harm experienced by Sandusky's victims.

The Penn State scandal was the largest sex abuse scandal at a university until the Michigan State scandal came to light in 2017. Larry Nassar, a sports medicine doctor at Michigan State University and former director for USA Gymnastics, was accused of sexually abusing more than 500 women and girls over a two-decade timeframe. A subsequent congressional investigation was critical of groups that failed to stop the abuse. Groups that lawmakers believed should have done more to protect victims included Michigan State University, the U.S. Olympic Committee, USA Gymnastics, and the FBI (Chavez, 2019).

Michigan State University President Lou Ann Simon resigned just after the spring semester began in 2018 as a result of the public outcry. Former Republican Governor John Engler was appointed interim president with the university hoping that he could help them navigate the uncharted public relations nightmare. That fall, Simon was criminally charged by the state attorney general on grounds that she lied during the investigation about her knowledge of Nassar's behaviors. The following year, Engler was removed as president after making comments suggesting that some of the victims were "enjoying" the spotlight (McLaughlin, 2019). In May 2020, a judge dismissed the criminal case against Simon (Banta, 2020).

Nassar eventually pled guilty to sexual abuse. Prior to being sentenced, Nassar's victims were given the opportunity to address the judge and Nasar. They described horrific experiences of being molested hundreds of times by the doctor over the years. Nassar was sentenced to 175 years in prison. During the sentencing hearing, the judge told Nassar, "I just signed your death warrant." In charges related to the case, a jury found that William Strampel, Nassar's boss and dean of the College Osteopathic medicine, was found guilty for failing to oversee Nassar appropriately. In charges unrelated to the Nassar case, Strampel also was found guilty of "using his power as dean . . . to proposition and control female medical students" (Banta, 2019, August 7). He was sentenced to a year in jail.

The university paid a total of $500 million to the victims, with $425 million of that total going to "332 current claimants [and] $75 million set aside in a trust fund for any future claimants who allege abuse by Nassar" (Held, 2018).

The Michigan House of Representatives conducted an inquiry into how MSU responded to the Nassar case. Findings from the state investigation were included in a U.S. Senate investigation, which the university critiqued on the following five grounds, as excerpted from the senate report:

- Nassar spent decades developing his ability to abuse patients without detection, exploiting loopholes in the policies that governed his conduct.

- MSU did not have an adequate informed consent policy during much of Nassar's tenure, which he methodically exploited.

- MSU policies did not require a chaperone or other person to be present in the exam room during sensitive examinations or treatments. Nassar took full advantage of this on multiple occasions.

- MSU did not adequately track Nassar's activities regarding payments from patients or their insurers for treatments performed at his home and at Twistars

- MSU Title IX Office failed to properly investigate Nassar in response to the Title IX complaint filed by Amanda Thomashow in 2014. In addition, the MSU Title IX Office provided Thomashow a materially different version of its report than what was given to Nassar and other MSU officials. Specifically, Thomashow was given an incomplete version of the "Conclusion" section. (U.S. Senate Olympics Investigation, 2019, p. 60)

The U.S. Senate report also cited a special counsel investigation that found 13 instances since 1997 when individuals reported seemingly inappropriate behavior by Nassar to MSU officials, with just one of those allegations resulting in an investigation.

After subsequent investigations by the Office of Civil Rights and the Department of Education's office of Federal Student Aid, the U.S. Department of Education was critical of the university's handling of the Nassar case. The following four findings were found in that investigation:

- Finding #1: Failure to Properly Classify Reported Incidents and Disclose Crime Statistics

- Finding #2: Failure to Issue Timely Warnings in Accordance with Federal Regulations

- Finding #3: Failure to Identify and Notify Campus Security Authorities and to Establish an Adequate System for Collecting Crimes Statistics From all Required Sources

- Finding #4: Lack of Administrative Capability (USDOE, 2019)

As a result of the investigation, the university was ordered by the U.S. Department of Education to

- employ an independent *Clery* Compliance Officer, who will report to a high-level executive;

- establish a new *Clery* Compliance Committee that includes representation from more than 20 offices that play a role in campus safety, crime prevention, fire safety, emergency management, and substance abuse prevention; and

- create a system of protective measures and expanded reporting to better ensure the safety of its student-athletes in both intercollegiate and recreational athletic programs. Similar steps will be taken to better ensure the safety of minor children who participate in camps or other youth programs that are sponsored by the University or that are held on its properties. (USDOE, 2019)

The OCR investigation substantiated Title IX violations and concluded that the university "failed to take appropriate interim measures to protect its students while complaints against Nassar and Strampel were pending, and failed to take prompt and effective steps to end any harassment, eliminate the hostile environment, and prevent any further harassment from recurring" (USDOE, 2019). The investigation also led to the largest Title IX fine ever—$4.5 million. Though it was the largest USDOE Title IX fine ever, the penalty was seen as insignificant by many. Tiffany Lopez, a former MSU softball player and one of the first to tell her trainers about Nassar, made the following comments about the USDOE announcement: "I fear that the inadequate penalty they imposed will not stop other universities from hiding the crimes of sexual abusers on their campuses" (Siemaszko, 2019).

DISCIPLINING PROFESSORS

Some professors actually ended up in prison for their wrongdoing, but these cases are typically ones where quite serious wrongdoing occurred. Even more rarely are criminal sanctions applied to researchers who fabricate research findings. Eric Poehlman, a former tenured professor at the University of Vermont, became the first scientist jailed for research misconduct in the United States after he "pleaded guilty to lying on a federal grant application and admitted to fabricating more than a decade's worth of scientific data on obesity, menopause, and aging" (Interlandi, 2006).

Incidentally, the fraud came to light when Walter DeNino, one of his former students who had become a lab worker for Poehlman, noticed some discrepancies in the lab reports. DeNino viewed his professor as a mentor but still notified university administrators about his concerns—which eventually panned out after an investigation. His former student was in the courtroom when Poehlman pleaded guilty. The disgraced professor apologized to his former student (Interlandi, 2006). Poehlman was sentenced to 366 days in federal prison. His case has been described as the "most extensive case of scientific misconduct in the history of the National Institutes of Health" (Kintisch, 2006). One can only imagine what DeNino went through as he mulled over the decision to report his former professor to administrators. Think about it— would you report your professor for misconduct?

As one journalist points out, "Rare is the scientist who goes to prison on research misconduct charges." (Reardon, 2015). But with increased congressional oversight from political leaders, including Iowa Senator Charles Grassley, we are beginning to hear of more prosecutions for these cases. In a recent prosecution, an Iowa State University biomedical scientist was sent to prison for nearly five years after pleading guilty for lying to the National Institutes of Health in his grant submissions and grant reports. The researcher falsified results of his research by spiking blood samples so that it appeared a vaccine made the blood immune to HIV (Reardon, 2015).

Obviously, lying about such a vaccine has enormous implications for the safety of individuals who might have eventually used the vaccine.

Very few professors end up prosecuted in the criminal justice system for their misdeeds; more often, administrative sanctions are applied by the university. Common types of discipline against professors include (a) oral reprimands; (b) written reprimands; (c) recorded reprimands; (d) loss of benefits for a period of time, such as forgoing a raise; (5) restitution; (6) fines; (7) salary reductions; (8) suspensions with or without leave; (9) dismissals; (10) tenure revocations; and (11) departmental reassignments (Euben & Lee, 2005). A number of court cases have focused on the appropriateness of these sanctions after professors sued for being disciplined. Table 7.1 provides an overview of some of these cases. One thing that stands out in these cases is that the courts have tended to uphold the sanctions unless it was clear that the professor's rights were violated. For example, the courts have said that professors cannot be placed on unpaid leave until after a hearing has occurred (Euben & Lee, 2005).

TABLE 7.1 ■ Legal Decisions Regarding Faculty Discipline

Case	Sanction	Action	Judicial Decision
Hall v. Board of Trustees of State Institutions of Higher Learning	Warning/reprimand	Faculty member touched a student's breasts after she asked a question about mammograms	Sanction did not violate the faculty member's rights
Newman v. Burgin	Public censure	Plagiarism	Sanction was upheld
Wirsing v. Board of Regents of Univ. of Colorado	One-time denial of salary increase	Professor refused to use departmental evaluation forms	Sanction upheld
Williams v. Texas Tech University Health Sciences Center	Permanent salary reduction	University told him to bring in more grants, but he didn't	The university could do this, particularly because the faculty member was given 6 months to do so.
Edwards v. California Univ. of Pennsylvania	Paid suspension	Bad language in classroom	No violation of the professor's rights
Bonnell v. Lorenzo	Unpaid suspension	Suspended without pay pending hearing on sexual harassment charges	University must pay salary before hearings
Klinge v. Ithaca College	Demotion in rank	Professor plagiarized and was demoted from professor to associate professor	No violation of rights
McClellan v. Board of Regents of the State Univ.	Modified teaching assignments	Made sexual comments to students, was told he couldn't teach specific class for years	No violation of rights
Bauer v. Sampson	Mandatory counseling	Alleged to have anger management issues because of temperament	Violated free expression rights

Source: Adapted from Euben, D. & Lee, B. (2005). Faculty misconduct and discipline. In Presentation to National Conference on Law and Higher Education, February 22, 2005. Available from http://www.aaup.org/AAUP/programs/legal/topics/misconduct-discp.html

Also, note that the type of discipline will vary according to the type of misconduct. Faculty who "blow off " class a little too often would be subjected to one form of discipline, whereas those who fabricate data would be subjected to another form of discipline. Also, even within specific types of misconduct, different forms of discipline are necessary. For example, "no single punishment is appropriate for all sexual harassment cases, but it is the faculty member's misconduct, not his ideas, that should be punished" (Knight, 1995, as cited in Euben & Lee, 2005). The key is that behaviors are disciplined, not beliefs or ideas.

OPERATION: VARSITY BLUES

Thus far, attention has been given to crimes committed by those working in the educational system. In some cases, the offenses include outsiders who either target the educational system in their offending or who work with those inside the educational system to commit criminal acts. Operation: Varsity Blues, or the college admissions scandal, is an example of the latter. The scandal was perhaps the most headline-grabbing set of crimes occurring in higher education in recent times. Hollywood celebrities Lori Loughlin and Felicity Huffman, as well as many other well-off individuals, ended up pleading guilty to a range of criminal law violations. It was likely the celebrity of the *Fuller House* and *Desperate Housewives* stars that put the case in the headlines of a wide range of news and entertainment shows.

William Singer, an owner of a college prep business, was at the center of the scheme. Singer guaranteed students admission to top colleges in exchange for fees ranging from tens of thousands to more than one million dollars in some cases. Parents paid the fees (through direct payments, stocks, or some other method) as donations to a fake charity Singer ran. One of the tactics Singer used to guarantee admission was to have the students admitted as athletes; he would then collaborate with admissions and athletics officials to facilitate the admission. Another tactic was to charge parents to have an impostor take the students' college entrance exams such as the SAT or ACT. Figure 7.3 shows how the money flowed in the scheme.

FIGURE 7.3 ■ Operation: Varsity Blues Money Flow

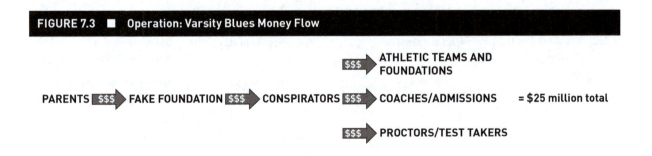

The scam was discovered almost by accident. A Los Angeles millionaire and financier, Morrie Tobin, was being investigated by federal authorities for securities fraud. Seeking leniency from the authorities, in March 2018, Tobin told justice officials about a Yale soccer coach he was bribing to help get his daughter admitted to the prestigious Ivy league school (Ormseth, 2020). Tobin agreed to meet with the coach and have the meeting recorded by law enforcement. During the meeting, Singer's name was mentioned, and the investigation unfolded from there.

The case eventually gained so much notoriety that the Department of Justice devoted an entire website to updates about it. The site posts public court materials including complaints, plea agreements, indictments, affidavits, and court decisions. Reading through the materials provides insight into the way that the rich and powerful can use their wealth to buy their way into elite universities. The following are a few highlights found in the case materials:

- Singer received $25 million in bribes over a seven-year timeframe.

- One tennis coach was paid $100,000 to designate a non-tennis player as a tennis recruit.

- Proctors were paid $10,000 to take or alter placement exams to improve the students' scores on those exams.

- A mother paid Singer $50,000 to arrange for a test taker to take the ACT in her son's name.

- One parent paid more than $550,000 in stocks to guarantee his son's admission to college.

- A father paid $300,000 to have his daughter identified as a basketball recruit in order to facilitate her admission into a prestigious university.

- Lori Loughlin paid $250,000 to get her daughter identified as a member of the crew team.

- Parents of one student paid more than $250,000 in Facebook stocks to have their daughter admitted to a prestigious university as a crew recruit. The father even asked Singer for a tax receipt so he could show that his "donation" was tax deductible.

- A father paid $220,000 to have his son recruited for the water polo team at a major university. Initially, the father was concerned that his son would not be very good at the sport. Singer assured him that the student would never actually join the team. After starting at the university, the son quit the water polo team.

- One father paid one million dollars to guarantee his daughter's admission to an elite institution.

- One of Singer's clients paid him $1.2 million to get his daughter admitted to an Ivy league school as a soccer player.

- Institutions where students were fraudulently admitted included USC, UCLA, Stanford, Wake Forest, Yale, University of San Diego, and others.

Fifty defendants—including parents, coaches, admissions officials, athletics representatives, test administration employees—were charged in the scheme. The evidence was so overwhelming and well-presented that the vast majority of them pled guilty. Huffman was sentenced to 14 days in prison, a year of probation, 250 hours of community service, and fined $30,000. Loughlin initially indicated that she was taking her case to trial, but she changed her mind and pled guilty in May 2020. She was sentenced to two months in jail, two years of probation, 100 hours of community service, and fined $150,000. Both actresses experienced the ancillary consequence of reputational damage. This was particularly significant for Loughlin who reportedly lost a lucrative contract with the Hallmark Channel, an informal sanction certainly more damaging than anything the justice system imposed.

CRIMES IN THE EDUCATIONAL SYSTEM BY STUDENTS

Some may question whether crimes by students are actually white-collar crimes. In this context, it is argued that a broad conceptualization of white-collar crime that views white-collar crime as offenses committed in various occupational systems allows one to consider student offenses as white-collar misconduct. Three types of behavior by students, in particular, can be seen as white-collar crimes: (1) offenses students commit on their jobs, (2) academic dishonesty, and (3) Internet or digital piracy by college and university students.

With regard to offenses committed on their jobs, note that many of the occupational offenses discussed in earlier chapters of the book might actually entail crimes committed by students employed in those professions. Restaurants and other service industries, for instance, routinely hire students as employees. In addition to students as occupational offenders in jobs outside of the college or university setting, students have opportunities to commit white-collar crimes in their positions as student workers or students affiliated with university workers.

Academic dishonesty can also be seen as a variety of white-collar crime. On one level, students are "pre-professionals" seeking an education that will, everyone hopes, prepare them for their future professional careers. On another level, students assume the role of a "worker" in their efforts to pursue an education. They perform "work-like" activities as part of their coursework. Just as some workers in legitimate occupations break occupational rules and criminal laws while performing their jobs, some students break college and university rules (and various laws) while performing as students.

In this context, academic dishonesty can be defined as "intellectual theft" (Petress, 2003). One author cites estimates suggesting that between 63% and 75% of students self-report cheating (Iyer & Eastman, 2006). Interviews with 31 undergraduates found that the "students did not seem to have any deep moral dilemmas about plagiarism" (Power, 2009, p. 643). Plagiarism using information copied from the Internet has been described as a "monumental problem" (Strom & Strom, 2007, p. 108), with researchers noting that of the 30,000 papers reviewed in one popular plagiarism detection tool each day, "more than 30 percent of [the] documents include plagiarism" (Strom & Strom, 2007, p. 112).

Research on academic dishonesty has focused on the characteristics of dishonest students, the connections between academic dishonesty and white-collar crime, the causes of academic dishonesty, the role of instructors in academic dishonesty, and the appropriate response strategies and policies for limiting academic dishonesty. To gain insight into the characteristics of students who engage in academic dishonesty, Iyer and Eastman (2006) compared 124 business students with 177 nonbusiness students and found that business students were more honest than nonbusiness students. They also found that males, undergraduates, and members of fraternities and sororities were more likely be dishonest than females, graduate students, and students who are not members of fraternities and sororities. Focusing specifically on types of business students, one research team surveyed 1,255 business students and found that accounting majors were more honest than management majors (Rakovski & Levy, 2007). This study also found that males and students with lower grade point averages were less honest than females and students with higher grade point averages.

Examining the connection between academic dishonesty and crime at work, R. L. Sims (1993) surveyed 60 MBA students, asking about various forms of academic dishonesty and workplace misconduct. Sims found that respondents "who engaged in behaviors considered severely dishonest in college also engaged in behaviors considered severely dishonest at work" (p. 207).

Researchers have identified a number of potential predictors of academic dishonesty. Reviewing prior studies on academic dishonesty, one author team cited the following causes: (1) low self-control, (2) alienation, (3) situational factors, and (4) perceptions that cheating is justified (Aluede, Omoregie, & Osa-Edoh, 2006). A survey of 345 students found that the more television they watched, the more likely it was that they would engage in academic dishonesty (Pino & Smith, 2003). Some have argued that academic dishonesty is part of a developmental process "in which students learn to behave professionally and morally by making choices, abiding by consequences, and (paradoxically) behave immorally" (Austin, Simpson, & Reynen, 2005, p. 143).

In a rather interesting study that may raise some critical-thinking questions among readers, one professor focused on the ties between opportunity and self-control (Smith, 2004). The professor had his students complete a self-control survey at the beginning of the semester. Later in the semester, the professor returned exams to the students and told them that he did not have time to grade the exams. Students were told they would have to grade their own exams and were given a copy of an answer key to complete this task. In reality, the professor had made copies of all students' exams before returning them ungraded to the students. This allowed the professor to grade the students' exams and compare their "earned" grade with the grades the students gave themselves. Of the 64 students in the class, 30 scored their exams higher than they should have. The author found that opportunity seemed to play a role in fostering the academic misconduct and that low self-control was related to academic dishonesty. Incidentally, the students received the "earned" grade on their exams, and the professor waited until the end of the semester to tell them about his experiment.

Some researchers have focused on the college professor's role in promoting (and preventing) academic dishonesty. This chapter's White-Collar Crime in the News outlines the way that federal scientists recommend new professors communicate with their students about expectations. Surveys of 583 students found that an instructor's perceived credibility influenced academic dishonesty (Anderman, Cupp, & Lane, 2010). If students perceived a professor as credible, they were less likely to commit academic dishonesty in that professor's course. Somewhat referring to this possibility, one author commented, "the value of individual and collective honesty has to be taught, role modeled, and rewarded in schools; to neglect or refuse to do so is malfeasance" (Petress, 2003, p. 624). Also highlighting the professor's role in preventing academic dishonesty, D. E. Lee (2009) advises professors to practice role modeling:

- Demonstrate to students why academic dishonesty is wrong.

- Develop assignments and class activities that make it virtually impossible for students to engage in academic dishonesty.

- Promote and foster values of respect and honesty between students and faculty.

WHITE-COLLAR CRIME IN THE NEWS
COMMUNICATING YOUR IDEAS TO YOUR LAB GROUP

The following is a blog post from the Office of Research Integrity.

Things to Think About: *Things to Think About* is a new section of the ORI blog where members of the ORI staff communicate about ideas we have about the responsible conduct of research.

After countless years at the bench, you have landed your dream job—running your own research group. You got here through your own hard work. You are proud of your achievements, but now you need to train students and trust them not only with your resources but also with your ideas. Things are going well for the first

(Continued)

(Continued)

year or so. You are still working in the lab, so you have your hand in every project. You are modeling ideal work practices for your students so they are meeting your expectations.

Now you are moving into a phase of your career that is taking you out of the lab more and more. As you withdraw from the bench, you notice that your new students are not putting out the work that you expect from them. It doesn't make sense to you. Everyone knows that graduate students basically live in the lab, right?

Do you have a problem? You may need to ask yourself some questions:

- What are my expectations for my students?

- Are my expectations for my students reasonable?

- How clearly have I communicated my expectations to my students?

- Have I listened to my students' responses to my expectations?

- Are my expectations in line with the expectations of other mentors in the department?

- Do I expect my students to spend 40-60 hours a week in the lab; do I expect 100 hours?

- Do I expect my students to work completely uninterrupted throughout the work day or do I encourage breaks throughout the day?

Possible Approaches

Defining what your expectations are and assessing whether they are reasonable might be an important first step. Your students are not you. You may have gladly worked 100 hours a week during your graduate education, but your students may have different priorities and circumstances. They may have children. They may have health conditions that require them to rest more. They may have service commitments that they are not willing to sacrifice. In addition, they might have very different career goals than you did when you were a student. A Ph.D. student who wants to continue in research after completing her degree likely will have a very different view of lab work than a student who plans to work in science communication.

It can be difficult for a student to meet your expectations when you have not communicated them. How you communicate your expectations is up to you, but there are several approaches, which might include the following:

- You could create a new group member handbook for your students, which outlines your expectations in a clear and concise manner. Your students can refer back to the handbook if they ever have questions. This method also lends weight to your expectations because your students see that you've taken the time to write the guidelines down.

- Meeting with new members to let them know what you expect from them (and what they can expect from you) is another equally useful method of communicating your expectations. One benefit of having this conversation is that the student has a chance to respond to your expectations.

A dialogue about your expectations can help clear up any misunderstandings. For instance, you may have told your students that you expect 80 hours a week in the lab and you have students who are having trouble meeting that goal. They may tell you that they cannot meet that expectation because of their teaching responsibilities. You realize that you meant to say 80 hours a week of lab and teaching combined. If you are expecting something different from other groups in the department, explaining your reasoning to the students might bring clarity. Are there particular demands for the project that require the extra hours? How might it affect the number of publications? Could it lead to publications in higher-tier journals? What are you willing to help them do to find postdoctoral employment in prestigious research groups? These benefits may seem obvious to seasoned researchers, but new graduate students might not be able to see that far ahead.

Reprinted from U.S. Department of Health and Human Services. US Government

---

Source: https://ori.hhs.gov/blog/communicating-expectations-your-lab-group

Some authors have noted that professors can prevent (or at least detect) these offenses by implementing aggressive academic dishonesty policies and using available tools to identify cases of academic dishonesty. For example, computer software is available that detects cheating on multiple choice exams that use scantrons to score the exams. The software detects similar wrong answer patterns and alerts professors to possible academic dishonesty (Nath & Lovaglia, 2008). A popular company, Turnitin, provides software that reviews papers submitted in classes and identifies plagiarized papers. Turnitin has been hailed as a "potent weapon against academic dishonesty" (Minkel, 2002, p. 25). Students filed a lawsuit against Turnitin, arguing that the collection tool violated students' copyright ownership rights over the papers they wrote because the tool stored their papers in order to compare them with past and future submissions to Turnitin, and the company made money off of the students' papers. In 2008, a federal judge ruled that the software program does not violate copyright laws (Young, 2008).

Perhaps the most extreme form of academic dishonesty (though infrequent) is lying about one's academic credentials. Believe it or not, it's quite easy to fake one's academic credentials. There are actually online businesses that sell fake diplomas and academic transcripts (just like some underage students are able to buy fake drivers licenses showing they are of age to drink!). The ease with which people can purchase fake academic transcripts is why most businesses require official copies of transcripts be sent from the college or university when hiring new employees. This chapter's Streaming White-Collar Crime highlights one television show focused on the topic.

STREAMING WHITE-COLLAR CRIME   *Suits*: Faking a Law Degree

Plot	What You Can Learn	Discussion Questions
The series begins with Mike receiving a dream job as a lawyer for Pearson Hardman. Mike has all the qualities of an effective attorney—he's intelligent, likable, witty, and hardworking. He lacks just one thing: a law degree. To overcome this barrier, Mike manufactures a fake degree from Harvard. The series follows the escapades of Mike, his love interest Rachel Zane (played by Meghan Markle), his boss Harvey, and the rest of the law office.	If you lie about your degree, you will likely get caught. Academic transcripts are meant to be safeguards to keep individuals from lying about their credentials. For some professions, lying about the presence of a degree could result in a criminal prosecution.	Should people who lie about their degrees be criminally prosecuted? What can higher education institutions do to keep people from fabricating degrees?

Internet and digital piracy is another type of white-collar crime believed to be particularly popular on college campuses across the United States. This topic will be addressed in detail in the chapter focusing on computer crime. At this point, it is prudent to warn you that the authorities take digital piracy by college students seriously. Not long ago, Michel Crippen, a student at California State University, Fullerton, was arrested by Homeland Security officers after he modified "Xbox video game consoles to play copied games" (Sci Tech Blog, 2009). So, if you are sitting in your dorm room or at home near your computer, make sure that you haven't illegally downloaded materials from the Internet or stored illegally copied software on your computer. The next knock on your door could be Homeland Security officers coming to take you away. The irony is that the Homeland Security officers were once college students themselves. One can't help but wonder if they broke any rules when they were college students.

Summary

- In this chapter, attention was given to crimes committed by professionals and students in the educational system.

- Four types of misconduct that appear to be among the more common types of academic misconduct are research misconduct, ghostwriting, pecuniary-oriented offenses, and sexual harassment.

- Research misconduct refers to a range of behaviors that centers on researchers (many of whom are faculty members) engaging in various forms of wrongdoing during the course of their research. These forms of wrongdoing include, but are not limited to, fabricating data, masking findings, plagiarism, and treating research subjects unethically. Experts have noted that research misconduct is "real and persistent" (Herman et al., 1994).

- Researchers have suggested that plagiarism by professors is more likely to occur in the humanities and social sciences than in the hard sciences due to the nature of the disciplines.

- Research misconduct has severe consequences on several different levels. These consequences include (1) consequences for the individual faculty member, (2) financial consequences for the college or university, (3) morale consequences for the college or university, (4) image consequences for science, (5) consequences for members of society, and (6) consequences for various cultures.

- Because of the potential role that mentors have in contributing to misconduct, some have argued that mentors should play an active role in training their students how to conduct research appropriately.

- Ghostwriting refers to situations in which professors or researchers have their work written by someone else, but the professor's name appears on the work.

- Pecuniary-based offenses include misbehaviors that are ultimately committed by professors for the economic gain that comes along with the commission of the offenses. Four varieties of pecuniary-oriented offenses are embezzlement, textbook fraud, double billing, and engaging in unapproved outside work.

- Embezzlement occurs when faculty members or university staff steal funds from an account to which they have access.

- Textbook fraud refers to instances where faculty members sell complimentary textbooks that they receive from publishers to book dealers who resell the books.

- Double billing occurs when professors bill more than one source for the same effort of work or reimbursement.

- Faculty members working full-time for a college or university also commit workplace offenses by engaging in outside work that is not approved by the institutions. Four overlapping types of conflicts arise with unapproved outside work: (1) research-based conflicts of interest, (2) teaching and service-based conflicts of interest, (3) time-based conflicts of interest, and (4) nation-based conflicts of interest.

- Sexual harassment refers to a range of behaviors whereby employees perform sexually inappropriate actions against their colleagues or students.

- Sexual harassment offenses committed by college professors include (1) sexualized comments, (2) sexualized behaviors, (3) academic incest, (4) sexual relationships with students in class, and (5) grades for sex.

- Sexual abuse refers to instances when employees of the educational system engage in sexual contact offenses with victims. Cases of white-collar crime, in this context, include those times when businesses/institutions fail to protect individuals from abuse.

- Common types of discipline against professors include (1) oral reprimands; (2) written reprimands; (3) recorded reprimands; (4) loss of benefits for a period of time, for example, no raise; (5) restitution; (6) fines; (7) salary reductions; (8) suspensions with or without leave; (9) dismissals; (10) tenure revocations; and (11) departmental reassignments.

- Three types of behavior by college students can be seen as white-collar crimes: (1) offenses students commit on their jobs, (2) academic dishonesty, and (3) Internet piracy by college and university students.

Key Terms

Academic dishonesty   194

Academic sexual
     relationships   185

Faculty double billing   182

Faculty embezzlement   181

Gender harassment   185

Ghostwriting   181

Grades for sex   186

Pecuniary-based
     offenses   181

Research misconduct   174

Seductive behavior   185

Sexual bribery   185

Sexual coercion   185

Sexual contact with
     students   185

Sexual harassment   184

Sexualized behavior   185

Sexualized comments   185

Textbook fraud   182

Discussion Questions

1. Should it be illegal for professors and students to engage in romantic relationships with one another? Explain.

2. What are some similarities and differences between crime in the educational system and crime in the health care system?

3. Should professors be fired for plagiarism? Explain.

4. If professors have their names listed on articles they didn't actually write, would this violate the honor code established for students? Explain.

5. Who is responsible for preventing research misconduct?

6. If you found out that one of your professors committed research misconduct, would it change the way you evaluated him or her on the teaching evaluations? Explain.

7. If you were a professor, what would you do to stop cheating in your courses?

8. How can academic dishonesty be categorized as white-collar crime? Explain.

CRIME IN THE ECONOMIC SYSTEM

Many readers likely have Facebook pages. When visiting your friends' pages, tagging their photos, making cute comments on their posts, and posting information yourself, you likely have given very little thought to how Facebook relates to white-collar crime. Believe it or not, the social networking site relates to white-collar crime in five ways. First, some people (when they are supposed to be working) spend time lurking through their friends' Facebook pages. Second, some workers have actually lost their jobs over information they posted on Facebook pages. Third, the computer technology that makes Facebook possible is the same technology that provides the opportunity for computer crimes by white-collar offenders. Fourth, most experts agree that the social media platform was used by Russians aiming to disrupt the 2016 presidential election. Finally, Mark Zuckerberg—the founder of Facebook—has been accused of various white-collar misdeeds related to his creation of the website and the administration of it.

As an undergraduate student at Harvard, Zuckerberg worked for Divya Narenda and Cameron and Tyler Winklevoss on a social network called ConnectU. After his experiences at ConnectU, Zuckerberg created Facebook but was sued by his former bosses on the grounds that he stole ConnectU's source code to create Facebook. So, his first accusation of white-collar

PHOTO 8.1 From student to creator of Facebook, Mark Zuckerberg has faced his share of accusations of white-collar misconduct.

©iStockphoto.com/COM & O

crime was for copyright infringement (or theft of computer codes). Eventually, the parties reached an out-of-court settlement where ConnectU was sold to Facebook, and the owners were given $65 million, with much of the payment being in the form of shares in Facebook. Later, however, it was learned that the stocks included in the settlement agreement were actually worth much less than what the ConnectU creators were led to believe (Thomas, 2010). It was eventually determined that the settlement was paid in cheaper shares (known as common shares) rather than the more expensive shares (known as preferred shares). The result—the original owners appealed the out-of-court settlement and accused Zuckerberg of securities fraud in 2010 (Thomas, 2010). The court subsequently found in favor of Zuckerberg. More recently, Facebook agreed to pay a $5 billion penalty to the Federal Trade Commission (FTC) for privacy violations related to the 2016 election, and a $100 million agreement to the Securities Exchange Commission (SEC) for "misleading disclosures" (Feiner & Rodriguez, 2019).

The securities fraud accusation against Zuckerberg is an example of the kind of white-collar crimes occurring in the economic system. Zuckerberg is not alone in being accused of misconduct in the economic system. Consider the following examples quoted verbatim from their original sources:

- +++++, the former Chief Information Officer of Equifax U.S. Information Solutions, has been sentenced to federal prison for insider trading. On Friday, August 25, 2017, +++++ texted a co-worker that the breach they were working on "sounds bad. We may be the one breached." The following Monday, +++++ conducted web searches on the impact of Experian's 2015 data breach on its stock price. Later that morning, +++++ exercised all of his stock options, resulting in him receiving 6,815 shares of Equifax stock, which he then sold. He received proceeds of over $950,000, and realized a gain of over $480,000, thereby avoiding a loss of over $117,000 (USDOJ, 2019, June 27).

- According to court documents and statements made in court, between approximately 2009 and July 2016, ++++++++ conspired to defraud investors through a stock "pump and dump" scheme. ++++++++ and his co-conspirators induced investors to purchase securities by making false and misleading representations in calls, emails and press releases concerning the securities and the issuing companies, thereby causing the price of those securities to become falsely inflated. . . thereby enriching the members of the conspiracy (USDOJ, 2018, November 29).

- ++++++, +++++++, and +++++++ conspired along with others to obtain home loans from mortgage lenders based upon false and fraudulent loan applications and supporting documents that falsely represented the borrowers' assets and income, liabilities and debts, and employment status. They provided money to the borrowers in order to inflate their bank account balances. Once the loans were secured, the borrowers returned the money to the defendants. . . . As a result of the conspiracy, mortgage lenders and others suffered losses of at least $4 million (USDOJ, 2019, September 30).

- ++++ and others working at her direction falsely promised victims that their investments were risk-free and 100 percent guaranteed by CES's "collateral account" at Wells Fargo. She lulled her victims by creating fictitious Wells Fargo bank statements to show that CES had an account with a balance of $7.2 million, as well as fabricating emails she claimed were from an employee of Wells Fargo Asset Management. ++++ also falsely told investors that her companies were investing in properties that had been evaluated by the international valuation firm of Duff & Phelps. (USDOJ, 2019, December 19).

These examples demonstrate the breadth of offenses that are committed in the economic system. When the term *white-collar offender* comes to mind, it is often images of offenders from the economic systems that come to mind. Prominent white-collar offenders who committed crimes against at least one of these systems include Bernie Madoff, Kenneth Lay, Martha Stewart, and Michael Milken. While many people recognize these names, the actual behaviors that got them into trouble are less understood.

CRIME IN THE ECONOMIC SYSTEM

The economic system includes banks; investment companies; stock markets across the world; commodities markets; and other exchanges and markets where individuals are able to make investments, purchase raw materials, and secure goods. Generally speaking, crimes in the economic system can be classified as investment frauds and banking frauds. In describing these behaviors, real examples are discussed in order to better illustrate each offense type.

INVESTMENT FRAUD

Investment fraud occurs when investments made by consumers are managed or influenced fraudulently by stockbrokers or other officials in the economic system. *Securities and commodities fraud* is a broad concept capturing a range of behaviors designed to rip off investors. At the broadest level, securities fraud refers to fraudulent activities related to stocks, bonds, and mutual funds. Consider a case where Andrew McKelvey, the former head of the employment recruitment firm, Monster Nationwide Inc., was charged with fraud and conspiracy after he backdated several employees' stock options. In doing so, he fraudulently changed the value of their stock options. In another case, four executives were convicted after backdating contracts and filing false SEC documents, lying in press releases, and being dishonest with the company's own auditors (Taub, 2006). Again, these actions were done to increase the value of the company's stocks.

Commodities fraud is defined as the "fraudulent sale of commodities investments" (FBI, 2009). **Commodities** are raw materials such as natural gas, oil, gold, agricultural products, and other tangible products that are sold in bulk form. Consider a case where one offender was convicted after he persuaded 1,000 victims to invest in commodities such as oil, gold, and silver. The problem was that the commodities did not exist ("Kingpin of Commodities Fraud," 2006).

While "securities and commodities" fraud is a general label given to fraud in the economic system, several specific varieties of these frauds exist, including these:

- Market manipulation

- Broker fraud and embezzlement

- Insider trading

- Futures trading fraud

- Foreign exchange fraud, high-yield investment schemes, and advance-fee fraud

Each of these is discussed in the following sections. Because most white-collar crime students have likely had little exposure to the workings of the stock market and other financial institutions, where appropriate, analogies to the experiences of college students are made in an effort to better demonstrate the context surrounding the offenses. After discussing these fraud types, attention will be given to Bernie Madoff's historic scheme and patterns surrounding these offenses, with a specific focus on the consequences of these frauds for individuals, community members, and society at large.

Market Manipulation

Market manipulation refers to situations where executives or other officials do things to artificially inflate trading volume and subsequently affect the price of the commodity or security. This is sometimes called *pump and dump* because participants will "pump" up the price of the stocks by sharing false information in chat rooms, e-mail messages, or other forums before "dumping" (or selling) the stocks that have been artificially inflated (FBI, 2009).

A scene from the classic 1986 Rodney Dangerfield film *Back to School* comes to mind. Thornton Melon (the likable nouveau riche character Dangerfield was playing) was standing in a long line with his son and two of his son's friends, waiting to register for classes, when he thought of a way to make the line shorter. He had his chauffer stand in front of his limousine with a sign that read "Bruce Springsteen" on it. Eventually, word spread through the registration area that "The Boss" was in the limo, and all of the students stampeded out of the registration hall to get to the limo. Melon and the other three were immediately at the front of the line and able to register for their courses. In effect, Melon's lie had manipulated others to behave differently. In terms of market manipulation, officials share false information to get others to invest differently, and by dumping their own stocks after prices increase, they profit from their lies.

Market manipulation is believed to be pervasive in the natural energy industry, particularly in the gas and electricity markets. Not surprisingly, market manipulation has been described as a "contentious topic" in energy markets (Pirrong, 2010). Energy industry leaders make a distinction between "market power" manipulation and "fraud-based" manipulation. Market power manipulation strategies manipulate the market through aggressive buying and selling strategies. Fraud-based manipulation strategies manipulate the market by distorting information (Pirrong, 2010).

The Enron scandal included fraud-based market manipulations. Among other things, the energy giant's operatives "used names such as 'Fat Boy,' 'Death Star,' 'Get Shorty,'" and 'Ricochet' for programs to transfer energy out of California to evade price caps and to create phony transmission congestion" (Bredemeier, 2002, p. A04). The strategies allowed the company to charge a higher price for the energy it was supplying than what the energy was worth. Enron executives unjustly profited more than $1.1 billion from these efforts.

Three federal statutes exist to "prohibit manipulation of various energy commodities and empower federal agencies to impose penalties" (Pirrong, 2010, p. 1). These laws include the Commodity Exchange Act, the Energy Policy Act of 2005, and the Energy Independence and Security Act of 2007. The latter act, in particular, calls on the FTC to treat market manipulations by petroleum and oil company insiders as false and deceptive business practices that could be subject to fines of up to $1 million.

Technology has changed the landscape of market manipulation, making it easier to manipulate markets and spread false information or "fake news" that may impact investors (Petcu, 2018). From social media to artificial intelligence, offenders have leveraged technological advances to their benefit. While Thornton Melon's limo driver used an actual sign to mislead students, today a fake post on Instagram or the Facebook would spread more quickly than the news on Melon's sign did! Here are some "new" ways that offenders manipulate markets:

- Mass misinformation—using social media to share faulty information about markets, erroneous news about regulatory actions or other "fake" news

- Pinging—making several small electronic orders of financial instruments and canceling them for the sole purpose of driving up the price

- Spoofing—using computerized platforms to submit orders at high prices with the sole purpose of driving up the cost and quickly canceling the orders

- Electronic front running—using electronic technology to get useful information to inform subsequent sales and purchases, with even a millisecond of advance notice providing opportunities for significant economic benefit (Lin, 2017)

Also related to the impact of technology are cryptocurrencies such as Bitcoin, which allow for online investments without going through a central bank or authority. Cryptocurrencies are believed to be ripe "pump and dump" schemes where offenders will pump up information about cryptocurrencies in chat rooms, get offenders to buy the currency, and then dump the cryptocurrency before the price drops (Kamps & Kleinberg, 2018).

PHOTO 8.2 Experts believe that the cryptocurrency market is ripe for manipulative behaviors.

Broker Fraud and Embezzlement

Broker fraud occurs when stockbrokers fail to meet their legal obligations to investors. It is believed that "one of the most common frauds is brokers omitting important types of information that investors need to make intelligent decisions about where to put their money" (Knox, 1997, p. 56). Imagine your professor failed to tell you about the due date for a paper and then held you accountable for not turning the paper in on time. Omitting useful information can create negative consequences for investors.

Broker embezzlement occurs when brokers take money that is supposed to be in an investment account and use it for their own personal use (Ackerman, 2001). Trust is an important element of these offenses. Investor-broker relationships are built on trust. It is not uncommon to hear of situations in which fraudulent brokers developed that trust through forming relationships at various institutions that have historically been seen as trustworthy. Consider the case of Gregory Loles, a broker accused of stealing more than $2 million from three parishioners of St. Barbara's Greek Orthodox Church in Easton, Connecticut. Loles "allegedly used the funds to support his private businesses" (McCready & Tinley, 2009).

Insider Trading

Insider trading occurs when individuals share or steal information that "is material in nature" for future investments. The notion of "material in nature" means that the information "must be significant enough to have affected the company's stock price had the information been available to the public" (Leap, 2007, p. 67). Information in insider trading cases typically is either bought, stolen, or created (Frankel, 2018). Media mogul Martha Stewart was accused of insider trading after it was learned that she sold some ImClone stocks upon hearing that one of the company's drugs was not going to be approved. Ultimately, Stewart was convicted of perjury and not insider trading.

In testimony before the U.S. Senate Judiciary Committee, Linda Chatman Thomsen (2006), who at the time was the Director of the Division of Enforcement for the SEC, provided this historical overview of insider trading:

- In the mid-1980s, information that was illegally traded focused on information about pending takeovers and mergers.

- In the late 1980s and early 1990s, due to the recession, illegally traded information tended to be "bad news" information about upcoming company closings or downsizings.

- In the mid-2000s, illegally traded information tended to involve illegally obtained or distributed information about technology, globalization, mergers, and hedge funds.

Somewhat reflecting Thomsen's assertions, in 2007, *Wall Street Journal* reporter Kara Scannell (2007) penned an article titled "Insider Trading: It's Back With a Vengeance." Not coincidentally, Thomsen described insider trading as "an enforcement priority" at the time. Figure 8.1 shows recent increases in allegations of insider trading. The number of insider training allegations in the securities/futures industry found in suspicious activity reports filed with the Financial Crimes Enforcement Network went up by more than 150% between 2014 and 2019.

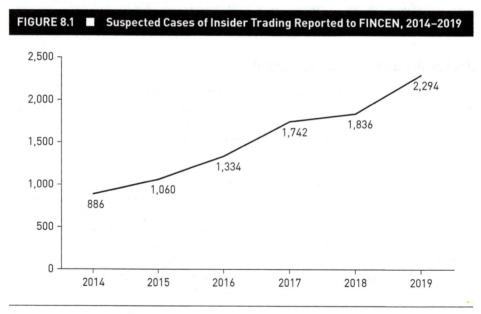

FIGURE 8.1 ■ Suspected Cases of Insider Trading Reported to FINCEN, 2014–2019

Source: Compiled from https://www.fincen.gov/fcn/Reports/SARStats

To put into perspective why insider trading is so unfair, imagine the student sitting next to you in your white-collar crime class is dating a student worker from the criminal justice department, and your classmate accesses copies of the exam ahead of time. In the end, the student would have an unfair advantage over the rest of the students in your class. In a similar way, those who receive material information about stocks and other investments have an unfair advantage over the rest of us. Of course, simply receiving the information is not in and of itself criminal; the action becomes illegal when the investor acts on the inside information.

By their very nature, these cases typically involve more than one offender, and in some cases, insider trading schemes may involve several offenders.

In a case demonstrating the "group" nature of insider trading, Yonni Sebbag was arrested along with his girlfriend, Disney employee Bonnie Hoxie, in May 2010. Hoxie, an administrative assistant at the resort, reportedly acquired insider information on Disney's quarterly earnings and shared that information with her boyfriend. He apparently anonymously contacted 33 different investment companies offering to sell the insider information. Several of the investment companies he called notified the authorities about Sebbag's offers (H. Johnson, 2010).

Insider trading is attributed to a number of factors, including an increase in the number of mergers, lightly regulated hedge funds, and more complex funding strategies (Scannell, 2007). Scannell also notes that the "rapid trading style" of hedge funds makes it "harder to pin trades on nonpublic information" (p. B1).

An ongoing issue making it harder to respond to these cases is the vagueness of insider trading laws (Gubler, 2020). There are times when use of nonpublic material information is not criminalized (La France et al., 2018). For instance, in some situations, investors and shareholders can act on information they have about a particular event or decision that may impact stock prices (Baumgartel, 2016). Consider the recent case where Moderna announced test results indicating that one of their products might be a successful COVID-19 vaccine. Shortly after the announcement, executives from the company sold some of their company shares and made millions from the sales. The sales were preplanned and legal, though they generated a great deal of attention from the press (Gandel, 2020). Had the executives shared their information with friends and relatives, and those friends and relatives acted on the information prior to the announcement, allegations of insider trading would have surely surfaced.

Insider trading concerns surfaced among Congress members when some congressional leaders made investment decisions prior to COVID-19; the investments appeared to be driven by information they received about the impending pandemic. One person facing scrutiny was former Senate Intelligence Committee Chair Richard Burr, who stepped down from this committee chair position after prosecutors executed a warrant searching for evidence of insider trading. The investigation reviewed stock sales potentially totaling $1.7 million that the senator and his wife made weeks before the pandemic wreaked havoc on the economy (Burns & Millhiser, 2020). In a tweet Burr sent on March 20, 2020, the senator claimed that his investing behavior was guided by public news, not news he got from his committee briefings.

Burr is not the only Congress person accused of insider trading during the 2020 pandemic. Senators Kelly Loeffler (GA–R), Dianne Feinstein (CA-D), and Jim Inhofe (OK-R) faced similar allegations at the same time Burr's allegations surfaced. The U.S. Department of Justice investigated the allegations and closed the insider trading investigation into these three senators without filing charges on May 26, 2020. The thrust of the investigation focused on the STOCK Act (Stop Trading on Congressional Knowledge), which guards against insider trading by political officials. The act provides guidelines that limit congressional officials' use of nonpublic information received in their governing capacity for economic gain (Frankel, 2018). Incidentally, when Congress passed the law in 2012, Senator Burr was one of three senators who voted against the legislation (Stockler, 2020).

Futures Trading Fraud

Futures trading fraud refers to fraud occurring in the trading of futures contracts and options on the futures trading market. **Futures contracts** are "agreement[s] to buy or sell a given unit of a commodity at some future date" (Schlegel, 1993, p. 60). Brokers "in the pits" buy and sell commodities based on a contract between the investor and the broker. The sale could be contingent on a specific date or a specific value of the commodity.

Schlegel (1993) describes several types of futures trading fraud, including prearranged trading, front running, and bucketing. Here is how he describes these schemes:

- **Prearranged trading**: "Brokers, or brokers and local brokers, first agree on a price and then act out the trade as a piece of fiction in the pit, thereby excluding other potential bidders from the offering. The prearranged deal ensures a given profit for the colluding traders while denying their customers the best possible price." (p. 63)

- **Front running**: "Broker takes advantage of the special knowledge about a pending custom order and trades on his or her own account before executing that order." (p. 63)

- **Bucketing:** "A floor trader will take a position opposite that of a customer's position, either directly or by using another floor trader, again in collusion." (p. 63)

In each of these actions, the broker unjustly profits from the fraudulent actions. To limit the extent of fraud in the futures markets, in 1974 the Commodity Futures Trading Commission (CFTC) was created.

Foreign Exchange Fraud, High-Yield Investment Schemes, and Advance-Fee Fraud

Other types of securities and commodities fraud include foreign exchange fraud, high-yield investment schemes, and advance-fee fraud. **Foreign exchange fraud** occurs when brokers or other officials induce "victims to invest in the foreign currency exchange market" through illegitimate and fraudulent practices (FBI, 2009). Typically, the frauds involve situations where offenders either don't provide the investor what was promised or simply take the funds and fail to perform the promised financial transaction.

High-yield investment schemes promise investors low-risk or even no-risk investment strategies, when in fact the funds are not actually invested (FBI, 2009). Sometimes offenders claim to the investor that the investment schemes are backed by the Federal Reserve or the World Bank, when they have no backing whatsoever (Behrmann, 2005). Investors are also told that they are being given access to a "prime" bank, thereby making investors falsely believe that they are a part of an exclusive group of investors in a "private club" (Welch, 2008). The offender fakes the investment and moves it through several international bank accounts, making "the chase futile for the original investors" (Behrmann, 2005).

Advance-fee fraud occurs when investors are promised certain actions in exchange for an up-front fee. Investors are pressured to invest and pay the broker and never receive any services. This is the top online scam reported to the SEC (Welch, 2008). Imagine your professor charging an advance fee for a study session—then, the professor doesn't show up for the event. Not only would you be ripped off, but you'd probably also be a bit angry at the professor.

PONZI AND PYRAMID SCHEMES

Ponzi and pyramid schemes scam investors by paying them from future investors' payments into the offender's scheme. Table 8.1 shows the differences between Ponzi and pyramid schemes. Pyramid schemes recruit individuals by promising them profits from getting others to invest, whereas Ponzi schemes do not require participants to recruit investors. In pyramid schemes, the participants' interactions are generally limited to interactions with the investor who got them to join the scheme; in Ponzi schemes, interactions are often with the individual who created the scheme. The source of payments in both schemes is from new participants—those in pyramid schemes know this, but those in Ponzi schemes do not. Pyramids collapse quickly, but Ponzi schemes may not (SEC, 2009). A recent study suggested that Ponzi and pyramid schemes are perpetrated through deliberate information delivered in trusting relationships, with the offender socially embedded in a high-status group, and technological changes and promises of high returns have increased the "lure" of these offenses (Nolasco, Vaughn, & del Carmen, 2013).

TABLE 8.1 ■ Differences Between Pyramid and Ponzi Schemes		
	Pyramid Scheme	**Ponzi Scheme**
Typical "hook"	Earn high profits by making one payment and finding a set number of others to become distributors of a product. The scheme typically does not involve a genuine product. The purported product may not exist, or it may be "sold" only within the pyramid scheme.	Earn high investment returns with little or no risk by simply handing over your money; the investment typically does not exist.
Payments/profits	Must recruit new distributors to receive payments.	No recruiting necessary to receive payments.
Interaction with original promoter	Sometimes none. New participants may enter scheme at a different level.	Promoter generally acts directly with all participants.
Source of payments	From new participants—always disclosed.	From new participants—never disclosed.
Collapse	Fast. An exponential increase in the number of participants is required at each level.	May be relatively slow if existing participants reinvest money.

Source: U.S. Securities and Exchange Commission

To illustrate how these schemes are developed, consider the basic definitions of the schemes. Here is how the SEC defines **Ponzi schemes**:

A Ponzi scheme is an investment fraud that involves the payment of purported returns to existing investors from funds contributed by new investors. Ponzi scheme organizers often solicit new investors by promising to invest funds in opportunities claimed to generate high returns with little or no risk. In many Ponzi schemes, the fraudsters focus on attracting new money to make promised payments to earlier-stage investors and to use for personal expenses, instead of engaging in any legitimate investment activity. (SEC, 2009)

Ponzi schemes have received a great deal of scrutiny in recent times. To understand the increase in these schemes in the United States, it is helpful to understand the history of the schemes. Charles Ponzi was the mastermind behind the first Ponzi scheme. He developed a scheme in 1919 in which he persuaded investors to invest in an international postage stamp program. He paid off early investors with funds contributed by new investors. His scheme was uncovered when *The Post* asked Clarence Barron, who published the *Barron's Financial Report* at the time, to review Ponzi's company. Barron learned that Ponzi's investors were making significant profits without Ponzi actually investing any money. A federal investigation followed, and Ponzi eventually pleaded guilty and served just under four years in federal prison. After his federal prison stay, he was convicted in state court and sentenced for seven to nine years as a "common and notorious thief" (Zuckoff, 2005, p. 305). Today, his legacy is not as a common offender but as a notorious white-collar criminal.

Today, Ponzi schemes seem to be so common in the United States that some have referred to the country as "a Ponzi nation" ("A Ponzi Nation," 2009). One author labeled 2009 as the "Year of the Ponzi" (C. Anderson, 2010). In 2009, 150 Ponzi schemes collapsed, as compared to 40 in 2008. Also, in 2009, one fifth of the SEC's workload was directed toward responding to Ponzi schemes. By comparison, in 2005, just one tenth of their workload was for Ponzi schemes. C. Anderson (2010) notes that the financial crisis brought the scams to light more quickly. Investors, in need of funds to respond to the economic downturn, tried to withdraw from their investments, only to learn that their investor was actually operating a Ponzi scheme.

Establishment and maintenance of trust have been identified as central components to Ponzi schemes (Carey and Webb, 2017). One-way offenders maintain trust is by falsifying documents to make it virtually impossible for victims to identify the scheme (Nash, Bouchard, & Malm, 2017). In fact, a study of 559 victims of one Ponzi scheme found that those who did their "due diligence in the beginning of the fraud increased [their] initial investments and also subjected them to greater losses" (Nash et al., 2017, p. 85). The maintenance of trust allows offenders to continue the scheme for years, with occasional "payments" that are actually just investments from new victims placing their trust in the offender.

This chapter's White-Collar Crime in the News describes a recent case where trust was central to these cases.

WHITE-COLLAR CRIME IN THE NEWS
LAWYER USES TRUST IN $2.7 MILLION PONZI SCHEME TO RIP OFF CLIENTS

The following is a press release from the Eastern District of Pennsylvania from April 23, 2020.

PHILADELPHIA—United States Attorney William M. McSwain announced that +++++++, 60, of Nazareth, PA, pleaded guilty today to one count of conspiracy to commit securities fraud and wire fraud, two counts of securities fraud, and four counts of wire fraud. United States District Judge Edward G. Smith presided over the guilty plea hearing in Easton via video teleconference.

+++++++, an attorney licensed to practice law in Pennsylvania, perpetrated a multiyear securities fraud scheme that targeted his own law clients. The scheme involved the fraudulent sale of the securities of two entities, THL Holdings, LLC and Ferran Global Holdings, Inc. +++++++ raised funds for the two companies by soliciting investments from his clients, telling them that their money would be used for a variety of business opportunities which were, in fact, non-existent.

+++++++ initially sold THL Holdings investments, promising that the money raised would be used to pursue specific business opportunities, including mining operations in Papua New Guinea and the acquisition of the shares of a penny stock. In reality, the money was used for +++++++'s personal expenses and to make Ponzi scheme payments to prior investors, among other things. Once +++++++ realized that he was running out of investor money to pay the THL Holdings investors, he sought investors for a second entity, Ferran. He told the Ferran investors that their money would be used for business opportunities, including even more mining in Papua New Guinea and residential property leases in Spain and England—but, in fact, these funds were used to repay the prior THL Holdings investors and for +++++++'s personal expenses to fund his lifestyle. Among these personal expenses were his home mortgage, his child's school tuition, utility bills, and other personal debt. Total investor losses are estimated to be over $2.7 million.

Even after he was caught, +++++++ continued his deception by lying in sworn testimony before the U.S. Securities and Exchange Commission (SEC). In this testimony, +++++++ denied writing checks to his personal accounts from the THL Holdings accounts, when, in fact, he had written at least 25 separate checks to himself over a three-year period.

In addition to these criminal charges, the SEC filed a parallel civil enforcement action in the Eastern District of Pennsylvania last month based on the same course of conduct. The SEC Complaint charges +++++++ and another individual, ++++++++, with multiple securities fraud violations and seeks disgorgement, prejudgment interest, civil money penalties, and injunctions against future violations of the federal securities laws against both defendants.

"+++++++ targeted the very people to whom he owed a duty of loyalty: his own law clients," said U.S. Attorney McSwain. "He stole millions of dollars from innocent victims who trusted him to serve as their lawyer and provide wise counsel. He betrayed them and served his own greedy impulses instead. My Office will continue to aggressively pursue securities and other financial frauds, particularly when perpetrated by lawyers and other industry professionals who are supposed to protect the rule of law, not defile it."

"+++++++'s clients felt comfortable investing with their trusted lawyer, expecting he would act in good faith," said Michael J. Driscoll, Special Agent in Charge of the FBI's Philadelphia Division. "In reality, +++++++ was inventing these great business opportunities, investing client funds only in himself and his teetering Ponzi scheme. The FBI is gratified to help bring to justice the perpetrator of such blatant and damaging fraud."

Reprinted from US Department of Justice.

Source: https://www.justice.gov/usao-edpa/pr/lehigh-valley-attorney-pleads-guilty-orchestrating-27-million-ponzi-scheme-targeted-his

Bernie Madoff's Ponzi Scheme: From Armani Suits to a Bulletproof Vest

Bernie Madoff was the mastermind behind what has come to be called the largest Ponzi scheme in the history of the United States. Madoff's scheme was simple. Figure 8.2 shows a timeline highlighting Madoff's scheme. Starting in the early 1990s, he marketed his scheme as an exclusive investment opportunity, with clients waiting a year to be given the opportunity to invest with him (Healy & Syre, 2008). It was seen as a privilege to have Madoff investing on an investor's behalf. Investors sent him millions, but instead of investing the money, he deposited it in a bank account at Chase Manhattan (Healy & Mandell, 2009). Eventually, thousands of investors had invested $65 billion in Madoff's accounts (Glovin, 2009a). Madoff had a few complaints about his activities, which opened up SEC investigations, but the investigations never substantiated wrongdoing.

Madoff's scheme continued for more than 17 years. Two elements of his scheme allowed it to continue for so long: (1) investors were receiving positive returns on their investments, and (2) Madoff was extremely secretive in sharing information about investors' accounts. In terms of positive returns, a hedge fund managed by Madoff averaged a 10.5% annual return over 17 years—at least it appeared to average those returns (Appelbaum, Hilzenrath, & Paley, 2008). With returns like that, investors were likely extremely satisfied with their interactions with Madoff.

Regarding his secretiveness, Madoff provided very little information about his "investments" to his investors. When he was asked questions by his investors about how his investment strategy paid so well, he told investors, "secrecy as to information is a key issue for everyone" (Glovin, 2009b, p. C4). Madoff was so extreme in his secrecy that he did not allow clients electronic "access to their accounts" (Appelbaum et al., 2008). This practice was described by the head of a consulting firm as "extremely secretive, even for the non-transparent world of hedge funds" (Appelbaum et al., 2008).

FIGURE 8.2 ■ Madoff Timeline

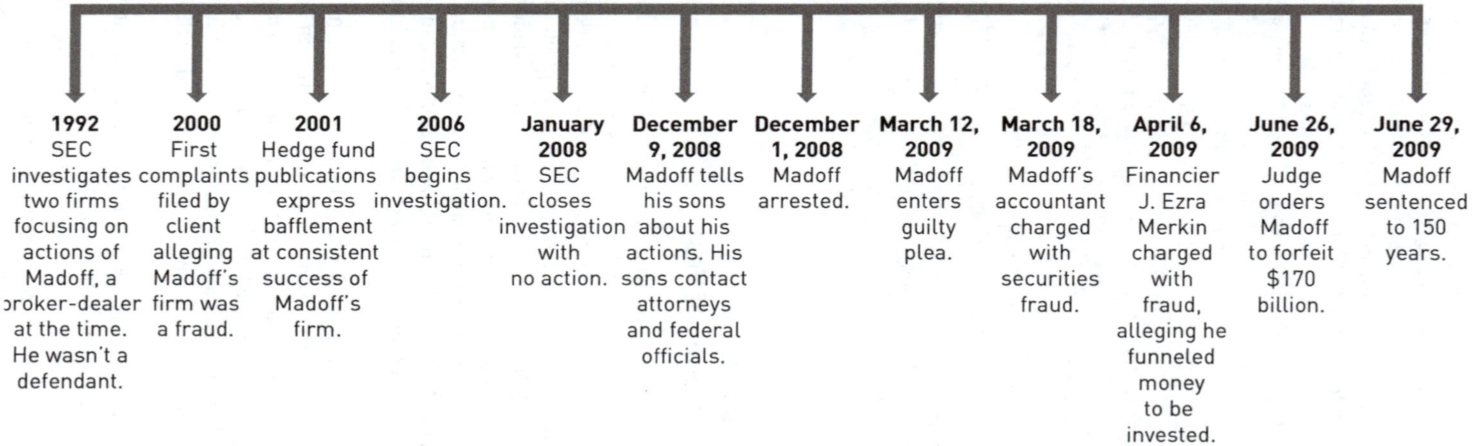

1992
SEC investigates two firms focusing on actions of Madoff, a broker-dealer at the time. He wasn't a defendant.

2000
First complaints filed by client alleging Madoff's firm was a fraud.

2001
Hedge fund publications express bafflement at consistent success of Madoff's firm.

2006
SEC begins investigation.

January 2008
SEC closes investigation with no action.

December 9, 2008
Madoff tells his sons about his actions. His sons contact attorneys and federal officials.

December 1, 2008
Madoff arrested.

March 12, 2009
Madoff enters guilty plea.

March 18, 2009
Madoff's accountant charged with securities fraud.

April 6, 2009
Financier J. Ezra Merkin charged with fraud, alleging he funneled money to be invested.

June 26, 2009
Judge orders Madoff to forfeit $170 billion.

June 29, 2009
Madoff sentenced to 150 years.

Source: Adapted from McCoy (2009)

One day in the fall of 2008, clients asked Madoff to withdraw $7 billion. His account, however, did not hold the funds. He called a meeting with his sons and told them about his scheme. The next day, his sons turned their father in to the FBI (Healy & Syre, 2008). Incidentally, his wife "withdrew ten million dollars from a brokerage account the same day her sons turned him in" (Healy, 2009a). On March 12, 2009, Madoff pleaded guilty to the largest Ponzi scheme to date. At his court hearing he very directly admitted, "I operated a Ponzi scheme through the investment advocacy side of my business" (Glovin, 2009b).

Madoff's victims were stunned by the revelations. Both individual and institutional investors lost huge amounts of funds. Victims included nonprofits and charities that had trusted Madoff to manage their foundation's finances. Several philanthropic organizations lost hundreds of millions, and charities experienced large losses. Madoff managed "nearly 45% of Carl and Ruth Shapiro's Family Foundation," which lost $145 million (Healy & Syre, 2008). Jewish charities, in particular, were hit quite hard. The Women's Zionist Organization of America lost $90 million, Yeshiva University lost $14.5 million, and the Eli Weisel Foundation for Humanity lost the $15.2 million it had invested with Madoff. Mark Charendoff, the Jewish Funders Network president, lamented, "It's an atomic bomb in the world of Jewish philanthropy" (Campbell, 2009, p. 70). Madoff's individual victims included well-known clientele such as Sandy Koufax (baseball Hall of Fame pitcher), Fred Wilpon (owner of the New York Mets), Larry King (Cable News Network, or *CNN*, anchor), Jeffrey Katzenberg (Hollywood mogul), Kevin Bacon (actor), Zsa Gabor (actress), and John Malkovich (actor) ("Madoff's Victims," 2009). Thousands of others also lost money to Madoff's scheme.

One task that has proven to be particularly difficult has been to accurately estimate the losses. Initially, Yeshiva University was believed to have lost $110 million to the scheme. However, when examining their losses, they found they had actually lost $14.5 million. Why the discrepancy? Because the university officials (and Madoff's investors) were basing their losses on amounts that Madoff told them they had in their accounts—fictitious amounts for his victims. Yeshiva never actually had $110 million. So, their loss was calculated as the actual amount it had invested. Beyond the economic losses, foundations and charities also experienced negative consequences from having their names attached to Madoff.

As an analogy, imagine that, unbeknownst to you, someone had broken into your white-collar crime professor's grade book online and changed all of the student's grades to make it look as if everyone had an A+. You would not know the other students' grades, but you would "know" (or assume) that you had a perfect score in the class. You would likely be feeling pretty good about the class. Then, if the professor became aware of the scheme and changed everyone's grades back to their actual grade, how would you feel? Would you think that you "lost" points? Many of you probably have legitimate A+ grades, but for those who would have the grade changed to something lower, understanding your actual grade in the class would be somewhat confusing. For Madoff's victims, understanding the precise extent of their losses was confusing—on both an economic level and an emotional level.

Not surprisingly, Madoff was not well liked by Americans. As an indicator of the hatred that Americans had for him, it is significant to note that Madoff wore a bulletproof vest when going to and from court. Somewhat telling of his betrayal to his friends and family, the judge in Madoff's case, Manhattan Federal Judge Denny Chin, "noted he had not gotten a single letter from friends or family testifying to Madoff's good deeds" during his sentencing hearing (Zambito, Martinez, & Siemaszko, 2009). In statements to the court, his victims called him "a psychopathic lying egomaniac," "ruthless and unscrupulous," and "a devil" (Dey, 2009, p. 10).

It is not entirely clear where all of the money went. Madoff lent millions to his family members and paid their corporate credit card bills, even for those family members who worked for a different corporation. He also paid bills for the captain of his boat (Efrati, 2009). But even these expenses would account for only a minuscule amount of the funds. Douglas Kass, a hedge fund manager himself, told a reporter, "It appears that at least $15 billion of wealth, much of which was concentrated in southern Florida and New York City, has gone to 'money heaven'" (Stempel & Plumb, 2008, p. B04).

The fallout from Madoff's fraud continues. Civil charges were filed against his broker, Robert Jaffe, for "knowingly and recklessly participating in Madoff's Ponzi scheme" (Healy, 2009b, p. 1). Stanley Chais, a California investment advisor, was charged with fraud for funneling his clients' funds to Madoff. Frank Dipascali, Jr., Madoff's top aide, pleaded guilty in August 2009 for his role in helping to deceive investors in the scheme. The U.S. Marshall's service auctioned off Dipascali's belongings in an effort to help make up for losses. During an auction preview, one woman attending the auction commented, "For someone who stole millions, this stuff isn't all that nice" (Debusmann, 2010).

The SEC has faced enormous criticism for not stopping the scheme sooner. After all, on six separate occasions, it had received complaints about Madoff's activities. A report by the SEC's Office of Investigations titled *Investigation of the Failure of the SEC to Uncover Bernard Madoff's Ponzi Scheme* noted that,

> the SEC received more than ample information in the form of detailed and substantive complaints over the years to warrant a thorough and comprehensive examination and/ or investigation of Bernard Madoff . . . for operating a Ponzi scheme, and that despite three examinations and two investigations being conducted, a thorough and competent investigation or examination was never performed. (SEC, 2010)

The 499-page report provides a scathing review of the SEC's failure, but it offers suggestions on how to avoid such a failure in the future.

Strategies for improving the investigation of these offenses will be discussed in a later chapter. At this point, one benefit that has come out of Madoff's actions is that increased attention is being given to the warning signs, or "red flags," of Ponzi schemes. These red flags include the following:

- Complicated trading strategies

- Irregular investment payments

- Unique customer statements

- Delays in withdrawals and transfers

- Promises of high investment returns with little or no risk

- Overly consistent returns

- Unregistered investments

- Unlicensed sellers

- Secretive strategies

- Issues with paperwork

- Difficulty receiving payments (SEC, 2009)

Recognizing that Ponzi schemes are more likely to be detected and stopped by individuals and forces outside of the scheme, some have recommended training investors to watch for signs such as an overemphasis on short-term gains and social engineering tactics investors often use to recruit victims (Raval & Raval, 2019). Wells (2010) suggests that "the flag that flies the highest is a rate of return for an investment that greatly exceeds the norm" (p. 6). Madoff's scheme flew this red flag as high as it could be flown. Recognizing patterns surrounding fraud in the securities and commodities industry should help prevent and facilitate response to these offenses in the future.

PATTERNS SURROUNDING INVESTMENT FRAUD

Several patterns characterize various dynamics surrounding investment fraud. Some of these patterns are similar to other forms of white-collar crime, while others seem more specific to cases of investment fraud. These patterns include the following:

- Significant press attention
- Attributions of greed
- Increasing punitiveness
- "White-collar gangs"
- Multiple offenses
- Regulatory changes
- Negative consequences

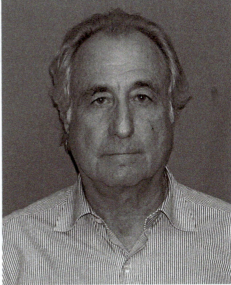

PHOTO 8.3 Bernie Madoff operated an enormous Ponzi scheme through the investment advocacy side of his business. When he was sentenced for it, few individuals spoke on his behalf.

Addressing these patterns will provide a full understanding of investment fraud.

First, several cases of investment fraud, or related offenses, receiving significant press attention were prominently highlighted in the national media over the past few decades. Table 8.2 shows 13 offenders that I would characterize as "infamous," the offenses they were accused of committing, the specific behaviors they performed, and the outcomes of these behaviors. Each of these individuals received a great deal of press attention for his or her misdeeds. In fact, so much press coverage focused on these scandals that some researchers have focused on how the press reported specific cases of investment fraud. One author team, for example, reviewed media reports about Enron and noted that the reports demonstrated four consistent themes about the scandal: risk, gratification, pride, and fantasy imagery (Knottnerus, Ulsperger, Cummins, & Osteen, 2006). Perhaps partly because of the press coverage given to the Enron fiasco, Friedrichs (2004) notes that Enron became a metaphor for a series of corporate scandals in the past decade. Cases involving executives from WorldCom, Adelphia, Tyco, Rite Aid, and other recognizable companies received significant press attention.

A second pattern has to do with attributions of greed that are used to explain cases of investment fraud. Reporters seemed either directly or indirectly to focus on greed explanations in explaining investment fraud. The high salary of executives has been a particular source of contention, both in the media and in private discussions. By focusing on their salaries when discussing the offenses by executives, it is as if the reporters are suggesting that the crimes are somehow tied to salary, when—in fact—the root causes of investment fraud are much more complex.

Still, the notion that greed causes investment fraud persists. The movie *Wall Street* (1987), starring Michael Douglas and Charlie Sheen, is illustrative. Douglas stars as Gordon Gekko—a white-collar criminal engaging in a variety of investment frauds, and Sheen plays Bud Fox—a character new to Wall Street and aiming to learn from Gekko. In one scene, Gekko tells a group of shareholders,

The point is, ladies and gentleman, that greed—for lack of a better word—is good.

Greed is right.

TABLE 8.2 ■ Top Thirteen Infamous Offenders Committing White-Collar Crime Against the Economic System

Name	Former Job Title	Offense Title	Offense Description
Ivan Boesky	Chairman of The Beverly Hills Hotel Corp.	• Insider trading	Boesky made several large stock purchases in the days before corporate takeovers, and he would sell the newly purchased stocks soon after the takeovers were complete and the value of the stock increased. The breadth of his purchases alerted investigators to possible wrongdoing.
Bernard Ebbers	WorldCom CEO	• Conspiracy • Securities fraud • False regulatory filings	Ebbers exaggerated WorldCom's earnings and hid company losses for 2 years. WorldCom went bankrupt, and the investigation uncovered $11 billion in false accounting entries. More than 17,000 employees lost their jobs, and the incident harmed investor confidence.
Andrew Fastow	Enron CFO	• Wire fraud • Securities fraud	Fastow helped hide Enron's debt and exaggerated the company's profits. He conspired with Jeffrey Skilling to lie to investors. Some see him as a scapegoat in the Enron fiasco. Fastow plead guilty and agreed to testify against Kenneth Lay and Skilling.
Walter Forbes	Cendant chairman	• False statements • Conspiracy to commit securities fraud	Forbes was involved in a scheme in which company stock was inflated by $500 million. Upon hearing of the fraud, public confidence dropped, and the company's market value decreased $14 billion in a 24-hour period.
Dennis Kozlowski	Tyco CEO	• Grand larceny • Conspiracy • Falsifying records	Kozlowski took $120 million in bonuses without the approval of the board of directors. He also lied about the value of his company to increase stock prices.
Kenneth Lay	Enron chairman and CEO	• Fraud • Conspiracy • Lying to banks	With other Enron executives, Lay lied about Enron's finances. Enron, a Houston-based company that was once the top energy trading company in the United States, eventually collapsed, and 20,000 employees lost their jobs and retirement packages. Lay was convicted but died of heart disease before his sentencing. The judge, following traditional policies in death of offenders presentence, vacated the conviction.
Bernie Madoff	Founder of Bernard L. Madoff Investment Securities and chairman of the NASDAQ Stock Market	• Securities fraud • Ponzi scheme	Madoff stole several million dollars from thousands of investors through a Ponzi scheme he developed. The scheme took place over years, as he did not rapidly increase the amount of positive returns to investors, but he increased the amounts slowly over time. Victims describe him as an angry man. Madoff was quoted by a fellow inmate who was badgering him about his victims: "F--k my victims," Madoff reportedly said. "I carried them for 20 years, and now I'm doing 150 years."

Name	Former Job Title	Offense Title	Offense Description
Michael Milken	Wall Street financier	• Securities fraud	Milken was involved in the crackdown on Wall Street misconduct in the late 1980s, early 1990s. He pleaded guilty to securities fraud after Boesky indicated he would testify against Milken. Some blame Milken for the savings and loan collapse 30 years ago, a charge he vehemently denies. Milken is now a philanthropist, consultant, and sought-after speaker. Some credit him with making several important changes to the medical field. He has raised hundreds of millions of dollars for medical research, particularly for cancer research. His net worth is $2.5 billion, which is just $200 million below Oprah.
Charles Ponzi	Founder of Old Colony Foreign Exchange Company	• Ponzi scheme	Ponzi persuaded thousands of individuals to invest in a postage stamp program that would provide, according to Ponzi, a 50% return in less than three months. Ponzi used international mail coupons to begin his scheme and then used incoming investments from new investors to maintain the scheme and pay former investors.
John Rigas	Adelphia CEO	• Securities fraud • Lying to investors • Conspiracy	Rigas hid $2.3 billion of his company's debt. He allegedly "helped himself" to so much of the company's funds that his son limited the elder Rigas's withdrawals to $1,000,000 a month.
Jeffrey Skilling	President and chief operating officer of Enron	• Fraud • Conspiracy • Lying to auditors • Insider trading	Skilling was second in command to Lay at Enron. Part of their scheme included reporting the value of their company based on future rather than current estimates.
Martha Stewart	Martha Stewart Living CEO	• False statements • Obstruction of justice	Stewart sold $228,000 worth of her ImClone stock the day before the Food and Drug Administration (FDA) announced it was not going to approve one of ImClone's cancer drugs. The investigation revealed that she had the same stockbroker as the CEO of ImClone. She was later convicted of lying to investigators (perjury) and obstruction of justice. Ironically, at the time of her sentencing, the stocks she sold had increased in value to $315,000.
Samuel Waksal	ImClone CEO	• Insider trading	Waksal unloaded 79,000 shares of ImClone stock upon hearing that the company's cancer drug, Erbitux, was not being approved by the FDA in 2001. Later, the drug was approved and was instrumental in the sale of ImClone to Eli Lilly for $6.5 billion. Waksal served five years in prison, but because he still owned stock options in ImClone, he profited from the sale.

Sources: Information from various news and governmental sources, including Associated Press ("Martha Stewart Reads," 2004), *MSNBC* ("Accused Dentist," 2007), Cosgrove-Mather (2003), Crawford (2005), Hays (2006), Johnson (2005), Johnson (2006), Kolker (2009), Masters (2005).

Greed works.

Greed clarifies, cuts through, and captures the essence of the evolutionary spirit.

Greed, in all of its forms—greed for life, for money, for love, knowledge—has marked the upward surge of mankind.

And greed—you mark my words—will not only save Teldar Paper, but that other malfunctioning corporation called the USA.

I won't spoil the end of the movie for those who have not yet seen it, but it is important to note that Gekko's speech has been linked to the following comments Ivan Boesky once told a group of University of California, Berkeley, students: "Greed is all right, by the way. I want you to know that. I think greed is healthy. You can be greedy and still feel good about yourself" (Boesky, n.d.).

A third pattern consistent in these investment frauds is that the criminal justice system has demonstrated increasing punitiveness toward these offenders (Payne, 2003b). It is a myth that white-collar offenders are always sentenced more leniently than conventional offenders, and this will be discussed in more detail in the chapter focusing on corrections. For now, it can simply be stated that judges and prosecutors seem intent on penalizing investment fraud offenders severely, particularly those investment fraud offenders who receive a great deal of attention from the media (Payne, 2003b). Some have attributed the increased punitiveness to the fact that the schemes often bilk elderly persons out of their life savings, as well as the fact that concern about white-collar crime in general has heightened (Hansard, 2007). The stiff "public sentence" allows judges to "send a message" that the (justice) system is not tolerant of these behaviors. In fact, judges and prosecutors often use the phrase "send a message" or some variation when describing the sentence given to investment fraud offenders.

Another pattern surrounding these offenses can be called **white-collar gangs**. The very nature of most investment frauds requires that offenders work with other offenders in ways that compare to nonviolent gang behavior. Highlighting the themes surrounding the investment scandals of the early 2000s, Friedrichs (2004) drew attention to the "cooperative involvement of a broad network of other parties" (p. 114) that was found in the scandals. While the behaviors of street gangs and white-collar gangs are substantively different, the point is that investment offenders almost always work with other conspirators in committing their crimes.

A related pattern has to do with the fact that investment offenders tend to commit multiple offenses. It is rare that these offenders engage in their illicit behaviors only once or twice, and rarely do they commit just one type of misconduct. As an example, one offender (a) lied to investors about funds, (b) falsely solicited payments from investors, (c) did not tell investors information they needed to know about their accounts, and (d) did not pay his taxes for four years (Mclaughlin, 2010). That investment offenders commit crimes in groups and commit these offenses on multiple occasions is useful information for investigators—if they find evidence of one offender committing one offense, by broadening the scope of their investigation, they can identify additional offenses and offenders.

Another pattern concerns regulatory changes enacted to address these offenses. For example, financial institutions have been called upon to help curb financial offenses through identifying customers, improved record keeping, verification processes, and disclosing information to the authorities (Fasanello, Umans, & White, 2011). Other regulatory changes have also been implemented in an effort to limit these crimes. However, it is believed by some that "regulatory gaps and continued lack of adequate oversight . . . [and] non-understanding of the role of fraud . . . virtually guarantee that future financial crises will occur due to fraud" (Pontell & Geis, 2014, p. 70). It is here that the connection between government power and Wall Street crimes becomes particularly evident. Decisions by government officials may either close or open the door to crimes in the economic system. This chapter's Streaming White-Collar Crime highlights how one television show captures this relationship.

STREAMING WHITE-COLLAR CRIME	*Billions*: Power, Greed, and Wall Street	
Plot	**What You Can Learn**	**Discussion Questions**
Seemingly titled in reference to the vast amount of wealth that the powerful are able to accumulate, *Billions* tells the story of the changing relationship between the politically motivated Chuck Rhoades and Wall Street investor and billionaire Bobby Axelrod. The two go from adversaries to peers and back. The series begins with Rhoades, a U.S. Attorney, focused on taking down Axelrod for trading misdeeds. At the same time, Rhoades's own quest for power and transgressions into political and banking malfeasance are uncovered. In the middle of this is Wendy Rhoades, who happens to be Chuck's wife and Bobby's most-trusted confidante, serving as Bobby's company's internal psychiatrist. As the series unfolds, viewers are treated to the innerworkings of banking investigations, with insight given to how criminal justice professionals and banking professionals rationalize their behaviors.	Corporate power and political power are interconnected. State-corporate crime thrives on interactions between corporations and political leaders. Investors use algorithms when making investment decisions. Those algorithms become problematic when they rely on insider information.	How might powerful corporate officials influence decisions made by politicians? Why is it unfair to use inside information to decide how to invest funds in the stock market? Why do you think investors engage in criminal behavior?

A final pattern surrounding investment frauds involves the negative consequences that stem from these offenses. Beyond the direct economic toll for society in general, the offenses negatively impact investors' confidence in their immediate aftermath, and this reduction in confidence may result in fewer investments and lower stock values (Friedrichs, 2004). For specific victims of the investment frauds, different consequences may surface, and these consequences may linger, at least for some victims.

To address the long-term consequences of investment frauds, Shover and his research team (Shover, Fox, & Mills, 1994) interviewed 47 victims of fraud a decade after their victimization. The sample included victims of the Southland Industrial Banking Commission collapse, which was a result of fraudulent and criminal activities committed by the commission's executives. The researchers found that the long-term effects were minimal for many victims, but some described significant effects. Elderly victims, in particular, seemed to experience more negative consequences from the victimization. One victim told an interviewer,

> it's destroying us. It's destroying us. She was trained to look up to and obey an authority figure. I don't necessarily agree with that. Sometimes the authority figures are wrong. So as a result, she's a walking bag of nerves, very short-tempered. (Shover et al., 1994, p. 87)

The results of the Shover research team's study showed that *delegitimation effects dissipated over time, suggesting that investor confidence can be restored.* They also found, though, that when these effects lingered, that tended to be a result of the actions of state officials responding to the misconduct more than the actual misconduct itself.

BANKING FRAUD

Whereas investment frauds center around investing strategies with the broader economic system, banking fraud includes illicit behaviors individuals engage in to take money from a bank. Figure 8.3 shows complaints the FTC received about banking behaviors between 2016 and 2019. While much could be written about different banking frauds, for our purposes, two types of bank fraud will be addressed: mortgage fraud and student loan fraud.

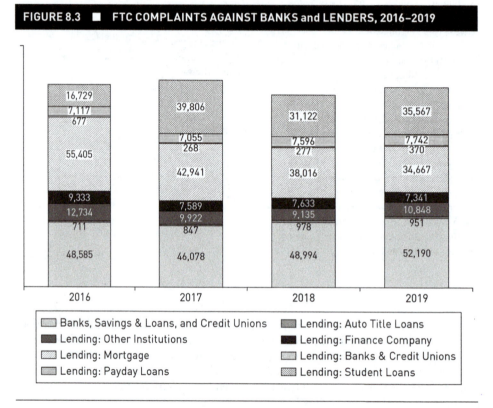

FIGURE 8.3 ■ FTC COMPLAINTS AGAINST BANKS and LENDERS, 2016–2019

Legend:
- Banks, Savings & Loans, and Credit Unions
- Lending: Other Institutions
- Lending: Mortgage
- Lending: Payday Loans
- Lending: Auto Title Loans
- Lending: Finance Company
- Lending: Banks & Credit Unions
- Lending: Student Loans

Source: United States Federal Trade Commission, http://www.ftc.gov

MORTGAGE FRAUD

Mortgage fraud involves cases of "intentional misrepresentation to a lender for the purpose of obtaining a loan that would otherwise not be advanced by the lender" (Financial Crimes Enforcement Network [FinCEN], 2009). Mortgage fraud has always been a problem in the United States, but it increased in the mid-2000s in response to a cooling real estate market. Suspected cases of mortgage fraud are reported by banking officials "through Suspicious Activity Reports (SARs) required under the Bank Secrecy Act" (FinCEN, 2009). SARs have been described as "one of the most important sources of lead information for law enforcement in fighting financial crimes" (FinCEN, 2010b). To put in perspective the increase in mortgage fraud cases (at least, suspected mortgage fraud cases), consider that in fiscal year 2004, banks across the United States filed 17,127 SARs about mortgage fraud. In fiscal year 2009, bank officials filed 67,190 SARs about mortgage fraud. This means that the number of suspected mortgage fraud cases nearly quadrupled within a five-year time frame! The number of suspected cases of mortgage fraud has dropped since then, but the problem remains a significant concern. Figure 8.4 shows the number of suspicious activity reports between 2014 and 2019.

It is important to stress that not all cases of mortgage fraud are necessarily white-collar crimes committed by employers. Some cases involve consumers scamming banks by committing fraud in order to benefit from deceiving the lender. Many cases of mortgage fraud, particularly those that are the most pervasive, can be classified as white-collar crimes.

Several different types of mortgage fraud exist: (a) straw buyer fraud, (b) short sale fraud, (c) appraisal fraud, (d) equity skimming, (e) reverse mortgage fraud, (f) builder bailout schemes, (g) faulty credit enhancements, (h) flipping, (i) qualifications fraud, and (j) real estate agent/investor fraud. Each of these is discussed in the following sections.

Straw buyer fraud occurs when people who do not plan on living in or even owning a house purchase the house and then deed it over to the person who will live there. The individual making the purchase is called a straw buyer. In many cases, straw buyers do this for a fee (Fannie Mae, 2007). In other cases, straw buyers do this with the intent of unloading the mortgage on an unsuspecting homeowner who is unaware of the true costs of the home and is probably unable to pay the actual mortgage amount. Based on these dynamics, Curry (2007) identified two types of straw buyers: (1) conspirator straw buyers who are in on the scheme and the (2) victim straw buyers who are not in on the scheme but who believe they will either legitimately own the home or be able to rent it. In the latter case, the victim is often an "unsophisticated buyer, without cash or good credit" (Martin, 2004).

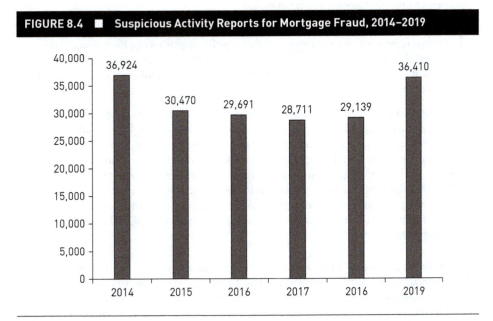

FIGURE 8.4 ■ Suspicious Activity Reports for Mortgage Fraud, 2014–2019

Source: Financial Crimes Enforcement Network (2020).

Short sale fraud occurs when parties involved in the short sale manipulate the process in order to persuade the lending institution to permit the short sale to occur. The phrase *short sale* refers to instances where lending institutions allow homes to be sold for amounts that are lower than what the homeowner owed on the home's mortgage. These sales typically occur for houses that have been foreclosed on or those that are nearing foreclosure. To put this in perspective, a homeowner might have a $400,000 mortgage. Unable to sell the home for that amount, the bank may allow the homeowner to sell it for less, even waiving any additional future costs to the homeowner in some cases. Short sales in and of themselves are entirely legal and offer homeowners a way to get out from a mortgage and home they are no longer able to afford. These sales allow lending institutions to avoid lengthy and costly foreclosure processes. Still, the lending institution loses money on a short sale. Consider the following example:

1. Tisha buys a home from Robert and gets a $300,000 mortgage.

2. The bank gives $300,000 to Robert as part of the transaction.

3. Tisha is unable to pay her mortgage and asks for a short sale.

4. The home is sold for $270,000 to Bryan.

5. The bank loses $30,000

Short sales are legal strategies when done this way. They become fraudulent when participants manipulate parts of the short sale process. Here is an example where an attorney admitted to conspiring with a real estate agent to steal more than $30 million in fraudulent short sales:

> From January 2011 through August 2017, ++++++++, his co-defendant, +++++++, and others engaged in a short sale mortgage fraud conspiracy targeting various New Jersey properties with mortgages that were in default.
>
> The conspirators arranged simultaneous fraudulent transactions on the same target property. In the first transaction, which involved the sale by the current owner, the conspirators convinced the financial institution holding the mortgage to accept the sale of the target property at a loss, usually to a buyer who was secretly a conspirator or an entity controlled by the conspiracy.
>
> In the second transaction, the conspirators flipped the same target property from the first buyer to a second buyer, who typically obtained a mortgage from another financial institution using false loan applications, pay stubs, bank account statements and title reports provided by members of the conspiracy. As a result, the second transaction frequently closed for significantly more or even double the price of the first transaction. +++++++ admitted that he, ++++++, and others rigged the short sale process at each step in order to maximize the difference in price between the two transactions and keep the victim financial institutions from detecting the fraud. (USDOJ, 2018, September 28),

Appraisal fraud occurs when appraisers misrepresent the actual value of a home (Curry, 2007). Appraisers are called upon to determine a home's value so the lending institution can determine if the home is worth the amount of money that the lending institution would need to lend the buyer for the purchase. Four types of appraisal fraud occur. First, **inflated appraisals** overestimate the value of a home in order to allow it to be sold at an inflated price. This is also known as value fraud (Rudra, 2010). Second, **deflated appraisals** underestimate the value of the home in order to force the seller to lower the home price. Third, **windshield appraisal fraud** occurs when appraisers fail to do a thorough appraisal of a home (and may not even go into the home to determine its value—hence they determine its value by looking through the windshield of their automobile) (FDIC, 2007). Fourth, **conspiracy appraisal fraud** occurs when appraisers work with other offenders as part of broader mortgage schemes. For example, for straw buying or flipping schemes to be successful, appraisers must provide inflated appraisals of targeted homes on a regular basis for their coconspirators.

Equity skimming occurs when investors persuade financially distressed homeowners to use their home equity to "hire" the investor to buy the home, or part of the home, from the homeowner and rent it back to the homeowner. The investor receives funds from the equity loan, collects fees for rent, and then defaults on the mortgage (Donohue, 2004). Figure 8.5 shows the stages of equity skimming. Here is the foundation of the equity skimming process:

> Homeowners facing foreclosure sell their homes to a third-party investor,
> typically located by a foreclosure consultant, but continue living in them for one year.
> The original homeowners use that time to build their credit or otherwise improve
> their financial position. Fees for the investor and the foreclosure consultant are paid
> from equity in the property, and at the end of the year, the property is sold
> back to the original owner if that person can obtain a new mortgage.
> (Londoño, 2007)

If the process unfolds as described, then fraud has not necessarily occurred. Fraud occurs when the investor decides not to pay the equity loan or the mortgage, resulting in the homeowner's losing their home to foreclosure.

Reverse mortgage fraud refers to situations where fraudulent activities occur as part of the reverse mortgage transaction. A reverse mortgage is a transaction whereby older homeowners sell their homes back to the lending institution and are able to live in their homes until they move or pass away. The homeowner can receive either a lump sum or monthly payments from the bank. (FBI, 2010a). One financial expert cites the following types of reverse mortgage fraud: charging for free information, misrepresenting preloan counseling, forgery of homeowner's signature, posing as government officials hired to help seniors get reverse mortgages, and bundling unnecessary services with reverse mortgage transactions (Paul, 2006). Another scheme occurs when closing agents fail to pay off the homeowner's original mortgage and pocket the funds from the reverse mortgage transaction instead of sending those funds to the lending institution (Tergesen, 2009).

FIGURE 8.5 ■ Stages of Equity Skimming

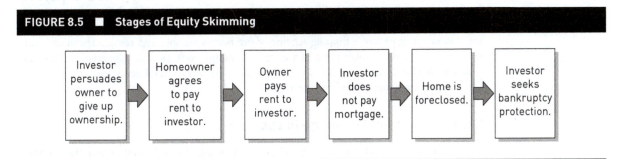

Source: Adapted from Donohue, K. (2004 October 7). *"Statement of Kenneth Donuhue, Inspector General Department of Housing and Urban Development."* Before the United States House of Representatives Subcommittee on housing and Community Opportunity Committee on Financial Services.

In **builder bailout schemes**, builders offer buyers "excessive incentives" but hide those offers from the mortgage company to make it appear that the property is worth more than it is (FBI, 2010b). It has become increasingly common, for example, for builders to give homeowners a new car to get them to purchase a new home. As long as the builder reports this incentive to the lender, such practices are legitimate. When builders hide these incentives, they are able to increase the amount of profit they actually get from the lender.

Faulty credit enhancements by builders occur when builders engage in measures that make it appear as if buyers have better credit than they actually have. They do this to ensure that buyers are able to secure a mortgage. For instance, builders might put money in a buyer's account to make it appear that the buyer has a strong credit rating and the funds needed for the down payment (Glink, 2009). The problem is that the buyers actually do not have good credit, and their risk of not being able to repay the mortgage is higher than the lending institution realizes. The builder sells the home, gets the money, and then the lending institution may in the not-so-distant future end up having to begin the foreclosure process on the home.

Flipping occurs when scammers buy and resell properties with inflated prices. Sometimes, the same home will be sold over and over at escalating prices as part of these schemes. This should not be confused with legitimate flipping businesses, whereby investors purchase homes, fix them up, and then sell the homes for a profit (Curry, 2007). In the illegal flip, the home is bought, sold, resold, resold, and so on, with no changes made to the property. Fraudulent appraisals are used to resell the property at inflated prices (FBI, 2009).

Qualifications fraud involves professionals lying about a buyer's qualifications in order to secure a mortgage that allows the buyer to purchase the home. Industry professionals will lie about or exaggerate any of the following: income, assets, collateral, length of employment, employment status, and property value (FBI, 2005). Those items most commonly misrepresented are "employment, income, and occupancy intentions" (FDIC, 2007). In some cases, professionals might help buyers appear to be qualified when they are not (IRS, 2010). For instance, real estate developers or agents might tell buyers to have their names added to a family member's or friend's bank account so they look as if they have more funds available for the home purchase than they do (FBI, 2009). Not surprisingly, income overstatement has been empirically tied to "poor performance during the mortgage credit boom" (Mian & Sufi, 2015, p. 1).

Real estate agent/investor fraud refers to a variety of scams committed by agents and investors. One example is **home improvement scams** in which agents or investors conceal problems with homes that should be disclosed to potential buyers. **Fraudulent loan origination** scams occur when professionals help buyers qualify for loans even though the buyers are not actually qualified. **Chunking** occurs when investors buy several properties without telling banks about properties other than the one the bank is financing. Believed to play a part in the 2008 recession, **liar loans** refer to situations where buyers or investors lie about loans they have or are trying to get (Edwards, 2020). **Churning** refers to "excessive selling [of the same property] for the purpose of generating fees and commissions" (Fannie Mae, 2007). Many of these scams occur as part of a broader scheme involving several coconspirators. As an illustration, churning may occur as part of a flipping scheme where homes are sold and resold. The agent's role in these schemes is to broker the deal and collect commissions. In many appraisal fraud cases, "unscrupulous real estate agents . . . conspire with appraisers to fraudulently declare artificially high market values for homes" (Bennett, 2007).

Consequences of Mortgage Fraud

The consequences of mortgage fraud are widespread. To fully understand these consequences, it is necessary to focus on the consequences for (a) individual victims of mortgage fraud, (b) business victims of mortgage fraud, (c) communities and neighborhoods where the frauds occur, and (d) the real estate market.

In terms of individual victims of mortgage fraud, homeowners victimized by mortgage fraud experience tragic consequences as a result of these crimes. Consumers who have lost their homes due to these offenses offer "stories of financial ruin" (J. C. Anderson, 2010). James Frois, director of the federal government's Financial Crime Enforcement Network, lamented that the most "troubling aspect" of some types of mortgage fraud is that the fraudulent actions "take advantage of senior citizens who have worked hard over their entire lives to own their homes" (FinCEN, 2010a).

PHOTO 8.4 Mortgage fraud cases can damage neighborhoods with rundown homes and lower home values.

When businesses are victimized by mortgage fraud, similar stories of financial ruin may surface. Beyond the dollar losses that lending institutions experience from fraud, many businesses face problems with morale and potential business failures. After Lee Farkas, chairman of the bankrupted mortgage lender Taylor, Bean, and Whitaker Mortgage Corporation, perpetrated a mortgage scheme that resulted in millions in overdrafts to the bank, the fraud "contributed to the downfall of Colonial Bank" ("Ex U.S. Mortgage Executive Charged," 2010). Many employees lost their jobs, and the bank ceased to exist because of the illicit actions of Farkas.

Communities will also experience negative consequences from mortgage fraud. Abandoned homes used in various mortgage frauds become targets of vandals (Fannie Mae, 2007), and the vandalism results in neighboring homes having lower property values (Creswell, 2007). The abandoned homes also increase levels of disorganization in the neighborhood, which may serve to breed conventional crime. Alternatively, as noted above, some types of mortgage fraud—such as variations of appraisal fraud—may artificially increase property values and subsequently raise homeowners' property taxes (Fannie Mae, 2007).

The real estate market also experiences consequences from mortgage fraud. At the simplest level, increased mortgage rates and fees as well as difficulties determining actual home values have been linked to fraud (Fannie Mae, 2007). Federal officials suggested that "a direct correlation between fraud and distressed real estate markets [exists]" (FBI, 2009). Others have suggested that the inflated home prices found during the real estate boom of the early to mid-2000s could be attributed to mortgage fraud (J. C. Anderson, 2010). In somewhat of a cyclical pattern, then, the current housing crisis can be seen as stemming at least partly from potentially fraudulent activities. In the past it was common that many homeowners had mortgages that were higher than the value of their homes. The high rate of foreclosures has dropped home values even further. Ironically, the lack of business for mortgage industry insiders is now being seen as a motivating factor for current fraudulent activities.

Patterns Surrounding Mortgage Fraud

Because mortgage fraud is a recent social and criminal problem, few criminological studies have examined the offense type. Still, news reports, government studies, and the few other studies that have been done reveal four patterns characterizing mortgage fraud offenses.

First, as with other white-collar crimes, the offenses generally involve large dollar losses. The offenses can range from thousands of dollars to millions of dollars, depending on the size of the mortgage and value of the home.

Second (and also similar to other white-collar crimes), mortgage fraud cases often occur over long periods of time. Offenders committing these schemes do not tend to commit the offense

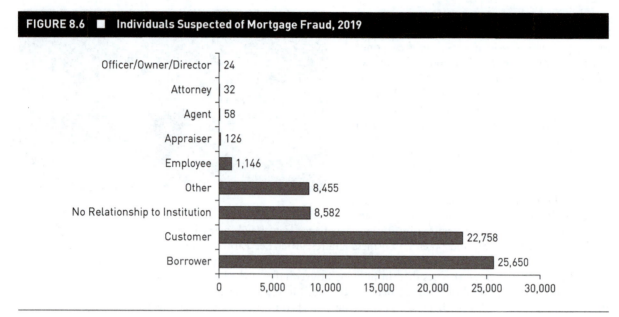

FIGURE 8.6 ■ Individuals Suspected of Mortgage Fraud, 2019

Source: Financial Crimes Enforcement Network: https://www.fincen.gov/fcn/Reports/SARStats

just once and stop. Rather, they appear to commit the offenses over time as a part of their occupational routines.

Third, these are offenses that typically involve coconspirators (Hales, 2016). The very nature of the mortgage process requires that individuals work with other professionals to process the mortgage loans. When fraud occurs, like other crimes committed in the economic system, more than one offender is likely involved in the incident. Figure 8.6 shows the range of people suspected of mortgage fraud in 2019.

Fourth, some criminologists have suggested that the practices underlying fraud in the housing crisis disproportionately impacted persons of color (Nguyen & Pontell, 2011). Through predatory loan practices, many African American and Hispanic families who could not actually afford homes were given loans after putting their life savings into the new home. Many of them later lost their homes and their livelihoods because they were given loans they were not able to repay. Nguyen and Pontell (2011) described opening up the home market to disadvantaged persons of color as a "latent and sinister element that has little to do with equality and more to do with continued victimization and exploitation" (p. 20). Other research shows that mortgage fraud is more prevalent in communities experiencing more racial segregation, higher property crime rates, increased loan volumes, and a larger number of loans originating through independent mortgage companies (Baumer, Ranson, Arnio, Fulmer, & De Zilwa, 2017). The same study identified a connection between mortgage fraud and the foreclosure crises with higher rates of mortgage fraud in a neighborhood translating to higher foreclosure rates. The researchers also found that property valuation fraud was more likely if the distance between the purchased home's location and the lender's location was greater. Based on the connection between community-level variables and mortgage fraud, the researchers highlighted the need to develop interventions at the community level rather than the state or national level.

STUDENT LOAN FRAUD

Students may think that crimes in the economic system do not closely relate to them. Such an assumption could not be further from the truth. One type of crime occurring in the economic system very closely relates to the lives of college students: fraud in the student loan and financial aid process. According to one author, "fraud schemes have been plaguing higher education for years and have been growing in notoriety" (O'Colmain, 2014). Federal authorities estimated that the number of recipients "potentially participating in this fraud activity had increased 82 percent from award year 2009 (18,719 students) to award year 2012 (34,007 students)" (U.S. Department of Education, 2014). It has also been estimated that during this time period, $187 million of federal aid funds was lost to fraud perpetrated by student aid fraud rings (U.S. Department of Education, 2014, November 14).

Various types of student loan/aid fraud exist. These varieties include the following: (1) lying about intent to take classes, (2) taking out loans with no intent to pay them back, (3) lying about qualifications/income, (4) schemes or fraud rings designed to enroll students in college, (4) identity fraud to enhance qualifications, and (5) schemes targeting students with fee-based financial aid seminars. When applying for loans and federal aid, students and their parents are expected to provide honest information that officials can use to make a determination on whether to award the loan/aid. It is also expected that the student will actually attend the college listed on the aid application. Perpetrators in these cases come from at least five different roles: (1) college officials trying to recruit students to their college, (2) consultants assisting students in college applications, (3) parents helping students apply for financial aid, (4) students applying for financial aid, and (5) traditional offenders organizing fraud rings.

Few studies have been conducted on student loan and student aid fraud, but this appears to be growing problem. In a study focusing generally on student loans, but not specifically on fraud, a financial aid counselor commented:

> All the advisors at my college are very concerned with the amount of what we consider to be loan fraud at our college. These are students who apply and take out loans and have no intention of getting an education or ever paying back these loans. The advisors here believe this is a silent killer that could sink not only our colleges, but [also] the ability for the federal government to continue to support these loans going forward. We all wish we had more discretion to STOP these students who we suspect and have cause to see [as] NOT serious students. (McKinney, Roberts, & Shefman, 2013, pp. 11–12)

In some cases, students may be targets of student aid fraud. Figure 8.7 shows the number of complaints received related to scholarship scams between 1996 and 2011. As shown in the figure, the number of complaints increased. Potential reasons for this increase include (1) more offenders may have been targeting students, (2) students and families became more aware of complaint processes, (3) a downturn in the economy made students more in need of aid and subsequently more vulnerable, (4) a reduction in the amount of government support given to public universities increased tuition costs and made it harder for students to pay for college (again making them more vulnerable targets), and (5) the market demand for college education expanded.

- Various strategies have been suggested for limiting student loan/aid fraud. One suggestion that some colleges have implemented is disbursing student loan funds twice a semester rather than once a semester (Queisser, Sutton, & Fultz, 2015).

- Another set of recommendations from another author team includes interdepartmental cooperation, training, policies to deny suspicious applications, deferring financial aid payment, and required orientation. (Lokken & Mullins, 2014, p. 6)

FIGURE 8.7 ■ Complaints About Scholarship Scams Made to Federal Trade Commission

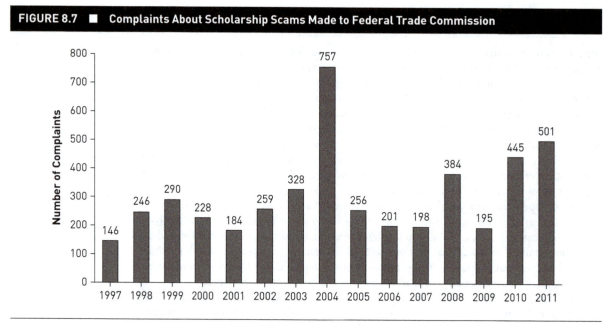

Source: United States Federal Trade Commission: http://www.ftc.gov

Summary

- A wide range of offenses are committed in the economic system.

- When the term *white-collar offender* is used, it is often images of offenders from the economic or technological system that come to mind.

- The economic system includes banks, investment companies, stock markets across the world, commodities markets, and other exchanges and markets where individuals are able to make investments, purchase raw materials, and secure goods.

- The phrase "securities and commodities fraud" covers a broad concept, capturing a range of behaviors designed to rip off investors.

- Several specific varieties of these frauds exist, including market manipulation, broker embezzlement, insider trading, futures trading fraud, foreign exchange fraud, high-yield investment schemes, advance-fee fraud, and Ponzi and pyramid schemes.

- Three federal statutes restrict market manipulation by energy companies: the Commodity Exchange Act, the Energy Policy Act of 2005, and the Energy Independence and Security Act of 2007.

- Bernie Madoff was the mastermind behind what has come to be called the largest Ponzi scheme in the history of the United States.

- One benefit that has come out of Madoff's actions is that increased attention is being given to the warning signs, or "red flags," of Ponzi schemes.

- Several patterns characterize various dynamics surrounding investment fraud, including significant press attention, attributions of greed, increasing punitiveness, white-collar gangs, multiple offenses, regulatory changes, and negative consequences.

- To address the long-term consequences of investment frauds, Shover and his research team interviewed 47 victims of fraud a decade after their victimization. The results of the Shover research team's study showed that delegitimation effects dissipated over time, suggesting that investor confidence can be restored.

- Types of fraud occurring in the student financial aid process include (1) lying about intent to take classes, (2) taking out loans with no intent to pay them back, (3) lying about qualifications/income, (3) schemes or fraud rings designed to enroll students in college, (4) identity fraud to enhance qualifications, and (5) schemes targeting students with fee-based financial aid seminars.

- Mortgage fraud involves cases of "intentional misrepresentation to a lender for the purpose of obtaining a loan that would otherwise not be advanced by the lender" (FinCEN, 2009).

- Not all cases of mortgage fraud are necessarily white-collar crimes committed by employers.

- Mortgage fraud includes (a) straw buyer fraud, (b) short sale fraud, (c) appraisal fraud, (d) equity skimming, (e) reverse mortgage fraud, (f) builder bailout schemes, (g) faulty credit enhancements, (h) flipping, (i) qualifications fraud, and (j) real estate agent/investor fraud.

- The consequences of mortgage fraud affect (a) individual victims, (b) business victims, (c) communities and neighborhoods where the frauds occur, and (d) the real estate market.

- Some research shows that mortgage fraud disproportionately impacted persons of color by targeting disadvantaged families with loans they actually could not afford.

- Research has shown a direct relationship between a community's rate of mortgage fraud and foreclosures.

Key Terms

Advance-fee fraud   208

Appraisal fraud   222

Broker embezzlement   205

Broker fraud   205

Bucketing   208

Builder bailout schemes   224

Chunking   224

Commodities   203

Commodities fraud   203

Conspiracy appraisal fraud   223

Deflated appraisals   223

Equity skimming   223

Faulty credit enhancements   224

Flipping   224

Foreign exchange fraud   208

Fraudulent loan origination   224

Front running   208

Futures contracts   207

Futures trading fraud   207

High-yield investment schemes   208

Home improvement scams   224

Inflated appraisals   222

Insider trading   205

Investment fraud   203

Liar loans   224

Market manipulation   204

Mortgage fraud   220

Ponzi schemes   209

Prearranged trading   208

Qualifications fraud   224

Real estate agent/investor fraud   224

Reverse mortgage fraud   223

Short sale fraud   222

Straw buyer fraud   221

Windshield appraisal fraud   223

White-collar gangs   218

Discussion Questions

1. Which crimes do you think do more harm—crimes against the economic system or street crimes? Explain.

2. How would you describe investment fraud to someone unfamiliar with the concept?

3. How can mortgage fraud be harmful to communities of color?

4. What are some patterns surrounding investment fraud?

5. How does mortgage fraud impact your life as a student?

6. How does student loan fraud impact your life?

7. Is it a crime for a student to register for a class simply so he or she can get federal aid? Explain.

CRIME IN THE CYBER SYSTEM

A few years ago, the dating site Ashley Madison faced the nightmare of a breach. Hackers accessed the names, contact information, and credit card numbers for those who used the dating site. This dating site differed in its clientele from other sites: It connected married people to those interested in committing adultery. The hackers, a group calling itself "The Impact Team," released the names and e-mail addresses of Ashley Madison customers on the dark web (which is a collection of websites accessible only when users have certain types of software). The hack received international attention. While many found the reports to be amusing, the real consequences were devastating for those exposed from the breach. Media reports suggested that at least a handful of suicides occurred as a result of the shame adulterers felt from being exposed internationally. For a timeline of this hack see Bisson (2015).

While the Ashley Madison breach received widespread attention, in reality, it represented just one of the many different types of cyber offenses that target businesses. A recent cyber intrusion effort targeted higher education via an e-mail sent to multiple colleges' and universities' faculty and staff. The e-mail message, purporting to be from the dean, told faculty/staff that the dean was in a bind and needed a certain amount of money. Instructions were given to the faculty/staff telling them how to help their dean in this apparent emergency. In reality, the e-mail was nothing more than a scam trying to get money and personal information from recipients. Several faculty members at my university received this e-mail, but none of them fell for the ploy.

Many different types of computer-related offenses are perpetrated in workplace settings. Consider the following examples quoted verbatim from their original sources:

- +++++++ who is not a pharmacist, has allegedly illegally operated as the Darknet vendor NeverPressedRX (NPRX) since at least August 2019. The NPRX vendor store claimed to sell authentic medications, including prescription opioids, sourced from United States pharmacies. NPRX had thousands of recorded sales on a major Darknet market. +++++++ allegedly laundered the proceeds of his criminal activity by cashing out his Bitcoin cryptocurrency drug payments into United States dollars and moving the funds through a variety of accounts, including his business bank accounts, in an effort to conceal and disguise the nature and source of his illicit proceeds (USDOJ, 2020, April 9).

- "[The company] maintained computer servers related to the dispensing machines at its facility in Niles. [The offender] worked at the facility as a contractor from November 2014 to February 2016, after which his access to Grainger's servers was deactivated. [The offender] hacked into the servers on several occasions in July 2016, the indictment states." (USDOJ, 2017, December 14)

- A 64-year-old man has admitted to conspiring to commit money laundering for his role in a complex email fraud scheme, announced U.S. Attorney Ryan K. Patrick. +++++++ engaged in a business email compromise scheme using "spoof" email addresses which have similar names to legitimate email accounts that +++++++ hacked. He would then use the addresses to create fictitious transactions or to hijack legitimate transactions to convince a victim company or individual to send funds to a bank account [he] actually controlled (USDOJ, 2020, June 2).

- A month after his departure, ++++++ conducted a multi-stage sabotage campaign targeting the company's network. Using information he gained in his employment, ++++++ logged into the network remotely without authorization and used encryption methods to hide his network connections. In mid-August 2018, ++++++ changed passwords for network routers located at dozens of company warehouses. Company employees were unable to access the routers, and the company replaced them shortly thereafter at a cost of roughly $100,000. (USDOJ, 2020, May 28).

In this chapter, attention is given to computer offenses in the workplace. In addressing these offenses, it is important to note that all types of computer crime are not necessarily white-collar crimes. For example, distributing child pornography on the Internet is a computer crime, but it is not a white-collar crime. As well, many computer crimes target businesses but are not necessarily committed by workers. In effect, one might broadly conceive these offenses as forms of white-collar victimization because they target businesses.

CONCEPTUALIZING CRIME IN THE CYBER SYSTEM

Our technological system has made massive strides during our lifetime. Cell phones, liquid crystal display (LCD) televisions, laptops, and handheld technological devices are relatively recent creations. These items all came about as the result of technological advancements. While technological advancements have resulted in new products, the same advancements have also resulted in new types of crimes. In particular, computer crime (or cybercrime) has become an international concern.

The terms **computer crime** and cybercrime refer to a range of computer-related behaviors that are criminally illegal or otherwise harmful. In cases of computer crime, the computer is either a target of the offense (e.g., sabotage) or a tool for the crime (e.g., cyber fraud, piracy), or is incidental to the crime (e.g., containing evidence about a crime; Hale, 2002; Sinrod & Reilly, 2000). While not all "computer crimes" are necessarily illegal—consider times when workers spend the day surfing the Internet rather than working—legal changes beginning in 1978 have provided criminal definitions that prohibit computer crime. In 1978, Florida and Arizona became the first two states to pass laws related to computer crime. Florida's Computer Crime Act

PHOTO 9.1 People are so reliant on technology that it is natural to ask whether technology is good for one's health. Many believe it is. On the other hand, the consequences experienced from cybercrime are hardly good for one's health.

"defined all unauthorized access as a third-degree felony regardless of the specific purpose" (Hollinger & Lanza-Kuduce, 1988, p. 114). Within 10 years, the majority of states and the federal government had followed suit.

Hollinger and Lanza-Kuduce (1988) note that the public was somewhat apathetic with regard to the creation of these new laws. They also note that, unlike other legal developments, the media's reporting was "indispensable to the criminalization process" (p. 113). They also wrote that unlike other legal developments that are promoted by advocacy groups, efforts to reform the criminal law so it would respond more directly to computer crimes was led by "computer crime experts and legislators rather than moral entrepreneurs" (p. 101). More than three decades after these laws were first developed, computer crime laws have expanded and are routinely enforced by state and federal authorities.

While the phrase "computer crime" was initially used to characterize offenses involving computers, over the past decade an assortment of terms has been used to describe these behaviors. Among these terms are cybercrime, cyber offense, cyber deviance, digital crime, e-crime, high-tech crime, and Internet crime (see Figure 9.1). In this chapter, the terms "cybercrime," "computer crime," and "cyber offense" will be used interchangeably. In addition, many different terms and concepts are used to describe various facets of cyber offending. Table 9.1 provides definitions of common terms as defined by the National Institute of Standards and Technology. These terms are frequently used to characterize different dimensions of offending in the cyber system.

The dynamic and changing nature of computer crimes will be demonstrated through this discussion, and the way that the systems approach relates to this form of white-collar crime will be particularly evident.

TYPES OF CYBERCRIME

Experts have identified a laundry list of different types of computer crimes. These include hacking, cracking, phishing, extortion, child pornography, software piracy, money laundering, fraud, corporate espionage, cyberterrorism, surveillance, identity theft, cyber trespassing, cyber hoaxing, cyber bullying, online stalking, and hate speech (Minnaar, 2008; Sinrod & Reilly, 2000; Yar, 2006).

For our purposes, the simplest way to understand computer crimes as white-collar crimes is to focus on general categories of computer crimes that target, or occur in, businesses. The following overlapping types of computer crimes warrant discussion: theft, unauthorized access, virus introduction, software crimes, and Internet crimes.

FIGURE 9.1 ■ Phrases Used to Describe Computer Crime

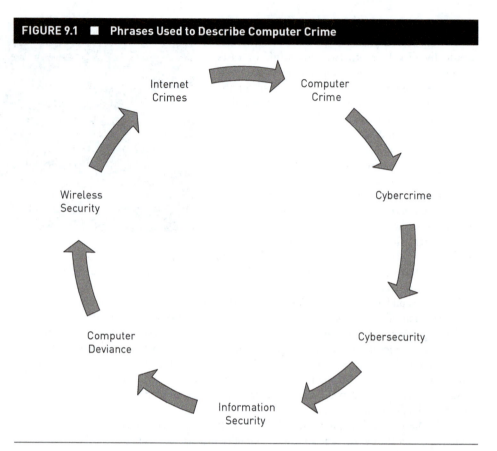

TABLE 9.1 ■ Key Terms in Cybersecurity

Antivirus Software	A program that monitors a computer or network to identify all major types of malware and prevent or contain malware incidents.
Backdoor	A malicious program that listens for commands on a certain Transmission Control Protocol (TCP) or User Datagram Protocol (UDP) port.
Blended Attack	An instance of malware that uses multiple infection or transmission methods.
Boot Sector Virus	A virus that infects the master boot record (MBR) of a hard drive or the boot sector of removable media, such as floppy diskettes.
Compiled Viruses	A virus that has had its source code converted by a compiler program into a format that can be directly executed by an operating system.
Cookie	A small data file that holds information regarding the use of a particular Website.
Deny by Default	A configuration for a firewall or router that denies all incoming and outgoing traffic that is not expressly permitted, such as unnecessary services that could be used to spread malware.
Disinfecting	Removing malware from within a file.
Egress Filtering	Blocking outgoing packets that should not exit a network.

False Negative	An instance in which a security tool intended to detect a particular threat fails to do so.
False Positive	An instance in which a security tool incorrectly classifies benign content as malicious.
File Infector Virus	A virus that attaches itself to executable programs, such as word processors, spreadsheet applications, and computer games.
Host-Based Intrusion Prevention System	A program that monitors the characteristics of a single host and the events occurring within the host to identify and stop suspicious activity.
Indication	A sign that a malware incident may have occurred or may be occurring.
Ingress Filtering	Blocking incoming packets that should not enter a network.
Interpreted Virus	A virus that is composed of source code that can be executed only by a particular application.
Keystroke Logger	A device that monitors and records keyboard usage.
Macro Virus	A virus that attaches itself to application documents, such as word processing files and spreadsheets, and uses the application's macro programming language to execute and propagate.
Malware	A program that is inserted into a system, usually covertly, with the intent of compromising the confidentiality, integrity, or availability of the victim's data, applications, or operating system or of otherwise annoying or disrupting the victim.
Mass Mailing Worm	A worm that spreads by identifying e-mail addresses, often by searching an infected system, and then sending copies of itself to those addresses, either using the system's e-mail client or a self-contained mailer built into the worm itself.
Memory Resident	A virus that stays in the memory of infected systems for an extended period of time.
Mobile Code	Software that is transmitted from a remote system to be executed on a local system, typically without the user's explicit instruction.
Multipartite Virus	A virus that uses multiple infection methods, typically infecting both files and boot sectors.
Network Service Worm	A worm that spreads by taking advantage of a vulnerability in a network service associated with an operating system or an application.
Network-Based Intrusion Prevention System	A program that performs packet sniffing and analyzes network traffic to identify and stop suspicious activity.
On-Access Scanning	Configuring a security tool to perform real-time scans of each file for malware as the file is downloaded, opened, or executed.
On-Demand Scanning	Allowing users to launch security tool scans for malware on a computer as desired.
Payload	The portion of a virus that contains the code for the virus's objective, which may range from the relatively benign (e.g., annoying people, stating personal opinions) to the highly malicious (e.g., forwarding personal information to others, wiping out systems).
Persistent Cookie	A cookie stored on a computer indefinitely so that a Website can identify the user during subsequent visits.
Phishing	Tricking . . . into disclosing sensitive personal information through deceptive computer-based means.

(Continued)

TABLE 9.1 ■ (Continued)

Precursor	A sign that a malware attack may occur in the future.
Proxy	A program that receives a request from a client, and then sends a request on the client's behalf to the desired destination.
Quarantining	Storing files containing malware in isolation for future disinfection or examination.
Remote Administration Tool	A program installed on a system that allows remote attackers to gain access to the system as needed.
Rootkit	A collection of files that is installed on a system to alter the standard functionality of the system in a malicious and stealthy way.
Session Cookie	A temporary cookie that is valid only for a single Website session.
Signature	A set of characteristics of known malware instances that can be used to identify known malware and some new variants of known malware.
Spyware	Malware intended to violate a user's privacy.
Spyware Detection and Removal Utility	A program that monitors a computer to identify spyware and prevent or contain spyware incidents.
Tracking Cookie	A cookie placed on a user's computer to track the user's activity on different Web sites, creating a detailed profile of the user's behavior.
Trigger	A condition that causes a virus payload to be executed, usually occurring through user interaction (e.g., opening a file, running a program, clicking on an e-mail file attachment).
Trojan Horse	A nonreplicating program that appears to be benign but actually has a hidden malicious purpose.
Virus	A form of malware that is designed to self-replicate; make copies of itself; and distribute the copies to other files, programs, or computers.
Web Browser Plug-In	A mechanism for displaying or executing certain types of content through a Web browser.
Web Bug	A tiny graphic on a Website that is referenced within the Hypertext Markup Language (HTML) content of a Web page or e-mail to collect information about the user viewing the HTML content.
Worm	A self-replicating program that is completely self-contained and self-propagating.
Zombie	A program that is installed on a system to cause it to attack other systems.

Source: Definitions Reprinted from Mell, P., Kent, K., & Nusbaum, J. (2005, November). Guide to malware incident prevention and handling: Recommendations of the national institute of standards and technology. *National Institutes of Standards and Technology*, Special Publication 800–83. Retrieved from http://csrc.nist.gov/publications/nistpubs/800-83/SP800-83.pdf

Theft as a Computer Crime

Theft as a type of computer crime refers to a variety of computer-related activities that result in the offender stealing something from the business. Items stolen include funds, information, and intellectual property (Carter & Katz, 1996). In terms of theft of funds, computer crimes include computer fraud and computer embezzlement. In computer fraud cases, offenders gain access to an account they are not supposed to enter and steal from the account. In computer embezzlement cases, the offender already has authorized access to the account by virtue of his or her position in the business.

Theft of information occurs when offenders steal information including (a) information that can be used to trade securities and stocks and (b) intellectual property (Carter & Katz, 1996). Technology has exacerbated the problem of information theft and made it easier for offenders to engage in espionage against businesses and government agencies (Rowe, 2016). One type of information theft, the theft of intellectual property, occurs when offenders steal information that is protected by copyright. Estimates suggest that 63% of computer theft of proprietary information in the United States is done by current employees or employees of other U.S. businesses (Sinrod & Reilly, 2000).

Cyber offenders sometimes use what are called phishing strategies to commit their offenses. **Phishing** refers to the distribution of a large number of e-mails to potential victims, inviting them to participate in a particular scheme. The schemes might include any of the following:

- Advance fee frauds, where victims are promised an extravagant item or service in exchange for a minimal upfront fee

- Refund scams, where victims are promised a refund for something they should have received in the past

- Fake greeting cards

- Fake reimbursements

- Fake lottery winnings

- Promises of assistance with a blocked inheritance (Minnaar, 2008)

Identity theft might also occur as a result of these cyber offenses. In these situations, offenders steal the identity of a victim and use that identity to receive credit, make purchases, and engage in business transactions. Identity theft has been characterized as more of a "social construction" than a "legal construction" on the basis that the behavior is not technically new behavior (Wall, 2013). Sometimes the size of these thefts may make them too small for authorities to investigate, and corporations are increasingly expecting victims to be responsible for protecting their identity (Wall, 2013). Also, according to one estimate, it may take more than two years for victims to recover any goods/funds they lost from identity offenses (Martin & Rice, 2011).

Not all criminologists define identity theft as a form of white-collar crime. The acts are often committed by unemployed and traditional offenders. Also, the behavior has been linked to terrorism, with one author team describing identity theft as "one of the most lucrative enterprises which terrorists have engaged in" (Perri & Brody, 2011, p. 55). In these situations, identity theft provides terrorists many items of value, including money, the ability to hide in plain sight, access across borders, and entrance into airports.

Unauthorized Access as a Computer Crime

Unauthorized access occurs when individuals break into various computer databases to which they do not have legitimate access. *Hacker* is a term used to describe those who have the skills to access various secure computer databases and programs but do so only out of a desire to experiment to see if they are able to access these programs. **Crackers** crack into computer systems "with [the intent] to sabotage and cause chaos to [the] corporation" (Wiggins, 2002, p. 20). Health care providers and utility companies are believed to be especially vulnerable to these incidents (Rogers, 2002).

Two types of crackers exist—those outside the targeted business and those inside the business. Crackers outside the business engage in their activities to "cause disruption to the networks for personal or political motives" (Sinrod & Reilly, 2000, p. 5 [e-version]). Hacktivism is the concept of politically motivated cracking and hacking. Some crackers may commit their acts in order to highlight security problems to the company. Others might commit electronic theft of credit card information, while some may engage in what is called netspionage (e.g., stealing confidential information) (Philippsohn, 2001).

When insiders are the crackers, a different set of concerns arise. Data breaches by insiders have been found to be more costly than breaches by outsiders (Ponemon Institute, 2015, May).

According to Sinrod and Reilly (2000), "disgruntled employees are the greatest threat to a computer's security" (p. 7 [e-version]). Another expert suggested that cyber intrusions are "usually not an 'outside' job" (Minnaar, 2013, p. iii). When insiders break into computer systems, they are believed to do so for any of the following reasons:

- Destroying information valuable to the company

- Finding secrets than can be sold

- Deleting client lists

- Destroying information that the company would find valuable

- Selling lists of clients/consumers to competitors (Minnaar, 2013)

The term *extrusion* specifically refers to instances when employees access information and provide that information to outsiders. Typically, companies are most vulnerable to this when employees are leaving a company (Finkel, 2014). As a result, companies frequently shut down data access of departing employees as soon as possible.

Even if insiders are not the offenders in the cyber intrusion, employees may be targeted for entry points into a company's databases. One cybersecurity advisor told a journalist, "hackers have increased their focus on trying to enter an enterprise network through 'soft' targets (i.e., users and employees) rather than trying to attack the servers, switches, and networks" (Meyer, 2015, p. 34). Indeed, sometimes the threat posed by insiders stems from unintentional but negligent actions. These threats include behaviors such as (1) keeping sensitive information on personal devices that are not safe (e.g., if your professor kept your grades on a public computer), (2) failing to understand how to respond to cyberattacks, (3) sharing passwords with friends or coworkers, and (4) selecting passwords that are easy to identify (Ritchie, 2014). Essentially, two types of insider threats exist: intentional insider attacks by employees and attacks by "inadvertent insiders" who make a mistake and place the company at risk (Mrcela & Vuletic, 2018).

There is no way of knowing how many data breaches occur each year. These are cases that are especially hard to detect. While virus protection software will alert companies to the introduction of viruses, it is not as easy to detect a cyber intrusion. One estimate suggests that it takes, on average, 243 days before breaches are detected (Kawalec, 2014). As well, the time it takes to "recover" from intrusions has grown from a two week "recovery time" in 2010 to a one month "recovery time" in 2013 (Kawalec, 2013).

After cyber intrusions occur, companies will decide whether to notify law enforcement. Reasons that companies choose to notify the police about these intrusions include the following:

- The police may be able to help catch the cyber offenders and keep them away from the company's computer systems.

- The police are in a position to help the company retrieve the stolen data, if possible. If it is not possible, the police may be helpful in minimizing losses.

- Working with law enforcement can strengthen the skills of the company security team.

- The company may have a legal obligation to report the intrusion (Chabinsky, 2013).

Alternatively, failure to report these incidents may be illegal, open the business up to civil lawsuits, increase their risk of cyber victimization, and lead to negative publicity (Davis, 2003). In some ways, being a victim of cybersecurity offenses, and failing to report that victimization, may actually result in a company committing a white-collar crime. In these situations, mistakes that companies might make include failing to notify the Securities Exchange Commission (SEC) of cyber incidents, failing to follow protocol established by the company, failing to follow comprehensive breach policies, and failing to monitor cyber risks that surface when working with other business partners or contractors (Reed & Scott, 2013). Companies and employees could be prosecuted for any of these failures.

One author team has identified four pragmatic actions that companies should perform after a data breach: (1) identify the attack, (2) manage the offense, (3) restore operations, and (4) communicate with stakeholders (McNerney & Papadopoulos, 2013). Another expert recommended answering a series of questions that should be asked in order to determine how to respond. These questions include (1) what kind of cyber-attack occurred?; (2) why did it occur?; and (3) who committed the intrusion? (Brenner, 2007). The answers to these questions will determine whether the action is defined as a type of cybercrime, a type of terrorism, or cyber warfare. In turn, this determination will dictate which officials should be notified about the intrusion.

Recent attention has been given to the confusion that surfaces surrounding data breaches. One issue that arises is that there is no central agency responsible for monitoring data breaches. Some researchers have called for "the creation of a federal agency to deal with national data breaches across all industries [as a] next logical step" (Collins, Saintano, & Khey, 2011, p. 807). In theory, such an agency would allow government resources to be allocated in a way that protects the most vulnerable industries in a fair way.

Virus Introduction as a Computer Crime

Virus introduction is another type of computer crime. Viruses are introduced for various reasons. Crackers typically introduce viruses for recreational reasons, pride, profit, protection, or cyberterrorism reasons. Recreationally, just as some unsupervised youth might vandalize public property, crackers find pleasure in "vandalizing" computer programs. In terms of pride, successfully sabotaging computer programs that are difficult to break into provides crackers a sense of accomplishment. In terms of profit, crackers can profit either from stealing funds themselves or from being paid by a coconspirator who is unable to carry out the crime alone. Also, viruses are introduced as a form of protection by employees to cover up evidence of their thefts and protect them from being identified (Carter & Katz, 1996).

With regard to cyberterrorists, crackers aim to use viruses to threaten public security. Note that the types of activities of cyberterrorists are much different from the virus introducing activities of traditional crackers. Consider the following two examples described by Barry C. Collin (2001) of the Institute for Security and Intelligence at the 11th Annual Symposium of Criminal Justice Issues:

- A CyberTerrorist will remotely access the processing control systems of a cereal manufacturer, change the levels of iron supplement, and sicken and kill the children of a nation enjoying their food. That CyberTerrorist will then perform similar remote alterations at a processor of infant formula. The key: the CyberTerrorist does not have to be at the factory to execute these acts.

- A CyberTerrorist will attack the next generation of air traffic control systems, and collide two large civilian aircraft. This is a realistic scenario, since the CyberTerrorist will also crack the aircraft's in-cockpit sensors. Much of the same can be done to the rail lines.

Some will question whether cyberterrorism is a form of white-collar crime. To be sure, not all cases would necessarily fit within the types of behaviors typically characterized as white-collar crimes. However, note that some companies might commit cyberterroristic activities against others, and when businesses are targeted, it can be suggested that they have experienced a form of white-collar victimization. The enormous threats that cyberterrorists pose for businesses and governments have led state and federal officials to develop cyberterrorism law enforcement units.

Viruses may also be introduced in the form of denial-of-service attacks. These attacks make programs or websites nonfunctional (Bartolacci, LeBlanc, & Podhradsky, 2014). Generally speaking, two types of denial-of-service attacks exist: permanent denial of service and personal denial-of-service attacks. Permanent denials (also known as phlashing) aim to make software or a computer system permanently inaccessible. In contrast, in personal denials, a specific individual or business is targeted. The differences in the two varieties center on the nature of the victim, the motivation, the consequences, and the processes used by the offender to carry out the attack (Bartolacci et al., 2014).

Ransomware is an example of a personal denial-of-service attack. With ransomware, offenders are able to stop a victim's computer from working and essentially hold that computer hostage until a ransom is paid or the virus is removed. One popular form of ransomware was the Moneypak virus. This virus attaches itself to the victim's computer and threatens to prosecute the victim for a copyright violation, child pornography, or some other offense unless the victim pays a "fine" using an untraceable prepaid Moneypak card. The FBI's seal appears on the frozen computer screen and, in some cases, the camera from the computer is activated and a video of the victim appears in the upper left hand of the computer screen. The official appearance of the virus led many victims to actually pay the offender. Victims would realize they were victimized when the offender never released the virus from the computer.

Software Crime as a Computer Crime

Software crimes refer to situations when computer software is central to the offense. Four overlapping types of software crimes exist: (1) theft of software, (2) counterfeiting software, (3) copyright violations of computer software, and (4) piracy (Wiggins, 2002). **Theft of software** refers to instances when workers steal computer software that their company owns and use it for their personal use. Imagine a situation where a worker has a copy of a photo editing program. The computer software is supposed to be loaded only on the worker's office computer. If the worker takes the software home and loads it on his or her home computer so family members can use the software for personal reasons, then misconduct has occurred.

Counterfeiting software crimes occur when individuals make counterfeit copies of particular software programs. Microsoft (2010) describes these crimes as resulting from "unauthorized copying, reproduction, or manufacture of software products." Once the counterfeit software is produced, it is sold to consumers (a) by fraudulent business owners, (b) through e-mail scams, (c) in online auction sites like eBay, (d) on websites like Amazon.com, and (e) by street vendors (Microsoft, 2010). In what was called the "most significant crackdown on software piracy," the FBI and Chinese authorities arrested more than two dozen individuals as part of an offense involving "more than $500 million worth of counterfeit Microsoft and Symantec software that was being made in China and distributed worldwide" (Barboza & Lohr, 2007).

Copyright violations of computer software occur when users use software for purposes beyond what was intended under the copyright agreement described on the software. This could include illegally reproducing, altering, selling, or misrepresenting software programs. Piracy is also seen as a type of copyright violation.

Electronic and software piracy refers to theft of copyright-protected electronic information, including software, electronic programs, and electronic files of movies and music. The

Digital Millennium Copyright Act of 1998 was passed in an effort to limit piracy and copyright violations. The law stipulates that it is illegal to possess, sell, or distribute codecracking devices and calls for stiff penalties for offenders (Higgins, 2006). Much more will be written about piracy when considering students and computer crime. At this point, it is significant to note that the government has been building its efforts to respond to piracy. These efforts are captured in a statement then-Vice President Joe Biden made to reporters: "Piracy is theft. Clean and simple. It's smash and grab. It ain't no different than smashing a window at Tiffany's and grabbing [merchandise]."

Internet Crimes

Internet crimes are a range of offenses committed by offenders through the use of the Internet. A decade ago, it was estimated that Internet crime losses totaled one trillion dollars across the world (Rataj, 2001). Examples of Internet crimes reported to the FBI (2010b) include the following:

- Fake e-mail messages from the FBI: scammers sending potential victims e-mail messages requesting funds as part of an FBI investigation

- Nondelivered merchandise: not receiving merchandise purchased on an Internet website

- Nonpayment for items sold on the Internet: not being paid for items sold through auction sites or other Internet websites

- Advance-fee fraud: requesting fees for goods or services that will never be provided

- Identity theft: stealing and falsely using someone's personal identity information

- Overpayment fraud: sending a counterfeit check for a purchase and asking for the difference to be returned

Figure 9.2 shows the number of complaints the FBI's Internet Crime Complaint Center received, and the losses attached to those complaints between 2015 and 2020. As shown in the figure, the number of crimes reported and the costs of the offenses have increased dramatically. In fact, these financial costs nearly quadrupled from $1.1 billion in 2015 to $4.2 billion in 2020. Note that 2020 saw a significant increase of more than 300,000 cybercrime incidents reported to the complaint center. The increase is at least partly attributed to Covid-19 given that so many individuals turned to cyberspace for their work and social needs in 2020. Figure 9.3 shows the age distribution among people reporting victimization. As shown in the figure, older victims lost more to Internet crimes, and victimization numbers increased with age for ages 30 and above. The most common Internet crimes reported in 2019 and 2020 were phishing and nonpayment/non-delivery (see Figure 9.4). Note the significant increase in each of these offense types between the two years.

WHITE-COLLAR CYBERCRIME

The discussion in the previous section shows the breadth of cybercrime and the numerous types of cyber offending. It is important to note that each of the other types of crime discussed in other chapters of this text could be forms of cybercrime if they are committed using cyber tools. Health care crimes, market manipulations, and insider trading cases, for example, have involved the use of cyber technologies in some cases (Collier, 2016). A cyber attack on offshore

FIGURE 9.2 ■ Number of Complaints Received by Internet Crime Complaint Center and Amount of Losses Reported, 2015–2020

+Losses rounded to the nearest million.

Year	Complaints	Losses+
2020	791,710	$4.2 Billion
2019	467,361	$3.5 Billion
2018	351,937	$2.7 Billion
2017	301,580	$1.4 Billion
2016	298,728	$1.5 Billion
2015	288,012	$1.1 Billion

Source: Internet Crime Complaint Center. (2021). *2020 annual report.* Retrieved from https://www.fbi.gov/news/pressrel/press-releases/fbi-releases-the-internet-crime-complaint-center-2020-internet-crime-report-including-covid-19-scam-statistics

FIGURE 9.3 ■ Age and Losses to Internet Crimes

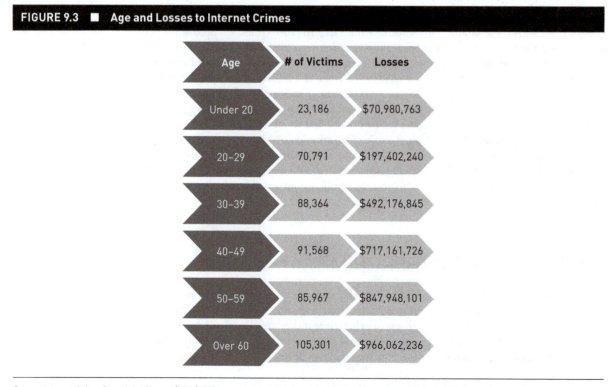

Age	# of Victims	Losses
Under 20	23,186	$70,980,763
20–29	70,791	$197,402,240
30–39	88,364	$492,176,845
40–49	91,568	$717,161,726
50–59	85,967	$847,948,101
Over 60	105,301	$966,062,236

Source: Internet Crime Complaint Center. (2021). *2020 annual report.* Retrieved from https://www.ic3.gov/Media/PDF/AnnualReport/2020_IC3Report.pdf

FIGURE 9.4 ■ Most Common Types of Victimization Reported to IC3

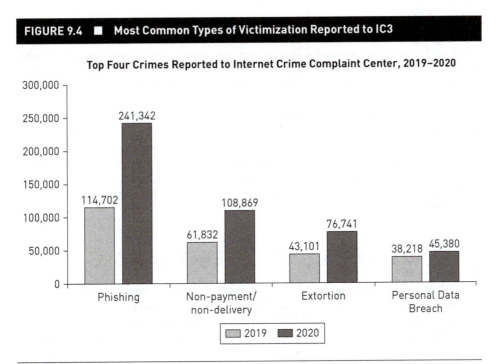

Top Four Crimes Reported to Internet Crime Complaint Center, 2019–2020

Source: Internet Crime Complaint Center. (2021). *2020 annual report.* Retrieved from https://www.ic3.gov/Media/PDF/AnnualReport/2020_IC3Report.pdf

FIGURE 9.5 ■ White-Collar Cybercrime

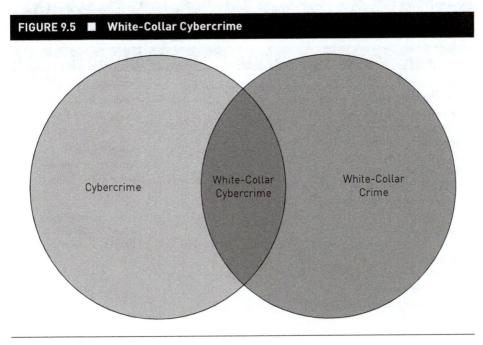

Source: Reprinted from Payne (2018)

oil rigs would be both a cybercrime and an environmental crime (Crandal, 2019). Sales crimes occurring online would be both a sales crime and a cybercrime. False advertising in online sales would be a cybercrime and a form of corporate crime. With these intersections, who should respond to the cases? Respondents are usually the Department of Justice, Securities Exchange Commission, Federal Bureau of Investigation, or authorities with cyber expertise (Collier, 2016).

Not all cybercrimes are actually white-collar crimes. Therefore, the phrase "**white-collar cybercrime**" describes situations when cybercrimes are committed at work by employees or employers (Payne, 2018). The term draws attention to the overlap and the similarities between white-collar crime and cybercrime. Distinguishing between the two types of crime helps to avoid conflating the extent of both crime varieties, their causes, and strategies to stop them. At the same time, scholars and practitioners alike must recognize that significant overlap exists between the two types (Payne, 2018).

CHARACTERISTICS OF CYBERCRIMINALS

Just as there are different types of cybercrimes, so too there are different types of cybercriminals. The most general characterization can focus on characteristics of cybercriminals in terms of their (1) roles in the offense and (2) the networks to which they are attached. In terms of their role in the offense, some cybercriminals may operate alone, while others may work with other offenders. One criminal justice scholar classified cyber offenders as loners, associates, and crime networks (Rege-Patwardhan, 2009). From this typology, loners include novice offenders, insiders, and professionals who work alone (Rege-Patwardhan, 2009). An example of professionals are *cyber mercenaries* or "specialists who sell their knowledge and training to whoever is willing to pay" (Valeri, 1998, p. 52). Services are even available online where hackers are rated based on how well they perform (Kawalec, 2014). Television shows and movies tend to sensationalize criminals, including cybercriminals (see this chapter's Streaming White-Collar Crime).

STREAMING WHITE-COLLAR CRIME *Mr. Robot*: Cybersecurity Engineer Turns Hacker		
Plot	**What You Can Learn**	**Discussion Questions**
Allsafe cybersecurity engineer and hacktivist Elliot Alderson is recruited by Mr. Robot to use his hactivism skills against E-Corp, his employer's largest client. Viewers see inside Elliot's mind and inside his computer. Elliot's hacking rationalizations are so convincing that viewers might feel envy about not being able to engage in similar heroic, albeit criminal, actions. Joining an underground hacking society, Elliot narrates his inner thoughts while going out of his way to protect coworker and childhood friend Angela, who wants to take down E-Corp through legitimate means.	A hacker subculture exists. Hackers tend to be younger than other types of white-collar criminals.	Why do you think hackers tend to be younger than other white-collar offenders? Are all types of cybercrime types of white-collar crime? Explain. How might hackers engage in behaviors helpful to society?

The concept of "network" is relevant to cybercriminals in three different ways: (1) these are offenders who are very familiar with computer networks, software, and technology; (2) cyber offenders often work in a network with other offenders; and (3) cyber offenders often are part of a broader distribution network that mimics the way traditional goods are distributed. Regarding their familiarity with computer networks, cyber offenders have the knowledge and skills to access various computer networks. Consider botnets as an illustration. A botnet is a group of infected computers under the simultaneous control of one offender while those computers are connected to the Internet. It is nearly impossible to determine the source of the botnet or the identity of the offender (van der Wagen & Pieters, 2015). It is important to note that their access to these computer networks is not immediate. According to one expert, "successful intrusions almost always occur by hackers who first got away with thousands of unsuccessful intrusion attempts" (Chabinsky, 2015, April 1, p. 46).

These actions frequently occur within an offender network. A review of Department of Justice cases from 2010 found that more than half of the cases involved offenders who collaborated with other offenders (Lusthaus, 2012). In these cases, offenders assume "cybercriminal identities" to maintain anonymity. This is different from conventional crimes where fake identities are rare. Some have drawn attention to "cybergangs" to describe the relationships between these offenders. According to G. S. Smith (2015), the characteristics of cybergangs are as follows:

- They are formed because of their expertise.

- They communicate online.

- They have strong technological skills.

- Whereas traditional gangs have reputations across neighborhoods, their reputation is online.

- While traditional gangs control a small part of a neighborhood, these gangs cover international areas.

- They tend to be more flexible than traditional gangs.

- Their motive is profit and information, not violence.

- They tend to have self-taught skills.

Organized crime networks have also been connected to cybercrime. First, in some situations, organized crime groups might use cyber technology to commit crimes such as prostitution, gambling, and so on. Second, some organized crime networks (such as those previously cited by Smith) might operate purely online. Third, some organized crime groups might use cyber technology to create havoc in order to promote their political or ideological beliefs.

With regard to the distribution network, when cyber offenders steal information for profit motives, they need to find ways to sell that information. Similar to the way that burglars and other thieves fence their goods, cyber offenders use different strategies to distribute their stolen information. One research team studied 300 threads in a web-based discussion forum to shed light on the way stolen data is marketed online (Holt & Lampke, 2010).

The items sold most often were dumps. Holt and Lampke (2010) explain that the term *dump* is used to refer to the credit card or bank account information being marketed. Track 1 "dumps" include the credit card number, name of cardholder, and some additional information, while Track 2 "dumps" include the card information, the encrypted pin, and some additional information. Track 2 dumps are more common.

Other items marketed included compromised bank accounts, compromised PayPal accounts, plastics (blank cards that could be converted into credit cards), e-mail databases, and hacking services. As with other online forums, buyers could even rate the data thieves as verified (they have sold before), unverified, or "rippers." Here is a review of a ripper:

THIS GUY IS A RIPPER HE RIP ME FOR A LOT OF MONEY AND SENT ME ALL

BOGUS DUMPS . . . WE HAVE TO HAVE HONOR WITH EACH OTHER IN

ORDER TO KEEP THIS BUSINESS FLOWING YOU HAVE TOOK MONEY

FROMA FEWLLOW CARDER KNOWING YOUR DUMPS ARE BOGUS . . . YOU'RE A MARK IN THE DARK AND A PUNK IN THE TRUNK F**K YOU! (Holt & Lampke, 2010, p. 44)

If you ever purchase stolen data, you are advised not to pay with your credit card! Incidentally, the authorities sometimes infiltrate these networks.

COSTS OF CYBERCRIME

As noted in Chapter 2, the costs of all white-collar crimes include physical, social, and economic consequences, and these consequences can be quite significant. The physical and social costs of cybercrime can be particularly devastating, but they are not well-studied. On one hand, imagine a time when you did not have access to technology and how that impacted you both personally and socially. We have become so dependent on technology that some psychologists have suggested that some individuals may, in fact, become addicted to technology. For those who are addicted, instances when cyber offending stops individuals from accessing their technology will cause both physical and social consequences. More pragmatically, instances when cyber offenses attack the critical infrastructure can also result in both physical and social losses for members of society.

The phrase **critical infrastructure** refers to parts of the public sector that societies rely on in order to provide basic services. The USA Federal Critical Infrastructure Protection Policy identifies the following sectors as critical infrastructures:

- Agriculture
- Banking
- Chemicals and hazardous wastes
- Defense industry
- Energy services
- Food
- Government
- Information technology/telecom
- Postal and shipping
- Public health and health care
- Transportation
- Water treatment and drinking water (Skylar, 2012)

The operations of each of these sectors rely heavily on technology. Depending on the types of services offered by the critical infrastructure, the consequences from attacks on these entities could range from food poisoning to freezing temperatures to pollution to heat exposure to traffic delays (Rege-Patwardhan, 2009). Concern about a cyberattack on the critical infrastructure led former Secretary of Defense Leon Panetta to warn about the possibility of a "cyber Pearl Harbor" (McNerney & Papadopoulos, 2013, p. 1244).

One of the first publicized cyberattacks on a critical infrastructure involved a teenager's attack on a computer system of the Worcester, Massachusetts computer system. The attack crippled the airport for six hours (Rege-Patwardhan, 2009). Cases can be true examples of white-collar offenses where employees commit crime as part of their job. In 2006, for example, two disgruntled engineers hacked into the Los Angeles Traffic Surveillance Center's computer system as part of a protest against the wage paid to city engineers. The hackers created havoc by programming traffic lights near major intersections so as to create gridlock (Rege-Patwardhan, 2009). While no injuries occurred from this critical infrastructure attack, the possibility existed. Of course, there were certainly economic costs arising out of the attack in terms of public safety efforts directed toward protecting motorists from the malfunctioning stoplights.

PHOTO 9.2 Health care providers rely heavily on computers to do their jobs. Cyberattacks on hospitals could be devastating.

FDA photo by Michael J. Ermarth

Hospitals may be especially susceptible to cyber attacks. Cases of ransomware place hospitals in a particularly vulnerable situation where they have no choice but to pay the ransom to the offender(s) holding the hospital's cyber system hostage (Mrcela & Vuletic, 2018). Compared to business and financial institutions, hospitals are relatively new to the cybersecurity world, placing them at a higher risk for victimization given their lack of experience in securing information (Vuletic, 2018). In addition, insiders are threats in hospital attacks because they know about the hospital's cyber infrastructure, and they are familiar with its vulnerabilities (Mrcela & Vuletic, 2018).

The Ponemon Institute (a cybersecurity think tank) categorizes the costs of cybercrime into internal and external costs. Internal costs refer to costs experienced within the company. These include detection costs, investigation costs, containment costs, recovering costs, and ex-post responding costs. External costs refer to costs involving parties or relationships outside the business. These include information loss, business disruption, damaged equipment, and revenue loss (Ponemon Institute, 2015, October).

The most recent estimates of the costs of cyber offending come from the Ponemon Institute's (2015, October) Cost of Cybercrime Survey. The institute interviewed 2,128 employees working in 252 companies across seven countries. The study found that, on average, the companies reported losing $7.7 million a year to cyberattacks. The United States had the highest average losses at roughly $15 million per company, while Russia had the lowest average cost at $2.37 million. While all types of organizations incurred losses, the losses were higher in the financial, utility, and energy industries.

The October 2015 Ponemon study also found that just over one third of the companies attributed some of their attacks to a malicious insider. There may be reason to believe that the role of insiders varies across countries. In terms of cost, in the United States, 10% of the costs from cyberattacks were attributed to insiders, while in Japan, 19% of the costs from cyberattacks were attributed to insiders. In Germany, 6% of the total costs were attributed to insiders. Another important pattern surrounding insider attacks is that they take longer to address than other attacks. Once identified, insider attacks took an average of 54.4 days to address, while other attacks took much less time: Web attacks took 27 days, phishing took 22 days, and denial of service attacks took 22 days. The average cost for insider attacks was also higher than all other attacks: They cost $144,542 on average in comparison to an average cost of $1,900 for viruses and **worms**.

Explaining Computer Crime

Although it is impossible to know for certain why computer crimes occur, a handful of explanations that are routinely cited will likely help clarify the source of many of these offenses. In particular, computer crimes are commonly attributed to human factors, opportunity, structural changes, peer associations, and cultural factors. Each of these explanations will be briefly reviewed here and discussed in more detail when causes of all forms of white-collar crime are considered later in this text.

The explanations of *human factors* focus on the types of activities individuals and businesses engage in and how those activities contribute to offending. For example, research shows that cyber intrusions against universities are more likely to occur during business hours and that the fewest intrusions occur between 5:00 p.m. and 12:59 a.m. (Maimon, Kamerdze, Cukier, & Sobesto, 2013). The same study found that attack patterns were related to foreign students' countries of origin, which suggests that "the human element is a key component when dealing with computer security" (p. 337). Another study of 600 students and faculty found that factors involved with cyber victimization included using someone's Internet without their permission, viewing pornography, pirating media, and cyber harassment (Holt & Bossler, 2013). Elsewhere, the same author team found that, for students, engaging in computer deviance may increase individuals' risk of being victimized by malicious software (Bossler & Holt, 2011). The authors suggest that because online behaviors may contribute to victimization risk, "crime and victimization in the real world may be replicated in online environments" (p. 338). In fact, for some types of cyber victimization, it has been found that behaviors and activities of victims are related to victimization, while presence of guardianship (e.g., malware) was not (Holt & Bossler, 2008).

Opportunity explanations center on the ease by which these offenses are committed, particularly for those who have a high degree of knowledge about computers. Offenders can target a high number of victims with great ease and relatively quickly—sometimes with a few key strokes on the computer keyboard. From this perspective, the steady availability of and access to computers provides offenders opportunities to commit all sorts of crimes. Many criminal justice sanctions for convicted computer criminals are based on the belief that opportunity contributes to the crime. As a condition of probation, many offenders are not allowed to own computers or live in a home where computers are present. The assumption is that restricting the opportunity for computer crime will prevent computer crimes from occurring.

Some experts attribute computer crimes to *structural changes*, an explanation that fits well within the ideals of the systems perspective. When I was born in the early 1980s (okay, I'm fibbing about the date), there was virtually no concern about computer crime. Technology was extremely limited. I have fond memories of playing Pong with my brother on our 26-inch black-and-white Zenith television. The television didn't have a remote control—unless you consider my brother and me as my father's remote control. In any event, changes in the technological, educational, social, and political systems resulted in technological advancements that have changed our society. One technological change entailed an increase in the use of computers to the point that virtually all businesses and most individuals in the United States now are computer literate. The increased presence of computers, then, provides new criminogenic opportunities. Consider that the advent of the Internet has resulted in different types of computer crimes (Yar, 2006). It is important to note that the crimes committed with computers are not all necessarily new crimes but that the technologies for committing the crimes are new (Montano, 2001). As shown previously, crimes such as theft, trespassing, and vandalism are committed with computers. These are not new crimes per se, though new laws are used to respond to instances where these crimes are committed with the use of computers.

These technological changes may, however, lead to different varieties of crime. Consider, for example "cyborg crime" (van der Wagen & Pieters, 2015). The hybrid nature of human/technological behavior may lead to new interactions, which have been labeled cyborg crime. While a human's actions might initiate a technological action, technology can now act or behave in a way that alters the crime or carries out additional violations. In other words, robots—in the near future— might actually commit crime! Whether one agrees with this possibility, most experts agree that in order to understand cyber offending, attention must be given to both network factors and human factors.

Computer crimes have also been explained by *peer association*, which suggests that the crimes occur as the result of individuals being associated with peers who might be more prone to commit these offenses. Studies of middle school students (Holt, Bossler, & May, 2012) and college students (Gunter, 2009) have supported these explanations. One study found that the seriousness of computer crimes committed by college students was tied to negative peer associations—the more negative peer associations students had, the more serious the types of computer misconduct they committed (Morris & Blackburn, 2009). In another study, a survey of 581 college students found that factors contributing to piracy and illegal access included differential associations, imitation, and differential reinforcement (Skinner & Fream, 1997). The same pattern has been found for cyber victimization: Having peers who engaged in cyber deviance has been found to increase the likelihood of experiencing cyber harassment (Holt & Bossler, 2008).

Cultural factors also impact cyber offending. Cybercrime is an international problem, but certain countries may be at a higher risk for different types of cyber offenses. One author, for example, has pointed to five factors that place China and Taiwan at a high risk for cyber offenses between the two countries:

1. Both countries have high populations of Internet users.

2. Residents are not fully aware of appropriate security precautions.

3. A similar language and culture between the two countries makes it easier for offenders to attack one another.

4. Security companies resist developed measures (e.g., malware) that would work only in Chinese systems.

5. Political tensions between the two countries may increase the likelihood of offending (Chang, 2013).

Of course, there is no definitive explanation for why computer crimes occur. Explanations vary across offenders and offense types. For example, factors that lead males to commit computer crimes might be different from the factors that contribute to females' decisions to commit these offenses. As well, the causes of virus introductions might be different from the causes of computer fraud or computer embezzlement. Unfortunately, few studies have focused on the motivations for computer crime. Being unable to accurately pinpoint the causes of these behaviors has made it more difficult for authorities to respond to computer crimes.

Problems Responding to Computer Crimes

In addition to the fact that the causes of computer crime are not clear, other factors have made it more difficult to respond to computer crimes. These problems stem from the dynamics of the offense, awareness issues, offender characteristics, jurisdictional issues, criminal justice dynamics, victim characteristics and decisions, and collaboration issues. With regard to the dynamics of the offense, four issues arise. First, computer crime is an offense that occurs very quickly (Carter & Katz, 1996). Some have referred to the crimes as "hit and run" offenses because of how quickly the offenses occur (McMullan & Perrier, 2007). Second, the offenses, by their very nature, are international in scope, making it difficult to even know where the crime actually occurred (Speer, 2000). Third, the technological nature of the crimes allows the offenses to occur without victims even realizing that they have been victimized until hours, days, weeks, or even months after the offense occurred. Fourth, the nature of computer offenses is constantly changing, making it more difficult to watch for signs of the crimes. Indirectly discussing these offense dynamics, one author wrote: "'Online' is a vast place that promises lots of anonymity as well as eager collectors and conspirators. There is little in the way of a paper trail in these cases, and hardly anyone around to recall a face" (Scullin, 2014, p. 91).This relates to awareness issues that make it difficult to respond to cybercrime. Common misconceptions about cybercrime are that only tech companies are targeted for these crimes, and only IT staff needs to respond (Chabinsky, 2015, April 1, May 1; Davis, 2003). One expert adds the following misconceptions that businesses and employees have about cybercrime:

- It is wrongly assumed that employees should be the first line of defense to cyberattacks, when they should be the last line of defense.

- Companies sometimes erroneously believe they are insulated against cyberattacks.

- Smaller business owners and employees might incorrectly assume they will not be targeted.

- If the federal authorities are notified, a raid will follow.

- Federal oversight will protect all businesses.

- Information sharing is simple and straightforward.

- Companies should devote their efforts toward defense, with little concern given to identifying offenders.

- Businesses can become invincible to attacks.

- Computer patches can be used to stop attacks (Chabinsky, 2015, April 1, May 1).

These misconceptions can leave businesses vulnerable to attacks. It has been suggested that the sources of many misconceptions about cyber offending include inaccurate reporting by the media, the failure of victims to report victimization, conceptual ambiguity regarding cybercrime, and jurisdictional differences in cybercrime definitions (Wall, 2013).

In terms of offender characteristics, computer offenders tend to be highly educated people who are able to go to great lengths to conceal their crimes and their identities. When a conventional offender robs a bank, witnesses see the offender, and cameras may even provide pictures of the suspect. When a computer criminal robs a bank, no one sees the criminal, and pictures are certainly not available. Offenders' technical knowledge is the equivalent of the stereotypical ski mask that conventional offenders wear in old cops-and-robbers movies.

Jurisdictional issues also surface and make it more difficult to address cybercrimes, particularly those that cross international borders. If a cybercrime starts in one country and ends in another country, which country has jurisdiction? What if the information "traveled through" the cyberspace of yet another country? These questions make it fundamentally more difficult to address cybercrimes (Bernate & Godlove, 2012). Legal expert Susan Brenner (2006) identified the following additional jurisdictional challenges that may surface in cybercrime cases:

- There may be cases where no government has jurisdiction.

- It may be impossible for a particular government to "assert" jurisdiction.

- Multiple countries might claim jurisdiction over the same offense.

Summarizing these challenges, Brenner (2006) writes that "pieces of the cybercrime occur in territory claimed by several different sovereigns" (p. 189).Criminal justice dynamics also contribute to problems in responding to computer crimes. Often, criminal justice professionals are not adequately trained in how to respond to computer crimes (Carter & Katz, 1996). Also, solving these offenses requires collaboration between criminal justice agencies, and such collaboration may be difficult to carry out at times (Montano, 2001). In some cases, international collaboration may be necessary (Speer, 2000). Criminal justice officials must grapple with resource deployment issues in deciding the amount of fiscal resources and workload to devote to responding to computer crimes (McMullan & Perrier, 2007).

Victim characteristics and behaviors inhibit the response to computer crimes. On one level, it is difficult in some cases to identify victims of computer crimes, especially when businesses and individuals do not even know they have been victimized (Speer, 2000). On another level, even when businesses are victimized by a computer crime, many will decide not to report the offense to the authorities. If the offense is not reported, authorities cannot respond to the offense.

Collaboration issues refer to problems that criminal justice officials confront in their efforts to work with other officials in responding to cybercrime. Workers from different agencies will often have their own goals, their own professional language, and limited interaction with those from other agencies (see Bolton, 2013). When called upon to work together in responding to cybercrime, collaboration barriers may arise that inhibit effective and efficient responses. In many ways, the bureaucratic "red tape" that surfaces potentially inhibits collaborative responses to crimes committed in the cyber system.

Reasons for this lack of cooperation include the clear lines of authority between different agencies, the "novelty" of cybercrime, the "blurred" jurisdictional lines, and a long history of animosity between organizations (Givens & Busch, 2013). This lack of cooperation is not just between public agencies. Indeed, private agencies may be even less willing to cooperate in cybercrime investigations. As one author notes, private companies providing critical infrastructure services (such as electricity) would be more concerned with continuing to provide services and less concerned with where the offense originated from (Zhang, 2011). Public agencies, on the other hand, would want to know who committed the attack. An unwillingness to share information makes the investigations even more difficult. In the public sector, some believe that information security specialists have the "tendency to over classify documents" (Bolton, 2013, p. 6).

Experts have identified strategies to improve collaboration between agencies in cybercrime investigations. One author suggested the following:

- Officials should avoid jargon, acronyms, and language specific to their profession.

- Interactions should be increased between parties.

- The focus should be on the goals rather than the process.

- Disconnects between parties should be identified (Bolton, 2013).

The federal government has taken a stronger role in promoting information sharing between agencies addressing cyber offenses. To promote communication between agencies and reduce the risk of attacks on government or public systems related to critical infrastructures, former President Obama signed Executive Order 12,636. The order, titled "Improving Critical Infrastructure Cybersecurity," was hailed as "an important step toward protecting critical infrastructures from cyber threats" (Broggi, 2014, p. 676). Strategies for promoting information sharing were described as necessary in order to reduce cyber threats. The order specifically stated,

> It is the policy of the United States Government to increase the volume, timeliness, and quality of cyber threat information shared with U.S. private sector entities so that these entities may better protect and defend themselves against cyber threats. Within

120 days of the date of this order, the Attorney General, the Secretary of Homeland Security (the "Secretary"), and the Director of National Intelligence shall each issue instructions consistent with their authorities and with the requirements of section 12(c) of this order to ensure the timely production of unclassified reports of cyber threats to the U.S. homeland that identify a specific targeted entity. The instructions shall address the need to protect intelligence and law enforcement sources, methods, operations, and investigations. (White House, 2013)

Each of the problems addressed in this section could be at least partially addressed by better preparing professionals for cybersecurity careers. Currently, few university programs focus on cybersecurity, meaning the professionals do not receive the preparation they need (Gogolin, 2011). It is important to note that some colleges and universities have developed academic programs focused on cybersecurity. These courses and programs, however, are sometimes too narrowly construed to effectively address cybercrime.

The Interdisciplinary Response to Cybercrime

Over the past two decades, higher education scholars have increasingly recognized the value of interdisciplinary efforts that provide a broad understanding of societal problems. For cyber-crime, experts have noted that cybersecurity curricula should include a focus on technology, people (e.g., human behavior), and processes (LeClair, Abraham, & Shih, 2013). In other words, cybersecurity professionals need to understand (1) the technology behind cyber offenses, (2) the way that human behavior contributes to cybersecurity incidents, and (3) the processes and poli-cies that are used to prevent and respond to cyber offenses.

Scholars have specifically called for more connections between those disciplines studying and teaching about the topic. In 2010, participants in a National Science Foundation (NSF) workshop on cybersecurity education offered the following conclusion:

Cyber security requires a multi-disciplinary approach. Efforts should be made to educate and partner with disciplines not always thought of as related to cyber security (e.g., decision sciences, forensic sciences, public policy, law). A holistic approach will foster more collaboration across disciplines, increase interest in cyber security as a necessary component of nearly all types of work, and increase resources and support for cyber security. (Hoffman, Burley, & Toregas, 2011, November 1, p. 5)

Three years later, a group of cybersecurity professionals and academics engaged in a simi-lar NSF workshop and made a similar conclusion: "There is need for a whole variety of aca-demic degree programs in cybersecurity from the technical aspects through to courses based on psychology, psychiatry, criminal justice, business (i.e., policy and economics) and more" (McGettrick, 2013).

The call for interdisciplinary cybersecurity programs is justified given the various types of issues that arise in efforts to prevent and respond to cybersecurity incidents. An early estimate suggested that less than 1% of cyberattacks are detected (Jefferson, 1997). There is little evidence that suggests an increase in our ability to detect cyberattacks.

One of the reasons that efforts lag behind is the death of academic training programs for cur-rent and future cybersecurity professionals. Particularly missing from those academic programs that exist are academic programs addressing cybersecurity from an interdisciplinary perspective. Interdisciplinary cybersecurity programs are justified on several practical grounds. Among the most salient justifications are the following:

- In general, interdisciplinary programs are focused on solving a real-world problem from a holistic perspective.

- The complex nature of cybersecurity makes it virtually impossible for one discipline to "claim ownership" over the topic.

- Certain careers that have recently been created, and some that will be developed in the future in response to increases in cybersecurity, will require an interdisciplinary understanding of cybersecurity.

- It is plausible that interdisciplinary programs will increase the number of women and minorities in cybersecurity programming.

This last point warrants additional discussion. It is clear that women and minorities are underrepresented in Science, Technology, Engineering, and Math (STEM) majors. Women received 57.3% of the bachelor's degrees in 2011 but received less than one fifth of the computer science, engineering, and physics degrees (National Science Foundation [NSF], 2015). As well, minority females graduating with a bachelor's degree appear to be four times more likely to graduate in the social sciences rather than engineering and three times more likely to graduate in the social sciences than in computer sciences. In 2012, 14.2% of awarded bachelor's degrees in the social sciences were received by female minorities. That same year, just 3.1% and 4.7% of bachelor's degrees in engineering and computer science were received by female minorities (NSF, 2015).

While there are fewer women in STEM majors than other majors, there is reason to believe that women may be particularly interested in interdisciplinary STEM initiatives. In general, research shows that females are more open to interdisciplinary research collaborations than males. This includes research in the United States (Payne, 2015), Italy (Abramo, D'Angelo, & Murgia, 2013), and the Netherlands (van Rijnsoever & Hessels, 2011). In some ways, some women might be drawn to opportunities to create new fields, while there is also a possibility that females are pushed away from traditional disciplines into interdisciplinary programs (Rhoten & Pfirman, 2007). Regardless of the mechanisms driving women into interdisciplinary initiatives, it seems reasonable to suggest that interdisciplinary cybersecurity programs are in a prime position to produce more female cybersecurity professionals.

As noted above, certain challenges arise when addressing cybersecurity through an interdisciplinary lens. Perhaps the strongest barrier is the structure of higher education institutions. The 2010 NSF cybersecurity workshop participants concluded the following:

> Academic silos prevent collaboration and integration. Cyber security is a relatively new field that does not always integrate neatly with other computing programs. Academic departments are notorious for guarding their resources and are justifiably resistant to giving up faculty spots, laboratory space, or funding opportunities. Most academic programs have tended to build their own tools rather than exchange resources with others, and they tend to hold firm ownership over whatever they create. (Hoffman et al., 2011, November 1, p. 6)

These challenges, however, can be overcome when professors from different academic disciplines work together in developing courses and academic programs focusing on the topic of cybersecurity from a holistic framework.

Colleges and Cybercrime

Colleges and universities are not immune from concerns about cybersecurity. For our purposes, there are two frameworks for understanding the relevance of cybersecurity for college campuses: a data framework and a behavioral framework. The data framework focuses on the various types of data available on college campuses, while the behavioral framework focuses on the behaviors of individuals on those campuses.

Regarding the data framework, it is important to understand the sheer amount of information that colleges store about students and employees (see Figure 9.6). Think about the types of information that your college has about you. In all likelihood they have the following:

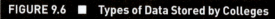

FIGURE 9.6 ■ Types of Data Stored by Colleges

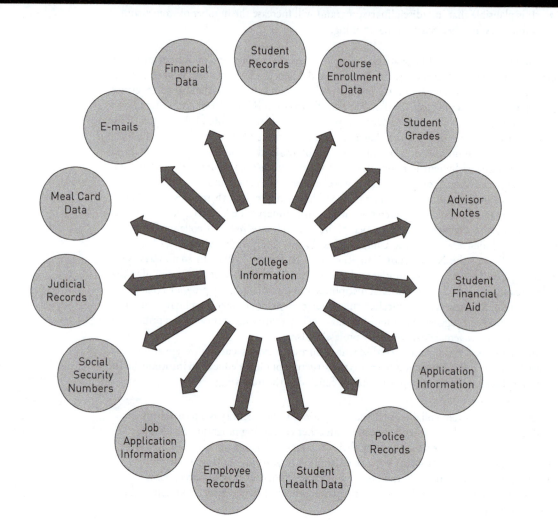

- Your social security number
- Your health records
- Your high school grades
- Your college grades
- Your disciplinary records (for the few of you who have them!)
- Your family's financial records
- Your current bills

Every time you swipe your identification card, your college is able to gather another piece of information about you. How often do you go to the library? How often do you login to your e-mail? How often do you eat at certain places? How often do you login to your online class? What websites did you go to on the college computer? How often did you go to sporting events? How much money do you have left on your account? All of this information (and more) is available on most college computer networks for their students.

Colleges and universities also store an equivalent amount of information about their employees. The sheer amount of information available on computer databases means that these institutions can be targeted for cyber offenses. The security specialists working at your college will not advertise their security strategies because they don't want everyone to know these measures. In some instances, security specialists may work with the campus police department to develop a collaborative information sharing network so the area agencies are prepared for breaches (Aeilts, 2005). In some ways, it's not a matter of if these breaches will occur, but when.

Regarding the behavioral framework as it relates to cybercrimes in colleges and universities in Chapter 7, it was briefly noted that a current concern on college and university campuses is digital and Internet piracy by students. Most colleges have specific policies that prohibit piracy by students. By developing these policies, colleges and universities are able to insulate themselves from blame when students are caught misusing college or university computers. In effect, officials can say that the student was violating an institutional policy, showing that the officials do not support the student's actions.

Internet piracy is "the illegal duplication and distribution of copyrighted materials from the Internet" (Hohn, Muftic, & Wolf, 2006), and digital piracy is the illegal duplication of copyright-protected software. These forms of piracy are believed to cost society between 25 and 30 billion dollars a year (Hohn et al., 2006). The music and movie industries have been particularly vigilant in their efforts to suppress Internet piracy. This chapter's White-Collar Crime in the News shows how large these cases become.

WHITE-COLLAR CRIME IN THE NEWS
DIGITAL PIRACY CONVICTION

The following is a press release from the Department of Justice from December 13, 2019.

Two Computer Programmers Plead Guilty in Connection with Operating Two of the Biggest Illegal Movie and Television Show Streaming Services in the United States

A resident of Las Vegas, Nevada, pleaded guilty yesterday to multiple criminal copyright and money laundering charges related to his running of iStreamItAll, one of the biggest illegal television show and movie streaming services in the United States, and to his working as a computer programmer with co-defendants to help build Jetflicks, a similarly large illegal television show streaming service. Today, a second defendant, who also resides in Las Vegas, pleaded guilty in the same court to a criminal copyright charge for his work as a computer programmer for Jetflicks.

++++++, aka djppimp, 36, pleaded guilty yesterday in the U.S. District Court for the Eastern District of Virginia to one count of conspiracy to commit criminal copyright infringement, one count of criminal copyright infringement by distributing a copyrighted work being prepared for commercial distribution, one count of copyright infringement by reproduction or distribution, one count of copyright infringement by public performance and one count of money laundering. In a separate proceeding today, co-defendant ++++++, 40, pleaded guilty to one count of conspiracy to commit copyright infringement. Sentencing for both defendants will be before U.S. District Judge T.S. Ellis III of the Eastern District

(Continued)

(Continued)

of Virginia, with +++++++'s on March 13, 2020, and +++++++'s on March 20, 2020.

According to +++++++'s plea agreement, +++++++ ran a site called iStreamItAll (ISIA), an online, subscription-based service headquartered in Las Vegas that permitted users to stream and download copyrighted television programs and movies without the permission of the relevant copyright owners. +++++++ admitted that he reproduced tens of thousands of copyrighted television episodes and movies without authorization, and streamed and distributed the infringing programs to thousands of paid subscribers located throughout the U.S. Specifically, +++++++ admitted that ISIA offered more than 118,479 different television episodes and 10,980 individual movies. In fact, according to the plea agreement, ISIA had more content than Netflix, Hulu, Vudu and Amazon Prime, and +++++++ sent out emails to potential subscribers highlighting ISIA's huge catalog of works and urging them to cancel those licensed services and subscribe to ISIA instead.

According to +++++++'s plea agreement, +++++++ obtained infringing television programs and movies from pirate sites around the world—including some of the globe's biggest torrent and Usenet NZB sites specializing in infringing content—using various automated computer scripts that ran 24 hours a day, seven days a week. Specifically, +++++++ used sophisticated computer programming to scour global pirate sites for new illegal content; to download, process, and store these works; and then make the shows and movies available on servers in Canada to ISIA subscribers for streaming and downloading. +++++++ also admitted to running

several other piracy services—including a Usenet NZB indexing site called SmackDownOnYou—and earning over $1 million from his piracy operations.

In addition, in +++++++'s and +++++++'s plea agreements, they each admitted that they separately worked as computer programmers at Jetflicks, another online, subscription-based service headquartered in Las Vegas that permitted users to stream and, at times, download copyrighted television programs without the permission of the relevant copyright owners. According to both plea agreements, +++++++, +++++++ and their co-conspirators at Jetflicks reproduced tens of thousands of copyrighted television episodes without authorization, and streamed and distributed the infringing programs to tens of thousands of paid subscribers located throughout the U.S.

Both +++++++ and +++++++ also admitted that at Jetflicks they and their co-conspirators used automated software programs and other tools to locate, download, process and store illegal content, and then quickly make those television programs available on servers in the U.S. and Canada to Jetflicks subscribers for streaming and/or downloading. In addition, as set forth in +++++++'s and +++++++'s plea agreements, both Jetflicks and ISIA were not only available to subscribers over the internet but were specifically designed to work on many different types of devices, platforms and software including myriad varieties of computer operating systems, smartphones, tablets, smart televisions, video game consoles, digital media players, set-top boxes and web browsers.

Reprinted from U.S .Department of Justice.

Source: https://www.justice.gov/opa/pr/two-computer-programmers-plead-guilty-connection-operating-two-biggest-illegal-movie-and.

Lars Ulrich, drummer from the heavy metal band Metallica, was among the most vocal critics of file-sharing programs that allowed computer users to illegally download and share music. After learning that his band's unreleased music was being distributed on Napster, the band sued Napster for copyright infringement and racketeering. Testifying before the Senate Judiciary Committee on downloading music on the Internet on July 11, 2000, Ulrich said,

We were startled to hear reports that five or six versions of our work-in-progress were already being played on some U.S. radio stations. We traced the source of this leak to a corporation called Napster. Additionally, we learned that all of our previously recorded copyright songs were, via Napster, available for anyone around the world to download from the Internet in a digital format known as MP3. In fact, in a 48-hour period, where we monitored Napster, over 300,000 users made 1.4 million free downloads of Metallica's music. Napster hijacked our music without asking. They never sought our permission. Our catalog of music simply became available for free downloads on the Napster system. I do not have a problem with any artist voluntarily distributing his or her songs through any means that artist so chooses. But just like a carpenter who crafts a table gets to decide whether he wants to keep it, sell or give it away, shouldn't we have the same options? We should decide what happens to our music, not a company with no rights to our recordings, which has never invested a penny in our music or had anything to do with its creation. The choice has been taken away from us. (Ulrich, 2000)

Metallica and Napster settled out of court.

Research shows that college students routinely engage in various forms of digital and Internet piracy. A study of 114 students found that 79.8% said they had illegally downloaded music, and more than a third said they had pirated software (Hohn et al., 2006). A 2007 survey by SurveyU found that two thirds of the 500 students surveyed were not concerned about illegally downloading music or repercussions from doing so. The survey also found that "only 57% of the students' total libraries had been purchased" (Yoskowitz, 2007).

Researchers have tested various theories in an effort to explain software piracy by students. One author team surveyed 342 students and found support for the idea that low self-control contributes to software piracy (Higgins, Fell, & Wilson, 2006). In another study, of 507 college students, a researcher found that broadband connections combined with prior experience using CD-ROMs increased the risk of Internet piracy (Hinduja, 2001).

RESPONDING TO CYBERCRIME

Different strategies are used to address cybercrime. Broadly speaking, these strategies can be characterized as police strategies, legislative strategies, retributive strategies, general prevention strategies, and hybrid strategies. Each of these strategies is addressed below.

Police Strategies

In this context, the phrase *police strategies* is used to describe a range of activities performed by law enforcement agencies in response to cyber offending. Depending on offense type, different law enforcement agencies may be called upon to respond to different types of cyber offending. Table 9.2. shows the federal law enforcement agencies that have jurisdiction over select types of cybercrimes. Each of these agencies has specific units dealing with different aspects of cybercrime. For instance, in 2018, the Internet Crime Complaint Center created the Recovery Asset Team to "streamline communication with financial institutions and assist FBI field offices with the recovery of funds for victims who made transfers to domestic accounts under fraudulent pretenses" (Internet Crime Complaint Center, 2020). In 2019, the team was involved in recovering more than $300,000,000 across 1,307 incidents.

While members of the public may expect the police to protect them against cyber offending, law enforcement officers may not be adequately prepared to respond to these crimes. A study of 268 patrol officers found that although nearly 80% of the officers viewed computer crime as serious, roughly only 10% of them had received computer crime training (Holt & Bossler, 2012). The officers demonstrated a great deal of uncertainty about the dynamics of computer crime. Echoing this concern, one author commented, "the structure within which law enforcement operates does not lend itself to effective investigations of digital crimes" (Gogolin, 2011, p. 469).

TABLE 9.2 ■ Federal Law Enforcement Agencies Responding to Different Types of Cybercrimes	
Type of Crime	**Appropriate Federal Investigative Law Enforcement Agencies**
Computer intrusion (i.e., hacking)	• FBI local office • U.S. Secret Service • Internet Crime Complaint Center
Password trafficking	• FBI local office • U.S. Secret Service • Internet Crime Complaint Center
Counterfeiting of currency	• U.S. Secret Service
Child pornography or exploitation	• FBI local office • If imported, U.S. Immigration and Customs Enforcement • Internet Crime Complaint Center
Child exploitation and Internet fraud matters that have a mail nexus	• U.S. Postal Inspection Service • Internet Crime Complaint Center
Internet fraud and SPAM	• FBI local office • U.S. Secret Service • Federal Trade Commission (online complaint) • If securities fraud or investment-related SPAM e-mails, Securities and Exchange Commission (online complaint) • Internet Crime Complaint Center
Internet harassment	• FBI local office
Internet bomb threats	• FBI local office • ATF local office
Trafficking in explosive or incendiary devices or firearms over the Internet	• FBI local office • ATF local office

Source: Adapted from Richardson, R. (n. d.). *15th Annual 2010/2011 cyber crime and security survey.* New York, NY: Computer Security Institute.

Some officers have described the response to cybercrime as "good, old fashioned police work" (Garrett, 2010, p. 45). While technology allows offenders access into spaces they would not have accessed in the past, law enforcement can gain access to those same spaces. One expert suggests that law enforcement authorities ask these questions in the early stages of their investigation:

- Was the attack launched from the Internet or from the internal network?

- Did the attacker have access to the [local] system?

- If the attacker was an outsider . . . how did he manage to have the first access?

- Did he take advantage of any vulnerability?

- Was he helped by any employee?

- Did he use some kind of blackmail? (Donato, 2009, p. 189)

Obviously, different types of cybercrimes will require different investigation techniques. Those crimes that involve e-mails, for example, might involve an analysis of the e-mails to determine if they were all written by the same suspect. Writers often use the same punctuation and characters in the same way. Investigators will review e-mails much as handwriting might be analyzed. How did the writer set the tab function? How long were the sentences? Were numbers spelled out or listed numerically? How many numbers were used? How many spaces were after the period? Were there common spelling errors? Asking these questions will allow investigators to group together anonymous e-mails to determine if they were written by the same suspect (Iqbal, Binalleeh, Fung, & Debbabi, 2010). Instant messages can also be analyzed to determine who wrote them. According to one author team, "the real time, casual nature of instant messages produces text that is conversational in style and reflects the author's true writing style and vocabulary" (Orebaugh, Kinser, & Allnut, 2016, p. 14).

Legislative Strategies

Legislative strategies are also used in an effort to respond to cybercrime. As noted previously, in the United States, the Computer Fraud and Abuse Act of 1984 was the first law to specifically address computer offenders. This law was initially passed to protect government information on government computers. It was broadened in 1996 to offer protections to the private sector (Davis, 2003). The act makes the following behaviors federal crimes:

- Hacking into government or bank computers

- Damaging computers through viruses, worms, or other software crimes

- Committing fraud through computer access

- Threatening computer damage against a bank or government computer

- Password trafficking related to government computers

- Using computers to spy on the government (Doyle, 2014)

Other countries have passed similar laws. England, for example, passed the Computer Misuse Act of 1990, which, among other things, made it illegal to create or possess certain hacking tools (Furnell, 2008). States have passed their own laws governing cybersecurity and other federal policies, and executive orders have followed. One federal policy, for example, now requires businesses receiving government contracts to demonstrate how the business protects information related to the government contract (Bancroft, 2013). In addition, an executive order issued by former President Barack Obama mandated that the National Institute of Standards and Technology (NIST) develop a framework to minimize cyber risks confronting critical infrastructures. NIST identified five functions that are a part of the government's comprehensive framework:

- Identifying systems, assets, and data that need protection

- Providing safeguards to protect those systems, assets, and data

- Detecting cyber offenses

- Responding to cyber events

- Recovering from cyber events (Levi, 2014)

The cybersecurity laws have been criticized on different grounds. For example, the information security regulations are seen as potentially making it more difficult for small businesses to compete for government contracts (Bancroft, 2013). Also, laws requiring Internet service providers to support law enforcement activities have been viewed as "a larger move by governments to establish policing networks 'beyond the state'" (Huey & Rosenberg, 2004, p. 599).

Retributive Strategies

Retributive strategies refer to efforts to punish individuals in order to keep them from committing cybercrimes. One philosophical question that arises is whether the punishment for cybercrimes should be proportionate to the pleasure/harm from the offense. This would mean that the penalties for these crimes would be far more severe than for conventional crimes. After all, the harm from cybercrimes can be quite severe. According to one scholar, proportional sanctions for some cyber offenders might potentially "offend our sense of justice" (Jetha, 2013, p. 20).

General Prevention Strategies

Three different types of strategies are used to prevent computer crimes by white-collar offenders. These include employer-based strategies, employee-based strategies, and situational crime prevention strategies. In terms of *employer-based strategies*, employers use a range of tactics to protect their businesses from computer crimes. Most commonly, these tactics include encryption, firewalls, employee training, routine audits, and physical surveillance (Carter & Katz, 1996). Many large private businesses have security personnel whose sole efforts are directed toward preventing and/or identifying cases of computer crime.

Employee-based strategies call upon employees to make active efforts to prevent computer crimes. The phrase "security hygiene" is used to characterize efforts where workers learn and carry out safe computer behaviors (Pfleeger, Sasse, & Furnham, 2014). Such strategies include updating virus protection programs, conducting employee-initiated audits of computer use, taking additional precautions to protect one's work computer from victimization, and initiating formal agreements whereby employees agree to use computers only for work-related activities (Carter & Katz, 1996). Including employees in prevention strategies ensures that well-rounded prevention programs are in place.

Situational crime prevention strategies refer to specific actions that can be taken that are directly related to those factors that promote offending. Companies can use specific strategies to limit opportunities for cyber offending. Examples relevant to cybercrime include the following:

- Requiring biometric credentials (eyes, fingerprints, voice recognition) for employees to gain access to certain types of data

- Using entry screening measures that grant access only to certain individuals

- Developing formal surveillance strategies that monitor the behavior of employees

- Identifying property with codes so the property can be recovered if misplaced or stolen

- Removing the temptation by hiding data systems

- Setting rules that are clear and enforceable

- Implementing target hardening strategies, such as information security standards, secure passwords, and encryption (Hinduja & Kooi, 2013)

Encryption refers to the process of coding information so that only the original codes are able to understand the information.

Other specific strategies that have been suggested include spam filters, honey nets, self-initiated Google hacking, and security banners. *Spam filters* are e-mail tools that catch unwanted bulk e-mails. One estimate suggested that 97% of all e-mail sent through the Internet was spam (Carucci, Overhuls, & Soares, 2011). Users set their spam filters so that e-mails scoring above a certain level or identified by the user as spam are sent to the user's spam folder. For some reason, the author receives an e-mail almost weekly from a user called "6 Pack Abs." It doesn't take a sophisticated spam filter to recognize that this e-mail is either spam or meant for someone else!

Honey nets (or honey pots) are websites or datasets that are designed to "attract and entrap offenders" (Wall, 2008, p. 57). These sites do not include any data of real value to the company. There are at least three reasons why honey nets are used by businesses. First, some businesses may do this so they can catch offenders and turn them in to law enforcement. Second, some businesses (including researchers) may create these honey nets so they can study the behavior of hackers. Third, some businesses may use honey nets simply as a decoy or distraction for hackers. In this case, the hope is that hackers would spend their time and energy on the "fake" site and stay away from the data that is truly of value to the company.

Self-initiated Google hacking refers to instances when companies or businesses google themselves in order to identify vulnerable networks that might be uncovered from Google searches. It is well accepted that hackers search certain terms in order to locate vulnerable networks.

PHOTO 9.3 Society has changed dramatically through the recent technological revolution led by masterminds such as Steve Jobs. These changes have had ramifications for the criminal justice system as well.

The presence or lack of certain features on a company's website increases its vulnerability. The phrase "Google Dork" characterizes "the search terms used to discover vulnerabilities" (Mansfield-Devine, 2009, p. 4). For instance, the following search would reveal files that contain passwords: inurl:wp-content/uploads filetype:xls | filetype:xlsx password (https://www.exploit-db.com/google-hacking-database). Security experts encourage companies to Google hack their websites in order to identify potential vulnerabilities (Mansfield-Devine, 2009).

Security banners or warnings have also been used by companies in an effort to prevent cybercrime. In these cases, a box appears on the computer screen advising workers they are in a part of the network that they should not be in. The usefulness of these banners is debatable. Some have suggested that workers ignore the banners unless there is an immediate consequence (Pfleeger et al., 2014). David Maimon and his colleagues (Maimon, Alper, Sobesto, & Cukier, 2014) conducted an experiment in which computers were set up with the expectation that they would be targeted for intrusions or trespassing. After cyber offenders hacked into the computers, they were randomly assigned to one of two groups. One group received a warning in the form of a banner, and the other did not receive anything. Maimon found that the banner did not reduce the number of intrusions, but it did reduce the amount of time that offenders spent in the targeted computer database. This research suggested that banners won't keep offenders from entering databases, but they won't stay as long. As an analogy, a "Stay Off the Grass" sign may not keep people from standing in my yard, but they won't stay as long!

Identifying prevention strategies can be problematic given the changing nature of cyber offenses. Efforts to develop prevention plans face financial, personnel, and structural barriers. In addition, it is believed by some that cybercrime has changed over time. Whereas past hackers more frequently committed offenses out of the desire to "brag," more cyber offenses are now committed for profit motives. Describing this shift, one author has suggested that "cybercriminals have become an international plague" (Smith, 2015, p. 104). Despite this change, others have argued that, in some ways, the presence of computers has only provided "a new medium . . . to commit traditional crimes" (Viano, 2006). As Viano notes, the advent of the phone, television, and audio resulted in different strategies to commit crime. Others agree that technology has simply provided new ways of committing "old" crimes. One author team explained, "health care fraud provides an example of a traditional crime that has been upgraded and enhanced by new computer and Internet technologies" (Gray, Citron, & Rinehart, 2013, p. 749).

That technological changes have enhanced traditional crimes has implications for the way that officials prevent and respond to cybercrime. New prevention and response strategies are not necessarily needed; instead, enhanced response strategies are justified. In line with this point, it has been suggested that cybersecurity efforts have been "iterative rather than linear" (Harknett & Stever, 2009, p. 2). Within this iterative change, it has been recognized that the key to successful cybersecurity efforts is cooperation between government agencies, citizens, and businesses.

Hybrid Strategies

Hybrid strategies include instances when a combination of the strategies discussed in the previous section of this book are used to respond to cyber offending. In many ways, hybrid strategies may be the most common. Given that 183 million personal records held by the United States were breached between 2005 and 2017, Burns (2017) calls for a hybrid approach to respond to breaches. Burns describes five different strategies the government might use to respond to data breaches (see Figure 9.7). Criminal prosecutions involve the legal system responding to breaches. Financial penalty calls for civil and administrative penalties against breachers; some point out that this penalty may actually prevent the breach in the first place (Goldman & McCoy, 2016). Diplomacy efforts call for peace-making efforts with the breacher to avoid escalating tensions between governments. Counter breaches refer to times when the United States might breach another country's cyber

FIGURE 9.7 ■. Possible Government Responses to Data Breaches

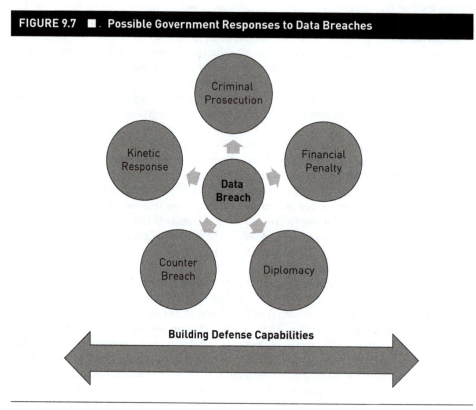

Source: Adapted from Burns (2017)

systems in response to a breach by the other government. This one, Burns says, is more "nuanced" because it "requires the U.S. to commit acts that it does not want committed against itself" (p. 984). Finally, kinetic responses are seen as a last resort to protect national security. These efforts involve the destruction of the attacker's cyber infrastructure. Underlying these efforts, Burns calls for a commitment to building national defense strategies through an understanding of how each of these responses can be used to respond to data breaches against the government.

Building a national defense to cyber policy is a balancing act for policy makers. Some have strongly critiqued the rhetoric of engaging in "cyberwar" as a strategy to respond to offenses. Specific concern centers on "overzealous responses," unnecessary and aggressive prosecutions (e.g., someone was prosecuted for downloading public information), and "counterproductive" consequences analogous to the negative aspects of the U.S. war on drugs (Rowe, 2016). Focusing on rhetoric and cybersecurity, Marion and Hill (2018) examined the comments about cybercrime that former presidents Clinton, Bush, and Obama made in various speeches. The research found that the presidents tended to make comments driven more by "crime control theatre" rather than actual policies or behaviors.

Some experts believe that cyber attacks are harder to stop than other types of behavior. Typically, it's not clear who the attacker is or where the attack came from, and businesses often choose not to report the victimization. In addition, it's not always clear if cyber incidents stem from attacks, human errors, or technological failure (Goldman & McCoy, 2016). Also, research shows that sentencing guidelines for cybercrime overemphasize areas such as the amount of loss and the target of the crime, while members of the public see motivations as more important for sentencing (Graves, Acquisti, & Anderson, 2019). This means that criminal penalties don't align well with public attitudes, and, as a result, the penalties have less deterrent potential.

Do as I Say, Not as I Do

In what can be filed under the category of "Do as I say, not as I do," an interesting anecdote about my own experience with computer victimization comes to mind. While working on this chapter for the first edition, I decided that I would search the Internet for additional information about computer viruses. I found a few useful websites and took some notes on the material I read. About two hours later, I realized that my computer had become infected by a computer virus called the *control center virus*. Somehow, during my search, I had clicked on a website that downloaded this virus to my laptop. I had to stop work immediately, save my work to that point, and shut down the computer. The next day I delivered my computer to one of the computer tech employees in my college. He confirmed that my computer had become infected and that he would need to take a few days to get rid of the virus and restore the computer to its appropriate state. Fortunately, I didn't lose any files or data—I just lost some time.

So, if you are writing a paper about computer viruses for your white-collar crime class, do not search the Internet for information—make sure you search your library database and rely on scholarly journal articles published by top publishing companies, such as SAGE. This little bit of advice will take you a long way in your academic career.

Summary

- The phrases *computer crime* and *cybercrime* refer to a range of computer-related behaviors that are criminally illegal or otherwise harmful.

- In 1978, Florida and Arizona became the first two states to pass laws related to computer crime.

- Not all computer crimes are white-collar crimes.

- The following overlapping types of computer crimes are often cases of white-collar crime: theft, unauthorized access, virus introduction, software crimes, and Internet crimes.

- Theft as a type of computer crime refers to a variety of computer-related activities that result in the offender stealing something from the business. Items stolen include funds, information, and intellectual property.

- Theft of information occurs when offenders steal information, including (a) information that can be used to trade securities and stocks and (b) intellectual property.

- Unauthorized access occurs when individuals break into various computer databases to which they do not have legitimate access.

- Crackers typically introduce viruses for recreational reasons, pride, profit, protection, or cyberterrorism reasons.

- Four overlapping types of software crimes exist: (1) theft of software, (2) counterfeiting software, (3) copyright violations of computer software, and (4) piracy.

- The phrase *Internet crimes* refers to a range of offenses committed by offenders through the use of the Internet.

- The phrase *white-collar cybercrime* refers to cybercrimes committed by workers during the course of work.

- Different types of cybercriminals exist, including loners, associates, and crime networks.

- The costs of cybercrime include physical, social, financial, and emotional.

- Computer crimes are commonly attributed to opportunity, structural changes, and peer associations.

- Problems in responding to computer crime stem from the dynamics of the offense, offender characteristics, jurisdictional issues, criminal justice dynamics, victim characteristics, and general crime prevention issues.

- The best way to respond to cybercrime involves an interdisciplinary response system.

- Colleges house a great deal of information that could be targeted by cyber offenders.

- Most colleges have specific policies that prohibit piracy by students. One author team surveyed 342 students and found support for the idea that low self-control contributes to software piracy (Higgins et al., 2006).

- Strategies used to prevent computer crimes by white-collar offenders include police strategies, legislative strategies, retributive strategies, and general prevention strategies.

Key Terms

Computer crime 233

Copyright violations of computer software 240

Counterfeiting software crimes 240

Crackers 237

Critical Infrastructure 246

Cybercrime 233

Electronic and software piracy 240

Internet crimes 241

Internet piracy 255

Phishing 237

Ransomware 240

Situational crime prevention 260

Software crimes 240

Theft of software 240

Unauthorized access 237

Virus 239

White-collar cybercrime 244

Worm 248

Discussion Questions

1. Which crimes do you think do more harm—crimes against the cyber system or street crimes? Explain.

2. Find an example of white-collar cybercrime in the news. Identify three patterns in the case that relate to this chapter's discussion.

3. How are crimes in the economic system similar to crimes in the technological system? What are some differences in the two categories of crime?

4. How is "being hacked" a crime rather than a form of victimization?

5. How does cybercrime impact your life as a student?

6. How serious are computer crimes on your campus?

7. What should businesses do to reduce cybercime?

8. How can individuals make money legally off of cybercrime??

10

CRIME BY THE CORPORATE SYSTEM

A student interested in learning more about a specific for-profit college completed a website registration form indicating interest in the college. Minutes later, the individual received a phone call from a marketing specialist from the college. The student told that marketer that he was interested in criminal justice. The marketer told the student that he should consider a medical assistant certificate instead because he would potentially earn $70,000 a year after just 9 months of course work. In reality, 9 out of 10 employees in the medical assisting field make under $40,000 a year. And the marketer knew this. What the marketer did not know, however, was that the "student" was actually an undercover employee working on an investigation focusing on the marketing practices of for-profit colleges for the U.S. Government Accountability Office (U.S. Government Accountability Office [USGAO], 2010).

In this case, the marketer's illicit actions were conducted to benefit the company for which he worked. This distinguishes the misconduct from those discussed earlier in this work. Indeed, all of the offenses discussed in the prior chapters were conducted by the employee and for the employee's benefit. Other white-collar offenses either benefit—or are committed by, an employer or business. Consider the following quotes from news articles:

- A 5-month-old baby boy was placed on his back to sleep toward the foot of an adult bed. He was lying on a bath towel. There were a bed comforter and several large stuffed animals on the bed also. There was a gap of 10 inches between the bed and the wall. One large plush bear had fallen into this opening. It appeared that the victim had rolled off the bed into the gap between the bed and the wall. The victim was found face down on top of the plush bear. The head of the victim was at the lowest point of the bear that was 11 inches below the side of the bed. The victim was transported to a local hospital where he was pronounced dead as a result of mechanical asphyxia (Consumer Product Safety Commission, 2019).

- Gerber made unsubstantiated claims that its Good Start Gentle formula prevented children who took it from developing allergies, a claim that could have significant consequences for children with allergies. The 2014 lawsuit filed by the Federal Trade Commission was settled in 2019, with Gerber agreeing not to make any similar claims for the product or imply the government authorized such a claim. (Suneson and Harrington, 2020).

- The FTC announced a settlement with Williams-Sonoma. The company has agreed to stop making false, misleading, or unsubstantiated 'Made in the USA' claims for several of their houseware and furniture product lines. As part of the settlement, Williams-Sonoma is required to pay $1 million to the FTC. According to the FTC's complaint, numerous Williams-Sonoma product lines, including Goldtouch Bakeware products, and Pottery Barn Kids furniture were wholly imported, or contained significant imported materials or components making Williams-Sonoma's representations false or misleading. (Kreidler, 2020).

- Twenty-six drug manufacturers were sued on Wednesday by the attorneys general of most U.S. states and several territories, which accused them of conspiring to reduce competition and drive up generic drug prices (Bartz and Stempel, 2020).

In this context, the phrase *crime by the corporate system* is used to characterize the body of offenses that are committed to benefit the corporation for which the employee (or employees) works. To provide an understanding of this body of offenses, this chapter gives attention to conceptualizing corporate crime, types of corporate crime, dynamics of corporate offending, and public concern about crimes by the corporate system. By addressing these areas, readers will see how corporations also commit, and benefit from, various types of misconduct.

CONCEPTUALIZING CORPORATE CRIME

As noted in Chapter 1, the term *corporate crime* was initially discussed by Clinard and Quinney (1973), who, in *Criminal Behavior Systems,* showed how white-collar crime can be classified into "corporate crime" and "occupational crime." From this perspective, the crimes discussed in the prior chapters can be seen as occupational crimes. To understand what is meant by corporate crime, it is useful to first define *corporation*.

The concept of corporation can be seen four different ways (see Figure 10.1). First, one can suggest that a corporation is a *business*. Second, one can also point to the *physical or structural location* where a business exists as a corporation (or an organization). Third, if businesses become incorporated, that *legally recognized status* can be seen as indicating the presence of a corporation that is separate from the presence of a specific person or persons owning or running an organization. Fourth, a corporation can be seen as a *collection of employees* who work for an employer.

The employment arrangement in a corporation is hierarchal in nature. At the bottom of the corporate hierarchy are workers with no supervisory responsibilities. Direct supervisors are at the next level of the corporation. Managers and administrators are above the supervisors. Many corporations also have a specific corporate board. A chief executive officer or president of the board is ultimately the highest ranking individual in a corporation. In theory, the corporation exists to meet its goals—which typically include profit, growth, and success.

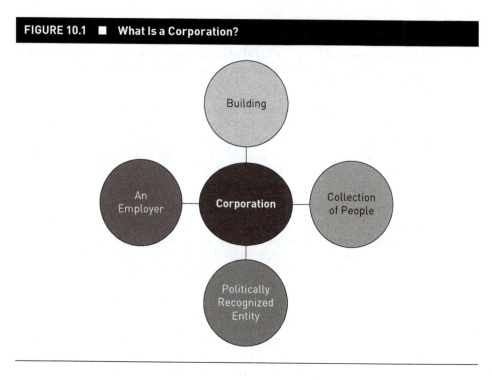

FIGURE 10.1 ■ What Is a Corporation?

Understanding these levels helps shed light on the concept of corporate crime and the persistence of misconduct in businesses. As Ermann and Lundman (2002) note, corporations are not technically "collections of people," but are collections of "replaceable people." What this means is that individuals can lose their jobs if they are not performing in a way that helps the corporation to meet its goals. Consequently, individuals—through direct or indirect pressures—might break rules or violate the law in order to promote corporate growth. In some cases, criminal decision making might be clearly intentional in nature. In other cases, harm arising from corporate misdeeds might be the result of organizational processes that do not actually intend for the harmful behavior to occur.

The abstract nature of corporate offending has resulted in an assortment of terms and definitions to describe these behaviors. One author has suggested that corporate crime "includes the vast majority of regulatory offenses subsumed under regulatory law" (Snyder, 1990, p. 439). Frank and Lynch (1992) describe corporate crime as including behaviors that are "socially injurious and blameworthy acts, legal or illegal that cause financial, physical, or environmental harm, committed by corporations and businesses against their workers, the general public, the environment, other corporations or businesses, the government, or other countries" (p. 17).

Some scholars have used phrases such as organizational crime (Schrager & Short, 1978), organizational deviance (Ermann & Lundman, 1978), and organizational misconduct (Vaughan, 2001) to describe similar behaviors. **Organizational misconduct**, for example, refers to "violations of laws, rules, or administrative regulations by an individual or group of individuals in an organization who, in their organizational role, act or fail to act in ways that further the attainment of organizational goals" (Vaughan, 2001, p. 46).

These behaviors can be distinguished from the other forms of white-collar crime (discussed earlier in this text) in at least four different ways. First, the offenses are committed either *for the organization* or *by the organization*. Many of the crimes discussed earlier are committed *against the organization* and *by an individual*. Second, many corporate crimes are committed in groups, as part of an organizational decision-making process. Third, while the consequences of all forms of white-collar crime are serious, the consequences of corporate misdeeds can be particularly devastating. Fourth, the misdeeds of corporations are more rarely defined as criminally illegal.

Because corporate crime is different from the other forms of white-collar crime, it is best seen as a distinct form of white-collar crime. As a distinct form of white-collar crime, one can point to several specific types of corporate crime.

TYPES OF CORPORATE CRIME

In a classic corporate crime study, Clinard and Yeager (1980) reviewed 1,553 corporate offenses and uncovered the following varieties: (1) administrative violations, (2) environmental violations, (3) financial violations, (4) labor violations, (5) manufacturing violations, and (6) unfair trade practices. Their research was useful in showing that the concept of corporate crime could be subdivided into types of corporate misdeeds. Depending on the level of analysis, it would be possible to list hundreds of different types of corporate misconduct. To keep the discussion manageable, it is useful to focus on general types of corporate wrongdoing. Therefore, the following seven types of corporate crimes warrant attention:

- Antitrust offenses
- False advertising
- Deceptive sales
- Unfair labor practices
- Unsafe work environments
- Harmful consumer products
- Harmful treatment of consumers

Antitrust Offenses

Our economy is based on principles of open market competition. The price of goods and services is tied to supply and demand. Businesses compete with one another by selling goods and services at prices that can be determined by a competitive marketplace. This helps keep prices low and stimulates new businesses that form to enter the competitive marketplace (USDOJ, n.d.a., p. 2). Such a process, in theory, ensures that consumers pay fair prices for goods and services. Some corporations, however, commit crimes known as antitrust offenses to control competition. Put simply, antitrust offenses are those that restrict competition. **Antitrust laws** are designed to promote and protect competition. In the United States, antitrust laws cover business activities in the areas of (1) pricing distribution, (2) mergers, (3) joint ventures, and (4) intellectual property use (Jacobsen, Seat, Shugarman, & Gildea, 1991).

The most prominent laws that control antitrust offenses are the Sherman Antitrust Act, the Clayton Act, and the Federal Trade Commission (FTC) Act (see Table 10.1). The **Sherman Antitrust Act**, often called the Sherman Act, passed in 1890, is the broadest antitrust law. This act makes it illegal for competitors to engage in activities that restrict competition. The Antitrust Division of the U.S. Department of Justice has the responsibility for prosecuting these crimes. Common types of antitrust offenses include the following:

- Price fixing
- Bid rigging
- Price discrimination

- Price gouging
- Market allocation
- Group boycotts

As will be shown later in the chapter, it is extremely difficult to determine whether these crimes occur or behaviors in the corporate system simply reflect fluctuations in the economy.

TABLE 10.1 ■ Major Antitrust Laws	
Law	Descriptions
Sherman Antitrust Act	The Sherman Act outlaws all contracts, combinations, and conspiracies that unreasonably restrain interstate and foreign trade. This includes agreements among competitors to fix prices, rig bids, and allocate customers. The Sherman Act also makes it a crime to monopolize any part of interstate commerce. An unlawful monopoly exists when only one firm controls the market for a product or service, and it has obtained that market power, not because its product or service is superior to others, but by suppressing competition with anticompetitive conduct.
Clayton Act	The Clayton Act is a civil statute (carrying no criminal penalties) that was passed in 1914 and significantly amended in 1950. The Clayton Act prohibits mergers or acquisitions that are likely to lessen competition. Under the Act, the government challenges those mergers that a careful economic analysis shows are likely to increase prices to consumers.
Federal Trade Commission Act	The Federal Trade Commission Act prohibits unfair methods of competition in interstate commerce but carries no criminal penalties. It also created the Federal Trade Commission to police violations of the act.
Other Laws	The Department of Justice also often uses other laws to fight illegal activities, including laws that prohibit false statements to federal agencies, perjury, obstruction of justice, conspiracies to defraud the United States, and mail and wire fraud.

Source: U.S. Department of Justice (USDOJ). (n.d.a). *Anti-Trust Enforcement and the Consumer.* Retrieved November 27, 2015 from http://www.justice.gov/sites/default/files/atr/legacy/2015/03/06/antitrust-enfor-consumer.pdf

Price Fixing

Price fixing offenses occur when competitors agree on a price at which goods or services should be sold. The competitors do not need to agree on the same price; they simply need to agree to set prices. Other examples of price fixing include instances where competitors agree to

(1) establish or adhere to price discounts; (2) hold prices firm; (3) eliminate or reduce discounts; (4) adopt a standard formula for computing prices; (5) maintain certain price differentials between different types, sizes, and quantities of products; (6) adhere to a minimum fee or price schedule (7) fix credit terms; and (8) not advertise prices. (USDOJ, n.d.b.)

A distinction can be made between horizontal and vertical price fixing. **Horizontal price fixing** involves situations where competing businesses conspire to charge prices at a similar level. **Vertical price fixing** refers to situations where parties from different levels of the production and distribution chain agree to set prices. Traditionally, vertical price fixing has been regarded as illegal. A manufacturer, for example, is not allowed to tell retailers and distributors how much to charge for products produced by the manufacturer. In a U.S. Supreme Court case, *Leegin Creative Leather Products, Inc. v. PSKS, Inc.* (2007), this premise was changed, and the Court ruled that the "rule of reason" should be used to determine whether agreements between various levels of the production distribution chain are illegal. The rule of reason refers to the premise that "courts must weigh all of the circumstances of the restraint, and the restraint's history, nature and effect in the market involved, in order to ascertain whether anti-competitive effects outweigh any pro-competitive benefits" (Martin, 2007, p. 1). The Court cited "a growing consensus in economic theory that vertical pricing agreements, while sometimes anti-competitive, can often have pro-competitive effects" (as cited in Martin, 2007).

Bid Rigging

Bid rigging (or collusion) occurs when competitors conspire to set specific bids for goods or services they would supply in response to a request for bids. At least four types of bid rigging exist. First, **bid suppression** refers to instances where competitors agree not to submit a bid for a particular job on the understanding that a specific competitor will likely be selected for that job. Second, **complementary bidding** exists when competitors submit bids with artificially high estimates or specific demands that cannot be met so that a specific competitor with a lower price or without the demands is selected. Third, **bid rotation** occurs when competitors agree to take turns submitting the lowest bid on different bids. Fourth, **subcontracting** occurs when competitors hire one another on subcontracts after the winning bid has been selected (USDOJ, n.d.b, p. 2).

It is believed that bid rigging is more likely to occur if (1) there are fewer competitors, (2) the products or services are standardized, (3) competitors know one another, and (4) bidders or businesses submit their bids in the same physical location at the same time (USDOJ, n.d.b, p. 5). This last item refers to the possibility that competitors will meet one another in the building when submitting their bids, and this "chance meeting" will give them the opportunity to "compare notes," or otherwise discuss their bids. Imagine a professor telling students to turn their take-home exams in at a specific time and in a specific location. The possibility that students might run into one another and engage in wrongdoing potentially increases by creating a situation where it is likely they will see one another.

Price Discrimination

On the surface, one might assume that the term **price discrimination** means that businesses cannot charge individuals two different prices based on protected classes such as gender, race, religion, and so on. While civil rights laws do prohibit charging for goods based on the characteristics of the consumer, price discrimination actually refers to practices where different prices are charged simply to restrict competition between competitors (Knopp, 1966). It is problematic, however, to determine whether different prices are being offered to limit competition or price differences are just a natural part of business. Indeed, in many instances consumers can legally be charged two different prices. Rakowski (2004) uses the example of charging business travelers more for airfare. One can point to several other examples where consumers are charged different prices:

- Two consumers buy the same car on the same day, with one paying more than the other.

- Two consumers stay in a hotel on the same day, with one paying more than the other.

- Two concertgoers pay two different prices to see Justin Bieber in concert.

- Two students in the same class are charged two different prices for the class (one student is a graduate student, and the other is an undergraduate student).

- A grocery store charges two consumers two different prices for the same goods because one of the consumers has a "grocer card" that allows discounts.

- On "Ladies'" night, women are admitted free to a bar, but men have to pay a cover charge.

What it comes down to is the fact that price discriminations "are generally lawful, particularly if they reflect the different costs of dealing with different buyers or are the result of a seller's attempts to meet a competitor's offering" (FTC, 2010). Made illegal under the **Robinson-Patman Act,** price discrimination is illegal if it is done to lessen competition.

Price Gouging

Price gouging refers to situations where businesses conspire to set artificially high prices on goods and services. Check cashing businesses have been implicated in price gouging. These businesses, which exist primarily in minority neighborhoods, charge consumers relatively high fees to cash their paychecks. Some states have passed laws capping the amount that these businesses can charge for cashing checks. Such laws have been found to reduce the number of minority households that do not have bank accounts (Washington, 2006).

Price gouging claims often surface after disasters because of seemingly inflated prices for goods and services such as gas, hotel rooms, food, and so on. After Hurricane Katrina, politicians were quick to blame the oil industry and local gas stations for the high gas prices consumers were forced to pay in the hurricane's aftermath. State attorneys general charged gas stations with gouging, although "it was later found by the FTC that gas prices were being set in competitive markets" (Carden, 2008, p. 531).

Some states have passed laws making it illegal for businesses to raise prices if a state of emergency has been declared. Critics of such laws suggest that selling commodities at prices below market value will actually create more problems and cause shortages on a quicker basis. The higher price, it is believed, helps to prevent shortages. Indeed, after Hurricane Katrina, a call for federal antigouging laws was opposed by FTC Chairwoman Deborah Platt Majoras because such a law "could hurt consumers by causing fuel shortages" (McNamara, 2006). Other experts have also warned against federally mandated price controls, suggesting that such practices harm consumers by increasing the amount of time it would take goods to reach consumers (Montgomery, Baron, & Weisskopf, 2007). Montgomery and his colleagues (2007) note that price controls on gasoline after Hurricanes Katrina and Rita would have increased economic damage by 1.5 to 2.9 billion dollars.

Other critics of federal price controls suggest that such laws and policies would keep many businesses from "providing goods and services after natural disasters" (Carden, 2008, p. 531). If there is no economic incentive to deliver goods to a disaster area where it may take more resources to deliver the goods, businesses may choose to deliver their goods elsewhere. Critics also suggest that the policies assume that the government better knows how to "allocate resources more efficiently than the market" (Culpepper & Block, 2008, p. 512). To these critics, price controls place artificial constraints on demand and supply, which makes it difficult to promote a free market economy. Culpepper and Block (2008) further suggest that "government regulation is nothing short of a disaster as far as satisfying customers is concerned" (p. 512).

Of course, some scholars support the use of price controls in responding to disasters. The assumption is that while natural laws of supply and demand exist during routine days,

in times of disaster, this assumption is often void. A gouger has a local monopoly on the scarce commodity and exploits this monopoly. Gougers violate social norms that dictate that one should help out in times of disaster, not seek profit from them. (Angel & McCabe, 2009, p. 283)

Finding prices repulsive does not mean price gouging occurred. Many were shocked to learn that Turing Pharmaceuticals CEO Martin Shkreli committed no crime when he "unapologetically raised the prices of an AIDS drug from $13.50 per pill to $750" (Smith & Horowitz, 2017). Based on the premise that gougers violate social norms, some have also suggested that gougers are immoral. Drawing on principles of supply and demand, one economist, however, argues that (1) antigouging laws are not morally justified, (2) price gouging is not necessarily morally reprehensible, and (3) gouging "offenders" are not necessarily immoral (Zwolinski, 2008). The ambiguity surrounding the utility of these laws reflects the general difficulties that arise when defining white-collar crime (discussed earlier in this text).

Market Allocation

Market allocation refers to dividing markets according to territories, products, goods, or some other service (USDOJ, n.d.b, p. 4). Perhaps an analogy can be made to drug dealing. It is well known that drug dealers have specific territories where they sell their drugs. Efforts to deal drugs in a rival drug dealer's neighborhood would likely be met with a violent response from the rival dealer. In effect, the drug dealers have engaged in market allocation. As regards legitimate goods and services, market allocation is illegal because it restricts competition and potentially allows one business to have a monopoly over the jurisdiction or territory it serves or the product or services it provides.

Group Boycotts

Group boycotts are situations where competitors agree not to do business with specific customers or clients. Consider a case in which a group of competing attorneys in the District of Columbia agreed not to provide services to indigent defendants unless the District paid the attorneys more for their services. The FTC investigated the case and found the attorneys in violation of antitrust laws, group boycotting in particular. The attorneys appealed the decision and the case eventually made its way to the Supreme Court. The Supreme Court upheld the FTC's decision (FTC, n.d.).

Dynamics Surrounding Antitrust Offenses

Several varieties of antitrust offenses exist, and four patterns are consistent across these offenses. These patterns include (1) the way that "agreement" is conceptualized, (2) the seriousness of harm arising from the offenses, (3) globalization, and (4) difficulties proving (and punishing) offenses.

First, in terms of the way "agreement" to limit competition is conceptualized, some might assume that agreements occur only through verbal or written agreements. This is not the case. In each of the antitrust offenses discussed above, agreements can be in writing, verbally agreed, or *inferred from the conduct of businesses*. As a result, to prove an antitrust offense, officials may rely on either direct evidence—such as testimony of participants or witnesses—or circumstantial evidence, such as expense reports, fluctuations, or bidding histories (USDOJ, n.d.b, p. 4). Note also that if the behaviors of competitors result in an antitrust offense, like price fixing, competitors can be found in violation of the laws. Consider the following example provided by the FTC (n.d.):

> A group of competing optometrists agreed not to participate in a vision care network unless the network raised reimbursement rates for patients covered by its plan. The optometrists refused to treat patients covered by the network plan, and eventually the company raised reimbursement rates. The FTC said that the optometrists' agreement was illegal price fixing, and that its leaders had organized an effort to make sure other optometrists knew about and complied with the agreement.

Second, it is important to draw attention to the serious harm that arises from antitrust offenses. Estimates suggest that antitrust offenses "can raise the price of a product by ten percent . . . and that American consumers and taxpayers pour billions of dollars each year into the pockets of [those participating in these schemes]" (USDOJ, n.d.a, p. 4).

One of the most prominent antitrust offenses involved vitamin producers in the late 1990s. Firms across the world conspired to set caps on how many vitamins each firm would produce, how much they should charge, and whom they should sell the vitamins to. The scheme was so large that the U.S. Department of Justice suggested that

> in the end, for nearly a decade, every American consumer—anyone who took a vitamin, drank a glass of milk, or had a bowl of cereal—ended up paying more so that the conspirators could reap hundreds of millions of dollars in additional revenue. (USDOJ, n.d.a, p. 4)

Those involved in the conspiracy included executives from F. Hoffmann-LaRoche, Ltd. and BASF AG.

A third pattern surrounding antitrust offenses centers on the globalization of our economy. As the world has become more global in nature, the types of antitrust offenses have become more globally oriented. The federal response to antitrust offenses has shifted to adjust to the types of issues arising in a global economy. For example, historically, the United States would apply only civil actions against businesses from other countries that engaged in violations of U.S. antitrust laws. In the 1990s, however, U.S. officials began to apply criminal sanctions to businesses in other countries. The criminalization of foreign antitrust cases through an application of the Sherman Act was upheld in *U.S. v. Nippon Paper Industries* (M. S. Lee, 1998).

The fourth pattern surrounding antitrust cases centers on the difficulties officials have establishing that crimes occurred and subsequently applying appropriate punishments. Interestingly, difficulties convicting antitrust offenders have been traced to efforts to "get tougher" against this group of offenders. In particular, some scholars have argued that it became harder to convict antitrust offenders in the 1980s after a 1970s law made offenses such as price fixing a felony rather than a misdemeanor (Snyder, 1989, 1990). The rationale for this argument is that offenders put a lesser defense when they were charged with misdemeanors. Facing a felony conviction, alternatively, potentially raises the bar for the kinds of penalties convicted offenders would receive and, as a result, may cause defendants to seek more remedies to avoid a conviction.

False Advertising

False advertising occurs when businesses make inaccurate statements about their products or services in order to facilitate the sale of those items or services. Put more simply, false advertising laws prohibit "untrue or misleading information given to you to get you to buy something, or to come to visit their store" (County of Los Angeles Department of Consumer Affairs, 2010). False advertising is illegal through the Federal Trade Commission Act, which stipulates the following:

- Advertising must be truthful and nondeceptive.
- Advertisers must have evidence to back up their claims.
- Advertisements cannot be unfair (FTC, 2001).

The concept of *deceptive* suggests that businesses cannot mislead or provide irrelevant information in their efforts to promote products. The concept *unfair* means that businesses cannot use advertisements to injure or harm consumers. Types of false advertising include the following:

- **Bait and switch practices**, where customers are lured into the store with the promise of a sale item that does not exist or is not available in an appropriate amount
- **Resale fraud**, where used items are sold as new
- Misuse of on sale phrases, where regular prices are presented as if they are sale prices

- Misrepresenting the product's capability, where consumers are told that the product can do things that it cannot

- Misrepresenting items as made in the United States, when parts of the product were made elsewhere (County of Los Angeles Department of Consumer Affairs, 2010)

The FTC regularly addresses cases of false advertising. A recent case involved a large for-profit higher education institution touting business relationships with high profile companies to market curricula that the companies helped design. Allegations were made, and questions surfaced about whether the identified companies actually had specific partnerships with the university and whether the companies were involved in developing the curricula as was represented by the university. After a five-year investigation, the university settled with the FTC and agreed to give students $50 million and cancel $141 million in debt owed by students (Fair, 2019). This was the largest FTC settlement ever with a for-profit higher education institution. As with most settlements, there was no admission of guilt on the part of the university.

Here are a few other recent examples of cases the FTC handled:

- On March 4, 2020, the FTC announced a settlement with the marketers of a pain relief device called Quell. The marketers "agreed to pay at least $4 million and stop making deceptive claims that the device treats pain throughout the body when placed below the knee and is clinically proven and cleared by the Food and Drug Administration (FDA) to do so" (FTC, 2020, March 4). This chapter's White-Collar Crime in the News includes the press release issued by the agency.

- On June 25, 2020, the FTC announced a settlement with the marketers of a product called Willow Cure. The marketers agreed to a multi-million dollar judgement and agreed "to stop making alleged deceptive claims that the device treats chronic, severe pain and associated inflammation" (FTC, 2020, June 25).

- On March 19, 2020, the FTC announced a settlement with a health company who agreed to a multi-million dollar judgement and promised to "halt their allegedly deceptive advertising claims about three 'cure-all' health and wellness products that targeted older consumers nationwide" (FTC, 2020, March 19).

WHITE-COLLAR CRIME IN THE NEWS
FALSE ADVERTISING

The following is a press release from the Federal Trade Commission from March 4, 2020.

Marketers of Pain Relief Device Settle FTC False Advertising Complaint

Under a settlement with the Federal Trade Commission, the marketers of an electrical nerve stimulation device called Quell have agreed to pay at least $4 million and stop making deceptive claims that the device treats pain throughout the body when placed below the knee and is clinically proven and cleared by the Food and Drug Administration (FDA) to do so.

The order settling the FTC's allegations bars the marketers of Quell from making such pain-relief claims unless they are true, not misleading, and supported by competent and reliable scientific evidence; prohibits misrepresentations about clinical proof or the scope of FDA clearance for any device; and requires them to pay redress.

(Continued)

[Continued]

"With the opioid crisis, consumers are searching for drug-free pain relief," said Bureau of Consumer Protection Deputy Director Daniel Kaufman. "Devices claiming pain relief without scientific support harm consumers and undermine the market for non-drug products. The FTC will act on empty promises of pain relief."

Since 2015, Massachusetts-based NeuroMetrix, Inc. and its CEO, Shai Gozani, have sold Quell, a transcutaneous electrical nerve stimulation device designed to be placed below a user's knee, according to the FTC's complaint.

The defendants marketed Quell nationwide, touting the device as "clinically proven" and "FDA cleared" for widespread chronic pain relief. The FTC alleged that the defendants lack scientific evidence to support widespread chronic pain relief claims, and their claims about clinical proof and the scope of FDA clearance are false.

In addition to barring the defendants' deceptive claims, the order imposes a $4 million judgment against the defendants, which must be paid to the FTC within 30 days, and requires them to turn over up to an additional $4.5 million in future foreign licensing payments.

NOTE: The Commission files a complaint when it has "reason to believe" that the named defendants are violating or are about to violate the law and it appears to the Commission that a proceeding is in the public interest. Stipulated final judgments and orders have the force of law when signed and entered by the District Court judge.

Reprinted from FTC.

Two common trends in advertising include going-out-of-business sales and the use of celebrities to promote goods. Laws exist to govern these advertising practices. For example, a business cannot advertise that it is going out of business unless it is actually going out of business. With regard to celebrity ads, the advertisement must accurately reflect the celebrity's view of the product. If a celebrity states that he or she uses a product in an ad, he or she must actually use that product. If the celebrity decides at a later date not to support the product any longer, the advertiser can no longer promote the product as if it were endorsed by the celebrity (FTC, 2001). For example, if Cardi B endorsed this book upon its release, the book could be promoted with her endorsement. If Cardi B later writes her own white-collar crime book and decides not to support this one, later promotions would not be able to use the music mogul's endorsement.

Some have suggested that the recession starting in 2008 contributed to an increase in false advertising by businesses trying virtually anything to offset the negative consequences of the downturn in the economy (A. Cooper, 2009). Another author suggested that the Internet provides easier opportunities to commit false advertising (Sarna, 2012). While these suggestions are speculative, they are in line with the assumption of the systems perspective, which suggests that changes in the one system (e.g., the economic system) will have ramifications for other systems (e.g., marketing practices in the corporate system).

One author team found that after false claims are sanctioned by federal authorities, it appears that the misleading claims "primarily affect newcomers and not the loyal users" (Rao & Wang, 2015, p. 5). This same author team estimated using a "back of the envelope" calculation that a company's false advertisement "gained $105 million in revenue because of the false claims [which is] a substantial amount compared to the $4 million it settled in a recent class action lawsuit" (p. 3).

Deceptive Sales

Deceptive sales are illicit sales practices that are driven by corporate policies and directives. Certainly, corporate policies and pressures can promote deceptive sales practices by employees. Wells Fargo's policies rewarding employees for new checking accounts illustrates how corporate officers' decisions influence wrongdoing by workers. In the early 2000s, the banking company—at the time, under the leadership of CEO John Stumpf and head of retail banking Carrie Tolstedt—developed policies that were subsequently labeled as "impossible sales goals" (Flitter, 2020). The policies promoted cross-selling by workers across the country. Cross-selling is the practice of getting current customers to purchase additional products. The company pushed cross-selling to employees who reported feeling intense pressure from their supervisors to meet those metrics. Officials believed that the goals and practices caused employees to create phony bank accounts without the customer's knowledge so that the employees would be paid more and avoid being reprimanded for not meeting their sales goals.

Concern about the practices first surfaced in 2013 when the scamming behaviors of a handful of employees came to light. The investigation grew into an international scandal over subsequent years when it found that 5,300 Wells Fargo employees had created fake bank accounts in order to meet their sales goals. For the investigation, the Department of Justice (DOJ) focused much of its attention on the "gaming" activities of the employees, a term widely used by those involved in the activities. Gaming referred to a wide range of behaviors that a large number of employees performed in order to fraudulently meet their sales goals. The DOJ Statement of Facts describes these behaviors in the following way:

- Gaming strategies varied widely and included using existing customers' identities—without the customers' consent—to open checking and savings, debit card, credit card, bill pay, and global remittance accounts. Many widespread forms of gaming constituted violations of federal criminal law. The following are examples of gaming practices engaged in by Wells Fargo employees during the period from 2002 to 2016:

  a. Employees created false records and forged customers' signatures on account opening documents to open accounts that were not authorized by customers.

  b. After opening debit cards using customers' personal information without consent, employees falsely created a personal identification number ("PIN") to activate the unauthorized debit card. Employees often did so because the Community Bank rewarded them for opening online banking profiles, which required a debit card PIN to be activated.

  c. In a practice known as "simulated funding," employees created false records by opening unauthorized checking and savings accounts to hit sales goals. They then transferred funds to the unauthorized account to meet the funding criteria required to receive credit for "selling" the new account. To achieve this "simulated funding," employees often moved funds from existing accounts of the customers without their consent. Millions of accounts reflected transfers of funds between two accounts that were equal in amount to the product-specific minimum amount for opening the later account and that thereafter had no further activity on the later account; many of these accounts were subject to simulated funding. In many other instances, employees used their own funds or other methods to simulate actual funding of accounts that they had opened without customer consent.

  d. Employees opened unauthorized consumer and business credit card accounts without customer authorization by submitting applications for credit cards in customers' names using customers' personal information.

  e. Employees opened bill pay products without customer authorization; employees also encouraged customers to make test or "token" payments from their bill pay accounts to obtain employee sales credit (which was only awarded for bill pay accounts that had made a payment).

  f. Employees at times altered the customer phone numbers, email addresses, or physical addresses on account opening documents. In some instances, employees did so to prevent the customers from finding out about unauthorized accounts, including to prevent customers from being contacted by the Company in customer satisfaction surveys. Millions of non-Wells Fargo-employee customer accounts reflected a Wells Fargo email address as the customer's email address, contained a generic and incorrect customer phone number, or were linked to a Wells Fargo branch or Wells Fargo employee's home address. (U.S. Department of Justice, Source: Reprinted from https://www.justice.gov/opa/press-release/file/1251346/download)

The fact that 5,300 employees across the company created fake accounts suggests that the motivations for offending were driven by corporate policies incentivizing the fraudulent behavior. In addition to creating thousands of fake bank accounts, employees created more than 560,000 credit card accounts without customers knowledge, resulting in significant fees for those customers (Egan, 2016).

In February 2020, the company signed a deferred prosecution agreement with the Department of Justice, including a settlement with the Securities Exchange Commission to settle criminal and civil charges arising from the employees' behavior. The settlement cost Wells Fargo $3 billion (Flitter, 2020). In separate actions, Stumpf and Tolstedt were fined $16.5 million and $25 million, respectively (Flitter, 2020).

In another case involving deceptive sales practices, and one many students might be able to relate to, a large for-profit college came under fire in 2004 after a federal investigation by the Department of Education (DE) revealed that the college recruiters systematically lied to students about how courses would transfer, the amount of financial aid available, and class size (Coutts, 2009). The DE report said that the college "based its recruiters' pay on the number of students they brought in, and punished underperforming recruiters by isolating them in glass-walled rooms and threatening to fire them if they failed to meet management goals" (E. Brown, 2004). Here's how a recruiter from the college described the process:

One thing we would be told to do is call up a student who was on the fence and say, "all right, I've only got one seat left. I need to know right now if you need me to save this for you, because this class is about to get full." Well, that wasn't true. We were told to lie. . . . One of the things we were to do was . . . say we are regionally accredited, which means that [credits] are transferred anywhere. (Coutts, 2009)

Those of you who have transferred know that transfer decisions are made by the college or university to which the student is transferring, not by an accreditation standard. Such deceptive practices were done to benefit the college, not the employee.

The DE ruled that the recruiting strategies violated Title II of the Higher Education Act. A subsequent audit found that other violations related to the use of financial aid funds were also allegedly committed by the college. The parent company of the for-profit college eventually paid the Department of Education $9.8 million. Later, it was ordered to pay shareholders $280 million because investors were reportedly fraudulently misled about the school's recruiting practices ("University of Phoenix Parent," 2008).

Problems with deceptive practices in recruiting students were not limited to this one for-profit college. In a U.S. Government Accountability Office (GAO) investigation, four undercover employees registered on the websites of 15 different for-profit colleges (USGAO, 2010). After registering on the websites, they began receiving phone calls from recruiters. Some calls were made within five minutes after the employee registered on the website. One received an average of six calls a day for an entire month.

The active recruiting by the for-profit recruiters was not problematic in and of itself. After all, they were hired to recruit students to their colleges. Instead, the problems arose when recruiters made deceptive statements about (1) accreditation, (2) graduation rates, (3) employment possibilities, (4) expected salaries, (5) program duration, and (6) cost. Four of the colleges encouraged the undercover applicant to lie about their income and savings in order to gain federal support for their education. All 15 of the colleges "made some type of deceptive or otherwise questionable statement to undercover applicants" (USGAO, 2010, p. 7).

The types of deceptive statements made by recruiters might resonate some with readers who, as students, have their own set of expectations about the value of their education. Consider the following examples quoted from the GAO report:

- A college owned by a publicly traded company told our applicant that, after completing an associate's degree in criminal justice, he could try to go work for the Federal Bureau of Investigation or the Central Intelligence Agency. While other careers within those agencies may be possible, a position as an FBI special agent or CIA clandestine officer requires a bachelor's degree at a minimum.

- A small beauty college told our applicant that barbers can earn $150,000 to $200,000 a year. While this may be true in exceptional circumstances, the Bureau of Labor Statistics (BLS) reports that 90% of barbers make less than $43,000 a year.

- A representative at a college in Florida owned by a publicly traded company told an undercover applicant that the college was accredited by the same organization that accredits Harvard and the University of Florida when in fact it was not. The representative told the undercover applicant: "It's the top accrediting agency— Harvard, University of Florida—they all use that accrediting agency. . . . All schools are the same; you never read the papers from the schools." (USGAO, 2010, p. 91)

The undercover investigation revealed that deceptive sales practices by college recruiters seemed to occur far too regularly. To date, no charges have been filed against the colleges, but charges remain possible. Go to https://www.gao.gov/products/gao-10-948t to view a video of the undercover applicants talking with recruiters.

Some for-profit colleges have also been accused of engaging in harmful practices that may not technically be illegal but may bend the rules. For example, attorneys general raised concerns that some for-profit colleges were pushing the envelope on the 90/10 rule, which states that no more than 90% of a student's education can be paid for with federal student aid funds from the Department of Education's Title IV program. The rule is based on the premise that someone other than the federal government should pay for at least some of a student's college education. The attorneys general expressed concern that for-profit colleges were aggressively targeting military students and using the student's military aid to count in the "10 percent" rather than the "90 percent" (Blumenstyk, 2012). Proponents of changing the rule argue that the application of the rule has placed "a dollar sign on the backs of veterans, service members and their families and led unscrupulous for-profit colleges to aggressively and deceptively recruit veterans, service members and their families to enroll in high-priced, low-quality programs" (Institute for College Access and Success, 2015).

A group of state attorneys general also recommended legislation limiting the amount of federal funds that for-profit colleges can use to advertise their services. In 2009, 15 for-profit education corporations received roughly 86% of their revenue from federal sources and spent $3.7 billion on marketing. This amount represented one fourth of the total budget for these colleges. In comparison, nonprofit colleges had marketing budgets that were less than 1% of their total budget (Wallack, 2013). In their defense, proponents of the for-profit schools pointed out that the schools provide access to education for a large number of nontraditional students who otherwise would not have education. Limiting marketing was viewed as limiting access. Steve Gunderson, president of the Association of Private Sector Colleges and Universities, told a reporter, "Advertising can shine a light on available opportunities for all citizens and should be encouraged rather than restricted. What this legislation does is limit information, and by doing so it limits access" (Wallack, 2013). The proposed law, while introduced in 2012, has yet to make it out of congressional committees. According to one author, these activities are expected to continue because "market structures and government policies play crucial roles in facilitating crime in these organizations and . . . such behavior is likely to continue despite tougher regulations, since the same elements will continue to influence for-profit colleges" (Beaver, 2012, p. 274).

In a more recent case, the second largest for-profit education company in the United States (Education Management Corporation) settled charges centering on deceptive recruiting practices where the company allegedly paid its recruiters based on the number of students they recruited. The company agreed to pay $95.5 million to settle the allegations. In the words of one of the deputy assistant attorneys general who worked on the case, "Improper incentives to admissions recruiters result in harm to students and financial losses to the taxpayers" (USDOJ, 2015, November 16).

Unfair Labor Practices

Unfair labor practices refer to corporate violations where workers are subjected to unethical treatment by their bosses and corporate leaders. Unfair labor practices are prohibited in the Fair Labor and Standards Act, which prohibits employers paying employees below a federal minimum wage, retaliating against employees who filed complaints against the corporation, exploiting child labor, not maintaining employee records, and paying protected classes unequally (Saba, 2019). In this context, two types of unfair labor practices can be identified: (1) exploitation and (2) systemic discrimination.

Exploitation

Exploitation refers to situations where businesses take advantage of their workers. Pay exploitation is an example.

An assignment I give my white-collar crime students asks them to write about types of white-collar crimes they have experienced. Each semester, at least a handful of students write about jobs where they work parts of their shifts for free. From my students' reports, this seems to be particularly popular in the restaurant industry—where waiters and waitresses stick around after their shifts to help clean the restaurants, being paid the standard waiter-waitress wage of $2.13 an hour if they are paid at all.

Sweatshops are examples of unfair labor practices. Such businesses "regularly violate both wage and child labor laws and safety or health regulations" (Foo, 1994, p. 2179). In many sweatshops, undocumented workers are hired and paid reduced wages. Such practices are criticized because they cheat the government out of tax dollars and deprive workers of necessary benefits (Foo, 1994). These activities are not simply a modern phenomenon. In 1892, Florence Kelley identified three types of sweatshops in the garment industry:

- *Inside shops* are those created by manufacturers inside a factory.

- *Outside shops* include contractors hired to produce goods or materials to be used by the manufacturer.

- *Home shops* (also known as family groups) are run out of the exploited worker's home (F. Kelley, 2005).

Even then, she drew attention to the problems of infection and disease that stemmed from such practices.

Some may point to greed and profit as the primary motivators for the creation and persistence of sweatshops. However, the reasons for the development of sweatshops are more complex than this. Foo (1994) cites a GAO report that attributed the existence of sweatshops to the following:

- The presence of a vulnerable population

- The presence of an exploitable population

- Labor intensive industries

- Low profit margin industries

- Lack of inspection staff

- Weak penalties

- Inadequate cooperation among enforcement agencies

Barnes and Kozar (2008) examined the types of exploitation targeted at pregnant workers in the textile industry in China, Mexico, Nicaragua, and the Philippines. Their research identified various types of exploitation, including forced abortions, unpaid overtime, forced job requirements harmful to the fetus, and lack of appropriate benefits. The authors note that U.S. firms are linked to these practices in that "governments of developing nations continue to lure [U.S. firms] in with promises of tax breaks, no duties, longer work weeks, and low minimum wage requirements" (p. 291). One study found that exploitation of labor is driven by profit motives, the lack of regulatory oversight, availability of a vulnerable labor pool, and the lack of unionization (Davies & Ollus, 2019).

Discrimination

Discrimination is another type of unfair labor practice committed in the corporate system. Some may question whether these offenses are actually corporate crimes. It is significant to note that Clinard and Yeager (1980) cited discrimination under the category of labor violations in their discussion of corporate crime. What this suggests is that discrimination has been considered a type of corporate misconduct ever since scholars first began to discuss these misdeeds.

Four federal statutes prohibit employment discrimination: Title VII, the Americans with Disabilities Act, the Age Discrimination Act, and the Equal Pay Act of 1963 (Goldman, Gutek, Stein, & Lewis, 2006). These laws prohibit the unfair treatment of employees based on their membership in a protected class including race, sex, religion, national origin, and disability status (Chien & Kleiner, 1999). Table 10.2 shows the total number of complaints filed with the Equal Employment Opportunity Commission between 2010 and 2019. A few patterns are worth highlighting. First, the number of complaints overall have dropped roughly 30% from 2010 to 2020. Second, disability and retaliation complaints increased. In 2020, retaliation complaints made up more than half of all complaints. In contrast, retaliation complaints made up 36% of all complaints in 2010. Across the board, equal opportunity violations disproportionately impact lower income workers. These workers work in isolated jobs lacking necessary protections and support to help them address work-related problems; these workers also have less access to justice mechanisms (Ditkowsky, 2019). The amount of time needed to file civil lawsuits, and problems finding attorneys who might help them, keeps lower income workers from seeking justice in these cases.

TABLE 10.2 ■ Complaints Filed With EEOC, 2010–2020 (FY)

Fiscal Year	2010	2011	2012	2013	2014	2015	2016	2017	20218	2019	FY 2020
Total charges	99,922	99,947	99,412	93,727	88,778	89,385	91,503	84,254	76,418	72,675	67,448
Race	35,890	35,395	33,512	33,068	31,073	31,027	32,309	28,528	24,600	23,976	22,064
	35.90%	35.40%	33.70%	35.30%	35.00%	34.7%	35.3%	33.9%	32.2%	33.0%	32.70%
Sex	29,029	28,534	30,356	27,687	26,027	26,396	26,934	25,605	24,655	23,532	21,398
	29.10%	28.50%	30.50%	29.50%	29.30%	29.5%	29.4%	30.4%	32.3%	32.4%	31.70%
National origin	11,304	11,833	10,883	10,642	9,579	9,438	9,840	8,299	7,106	7,009	6,377
	11.30%	11.80%	10.90%	11.40%	10.80%	10.6%	10.8%	9.8%	9.3%	9.6%	9.50%
Religion	3,790	4,151	3,811	3,721	3,549	3,502	3,825	3,436	2,859	2,725	2,404
	3.80%	4.20%	3.80%	4.00%	4.00%	3.9%	4.2%	4.1%	3.7%	3.7%	3.60%
Color	2,780	2,832	2,662	3,146	2,756	2,833	3,102	3,240	3,166	3,415	3,562
	2.80%	2.80%	2.70%	3.40%	3.10%	3.2%	3.4%	3.8%	4.1%	4.7%	5.30%
Retaliation–all statutes	36,258	37,334	37,836	38,539	37,955	39,757	42,018	41,097	39,469	39,110	37,632
	36.30%	37.40%	38.10%	41.10%	42.80%	44.5%	45.9%	48.8%	51.6%	53.8%	55.80%
Retaliation–Title VII only	30,948	31,429	31,208	31,478	30,771	31,893	33,082	32,023	30,556	30,117	27,997
	31.00%	31.40%	31.40%	33.60%	34.70%	35.7%	36.2%	38.0%	40.0%	41.4%	41.50%
Age	23,264	23,465	22,857	21,396	20,588	20,144	20,857	18,376	16,911	15,573	14,183
	23.30%	23.50%	23.00%	22.80%	23.20%	22.5%	22.8%	21.8%	22.1%	21.4%	21%
Disability	25,165	25,742	26,379	25,957	25,369	26,968	28,073	26,838	24,605	24,238	24,324
	25.20%	25.80%	26.50%	27.70%	28.60%	30.2%	30.7%	31.9%	32.2%	33.4%	36.10%
Equal Pay Act	1,044	919	1,082	1,019	938	973	1,075	996	1,066	1,117	980
	1.00%	0.90%	1.10%	1.10%	1.10%	1.1%	1.2%	1.2%	1.4%	1.5%	1.50%
GINA	201	245	280	333	333	257	238	206	220	209	440
	0.20%	0.20%	0.30%	0.40%	0.40%	0.3%	0.3%	0.2%	0.3%	0.3%	0.70%

Source: U.S. Equal Employment Opportunity Commission. (n. d.). *Charge statistics FY 97 to FY 2019.* Retrieved from http://eeoc.gov/eeoc/statistics/enforcement/charges.cfm

Women are more likely than men to experience discrimination because of stereotypes, perceptions of a lack of fit in the workforce, and the inability of recruiters to identify with women (Chien & Kleiner, 1999). Chien and Kleiner (1999) argue that these factors "inhibit women's career development and advancement and subsequently undermine women's contributions to the labor market" (p. 34).

Basing employment decisions on stereotypes has been regarded as a form of discrimination. In *Price Waterhouse v. Hopkins* (1989), a woman was denied a promotion in an accounting firm because she was seen as "too macho" (Malos, 2007, p. 97). Managing partners of the company said she needed to act more feminine and wear more makeup. The Supreme Court ruled that businesses could not base promotion decisions on gender stereotypes. Courts have also held that employers can be held liable for discrimination if they make employment decisions based on a woman's status as a mother. If employers assume, for instance, that a job would be too difficult because the employee is a new mother, the employer could be held liable for discrimination (Malos, 2007).

Discrimination does not just stem from employment decisions; instead, hostile or harassing behaviors of employees against other employees can be seen as discriminatory. Consider the following illustration:

> An African American employee at an East Coast Company took the day off to celebrate Martin Luther King Jr. Day. Upon returning from work, he discovered a note that had been scribbled on his desk calendar. It read: "Kill four more, get four more days off." (Solomon, 1992, p. 30)

In many cases, such attitudes stem from the top of the corporation and reflect corporate culture. Indeed, one court has recognized that "top level officials are 'in a position to shape the attitudes, policies, and decisions of corporate managers'" (Sorensen, 2009, p. 194, citing *Ercegovich v. Goodyear Tire and Rubber Co.,* 1998). It is through this perspective that corporations can be held accountable for discriminatory practices of its employees. Consider, as an illustration, a survey of nearly 700 business leaders focusing on hiring disabled workers that found that "86% agreed that employers would pick a non-disabled candidate, while 92% said there was still discrimination against disabled people in employment and recruitment" (Faragher, 2007, p. 22).

In a case highlighting how corporate leaders are involved in discrimination, an investigation by the Office of Inspector General (USOIG) and the Office of Professional Responsibility found that U.S. Deputy Assistant Attorney General Bradley S. Schlozman "considered political and ideological affiliations in hiring career attorneys and in other personnel actions affecting career attorneys in the Civil Rights Division" (USOIG, 2008, p. 64). As part of the evidence to substantiate the investigation, investigators found e-mail messages with comments such as "I have an interview with some lefty who we'll never hire but I'm extending a courtesy interview as a favor," "[I] just spoke with [the attorney] to verify his political leanings and it is clear he is a member of the team," (p. 24) and in response to a request to hire an attorney, Schlozman e-mailed, "Conservative?" Ironically, while the Civil Rights Division exists to protect against civil rights violations, in this case a top-ranking official from the division committed multiple civil rights violations.

Discrimination has negative consequences for individuals, groups, and organizations. At the individual level, discrimination can negatively impact one's health, self-esteem, and job performance. At the group level, groups receive unfair pay differences and are assigned to different jobs based on group identities. At the organizational level, the corporation suffers from a negative reputation, lawsuits, and fines from the Equal Employment Opportunity Commission (EEOC; Goldman et al., 2006).

Unsafe Work Environments

Crime also occurs in the corporate system when employers place employees at risk of harm in *unsafe work environments*. Labeled corporate violence by Frank and Lynch (1992), unsafe work environments can result in death, illnesses, and injuries. In terms of death, one author describes corporate murder as including deaths from industrial "accidents" and "occupationally related diseases, the majority of which are caused by the knowing and willful violation of occupational health and safety laws by corporations" (Kramer, 1984, p. 7). One scholar has suggested that "managers and corporations commit far more violence than any serial killer or criminal organization" (Punch, 2000, p. 243). The ability of corporations to hide violence has led some to refer to their behavior as "the invisible harm" (Forti & Visconti, 2020, p. 70).

Prior to the creation of the Occupational Safety and Health Administration (OSHA) in 1971, roughly 14,000 workers in the United States were killed on the job annually. This has improved dramatically, with 5,250 workers dying on the job in 2018. The 2018 numbers are up 2% from the 2017 total of 5,147 (OSHA, 2019). Figure 10.2 shows the causes of workplace deaths in 2018. Roughly 40% of the deaths involved transportation incidents, and another 16% were caused by violence either from an individual or an animal.

While the number of workplace fatalities from physical factors can be tracked, it is difficult to track the number of workplace deaths stemming from illnesses caused by the workplace. Consider stress-induced illnesses, for example. Did the stress come from the workplace or some other aspect of the individual's life? One author points to three issues that make it difficult to link illness to the workplace. First, determining the precise cause of illnesses and linking the illness to the workplace are difficult. Second, disease is seen as a normal part of the aging process. If individuals develop a workplace illness after years of work, the assumption is that the illness came from "getting old" rather than working. Third, and somewhat related, diseases are "considered normal" and accepted as a part of our lives (Frank, 1993, p. 110).

FIGURE 10.2 ■ Causes of Workplace Fatalities, 2018

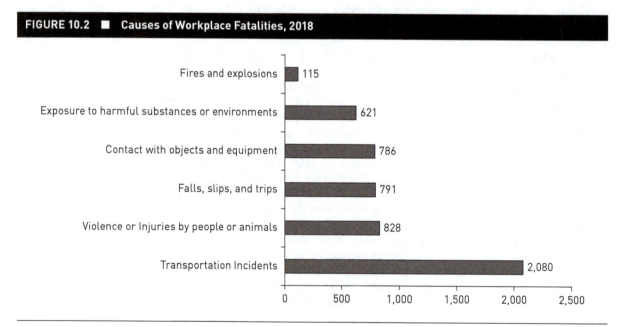

Source: Bureau of Labor Statistics: https://www.bls.gov/charts/census-of-fatal-occupational-injuries/fatal-occupational-injuries-by-event-drilldown.htm

Workplace injuries can be either acute or chronic. Acute injuries are immediate injuries that one might experience on the job. Chronic injuries refer to those that occur over time. The nature of some types of jobs can lead to long-term injuries. Standing on a cement floor and packing boxes in a 100°F factory for 40 hours a week over 30 years (a job my dad had) can lead to knee and shoulder problems. Bending over and serving schoolchildren lunch for 22 years (a job my mom had) can lead to back problems. Typing on a computer over several years (a job I have) can result in carpal tunnel syndrome, a disease that makes it difficult to move one's hands (see Frank, 1993).

In terms of acute injuries, in 2019, 2.8 million incidents of nonfatal workplace injuries or illnesses occurring in private industry were reported to OSHA. Roughly the same number was reported the prior year. In all, 888,220 of the cases required time off work with sprains, strains, and tears being the most prevalent injuries. In private industries, 90 out of 10,000 full-time workers missed at least one day of work in 2019 as the result of an occupational injury or illness (Bureau of Labor Statistics [BLS], 2020).

Figure 10.3 shows the rate of injuries and illnesses between 2003 and 2019. Overall, incidence rates per 100 full-time workers dropped dramatically since 2003. The rates for injuries requiring missed work, transfers, or other restrictions also dropped, but not quite at the same rate. Generally speaking, the older the workers, the more days of work that were missed from injuries or illnesses attributed to the workplace (see Table 10.3). In 2018, those over the age of 55 missed nearly three times as many work days due to workplace injuries and violence as did those between the ages of 20 and 24.

Despite the overall reduction in occupational injuries and illnesses, certain industries seem to be more at risk for workplace injuries than others. Table 10.4 shows the number of injuries in

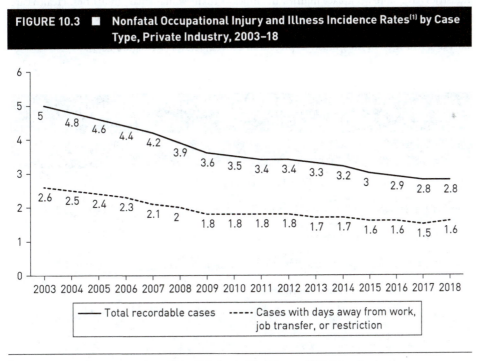

FIGURE 10.3 ■ Nonfatal Occupational Injury and Illness Incidence Rates[1] by Case Type, Private Industry, 2003–18

Total recordable cases: 5, 4.8, 4.6, 4.4, 4.2, 3.9, 3.6, 3.5, 3.4, 3.4, 3.3, 3.2, 3, 2.9, 2.8, 2.8

Cases with days away from work, job transfer, or restriction: 2.6, 2.5, 2.4, 2.3, 2.1, 2, 1.8, 1.8, 1.8, 1.8, 1.7, 1.7, 1.6, 1.6, 1.5, 1.6

—— Total recordable cases   ----- Cases with days away from work, job transfer, or restriction

[1] The incidence rates represent the number of injuries and illnesses per 100 full-time workers.

Note: Components may not add to totals due to rounding.

Source: Bureau of Labor Statistics. (2009–2019). *Nonfatal occupational injuries and illnesses: Private industry, state government, and local government.* Available online.

TABLE 10.3 ■ Median Days Away From Work due to Injuries and Illnesses and Incidence Rate by Age of Worker, All Ownerships, 2018			
Year	Age Group	Median Days Away From Work[1]	Incidence Rate per 10,000 Full-Time Workers
2018	16 to 19 years	5	111.4
2018	20 to 24 years	5	100.9
2018	25 to 34 years	6	86.5
2018	35 to 44 years	8	91.7
2018	45 to 54 years	11	104.5
2018	55 to 64 years	14	113.4
2018	65 years and older	14	98.3
2018	Total	9	98.4

Source: Bureau of Labor Statistics. (2019). https://www.bls.gov/iif/soii-chart-data-2018.htm

various industries. One clear pattern, and one that is not entirely surprising, is that "blue-collar" industries have more workplace injuries and illnesses than "white-collar" industries. Health care jobs, manufacturing jobs, and transportation jobs have the highest incidence rates of nonfatal injuries. There are also geographical patterns to workplace injury cases; these patterns may be more of a reflection of the industries present in different states (see Figure 10.4).

TABLE 10.4 ■ Highest Incidence Rates[1] of Total Nonfatal Occupational Injury Cases, 2019	
Industry	Incidence Rate[2]
Nursing and residential care facilities (State government)	6.0
Prefabricated wood building manufacturing (Private industry)	5.1
Scheduled passenger air transportation (Private industry)	4.2
Elevator and moving stairway manufacturing (Private industry)	3.8
Correctional institutions (State government)	3.7
Hospitals (State government)	3.5
Couriers and express delivery services (Private industry)	3.4
Urban transit systems (Private industry)	3.2

Industry	Incidence Rate[2]
Other support activities for transportation (Private industry)	3.2
Seafood product preparation and packaging (Private industry)	3.1
Marine cargo handling (Private industry)	3.1
Bituminous coal underground mining (Private industry)	3.0
Solid waste collection (Private industry)	3.0
Ambulance services (Private industry)	3.0
Siding contractors (Private industry)	2.8
Steel foundries (except investment) (Private industry)	2.7
Interurban and rural bus transportation (Private industry)	2.7
Framing contractors (Private industry)	2.6
Reconstituted wood product manufacturing (Private industry)	2.5
Psychiatric and substance abuse hospitals (Private industry)	2.5
Nursing and residential care facilities (Local government)	2.5
Dairy cattle and milk production (Private industry)	2.4
Water supply and irrigation systems (Private industry)	2.4
Skiing facilities (Private industry)	2.4
Truss manufacturing (Private industry)	2.3
Concrete block and brick manufacturing (Private industry)	2.3
All industries including state and local government[3]	0.9

[1]The incidence rates represent the number of injuries and illnesses per 100 full-time equivalent workers and were calculated as: (N/EH) x 200,000, where

N = number of injuries and illnesses

EH = total hours worked by all employees during the calendar year

200,000 = base for 100 full-time equivalent workers (working 40 hours per week, 50 weeks per year)

[2]Days-away-from-work cases include those that result in days away from work with or without job transfer or restriction.

[3]High rate industries were those having the highest incidence rate of injury and illness cases with days away from work and at least 500 total

Recordable cases at the most detailed level of publication based on the North American Industry Classification System—United States 2017

Source: U.S. Bureau of Labor Statistics, U.S. Department of Labor https://www.bls.gov/iif/oshsum.htm #19Supplemental_News_Release_Tables

FIGURE 10.4 ■ Number of Fatal Work Injuries by State, 2018

Number of fatal work injuries by state, 2018

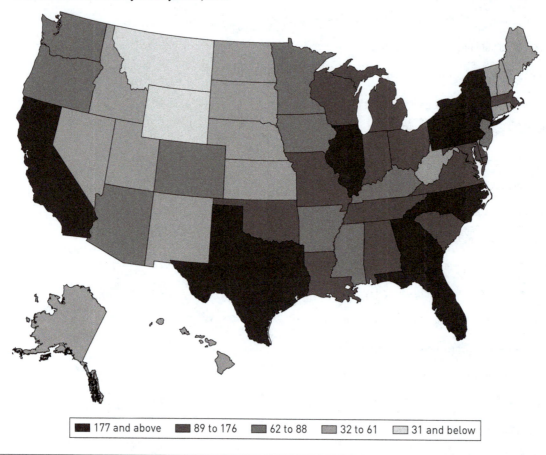

| ■ 177 and above | ■ 89 to 176 | ■ 62 to 88 | □ 32 to 61 | □ 31 and below |

Source: Bureau of Labor Statistics: https://www.bls.gov/charts/census-of-fatal-occupational-injuries/state-fatal-work-injuries-map.htm

The top 10 most frequently cited OSHA standards in fiscal year 2018 included the following:

(1) Fall protection, construction

(2) Hazard communication standard, general industry

(3) Scaffolding, general requirements, construction

(4) Respiratory protection, general industry

(5) Control of hazardous energy (lockout/tagout), general industry

(6) Ladders, construction

(7) Powered industrial trucks, general industry

(8) Fall protection–training requirements

(9) Machinery and machine guarding, general requirements

(10) Eye and face protection (OSHA, 2019)

Where these problems exist, the possibility of workplace injuries increases. Note that I made an intentional decision not to refer to injuries as "accidents." As will be shown below, injuries occurring in the corporate system are often far from accidental.

Beyond the physical costs, the costs of workplace injuries and illnesses are significant. These costs include (1) settlement costs to victims and family members, (2) negative publicity, (3) increases in insurance premiums, (4) higher worker compensation rates, and (5) increased attention from government agencies (Yakovlev & Sobel, 2010). In terms of economic costs, it is estimated that "the cost of occupational injuries and illnesses totals more than $156 billion" (OSHA, 2006, p. 5).

Some authors have suggested that corporations are more concerned with profit than worker health and safety. One author even suggests that such a statement "seems incontrovertible" (Tombs, 2008, p. 26). However, economists have found that companies actually maximize profit if they provide safer working environments for their employees.

In some cases, this means replacing workers with technological devices that are safer and "reduce worker exposure to danger and lead to lower injury rates over time" (Yakovlev & Sobel, 2010, p. 435). This may mean fewer jobs in "dangerous" occupations but more jobs in technologically oriented occupations that develop the technologies to make work-places safer.

A summer job I had in college comes to mind. For four years, I spent my summers work-ing in the bottle factory where my dad worked. College students had various summer jobs in the factory, including painting, packing bottles in boxes, driving forklifts, cleaning, and so on. One job was called "snapping." In this job, workers waited on the basement floor of the factory to stack packed boxes of bottles on a pallet. The packed boxes were carried on a conveyor belt, with as many as 30 boxes a minute coming before the "snapper." The snapper would grab several boxes at once, "snap" the lids of the boxes strategically, and flip them over while turning around to place them in a predetermined pattern on a pallet. The job was actually somewhat exciting to those of us who rarely did it. Trying to stack all of the boxes without creating a mess made the task more like a game than a job. If we fell behind, a full-time worker was there to help us out (while making fun of us for being unable to keep up). Each summer, someone got hurt from either dropping boxes (filled with bottles—which would become broken bottles) or from trying to lift too many boxes at once.

Years later, I learned that the snapper job no longer existed. A machine was created that would simultaneously pack the bottles in boxes and then stack the packed boxes on a pallet. A worker had to watch the machine to make sure it was working properly. Sitting and watching a machine stack boxes is much safer than stacking the boxes yourself!

OSHA, situated in the Department of Labor, is the federal agency charged with address-ing health and safety issues in businesses. OSHA exists to "ensure safe and healthful work-ing conditions for working men and women by setting and enforcing standards and by providing training, outreach, education, and assistance" (OSHA, 2011a). About 2,400 inspectors work for OSHA and related state agencies. In 2018, OSHA completed 32,023 inspections, with more than half of the inspections "unprogrammed" (i.e., unplanned) and resulting from referrals, injuries, complaints from employees, or other types of information warranting an inspection (OSHA, 2019). The types of violations OSHA issues citations for are outlined in Table 10.5.

TABLE 10.5 ■ Types of OSHA Violations	
Violation	**Definition**
Willful	The employer knew that a hazardous condition existed but made no reasonable effort to eliminate it, and the hazardous condition violated a standard, regulation, or the OSH Act.
Serious	The workplace hazard could cause injury or illness that would most likely result in death or serious physical harm, unless the employer did not know or could not have known of the violation.
Other-than-serious	A situation in which the most serious injury or illness that would be likely to result from a hazardous condition cannot reasonably be predicted to cause death or serious physical harm to exposed employees but does have a direct and immediate relationship to their safety and health.
De minimis	Violations that have no direct or immediate relationship to safety or health.
Failure to abate	The employer has not corrected a violation for which OSHA has issued a citation, and that abatement date has passed.
Repeated	Employer may be cited for a repeated violation if that employer has been cited previously for a substantially similar condition.

Source: Occupational Safety & Health Administration (OSHA), United States Department of Labor. (2015). *Employer rights and responsibilities following an OSHA inspection.* Available from https://www.osha.gov/Publications/osha3000.pdf.

OSHA was created in 1970 as part of the Occupational Safety and Health Act. This act covers all employees working in the private sector. State and local government workers are covered under specific state occupational acts, which by law must be similar to the federal law. The act does not cover (1) self-employed workers, (2) immediate family members of self-employed farmers, and (3) workers covered by another federal agency (OSHA, 2010a). The act stipulates that workers have the following rights (see OSHA, 2011b):

1. Receive information and training about hazards, methods to prevent harm, and the OSHA standards that apply to their workplace

2. Observe testing that is done to find hazards in the workplace and get the testing results

3. Review records of work-related injuries and illnesses

4. Get copies of their medical records

5. Request that OSHA inspect their workplace

6. Use their rights under the law to be free from retaliation and discrimination

Under this last provision, employees cannot be punished by employers for exercising their rights. If employers engage in any form of adverse action, the corporation or business could face additional penalties from OSHA. Types of adverse actions that would warrant a response from OSHA include any of the following actions directed toward the employee who reported a concern to OSHA: firing or laying off, making threats, blacklisting, reassigning, reducing pay or hours, demoting, denying overtime, disciplining, denying benefits, failure to rehire, and intimidation (OSHA, 2010b).

Workplace injuries and illnesses are rarely treated as crimes. A study of Finnish police officers found a systematic lack of interest in responding to workplace safety offenses (Alvesalo & Whyte, 2007). In this study, one officer told an interviewer that such cases were "worthless shit" that should not receive police intervention.

Typically, workplace injuries and illnesses are handled within the regulatory environment. This presents problems in that victims' needs may not be fully addressed through an administrative response system. One expert has suggested expanding workers' compensation policies as well as filing civil lawsuits and criminal prosecutions in cases where companies harm their workers.

With regard to workers' compensation, the specific features of the policies are not "worker friendly" policies. Under worker compensation systems, it is up to workers to prove that their ailment was caused by the occupational setting.

If workers agree to the compensation, they typically give up their right to sue their company for negligence (Frank, 1993). The pursuit of criminal remedies is complicated by perceptions of workplace injuries as accidents rather than avoidable injuries inflicted by the corporate system employing the injured employee.

Some have criticized the use of the word *accidents* to describe workplace injuries (Alvesalo & Whyte, 2007). The basis for the criticism is fourfold. First, many of the injuries are foreseeable and can be attributed to decisions made by managers and supervisors to place workers at risk. Second, the term *accident* implies that the injured party is to blame. Keep in mind that injured parties more often work in blue-collar occupations. Third, by construing injuries as accidents, the managers increase their power over the workers, who get blamed for getting hurt on the job. Finally, by defining injuries as accidents, workers are less likely to pursue civil and criminal remedies to address their injuries. As an example of how defining workplace injuries as accidents helps keep the cases out of the justice system, consider the following comments from one police officer: "It's not the responsibility of the employer if some idiot blunders by oneself, does something stupid. There cannot be someone looking over every Tom, Dick, and Harry" (Alvesalo & Whyte, 2007, p. 69).

Reflecting the connections between constructions of definitions of deviance, workplace injury, and the system's response, author Maurice Punch (2000) observed the following: "Corporations can create an environment that leads to risk-taking, even recklessness, resulting in high casualties and severe harm. Companies then get away with 'murder' because the courts are not geared to organizational deviance and corporate violence" (p. 243).

Discussing these ideas in the abstract may make it difficult for some students to fully appreciate the dynamics of workplace injuries and illnesses. However, many students are likely already employed in either full- or part-time jobs. Students must recognize that in their role as "worker" they too have certain rights that their employer is expected to recognize.

Harmful Consumer Products

Crimes also occur in the corporate system when corporations create **harmful consumer products**. Companies produce all sorts of goods for our use. In most cases, these goods are safe. Occasionally, however, goods enter the marketplace that create significant harm to consumers. Consider that in 2019, the U.S. Consumer Product Safety Commission (USCPSC) issued 241 recalls for millions of goods that were deemed to be unsafe (Frankel, 2020).

While virtually any product can be unsafe if used inappropriately, goods that have been linked to serious harm include certain types of the following:

- Toys
- Automobiles
- Food
- Construction material
- Recalled goods from China

These goods are discussed further in the following sections.

PHOTO 10.1 The number of children requiring emergency room treatment for injuries they experienced from playing with toys in the United States nearly doubled between 1996 and 2014.

Harmful Toys

Children's products are those that are often found to be the least safe. One advocacy group, Kids in Danger, lamented that children are "used as guinea pigs for unsafe products" because government "safety tests aren't required for children's products" (Sorkin, 2008). Interestingly, the number of toy-related injuries has continued to consistently grow since 2005. Table 10.6 shows the number of toy injuries requiring emergency room treatment between 2010 and 2018. The number of toy injuries remained relatively stable until 2018 when the number dropped by roughly 10%. Incidentally, approximately 130,000 toy injuries requiring emergency room treatment occurred in 1996. This means that the number of injuries is still far from the 1996 amount. Among specified tools, in 2018, nonmotorized scooters caused the most injuries. They accounted for 17% of the injuries (Tu, 2019). Seventeen children (all under the age of 12) died as a result of toy-related injuries in 2018 (Tu, 2019).

TABLE 10.6 ■ Number of Toy-Related Injuries Requiring Emergency Room Intervention, 2010–2018			
Year	All Ages	Under 15	Under 5
2010	242,000	177,500	88,900
2011	252,600	188,500	92,000
2012	253,500	187,300	89,300
2013	246,300	184,500	83,300
2014	240,900	179,700	84,000
2015	244,400	181,600	88,400
2016	240,000	174,100	85,200
2017	251,700	184,000	89,800
2018	226,100	166,200	83,800

Source: Tu, Y. (2019). *Toy-related deaths and injuries calendar year 2018.* Bethesda, MD: U.S. Consumer Product Safety Commission.

Certain Automobiles

On August 28th, 2009, a 911 operator received a call from Mark Saylor, an off-duty California highway patrol officer. He told the operator,

> We're in a Lexus . . . and we're going north on 125 and our accelerator is stuck . . . we're in trouble . . . there's no brakes . . . we're approaching the intersection . . . hold on . . . hold on and pray . . . pray. (Frean & Lea, 2010)

He and three family members were killed in what was later attributed to a problem with the accelerator sticking to the floor mat.

Initially, National Highway Traffic Safety Administration (NHTSA) investigators found that the mat in Saylor's vehicle was longer than it should have been, and it was believed that this potentially contributed to the crash. Until Toyota found a fix, owners of certain models were advised to remove the mats from the driver's side ("Fatal Crash Spurs Review," 2009). Another review of the incident found that the design of the gas pedal could have forced it to get lodged with the mat (Bensinger & Vartabedian, 2009). A subsequent investigation revealed that similar problems in other cars made by Toyota "led to thousands of accidents and nineteen deaths" (Frean & Lea, 2010).

In response to these concerns, in 2009 Toyota recalled 4.26 million automobiles. The recall resulted in Toyota's shares dropping 0.9% (Keane & Kitamura, 2009). It is estimated that the recall cost Toyota $900 million (Glor, 2010), and U.S. sales of Toyota vehicles dropped to under 100,000 vehicles for the first time since the late 1990s ("There's No Brakes," 2010). Obviously, this drop in sales was the result of a reduction in consumer confidence.

Toyota was not the first automobile company to face concerns about safety; the automobile industry has a long history of compliance problems related to safety issues (Diehl & Batsford, 2019). In the early 2000s, the Ford Explorer faced public scrutiny after it was found that tread separation problems on the Explorer's Firestone tires resulted in the deaths of 134 individuals in the United States. The investigation found that separately the tires and the vehicles were safe. However, when combined, they were a "toxic cocktail," according to Rep. Edward Markey (D-MA) (White, Power, & Aeppel, 2001). Ford and Firestone recalled more than 27 million tires in a 10-month time frame, and in 2001, Ford cut its 100-year supply relationship with Firestone (Ackman, 2001).

Of course, this was not the first time that the safety of a Ford vehicle was called into question. Recall the discussion of the Ford Pinto case earlier in this text. The Pinto was linked to a series of deaths "because of gas-tank explosions in rear-end collisions" (Glazer, 1983, p. 37). Ford was sued in 50 different lawsuits between 1971 and 1978 as a result of these collisions. One employee, Frank Camps, a design engineer,

> questioned the design and testing procedure and later charged publicly that his superiors who knew of this danger were so anxious to produce a lightweight and cheap car . . . that they were determined to overlook serious design problems. (Glazer, 1983, p. 36)

An automotive compliance scandal in 2017 involved Volkswagen. Engineers for the company developed a computer algorithm that could fool emissions tests designed to control automobile pollution. The engineers installed the algorithm on more than 11 million cars (Haugh, 2017). In March 2016, the FTC charged Volkswagen with using deceptive practices to market more than 550,000 automobiles in the United States as environmentally friendly. The company eventually settled the case with the FTC and agreed to give car owners the option to either return the car for payment in a buyback program, terminate their leases, or have their car repaired so the emissions tests would be accurate. In total, 86% of the car owners returned their automobiles. The FTC case alone cost the company $8.6 billion (FTC, 2020, July 27). This is in addition to a $4.3 billion penalty the company agreed to pay to resolve allegations initiated by the Environmental Protection Agency and adjudicated by the U.S. Department of Justice (USDOJ, 2017, January 11).

Types of Food

Certain types of food can also be seen as unsafe consumer products. Walters (2007) notes that genetically modified food has the potential to harm consumers. He also draws attention to the "sale of contaminated meat" and "the illegal use of chemicals" on food items. Whereas the Consumer Product Safety Commission has the authority to recall many products, consumable products, such as food, are under the authority of the Food and Drug Administration (FDA).

In September 2008, concern surfaced over potentially contaminated peanut butter. An investigation revealed that Peanut Butter Corporation of America, a peanut butter producer in Georgia, had distributed peanut butter contaminated with salmonella. Initially, the FDA concluded that the company actually knew about the tainted peanut butter but engaged in "lab shopping" to find another lab that would approve the peanut butter before distribution. A subsequent report by the FDA found that the company had actually distributed the peanut butter before even receiving approval from the second laboratory. Congress held a hearing, inviting food safety experts and subpoenaing representatives from Peanut Butter Corporation. Officials from the corporation did not testify, invoking their Fifth Amendment right against self-incrimination ("FDA: Georgia Plant Knowingly Sold," 2009). By April 2009, at least nine individuals had allegedly died from eating the peanut butter, and more than 700 had become seriously ill (Centers for Disease Control [CDC], 2009). The company filed for bankruptcy, and the entire peanut butter industry experienced economic losses as consumers cut back on their peanut butter consumption. In September 2015, the CEO was sentenced to 28 years in prison after a jury found him guilty of 72 fraud and conspiracy charges the year before. This was reportedly the first time a food safety case resulted in a felony conviction, let alone a prison sentence. The company's food broker and quality assurance manager received prison sentences of 20 and 5 years respectively.

Many cases of food poisoning from harmful food products likely go unnoticed. A report from the World Health Organization (2015) estimates food poisoning contributed to 420,000 deaths and 600 million illnesses. Criminologists have shown how the lax regulatory efforts in the food industry have contributed to the growth of harmful food products (Leighton, 2016; Leon & Ken, 2017; Tombs & Whyte, 2020).

PHOTO 10.2 In general, consumers expect their food to be safe, and most give little thought to the possibility that they could be consuming unsafe meals.

©iStockphoto.com/EXTREME-PHOTOGRAPHER

Specific Types of Construction Material

Certain types of construction materials have also been shown to be unsafe products. Asbestos is perhaps the most well-known construction material deemed to be unsafe. Asbestos is a mineral used in the past in various construction processes and products, including insulation, siding, roofing materials, shipyard construction materials, and so on. Initial concern about asbestos can be traced to the 1920s, when physicians wrote about the potential for harm from exposure to this product. It was not until the mid-1970s, however, that widespread concern about the product surfaced. Workers in various industries exhibited different illnesses that were traced to exposure to asbestos. It is now known that asbestos exposure can lead to asbestosis (an illness making it difficult to breathe), lung cancer, and mesothelioma. Between the early 1970s and 2002, 730,000 individuals filed asbestos claims at a cost of $70 billion. Estimates suggest that by 2029, a half million Americans will have died from asbestos-related diseases (J. Morris, 2010).

Asbestos is rarely used in building products today, though materials containing it are still found in older buildings and homes. Left alone in the construction material, the asbestos poses little harm. However, when cut, damaged, or moved, the asbestos fibers can become airborne and cause health problems.

Chinese drywall is another type of unsafe building material. In 2008, the U.S. Consumer Product Safety Commission began receiving complaints about problems homeowners were having with drywall installed in their homes. The drywall was imported from manufacturers in China between 2003 and 2007 when the U.S. levels of drywall were low because of the building boom and the need for drywall to repair homes after Hurricanes Katrina and Rita. Residents with the drywall in their homes reported (1) rotten egg smells or odors that smelled like fireworks, (2) corroded or black metals, (3) corroded electrical wiring, and (4) an assortment of health problems. The health problems they described included "irritated and itchy eyes, difficulty breathing, persistent coughing, bloody noses, runny noses, headaches, sinus infections, fatigue, asthma attacks, loss of appetite, poor memory, and irritability;" testing of the homes with the drywall found that the Chinese drywall emitted 100 times the amount of hydrogen sulfide emitted from non–Chinese drywall emitted (USCPSC, 2010a; Hernandez, 2010).

It is estimated that 7 million sheets of the tainted drywall were installed in thousands of homes in the United States and that property damage from the defective drywall will rise to $3 billion. By March 2010, approximately 2,100 homeowners had filed lawsuits over the drywall against builders, insurers, manufacturers, and others ("Insurers' Recent Success," 2010). Around the same time, the USCPSC recommended that homeowners remove the drywall from their homes, an expense that would need to be covered by the homeowners. Estimates suggested that such a process would cost an average of $100,000 per home (Hernandez, 2010).

In the fall of 2010, a judge held that insurers could not be held liable because of traditional exclusions found in insurance policies ("Insurers' Recent Success," 2010). In October 2010, Knauf Plasterboard Tianjin Co., the company responsible for some of the tainted drywall, agreed to fix the homes that had its drywall installed in them (Burdeau, 2010). By January 2011, the USCPSC had received 3,770 complaints from consumers in 41 states saying that the defective drywall caused problems in their homes. By the end of the investigation, the USCPSC had received 4,051 complaints about illnesses from the tainted drywall (USCPSC, n.d.). The protection hailed the investigation at the time as "the largest compliance investigation in agency history" (USCPSC, 2010b).

Recalled Goods From China

The drywall was not the first imported good from China deemed to be unsafe. The year 2007, deemed "Year of the Recall," saw a particularly high number of Chinese goods recalled by the USCPSC. To put this in perspective, in 2007, the USCPSC issued 473 recalls. Of those 473, 82% were for imported goods, most of which included toys and jewelry from China (USCPSC, 2010c). Many of the recalls centered on what was deemed to be an unsafe level of lead paint in the goods. In September 2007, the USCPSC signed an agreement with China's equivalent agency stipulating that China would no longer export toys containing lead paint to the United States ("Chinese Goods Scare Prods Regulators," 2007). The USCPSC's Office of International Programs and International Affairs enhanced its efforts to work with China and other foreign manufacturers to focus on product safety. Part of their efforts entailed the coordination of U.S.–China Consumer Product Safety Summits. The agency also staffed an employee in China for the first time beginning in December 2009 (USCPSC, 2010c).

To be sure, globalization has had ramifications for the way that corporations create and distribute unsafe products. On the one hand, it is hard to hold manufacturers in other countries accountable "because attorneys can't establish jurisdiction" (PR Newswire, 2007). On the other

PHOTO 10.3 The FDA trains Chinese manufacturers and regulators how to promote safety. In this photo, the FDA's Daniel Geffin is showing Chinese regulators the way he inspects manufacturing equipment designed to sterilize canned foods.

hand, the way that goods are now created, a specific product may include parts that were created in several different countries. It becomes particularly difficult to determine where the faulty part of an unsafe product was made (Wahl, 2009).

Harmful Treatment of Consumers

Harmful treatment of consumers refers to situations where businesses either intentionally or unintentionally put consumers who are using their services at risk of harm. Institutional neglect in nursing homes is one example. Offenses that have been known to occur in nursing homes include instances where nursing homes fail to meet regulatory standards such as feeding residents a healthy diet, monitoring their health needs, and administering appropriate medications. (Payne, 2011). Note that these offenses in and of themselves may not produce harm. However, they raise the likelihood that consumers might experience harm. Other times, the failure to provide care can be deadly. During the Covid-19 pandemic, a large number of deaths in nursing homes occurred, and some of those were attributed to neglect. In September 2020, for instance, two nursing home administrators were charged with criminal neglect "for their roles in the deadly COVID-19 outbreak that contributed to the death of at least 76 residents" (Office of Attorney General Maura Healey, 2020).

Businesses have a duty to ensure that consumers are as safe possible. A landmark case demonstrating this involved pop singer Connie Francis. In 1974, she was raped at a Howard Johnson's hotel in New York. After her victimization, she sued the hotel for failing to provide her adequate security after learning that the lock on the door of the room where her rape occurred had not been fixed six months after she was raped (Barrows & Powers, 2009; Shuler, 2010).

Another case demonstrating how businesses and corporations can commit misconduct by failing to keep consumers safe involves the band Great White. The 1980s band is best known for its hit, "Once Bitten, Twice Shy." Like many 80s bands, Great White was still entertaining audiences two decades later by playing in nightclubs and local establishments across the country. On February 20, 2003, they were playing at The Station, a popular nightclub in West Warwick, Rhode Island. To start the show, the band's tour manager, Dan Biechele—with the approval of the owners of the establishment— set off a fireworks display that shot flames into the soundproofing foam installed in the ceiling (Kreps, 2010; Kurkjian, S. Ebbert, T. Ebbert, & Farragher, 2003).

The establishment erupted in fire. Concertgoers could not even see the exit signs at the doors because of the smoke. Some of them had problems getting past a local television camera person who was there, ironically, to film a story about nightclub safety. Within three to five minutes, The Station was engulfed in flame. By the time the fire was over, 100 people had been killed (Kurkjian et al., 2003).

Band manager Biechele later pleaded guilty to 100 counts of manslaughter. In May 2006, he was sentenced to 15 years in prison with 11 years suspended. He was paroled in March 2008. The owners of the club—brothers Michael and Jeffery Derderian—pleaded no contest after Biechele, while still claiming that they did not know that the soundproofing was flammable. Several entities involved in the concert were sued, including the band, the installer of the soundproofing foam, the promoters, alcohol suppliers, the owners, their insurance companies, and the television station doing the story on nightclub safety. In 2010, the case was settled for $176 million ("Great White Band Manager," 2006; Kreps, 2010). That so many defendants were listed in the lawsuit demonstrates the complexity of these cases. The Great White case also shows that the failure to keep consumers safe is defined as a criminal wrong for those directly involved in the event and a civil wrong for those indirectly involved.

DYNAMICS OF CORPORATE OFFENDING

It is clear that several varieties of corporate crime exist. At least four patterns run through these varieties of crime. These patterns include the following:

- The benefits of corporate crime

- The complexity of intent

- The breadth of victimization

- Problems responding to corporate crime

With regard to the *benefits of corporate crime*, it is clear that corporations benefit from wrongdoing, assuming they don't get caught. Even when they get caught, many believe that the low penalties given to offenders result in corporations still benefiting from the misconduct. It is important to stress that some individuals benefit from corporate offending. The discussion has tended to suggest that it is the corporation that benefits from these misdeeds (Glasberg & Skidmore, 1998a). However, employees may also benefit, particularly if the misdeeds result in promotions, favorable job evaluations, and bonuses.

The *complexity of intent* is another dynamic of corporate crimes. Intent is a tricky legal concept in all types of crimes, but it is especially complex in corporate crime (Yeager, 2016). The phrase "responsibility gap" has been used to describe problems assigning criminal culpability to corporate leaders for actions occurring in their organization (Buell, 2018). The responsible corporate office doctrine stipulates that corporate officers can be held liable for the behavior of employees, but when the doctrine is applied, it often seems unfair, unnecessary, or unjust (Lerner, 2018). Punch (2000) categorized three levels of knowledge to describe managerial involvement in corporate violence: (1) fully conscious conspiratorial behavior over time; (2) incompetent and negligent; and (3) unaware of criminal risks, or perceived as legitimate behavior. This third level may be particularly difficult to grasp. In effect, it is entirely reasonable that no one did anything wrong, but a corporate harm nonetheless occurred. Combined with the technical nature of corporate crime, the difficulty that arises in assigning blame hinders the system's response to corporate misdeeds (Yeager, 2016).

As Vaughan (2001) notes, "traditionally, when things go wrong in organizations, individuals are blamed." Vaughan goes on to say that organizations "have their dark side" and that organizational processes can produce "harmful outcomes, even when personnel are well-trained, well-intentioned, have adequate resources, and do all the correct things" (p. 57). Ermann and Lundman (2002) offer a similar perspective: "Well-intentioned individuals in organizational settings may produce deviant actions, even though none of them have deviant knowledge, much less deviant motivations. Indeed, individuals may do their jobs well and nevertheless produce deviance" (p. 9).

Consider the Ford Pinto case, the first time a prosecutor tried to criminally prosecute an automobile company for corporate misconduct tied to the gas tank explosions of the Pinto. While many may want to place blame on the Ford executives and attribute the misdeeds to profit-seeking motivations, Lee and Ermann (1999), after a thorough review of the case, "argue[d] that institutionalized norms and conventional modes of communication at the organizational and network level better explain available data" (p. 33). They also note that "routine processes can generate unintended tragedy" (p. 43) and concluded that the accidents were the result of "unreflective action," writing, "the Pinto design emerged from social forces both internal and external to Ford. There was no 'decision' to market an unsafe product, and there was no decision to market a safe one" (p. 45).

As another example, recall the Great White tragedy. The tour manager and bar owners were simply doing their jobs—trying to entertain the concertgoers. They did not intend to create the harm that arose that winter night. But their actions did, nonetheless, result in harm.

One can also point to the **breadth of victimization** as another corporate crime dynamic. One single corporate offense could harm thousands, if not millions, of individuals. One author has classified corporate crime victims into primary, secondary, and tertiary victims (Shichor, 1989). Primary victims are those directly harmed by the corporate offense (i.e., the individual who used the unsafe product). Secondary victims are impersonal victims, typically not individuals (e.g., businesses that are harmed by the misdeeds of a corporation). Tertiary victims include members of the community harmed by victimization. Another author has noted that victims of corporate crime include workers, consumers, investors, taxpayers, and other corporations (H. C. Barnett, 1981). In addition, scholars have noted that corporations can victimize themselves through what is called collective embezzlement, defined as "crimes by the corporation against the corporation" (Calavita & Pontell, 1991, p. 94). Instances where top executives allow a corporation to fail, knowing that they will profit from the failure, are examples of collective embezzlement.

Another dynamic surrounding corporate crime has to do with *problems responding to corporate crime.* Generally speaking, four responses are used to address corporate offending: (1) criminal or civil charges are levied against wrongdoers, (2) punitive sanctions are administered to the offenders, (3) regulatory policies are enforced against companies, or (4) a combination of the first three occur (Schell-Busey, Simpson, Rorie, & Alper, 2016). These responses are more difficult to administer for corporate crimes than they are for conventional crimes. Corporations "possess an economic and political power that is great relative to that generally possessed by victims of corporate crime" (H. C. Barnett, 1981, p. 4). With this power, corporations are believed to be able to influence criminal justice decision making and use their resources to "manipulate politicians and the media" (Garoupa, 2005, p. 37). As an example, one expert has shown how some types of corporate misconduct are not defined as crime but as "risky business" by various parties (Pontell, 2005). In addition, because many of these companies play a critical role in the economy, concern exists that too strict of a response might end up damaging a community's economic system (Buell, 2018). This chapter's Streaming White-Collar Crime describes an Amazon Prime show depicting the difficulties that the legal system has in corporate crime cases.

STREAMING WHITE-COLLAR CRIME	*Goliath*: Corporate Crime	
Plot	**What You Can Learn**	**Discussion Questions**
Billy Bob Thorton stars as Billy McBride, a has-been lawyer who spends more time in the bar than the courtroom. As a solo practitioner, his law practice turns around when he has the chance to defend a client in a case against his former law firm, Cooperman McBride. The first three seasons have connections to white-collar crime, with seasons one and three focused on white-collar crime cases (wrongful deaths and pollution) and season two integrating public corruption into a murder case Thornton is working. The not-so-subtle theme of each season is captured in the show's description: An underdog lawyer goes up against powerful companies and entities to bring justice to the average client.	It is difficult to hold corporations accountable for their misdeeds. Major corporations often see penalties from wrongdoing as a cost of doing business. Very serious consequences arise from corporate offending.	Why is it difficult to hold corporations responsible for misconduct? Describe some types of corporate wrongdoing that corporations might engage in simply because it's cheaper to break the law than it is to abide by the law. In what ways are corporate crimes more serious than other types of white-collar crime?

Another difficulty in responding to these crimes is the fact that there is no ideal response process or system. Responses vary or are impacted by country-level factors, organizational cultures, timeframes, and company size (Yeager, 2016). Yeager (2016) notes that "the consequences of such variability in enforcement are costs to both justice and enforcement" (p. 644).

PUBLIC CONCERN ABOUT CRIMES BY THE CORPORATE SYSTEM

Corporate crimes do not typically receive the same level of public scrutiny that other crimes do. One author attributed this to the belief that these offenses "are usually less sensational, better concealed, and harder to prove" (Minkes, 1990, p. 128). Members of the public often do not know they have been victims of corporate offenses, nor are they aware of the harm from these offenses or of possible strategies for recovering the costs of the harm (Tombs, 2008).

Some have attributed the lack of understanding about corporate crime to media coverage of these offenses. Research by R. G. Burns and Orrick (2002) suggested that (1) corporate crime coverage is less frequent than traditional crime coverage, (2) when corporate crime is covered in the media, the coverage will influence policy makers, (3) the public receives a distorted image of corporate crime, and (4) reporters do not define corporate misconduct as deviant or criminal. The authors also suggested that when corporate crime is addressed in the media, the focus is on the harm and the incident—but not on the criminal or the factors contributing to the crime.

A study by Cavender and Miller (2013) confirms this suggestion. They examined how three newspapers—the *New York Times*, the *Washington Post*, and the *Wall Street Journal*—reported on the 2002 corporate crime scandals. Analyzing 227 articles published in the three newspapers, they found that the media tended to focus narrowly on the offense and assign blame on the individual level. They wrote, "The media covered the scandals to be sure, but the newspapers that we analyzed did not connect the dots that would have revealed how these scandals were emblematic of the larger economy" (p. 926). Others have argued that the portrayal of fraud in this way "deflects attention to one of the actors, the business and its directors, without clear recognition of the role played by the government itself" (Haines, 2014, p. 1). News reporters are not the only ones to ignore corporate crime.

While the public may hold ambivalent views towards corporate crime, corporations engage in a number of actions to make sure that thoughts about the corporation's criminal behavior are removed from the minds of future consumers and customers. Sometimes, corporations change their names following corporate scandals. In the aftermath of a very public debacle involving accusations of price gouging, for example, Valeant changed its name to Bausch Health. Similarly, after Lance Armstrong's doping practices came to light, the Lance Armstrong Foundation renamed itself the LiveStrong Foundation (Court, 2017). It's comparable to the way that the crime show *Dateline* occasionally shows stories about people who changed their names to distance themselves from their scrupulous pasts. Very few *Dateline* episodes focus on corporate scandals, however, probably because the topic doesn't interest audiences as much as other crimes.

Summary

- The phrase *crimes by the corporate system* is used to characterize the body of offenses that are committed to benefit the corporation for which the employee (or employees) works.

- The concept of corporation can be seen four different ways—as a business, a location, a legally recognized status, and a collection of employees.

- Frank and Lynch (1992) describe corporate crime as including behaviors that are "socially injurious and blameworthy acts, legal or illegal that cause financial, physical, or environmental harm, committed by corporations and businesses against their workers, the general public, the environment, other corporations or businesses, the government, or other countries" (p. 17).

- Antitrust offenses are offenses that restrict competition. Antitrust laws are designed to promote and protect competition.

- Price fixing offenses occur when competitors agree on a price at which goods or services should be sold.

- Bid rigging (or collusion) occurs when competitors conspire to set specific bids for goods or services they would supply in response to a request for bids.

- Made illegal under the Robinson-Patman Act, price discrimination is illegal if it is done to lessen competition.

- Price gouging refers to situations where businesses conspire to set artificially high prices on goods and services.

- Market allocation occurs when competitors agree to divide markets according to territories, products, goods, or some other service (U.S. Department of Justice, n.d.b., p. 4).

- Group boycotts refer to situations where competitors agree not to do business with specific customers or clients.

- Four patterns are consistent across these antitrust offenses—(1) the way that "agreement" is conceptualized, (2) the seriousness of harm arising from the offenses, (3) globalization, and (4) difficulties proving (and punishing) offenses.

- False advertising occurs when businesses make inaccurate statements about their products or services in order to facilitate the sale of those items and services.

- Two common trends in advertising include going-out-of-business sales and the use of celebrities to promote goods.

- Deceptive sales refers to illicit sales practices that are driven by corporate policies and directives.

- Unfair labor practices refer to corporate violations where workers are subjected to unethical treatment by their bosses and corporate leaders. Two general types of unfair labor practices can be identified: (1) exploitation and (2) systemic discrimination.

- Discrimination has negative consequences for individuals, groups, and organizations.

- Labeled corporate violence by Frank and Lynch (1992), unsafe work environments can result in death, illnesses, and injuries.

- The year 2007, deemed "Year of the Recall," saw a particularly high number of Chinese goods recalled by the Consumer Product Safety Commission.

- Globalization has ramifications for the way corporations create and distribute unsafe products.

- *Harmful treatment of consumers* refers to situations where businesses either intentionally or unintentionally put consumers who are using their services at risk of harm.

- At least four patterns run across these varieties of crime—the benefits of corporate crime, the complexity of intent, the breadth of victimization, and problems responding to corporate crime.

- Corporate crimes do not typically receive the same level of public scrutiny that other crimes receive.

Key Terms

Antitrust laws   269

Bait and switch practices   274

Bid rigging   271

Bid rotation   271

Bid suppression   271

Breadth of victimization   298

Complementary bidding   271

Deceptive sales   276

Exploitation   280

False advertising   274

Group boycotts   273

Harmful consumer
products   291

Harmful treatment of
consumers   296

Horizontal price fixing   271

Market allocation   273

Organizational misconduct   268

Price discrimination   271

Price fixing   270

Price gouging   272

Resale fraud   274

Robinson-Patman Act   272

Sherman Antitrust Act   269

Subcontracting   271

Unfair labor practices   280

Vertical price fixing   271

Discussion Questions

1. Watch the GAO video showing college recruiters lying to undercover applicants available online at http://www.gao.gov/products/gao-10-948t. Do you think any crimes were committed? How can the recruiters' behaviors be characterized as corporate crime?

2. Write two personal ads for yourself: one that is accurate and one that is a "false advertisement." What is it that makes the advertisement false?

3. Visit the Federal Trade Commission's website, and find an example of an antitrust offense. Search the World Wide Web to find how often the specific offense was discussed on various websites. How does the attention given to the antitrust offense compare to the attention given to other offenses?

4. What do you think should be done to companies that produce unsafe products? Explain.

5. How can companies save money by providing a safer work environment? What factors would influence a business leader to provide an unsafe environment?

6. Is food poisoning a crime? Explain.

7. What would you tell a consumer who asked you how to avoid falling victim to corporate misconduct?

8. Describe a way that you have been a victim of a corporate crime.

9. Should corporate leaders be punished criminally for the behavior of employees?

ENVIRONMENTAL CRIME

On April 20th, 2010, an explosion on British Petroleum's (BP's) *Deepwater Horizon* rig occurred in the Gulf of Mexico. Eleven rig workers were killed, and oil began to spill out of the Macondo well into the Gulf of Mexico. The oil poured into the Gulf for three months, with some estimates suggesting that a million gallons of oil flowed into the Gulf every day. By most measures, this seemed to be the "world's worst oil spill" (Randall, 2010). Referring to the harm from the spill, one reporter called the Gulf an "unsolved crime scene" (Sutter, 2010).

It is still too early to know all the consequences of the spill. As of August 2010, the National Science Foundation provided $7 million in research funding to study the long-term effects of the disaster. BP pledged to spend $500 million to address the consequences of the disaster, though it may be some time until we fully understand the effects of the unprecedented spill. After all, the consequences of the *Exxon Valdez* disaster are still being identified two decades after that oil spill occurred (Sutter, 2010).

Some consequences are obvious. Eleven men died. Fishermen in the Gulf were forced to give up their livelihoods. Birds, fish, and oysters died from the exposure to oil. Some have argued that the disaster will impact ecosystems across the world (M. Adams, 2010). Said the editor of naturalnews.com, "We may have just done to ourselves . . . what a great meteorite did to the dinosaurs" (M. Adams, 2010). The cleanup effort cost an estimated $6 million a day, and a long-term focused financial analysis estimated that cleanup costs alone would amount to $7 billion (Condon, 2010).

BP received criticism on a daily basis. The criticism targeted BP for misrepresenting various aspects of the response, underestimating the extent of the problem, paying out claims too slowly to affected workers, and having a flawed response plan (Searcey, 2010;

Webb & Pilkington, 2010). The response plan received the brunt of the criticism. One rather disturbing criticism was that the response plan listed "a wildlife expert who died in 2005" (Webb & Pilkington, 2010). Also, the response plan listed marine animals (walruses, seals, etc.) as "sensitive biological resources," despite the fact that these mammals do not "[live] anywhere near the Gulf " (Mohr, Pritchard, & Lush, 2010). Mohr and his coauthors (2010) referred to BP's response as "on-the-fly planning." It did not help when the world saw BP Chief Executive Tony Hayward vacationing on his 52-foot yacht just weeks after the explosion. Hayward explained that he just "wanted to get [his] life back." He was removed as chief executive not long after making those comments.

One news headline that comes to mind read "Officials dismayed with BP's response." A colleague of mine cut this headline from the paper and hung it on my door, referring to my own initials (and maybe my own response to departmental issues). Suddenly, my initials weren't as cool as they used to be.

BP established a $20 billion fund that was to be used to respond to claims that individuals brought against the company (Searcey, 2010). The confusing nature of the claims process made it difficult to process the claims. Ironically, those involved with administering the fund on behalf of BP noted that they "had to sift through fraudulent claims" against the company (Searcey, 2010).

Some have argued that the blame for the disaster cannot be placed solely on BP. One author noted that it was "American firms that owned the rig AND the safety equipment that failed" (Pendlebury, 2010). This same author noted that the United States uses more oil than any other country and that the United States leased drilling rights in coastal waters to BP to generate revenue. It is safe to suggest that several companies were involved in the disaster.

On December 15, 2010, the U.S. Department of Justice filed a lawsuit against BP and eight other companies for their role in the rig explosion. Filed under the Oil Pollution Act and the Clean Water Act, the lawsuit alleged the following:

- Failure to take necessary precautions to secure the Macondo well prior to the April 20th explosion

- Failure to use the safest drilling technology to monitor the well conditions

- Failure to maintain continuous surveillance of the well

- Failure to utilize and maintain equipment and materials that were available and necessary to ensure the safety and protection of personnel, property, and the environment ("Attorney General Holder Announces," 2010)

The lawsuit sought costs for governmental removal efforts, the damage to the environment, and the impact on the economy. On July 2, 2015, it was announced that BP settled with the government and agreed to pay an $18.7 billion penalty. This penalty made it the largest penalty ever given in the United States for an environmental crime (Gilbert & Kent, 2015). Previously, the company had pleaded guilty to criminal manslaughter charges and was fined $4.5 billion for those charges. In all, the company had incurred settlement and legal costs totaling $54 billion "pushing its tab for the spill higher than all the profits it has earned since 2012" (Gilbert & Kent, 2015).

In terms of specific criminal charges against workers, charges were filed against some of the workers. Manslaughter charges against two of the rig supervisors were dropped in December 2015, prompting one of the parents of a worker killed in the spill to say, "As a result of this court proceeding today, no man will ever spend a moment behind bars for killing 11 men for reasons based entirely on greed" (McConnaughey & Kunzelman, 2015). In the end, it appears that just two criminal convictions were obtained against individuals for the offense, and those were for charges related to obstructing justice after the investigation began.

A decade after the oil spill, communities and wildlife are still experiencing consequences from the spill. Among other things, cleanup works responding to the spill are exhibiting lung and heart problems and only one fifth of dolphin pregnancies in the areas most affected by the spill are successful (Meiners, 2020). One study found that home values in Gulf of Mexico communities fell between 4% and 8%, potentially costing between "$3.8 to 5 billion in capitalized damage" (Cano-Urbina, Clapp, & Willardsen, 2019, p. 131).

BP and the other companies implicated in the spill are not the only businesses to harm the environment. Consider the following, quoted verbatim from press release for three different environmental crime cases:

- ++++++ was ordered today to pay $369,693.58 in restitution to the United States Environmental Protection Agency (EPA) to reimburse it for its expenses incurred in removing hazardous waste that ++++++ stored without a permit at the former ++++++ National Leather Corporation building in Johnstown. (USDOJ, 2020, May 15).

- Over a dozen workers were interviewed and confirmed they were supposed to put the poison in the holes, but due the high demand on the amount of poison that needed to be dispensed and the large land tract, workers got sloppy and the poison was not dispensed as required by the label. Because of the misapplication, the EPA emergency response team was dispatched to oversee the cleanup of the ranch land by Meyer. During the course of the investigation, six bald eagles were recovered and confirmed to have died as a result of the poison. (USDOJ, 2020, April 28).

- Suffolk County District Attorney Timothy D. Sini was joined by the New York State Department of Environmental Conservation ("DEC") and the Suffolk County Police Department today to announce the sentencing of a self-proclaimed "dirt broker" who was indicted as part of the District Attorney's Office's "Operation Pay Dirt" investigation into an illegal dumping conspiracy on Long Island. "The defendant, with no regard for the safety and wellbeing of Suffolk County residents, facilitated the dumping of solid waste on residential properties, properties near schools, and other sites," District Attorney Sini said. "Many of the sites contained materials that were hazardous or acutely hazardous. This is a major issue for those individual homeowners who were affected and a major issue for the general public." ++++++ was sentenced today by Suffolk County Court Judge Timothy Mazzei to two to four years in prison (Suffolk County New York, 2019).

In each of these cases, businesses or employees harmed the environment as part of their work efforts. To fully understand environmental crime within the context of white-collar crime, it is necessary to consider the following topics: the conceptualization of environmental crime, varieties of environmental crime, consequences of environmental crime, the EPA and environmental crime, and problems addressing environmental crime. A full understanding of these topics will help students understand how environmental crime fits within the broader concept of white-collar crime.

CONCEPTUALIZING ENVIRONMENTAL CRIME

Pollution is a problem that affects all of us. Several different types of pollution exist, including water pollution, air pollution, noise pollution, soil pollution, waste disposal, and so on. Concern about environmental pollution escalated in the United States in the 1970s, a decade labeled the "environment decade in reference to the increase in environmental legislation and political support for laws regulating pollution" (H. C. Barnett, 1993, p. 120). Elsewhere, H. Barnett (1999) refers to this time period as "a decade long surge of environmental concern" (p. 173). As a result of this public and political concern, hundreds of environmental protection laws were passed by state and federal governments. At the federal level, the best-known environmental protection laws include the following:

- Atomic Energy Act

- Chemical Safety Information, Site Security, and Fuels Regulatory Relief Act

- Clean Air Act

- Clean Water Act

- Comprehensive Environmental Response, Compensation, and Liability Act

- Emergency Planning and Community Right to Know Act

- Endangered Species Act

- Energy Independence and Security Act

- Energy Policy Act

- Federal Food, Drug, and Cosmetic Act

- National Environmental Policy Act

- Noise Control Act

- Occupational Safety and Health Act

- Ocean Dumping Act

- Oil Pollution Act

- Pollution Prevention Act

- Safe Drinking Water Act

- Resource Conservation and Recovery Act

- Shore Protection Act

- Toxic Substance Act (US-EPA, 2010d)

U.S. Coast Guard photo

PHOTO 11.1 Emergency responders work to put the fire out that was caused by the explosion on BP's *Deepwater Horizon* rig.

These acts provide a foundation from which one can consider criminal and civil definitions of environmental crime. In particular, violations of these acts are environmental crimes. Some environmental crime scholars have called for broader, more philosophical conceptualizations of environmental crime. H. Barnett (1999) used Aldo Leopold's land ethic to conceptualize environmental crime: "A thing is right when it tends to preserve the integrity, stability, and beauty of the biotic community. It is wrong when it tends otherwise" (p. 161). Such an approach highlights the fact that many behaviors that harm the environment are often not codified in law. As a result, some authors have argued that a need exists to distinguish between those behaviors labeled as environmental crime and those that are "serious instances of ecological destruction" (Halsey, 1997, p. 121).

Two fundamental statements about environmental crime need to be made to adequately discuss this concept within the context of white-collar crime. First, pollution in and of itself is not an environmental crime. Many individuals and businesses routinely pollute the environment without actually committing environmental crimes. When we drive our automobiles to get to class, we pollute the environment. If we are running late for our white-collar crime class and speed to make up for lost time, we pollute the environment even more, but we have not committed an environmental crime. Indeed, routine activities we engage in on a daily basis produce different levels of pollution or destruction. Here is how one author described the seemingly routine nature of environmental harm:

> Not only is it profitable to be environmentally destructive (in the sense of mining, manufacturing cars, clear felling forests), it feels good too (in the sense of purchasing a gold necklace, driving on the open road, looking at a table, chair, or house constructed from redwood, mahogany, mountain ash, or the like). (Halsey, 2004, p. 844)

Second, it is important to understand that not all environmental crimes are white-collar crimes. If an individual throws an old washer and dryer away along the side of a rural road, that person has committed an environmental crime but not a white-collar crime because the offense was not committed as part of work efforts. As another example, if an individual buys new tires for his or her automobile, asks to keep the old tires, and then dumps the old tires in an empty field, the individual has committed an environmental crime but not a white-collar crime.

White-collar environmental crimes, then, involve situations where individuals or businesses illegally pollute or destroy the environment as part of an occupational activity. Here are a few examples quoted from the U.S. Environmental Protection Agency (2010d) that demonstrate what is meant by white-collar environmental crimes:

- A plant manager at a metal finishing company directs employees to bypass the facility's wastewater treatment unit in order to avoid having to purchase the chemicals that are needed to run the wastewater treatment unit. In so doing, the company sends untreated wastewater directly to the sewer system in violation of the permit issued by the municipal sewer authority. The plant manager is guilty of a criminal violation of the Clean Water Act.

- In order to avoid the cost of paying for proper treatment of its hazardous waste, the owner of a manufacturer of cleaning solvents places several dozen 5-gallon buckets of highly flammable and caustic waste into its Dumpster for disposal at a local, municipal landfill that is not authorized to receive hazardous waste. The owner of the company is guilty of a criminal violation of the Resource Conservation and Recovery Act.

- The owner of an apartment complex solicits bids to remove 14,000 square feet of old ceiling tiles from the building. Three bidders inspect the building, determine that the tiles contain dangerous asbestos fibers, and bid with understanding that, in doing the removal, they would be required to follow the work practice standards that apply to asbestos removal. The fourth bidder proposes to save the owner money by removing the tiles without following the work practice standards. The owner hires the fourth bidder on this basis, and, so, the work is done without following the work practice standards. The owner is guilty of a criminal violation of the Clean Air Act (no pagination, available online; see US-EPA, 2010e).

In each of these cases, the offender committed the offense as part of an occupational routine. Note that although each of these cases could be handled as violations of criminal law, in many cases white-collar environmental offenses are handled as civil wrongs or regulatory violations.

As you read through these types of environmental white-collar crimes, one point to bear in mind is that many careers are available for criminal justice students battling these offenses.

VARIETIES OF ENVIRONMENTAL WHITE-COLLAR CRIME

Recognizing the distinction between environmental crime and environmental white-collar crime helps to identify the roles of workplace and class status in the commission of these offenses. The distinction also helps us recognize that several varieties of environmental white-collar crimes exist. These varieties include the following:

- Illegal emissions

- Illegal disposal of hazardous wastes

- Illegal dumping

- Harmful destruction of property and wildlife

- Environmental threats

- Environmental state crime

- International environmental crimes

It is important to note that these varieties are not mutually exclusive because there is overlap between them.

Illegal Emissions

Illegal emissions, as a variety of environmental white-collar crime, refer to situations where companies or businesses illegally allow pollutants to enter the environment. Water pollution and air pollution are examples of illegal emissions. Sometimes, water and air pollution occur as a result of the production process. The smoke billowing out of factory towers contains pollutants that are the result of the production process. Companies are permitted to allow a certain amount of pollutants into the environment. They pay what is called a *sin tax* to cover the perceived costs of polluting the environment. If they exceed the "permissible" amount of pollution, then civil and criminal laws can be applied.

Other times, the pollution might be the result of unintended processes or neglectful behavior by employees. Consider the *Exxon Valdez* incident in March 1989, when the ship ran aground on Bligh Reef off the Alaskan shore. The crash spilled more than 11 million gallons of oil into Prince William Sound. It has been reported that the ship was on autopilot while the ship's captain was sleeping off a drunken stupor below deck and the third mate ran the ship on less than 5 hours of sleep. Exxon did not technically intend for the disaster to occur, but because the company overworked ship employees (not giving them enough rest) and allowed someone with an alcohol problem to serve as the captain of the ship, the company eventually settled both criminal and civil charges resulting from the incident.

Under the **Federal Water Pollution Control Act**, companies are required to self-disclose to the EPA instances when they have discharged potentially harmful substances into navigable waters. After disclosing the incident, they can still be assessed civil penalties, like fines. Criminal justice students might quickly ask if this is a violation of the Fifth Amendment right against self-incrimination. In an early test of the self-disclosure rule, the owner of an oil refinery in Arkansas, who had self-disclosed that oil from his property had leaked into a nearby tributary, appealed a $500 fine on the grounds that his Fifth Amendment right had been violated (*U.S. v. Ward*). The U.S. Supreme Court upheld the fine on the grounds that the self-disclosure resulted in a civil penalty and not a criminal penalty (D. G. Beck, 1981; Melenyzer, 1999).

Illegal Disposal of Hazardous Wastes

Illegal disposal of hazardous wastes involves situations where employees or businesses dispose of wastes in ways that are potentially harmful to individuals and the environment. These offenses are actually quite easy to commit. For example, it is easy to mix hazardous substances with nonhazardous substances, but it is difficult to detect (Dorn, Van Daele, & Vander Beken, 2007). Often, the cases are detected through witnesses who anonymously report the misconduct. In one case, for instance, an anonymous caller contacted the Maryland Department of Environment to reveal "that asbestos debris was being dumped [by contractors] through a trash chute into an open [D]umpster on the street below, potentially exposing both workers and the community to toxic asbestos fibers" ("Maryland Contractor Fined," 2010). Officials recovered 7,000 bags full of asbestos debris. The contractor was fined $1.2 million. In another case, a company was fined $819,000 after its workers threw asbestos into public trash receptacles, including one located at a high school (Hay, 2010).

In the past, illegal hazardous waste disposal cases were attributed to private truckers or waste management contractors hired to get rid of waste via illegally dumping of the waste, and there were no repercussions for the businesses that created the waste. The Resource Conservation and Recovery Act, passed in 1976, provided greater controls over the way that hazardous waste was created, monitored, and discarded. Of particular relevance is the "Cradle to Grave" provision of the act, which requires a "manifest system" to keep track of the waste from the time it is created through its disposal. The *manifest system* refers to the record-keeping process used to monitor the waste. The creator of the waste must monitor the waste when it is created and keep track of the waste all the way through its disposal. The law states that those who create the waste are accountable for all aspects of the disposal of the waste. The business can be held liable if it doesn't complete the manifest forms, if it hires an unlicensed contractor to get rid of the waste, or if the waste is eventually dumped illegally by the contractor hired to dispose of it (Stenzel, 2011).

One of the most well-known environmental crimes involving hazardous wastes is the Love Canal tragedy. Located in Niagara Falls, New York, the Love Canal was initially designed to be a canal, but it ended up being a waste disposal site for Hooker Chemical. After Hooker filled the canal with waste—and covered the waste in ways the company thought were safe, it sold the property to the Niagara Falls school board for one dollar in the mid-1950s. The company never hid the fact that the property was on top of a waste site (E. Beck, 1979).

The school board developed a school, and several homes were built on and around Love Canal. In the late 1970s, chemicals from the abandoned site leaked into the homes, and residents began to experience a number of different health problems (Baldston, 1979). An EPA report cited "a disturbingly high rate of miscarriages" among pregnant women in the neighborhood (E. Beck, 1979). One EPA administrator wrote:

> I visited the canal area. Corroding waste disposal drums could be seen breaking up through the grounds of backyards. Trees and gardens were turning black and dying . . . puddles of noxious substances were pointed out to me by the residents. . . . Everywhere the air had a faint, choking smell. Children returned from play with burns on their hands and faces. (E. Beck, 1979)

Eventually, the federal government and the State of New York declared an emergency and provided a temporary relocation of 700 families

In 1979, the EPA and U.S. Department of Justice (USDOJ) filed four suits against Hooker Chemical alleging violations of Resource Conservation and Recovery Act, the Clean Water Act, the Safe Drinking Water Act, and the Refuse Act. The basis for the suits was that Hooker had illegally disposed of its waste, which included 21,000 tons of chemical waste. The State of New York filed a similar lawsuit against the company. By the mid-1990s, the company had settled for $20 million, and its parent company agreed to pay $129 million to the federal government and $98 million to the State of New York to support cleanup efforts (W. Moyer, 2010).

Illegal Dumping

Illegal dumping, in this context, is different from illegal disposal of hazardous waste. Also known as "fly dumping," "wildcat dumping," and "midnight dumping," **illegal dumping** refers to situations where employees or businesses dump products they no longer need in sites that are not recognized as legal dump sites (US-EPA, 1998). Common products that are illegally dumped include automobile tires, construction waste (such as drywall, roofing materials, plumbing waste), landscaping waste, and automobile parts.

These materials present different types of risk than might be found with the illegal disposal of hazardous wastes. For example, many of the products are not biodegradable and will destroy the usefulness of the land where they are dumped. Also, the site where offenders dump these products will become an eyesore and attract future illegal dumpers. In addition, some of the products such as tires will trap rainwater and attract mosquitoes, thus becoming a breeding ground for disease (US-EPA, 1998). In one case, the owner of a used tire shop in Ohio was sentenced to six years in prison after he was caught illegally dumping tires on five separate occasions (Futty, 2010).

Illegal dumping is primarily done for economic reasons. Business owners wanting to avoid the costs of waste disposal dump their goods in the unregulated open dump areas. The offenses also present significant economic costs, particularly in terms of cleanup costs. In Columbus, Ohio, for example, city crews "cleaned up 621 tons of illegally dumped tires in 2009" (Futty, 2010). Assuming that the average city worker makes $30,000 a year, this suggests that three full-time employees were hired solely to clean up illegally dumped tires in Columbus. And this estimate accounts for only one type of illegal dumping.

Harmful Destruction of Property/Wildlife

Harmful destruction of property and wildlife by companies or workers during the course of their jobs can be seen as environmental white-collar crime. Before businesses can clear land for development, thus destroying habitat, they must gain approval from the local government. Failing to gain such approval would be a regulatory violation. Also, instances where workers destroy wetlands are examples of environmental crimes. Additional examples of harmful destruction of property include using unsafe chemical pesticides, using chemical fertilizers, and logging on public land (H. Barnett, 1999).

Harmful treatment of animals can be seen as an environmental white-collar crime. This could include illegal trading of wildlife or illegal fishing by companies or sailors (Hayman & Brack, 2002) and overharvesting sea life (H. Barnett, 1999). Illegal trading of wildlife involves trafficking rare and protected species and selling those for profit. These crimes will impact the communities relying on wildlife for their jobs and economic development. One author cites estimates suggesting that illegal wildlife trafficking costs society up to $10 billion a year (Pathal, 2016). This chapter's Streaming White-Collar Crime describes a Netflix hit documentary about one zoo owner's involvement in environmental offenses.

STREAMING WHITE-COLLAR CRIME	Tiger King: White-Collar Criminal?	
Plot	**What You Can Learn**	**Discussion Questions**
The documentary series Tiger King: Murder, Mayhem, and Madness explores how zookeeper, tiger breeder, and one-time gubernatorial candidate Joe Exotic went from putting tigers in cages to being incarcerated himself. Though much of the series focuses on his troubled relationship with his archnemesis, tiger advocate Carol Baskin—whose murder he was convicted for plotting—Joe Exotic was also convicted for falsifying wildlife records and violating the Federal Endangered Species Act. These latter violations were committed in his role as a businessperson.	Offenders who engage in one type of crime frequently engage in multiple types of crime. Crimes against animals and the environment can be classified as white-collar crimes. Anyone can run for governor.	Are all environmental criminals white-collar criminals? Explain. Who are the victims in cases when animals are harmed? Explain.

Harmful treatment of animals, as an environmental white-collar crime, includes instances where those whose work centers on animals do things to harm the animals. Two examples include harmful treatment of animals in zoos and crimes by big-game operators. In one case of the former, a zoo owner was fined $10,000 and ordered to shut down his zoo for 30 days after the U.S. Department of Agriculture found the owner in violation of the Animal Welfare Act for failing to build appropriate fences around the animals, failing to keep the food safe from contamination, and failure to provide the animals proper housing (Conley, 2007). Just three years before, the same owner was fined after two Asiatic bears that escaped from the zoo had to be shot and killed (Chittum, 2003).

Illegal fishing also includes unregulated and unreported fishing. These activities include "fishing in an area without authorization; failing to record or declare catches, or making false reports; using prohibited fishing gear; re-supplying or re-fueling illegal, unregulated, or unreported vessels" (National Oceanic and Atmospheric Administration, 2010). In October 2010, a new federal rule was passed stipulating that the United States would deny foreign vessels suspected of illegal fishing entry into U.S. ports.

Crimes by big-game operators include situations where they or their clients kill endangered species or hunt on protected land. In one case, a big-game operator and his sons pleaded guilty "for illegally guiding clients on Brown bear hunts on federal property" (U.S. Department of Justice, Environment and Natural Resources Division, 2010, p. 28).

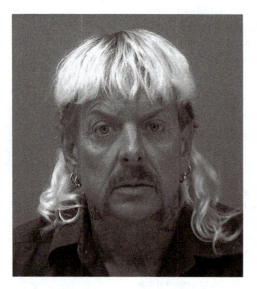

PHOTO 11.2 Joe the Tiger King gained instant fame after the Netflix series aired. Locked away for several charges, including some we can classify as white-collar offenses, the Tiger King has had to enjoy his fame from prison.

The owner was fined $71,000, and his sons were sentenced to three months of house arrest. Those getting paid to help individuals in these hunts commit a white-collar crime when they intentionally perform activities that harm animals. For the hunters (e.g., clients involved in a big-game hunt), a crime is also committed, but it would not be characterized as a white-collar crime because the activities were not committed during work. Note that the crime is not when the hunters actually harm the animals, but it is the act of intending to harm the protected animals that is illegal (USDOJ, Environment and Natural Resources Division, 2010, p. 28).

Animal fighting in illegal gambling efforts can also be seen as a variety of environmental crime. A study by J. S. Albanese (2018) found five illegal gambling businesses involved in animal fighting. The gambling rings involved five to eight people per ring. Albanese indicated that sentences given in these cases were more severe than those given in other small-scale illegal gambling operations. Here is a verbatim summary of one of the cases reviewed by Albanese:

> In a Virginia case, which was typical of others of this kind, a private club in Kentucky called "Big Blue" operated for years in which roosters were transported across state lines and spectators and handlers came from 8 surrounding states to participate. Each person was charged a $20 fee for a membership card, and this club had 5,000 members. Entry fees for birds to fight were $250 and there were between 40 and 100 total entries per derby. Entry fees for the "World Championship" in 2013 sold for $2,500 each. The couple and their son who led the ring were sentenced to 10 to 18 months in prison, and the court ordered them to forfeit $905,000, which was paid in part by seizing all their assets. Three other participants in the ring received lesser prison sentences and forfeitures. (Albanese, 2018, n.p.)

Environmental Threats

A number of environmental threats exist that have the potential to harm the environment. The federal government has identified five "significant threats" to the environment. First, **knowing endangerment** refers to situations where individuals or businesses intentionally mishandle hazardous wastes or pollutants that pose risks to their workers or community members. Second, *repeat offenders* are a threat inasmuch as the government recognizes that some businesses repeatedly violate environmental laws on the assumption that it is cheaper to pay the fine and harm the environment rather than fix the problem. Third, the federal government closely monitors *misuse of federal facilities and public lands* to protect properties from further environmental harm. Fourth, the government has called attention to the need to be prepared for *catastrophic events*. Finally, *organized crime entities* like the Mafia are believed to be intimately involved in the waste disposal industry (USDOJ, 1994).

Scholars have drawn attention to the way organized crime groups are involved in illegal waste offenses. In fact, some have used the phrase "environmental organized crime" to describe the Mob's involvement in these crimes (T. S. Carter, 1999). The organized nature of the illegal waste disposal enterprise has allowed authorities to use Racketeer Influenced and Corrupt Organization (RICO) statutes to prosecute environmental offenders.

In New York City, the Mafia had such a strong hold on the waste disposal industry that other businesses rarely tried to enter the waste disposal marketplace. In the early 1990s, Browning Ferris Industries (BFI) began its efforts to become one of the businesses responsible for collecting waste in the city. T. S. Carter (1999) quotes a *Fortune* magazine writer who described the Mob's reaction shortly after learning of BFI's intentions:

> The freshly severed head of a large German Shepherd [was] laid like a wreath on the suburban lawn of the one of the company's top local executives. A piece of string tied to the dog's mouth around a note . . . read, "Welcome to New York." (p. 19)

Fans of the former Home Box Office (HBO) hit *The Sopranos* might recall the following exchange between Tony Soprano and his daughter Meadow in an episode where the crime boss and his daughter were visiting colleges during Meadow's senior year in high school:

Meadow Soprano: *Are you in the Mafia?*

Tony Soprano: *Am I in the what?*

Meadow Soprano:	*Whatever you want to call it. Organized crime.*
Tony Soprano:	*That's total crap, who told you that?*
Meadow Soprano:	*Dad, I've lived in the house all my life. I've seen the police come with warrants. I've seen you going out at three in the morning.*
Tony Soprano:	*So you never seen Doc Cusamano going out at three in the morning on a call?*
Meadow Soprano:	*Did the Cusamano kids ever find $50,000 in Krugerrands and a .45 automatic while they were hunting for Easter eggs?*
Tony Soprano:	*I'm in the waste management business. Everybody immediately assumes you're mobbed up. It's a stereotype. And it's offensive. And you're the last person I would want to perpetuate it. . . . There is no Mafia. (Manos, Chase, & Coulter, 1999)*

A braver white-collar crime text author might follow up this exchange with a joke about the Mafia and the waste management industry. This author does not want to find the head of a German shepherd in his front yard, so he will pass on the opportunity for a joke.

Environmental State Crime

In Chapter 6, the way that governments are involved in corporate offending was discussed. One type of crime that governments can commit can be called **environmental state crimes**. In this context, environmental state crime refers to criminal or deviant behaviors by a governmental representative (or representatives) that result in individuals and/or the environment being harmed by pollutants and chemicals. Examples include situations where government officials illegally dispose of waste or use harmful chemicals in unjustified ways.

As an illustration, R. White (2008) describes how depleted uranium was used in the Gulf Wars. The product was used in armor and as weapons, and it has been linked to various illnesses in Iraq and Gulf War veterans. Government officials have denied that the use of the product was criminal, which is not surprising given that, as White notes, "one of the features of state crime is in fact denial on the part of the state that an act or omission is a crime" (p. 32). White quotes the former director of the Pentagon's Depleted Uranium Project, Dough Rokke, to highlight the criminal nature of the use of depleted uranium. Rokke remarked,

This war was about Iraq possessing illegal weapons of mass destruction, yet we are using weapons of mass destruction ourselves. Such double standards are repellent. . . . A nation's military personnel cannot willfully contaminate another nation, cause harm to persons and the environment, and then ignore the consequences of their actions. To do so is a crime against humanity. (p. 42)

White points out that Rokke has, himself, suffered negative health effects from exposure to depleted uranium.

International Environmental Crimes

International environmental crimes include environmental offenses that cross borders of at least two different countries or occur in internationally protected areas. Instances where companies ship their waste from an industrialized country to a developing nation are an example (Dorn et al., 2007). In some cases, companies might bribe "Third World government officials to establish toxic waste dumps in their countries" (Simon, 2000, p. 633).

Other examples of international environmental crimes include illegally trading wildlife, illegally trading substances harmful to the ozone, illegal fishing, and illegal timber trading and logging (Hayman & Brack, 2002). Drug trafficking has also been identified as a course of environmental harm in the transnational space. The term "narco-deforestation" describes the "process by which forests are cut for covert roads and landing strips" to be used for drug trafficking (Gore et al., 2019, p. 784). International environmental crimes are potentially more difficult for regulatory agencies to address because of issues surrounding jurisdiction, economic competition, and language barriers. Weak investigations, legal ambiguity, and contradictory policies also create obstacles for addressing these crimes (Ungar, 2017). In addition, public corruption and the willingness of impoverished communities to accept these offenses because of their economic benefits hinder investigations (Derri & Popoola, 2017). Still, it is clear that environmental crime has become an international issue that has evolved as the process of globalization has unfolded in our society.

Consequences of Environmental Crime

It is overly simplistic to say that the consequences of environmental crime are devastating. But it must be stated that these crimes threaten the existence of human life (Comte, 2006). Not surprisingly, environmental crime has more victims than other crimes, but these victims are often not aware of their victimization (Hayman & Brack, 2002). O'Hear (2004) provides a useful taxonomy that outlines the following types of harm potentially arising from environmental crime: (1) immediate physical injury from exposure to harmful products that may burn or kill individuals, (2) future physical injuries, (3) emotional distress, (4) disrupted social and economic activities, (5) remediation costs, (6) property damage, and (7) ecological damage. In general, the types of consequences can be classified as *physical costs, economic costs*, and *community costs*.

With regard to physical costs, there are absolutely no studies that show that pollution is good for one's health. It is impossible to accurately determine the precise extent of physical injuries from environmental crimes, but estimates are somewhat startling:

- Recent estimates suggest that 100,000 people die each year in the United States from air pollution (Neuhauser, 2019).

- Deaths from exposure to small particle matter in the United States occur more among minorities living in poorer communities (Bowe, XieYan, & Al-Aly 2019).

- Estimates suggest that worldwide seven million people die each year prematurely because of air pollution exposure (United Nations, 2019).

- Ambient air pollution was attributed to 7.6% of deaths across the world in 2016 (World Health Organization, 2018).

There are also physical costs experienced by those trying to protect the environment through protests and other environmental advocacy strategies. Those participating in these efforts are known as **environmental defenders**. Global Witness (2017) found that 200 environmental defenders were murdered in 2016. Victims were killed in 24 different countries with two thirds of those being Latin American countries. Global Witness (2019) identified mining as the most dangerous sector for environmental defenders: 164 environmental defenders were killed in 2018, and one fourth of those killings involved the mining industry. Figure 11.1 shows the countries with the highest death count among environmental defender killings in 2018. The Philippines had the highest number of environmental defender killings at 30.

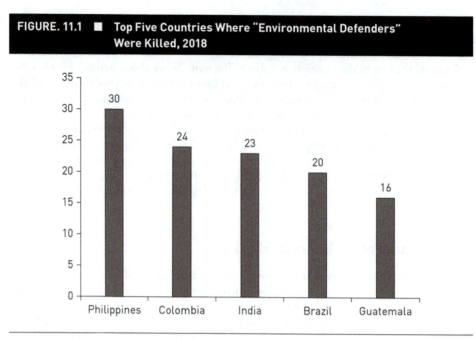

FIGURE. 11.1 ■ Top Five Countries Where "Environmental Defenders" Were Killed, 2018

Source: Global Witness. (2019). Available online at https://www.globalwitness.org/en/campaigns/environmental-activists/enemies-state/.

Of course, it is not just deaths that increase with environmental harm; physical illnesses are also tied to the problem. Research shows a connection between heart attacks and strokes and air pollution, with health issues spiking on days when air pollution spikes (Williams, Evangelo-poulos, Katsouyanni, & Walton, 2019), As well, research shows that lead exposure is related to developmental disabilities in children (Delgadot, Ullery, Jordan, Duclos, Rajagopalan, & Scott, 2018). Research also shows a connection between long-term exposure to air pollution and the onset of dementia (Grande, Ljungman, Eneroth, Bellander, & Rizzuto, 2020). Rather than list-ing ill effects from all pollutants, it can be stated that for virtually any pollutant, researchers can point to potentially harmful health effects.

Like other forms of white-collar crime, environmental crime has enormous economic costs. A study by a research team at California State University, Fullerton, found that the state of Cali-fornia loses $28 billion a year to the consequences of pollution (Hall & Brajer, 2008). Costs stem from a variety of sources, including missed work, missed school days, visits to the doctor, and visits to the emergency room. One can also note that taxpayers pay for enforcement and cleanup costs associated with white-collar environmental crime. In addition, employees end up "paying for" the violations of corporations and businesses when—after a company is caught engaging in environmental offending—they lose their jobs and must find other ways to make a living (H. C. Barnett, 1981). These costs together yield an estimate that pollution costs more than $5 trillion annually across the world (United Nations, 2019).

Environmental crime presents different costs to the community. In communities where these crimes occur, quality of life is reduced. These offenses create public eyesores and reduce property values around the areas exposed to environmental pollution. Also, consistent with other corporate crimes, environmental crimes have the potential to "erode the moral base" of the community (Kramer, 1984, p. 8). While not specifically tested, it is plausible that envi-ronmental crime is correlated with traditional crimes. Criminologists have noted that socially disorganized communities have higher crime rates than other communities. Environmental pollution has the potential to produce social disorganization and, therefore, potentially contributes to conventional crimes.

Environmental crimes also harm the community by posing a number of risks to those around the "environmental crime scene." For example, illegal waste disposals create the following risks for the immediate area surrounding the site where the illegal disposal occurred:

- Fire and explosion

- Inhaling toxic gases

- Injury to children playing around the site

- Soil or water contamination

- Plant or wildlife damage (Illinois Environmental Protection Agency, 2010)

A large body of research has shown that minorities and minority communities are more at risk for experiencing the ill effects of environmental crime (Nobles, 2019; Thomson, Espin, & Samuels-Jones, 2020). The term **environmental racism** is used to describe this heightened risk of victimization for minorities. Consider, for example, that research shows that minority children are significantly more likely than nonminority children to have higher levels of lead in their blood (Schwemberger et al., 2005). One author describes the placement of environmentally unsafe companies near minority communities as "the path of least resistance" (McDowell, 2013, p. 395). These situations do not go unnoticed by residents. McDowell (2013) provides the following quote one resident made to the county board of supervisors:

I personally feel our area has more than done its share. This area they are proposing has historic value, a fact that needs to be considered. . . . I feel it's extremely unfair to push another landfill on a small, poor rural area, simply because they most likely haven't the means to fight back. We are a small rural area, but there are enough of us to stand up and be heard! Please hear our voices! [Email communication to MCBS] (p. 400)

Because some businesses and companies locate high polluting industries in poorer communities where there is less political resistance to the businesses, environmental crime has a disproportionate impact on those communities (Greife, Stretesky, Shelley, & Pogrebin, 2017).

Some experts have called for "reparative justice" as a strategy to respond to environmental crimes (White, 2017). Such an approach would punish offenders while repairing the harm caused by the environmental corporate offender. The combination of reparations and punishments, along with strong enforcement of regulatory practices, is seen as enhancing the deterrent effect of responses to environmental crime. The costs of "repairing harm" are passed on to corporations in this model (White, 2017). In turn, this would protect all communities, including those minority communities disproportionately targeted in environmental crime cases.

The EPA has addressed concerns about environmental racism by developing an Office of Environmental Justice in the early 1990s and giving the office the responsibility of promoting environmental justice activities in the agency. According to the US-EPA (2010c), environmental justice is "the fair treatment and meaningful involvement of all people regardless of race, color, national origin, or income with respect to the development, implementation, and enforcement of environmental laws, regulations, and policies." The two assumptions of the federal Environmental Justice Initiative are fair treatment and meaningful involvement. Fair treatment refers to the notion that no group should be disproportionately impacted by pollution. In the words of the EPA, meaningful involvement refers to the following assumptions:

- People have an opportunity to participate in decisions about activities that may affect their environment and/or health.

- The public's contribution can influence the regulatory agency's decision.

- Their concerns will be considered in the decision-making process.

- The decision makers seek out and facilitate the involvement of those potentially affected (US-EPA, 2010b).

Some saw the EPA's environmental justice program as limited under the Trump administration. Prior to the 2020 presidential election, a former EPA attorney characterized Trump's EPA as "barely a shell of what the agency needs to play a leadership role—or any meaningful role—in ensuring fair environmental treatment for our nation's communities of color and lower income communities" (Coursen, 2020). As one author team points out, "a socially fair distribution of the costs and benefits of climate action will require deliberate action, but it is both possible and essential" (Hagedorn et al., 2019, p. 139). Strong leadership from policy makers is needed in order to address the negative impact of environmental harms on lower socioeconomic communities and communities of color. President Joe Biden campaigned on the need to address climate change and strengthen environmental regulations, leading many activists to anticipate more support for environmental protection measures under Biden's administration. To be sure, the consequences of environmental crime are serious and warrant a response from formal control agencies. Local police are not trained or equipped to respond to these offenses, which are complex and potentially harmful to those responding to environmental crimes involving hazardous materials (Dorn et al., 2007). Some have noted that criminal penalties are rarely applied and that while enforcement is done by local, state, and federal regulatory agencies, the law enforcement response is not as aggressive as compared to other crimes (Shover & Routhe, 2005). At the federal level, the U.S. Environmental Protection Agency (EPA) is the largest agency, with 17,000 employees, responsible for addressing environmental crimes.

THE U.S. ENVIRONMENTAL PROTECTION AGENCY (EPA)

The **Environmental Protection Agency** was created in 1970 when President Richard Nixon reorganized several federal agencies to create one federal agency responsible for addressing environmental pollution. In developing his message to Congress about the US-EPA, President Nixon stated that the agency's roles and functions would include the following:

- The establishment and enforcement of environmental protection standards consistent with national environmental goals

- The conduct of research on the adverse effects of pollution and on methods and equipment for controlling it, the gathering of information on pollution, and the use of this information in strengthening environmental protection programs and recommending policy changes

- Assisting others, through grants, technical assistance, and other means in arresting pollution of the environment

- Assisting the Council on Environmental Quality in developing and recommending to the president new policies for the protection of the environment (US-EPA, 1992)

Five decades later, the roles and functions have not changed a great deal, though the authority of the agency has expanded significantly. Today, the EPA can be understood in five overlapping ways: (1) as an enforcer of criminal and civil laws, (2) as a part of political machine, (3) as an agency trying to protect public health, (4) as an agency aiming to deter future misconduct, and (5) as a facilitator of fund generation and cost savings. As you read about these areas, consider whether you would want to work in environmental protection careers. Each of these areas is addressed below.

EPA as an Enforcer of Criminal and Civil Laws

The EPA works with other federal and state agencies to enforce environmental crime laws. Created in 1982, the EPA's Office of Criminal Enforcement responds to (1) Clean Water Act and Clean Air Act violations, (2) Resource Conservation and Recovery Act (RCRA) violations, (3) illegal disposal of waste, (4) exporting hazardous waste, (5) illegal discharge of pollutants, (6) illegal disposal of asbestos, (7) illegal importation of chemicals, (8) tampering with drinking water supplies, (9) mail fraud, (10) wire fraud, and (11) money laundering (US-EPA, 2010e). According to their webpage, the EPA's Office of Criminal Enforcement responds to those who have committed "serious environmental crimes and provides evidence to support prosecutions, environmental forensic analyses, digital forensic analysis of computer evidence, and legal advice to federal agencies." Note that the EPA does not prosecute environmental crime cases like the U.S. Department of Justice does with federal prosecutions.

The EPA takes an active stance toward detecting environmental criminals. In 2008, it borrowed from the traditional fugitive posters that other federal agencies used and began to publish fugitive posters of "wanted" environmental offenders. Figure 11.2 shows the wanted poster of environmental crime suspect Richard Dorenkamp, a former Volkswagen employee working in the company's engine development department. Dorenkamp was accused of working with coconspirators

> to sell approximately 585,000 diesel vehicles in the U.S. by using a defeat device, that is, a software function designed to cheat on emissions tests mandated by the Environmental Protection Agency (EPA) and the California Air Resources Board (CARB), and lying and obstructing justice to further the scheme. (US-EPA, n.d., June 7)

You can check out other wanted environmental crime fugitives on the EPA "Fugitives" webpage.

The EPA works with other agencies in its efforts to enforce criminal and civil laws. As Ristovic (2018) notes, environmental crime "requires solving a series of questions which are political, social, economical, and cultural [issues] outside the jurisdiction of the police" (p. 82). The cases are adjudicated by the Department of Justice. The EPA must work with regulators, law enforcement, the fire department, public health officials, insurance representatives, economic development officials, city leaders, representatives from the water and electric departments, and others (Barrett & White, 2017). The process for criminally prosecuting these types of crimes will be discussed later in the text.

EPA as a Part of the Political Machine

Ever since President Nixon's administration created the Environmental Protection Agency in 1970, every presidential administration has expressed support for efforts to protect the public. While they may have differed in their approach to specific climate issues, there was apparent consensus about the need to have a strong federal agency to promote environmental protection. The commitment to environmental protection changed under the Trump administration. In

FIGURE 11.2 ■ Environmental Protection Agency Wanted Poster

Source: U.S. Environmental Protection Agency. (n.d.). Available on p. 55 of https://www.epa.gov/sites/production/files/2020-03/documents/richard_dorenkamp_final.pdf.

an early sign of its environmental beliefs, the Trump administration removed all references to global warming from government websites soon after Trump took office (Kramer, 2020). The administration also withdrew from the Paris Agreement, which was an international treaty industrialized nations signed in an effort to combat climate change through a global framework. Also disconcerting to environmental activists was the fact that Trump selected former Oklahoma Attorney General Scott Pruitt as head of the EPA. For some, the selection confirmed Trump's desire to dismantle the agency given that Pruitt is a long-time critic of Obama's climate policies and a "close ally of the fossil fuel industry" (Davenport and Lipton, 2016). Pruitt's term as EPA head was cut short when accusations arose that he excessively spent EPA money on business travel, spent $1,560 of EPA money on a dozen fountain pens, hid controversial meetings in a secret calendar, had staff run personal errands for him, and obtained a low-cost rental from a lobbyist (Diamond, Watkins, & Summers, 2018; Watkins & Foran, 2018). Pruitt's term at the EPA lasted less than a year and a half. Trump's next pick, Andrew Wheeler, had previously served as a lobbyist for the fossil fuel industry. At the EPA, Wheeler continued to roll back environmental protection policies that had been developed under prior presidential administrations.

Figure 11.3 shows the number of EPA criminal cases opened each year between Fiscal Year 2007 and Fiscal Year 2019. The number of new cases began declining during the Obama administration; during the Trump administration, the numbers reached their lowest point in the 13-year span in 2017. Between 2018 and 2019, the number of new cases increased from 125 to 170. A similar pattern was found in civil investigations. In 2016—Obama's last year as president—the EPA conducted 125 civil investigations; in 2017 and 2018—during the Trump administration—the EPA conducted 40 and 22 civil investigations, respectively (Knickmeyer, 2019). While some may wonder whether fewer investigations reflected the possibility that fewer environmental crimes were occurring, there is no evidence to support such an assertion. The Trump administration has said these drops are a result of giving states more of the responsibility for environmental protection. However, a review by the Capitol Forum (2019) identified 20 states with no dedicated staff for criminal enforcement of environmental violations. It is important to note that data released just before Trump left office showed that in fiscal year 2020 the Trump administration had opened 247 new criminal cases, which was the highest number of new cases since 2014 (US-EPA, 2021). Incidentally, 60 of those cases dealt with allegations that individuals were selling or distributing pesticides to respond to Covid-19.

Table 11.1 shows the penalties that were given in EPA cases between 1989 and 2019. The years 2013 and 2016 had inflated amounts due to large penalties against BP (for the oil spill), and 2017 had inflated amounts as a result of penalties given to Volkswagen (for its Clean Air Act violations). Note the low total amount of penalties given in 2018. This number was offset by a significant increase the following year.

Jim Watson/AFP/Getty Images

PHOTO 11.3 Political leaders are expected to protect the environment and are held accountable in the media when they appear to respond too lightly to environmental disasters. Former President Bush took a lot of flack in the media for this picture of him flying over New Orleans in the aftermath of Hurricane Katrina. President Obama received similar criticism from members of the media for his response to the BP oil spill.

FIGURE 11.3 ■ Number of EPA Crime Cases Opened, 2007–2019

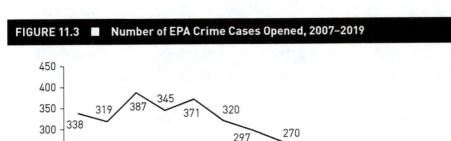

Source: Data compiled from EPA Office of Enforcement and Compliance. (n.d.). In *Annual Reports.*

TABLE 11.1 ■ EPA, FY 1989-FY 2019 Penalties Assessed

Fiscal Year	Civil Judicial	Administrative	Criminal	Total
1989	$21,473,087	$13,778,859	$11,601,241	$46,853,187
1990	$38,542,015	$22,747,652	$5,513,318	$66,802,985
1991	$41,235,721	$31,868,407	$14,120,387	$87,224,515
1992	$50,705,071	$28,028,260	$62,895,400	$141,628,731
1993	$85,913,518	$29,219,896	$29,700,000	$144,833,414
1994	$65,635,930	$48,020,941	$36,812,000	$150,468,871
1995	$34,925,472	$35,933,856	$23,221,100	$94,080,428
1996	$66,254,451	$29,996,478	$76,660,900	$172,911,829
1997	$45,966,607	$49,178,494	$169,282,896	$264,427,997
1998	$63,531,731	$28,041,562	$92,800,711	$184,374,004
1999	$141,211,699	$25,509,879	$61,552,874	$228,274,452
2000	$54,851,765	$29,258,502	$121,974,488	$206,084,755
2001	$101,683,157	$23,782,264	$94,726,283	$220,191,704
2002	$63,816,074	$25,859,501	$62,252,318	$151,927,893
2003	$72,259,713	$24,374,718	$71,000,000	$167,634,431
2004	$121,213,230	$27,637,174	$47,000,000	$195,850,404
2005	$127,205,897	$26,731,150	$100,000,000	$253,937,047
2006	$81,807,757	$42,007,029	$43,000,000	$166,814,786
2007	$39,771,169	$30,696,323	$63,000,000	$133,467,492
2008	$88,356,149	$38,197,194	$63,454,493	$190,007,837
2009	$58,496,536	$31,608,710	$96,000,000	$186,105,246
2010	$70,200,000	$33,400,000	$70,200,000	$175,800,000
2011	$104,390,628	$47,800,937	$41,000,000	$193,191,565
2012	$155,539,269	$52,022,612	$44,000,000	$251,461,881
2013	$1,100,000,000	$48,000,000	$1,500,000,000	$2,648,000,000
2014	$56,000,000	$44,000,000	$63,000,000	$163,000,000
2015	$163,000,000	$42,000,000	$200,000,000	$405,000,000
2016	$5,746,000,000	$44,000,000	$207,000,000	5,746,251,000
2017	$1,584,000,000	$48,000,000	$2,977,000,000	4,561,048,000
2018	$29,282,000	$40,192,000	$86,294,000	155,768,000
2019	$320,411,000	$40,384,000	$109,000,000	469,795,000

Source: Compiled from EPA Office of Enforcement and Compliance. *Enforcement and compliance numbers at a glance.*

Both the Obama and Trump administrations downsized the EPA workforce (see Figure 11.4). In 2011, the agency employed 17,359 employees. By 2015, the EPA employed 14,725, and by 2019, they employed 14,172—the lowest number in the 11-year span. In addition, the Trump administration's 2020 budget proposed a 31% budget cut (totaling more than 2 billion dollars) to the EPA. The cuts were not approved by Congress. In fact, Congress's involvement resulted in a budget increase of nearly $800 million. Trump inherited an EPA budgeted at $8.06 billion; in fiscal year 2019, the EPA's enacted budget was $8.85 billion, which was the highest the budget had been since 2010 (US-EPA, 2019b). Environmental advocates oppose EPA budget cuts on the grounds that resource reductions limit the ability of environmental protection agencies to adequately protect the environment (Gibbs & Pugh, 2017).

Despite an increased EPA budget, the Trump administration relaxed environmental laws and rolled back environmental protections, causing alarm among environmental advocates. In May 2020, the *New York Times* identified 100 regulations that the Trump administration had either reversed, revoked, relaxed, or for which the administration had begun seeking one of these outcomes. Figure 11.5 summarizes the areas targeted by these rule changes (Knickmeyer, 2019). Given Trump's pro-business policies, some believe these rollbacks were executed to help businesses increase their profits at the expense of environmental protections. Research shows that certain types of environmental crimes are driven by profit motives (Patten, 2019). With these rollbacks, one might wonder whether future environmental harms or breaking relaxed regulations will continue to be driven by profit.

Former EPA heads from the administrations of Presidents George W. Bush, George H. W. Bush, and Ronald Reagan spoke out against the environmental rollbacks by the Trump administration (Knickmeyer, 2019). It is the actions of those with the power to control the agency that characterize the EPA as part of the political machine. Many scientists, researchers, staff, attorneys, regulators, and others working in the EPA are committed to environmental protection, but they are restricted by political leadership who set priorities and budgets.

FIGURE 11.4 ■ EPA Workforce Numbers, 2009–2019 (FY)

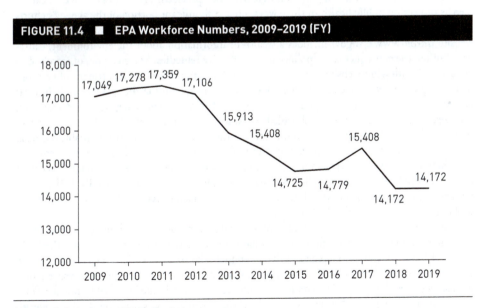

Source: U.S. Environmental Protection Agency

FIGURE 11.5 ■ Areas Targeted for Environmental Policy Reversals/Rollbacks by Trump Administration

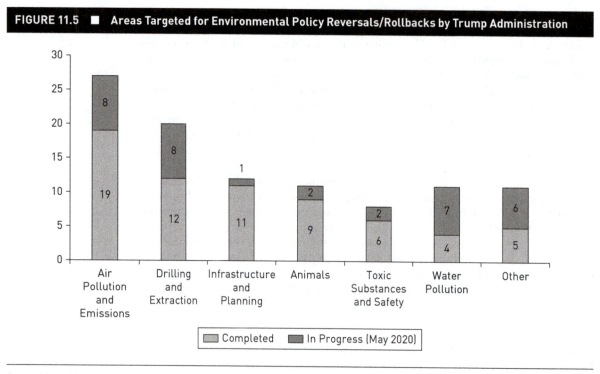

Source: Adapted from Knickmeyer, 2019

EPA as a Protector of Public Health

The adverse health effects of pollution were discussed previously. Activities of the EPA can be seen as protecting public health in three ways. First, a significant portion of the agency's efforts are directed toward educating members of the public about environmental issues. The agency's website (http://www.epa.gov) includes a wealth of information about the environment, causes of pollution, the consequences of pollution, and effective remedies. Various types of search tools are available, allowing website visitors to gather information about an assortment of environmental topics. As well, one search tool allows visitors to determine the quality of air in their city, county, or state. Many of you have likely heard of sex offender registries and may have even searched them. A similar tool, called AirNow, exists for air pollution. The tool provides users insight into the quality of air in different locations across the year. It is available online at airnow.gov. Another tool includes a mapping tool that provides users details on EPA enforcement actions each year. Users can use the map to click on the location where each enforcement action occurred. When doing so, they will access the address of the business/individual charged with the action, a detailed case enforcement report, and facility report. The 2015 data for this tool is available online at the AirNow website.

A second way that the agency protects public health is through research programs that investigate how various chemicals and pollutants harm individuals and the environment. The EPA's Office of Research and Development (ORD) conducts and oversees various scientific studies on different aspect of pollution. ORD oversees several research centers, laboratories, and research programs, including the National Center for Environmental Research, the National Center for Computational Toxicology, the National Center for Environmental Assessment, the National Health and Environmental Effects Research Laboratory, and the National Homeland Security Research Center. Research by ORD is focused on assessing environmental risks, characterizing harm from the pollutants, and developing management practices to deal with risk (US-EPA, 2010a).

Environmental risk assessment research encompasses three domains. *Hazard identification* refers to efforts to identify the negative health consequences of various pollutants. *Exposure assessment* refers to efforts to identify specific locations where the pollutants exist, how much of the pollutants exist, and how long they have existed. *Dose-response assessment* refers to efforts to determine how much of specific pollutants produce specific effects (US-EPA, 2010a). Using this risk assessment process as a foundation, researchers can then assess how to characterize environmental risks and how best to manage them.

A third way that EPA protects public health is through its enforcement efforts. When cases are resolved, agency representatives include a discussion on the way various chemicals or pollutants involved in that particular settlement or case harmed individuals and the environment. For example, in January 2020, the EPA and State of California announced a settlement with engine manufacturer Kohler Co. for allegations that the company was violating California law and the federal Clean Air Act. The company agreed to pay $20 million in a civil penalty and to change its practices to reduce pollution. In the announcement, the US-EPA provided the following summary about the health benefits:

> Generated hydrocarbon (HC) + oxides of nitrogen pollution contributes to the formation of harmful smog and soot, exposure to which is linked to a number of respiratory- and cardiovascular-related health effects as well as premature death. Children, older adults, people who are active outdoors (including outdoor workers that use the equipment at issue in this case), and people with heart or lung disease are particularly at risk for health effects related to smog or soot exposure. Nitrogen dioxide formed by NO_x emissions can aggravate respiratory diseases, particularly asthma, and may also contribute to asthma development in children. (US-EPA, 2020, January 30)

The announcement also indicated that the settlement would lead to a 3,600-ton reduction in harmful emissions.

EPA as a Deterrent

Settlements are designed not just to punish environmental offenders but also to ensure that the offenders develop measures to stop future offending. Consider the case of Dyno Nobel, an explosives manufacturing company operating in Missouri. In February 2020, the US-EPA announced a consent decree resolving allegations that the company had violated the Clean Water Act and the Resource Conservation and Recovery Act by discharging pollutants and operating facilities without appropriate permits. Like other consent decrees, this was not an admission of liability (or guilt). The company agreed to pay the U.S. government a $2.9 million fine. In addition, per the consent decree, the company agreed to make a number of changes to its operations. Among others, those changes included the following:

Carthage Facility Sewer Separation

a. By August 1, 2020, Dyno shall separate stormwater flow from process wastewater flow and consolidate piping to (1) four discharge points for stormwater and (2) a separate single discharge point for process wastewater, reached via hard-piped, underground pipe.

b. Following the outfall consolidation described above, any remaining Legacy Outfalls from which discharge is observed will be permanently closed.

Carthage Facility Process Wastewater Treatment

a. Beginning no later than August 1, 2020, Dyno shall ship high-strength wastewater from the Chub Emulsion Building and Paperwrap Building (identified in Appendix C) off-site to the Springfield publicly owned treatment works (POTW) and shall route all remaining process wastewater to the discharge point for process wastewater described in Paragraph 12.

b. By January 15, 2020, Dyno shall provide to EPA for approval pursuant to Paragraph 26, its plan for the treatment of its process wastewater in accordance with Paragraphs 12.a and 13.a, including the on-site changes that will take place.

c. By June 1, 2020, Dyno shall provide to EPA for approval, pursuant to Paragraph 26, a plan for a contingency option that could be implemented within 90 Days if the Missouri Department of Natural Resources ("MDNR") does not approve Dyno's plan or the Springfield facility no longer accepts Dyno's wastewater. Upon EPA's approval of the contingency plan, if at any future date either of the foregoing conditions occurs, Dyno will implement the contingency plan within 90 Days.

Complete Sewer Survey at the Louisiana Facility. By October 1, 2020, Dyno shall perform a Sewer Survey that includes:

a. camera inspection from outfall 008 out to former outfall 001 (the Mississippi River discharge point) as is practicable; and dye testing on the remainder of the Louisiana Facility process and stormwater sewers from the production area (which includes the truck and rail loadout and storage areas).

Within 6 months after completion of the sewer survey, Dyno shall submit to EPA a Sewer Survey Report that 1) describes in detail the findings and identifications of the Sewer Survey required above, 2) describes any corrective actions to be taken in response to the findings to minimize any unpermitted releases of materials to Buffalo Creek or the Mississippi River revealed by the sewer survey and to route any unpermitted flows of such materials from the Louisiana Facility production area to the outfalls consistent with the NPDES permit. The Sewer Survey Report shall be prepared and signed by a professional engineer and shall provide estimates of the capital cost of each proposed corrective measure and a schedule for the construction and implementation of all proposed corrective measures. EPA, after consultation with the State, shall approve, approve with modifications, or disapprove the proposed corrective measures and the proposed schedule in the Sewer Survey Report. (US-EPA, 2020, February 27)

Most consent decrees between the EPA and offending companies include similar stipulations targeting the harmful actions of the company. By reducing their ability to commit harmful actions, future harm is deterred. In theory, these initiatives would reduce the likelihood of future offending.

On another level, it is important to note that the ability of the EPA (and other agencies for that matter) extends beyond stopping specific offenders from committing new offenses. Indeed, the hope is that these agencies will keep businesses who have never offended from doing so as well. Surveys of 70 workers from two companies (a steel business and a paper/pulp business) and 91 environmental decision makers found that the likelihood of an environmental crime is lowest when "there is a credible legal threat for non-compliance and/or when one perceives information consequences associated with offending, such as losing the respect of one's significant others, to be certain and costly" (Simpson et al., 2013, p. 266). As Sally Simpson and her coauthors (2013) point out, "formal sanctions do not work in isolation" (p. 65).

EPA as a Fund Generator and Cost-Saving Entity

The EPA can be seen as a resource generator and a cost-saving entity. The agency generates resources through the fines that are imposed in cases it investigates. As shown in Table 11.1, the EPA routinely collects hundreds of millions, if not billions, of dollars in penalties each year.

Their collections come from legislation authorizing them to respond to cases and to use financial penalties to punish organizations.

The EPA is also instrumental in collecting fines to help with cleanup costs of environmental pollution sites in the United States. The **Comprehensive Environmental Response Compensation and Liability Act**, also known as the Superfund Act, was passed in 1980 "to clean up past environmental sins" (H. C. Barnett, 1993, p. 120). This law placed the economic onus of fixing environmental harm on corporations and provided a legislative remedy that assisted in determining how funds should be collected and distributed. Funds come from taxes and enforcement-initiated penalties on corporations and companies (H. C. Barnett, 1993). In fiscal year 2015, the EPA received commitments of $2.2 billion to support the investigation and cleanup of environmental crime sites. Sites selected to use Superfund dollars are referred to as Superfund sites.

The EPA also helps save future costs through its compliance efforts. By ensuring that companies are in compliance with environmental laws, in theory, the agency is reducing future costs of pollution. Though it is difficult to gauge the degree to which these savings occur, it nonetheless seems safe to suggest that fewer environmental crimes in the future means reduced costs of environmental crimes (controlling for business growth and inflation). The EPA announcement of the agency's 2019 enforcement efforts boasted the following items quoted verbatim from the press release (US-EPA, 2019a):

- Investment of over $4.4 billion in actions and equipment that achieve compliance with the law and control pollution, an increase of over $400 million from FY 2018.

- $471.8 million in combined Federal administrative and judicial civil penalties and criminal fines, the highest total of all but four of the past ten years.

- Commitments for $570.4 million in new site cleanup work, $283 million in reimbursement of EPA's costs, and more than $108 million in oversight billed, totaling $961 million, an increase of over $349 million from FY 2018.

Criticisms of EPA

In discussing the functions of the EPA, it is important to draw attention to the criticisms that individuals and groups have made about the agency. In particular, the EPA has been criticized for the following:

- An ineffective response to the September 11, 2001 terror attacks

- Overregulating rural areas

- Overstepping its boundaries regarding state issues

- Politicizing the science process

In terms of an ineffective response to September 11, the EPA was criticized for not providing enough information about the harmful effects of the air around New York City's "Ground Zero" after the September 11 terror attacks. The agency was also criticized for not providing enough assistance in cleanup efforts. Rep. Jerrold Nadler (D-NY) commented that "New York was at the center of one of the most calamitous events in American history and the EPA has essentially walked away" (Lyman, 2003b). The EPA's Office of Inspector General conducted its own investigation into the EPA's response to September 11. The report claimed that "the White House reviewed and even changed EPA statements about public health risks to make them sound less alarming" and that the EPA understated the potential health effects of the attack (Lyman, 2003a).

The EPA has been accused of overregulating in rural areas and making it difficult for farmers to make a living by producing goods they have been producing for centuries. With changes in rules, including one proposed rule that would have supposedly allowed the EPA to regulate dust, farmers and their advocates were in an uproar about the EPA's actions. Tamara Thies, the National Cattlemen's Beef Association chief environmental counsel, accused the EPA of "waging an unprecedented war to end modern production of animal agriculture" (K. Anderson, 2010). In September 2010, Senate Agriculture Committee Chairman Blanche Lincoln (D-AR) held a committee hearing to "examine the impact of the U.S. Environmental Protection Agency regulation on agriculture" (Clayton, 2010). At the hearing, Lincoln was critical of the EPA, stating, "Farmers need certainty and stability, not additional burdensome and costly regulation" and said that many of EPA's initiatives reflected "dubious rationales and . . . they will be of questionable benefit" (Kopperud, 2010).

Critics have also claimed that the EPA oversteps its boundaries into states' issues all too often. Texas Governor Rick Perry has been especially critical of the EPA. In a statement released on May 26, 2010, Perry made the following comments:

> An increasingly activist EPA is ignoring the 22 percent reduction in ozone and 46 percent decrease in NO_x emissions that Texas has achieved since 2000. On behalf of those Texans whose jobs are threatened by this latest overreach, and in defense of not only our clean air program but also our rights under the 10th Amendment, I am calling upon President Obama to rein in the EPA and instruct them to study our successful approach for recommended use elsewhere. (Office of the Governor Rick Perry, 2010)

In fall 2010, federal regulations changed in terms of how greenhouse gas permits should be issued to businesses, a task that had been done by state agencies previously. A spokesman from Perry's office told reporters,

> The existing permits in Texas have helped our state achieve dramatic improvements in air quality and we believe they will ultimately be upheld in the courts. In their latest crusade, the EPA has created massive job-crushing uncertainty for Texas companies. (Plushnick-Masti, 2010)

In December 2010, Perry vowed to "defend Texas' freedom to continue our successful environmental strategies free from federal overreach" (Powell, 2010). The battle reached the point where six Texas legislators developed a proposal to establish autonomy from the federal government.

The EPA has faced criticisms of politicizing the science process. A 2008 survey of 1,586 EPA scientists administered by the by Iowa State University's Center for Survey Statistics and Methodology on behalf of the Union of Concerned Scientists found that 889 of the scientists (60%) "reported personally experiencing what they viewed as political interference in their work over the last five years" ("Meddling at EPA?" 2008). Additional findings from the survey showed that about one fourth of the scientists witnessed EPA officials misrepresenting findings, 284 witnessed situations where officials selectively used data, and 224 scientists said they had been told to engage in such activities. One EPA scientist made the following comments in the study: "Do not trust the Environmental Protection Agency to protect your environment. Ask questions. Be aware of political and economic motives. Become politically active. Elect officials with motives to protect the environment and hold them accountable" (Union of Concerned Scientists [UCS], 2008, p. 6). Francesca Grifo, senior scientist with the Union of Concerned Scientists, presented a summary of the findings in a hearing titled *Oversight Health on Science and Environmental Regulatory Decisions* before the U.S. Senate Committee on Environment and Public

Works Subcommittee on Public Sector Solutions to Global Warming, Oversight, and Children's Health Protection. In her testimony, Grifo said,

> Science is not the only element of effective policy making. However, because science enjoys widespread respect, appointed officials will always be tempted to manipulate or suppress scientific findings to support predetermined policies. Such manipulation is not only dishonest; it undermines the EPA's credibility and affects the health and safety of Americans. (UCS, 2008, p. 8)

PROBLEMS ADDRESSING ENVIRONMENTAL CRIMES

Like other white-collar crimes, environmental white-collar offenses are complex, with a number of barriers making it difficult for control agencies to respond to the problem. In general, the three barriers are (1) media portrayals of environmental crime, (2) evidentiary issues, and (3) an empirical void.

Media Portrayals of Environmental Crime

With regard to the *media portrayals of environmental crime,* it is safe to suggest that the media provide little information about environmental crimes, and the information provided may give the public and policy makers a distorted image of environmental crime. One author team examined how often chemical spills were reported in the *Tampa Tribune*—the largest newspaper in Hillsborough County, Florida—between 1987 and 1997 (Lynch, Stretesky, & Hammond, 2000). The study showed that 878 chemical spills were reported to the EPA in the county over the decade. Of those 878, nine were reported in the newspaper. The authors note that newspapers fail to focus on environmental crimes because they do "not fit the public's image of crime" (Lynch et al., 2000, p. 123). Another study, this one of 162 EPA cases between 2001 and 2002, showed that the cases received little scrutiny from the press. The cases that did receive press attention were deemed as more serious, which was determined by the penalty given to the offender (Jarrell, 2007).

Another problem related to the media and environmental crime is that environmental disasters tend to be politicized by commentators in the media. After the BP disaster, President Barack Obama was criticized for not doing enough to respond to the environmental situation in the Gulf. Fox News showed a daily description of Obama's White House schedule and compared the president's schedule with the daily activities in the Gulf in the aftermath of the oil spill ("Disaster in the Gulf," 2010). In a similar way, President George W. Bush was vilified by commentators for what was perceived to be a lackadaisical response to Hurricane Katrina. One photo that created controversy showed President Bush looking out of the window of *Air Force One* as it flew over New Orleans. Five years later, in his memoir, the former president said he regretted having that photo taken.

Evidentiary Issues and Environmental Crime

Evidentiary issues also make it difficult to address environmental crimes. Environmental crime pioneer Gerhard Mueller (1996) identified 10 such problems that hindered the criminal justice response to environmental crime (see Table 11.2). These problems include the following:

- Identifying the harm from environmental crimes
- Determining the amount of "permissible" pollution

- Identifying liability
- Issues around vicarious liability (e.g., holding an employer responsible for an employee's actions)

TABLE 11.2 ■ Problems Responding to Environmental Crime		
Problem	**Why It's a Problem**	**Can This Problem Be Addressed?**
Problem of qualification	Harm is not always immediately visible, causing some criminal justice officials and policy makers to misunderstand the problem.	Through education and awareness, improved response systems have evolved.
Problem of quantification	It is difficult to determine how "much" pollution is permissible, and how much harm is appropriate, with decisions somewhat arbitrary.	Laws have placed a "sin tax" on companies exceeding permissible pollution, but this may not help.
Problem of strict liability	Laws too narrowly defined on intent make it difficult to prove intent.	Laws became more flexible in the United States, focusing on mens rea, but not in other countries.
Problem of vicarious liability	It can be counterproductive to deterrence if offenders are held accountable for things they did not intend.	Responsible corporate officers can be held accountable for environmental offending.
Corporate criminal liability	Identifying specific corporate officers with the decision-making power that was abused is difficult, with "blame passed downward."	Through complex investigations and plea bargains, officers can be identified.
Problem of proof	It is hard to prove damage, effects, guilt, mens rea, and connection between the crime and the consequences.	With time and resources, cases can be proven, but it is complex. Also, corporations can't plead the fifth (must provide information)
Problem of abuse of power	Powerful businesses might control policy makers and regulators.	Must be addressed on a case-by-case basis.
Problem of inadequate enforcement	In the 1970s, only 130 cases were referred by EPA to DOJ for criminal prosecution.	The EPA has been opening more criminal investigations this decade.
Problem of changing priorities	Industrialization is seen as progress, and consequences are virtually ignored.	Advocates must continue efforts to generate awareness about environmental issues.
Problem of decriminalization	Cases were routinely kept out of the justice system in the past.	The criminal justice system has increased its efforts in responding to environmental crime cases.
Problem of penalization	Mixed evidence on the deterrent potential of punitive policies.	Need more research to determine appropriate sentences.

Source: Adapted from Mueller, G. (1996). "An essay on environmental criminality." In S. M. Edwards, T. D. Edwards, & C Fields, *Environmental crime and criminality* (pp. 3–32). New York: Garland.

- Determining ways to hold corporations liable

- Establishing proof

- Lack of enforcement

- Power abuses

- Changing priorities

- Decriminalization and/or determining the appropriate penalty

Another evidentiary issue is that offenders will engage in behaviors which make it nearly impossible to get caught. Research shows that some types of environmental offenders, for example, choose a specific time of the day to pollute in order to avoid detection (Vollaard, 2017). Of course, the criminal justice system cannot respond to environmental crime by itself. Some have argued that better controls in the form of self-regulation, improved marketing of safe products, and improved communication about environmental risk will help address environmental crime (Grabosky & Gant, 2000). In fact, it has been noted that overcriminalization of environmental crimes could negatively impact rural populations (Neimark, 2019). It is important to note that these issues can be addressed through concerted efforts by criminal justice professionals. White-Collar Crime in the News shows how evidence was used to find the "Tiger King" guilty of environmental offenses.

WHITE-COLLAR CRIME IN THE NEWS

"JOE EXOTIC" CONVICTED OF MURDER-FOR-HIRE AND VIOLATING BOTH THE LACEY ACT AND ENDANGERED SPECIES ACT

The following is a press release from the Western District of Oklahoma from April 2, 2019.

OKLAHOMA CITY—A federal jury has found JOSEPH MALDONADO-PASSAGE, also known as Joseph Allen Maldonado, Joseph Allen Schreibvogel, and "Joe Exotic," 56, formerly of Wynnewood, Oklahoma, guilty on two counts of hiring someone to murder a woman in Florida, eight counts of violating the Lacey Act for falsifying wildlife records, and nine counts of violating the Endangered Species Act, announced First Assistant U.S. Attorney Robert J. Troester.

"The self-described Tiger King was not above the law," said Mr. Troester. "Rather, the jury only needed a few hours of deliberation before finding him guilty of engaging in a murder-for-hire plot to kill a rival and violating federal laws intended to protect wildlife when he killed multiple tigers, sold tiger cubs,

and falsified wildlife records. We are thankful for the jury's careful attention, deliberation, and verdict in this case."

"We would like to thank the U.S Attorney's Office for prosecuting this case and holding individuals accountable for these crimes," said Phillip Land, Special Agent in Charge of the U.S. Fish and Wildlife Service, Office of Law Enforcement for the Southwest Region. "We appreciate our state and federal law enforcement partners working together in this investigation."

On September 5, 2018, a federal grand jury returned an indictment that accused Maldonado-Passage of hiring an unnamed person in November 2017 to murder "Jane Doe" in Florida and also hiring a person who turned out to be an undercover FBI agent to commit that murder. A superseding indictment handed down on November 7, 2018, further alleged

(Continued)

(Continued)

Maldonado-Passage falsified forms involving the sale of wildlife in interstate commerce, killed five tigers in October 2017 to make room for cage space for other big cats, and sold and offered to sell tiger cubs in interstate commerce. Because tigers are an endangered species, these alleged killings and sales violated the Endangered Species Act.

During a trial that began on March 25, a jury heard evidence that Maldonado-Passage gave Allen Glover $3,000 to travel from Oklahoma to South Carolina and then to Florida to murder Carole Baskin, with a promise to pay thousands more after the deed. Baskin, a critic of Maldonado-Passage's animal park, owns a tiger refuge in Florida and had secured a million-dollar judgment against Maldonado-Passage's park.

The evidence further showed that beginning in July 2016, Maldonado-Passage repeatedly sought someone to murder Baskin in exchange for money, which led to his meeting with an undercover FBI agent on December 8, 2017. The jury heard a recording of his meeting with the agent to discuss details of the planned murder.

In addition to the murder-for-hire counts, the trial included evidence of violations of the Lacey Act, which makes it a crime to falsify records of wildlife transactions in interstate commerce. According to these counts, Maldonado-Passage designated on delivery forms and Certificates of Veterinary Inspection that tigers, lions, and a baby lemur were being donated to the recipient or transported for exhibition only, when he knew they were being sold in interstate commerce.

Finally, the jury heard evidence that Maldonado-Passage personally shot and killed five tigers in October 2017, without a veterinarian present and in violation of the Endangered Species Act.

After only a few hours of deliberation, the jury returned guilty verdicts on both murder-for-hire counts, eight Lacey Act counts, and nine Endangered Species Act counts.

Reprinted from U.S. Department of Justice.

Source: https://www.justice.gov/usao-wdok/pr/joe-exotic-convicted-murder-hire-and-violating-both-lacey-act-and-endangered-species

Empirical Issues and Environmental Crime

Empirical issues have made it difficult to address environmental crime. On a general level, one can point to a dearth of research on the topic, which is surprising given the wealth of compliance and violations data available from the EPA that could be used to study various types of white-collar crime (Burns & Lynch, 2004). Indeed, the data available are virtual gold mines for future researchers. Perhaps those of you doing theses or dissertations in the near future could "mine" some of the EPA data to help generate empirical understanding about environmental crime. In the meantime, according to Lynch (2020), environmental crime "is marginalized within criminology, treated as if it were a curiosity rather than a field of research focusing on a tremendously important set of global concerns" (p. 50).

A related empirical issue has to do with the way that environmental crime is conceptualized. Focusing solely on a legal orientation may ignore much of the harm done by corporations. Some researchers who see pollution as contributing to climate change define the behavior of the government—its reluctance to address the problem in particular—as a form of state-corporate crime (Kramer, 2013). Recall from Chapter 6 that state-corporate crimes are defined as harmful acts perpetrated by the government.

On a related point, the existing environmental crime research has given limited attention to "the place of the upper class in environmental research" (Simon, 2000, p. 633). What this means is that the research has failed to adequately address environmental crime *as a white-collar crime*. In doing so, opportunities for contextualizing, characterizing, and explaining "environmental white-collar crime" have been missed.

Another issue that surfaces concerns a lack of research on why certain companies do an outstanding job in terms of environmental compliance. Carole Gibbs (2012) reminds us of this important fact. She writes that "many companies comply and even overcomply with environmental regulations by polluting significantly less than legally allowed" (p. 345). Gibbs offers several reasons for this compliance. Some companies may have installed incredibly effective pollution equipment. Other companies may "over abide" in an effort to develop positive relationships with policy makers and thereby influence the way that regulations are developed in the future. Still others might over abide in order to avoid any harm to their reputation. Or, some might overestimate the risk of prosecution and be cautious to avoid getting in trouble. Regardless of the reason, research is needed to focus on why many corporations do not break environmental laws.

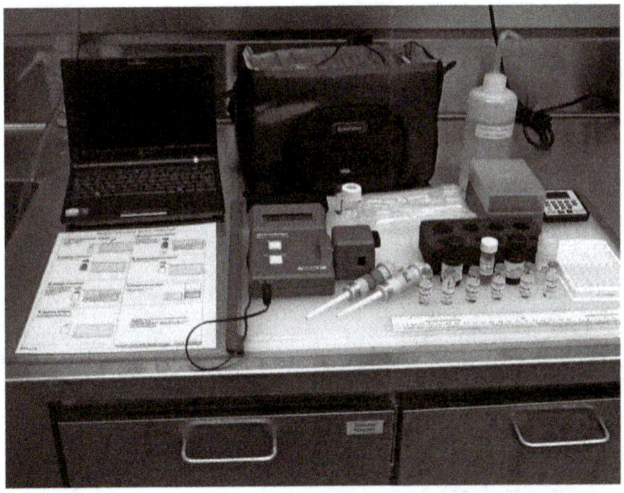

Simon (2000) also draws attention to the lack of research on global aspects of environmental offending. In a similar way, one can point to a lack of research on the way that environmental crime is influenced by various societal systems. Certainly, the environmental system can be seen as a system that interacts with other societal systems on various levels. As noted earlier in this text, the interrelated nature of systems is central to the systems perspective. Put another way, changes in one system will lead to changes in other systems. Some have argued that as our industrial system developed, the environmental system "has been cast in the role of a commodity for use in the production and consumption" (H. Barnett, 1999, p. 167). Then, as our technological system grew, new forms of chemical wastes were created, an increased need for certain raw materials surfaced, and new areas of concern for the environmental system arose. Little thought has been given to the way that technological advancements require raw materials and that accessing those materials damages the environment (Bohm, 2020). The task at hand is to recognize how our changing societal systems have changed the nature of environmental white-collar crimes occurring in communities across the world.

U.S. Government Work

PHOTO 11.4 Evidence-gathering in environmental crime cases is different from that in other types of crime. Environmental crime agents have a different tool kit from that of other law enforcement officers.

Summary

- On April 20, 2010, an explosion on BP's *Deepwater Horizon* rig occurred in the Gulf of Mexico. Eleven rig workers were killed, and oil began to spill out of the Macondo well into the Gulf of Mexico.

- On December 15, 2010, the U.S. Department of Justice filed a lawsuit against BP and eight other companies for their role in the rig explosion.

- Concern about environmental pollution escalated in the United States in the 1970s, a decade labeled the "environment decade in reference to the increase in environmental legislation and political

  support for laws regulating pollution" (H. Barnett, 1993, p. 220).

- It is important to understand that not all environmental crimes are white-collar crimes.

- White-collar environmental crimes involve situations where individuals or businesses illegally pollute or destroy the environment in the course of occupational activity.

- The varieties of environmental white-collar crime include illegal emissions, illegal disposal of hazardous wastes, illegal dumping, harmful destruction of property and wildlife, environmental threats, environmental state crime, and international environmental crimes.

- Illegal emissions, as a variety of environmental white-collar crime, refer to situations where companies or businesses illegally allow pollutants to enter the environment.

- Illegal disposal of hazardous wastes involves situations in which employees or businesses dispose of harmful wastes in ways that are potentially harmful to individuals and the environment.

- One of the most well-known environmental crimes involving hazardous wastes is the Love Canal tragedy.

- Also known as "fly dumping," "wildcat dumping," and "midnight dumping," illegal dumping refers to situations where employees or businesses dump products they no longer need in sites that are not recognized as legal dump sites (US-EPA, 1998).

- Harmful destruction of property and wildlife by companies or workers during the course of their jobs can also be seen as environmental white-collar crimes.

- The federal government has identified five "significant threats" to the environment: knowing endangerment, repeat offenders, misuse of federal facilities, catastrophic events, and organized crime.

- Environmental state crime refers to criminal or deviant behaviors by a government representative (or representatives) involving the intentional use of pollutants and chemicals to harm individuals and the environment.

- International environmental crimes include those environmental offenses that cross borders

of at least two different countries or occur in internationally protected areas.

- Environmental crime has more victims than other crimes, but victims are often not aware of their victimization (Hayman & Brack, 2002). In general, the types of consequences can be classified as *physical costs*, *economic costs*, and *community costs*.

- Between 2012 and 2018, more than 1,000 environmental defenders were killed across the world in their efforts to protect the environment.

- The Environmental Protection Agency has addressed concerns about environmental racism by developing an Office of Environmental Justice in the early 1990s and giving the office the responsibility of promoting environmental justice activities in the agency.

- The EPA was created in 1970 when President Richard Nixon reorganized several federal agencies to create a single federal agency responsible for addressing environmental pollution.

- The EPA can be characterized in five overlapping ways: (1) as an enforcer of criminal and civil laws, (2) as a part of the political machine, (3) as an agency trying to protect public health, (4) as an agency aiming to deter future misconduct, and (5) as a facilitator of fund generation and cost savings.

- The EPA has been criticized for the following: an ineffective response to the aftermath of September 11, overregulating rural areas, overstepping its boundaries regarding state issues, and politicizing the science process.

- Three barriers to addressing environmental crime include (1) media portrayals of environmental crime, (2) evidentiary issues, and (3) an empirical void.

Key Terms

Animal fighting 311

Comprehensive Environmental
Response Compensation
and Liability Act 325

Crimes by big-game
operators 310

Environmental Protection
Agency (EPA) 316

Environmental defenders 313

Environmental racism 315

Environmental state crime 312

Federal Water Pollution Control
Act 307

Harmful treatment of
animals 309

Illegal dumping 309

Illegal emissions 307

Illegal fishing 310

International environmental
crimes 312

Knowing endangerment 311

White-collar environmental
crimes 306

Discussion Questions

1. Do an Internet search for "EPA fugitives" to find the webpage for the EPA's wanted environmental fugitives. Categorize them based on (a) whether they are white-collar offenders, (b) the type of offense they committed, and (c) the harm from their offenses. What patterns do you see regarding gender, race, age, and geography? Explain.

2. Do an Internet search for "EPA air topics" to find the webpage on air pollutants, data, research, and more. Check to see how much air pollution exists in your hometown as well as your college town (if it is different from your hometown). Compare and contrast the amount of pollution in the two places.

3. Watch Doug Rokke's presentation about depleted uranium on YouTube called "Talk–Dr. Doug Rokke—Depleted Uranium (DU)" from

talkingsticktv. How can depleted uranium be characterized as white-collar crime? Is its use an environmental crime?

4. What is it that makes big-game hunting illegal in some situations? Do you think these crimes are serious? Explain.

5. Rank the various types of environmental crime from least serious to most serious. Explain your rankings.

6. Would you be interested in working for the Environmental Protection Agency? Explain.

7. How can scientists commit environmental crime? Explain.

8. Imagine the world 20 years from now. What do you think environmental crime will be like then?

EXPLAINING
WHITE-COLLAR CRIME

In the movie *Office Space,* the workplace experiences of a group of coworkers who are not entirely enthusiastic about their employer are chronicled in a rather humorous manner. The lead character Peter Gibbons, played by Ron Livingston, decides to put in as little effort as possible at his job and is rewarded for this effort with a significant promotion. Later in the movie, he and his disgruntled coworkers, who learn they are going to be fired, concoct a scheme to embezzle a small amount of money that should go unnoticed from the company on a regular basis until they have collected millions over time. The plan goes awry when they embezzle a large amount of funds that is noticed by company officials. Fearing the repercussions that they will experience once they are caught, they write a letter confessing their workplace misconduct and telling where the embezzled funds are located. After they slide their confession under their boss's door, Milton Waddams, another disgruntled coworker, played by movie director Mike Judge, decides to burn the business to the ground because he is fed up with the emotional abuses perpetrated by his bosses. Subsequent scenes show Milton enjoying the spoils of the embezzlement scheme and the offending team moving on in their respective careers.

A close look at the movie shows how various criminological theories can be used to explain the behaviors of workers in the movie. According to Sutherland (1941), "many white-collar crimes are made possible because a businessman holds two or more incompatible and conflicting positions of trust, and is analogous to a football coach who umpires a game in which his own team is playing" (p. 112). In the *Office Space* example, the workers used the trust placed in them by their employers to steal money from company accounts. In reviewing the movie, readers can likely identify how several other theories are relevant to the story line. This chapter's Streaming White-Collar Crime provides additional details about the classic movie.

STREAMING WHITE-COLLAR CRIME   Office Space: Excuse Me, I Believe You Have My Stapler and Criminological Theory

Plot	What You Can Learn	Discussion Questions
White-collar crime students should watch the movie to see how their coursework, and criminological theories in particular, relate to the plot. Filmed more than 20 years ago, Office Space tells a tale that could be found in many offices two decades later. Frustrated with his job at IniTech, Peter Gibbons becomes the ultimate unapologetic slacker at his job. He is rewarded with a promotion after consultants are inexplicably impressed with his leadership skills. Meanwhile, long-term employee Milton Waddams, who is indelibly attached to his red stapler, is moved to the basement and hard-working coworkers (Samir and Michael) hatch a plan with Peter to embezzle pennies from every paycheck after they learn about their layoffs despite their strong work ethics. A misplaced decimal point wreaks havoc.	People make rationalizations before stealing. In some careers, job satisfaction is connected to crime at work. At some point in your life you may work with a slacker who your boss thinks is the best worker ever.	Why do you think people steal at work? How can understanding motives for stealing help a business stop crimes from occurring in the workplace?

Criminological theory is central to the study of white-collar crime. Five comments about using criminological theory to understand and explain white-collar crime will help create a foundation from which readers can gain an appreciation of white-collar crime explanations. First, it is important to stress that theories are potential explanations of behaviors or phenomena. Recall the principle of skepticism discussed in Chapter 1: There are no truths when it comes to social science theories. Or, maybe there is one truth: We do not know for certain what causes white-collar crime. Still, theories are useful because they help us research white-collar crime and determine appropriate responses to the problem.

Second, for white-collar crime explanations to have practical utility, the theories or explanations must point to changes that would reduce (rather than increase) white-collar misconduct. For example, based on his review of the multidimensional causes of white-collar crime, Passas (2001) identified the need to (1) watch for fraud among high-level managers—especially when competition and corporate pressures are high, (2) develop strong internal control mechanisms to strengthen companies, (3) institutionalize internal and external strategies that can limit the ability of offenders to make excuses for or rationalize their misconduct, (4) improve publicity surrounding incidents of white-collar crime victimization, and (5) increase the amount of accountability given to external auditors. In essence, his explanations for white-collar crime led to specific policy implications.

Third, it is important to realize that multiple factors likely contribute to white-collar crime. We cannot say that one variable or one event automatically leads to white-collar misconduct. Although theories are discussed separately below, the most accurate explanations combine various theoretical assumptions and explanations to address human behavior.

Fourth, a great deal of theory building centers on explaining individual motivations for white-collar crime. Attempts to explain white-collar crime often center on identifying individual motivations for white-collar offending (Klenowski, 2012). Studying specific individual motivations for white-collar misconduct provides important insight for theory, policy, and future research on the topic.

Fifth, while explanatory attempts often focus on individual behavior, it is important to realize that structural variables and macrolevel features are useful in explaining and understanding white-collar crime. Consider, for example, that structural factors of the medical profession have been used to explain health care fraud (Wilson, Lincoln, Chappell, & Fraser, 1986). As well, structural features of other occupations might promote or inhibit white-collar offending in those occupations. Put another way, reasons that one occupational group engages in wrongdoing might be different from the reasons that other occupational groups engage in wrongdoing. Of course, some criminologists would dispute this statement vehemently and suggest that the phenomena that cause any specific type of crime are that same phenomena that cause all types of crime (Hirschi & Gottfredson, 1987). The key to keep in mind is that microlevel theories will address individual-level motivations for white-collar offending while macrolevel theories will address societal factors that contribute to rates of white-collar offending.

Criminologists have devoted a great deal of effort to trying to identify the causes of white-collar crime. In this chapter, the following topics are addressed to provide readers with a basic understanding about the potential causes of white-collar crime: culture, deterrence theory and rational choice theory, strain theory, learning theory, neutralizing and justifying white-collar crime, control theory, self-control, routine activities theory, conflict theory, an explanation of corporate crime, theories ignored in the white-collar crime literature, integrated efforts to explain white-collar crime, and systems theory. This should give readers a general understanding of the efforts to explain white-collar misconduct.

CULTURE AND WHITE-COLLAR CRIME

Some criminologists attribute white-collar crime to cultural influences that seemingly promote wrongdoing by workers and corporations. James Coleman (1987), for example, argued that industrial capitalism promotes a "culture of competition." Within the social structure that has developed in our industrialized capitalist society, upper-class workers are presented with various types of opportunities for white-collar crime. Based on this, Coleman suggested that white-collar crime "results from a coincidence of motivation and opportunity" (p. 407). The culture of competition is not just about competing to succeed; it is also reflective of a fear of failing that rests on apparent insecurities individuals have about their careers and their roles in their respective organizations. In effect, workers might bend, or even break, workplace rules in an effort to compete in the workplace.

As evidence of the presence of this culture of competition, consider a study in which Jenkins and Braithwaite (1993) reviewed violations in 410 nursing homes in Australia. They found that for-profit nursing homes had more violations than nonprofit nursing homes, and that nonprofit homes, when they do commit violations, often do so in response to the broader goals of the nursing home (e.g., their violations result from competing toward the organization's goals).

Greed is an often-cited explanation for white-collar misconduct that fits within this notion of a culture of competition. Both practitioners (Miller, 1993) and researchers (Braithwaite, 1991; Robinson & Murphy, 2009) have attributed corporate wrongdoing to greed that stems from cultural influences. Braithwaite (1991) wrote that "greed motivates crime even after a need has been satisfied" (p. 42). Miller (1993), a former federal probation officer who worked extensively with white-collar probationers, wrote the following reflections upon his retirement after a career that spanned 30 years:

> I am often asked what the offenders I supervised had in common. A large portion were professionals—doctors, pharmacists, lawyers, accountants, stockbrokers, and even a few former judges and high-level politicians. And the one common thread I noted, year after year, was greed. . . . This common denominator has changed society's priorities and damaged the nation's value system. One goal now dominates—to achieve material at any cost. (p. 22)

Tied into this competitive culture is ego seeking by workers. As Wheeler, Weisburd, Waring, and Bode (1988) wrote, the corporate "ladder is shaped like a pyramid," and competition for advancement becomes stiffer as employees move up the workplace ladder (p. 356). When the competition becomes extremely tight, some individuals might "slip over the boundary of legality" (p. 356). Also reflective of the ties between a competitive culture and greed, a study of 91 companies over a three-year period found that executive compensation was a factor in manager-controlled firms. In particular, more compensation for executives meant more crime in these firms (Bilimoria, 1995).

Poverty can be seen as a cultural influence that potentially promotes white-collar crime. Criminologists have long suggested that a culture of poverty is correlated with street crime. Historically, though, it has been assumed that poverty explanations were not relevant in terms of white-collar crime. Indeed, when Sutherland first discussed white-collar crime, he rejected poverty explanations as causes of the behavior because poverty, on the surface, does not seem to cause white-collar offending. After all, white-collar offenders are not impoverished. In an effort to broaden our understanding of poverty and crime, criminologist John Braithwaite (1991) has argued that poverty explanations may actually be useful in explaining how power is used to perpetrate white-collar crime if one considers the ties between poverty and inequality. He explained:

> When needs are satisfied, further power and wealth enable crime motivated by greed. New types of criminal opportunities and new paths to immunity from accountability are constituted by concentrations of wealth and power. Inequality thus worsens both crimes of poverty motivated by need for goods for use and crimes of wealth motivated by greed enabled by goods for exchange. (p. 43)

In other words, poverty is correlated with both street crime and white-collar crime. For poor individuals, crimes are motivated by a need for goods that arises out of poverty. For white-collar offenders, crimes are motivated by greed, and poverty provides them power to commit offenses. The more powerful those wealthy individuals become, the more pathways they have to white-collar crime, particularly in the face of limited responses to crimes committed by those with power.

Some authors have been extremely critical of cultural theories. One author team argues that culture's role is oversimplified given that opportunity structures, motivations, and other factors seem to play a role in white-collar offending (Jou, Hebenton, & Chang, 2016). Hirschi and Gottfredson (1987) argue that white-collar crime is far rarer than would be expected if culture actually caused white-collar crime. From their perspective, if a culture of competition or culture of poverty led to white-collar crime, then more professionals should be involved in workplace offending. Most doctors do not commit crime. Most accountants are honest. Most textbook authors do not plagiarize. Most lawyers are ethical. Most investors are law abiding. They also implied that if white-collar crime were caused by cultural values, then coworkers and citizens should be more accepting of the offenders, and the offenders would not feel the need to hide their crimes or their criminal identities. To Hirschi and Gottfredson, if white-collar crime emanated from values central to our society, then we would not expect the offenders to experience shame, embarrassment, or stigma when their crimes are exposed.

DETERRENCE THEORY/RATIONAL CHOICE THEORY AND WHITE-COLLAR CRIME

Deterrence theory can be traced to Cesare Beccaria's *On Crimes and Punishments* (1764), a work that many have defined as the foundation of the classical school of criminological thought. In this brief work, Beccaria outlined his theory of punishment, which was based on the assumption that punishment can stop individuals from offending. For punishment to be effective, however, he argued that it must meet three criteria: (1) Punishment must be swift so that the offender links the behavior of crime with the response of punishment in his or her mind; (2) punishment must be certain so that offenders know if a crime is committed, then a negative consequence will occur; and (3) punishment must be proportional to the crime so that the punishment outweighs the positive benefits individuals experience from committing crime.

PHOTO 12.1 Deterrence theory suggests that punishing individuals quickly, with certainty, and with the right amount of severity will prevent future misconduct.

The underlying assumption of deterrence theory is that individuals are rational beings. This assumption has direct bearing on the theory's applicability to white-collar crime. John Braithwaite (1982) wrote, "White-collar criminals are more deterrable than common criminals because their crimes are more rational and calculating and because they have more of all of the things that can be lost through criminal justice sanctions" (p. 760). Somewhat in line with this assumed rationality, interviews with judges found that the judges tended to view punishment as necessary in order to deter white-collar misconduct (Pollack & Smith, 1983).

Research by Sally Simpson and various colleagues (Elis & Simpson, 1995; Piquero, Exum, & Simpson, 2005; Simpson & Koper, 1992) has been instrumental in demonstrating how deterrence ideals can be used to explain various forms of workplace misconduct. One of her studies found some evidence that stiffer sanctions might deter corporations from future wrongdoing, though the likelihood of repeat offending in corporate crime cases was found to be more influenced by industry type than sanction severity (Simpson & Koper, 1992). In particular, automobile and oil industry firms were found to be more likely to reoffend than firms in the aircraft industry. Other scholars note that the question as to whether corporate prosecutions deter (or possibly negatively impact) corporate behavior remains unanswered (M. Cohen, 2020).

Many criminologists would agree that punishment, by itself, will not deter white-collar misconduct. In deterrence theory, one must consider the likelihood of getting caught, prosecuted, and convicted; another consideration is societal norms about different types of behavior (Gottschalk, 2020). If prevailing norms suggest that certain behaviors are appropriate, individuals will engage in those behaviors regardless of the prescribed penalties. Alternatively, if norms identify those behaviors as inappropriate, individuals will be less likely to violate those norms.

Because white-collar professionals "work in contexts that promote product decision making," (Hochstetler & Mackey, 2016, p. 163), theoretically their decisions could be swayed by the presence of law enforcement. Deterrence theory policy recommendations tend to focus on punishment to prevent crime, but other strategies can be employed to deter white-collar crime. For instance, ethical decision-making and moral education have been identified as strategies to limit white-collar crime (Jordanoska, 2018), as have ethics programs integrating training, enforcement, and support from leadership (Tomlinson & Pozzuto, 2016). In addition, leadership styles have been shown to deter workplace misconduct, with authoritarian leadership styles identified as more likely to deter misbehavior by employees (Zheng, Huang, Redman, Graham 2020). In a similar way, business practices are used to deter workplace crimes. As an illustration, Amazon reportedly publicized terminations due to theft on flat-screen televisions hung in warehouses. The name of the offender is not included, but the details surrounding the thefts are. The aim is to send a clear message to employees (Eidelson & Soper, 2016). At the same time, research suggests that it is important to find the right amount of control to exercise over employees because too much control has been found to potentially lead to certain types workplace deviance (Hunt & Topalli, 2019).

Rational choice theory, the modern variation of deterrence theory, considers the limits of human rationality while still considering humans as rational and suggests that offenders will consider the benefits of offending and weigh those benefits against possible negative consequences that arise from misconduct (Clarke & Cornish, 1985). Piquero et al. (2005) integrated rational choice theory with the idea of "desire for control" to explain how such a desire influences decision making that may lead to corporate offending. To test this premise, Piquero and her research team surveyed 13 business executives and 33 master of business administration (MBA) students. They found that desire for control was related to support for white-collar misconduct. From this finding, they suggested that corporate crime is committed to "gain control over environments that are uncertain or irrational" (p. 272). They also found a vicarious effect of internal reprimands. If coworkers were reprimanded, individuals were less likely to indicate intentions to engage in white-collar crime. In addition, they found that informal sanctions deterred intentions to offend, but formal sanction threats did not.

STRAIN THEORY AND WHITE-COLLAR CRIME

In general, **strain theory** focuses on the way stresses and strains contribute to offending. The source of strain varies across types of strain theories. Some theories point to the social and economic structures as the source of strain, others point to the individual, and others point to the organization. In terms of white-collar offending, three types of strain theories warrant discussion: classical strain theory, institutional anomie theory, and general strain theory.

Classical Strain Theory

Classical strain theory traces the source of strain to interactions between the social and economic structures. As a macrolevel theory, classical strain theory addresses how macrolevel variables influence individual behavior. Robert Merton (1938) developed his version of strain theory in "Social Structure and Anomie," a brief article published in *American Sociological Review*. Merton based this theory on four assumptions:

- Capitalism promotes financial success as a goal.

- Individuals are socialized to follow legitimate means such as working hard and getting an education to meet financial goals.

- Some individuals face barriers or strain in their efforts to attain financial success.

- When individuals experience strain, they change either the goals or the means to address the strain.

Merton's theory was developed to explain why poor individuals engage in crime, and this has led some to question whether the theory can be used to explain crimes by white-collar workers. The assumption of Merton's theory is that being unable to achieve economic success makes some individuals engage in illegitimate activities. White-collar workers have already achieved economic success. As Langton and Piquero (2007) wrote, "the basic focus on the stresses associated with being poor was incompatible with studies of white-collar crime" (p. 1). Despite this focus of Merton's theory, Langton and Piquero demonstrate how the theory can explain white-collar offending.

According to Merton, five modes of adaptation characterize how individuals adapt to the way goals and means are prescribed. **Conformists** accept the goals prescribed by society and follow legitimate means to attain the goals. Most white-collar professionals can be characterized as conformists. I am a conformist. I want material success, and I am awfully concerned about doing things the right way to attain it.

Innovators accept the goal of financial success but replace legitimate means with illegitimate means. Consider how embezzlers steal funds after experiencing strain caused by financial problems (Cressey, 1953; G. S. Green, 1990). Or consider how computer criminals find ways to get around the rules to attain material success. They maintain the goal of financial success but use illegitimate means to attain their goals. Interviews with 16 convicted white-collar offenders showed that some of the offenders attributed their misdeeds to the economic climate (Gill, 2011). In particular, when times were "bad," they said the likelihood of offending increased. In other words, they had to be innovators to deal with the "bad" times.

Ritualists are white-collar workers who do not accept the goals of society but go through the motions of engaging in the means prescribed by society. Companies that violate the law repeatedly and pay fines because the fines are seen as costs of doing business have been described as ritualists (Braithwaite, 1993). These companies go through the motions with regulators in a ritualistic way to make it seem as if they are playing by the rules, but in reality, they have no intention of actually following the rules.

Retreatists are white-collar workers who accept neither the goals of society nor the means to attain those goals. Merton noted that this is the least common adaptation. He wrote that retreatists are "*in* the society, but not *of* it" (1938, p. 677). To Merton, ritualists included those with drug and alcohol addictions. One could also suggest that workers who allow their drug and alcohol problems to influence their workplace activities are retreatists. Also, one could point to workers who show up for work but do not do any work as retreatists. They are "*in* the workplace," but they are not a part "*of* the workplace."

Rebels are workers who reject the goals and means of society and replace the societal-prescribed goals and means with their own goals and means. Recall the notion of collective embezzlement developed by Kitty Calavita and her coauthors (Calavita, Pontell, & Tillman, 1997). They described **collective embezzlement** as crime committed by the organization against the organization. Rather than focusing on success as the goal, workers developed failure as the goal so that the government insurance programs would bail out the failed business. As I have noted elsewhere, "those participating in collective embezzlement reject the standard goal of success, replace it with the goal of failure, and reject the legitimate ways to attain success" (Payne, 2003b, p. 45).

Merton's strain theory can be used to understand deviance by Olympic athletes, which, with a bit of a stretch, can be conceptualized as occupational deviance (Payne & Berg, 1999). Most Olympic athletes can be described as conformists—they want success, and they work hard in legitimate ways to attain success. Those who use performance-enhancing strategies like blood doping and the consumption of illegal substances can be seen as innovators. Ritualists would be those athletes who have little interest in winning or succeeding. Retreatists include former athletes who "drop out of organized sports to become 'beer-belly' softball players" (Payne & Berg, 1999, p. 139) or develop substance abuse problems. Rebels include athletes who defy the rules of the sport and replace the sport's rules with their own. Consider examples of "podium politics" where athletes make symbolic gestures while they are receiving their Olympic medals (Cardinal, 2010). Such gestures, prohibited by Olympic rules, are committed with the aim of meeting the athlete's own political or social goals (rather than the Olympic Games' apolitical and prosocial goals). In 1968, for example, gold medalist Tommie Smith and bronze medalist John Carlos were suspended from the U.S. Olympic team after they raised their fists on the Olympic podium to protest against racism.

Institutional Anomie Theory

Another variety of strain theory, **institutional anomie** theory, is a more modern macrolevel approach to explaining how societal institutions promote crime (Messner & Rosenfeld, 2007). In *Crime and the American Dream,* Steve Messner and Richard Rosenfeld describe how society promotes values related to financial success but fails to promote values consistent with using legitimate means to attain financial success. Culture, as it is described by the authors, affects societal institutions. Messner and Rosenfeld (2007) note that four values central to the American culture are a breeding ground for crime (see Table 12.1). First, the focus on achievement encourages Americans to always want more. Once we achieve a goal, new goals are developed. Second, universalism suggests that everyone should want material success, despite the fact that such a goal is unrealistic. Third, individualism suggests that we should be able to attain our financial goals on our own, which is also unrealistic. Fourth, materialism refers to the way that our society encourages us to be enamored of material goods and the acquisition of the best new products.

The underlying assumption of institutional anomie theory is that individuals are socialized to succeed at any cost, but not all individuals are (1) given the opportunities to succeed or (2) socialized in how to succeed in legitimate ways. Hence, anomie (e.g., normlessness) exists at the institutional level between the prescription of societal goals and legitimate means. The result of this anomie is unbridled aspirations to "get rich." According to one white-collar crime scholar, "regardless of their social background and social capital available to them, people are encouraged to desire more than they presently have" (Passas, 2001, p. 122). Describing these aspirations, one author team wrote,

Monetary success has no limit. There are always possibilities to acquire more. When money has inherent value as it does in America, and a person's "success" is measured in financial terms, there is also no limit to a person's status. American culture perpetuates these assumptions because to do so is productive to its advancement as a corporate nation. If American citizens become satiated with wealth at a certain level, American industry can move no further than this limit. (Trahan, Marquart, & Mullings, 2005, p. 606)

TABLE 12.1 ■ Values That Are Central to the American Dream		
Value	**What It Means**	**How It Relates to White-Collar Crime**
Achievement	Individuals are socialized to work hard and direct their efforts toward achieving financial goals. Once certain goals are achieved, new goals are developed.	Individuals keep working toward getting more and more. Eventually a fear of failure may cause some individuals to engage in wrongdoing in the workplace.
Universalism	All individuals are encouraged to strive for monetary success regardless of whether that is realistic.	As individuals move up the workplace ladder, advancement becomes more competitive. It is unrealistic to assume that everyone can be promoted. Individuals might engage in wrongdoing to increase their likelihood of advancement.
Individualism	Individuals are socialized to believe that they can succeed on their own.	Efforts to build careers on one's own can be stressful and counterproductive. Individuals might resort to wrongdoing to address the shortfalls of working alone.
Materialism	Individuals are socialized to want material goods.	The desire for better and new goods in order to "keep up with the neighbors" might cause individuals to engage in wrongdoing to have the finances needed to acquire the goods and services, and it may cause corporations to use shortcuts and provide products desired by the public but that are unsafe.

Messner and Rosenfeld's early editions of their work made little mention of white-collar crime, though they began their book with a description of Michael Milken's experiences as a white-collar offender. Schoepfer and Piquero (2006) point out that because institutional anomie theory "assumes that criminal activity relates to the pursuit of monetary success . . . white-collar crimes should not only be able to be explained under this theoretical framework, but also should expand the generalizability of the theory" (p. 228). In later editions, Messner and Rosenfeld (2007) added a significant amount of discussion about the way white-collar crime was tied to the American dream, and they began their book with a discussion of how the Enron scandal created a foundation for understanding institutional anomie theory. They also noted that "the same social forces that lead to higher levels of serious crime also produce the contrasting social responses to street crime and suite crime" (p. 32).

Schoepfer and Piquero (2006) tested institutional anomie theory through a consideration of embezzlement cases included in the FBI's *Uniform Crime Reports* in 1991. They used 1990 census data to determine how well structural variables related to institutional anomie predicted embezzlement cases in 1991. The researchers found some support for institutional anomie: More high school dropouts (a sign of increased anomie) meant more embezzlement, and more voters (a sign of decreased anomie) meant less embezzlement.

Theoretically, one might expect corporate offenses to increase during difficult economic times. A bad economy would theoretically be a source of strain or anomie for corporate institutions. No such relationship, however, has been found. In fact, "profit-oriented crimes by corporations occur during both recessions and times of economic euphoria" (Simpson & Rorie, 2016, p. 340). In other words, bad corporate actors are going to be bad regardless of the amount of strain or anomie in the economy.

General Strain Theory

Developing what is known as **general strain theory**, Robert Agnew (1985, 1992) used a social psychological approach to explain how crime is an adaptation to stress and frustration. Agnew highlighted three sources of strain that could lead to crime:

1. The failure to achieve positively valued goals

2. The removal or expected removal of positively valued stimuli

3. Confronting or expecting to confront negative stimuli

Agnew argued that stress leads to crime if the stress leads to negative affective states, such as anger.

First, the *failure to achieve positively valued goals* could lead to strain. In terms of white-collar crime, not being promoted, given raises, or paid fairly could result in offending. White-collar workers direct a great deal of effort toward meeting the organization's goals. If the organization meets its goals but the worker is not rewarded for his or her efforts in working toward those goals, strain occurs, and this strain could result in offending.

Second, *the removal or expected removal of positively valued stimuli* results in strain because individuals must confront losing something they find valuable. With regard to white-collar crime, individuals, who have invested so much in their careers and moved up the organizational ladder, might face stress maintaining their status. Donald Cressey's (1953) classic study of embezzling found that the embezzlers engaged in offending because they developed an "unshareable financial problem." In other words, they lost the amount of "positively valued stimuli" they needed to address their financial needs. Wheeler and his coauthors (Wheeler, Weisburd, & Bode, 1988) noted that the "fear of failing"—the fear of "losing what they have worked so hard to gain" (p. 356)—might lead these offenders to engage in misconduct. They also suggested that these types of offenders feel remorse (or "social pain") when they are caught.

Third, *confronting or expecting to confront negative stimuli* refers to instances where individuals confront negative events in their lives. Those who experience unpleasant work settings, for example, would be more prone to commit misconduct from this perspective (Van Wyk, Benson, & Harris, 2000). Surveys of 1,116 nursing home employees found that employees who reported being abused by patients were more likely to steal from patients and physically abuse them (Van Wyk et al., 2000). The authors found that motivations (confronting negative stimuli) were more important than opportunities because offenders would find or create the opportunities to commit the misconduct if they wanted to.

Langton and Piquero (2007) used data from the *Nature and Sanctions of White-Collar Criminals Study* (see Wheeler, Weisburd, & Bode, 2000) to assess the ties between strain and white-collar offending. They found that the presence of strain was related to financial motivations to offend. In addition, they found that types of strain experienced by white-collar offenders possibly vary across white-collar offenders by status. Lower status white-collar offenders might respond more to one type of strain while higher status white-collar offenders might respond more to other types of strain. For lower status offenders, financial motives seemed to be more likely types of strain. For white-collar offenders, like security violators, strain appeared to be linked more often to the fear of losing one's status. The authors compared this suggestion to Wheeler et al.'s (2000) conclusion that a "fear of failing in their professional careers" might lead some upper-status workers to engage in wrongdoing.

The role that "fear of failing" plays is somewhat complex. More recently, N. L. Piquero (2012) suggested that the impact the "fear of failing" has on an offender's intentions to offend may depend on situational factors. In particular, she noted that if offenders perceive negative consequences from the offense, the "fear of failing" may actually stop individuals from offending because the negative consequences would themselves be signs of failure.

LEARNING THEORY AND WHITE-COLLAR CRIME

Some criminologists have focused on the way that white-collar crime can be understood as learned behavior. The most prominent learning theory is **differential association theory**, which was developed by Edwin Sutherland. Differential association theory includes a series of nine propositions that describe how individuals learn criminal behavior. The general thrust of the theory is that individuals learn from their peers through a process in which they learn how to commit crimes, why to commit those crimes, and why laws restricting those crimes are inappropriate. An often-cited example of the way that Sutherland (1949) viewed his differential association theory as explaining crime in the workplace is the comment of a shoe salesman who said that his manager conveyed the following message to him when he was hired:

> My job is to move out shoes, and I hired you to assist in this. I am perfectly glad to fit a person with a pair of shoes if we have his size, but I am willing to misfit him if it is necessary in order to sell him a pair of shoes. I expect you to do the same. If you do not like this, someone else can have your job. While you are working for me, I expect you to have no scruples about how you sell shoes. (p. 238)

Although Sutherland created both the concept of white-collar crime and the differential association theory, few studies have tested the theory's ability to explain white-collar crime. In one of the few studies, Nicole Piquero and her colleagues (Piquero, Tibbetts, & Blankenship, 2005) used data from a survey of 133 MBA students to see whether the theory would explain students' decisions to market and produce a hypothetical drug that was about to be recalled (and respondents knew this about the drug). They found support for differential association. Decisions to market the drug even though it was going to be recalled were tied more to corporate climate and coworkers' attitudes and were not tied to connections with peers and friends outside the workplace. Put simply, if I am Bernie Madoff's coworker, I would be more likely to offend than if I were his friend or family member.

Learning theory is relevant in terms of the skills needed to commit white-collar offenses and the motives for offending. In terms of skills, many white-collar crimes involve "highly complex and technically skilled acts" (Robin, 1974, p. 259). Computer crimes, for example, often require a level of technological skills that many do not possess. Cases of embezzlement involving computers might require a similar level of skills. Physicians need certain skills to commit unnecessary surgery. Researchers need skills to fudge data. In essence, one needs the skill set required to do a job in order to commit crime on that job.

Learning theorists have suggested that in addition to learning the skills to commit white-collar crimes, white-collar offenders learn motives or reasons for committing crime on the job. Some researchers have examined how academic training influences attitudes supportive of white-collar offending. As an illustration, one author team surveyed 350 medical students to examine how the students perceived public health insurance programs and found that "the students viewed Medicare and Medicaid in the same unflattering light as physicians" (Keenan, Brown, Pontell, & Geis, 1985, p. 171). One third of the students attributed health care fraud to structural aspects of health care programs, and many students called for structural changes of the programs to improve the ability of doctors to deliver health care to impoverished groups. What this suggests is that the students had learned to attribute fraud to an external source even before they became practicing health care professionals.

In another study, a survey of 537 students compared MBA students to nonbusiness students and found that the business students "were more likely to be tolerant of business practices with ethical issues" (Yu & Zhang, 2006, p. 185). Business students tended to follow "a law-driven approach to business ethics," which suggests that "if it is legal, it is ethical" (p. 185). Somewhat ironically, the authors suggest that teaching business law classes may result in students becoming more accepting of unethical practices (e.g., if they learn that certain behaviors are technically legal, they would be more supportive of those behaviors regardless of whether the behaviors are ethical).

Learning theory has been criticized on a number of grounds. Some have questioned the source of learning: Whom did the first "white-collar criminal" learn the skills and motives from (see R. Martin, Mutchnick, & Austin, 1990)? Randy Martin and his colleagues (1990) also note that learning theory, differential association in particular, is difficult to test empirically. Researchers have found that the actual relevance of learning from coworkers is overstated. Research by Spahr and Alison (2004) on 481 fraud offenders found that most offenders worked alone, and when there were collaborators, the co-offenders tended to come from outside the white-collar offenders' workplace.

NEUTRALIZING AND JUSTIFYING WHITE-COLLAR CRIME

Neutralization theory was developed by Gresham Sykes and David Matza (see Matza, 1964; Sykes & Matza, 1957) in an effort to explain how juvenile delinquents drift in and out of delinquent behavior. They argued that juveniles understand right from wrong and that before they commit delinquent acts, they neutralize or rationalize their behavior as appropriate. Researchers have highlighted the difference between neutralization and accounts. Neutralizations occur before the criminal act and provide offenders the mental strength they need to commit the crime. Accounts are offered after the act and allow the offender to minimize the criminal label (Benson, 1985a). After an examination of how neutralizations are used to commit white-collar misconduct, attention will be given to the types of accounts offered by white-collar offenders to describe their behaviors and the purposes served by these accounts.

Neutralizations and White-Collar Offending

Sykes and Matza (1957) described five techniques of neutralization they believed juveniles used to rationalize their misconduct. Given that white-collar workers are rational beings, it is plausible that white-collar offenders use similar types of neutralizations. First, denial of injury refers to situations where offenders justify their actions on the grounds that no one was harmed or injured as a result of their misconduct. One study found that individuals neutralized the marketing of unsafe products by suggesting that the government overstates the degree of harm to consumers (Piquero et al., 2005).

Denial of victim refers to situations where the offenders convince themselves that victims deserve the harm they experience. As an illustration, Bernie Madoff told a fellow inmate about his misdeeds: "F*ck my victims. I carried them for 20 years and now I'm doing 150 years"

(Ruiz, 2010). In embezzlement cases, this denial arises when offenders convince themselves that "the victim mistreated the offender and deserved to be victimized, the money belonged to the offender anyway" (G. S. Green, 1993, p. 102).

Appeal to higher loyalties neutralizations occur when offenders justify their wrongdoing by suggesting that the misbehavior was done for the good of a larger group. Instances where white-collar offenders attribute their misdeeds to efforts to help their company make a profit are indicative of an appeal to a higher loyalty (Piquero, Tibbetts, & Blankenship, 2005). As another example, situations where prosecutors allow witnesses to lie on the grounds that the lie will help achieve justice can be seen as appeals to higher loyalties. In these cases, prosecutors possibly "neutralize misconduct because they believe they are prosecuting guilty defendants" (Schoenfeld, 2005, p. 258).

Denial of responsibility refers to situations where offenders neutralize their behaviors by suggesting that they are not responsible for their misconduct. An auto repair shop owner, for example, told a colleague: "You can't be honest in this business and make a decent living" (Seibel, 2009). In another example, an offender involved in a complex fraud told investigators,

> My mandate was to keep the bank running until a final solution to the financial problems is found. That was the mandate given to me by the president . . . when the security is involved . . . you do not always go by the rule of the book.
> (Passas, 2001, p. 130)

Condemnation of condemners is a neutralization where offenders blame the criminal justice and social control systems for their misdeeds. They argue that those who are persecuting them for their misdeeds also engage in wrongdoing. This rationalization is closely aligned with "claims that everyone does it" rationalizations. In addition, from their perspective, lenience would be a natural response from a system that is perceived to be run by individuals who engage in misconduct themselves. One offender convicted after defrauding victims in a $14 million commodities fraud scheme said that "he deserved mercy for helping fellow alcoholics like himself" ("Kingpin of Commodities Fraud," 2006).

Several studies have considered how different types of white-collar offenders justify their misdeeds with neutralizations. Paul Klenowski (2012) interviewed 40 convicted white-collar offenders (20 men and 20 women) and found that each offender offered at least one neutralization, with appeal to higher loyalties being the most commonly used neutralization. Other research shows that older individuals are more likely to neutralize their misconduct than younger workers are (Piquero, Tibbetts, & Blankenship, 2005). Research also shows that workers learn the types of rationalizations to use on the job from their coworkers (Dabney, 1995; Klenowski, 2012) or from family and friends (Klenowski, 2012). Incidentally, of the 40 white-collar offenders interviewed by Klenowski, just over one fourth of them learned their neutralizations on the job.

One team of researchers conducted an ethnographic study using participant observation, in-depth interviews, and survey methodologies to examine how speech therapists, occupational therapists, and physical therapists neutralized Medicaid fraud (Evans & Porche, 2005). Findings showed that "claims everyone else does it" were the most common neutralizations offered. Denials of responsibility and injury were the second and third most commonly used types of neutralization.

An ethnographic study of three private veterinary practices over a five-year time span focused on "ethical lapses" made by workers in this industry and the role of various neutralizations in promoting these misdeeds (Gauthier, 2001). The study found evidence of rationalizations paralleling those offered by Sykes and Matza (1957). For example, like a denial of responsibility, the defense of necessity was found to be "the primary justification invoked for professional lapses" (Gauthier, 2001, p. 475). This defense was frequently used to justify dishonest billing procedures. For instance, in one case, a veterinarian billed a client for euthanizing a dog when the dog had in fact died on its own. The vet wanted the dog owner to feel that the owner had made the decision to put the dog down.

Gauthier also found claims of "everyone else is doing it," particularly with regard to price fixing. The vets engaged in denial of injury, denial of victim, claims of entitlement, condemnation of condemners, and appeal to higher loyalties. In the latter case, Gauthier provides the example of billing for euthanizing a healthy animal when in fact the vet had put the pet up for adoption. Gauthier suggested this happened on at least a few occasions. In these cases, vets did not believe it was appropriate to put down a healthy animal, and their loyalty to animals led them to not euthanize the animal, even though they billed for it.

Some researchers have found that white-collar offenders' use of neutralizations does not vary from that of traditional offenders (Stadler & Benson, 2012). In addition, researchers have explored whether there are gender differences in the use of neutralizations by white-collar offenders. Results are somewhat mixed. Surveys of 133 MBA students asking about their intentions to offend for a hypothetical corporate crime found that denial of injury impacted men's intentions more than women's, while condemnation of condemners had a stronger influence on women's intentions to offend (Vieraitis, Piquero, Piquero, Tibbetts, & Blankenship, 2012). These relationships existed at the bivariate level but disappeared when other variables were entered into the equation. The authors concluded that "there were more similarities than differences found between men and women" (p. 487).

PHOTO 12.2 One study examined how veterinarians use neutralizations to engage in workplace offending.

Lori Iverson/USFWS

Others have suggested that there may be qualitative differences underlying the nature of the neutralization offered by men and women (Klenowski, Copes, & Mullins, 2011). For instance, research on the data collected by Klenowski showed that when offering appeals to higher loyalties, men tended to describe their need to fill a role of breadwinner, and females tended to use narratives describing a caregiver role. The accounts paralleled gendered expectations. Consider the following two appeals to higher loyalty from a man and woman respectively (Klenowski et al., 2011):

- I guess when I was committing my acts, I believed that maybe I was doing some of this for my family. I wanted to have the time and the financial security to be around my family to make sure I would be there for my children, so I guess family also subconsciously played into why I did what I did. It all boils down to power and greed and decisions you make in life, in my case, my family was part of my decision making for why I did what I did. (p. 55)

- Well what really happened is my two daughters when they were three and five years old in 1990, 1991 they were sexually abused by their father and I aligned myself with somebody that was able to pay my legal bills to fight for custody and to fight for justice in that regard so I guess I'm here because of what I did and I should be here but I don't think I should be here because of my motive. I feel like I was only doing what I had to do as a mother. (p. 59)

Another white-collar crime researcher examined how corporations use denials to explain or justify their behavior when accused of corporate wrongdoing. The researcher found that while the corporations used the same rationalizations that were found in prior research, they also used two additional "corporate techniques of neutralization"—denial of deviance and denial of cause (Whyte, 2016). The denial of deviance neutralization occurs when officials define the behavior as normal in the business practices. Denial of cause occurs when officials claim that the negative consequences experienced by victims cannot be attributed to the corporate behavior. These sorts of neutralizations, as well as the ones highlighted previously, help to explain why individuals who claim to have high morals occasionally break the law (Jordanoska, 2018).

Accounts and White-Collar Crime

While offenders use neutralizations to give them the mental fortitude to engage in wrongdoing, accounts are offered after the fact to describe their behaviors. An account is "a statement made by a social actor to explain unanticipated or untoward behavior" (Scott & Lyman, 1968, p. 46). Three types of accounts exist: denials, justifications, and excuses. Denials involve situations where offenders deny a specific aspect of the crime: They deny that they committed the crime, or they deny knowing anything about the crime. Types of denials attributed to white-collar offenders include the following:

- Denial of crime: Offenders say they did not commit the crime they are accused of.

- Denial of fact: Offenders deny specific aspects of the crime.

- Denial of awareness: Offenders indicate that they did not understand that their actions were violations of workplace rules.

- Denial of guilt: Offenders admit doing something but deny that the action was criminal (Payne, 2003b).

The denial of guilt may be particularly common among white-collar offenders. For example, former governor of Illinois Rod Blagojevich was convicted of using his position to "sell off" Barack Obama's senate seat, which he was charged with filling after Obama was elected president. Blagojevich never denied having conversations about filling the seat. He argued that his actions were "business as usual" in the political arena and that he was being persecuted. As another example, John Rigas, the former chairman of Adelphia Communications, was sentenced to 15 years in prison for fraudulent accounting practices. After his conviction, he maintained that his case was not "about fraud" (Cauley, 2007). He told a reporter, "because you know, there was no fraud. . . . It was a case of being in the wrong place at the wrong time. If this had happened a year before, there wouldn't have been any headlines" (Cauley, 2007, p. 1B).

Interviews with 30 white-collar offenders by Benson (1985a) focused on the types of denials offered by white-collar offenders for their misconduct. Within the context of "denying the guilty mind," Benson showed how different types of white-collar offenders used different denials that, on the surface, seemed to be tied to the nature of each occupation where the misdeeds occurred. Antitrust offenders, for example, told Benson about the "everyday character and historical continuity of their offenses" (p. 591). They described their actions as "blameless" and condemned prosecutors, while showing how their alleged crimes were not like street crime. Tax offenders, on the other hand, commonly made claims that everyone engages in the offenses. Those who committed financial trust violations were more likely to accept responsibility for their behavior. Fraud and false statement offenders denied "committing any crime at all," and suggested that prosecutors were politically motivated and inept. Because of the nature of fraud, Benson suggested that "defrauders are most prone to denying any crime at all" (p. 597). The nature of fraud is such that offenders lie to commit the crime. They continue to lie after the crime in an attempt to conceal their offending.

In contrast to denials where offenders reject responsibility for the act, justifications are "accounts in which one accepts responsibility for the act in question but denies the pejorative quality associated with it" (Scott & Lyman, 1968, p. 47). Types of justifications offered by white-collar offenders include the following:

- Denial of law: Professionals describe the law as unfair (Coleman, 1994).

- Defense of entitlement: Workers indicate that they are underpaid, overworked, and entitled to the funds.

- Borrowing: Workers say that they planned to return the money (Coleman, 1987).

- Metaphor of the ledger: Workers suggest that occasional wrongdoings are okay (Minor, 1981).

- Denial of wrongfulness: Offenders suggest that there was nothing wrong with their behavior (Payne, 2003b).

Excuses are different from justifications and denials. Scott and Lyman (1968) defined excuses as "socially approved vocabularies for mitigating or relieving responsibility" (p. 47). Examples of excuses Scott and Lyman described that are relevant to white-collar crime include appeal to accidents, appeal to defeasibility, and scapegoating. Appeal to accidents refers to excuses where offenders describe the outcome as an accident. The portrayal of the BP oil spill by BP executives and the way that OSHA violations are constructed as accidents are examples of the "appeal to accidents" excuse type.

Appeal to defeasibility includes situations where offenders deny intent, deny knowledge, or minimize the harm surrounding the offense. Consider a case where a white-collar offender said, "I would never have done this business if I wasn't told by my lawyers that it was legal. I didn't believe in my heart of hearts that I did anything wrong" ("Kingpin of Commodities Fraud," 2006). At his sentencing, Madoff tried to minimize his intent. He told the court: "When I began the Ponzi scheme, I believed it would end shortly and I would be able to extricate myself and my clients. But, that ended up being impossible" (Healy, 2009b, p. 1).

Scapegoating refers to excuses where white-collar offenders blame others for their wrongdoing. In some cases, for example, white-collar offenders blame their billing directors and administrative staff for wrongdoing. Also, cases where corporate executives blame lower level workers or "disgruntled" workers for corporate harm can be seen as examples of scapegoating.

Gibson (2000) discussed four types of excuses that workers make for workplace misconduct:

- "I was told to do it" (let's call this the authority excuse).

- "Everybody is doing it" (we can call this the institutional excuse).

- "My actions won't make a difference" (this can be called the minimization excuse).

- "It's not my problem" (the ostrich excuse) (p. 66).

Those who use the authority excuse might actually believe that their misconduct was the result of their being ordered by their boss to engage in the wrongful behavior. Gibson (2000) cites the power of authority as demonstrated in Stanly Milgram's *Obedience to Authority* study as an example of this power.

With regard to institutional excuses, Gibson (2000) notes that offenders know their actions are wrong, so they look around the workplace to find others who are engaging in similar acts. The minimization excuse parallels Sykes and Matza's (1957) denial of injury neutralization. Finally, the "ostrich" excuse refers to situations where workers ignore their coworkers' misdeeds because they believe that is not their responsibility to stop misconduct.

Purposes of Rationalizations and Accounts

Rationalizations and accounts serve four purposes for white-collar offenders (Payne, 2003b). First, given that white-collar offenders know right from wrong, rationalizing behavior allows them to engage in behavioral drifting: They can drift in and out of acceptable and unacceptable behavioral patterns (see Matza, 1964). Second, rationalizations and accounts promote intrinsic identity management, which simply means that they allow offenders to "maintain a positive self-image" (Payne, 2003b). Third, rationalizations and accounts promote extrinsic identity management, meaning that offenders are able to control that others see them in a positive way. Fourth, accounts allow offenders to try to minimize the types of sanctions given to them. In effect, by making excuses or using justifications, offenders can avoid punishment, reduce the sanction, and delay the sanction altogether (Payne, 2003b).

CONTROL THEORY AND WHITE-COLLAR CRIME

Control theory approaches the question of crime causation somewhat differently than other criminological theories. Rather than asking "why do people commit crime," the question from a control theory perspective is "why don't people commit crime" (Hirschi, 1969). Travis Hirschi (1969) answered this question in *Causes of Delinquency* by suggesting that individuals' bonds to society keep them from engaging in criminal behavior. According to Hirschi, four elements make up an individual's bond to society: attachment, belief, involvement, and commitment. Attachment refers to the degree of attachment that individuals have to their parents, schools, and other prosocial institutions. Belief refers to whether individuals believe in social rules and laws. Involvement refers to whether individuals are involved in prosocial activities, because those who are would have less time to commit criminal or delinquent acts. Commitment refers to whether individuals are committed to the values and goals prescribed by society. According to Hirschi, society is largely organized around conventional behavior, with supports and rewards given to promote conventional behavior. The theory is quite simple—the stronger an individual's societal bond is, the less likely the person will engage in criminal behavior; the weaker the bond, the more likely criminal behavior will follow. Hirschi's research confirmed his theory with the exception of his focus on involvement. He found that involvement in prosocial activities does not reduce likelihood of offending, possibly because it does not take that much time to commit a crime.

Finding that involvement in prosocial activities does not reduce criminal activities has direct implications for applying his theory to crime in the workplace. In particular, having a job is a prosocial activity, yet the fact that one has a job does not reduce the likelihood that one will commit a white-collar crime. In fact, the very definition of white-collar crime requires that individuals have jobs at which to commit crimes. Also, one does not have to be involved in a number of outside activities in order to keep from engaging in white-collar crime (Makkai & Braithwaite, 1991).

Lasley (1988) conducted surveys of 435 executives employed by a large multinational auto manufacturing company to consider how well Hirschi's control theory explained white-collar crime. He used Hirschi's theory to develop four "theorems of white-collar offending." These theorems included the following:

- Executives with stronger attachments to their company and coworkers will have lower workplace offending rates.

- Executives with stronger commitments to "lines of action" will have lower workplace offending rates.

- Executives with stronger involvement in corporate activities will be less likely to engage in white-collar crime.

- Executives who believe in workplace rules will be less likely to violate those rules.

The results of Lasley's (1988) study showed support for Hirschi's control theory. Executives with stronger (1) attachments to their corporation, (2) commitment to "corporate lines of action," (3) stronger involvement in corporate activities, and (4) stronger belief in organizational rules were less likely to commit white-collar crime. Lasley emphasized the importance of attachment to one's organization (or the lack of attachment) as being problematic for organizations.

Mixed support exists regarding the application of control theory to white-collar crime. One study found that white-collar offenders have stronger social bonds to society, as is evidenced through participation in religious activities and membership in community organizations (Benson & Kerley, 2001). Another study of a sample of convicted white-collar offenders found that higher rates of capital (defined by social, personal, and employment capital) translates into lower rates of offending (Piquero, Piquero, & Weisburd, 2016). While some research shows support for control theory, other studies raise questions about the theory's applicability to the topic. To some, bonds to a company might actually promote lawbreaking rather than inhibit it. This would be particularly likely in cases where individuals commit crime on behalf of their business. Some regard loyalty as central to corporate decision making. According to Robinson and Murphy (2009), "the reason loyalty is so important . . . is simple: loyalty means moving up in the corporate organization; disloyalty means failing" (p. 63).

SELF-CONTROL THEORY AND WHITE-COLLAR CRIME

Self-control theory was created by Michael Gottfredson and Travis Hirschi (1990), who argued in *A General Theory of Crime* that all types of crime were caused by the presence of low self-control. Self-control was described by the theorists as "the individual characteristic relevant to the commission of criminal acts" (p. 88). They characterized individuals with low self-control as "impulsive, insensitive, physical (as opposed to mental), risk-taking, short-sighted, and non-verbal" (p. 90). According to Gottfredson and Hirschi (1990), self-control levels are tied to parenting, with bad parenting resulting in low self-control, and levels of self-control are stable throughout one's life after early childhood.

The authors put a great deal of effort into arguing that their theory explains white-collar crime and street crime, and they critiqued white-collar crime theories for being narrow in scope (see Hirschi & Gottfredson, 1987). In their first effort to describe how their general theory of crime explained white-collar crime, the authors used the concept of "criminality" to describe what is now known as self-control. They wrote that,

> criminality is the tendency of individuals to pursue short-term gratification with little consideration for the long-term consequences of their act. . . . People high on this tendency are relatively unable or unwilling to delay gratification; they are relatively indifferent to punishment and to the interests of others. (Hirschi & Gottfredson, 1987, p. 960)

As evidence of the ties between criminality and white-collar crime, and their suggestion that white-collar crime and street crime are caused by criminality, Hirschi and Gottfredson compared arrest data for fraud and embezzlement with murder arrests. They suggested that similar age distributions for offenders across offense types showed evidence for a general theory, with their premise being that "a major correlate of ordinary crime is similarly correlated with white-collar crime" (Hirschi & Gottfredson, 1987, p. 966). They also compared gender and race data for the three offense types and found that arrest rates were similar across the offenses.

Hirschi and Gottfredson (1987) were extremely critical of white-collar crime theories that explained the behavior by focusing on the nature of the occupation rather than the characteristics of the individual offender. They argued that focusing on motives and opportunities limited to the workplace "confuse[s] social location with social causation" (p. 971). In their view, the cause of white-collar crime lies within the individual: Those with low self-control should be more prone to engage in white-collar misconduct. They also suggested that when low self-control interacts with opportunity, misconduct results (Gottfredson & Hirschi, 1990).

Several different studies have examined the utility of self-control theory in explaining various forms of occupational misconduct. Some of these studies offer support for self-control theory's applicability to white-collar crime. For example, one study found that low self-control of corporate managers was tied to corporate crime (Mon, 2002). As well, a study of 522 "fraud" and "force" offenders examined the self-control levels of the offenders and found that lower levels of self-control were more likely among those who committed more offenses (Longshore & Turner, 1998). The authors of this study found an important distinction between the two offense types: self-control was tied to fraud by the presence of criminal opportunity, but opportunity was not a factor in force crimes. In another study, surveys of 342 undergraduates revealed that the tie between low self-control and digital piracy was mediated by learning theory (Higgins, Fell, & Wilson, 2006). The authors suggested that those with low self-control must learn how to commit white-collar crimes, and they must also be presented with opportunities to offend.

Alternatively, research by Grasmick, Tittle, Bursik, and Arneklev (1993) found that self-control predicted fraud, but the presence of opportunity had independent effects on fraud. They noted that opportunity is tied to social structure and that their findings "direct attention back toward features of the social environment that influence the number and distribution of criminal opportunities" (p. 24). The authors suggested that researchers look more closely at motivations and cautioned not to assume that motivations are the same for all low self-control offenders.

In addition to being linked to offending, low self-control has been described as "a powerful predictor of victimization" (Holtfreter, Reising, & Pratt, 2008, p. 208). In terms of white-collar crime victimization, a study of 922 Florida residents by Holtfreter and her colleagues found that low self-control increases consumers' risks of fraud victimization (Holtfreter et al., 2008). The authors explained that "individuals who lack self-control tend to make impulsive decisions that are associated with negative life outcomes" (Holtfreter et al., 2008, p. 207). Another study found that some types of cybercrime victimization (cyber harassment, computer viruses, and stolen passwords) are tied to a low self-control among victims (Holt & Bossler, 2012).

Some studies offer mixed support for using self-control theory to explain white-collar crime. Benson and Moore (1992) analyzed presentence reports to compare 2,462 convicted white-collar offenders to 1,986 convicted conventional offenders, all of whom were convicted in federal court between 1973 and 1978. Addressing Gottfredson and Hirschi's (1990) assumption that white-collar offenders and conventional offenders share similar characteristics, Benson and Moore uncovered several differences between the two types of offenders. For instance, white-collar offenders exhibited fewer past problems in school and less excessive drinking. However, they found that white-collar offenders with more extensive criminal histories were, in fact, similar to conventional offenders.

Based on their findings, Benson and Moore (1992) suggested that self-control operates differently based on circumstances and situational factors. First, some occupational offenders with low self-control levels engage in misconduct just as conventional offenders do. These offenders commit criminal and delinquent acts somewhat frequently in the workplace. Second, high self-control offenders commit white-collar crime in order to meet organizational-economic goals that arise from our culture of competition. Third, opportunistic self-control offenders engage in misconduct as a result of personal situations (like unshareable financial problems) and do so only when opportunities are presented. Benson and Moore (1992) described this group of offenders in the following way: "If their positions in life are somehow threatened, a formerly adequate level of self-control may become inadequate and criminal opportunities that once were resisted are now accepted" (p. 257).

At least a handful of studies have found limited, if any, support for using self-control theory to explain various types of white-collar crime. One study found that the impact of self-control is moderated by morality, suggesting that individuals with high morality are less likely to offend regardless of their self-control level (Craig, 2019). Another study found that intentions to engage in white-collar misconduct were explained by unsocialized sensation thinking, which includes traits related to boredom susceptibility, experience seeking, and disinhibition; sensation thinking was found to be independent from self-control (Craig & Piquero, 2017). In addition, research shows that the theory does not explain corporate offending (Simpson & Piquero, 2002). In another study, N. L. Piquero and her coauthors (Piquero, Schoepfer, & Langton, 2010) surveyed 87 working adults enrolled in business courses using a vignette survey to determine how well self-control and desire for control explained "intentions to destroy damaging workplace documents" (p. 640). While they found that desire for control predicted intentions to offend, they also found that self-control level was not a significant predictor of offending intentions. They suggested that "self-control offers little by way of helping criminologists better understand corporate offending" (p. 642).

More recently, Schoepfer and her coauthors (Schoepfer, Piquero, N. L., & Langton, 2014) found that the desire for control—in comparison to low self-control— is a stronger predictor of corporate and white-collar crime but not traditional crime. They also found that those who have a high self-control also tended to have a high desire for control. Based on this, the authors suggest that the way that self-control interacts with other variables (such as desire for control) may be a stronger predictor of white-collar crime.

Several criticisms have been cited regarding the theory's application to white-collar crime. In general, these criticisms can be classified as conceptualization issues, empirical concerns, and problems with logical consistency. With regard to conceptualization issues, scholars have noted that Gottfredson and Hirschi conceptualize crime as an irrational act, though white-collar crime is generally rational behavior (Simpson & Piquero, 2002). Also, Gottfredson and Hirschi have been critiqued for oversimplifying the complex nature of white-collar crime in their efforts to conceptualize the relationship between self-control and workplace offending (Geis, 2000; Simpson & Piquero, 2002). Criminologist Gilbert Geis (2000) noted the complexities of explaining white-collar crime and highlighted the fact that many workplace decisions are driven by complex organizational processes and structural factors. He said, "to say an absence of self-control prods the decisions of top-level business officers who violate the law is to trivialize the roots of their actions" (p. 44).

Empirical criticisms of Gottfredson and Hirschi's efforts to explain white-collar crime as based on self-control centered on the way that the authors operationalized white-collar offending (Geis, 2000; G. E. Reed & Yeager, 1996). In particular, their reliance on arrest data and their focus on the offenses of fraud and embezzlement were seen as both narrowly and ambiguously defining white-collar crime. Their empirical effort was regarded as narrow because it focused only on arrests (excluding acts that did not result in arrests) for two specific types of offenses. Their effort was also seen as ambiguous because many offenders arrested for these crimes were likely not actually white-collar offenders.

Self-control theory's application to white-collar crime has been criticized on the grounds of logical consistency. In effect, it is illogical to some to suggest that white-collar crime can be caused by low self-control because most white-collar workers would not achieve their levels of status unless they possessed high self-control (Piquero, Exum, & Simpson, 2005; Spahr & Alison, 2004). Employees higher up in the workplace theoretically should have higher levels of self-control and more job stability, and they tend to be older than conventional offenders described by Gottfredson and Hirschi (Spahr & Alison, 2004). In other words, white-collar offenders are different from conventional offenders.

Gottfredson and Hirschi (1990) addressed the issue of whether executives have high levels of self-control by critiquing white-collar crime studies. They noted that their theory would not predict a great deal of offending by white-collar employees because they recognized that most white-collar employees need a high level of self-control to ascend the workplace ladder. They suggested that some white-collar crime authors misinterpret statistics and exaggerate the extent of the problem to make white-collar crime seem more prevalent than it actually is. They also follow a strictly "legal" approach in defining white-collar crime.

ROUTINE ACTIVITIES THEORY AND WHITE-COLLAR CRIME

Routine activities theory was developed by L. E. Cohen and Felson (1979) as a structural theory to explain how different societal changes work together to impact crime rates. In particular, the theorists contended that crime occurs when the following three elements exist at the same time and place: (1) the presence of motivated offenders, (2) the absence of capable guardians, and (3) the availability of suitable targets. As an example of their theory, they described how changes in the 1960s involving more televisions in homes (as a result of technological influences) and fewer individuals at home during the day (as a result of more women entering careers) resulted in an increase in burglaries by motivated offenders.

Various features of different types of white-collar crime discussed earlier in this text can be understood through an application of routine activities theory. Consider, for example, the following:

- A decrease in the number of workers in retail settings means that more workers are working alone in retail jobs. This means that there will not be as many capable guardians available to keep the workers from engaging in misconduct.

- The number of individuals injured in the workplace decreased significantly between 2007 and 2010. This decrease is potentially attributed to fewer individuals in manufacturing jobs. This means that there are fewer vulnerable targets for workplace injuries.

- With a downturn in the economy, businesses have been forced to become more competitive. This may mean that some businesses are more motivated to engage in such wrongdoing as false advertising or price fixing.

The theory is particularly useful for analyzing specific occupational situations to determine the likelihood of workplace crime. For example, experts have noted that the "presence of other employees close by is assumed to act as a form of guardianship" (Van Wyk et al., 2000, p. 35). In addition, research has shown that higher rates of unemployment are tied to lower rates of embezzlement (suggesting there are fewer motivated offenders available to embezzle when fewer individuals are employed) (Schoepfer & Piquero, 2006). Also, researchers have noted that consumers who engage in certain types of risky behaviors (like remote buying on the phone or Internet) are more at risk for fraud victimization (Holtfreter et al., 2008). Another study found that the types of activities businesses are engaged in along with the presence of guardianship is connected to white-collar cybercrime (Williams, Levi, Burnap, & Gundur, 2019). The value of these research findings is that they provide information that can be used to target opportunity structures that can reduce or prevent crime. At the same time, behaviors of policy makers, regulators, and law enforcement might increase opportunities for crime (Madensen, 2016).

Scholars have used the theory as a guide to determining how vulnerable different groups are for white-collar victimization and which strategies to use to reduce vulnerability (either by developing capable guardians or limiting the presence of motivated offenders). For example, several researchers have suggested that elderly persons are more likely to be vulnerable targets or "attractive targets for consumer fraud" (Braithwaite, 1991, citing research by Fattah & Sacco, 1989). A study of medical fraud found that the vast majority of the fraudulent acts were "directed at elderly persons, regardless of whether they were receiving therapy in nursing homes, hospitals, or through home health agencies" (Evans & Porche, 2005, p. 266). Evans and Porche (2005) went on to state, "this population seemed to be viewed as the ideal population to defraud," primarily because they are seen as unlikely to report fraud.

PHOTO 12.3 Older persons are believed to be more vulnerable to fraud than younger persons.

CONFLICT THEORY AND WHITE-COLLAR CRIME

Conflict theorists explain white-collar crime from a more critical perspective, focusing on the way that those with power exert influence in order to use the law as an instrument of power. Several different types of conflict theory exist, including but not limited to Marxist conflict theory, conservative conflict theory, radical conflict theory, anarchist criminology, left realist theory, feminist criminology, critical criminological theory, and peacemaking criminology (Bohm & Vogel, 2011; F. P. Williams & McShane, 2008). These theories tend to be macrolevel theories, focusing on the way institutional forces (controlled by those with power) shape wrongdoing. While various themes are presented with these different types of conflict theories, one common theme is an assumption that power differences between classes (upper vs. lower) result in differential treatment of those without power.

Richard Quinney's *The Social Reality of Crime* (1974) is a classic work that accurately shows how class differences potentially result in differential applications of the law. In this work, Quinney outlines six propositions that demonstrate how the powerful classes exert their power to define behaviors as criminal. These propositions are as follows:

Proposition 1: Definition of crime: Crime is a definition of human conduct that is created by authorized agents in a politically organized society.

Proposition 2: Formulation of criminal definitions: Criminal definitions describe behaviors that conflict with the interests of the segments of society that have the power to shape public policy.

Proposition 3: Application of criminal definitions: Criminal definitions are applied by the segments of society that have the power to shape the enforcement and administration of criminal law.

Proposition 4: Development of behavior patterns in relation to criminal definitions: Behavior patterns are structured in segmentally organized society in relation to criminal definitions, and in this context persons engage in actions that have relative probabilities of being defined as criminal.

Proposition 5: Construction of criminal conceptions: Conceptions of crime are constructed and diffused in the segments of society by various means of communication.

Proposition 6: The social reality of crime: The social reality of crime is constructed by the formulation and application of criminal definitions, the development of behavior patterns related to criminal definitions, and the construction of criminal conceptions (Quinney, 1974, pp. 15–23, as cited in R. Martin et al., 1990, pp. 389–390).

Quinney's (1974) thesis is that powerful classes use the law to exert influence over less powerful classes. In particular, the way law is developed, enforced, and applied is seen as a tool for increasing the amount of power that controlling groups have over minority groups. This assumption parallels many aspects of white-collar crime. Consider that many types of white-collar offending are not typically defined as criminally illegal. Doctors, for example, do not go to jail for making medical errors. Corporate executives are not sent to prison for creating unsafe products. Environmental pollution is defined as a cost of doing business, and those exposed to the pollutants are defined as unfortunate but are not defined as crime victims. As criminologist Ronald Kramer and his colleagues (Kramer, Michalowski, & Kauzlarich, 2002) note, "the social process of naming crime is significantly shaped by those who enjoy the economic and political power to ensure that the naming of crime . . . will reflect . . . their worldview and interests" (p. 266).

Conflict theorists are concerned not only with how crime is defined but also with how crime is perceived and addressed by criminal justice officials. With regard to perceptions about crime, conflict theorists would draw attention to the misguided perception that white-collar offenders are less serious offenders than conventional offenders. For example, some criminal justice officials have justified shorter prison sentences for white-collar offenders in the following two ways: (1) "Prison is much harder" on white-collar offenders than it is on conventional offenders, and (2) "it is not class bias to consider prison a greater hardship for the middle class because the loss of reputation is very serious" (Pollack & Smith, 1983, p. 178). To conflict theorists, such perceptions are inaccurate, unfair, and reflective of the influence that powerful classes have over those that are less powerful.

In a similar way, conflict theorists are critical of the criminal justice system's response to white-collar offending. Some criticize the system for punishing white-collar offenders too leniently, though it will be shown in a later chapter that convicted white-collar offenders may not be receiving sentences as lenient as believed. Others point out that most white-collar offenders commit a "prison escape" by preventing their cases from being brought into the criminal justice system in the first place (Gerber, 1994). Conflict theorists also point out that the overemphasis on street crimes (like the war on drugs) and lack of emphasis on white-collar crimes are indicative of unfair treatment of less powerful groups. They further stress that large companies control how laws are made, how businesses are regulated, and the amount of resources devoted to battling different types of crime (Bittle, 2020; Pontell, Black, & Geis, 2014).

The notions of regulation and deregulation, topics ignored by mainstream criminologists, are particularly relevant (Friedrichs, 2019). By ignoring the topic, deregulation becomes more like an economic and political decision rather than a legal decision. Hence, the Trump administration's calls for deregulation of federal policies were justified by supporters on economic and political grounds. One author team observes that deregulation is not "withdrawal of power" on the part of the government (Wonders and Danner, 2020, p. 104). Instead, deregulation is a transfer of power from the government to the corporation. Another way to think about it is that deregulation is, in effect, legalization. So, when rules and policies that prohibited certain types of behaviors are relaxed, those behaviors (for example, certain types of pollution) become "legal." To conflict theories, the basic point is that definitions matter, and, as a society, we allow those who have corporate power to decide how to define and respond to white-collar crime.

EXPLAINING CORPORATE CRIME

Thus far, the discussion of theories has focused primarily on explaining individual behavior in white-collar crimes. Recall from the discussion in the corporate crime chapter that, in some cases, the crime is committed either by the organization or for the good of the organization. The nature of corporate crime is such that individual-level variables may not sufficiently explain the misconduct. As a result, several theorists have devoted specific attention to explaining corporate crime. One thing is clear from these efforts—while it is difficult to explain individual behavior, it may be even more difficult to explain corporate behavior (Albanese, 1984). Describing the conceptual roadblocks that arise when trying to explain corporate crime, Tillman and Pontell (1995) said that organizations "have a dual nature." They explained organizations this way: "They both structure and constrain action by providing a context in which decisions are made, while at the same time existing as resources to be used by individual actors or groups to further their interests" (p. 1459).

Punch (2008) suggested that the "corporate setting provides MOM—motive, opportunity, and means." He described motives as including power, growth, profit, and so on. He said that the opportunity for offending occurs in boardrooms and executive offices that are not policed. The means for offending refers to the strategies employers use to carry out corporate offending. While Punch provides a simple framework for explaining corporate crime, the nature of the offending is so complex that identifying precise predictors of the behavior is not a simple task. In general, explanations of corporate crime have focused on (1) the structure of the organization, (2) organizational processes, and (3) dynamic organizational explanations.

Organizational Structure and Corporate Crime

Some theorists have noted how variables related to an organization's structure are also related to corporate crime. For example, Tillman and Pontell (1995) suggested that corporate crime is more often found in larger organizations, organizations growing quickly, and organizations with complex ownership structures. Other authors have also suggested that size and complexity influence corporate crime (Punch, 2008). One author suggested that corporate crime is more likely in larger organizations because larger businesses (1) see penalties as a cost of doing business and (2) are more resistant to any stigma that arises from misconduct (Yeager, 1986).

Organizational Processes and Corporate Crime

Theorists have also described the way that organizational processes influence wrongdoing. From this orientation, one can consider the definition of corporation offered by Ermann and Lundman (2002): "Organizations are collections of positions that powerfully influence the work-related thoughts and actions of the replaceable people who occupy positions in them" (p. 6). The notion of "replaceable people" is particularly important. Coleman (1982) described the "irrelevance of persons," writing that "persons have become, in a sense, that [which] was never before true, incidental to a large fraction of the productive activity in society" (p. 26).

Corporations have goals, and rules are assigned that prescribe behaviors corporate actors are expected to follow in their efforts to attain corporate goals. Although goals and rules are prescribed, there is evidence that pressure from the top of an organization may encourage wrongdoing by employees. Describing this top-down pressure, it has been suggested that "organizations, like fish, rot from the head down" (Jenkins & Braithwaite, 1993, p. 220). Others use the phrase "tone at the top" to demonstrate how corporate leaders foster misconduct (Diehl and Batsford, 2019). Another way to suggest it is that those with power influence "replaceable people" to engage in misconduct so that they, the replaceable people, do not become *replaced*. Simpson and Piquero (2002) note that "when employees are ordered to do something by a supervisor, most will do what is expected of them because they are only partial moral agents, limited in their responsibility and liability" (p. 537).

Figure 12.1 shows the cycle of corporate crime following a process-oriented explanation of corporate crime. Employees learn rules of what is expected in their corporation. In some cases, organizational rules may come into conflict with societal laws. The employees' behaviors, because the employees are replaceable, may break societal laws to further the organization's goals. Employees are rewarded for helping the organization move toward its goals. If they are caught breaking the rules, they may be fired. In such cases, new employees are hired into the position (after all, employees are replaceable people), and the cycle begins anew.

Dynamic Organizational Explanations and Corporate Crime

Dynamic organizational theories explore the links among societal factors, organizational processes, and individual motivation. These approaches recognize the limited nature of other organizational theories in explaining corporate crime. Simpson and Piquero (2002) called for an integration of organizational theories in order to develop stronger explanations of corporate misconduct. They theorized that less successful firms might engage in misconduct in order to become more successful; however, individuals in those firms must accept and conduct wrongdoing in order for misconduct to occur. Based on this, they call for the integration of macro- and microlevel theories and develop their own organizational contingency theory to "explain the circumstances and conditions under which corporate crime is likely" (p. 515). In line with this thinking, Simpson and Koper (1997) demonstrated how both external (political changes, market pressures, competition levels, legal changes) and internal dynamics (changes in organizational management) potentially influence corporate wrongdoing.

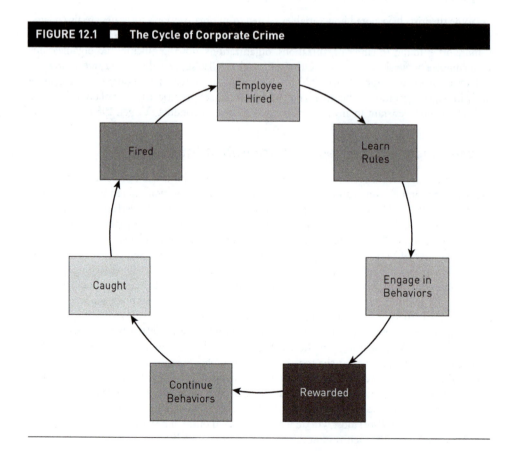

FIGURE 12.1 ■ The Cycle of Corporate Crime

Simpson and Piquero (2002) conducted a factorial survey with 96 students to examine the impact of organizational factors and self-control on attitudes about offending. They found that self-control and organizational factors (e.g., corporate offending propensity) were not tied together; however, they also found that "variables consistent with an integrated materialistic and cultural organizational theory predicted managers' offending intentions" (p. 309). They found additional support for integrating macro- and microlevel explanations. Managers were more likely "to offend if they perceived career benefits," and concerns about job security kept some from offending. They summarized their findings as follows:

> Offending is more likely when companies are not doing well economically and when illegality is apt to garner significant financial gains for the firm. . . . Managers who believed their illegal act would negatively affect the firm's reputation were significantly less willing to offend. (p. 536)

Diane Vaughan (1992) has also noted the importance of bringing together the micro- and macrolevels to explain corporate offending. According to Vaughan, "the link between individual choice and the structural determinants of those choices is paramount to understanding misconduct both in and by organizations" (p. 134). Vaughan's theory of organizational offending uses Merton's theory as a framework to link together individual and institutional motivations. According to Vaughan, three features of the interactions between individuals and the organizations where they work promote crime in the organization:

- A competitive environment generating pressures for organizational law violations

- Organizational characteristics, including processes that provide opportunities for offending

- A relationship with regulators that minimizes the likelihood of detection and prosecution

When these elements are present in an organization, the likelihood of corporate misconduct increases. If a corporation, for example, places a great deal of pressure on its employees and there is little likelihood that regulators will catch employees breaking rules for the good of the organization, then employees will be more prone to commit wrongful acts.

THEORIES IGNORED IN THE WHITE-COLLAR CRIME LITERATURE

At least a handful of criminological theories have received very little, if any, attention in white-collar crime studies. This is unfortunate because the strength of these "ignored" theories can be assessed by determining whether the theories explain white-collar crime, and our understanding about white-collar crime could be advanced through an application of different theories to the behavior. Theories that warrant more attention in the white-collar crime literature include the following:

- Life course theory

- Social disorganization theory

- Gender theories

- Labeling theory

- Biological theories

Life Course Theories and White-Collar Crime

Life course theory uses a social psychological orientation to identify how events early in one's life course shape experiences later in one's life (Payne & Gainey, 2009). The theory is regularly used to explain violence, with a great deal of research showing that many, but not all, individuals who have violent childhoods also have violent adulthoods. As Michael Benson and Kent Kerley (2001) note, white-collar crime researchers have not used life course theory to address white-collar crime, and life course theorists have not used white-collar crime to test the theory. Part of the reason for this lack of research is that it is more difficult to apply life course theory to white-collar crime than it is to apply other theories (Benson, 2016; Piquero & Piquero, 2016). Benson and Kerley (2001) note that such a gap between the two areas of research is problematic because of research showing relatively lengthy criminal histories among many white-collar offenders and evidence that white-collar offenders do not fit "the stereotypical image of the white-collar offender as a person who comes from the privileged sectors of society" (p. 121). In other words, a need exists to consider the past lives of white-collar offenders in order to understand how past experiences influenced decision making in offending.

To address this obvious gap in the white-collar crime literature, Benson and Kerley (2001) compared the life histories of a sample of convicted conventional offenders with a sample of convicted white-collar offenders. The authors culled data from the presentence investigation reports of offenders convicted in eight federal districts between 1973 and 1978. Their analysis showed that the life histories of white-collar and conventional offenders were different. White-collar offenders were much more likely to come from intact families and less likely to have problems in school. They were more likely to be involved in prosocial activities, had fewer prior arrests, and were older when their criminal careers began.

Benson and Kerley (2001) point to the need to consider how turning points later in life contribute to white-collar offending. Possible turning points they identify include dire family consequences, stressors related to occupational dynamics, and changes in business revenues. In addition to calling for more attention being directed toward the causes and consequences of white-collar crime for individual offenders, the authors suggest that white-collar crime be examined "as a social event in the life course" (p. 134).

Piquero and Benson (2004) described the need to expand the use of life course theory to address white-collar crime. They highlighted the differences between white-collar and conventional offenders, and also the similarities, to provide a framework that future researchers could use to address white-collar crime from a life-course perspective. As Piquero and Benson (2004) pointed out, "we simply need more information about the life histories of white-collar offenders" (p. 160).

In an effort to fill this void, R. G. Morris and El Sayed (2013) used longitudinal data over a 16-year time frame from the National Youth Survey Family Study in order to identify white-collar crime patterns over the life course. In general, the authors identified three patterns of white-collar offending: intermittency, periodic amplified offending, and persistent offending. They found that intermittency was a particularly common characteristic with rates of offending going up and down over time.

One researcher posits that "adult white-collar criminals developed their techniques of deception early in their lives" (Singer, 2016, p. 218). Singer uses the phrase "white-collar delinquency" to refer to workplace misconduct committed by young people and suggests that a connection may exist between the way individuals behave in the workplace when they are younger and when they are older. At its core, it's a simple question: If someone steals from work as a 16-year-old, are they more likely to steal from work when they are older? The answer to the question needs to be addressed in future research. Singer (2016) calls for more biographical research on the adolescent experiences of white-collar criminals to shed some light on the developmental experiences of those offenders.

The late onset of offending for many offenders and the lack of a clear criminal trajectory have been highlighted as inconsistent with life course theory, though the impact of turning points (e.g., business problems, financial issues, exposure to leadership cultures) helps to identify specific triggers for white-collar offenders (Piquero & Piquero, 2016). As Piquero and Piquero (2016) point out, focusing on the way these triggers vary between white-collar crime and traditional offenders through a life course lens provides valuable insight into white-collar behavior. If white-collar and blue-collar workers face comparable problems later in the life course, do they respond differently? Answering this, and related questions, would provide valuable insight into life course theory and white-collar crime.

Social Disorganization Theory and White-Collar Crime

Social disorganization theory suggests that a neighborhood's crime rate is shaped by the ability of its members to agree on and work toward a common goal, such as crime control. The ability of a neighborhood to be organized is predicted to be determined by neighborhood structural characteristics, in particular the mobility of its population, racial and ethnic heterogeneity, and poverty. Thus, neighborhoods that are less able to agree to work together toward controlling criminal behavior tend to have the following in common: A large percentage of the residents do not stay very long (a mobile population), residents are a diverse mix from different racial and ethnic origins, and many of the residents are poor. Many studies have found strong support for the idea that social disorganization breeds street crime.

At least one study used social disorganization theory to assess the factors that business owners take into account when deciding which types of crime prevention tools to use (Casten & Payne, 2008). Not surprisingly, business owners consider neighborhood factors in deciding how to develop loss-prevention strategies.

Another study applying social disorganization theory to white-collar crime examined mortgage fraud's distribution across Chicago (Ranson, Arnio, & Baumer, 2019). Findings supported the tenets of social disorganization theory, and the authors identified a connection between neighborhood structural factors and mortgage fraud. Criminologists use the phrase "disadvantaged neighborhoods" to describe those neighborhoods with high levels of poverty. Disadvantaged neighborhoods, which have fewer government sponsored agencies available to promote safer lending practices, had a higher level of subprime lending practices. The authors of the study attribute the higher estimates of mortgage fraud in disadvantaged neighborhoods to the lack of formal public control mechanisms in those disadvantaged communities (Ranson et al., 2019).

What is not clear is whether social disorganization contributes to white-collar crime. Such a question could be addressed several different ways. For example, it would be useful to identify whether retail settings in disadvantaged areas have more employee theft than retail settings in more advantaged areas. In addition, it would be interesting to determine whether corporations located in disadvantaged areas have different rates of regulatory violations than corporations located in nondisadvantaged areas. As well, more research needs to be done on the way white-collar crime promotes social disorganization in disadvantaged communities. It seems as though the application of social disorganization theory to white-collar crime is an area ripe for empirical efforts.

Gender Theories and White-Collar Crime

Gender theories are also underrepresented in the white-collar crime literature. These theories call attention to the need to consider crime from the perspective of women (M. J. E. Danner, 1998). In "Three Strikes and It's *Women* Who Are Out: The Hidden Consequences for Women of Criminal Justice Policy Reforms," Mona Danner outlines the way that laws such as three strikes policies negatively impact women. Similar questions arise with regard to white-collar crime theories and policies: (1) How do white-collar crime policies impact women? (2) Do patri-archal values contribute to white-collar crime? (3) Are women disproportionately victims of certain types of white-collar crime? and (4) How can the feminist perspective promote under-standing about white-collar crime?

Research by Kathleen Daly (1989) shows that theories used to explain women's involve-ment in white-collar crime may need to be different from those traditionally used to explain men's involvement in workplace offending. Reviewing data from Wheeler et al.'s data set of white-collar offenders, Daly found significant differences between male and female white-collar criminals. She found that many of the women did not fit the image of the typical upper-class, white-collar offender. A third of the women were unemployed, and many who worked were in clerical positions, while many of the men worked in managerial positions.

In addition, the women were less likely to have college degrees and more likely to be non-white. Daly (1989) found that that their crimes were better described as "occupational marginal-ity" as opposed to mobility (the women worked on the fringes of the organization rather than in its upper echelons). She also found that women were more likely to work alone in their offend-ing, and financial need was more commonly a motive for them. Daly notes that individuals do not need a white-collar job to commit the crimes of embezzlement, fraud, and forgery. Citing research by Howe (1977), she notes that a "'pink-collar world' suffices, as does having no ties to the labor market" (p. 179). Daly argues that white-collar crimes by women should be addressed with theories—not with a focus on how the crimes "deviate" from men's white-collar crimes; instead, "women's illegalities should be explained on their own terms" (p. 790).

Recent research shows that women are more likely to (1) support regulations in the corporate environment (Piquero, Vieraitis, Piquero, Tibbetts, & Blankenship, 2013) and (2) have lower intentions to commit corporate crime (Vieraitis et al., 2012). In the most comprehensive study on the topic to date, Darrell Steffensmeier and his coauthors (Steffensmeier, Schwartz, & Roche, 2013) developed a database including 436 defendants from 83 corporate crimes. They found that women were infrequently involved in these offenses and pointed to two pathways that brought women into the offenses: (1) relational pathways where women were involved because of a personal relationship with a coconspirator and (2) utility pathways where women held a "financial-gateway corporate position" that offenders had to go through in order to commit the offense (p. 448). In all, 91% of the offenders were men, and three fourths of the corporate crime groups were all-male groups. Mixed-sex offending groups were more common in industries where women tended to be employed more, such as health care, real estate, and insurance. Over half of the female corporate offenders received no profit from their offenses. Those women were primarily in the "utility role" because the male offenders had to "go through" them to commit the crime. Prosecutors then appeared to also use women in a "utility role," using them to make a case against other offenders.

Part of the explanation for fewer white-collar crimes by women may be the glass ceiling that keeps women from advancing to the highest levels of organizations (Dodge, 2016). Dodge points out an interesting criminological irony: "Women are still blocked from many workplace opportunities, which restricts their access to white-collar crime" (p. 205). It is important to clar-ify that women are also less likely to commit conventional crimes. While women are less likely to engage in any type of crime, some research shows that women are more likely to be involved in white-collar crimes than conventional crimes (Hochstetler & Mackey, 2016).

Labeling Theory and White-Collar Crime

Labeling theory focuses on the way that individuals develop criminal labels. Some labeling theorists have suggested that the process of labeling individuals certain ways results in behav-iors consistent with those labels. The notion of "self-fulfilling prophecy" comes to mind. It is widely accepted, for example, that if children are treated as intelligent, then they will be more likely to show signs of intelligence. If children are labeled as bad, then they will be more likely to misbehave. Criminologist Ruth Triplett (1993) has noted that it is not simply the process of being labeled that results in deviant outcomes; instead, negative labels increase the number of delinquent peers one has, which can increase support for subsequent misconduct. In other words, some individuals are able to reject negative labels, while others might respond to the labels by joining forces with others who have the same delinquent or criminal label.

The way labeling relates to white-collar crime has been only tangentially addressed in the literature. Research by Benson (1985a) shows how white-collar offenders reject the criminal label and use that as a coping strategy to deal with the consequences of their sanction. Elsewhere, Benson (1990) wrote the following:

> Few events produce stronger emotions than being publicly accused of a crime. Especially for the individual who has a stake in maintaining a legitimate persona, the prospect of being exposed as a criminal engenders "deep emotions" (Denzin, 1983): shame, humiliation, guilt, depression, and anger. (p. 515)

Consistent with Triplett's hypothesis, if convicted white-collar offenders avoid contacts with other offenders and reject the criminal label, they should be less prone to reoffend. Alternatively, the labeling of white-collar offenders as criminals may serve to increase their offending if the strength of the labeling is such that white-collar offenders are not able to reject the label. Such a label could create additional opportunities for offending. David Weisburd and his colleagues (Weisburd, Waring, & Chayet, 1995) described this process in the following way:

> Once prestige and status are lost, they may be perceived as difficult to regain. Once the cost of illicit behavior has been minimized, recidivism may be more likely. In some sense, the model of a spiraling process of deviance set into play by a labeling experience (Wilkins, 1965, cited in Weisburd et al., 1995) may be more appropriate for white-collar criminals than for the common criminals for whom the concept was initially developed. (p. 590)

It is plausible that labels attach differently based on offender type. Labeling a young male in a disadvantaged community as a gang member or criminal may serve to increase his social status in his community, and the rewards that come along with being labeled a criminal could perpetuate wrongdoing (Triplett, 1993). Labeling an older male in an affluent community a white-collar criminal would not increase his social status in his neighborhood. The negative consequences of the "white-collar criminal" label, as opposed to the rewards that others might get from the criminal label, might actually serve to promote future wrongdoing. Such an assumption has not yet been addressed in the white-collar crime literature. Indeed, research on how labels affect white-collar criminality is needed.

Biological Theories

Early explanations of crime cited biological factors as contributing to criminal behavior among traditional criminals. These **biological theory** explanations fell out of favor in the early 1900s when sociological theories became the more preferred explanations. In recent years, a small group of criminologists have reintroduced the possibility that biological factors contribute to criminal behavior (see Armstrong & Boutwell, 2012; Madden, Walker, & Miller, 2008; Rader, 2008; M. B. Robinson, 2004; Walsh, 2002; D. E. Wright, Titus, & Cornelison, 2008; J. P. Wright, Tibbetts, and Daigle, 2008). It makes sense that biological explanations might contribute to criminal behavior; after all, our biological makeup contributes to "normal" behavior. Why wouldn't it then contribute to criminal behavior?

A study conducted on white-collar crime and biological factors was recently conducted by Adrian Raine and his coauthors (2012). The research team compared neurobiological traits of 21 white-collar offenders and 21 nonoffenders, who were matched based on demographic variables.

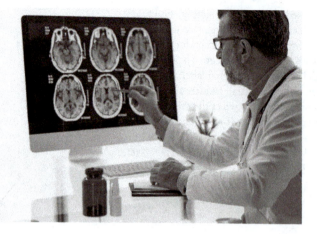

PHOTO 12.4 Do you think white-collar offenders' brains are different from nonoffenders' brains?

They hypothesized that certain neurobiological factors might make it easier for white-collar individuals to offend. These included superior executive functioning, attentional functions, and enhanced brain cortical thickness. The researchers conducted a series of medical tests, including MRIs, on the sample group. Interestingly, their research found that white-collar offenders' neurobiological factors (and brains) were different from nonoffenders. In particular, the researchers found "White-collar criminals demonstrate better executive functions, increased and sustained orienting, increased arousal, and increased cortical thickness in multiple brain regions subserving decision-making, social cognition, and attention" (Raine et al., 2012, p. 2937).

This study marked one of the first (if not the first) study applying biological factors to white-collar crime. Subsequent studies have begun to explore connections between biology and white-collar crime. Based on prior research showing that conventional offenders have lower resting heart rates than nonoffenders, one study examined the resting heart rates of white-collar offenders and found that their heart rates were no different than the heart rates of nonoffenders (Piquero, Ling, Raine, & Piquero, 2019).

Similarly, Benson and Cullen (2018) note that self-deception is a biosocial process combining cognitive and behavioral dynamics. Self-deception involves white-collar offenders convincing themselves that their criminal behavior is appropriate. Benson and Cullen write that "self-deception may have neurological roots, but it is expressed in a social environment and manifested in particular culturally appropriate behavior choices" (p. 118). Acknowledging the high percentage of white-collar misconduct driven by self-deception, the authors point to the possibility that a connection may exist between those neurological factors driving self-deception and social factors resulting in white-collar crime. Some have taken this a step further and—pointing to the relationship between thinking patterns conducive to white-collar crime and the presence of certain biomarkers—called for the use of biomarkers in hiring decisions for certain white-collar positions (Zohny, Douglas, & Savulescu, 2019).

INTEGRATED EFFORTS TO EXPLAIN WHITE-COLLAR CRIME

Thus far, the various theoretical perspectives addressing white-collar crime have been discussed separately. Many scholars, however, have suggested that the best way to explain white-collar crime is to use an integrated approach that brings together multiple perspectives (Gerber, Jensen, & Fritsch, 1996). Even among specific types of occupations, misconduct by employees is likely not "a unidimensional phenomenon" (Hollinger, Slora, & Terris, 1992, p. 155).

The call for integrated theories gained popularity in criminology in the mid- to late-1980s, so the importance of bringing together multiple perspectives is not a new idea. The value of theoretical integration is demonstrated in the way that Donald Cressey (1953) explained the causes of embezzlement in *Other People's Money*. Later, summarizing Cressey's research, Green (1993) highlighted four steps that Cressey saw as leading to embezzlement:

- An unshareable financial problem

- Embezzlement defined as a means to fix the financial problem

- An offender with the skills to commit the crime

- Neutralizations to give the offender the mental strength to commit the crime

In these steps, one can point to the linking together of four different theoretical perspectives: (1) The unshareable financial problem relates to strain theory, (2) the values suggesting that it is OK to steal can be linked to cultural theory, (3) the skills needed to steal can be linked to learning theory, and (4) the neutralization can be linked to neutralization theory.

Other researchers have noted the need to use integrated models to explain different forms of white-collar misconduct. Makkai and Braithwaite (1991) conducted a multimethod study involving interviews with regulatory officials, surveys of nursing home directors, and reviews of compliance data to determine how well four theories addressed violations by nursing homes: control theory, opportunity theory, subcultural theory, and differential association theory. They found that none of the theories on their own predicted compliance rates and called for theory integration to explain regulatory violations by nursing homes. Headworth and Hagan (2016) also promote an integrated approach, combining various explanations for misconduct. They suggest that security offenses and other financial crimes stem from "combinations of opportunity, rationalizations, and 'collective delusion'" (p. 277). Collective delusion seemingly refers to institutional and societal beliefs and practices protecting white-collar offenders from being defined or treated as criminals. Along with opportunity and rationalizations, the willingness of society to normalize harmful behavior of securities and financial professionals is believed to result in offending.

SYSTEMS THEORY

As noted throughout this book, **systems theory** offers a foundation from which white-collar crime can be addressed. The theory does not explain why white-collar crime occurs on an individual level; instead, it provides insight into the interconnections among various societal systems and the way that various systems influence white-collar wrongdoing.

As an illustration, activities in the political system have a direct influence on white-collar misconduct. For example, changes in the political system routinely lead to changes in the health care system. These systemic changes are tied to changes in the social, educational, and technological systems. Together, these changes influence the types of crimes committed in the health care system. Consider the nature of crimes committed in the home health care field:

> In the late 1980s and early 1990s, changes in health care payment plans encouraged hospitals to shorten hospital stays, technological advancements allowed hospital equipment to be mobile, and a graying population led to an explosion in the use of home health care services. . . . In the state-operated Medicaid system, which serves the impoverished population, home health care spending quadrupled between 1985 and 1992. (Payne & Gray, 2001, p. 210)

During this same time frame, the amount of fraud occurring in the home health care industry increased dramatically as well.

Also, showing how the political system influences white-collar crime, some have attributed white-collar crime to types of economic policies developed in legislation (Mon, 2002). From this perspective, researchers have blamed the rampant fraud found in the savings and loan industry in the late 1980s on federal policies promoting deregulation (Glasberg & Skidmore, 1998a). Under deregulation policies, rules governing thrifts and savings and loan companies were changed "so that the behaviors that previously fell within the definition of corporate or executive crime were no longer violations but, rather, were enabled by the structure of the legislation" (Glasberg & Skidmore, 1998b, p. 124). Among other things, deregulation policies relaxed federal control over interest rates, provided federal insurance on deposits up to $100,000 for thrift institutions, and removed "restrictions on the intermingling of commercial banking, real estate, and securities investing," thereby encouraging the institutions to engage in risky behaviors (Glasberg & Skidmore, 1998a, p. 432). Indeed, scholars argued that the deregulation policies resulted in the collapse of the thrift industry, with billions lost to fraud perpetrated by those employed in the industry (Calavita et al., 1997).

Glasberg and Skidmore (1998a) attributed the failure of deregulation and the fraud that resulted to "unintended consequences of the dialectics of state projects" (p. 424). They pointed to the need to look at how external factors came together to foster misbehavior by organizations in the thrift industry and called attention to the need to address how policies are implemented and the consequences of those policies (Glasberg & Skidmore, 1998b). In other words, in line with systems theory, they recognized that policy making in the political arena will impact other societal systems.

The justice system's response to misconduct during the COVID-19 pandemic as well as the changing nature of white-collar crime can be understood through a systems theory framework. In short, the types of white-collar crime occurring during the pandemic and the behavior of justice professionals working during the pandemic changed. In fact, virtually all of the white-collar crimes and topics discussed in this text were impacted by the pandemic. Consider, for example, the following:

- Those working in sales and services industries were asked to follow new rules adhering to new public health standards. Countless businesses broke those rules.

- Health care crimes related to the sale of fraudulent medicines to protect against the virus soared.

- Riots and protests during the pandemic were driven by frustrations about police brutality and concerns about the government's response to the health crisis.

- Political leaders were accused of politicizing a public health crisis; some were accused of insider trading based on their stock sales after receiving inside information about the pending pandemic.

- Educational institutions were criticized on numerous grounds. Some were sued for failing to reimburse students after sending them home in the spring with minimal refunds; other institutions were questioned for deciding to bring students back for in-person classes in the fall.

- False advertising accusations against companies selling products related to the pandemic soared.

- Reports of cybercrimes related to fraudulent online sales spiked during the pandemic.

- The Environmental Protection Agency was called upon to use its enforcement mechanisms to help promote public health.

- The police and courts started using more digital technologies, like virtual arraignments and trials, to process white-collar crime cases (and other cases for that matter).

- To minimize the spread of the virus in institutions, correctional inmates were released into the community, with nonviolent white-collar inmates among those initially released.

This chapter's White-Collar Crime in the News shows an example of one of the many crimes occurring during the pandemic. Bear in mind that broader societal and systemic changes led to changes in criminal behavior and changes in the way the system processed the cases. This is the basic tenet of systems theory.

WHITE-COLLAR CRIME IN THE NEWS
DEFENDANT ALLEGEDLY RAN WEBSITE THAT FRAUDULENTLY SOLD BUT FAILED TO DELIVER N95 MASKS TO CUSTOMERS

The following is a press release from the Norther District of California from April 28, 2020.

SAN FRANCISCO—The United States Attorney's Office for the Northern District of California unsealed charges today in a criminal complaint charging ++++++ with wire fraud for his operation of an e-commerce website that allegedly scammed customers into paying for N95 masks that they never received.

"Hospitals, healthcare providers and everyday people are understandably anxious to obtain N95 masks, N99 filters and other PPE," said U.S. Attorney Anderson. "The criminal element is always ready to prey on fear and uncertainty, and it is all too easy to lie over the internet. While sheltering in place, Americans are shopping on the internet like never before. The complaint alleges a consumer's nightmare of fake webpages and false promises."

"The United States Postal Inspection Service has a long history of successfully investigating complex fraud cases," stated San Francisco Division Inspector in Charge Nuñez. "Anyone or any organization engaging in deceptive practices, especially if they are attempting to exploit the COVID-19 pandemic emergency, should know they will not go undetected and will be held accountable. The collaborative investigative work on this case conducted by Postal Inspectors, our law enforcement partners, and the United States Attorney's Office illustrates our efforts to protect consumers."

According to the complaint, ++++++, of Muskegon, Michigan, controlled EM General, a Michigan limited liability company created in September 2019. EM General operated a website that purported to sell an available inventory of "Anti-Viral N95" respirator masks. An N95 respirator mask is a particulate-filtering facepiece respirator that meets the U.S. National Institute for Occupational Safety and Health N95 standard of air filtration. N95 masks, which cover the user's nose and mouth, are required to filter at least 95% of airborne particles.

The complaint alleges that ++++++, through its website, falsely claimed to have N95 respirator masks "in stock" and available for sale and shipment during the shortage caused by the COVID-19 pandemic. Based on these and other representations, customers bought masks from the website, sometimes paying EM General more than $40 or more per mask. Stevenson is alleged to have taken several steps to fraudulently make EM General appear to be a legitimate company. For example, Stevenson invented a fictional Chief Executive Officer, "Mike Thomas," from whom fraudulent emails were sent, as well as several other fake officers or employees of the company. Stevenson also used stock photographs from the internet to create a page depicting this team of fake professional management staff. After customers made their first purchase, the defendant offered additional masks to those customers at discounted prices.

The complaint describes how four victims paid for, but did not receive, N95-compliant masks. Three of the four victims reside in the San Francisco Bay Area, including one hospital employee. Also described in the complaint are follow-up emails from EM General to customers in which false excuses about supply and shipping issues were made. Three of the four customers in the complaint never received the promised products at all despite multiple representations that the masks had been shipped. The fourth customer paid over $400 on March 2, 2020, for N95 masks represented to be "in stock," and, after raising several complaints, on March 27, 2020, received cheaply made fabric masks. The masks, delivered in a white envelope with no return address, did not comply with the N95 standard that EM General purportedly sold.

++++++ was arrested at his home in Muskegon, Michigan, made his initial appearance before the United States District Court for the Western District of Michigan in Grand Rapids, and was released on supervised bond.

Reprinted from U.S. Department of Justice.

Source: https://www.justice.gov/usao-ndca/pr/michigan-man-charged-covid-19-related-wire-fraud-scheme

Systems theory is not fully embraced by criminologists studying white-collar crime. Even so, the theory clearly helps to understand how white-collar crime is driven by broader structural and societal changes as well as how the justice system operates to respond to white-collar crime. The remaining chapters provide a detailed overview of the criminal justice system's response to white-collar crime.

Summary

- Criminological theory is central to the study of white-collar crime. It is important to stress that theories are potential explanations of behaviors or phenomena, and for white-collar crime explanations to have practical utility, the theories or explanations must point to changes that would reduce (rather than increase) white-collar misconduct.

- Some criminologists attribute white-collar crime to cultural influences that seemingly promote wrongdoing by workers and corporations. James Coleman (1987), for example, argued that industrial capitalism promotes a "culture of competition."

- Deterrence theory can be traced to Cesare Beccaria's *On Crimes and Punishments*, a work that many have defined as the foundation of the classical school of criminological thought.

- Three types of strain theories were discussed: classical strain theory, institutional anomie theory, and general strain theory.

- Classical strain theory traces the source of strain to interactions between the social and economic structures.

- In *Crime and the American Dream*, Steve Messner and Richard Rosenfeld (2007) describe how society promotes values related to financial success but fails to promote values consistent with using legitimate means to attain financial success.

- Developing what is known as general strain theory, Robert Agnew (1985, 1992) used a social psychological approach to explain how crime is an adaptation to stress and frustration.

- Some criminologists have focused on the way that white-collar crime can be understood as learned behavior. The most prominent learning theory is differential association theory, which was developed by Edwin Sutherland.

- Sykes and Matza (1957) described five techniques of neutralization they believed juveniles used to rationalize their misconduct. Given that white-collar workers are rational beings, it is plausible that white-collar offenders use similar types of neutralizations.

- While offenders use neutralizations to give them the mental fortitude to engage in wrongdoing, accounts are offered after the fact to describe their behaviors.

- Rather than asking, "why do people commit crime," the question from a control theory perspective is, "why don't people commit crime" (Hirschi, 1969).

- Some have regarded loyalty as central to corporate decision making.

- Self-control theory was created by Michael Gottfredson and Travis Hirschi (1990), who argued in *A General Theory of Crime* that all types of crime are caused by the presence of a low self-control.

- Routine activities theory suggests that crime occurs when the following three elements exist at the same time and place: (1) the presence of motivated offenders, (2) the absence of capable guardians, and (3) the availability of suitable targets.

- Conflict theorists explain white-collar crime from a more critical perspective, focusing on the way those with power exert influence in order to use the law as an instrument of power.

- The nature of corporate crime is such that individual-level variables may not sufficiently explain the misconduct. In general, explanations of corporate crime have focused on (1) the structure of the organization, (2) organizational processes, and (3) dynamic organizational explanations.

- Theories that warrant more attention in the white-collar crime literature include life course theory, social disorganization theory, gender theories, labeling theory, and biological theories.

- Many scholars have suggested that the best way to explain white-collar crime is to use an integrated approach that brings together multiple perspectives.

- As noted throughout this book, systems theory offers a foundation from which white-collar crime can be addressed.

Key Terms

Appeal to higher loyalties   346
Biological theory   363
Collective embezzlement   340
Condemnation of
   condemners   346
Conflict theorists   355
Conformists   340
Control theory   350
Denial of responsibility   346
Denial of victim   345
Deterrence theory   338

Differential association
   theory   344
General strain theory   343
Innovators   340
Institutional anomie   341
Labeling theory   362
Learning theory   344
Life course theory   360
Neutralization theory   345
Rational choice theory   339
Rebels   340

Retreatists   340
Ritualists   340
Routine activities theory   354
Scapegoating   349
Self-control theory   351
Social disorganization
   theory   361
Strain theory   339
Systems theory   365

Discussion Questions

1. Which theory do you think most accurately explains white-collar crime? Which one is least effective? Why?

2. Watch the movie *Office Space*, and apply four different theories to the movie.

3. How can theory influence the criminal justice system's response to white-collar crime? Explain.

4. How would you convince someone that it is important to study theory in a white-collar crime class?

5. Are white-collar offenders born to be bad? Explain.

6. Do white-collar workers have complete free will? Explain.

7. Which types of rationalizations do you think are most commonly used by white-collar offenders? Are there any rationalizations that you think justify white-collar misconduct?

8. Do you think corporations cause people to commit crime? Explain.

13

POLICING WHITE-COLLAR CRIME

CHAPTER HIGHLIGHTS

- Agencies Involved in Responding to White-Collar Crime
- Law Enforcement Strategies and White-Collar Crime
- Suggestions for Improving the Law Enforcement Response to White-Collar Crime
- Self-Policing and White-Collar Crime
- Regulatory Policing and White-Collar Crime
- The Global Police and White-Collar Crime

Few of us like go to the doctor. But would you like to go to the doctor for your job? In 2020, two patients went to see a doctor in Boca Raton, Florida. The visits seemed ordinary. The patients met with the doctor and answered questions they were asked. While the visits were ordinary, the patients were not. They were undercover agents going to the doctor to look into concerns that the doctor was wrongfully prescribing drugs. During one of the visits, the doctor told the "patient" that she needed to have an allergy screening, even though the patient never indicated any type of allergy problem whatsoever. No results of an allergy screening were provided, but the doctor billed an insurance company roughly $20,000 for the allergy screening. A subsequent investigation alleged that the doctor had fraudulently billed three insurance companies nearly $900,000 for allergy treatments given to 78 patients over a two-and-a-half year timeframe (Milian, 2020). The investigation was somewhat typical in white-collar crime investigations. Police received information, gathered evidence through undercover operations, reviewed records, and interviewed witnesses before arresting the doctor.

Police investigations of white-collar crime can be quite complex, addressing a wide range of behaviors. Consider the following cases excerpted from their original sources:

- On September 27, 2019, the HCF Unit announced a coordinated federal law enforcement action involving fraudulent genetic cancer testing that resulted in charges in 5 federal districts against 35 defendants associated with dozens of telemedicine companies and cancer genetic testing laboratories (CGx) for their alleged participation in one of the largest health care fraud schemes ever charged. According to the charges, these defendants fraudulently billed Medicare more than $2.1 billion for these CGx tests. Among those charged were 10 medical professionals, including 9 doctors. (USDOJ Fraud Section, 2020, p. 25)

- According to evidence presented at trial, +++++ and ++++++ solicited bribes from undercover FBI agents posing as potential investors in connection with a proposed project to develop a port in the Môle St. Nicolas area of Haiti. The proposed project was expected to cost approximately $84 million and was to involve several very large infrastructure construction projects. During a recorded meeting at a Boston-area hotel, +++++ and ++++++ told the agents that, in order to secure Haitian government approval of the project, they would funnel the bribes to Haitian officials through a non-profit entity that ++++++ controlled, which was based in Maryland and purported to help impoverished residents of Haiti. (USDOJ Fraud Section, 2020, p. 13)

- An investigation into the City of Neola has revealed more than $230,000 in city funds were allegedly misspent over a five-year period, with a former city clerk now running for mayor at the center of the controversy. State Auditor Mary Mosiman released a report Tuesday investigating transactions from Jan. 1, 2009 through Dec. 31, which found $230,795.55 of improper and unsupported disbursements and undeposited utility collections. (Brownlee, 2015)

These examples highlight four important themes regarding the policing of white-collar crimes. First, white-collar crimes come to the attention of the police through several different avenues. Second, a number of different agencies are involved in the police response to white-collar crime. Third, the notion of "police response" describes different forms of policing, including criminal policing, private policing, and regulatory policing. Fourth, the specific police techniques used to address white-collar crimes are tied to the types of white-collar crime under investigation. An official responding to pollution, for example, performs one set of activities, while an officer responding to stock fraud would perform another set of activities.

AGENCIES INVOLVED IN RESPONDING TO WHITE-COLLAR CRIME

Generally speaking, three types of agencies are involved in responding to white-collar crime. These include private agencies (or self-policing by corporations or businesses), formal criminal police agencies, and governmental regulatory agencies. Private agencies are involved in policing misconduct inasmuch as a specific business guards against employee misconduct through the development of security and prevention measures. Formal criminal policing agencies at all levels of government respond to white-collar crime, though local police more rarely respond to these cases. State police agencies may become more involved, while federal law enforcement is engaged in even more policing of white-collar misconduct (see Figure 13.1). Typically, but not always, more serious cases are handled by federal officials and less serious cases are handled by state or local authorities (Berdejo, 2017). With regard to regulatory responses, at the local level, different government agencies have responsibility for ensuring that businesses are not in violation of local ordinances. At the state level, regulatory agencies enforce state health-, safety-, and sales-related laws. The federal government has several regulatory agencies whose purpose is to make sure that businesses and their workers are abiding by federal laws and regulations.

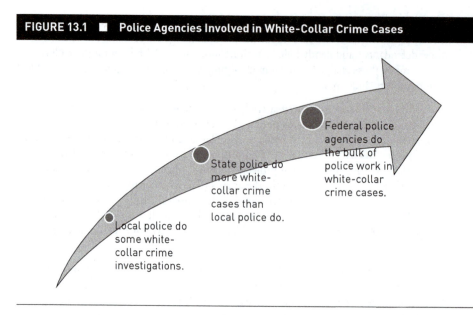

FIGURE 13.1 ■ Police Agencies Involved in White-Collar Crime Cases

Local police do some white-collar crime investigations.

State police do more white-collar crime cases than local police do.

Federal police agencies do the bulk of police work in white-collar crime cases.

It is important to note that many white-collar crime cases are addressed through joint policing efforts by agencies from each level of government (local, state, and federal) and each type of policing agency (criminal policing, regulatory policing, and self-policing). Table 13.1 shows some of the federal agencies involved in responding to white-collar crime. Note that this list is not exhaustive. Dozens of other federal agencies are involved in responding to different forms of white-collar crime. Perhaps one way to think of it is to recognize that for each profession and industry, a different type of policing or regulatory agency guards against occupational misconduct in that occupation.

TABLE 13.1 ■ Some Federal Agencies Involved in Policing/Regulating White-Collar Crime

Agency	What the Agency Does That Is Related to White-Collar Crime	White-Collar Crime* Where to Learn More
Consumer Product Safety Commission	Regulatory agency responsible for protecting the public from unreasonable risk of injury from thousands of products	www.cpsc.gov
Commodities Futures Trading Commission	Regulatory agency responsible for regulating U.S. commodities and futures markets and preventing fraud and abuse in the markets	www.cftc.gov
Environmental Protection Agency	Government agency responsible for protecting the environment through compliance efforts and criminal and civil law enforcement practices	www.epa.gov
Equal Employment Opportunity Commission	Federal agency responsible for enforcing federal employment discrimination laws; it has authority to file lawsuits if necessary	www.eeoc.gov
Federal Bureau of Investigation	Federal law enforcement agency that addresses white-collar crime through its financial crimes section	www.fbi.gov

Agency	What the Agency Does That Is Related to White-Collar Crime	White-Collar Crime* Where to Learn More
Federal Deposit Insurance Corporation	Independent agency that insures bank deposits, supervises financial institutions and examines their activities, and manages failed banks	www.fdic.gov
Federal Trade Commission	Addresses antitrust laws, anticompetitive practices, and false advertising practices by businesses	www.ftc.gov
Financial Crimes Enforcement Network (FinCEN)	Has regulatory duty to administer the Bank Secrecy Act; Assists law enforcement through analysis of information gathered as part of the Bank Secrecy Act	www.fincen.gov
Financial Industry Regulatory Authority	Independent regulatory agency regulating more than 4,500 securities firms operating in the United States (largest of its kind)	www.finra.org
Food and Drug Administration	Ensures safety and effectiveness of certain food and drug products and investigates potential manufacturing violations	www.fda.gov
HHS Center for Medicare and Medicaid Services (CMS)	Administers nursing home inspections by contracting with states, which hire inspection teams and provide inspection data to CMS	www.cms.gov
HHS Office of Research Integrity	Has regulatory authority to promote the responsible conduct of research and monitors college and university reviews of research misconduct cases	http://ori.hhs.gov/
Internal Revenue Service	Federal agency enforcing tax laws; becomes involved in white-collar crime cases when businesses/ corporations break tax laws	www.irs.gov
National Labor Relations Board	Independent agency administering the National Labor Relations Act, addressing unfair labor practices	www.nlrb.gov
National Highway Traffic Safety Administration	Federal agency that develops and enforces motor vehicle performance standards, including gas mileage standards, investigates motor vehicle safety, and detects odometer fraud	www.nhtsa.gov
Occupational Safety and Health Administration	Federal agency that sets and enforces safety and health standards for work settings and maintains data on workplace injuries and illnesses	www.osha.gov
Office of the Comptroller of the Currency	Independent agency responsible for chartering and regulating national banks and for ensuring fairness and equal access to the banks	www.occ.treas.gov
Office of Thrift Supervision	Independent agency that regulates savings associations and their holding companies	www.ots.treas.gov
Public Company Accounting Oversight Board	Ensures that publicly registered accounting firms are in compliance with various federal laws	http://pcaobus.org/Pages/ default.aspx

(Continued)

TABLE 13.1   ■   (Continued)

Agency	What the Agency Does That Is Related to White-Collar Crime	White-Collar Crime* Where to Learn More
Securities and Exchange Commission	Regulates the U.S. securities market, using civil enforcement actions and administrative proceedings	www.sec.gov
U.S. Army Corps of Engineers	Has responsibility of protecting nation's water from harmful and illegal discharge of dredged and fill material	https://www.usace.army.mil/
U.S. Department of Agriculture	Inspects and monitors poultry, eggs, and meat products sold in the United States	www.usda.gov
U.S. Department of Education (DE), Office of Inspector General	Conducts independent investigations, audits, and inspections of DE personnel, activities, and programs receiving DE funding	https://www2.ed.gov/about/offices/list/oig/index.html
U.S. Department of Health and Human Services, Office of Inspector General (OIG)	Conducts independent audits, investigations, and inspections to guard against fraud and abuse in Health and Human Services programs and to protect program beneficiaries	http://oig.hhs.gov/
U.S. Department of the Interior, Office of Inspector General	Provides oversight of programs, employees, and operations occurring in the Department of Interior	www.doioig.gov
U.S. Department of Justice Office of Inspector General	Conducts independent investigations of DOJ personnel and programs to determine whether fraud, abuse, or waste is occurring	www.justice.gov/oig
U.S. Fish and Wildlife Service	Administers Endangered Species Act and responds to white-collar crimes when businesses/corporations harm endangered species	www.fws.gov
U.S. Postal Inspection Service	Federal law enforcement agency addressing fraud conducted through the mail	https://postalinspectors.uspis.gov/
Wage and Hour Division of Department of Labor	Enforces federal labor laws, including minimum wage laws, overtime laws, and family and medical leave laws	www.dol.gov/whd

Source: *Information in this column adapted from agency's website. All agencies do activities other than those listed here.

Each of the agencies in Table 13.1 have individuals charged with "policing" misconduct in the businesses/industries under the authority or jurisdiction of the agency. In many cases, agencies work together on specific cases. The Federal Bureau of Investigation's (FBI's) White-Collar Crime (2020) website page, for example, says

FBI special agents work closely with partner law enforcement and regulatory agencies such as the Securities and Exchange Commission, the Internal Revenue Service, the U.S. Postal Inspection Service, the Commodity Futures Trading Commission, and the Treasury Department's Financial Crimes Enforcement Network, among others, targeting sophisticated, multi-layered fraud cases that harm the economy.

As an example of one of these partnerships, the FBI and Department of Health and Human Services work closely together responding to health care fraud. Figure 13.2 shows the number of new health care fraud investigations opened by the FBI between 2011 and 2019. As part of these joint operations, the FBI has a Health Care Fraud Unit focused on initiatives related to prescription fraud, conspiracies, major provider fraud, and health care fraud and prevention. This final initiative is carried out by the Health Care Fraud Prevention and Enforcement and Action Team (HEAT). Here is how the FBI describes the agency:

> HEAT is a DOJ, FBI and HHS Cabinet-level commitment to prevent and prosecute HCF. HEAT, which is jointly led by the Deputy Attorney General and HHS Deputy Secretary, is comprised of top-level law enforcement agents, prosecutors, attorneys, auditors, evaluators, and other staff from DOJ, FBI and HHS and their operating divisions, and is dedicated to joint efforts across government to both prevent fraud and enforce current anti-fraud laws around the country. The Medicare Fraud Strike Force (Strike Force) teams are a key component of HEAT. As part of the HEAT Initiative, the FBI coordinates with the DOJ and HHS-OIG on funding, resource allocation, Strike Force expansion, target identification, training, and operations. The FBI supports eleven Strike Forces located in Miami, Detroit, Houston (also includes McAllen, Texas), New York City (Brooklyn), Tampa, Los Angeles, Chicago, Dallas, Philadelphia, Newark, and Southern Louisiana (Baton Rouge and New Orleans). In addition to funding agent resources, the FBI funds undercover operation expenses, financial and investigative analysis support, offsite and evidence storage locations, operational travel, and other investigative costs. The Strike Forces have effectively investigated and prosecuted individuals and entities that do not provide legitimate health care services, but exist solely for the purpose of defrauding Medicare and other federal health care programs. In FY19, the FBI participated in ten DOJ regional HCF takedowns charging 268 subjects, including 101 doctors, nurses and other licensed medical professionals, for their alleged participation in HCF schemes involving approximately $2.6 billion in false billings. (DHHS & DOJ, 2020)

A few points about the agencies involved in responding to white-collar crime need to be stressed. First, a plethora of different agencies are involved in controlling and responding to white-collar crimes, and these agencies go by different names depending on the state or locality

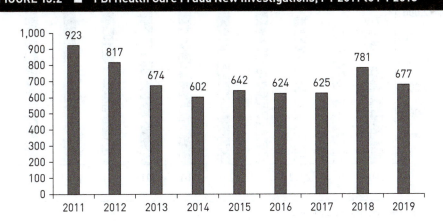

FIGURE 13.2 ■ FBI Health Care Fraud New Investigations, FY 2011 to FY 2018

Source: Department of Health and Human Services

where they exist. It can be somewhat confusing to keep track of jurisdictional issues and determine who is responsible for preventing and policing specific types of white-collar crime.

Let's return to health care fraud as an example. As shown previously, the FBI handles a large number of federal health care fraud cases. But, states also have agencies (known as Medicaid Fraud Control Units) responsible for prosecuting health care fraud cases targeting the Medicaid system. Figure 13.3 shows the number of open investigations in Medicaid Fraud Control Units between 2010 and 2019. The numbers increased over time, suggesting different trends than those found at the federal level. Inquisitive readers will ask why some health care fraud cases are investigated and prosecuted at the federal level while others are handled at the state level. The answer in surprisingly simple. On the one hand, Medicaid is a state-operated health program, so any offenses against that program would require state-level interventions (though federal authorities will provide resources and support to administering Medicaid and responding to fraud against the program). On the other hand, Medicare operates at the federal level, so any offenses against it would be federal offenses requiring federal intervention. In addition, billing strategies by health care providers can be treated as federal offenses when those offenses involve false claims submitted through the U.S. mail (or electronically for that matter).

It is important to consider the enforcement capabilities of different federal agencies. Some of the agencies, like the FBI, can enforce criminal law. Others direct their efforts toward civil and administrative investigations and rely on the Department of Justice (DOJ) for the enforcement of criminal law. The Securities Exchange Commission (SEC), for example, is not able to initiate criminal proceedings and must rely on the DOJ in that area. This has been highlighted as a shortcoming of U.S. efforts to battle financial offending (Francis & Ryder, 2020). Despite their inability to conduct criminal investigations, the SEC has a number of officials dedicated to enforcement actions, and those individuals stay busy enforcing regulations under the agency's authority.

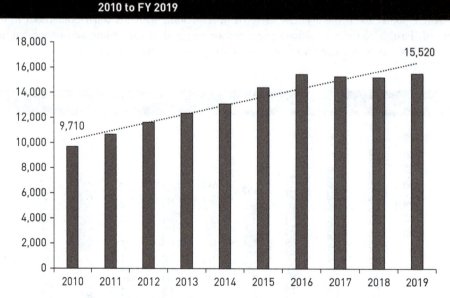

FIGURE 13.3 ■ Open Fraud Investigations of Medicaid Fraud Control Units, FY 2010 to FY 2019

Source: Department of Health and Human Services

Figure 13.4 shows the number of SEC enforcement actions and enforcement staff between 2015 and 2019. Note the relatively steady number of enforcement actions over the five years, with the exception of the drop in 2017. In addition, the number of enforcement staff in the SEC has dropped consistently since 2017, which coincides with the timing of President Trump entering office. The fact that enforcement actions remained stable counters claims that the new administration was ignoring securities offenses.

The number of enforcement staff in relation to the number of enforcement actions also warrants attention. At first look, one might question the success of an agency that has more enforcement employees than enforcement actions. Imagine if a police department had a higher number of officers than the number of crimes in their jurisdiction! The distinction here, however, has to do with the types of enforcement actions addressed by SEC staff, which are comparable to other white-collar crime varieties. In 2019, those 1,472 employees participated in enforcement actions resulting in businesses being ordered to pay $4.3 billion in penalties, with $1.2 billion being returned to victimized investors (SEC, 2020). In other words, the agency recovered $3.1 million per employee. Not bad for a year's work! Similar patterns are found in other agencies responding to white-collar crime. On the surface they might seem to be processing a small number of cases in comparison to the number of staff they employ. The cases they are handling, however, involve significant financial, physical, and emotional losses to victims.

PHOTO 13.1 The majority white-collar crime law enforcement is done at the federal level.

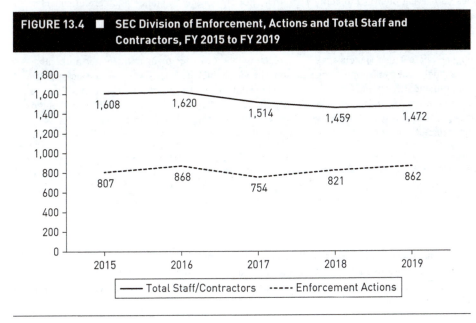

FIGURE 13.4 ■ SEC Division of Enforcement, Actions and Total Staff and Contractors, FY 2015 to FY 2019

Source: U.S. Securities and Exchange Commission

LAW ENFORCEMENT STRATEGIES AND WHITE-COLLAR CRIME

A major portion of the police response to white-collar crime involves law enforcement strategies carried out by officials in the justice system. The law enforcement response to white-collar crime is similar to how the police respond to traditional crimes in several ways. For example, police use both reactive and proactive strategies in both types of cases. **Reactive strategies** entail situations where the police respond to reports of criminal incidents, and **proactive strategies** entail situations where the police develop criminal cases in an active way. An enormous amount of power is afforded police officers who respond to both types of cases. In addition, law enforcement officers have an enormous amount of discretion in deciding how to proceed in both types of cases. In addition to the reactive and proactive strategies, law enforcement officials are also involved in educating about possible white-collar crimes in order to prevent those offenses (see this chapter's White-Collar Crime in the News).

WHITE-COLLAR CRIME IN THE NEWS
FBI WARNS POPULAR SOCIAL MEDIA TRENDS CAN LEAD TO FRAUD

The following is a post from the FBI San Francisco Media Office from April 23, 2020.

SAN FRANCISCO—The FBI San Francisco Division warns social media users to be cautious when sharing information online. Many trending social media topics that seem like fun games can reveal answers to common password retrieval security questions. Fraudsters can leverage this personal information to reset account passwords and gain access to user data and accounts.

The high school support photo trend encourages users to post their high school photo to support the class of 2020. Many people include the name of their schools, mascots, and graduation years, which are also often answers to common password retrieval security questions. Other examples include posting a picture of your first car; answering questions about your best friend; providing the name of your first pet; identifying your first concert, favorite restaurant, or favorite teacher; and tagging your mother, which may reveal her maiden name.

The FBI encourages vigilance and careful consideration of sharing too much personal information online. Social media users should check both their privacy and security settings to reduce vulnerability. The FBI recommends enabling two-factor or multi-factor authentication when available, especially when accessing sensitive personal data such as primary email accounts, financial information, and health records. The FBI urges potential victims to report cyber fraud to the Internet Crime Complaint Center at www.IC3.gov

Source: https://www.fbi.gov/contact-us/field-offices/sanfrancisco/news/press-releases/fbi-warns-popular-social-media-trends-can-lead-to-fraud

Despite these similarities, as will be shown later, a number of specific features of white-collar crime investigations make them substantively different from responses to traditional forms of crime. To provide insight into the law enforcement response to white-collar crimes, attention is given to the following:

- Stages of the white-collar crime investigation
- Evidence-gathering strategies

- Problems addressing white-collar crime through a law enforcement response

- Suggestions for improving the law enforcement response to white-collar crime

Stages of the White-Collar Crime Investigation

White-collar crime investigations can be discussed as part of the broader criminal justice process. In discussing investigations from this perspective, one can point to the fact that white-collar crime investigations begin one of two ways. First, some white-collar crime investigations begin when cases are referred to law enforcement agencies that are responsible for addressing specific forms of white-collar crime. Such referrals come from consumers who are victims of white-collar crime; coworkers of the individual or individuals committing white-collar crime; competitors of the white-collar or corporate offender; the suspect's employer; and local, state, and federal agencies that uncover evidence of wrongdoing (Payne, 2003a). With regard to local agencies in particular, in some cases, individuals might contact the local police to report white-collar offenses. In these situations, it is entirely likely that the local police do not have the resources to investigate or jurisdiction over the misconduct. In these cases, the local police will refer the report to the appropriate agency charged with addressing that specific form of misconduct, which could be a state or federal agency.

A second way that white-collar crime investigations begin is as the result of evidence uncovered as part of routine reviews of financial records by agencies proactively searching for evidence of wrongdoing. For example, auditors in Medicaid Fraud Control Units routinely review insurance claims submitted by health care providers in an effort to identify signs of misconduct. If the auditor finds signs of fraud, the investigation officially begins.

Once a white-collar crime investigation begins, a series of stages are followed. One expert suggested that white-collar crime investigations be conducted in the following stages:

- Identify target, including conspirators

- Locate documents

- Review and confirm false statements in the records

- Interview participants (Bradley, 2008, p. 4)

Bradley draws attention to the need to gather information through records reviews before interviewing participants. This is somewhat different from traditional investigations, perhaps because of the how the crimes are reported.

Compare a domestic violence incident to a white-collar crime, for example. In the domestic violence incident, the police are called, they arrive on the scene, and they immediately question participants about the incident. Records (e.g., threatening notes the offender wrote, phone records), if needed, might be gathered at a later date. If a banking employee is suspected of embezzling money from the bank, however, the investigators will wait until they have reviewed the records before interviewing participants.

In many white-collar crime cases, multiple suspects might be involved. For example, mortgage fraud cases might involve appraisers, real estate agents, mortgage brokers, developers, home builders, and other conspirators. In these situations, Bradley (2008) suggests that investigators "begin with the least culpable and work . . . toward the primary suspects" (p. 5). There are a number of possible reasons to start with the "least culpable" participant. For example, the person who has done the "least amount of harm" is not going to want to take the blame for the harm committed by conspirators. Somewhat related, the least culpable suspect will be in a better position to receive plea bargain offers later in the criminal justice process.

As an illustration of the *least culpable* recommendation, consider an incident of academic dishonesty that occurred in my class not long ago. Two students had written exactly the same wrong answers on their quizzes. Their wrong answers were so preposterously incorrect that it was clear to me that academic dishonesty had occurred. It was also clear that student B had copied from student A (because student A was an "A" student and student B . . . well, let's just say it was obvious). I asked student A to come by my office and asked her about the situation. In my view, student A was the least culpable because this student was not the "copier" but was the "supplier" who had the answers correct on her own. After I asked her about the incorrect answers, student A immediately confessed that student B had copied her answers. I asked student B to come by my office. Initially, he insisted that he did not copy but that he and student A had simply studied together. I asked if he really wanted to stick with that story. Shortly later, he confessed to the academic dishonesty. Had I started my "investigation" with student B, it is entirely likely that the process would not have flowed as smoothly.

Evidence-Gathering Strategies

White-collar crime investigations differ from traditional crime investigations in the way that evidence is gathered. Common strategies for gathering evidence in white-collar crime cases include (1) audits, (2) record reviews, (3) undercover strategies, (4) the use of whistle-blowers, and (5) the use of technological devices. Each of these strategies is discussed in the following sections. Bear in mind that most white-collar crime cases involve multiple strategies (Lokanan, 2019).

Audits

As noted above, some agencies routinely conduct **audits** in search of evidence of white-collar misconduct. Sometimes audits are done through data-mining techniques, which involve searching data sets for patterns that might indicate fraud (Rejesus, Little, & Lovell, 2004). Whether conducted in a proactive or reactive manner, audits are typically conducted by financial fraud accountants with specific skills designed to enhance their abilities to identify fraud.

Recall once again the principle of skepticism discussed in Chapter 1. This principle encourages individuals to have an open mind and to question and requestion everything, to never assume that anything is true. Financial fraud investigators are skeptical by nature and review cases from the perspective that the records are not accurate (Wells, 2003b). Such a perspective is believed to help find evidence of wrongdoing. Describing this skeptical approach to conducting audits, one investigator said, "audits are like an onion. You keep peeling away the different levels until you get to that level where you know what happened" (Payne, 2003a, p. 121).

Audits can be complex and time consuming, but the payoff is significant. In most cases, however, an audit by itself is not necessarily enough to establish that a white-collar crime was committed or to identify who the white-collar offender is. Instead, as one investigator said, audits are "an indicator of the problem; . . . they do not indicate automatically that a crime occurred" (Payne, 2003a, p. 121). While not always sufficient by themselves, when combined with other forms of evidence-gathering strategies, audits can provide the evidence needed to substantiate wrongdoing.

Record Reviews

White-collar crime investigators will review an assortment of records in building their case. The number of records law enforcement investigators will need to review in these cases can be enormous. Investigators conducting **record reviews** will review all sorts of records, including financial records, banking records, sales records, e-mail correspondence, phone records, property deeds, loan applications, and any other records that are relevant to the case under investigation.

As part of the search for records, white-collar crime investigators will examine whether suspects tried to destroy records, which would be a separate offense, as well as evidence supporting the belief that they engaged in the offense under investigation. In one case, for example, nine employees were convicted of neglecting an at-risk child who was in their care. An autopsy revealed that the child had starved to death. In the course of the investigation, officials from the HHS Office of Inspector General found that the employees "attempted to conceal the incident by destroying old records and creating new false records" (U.S. Department of Health and Human Services [HHS], 2010, p. v). The fact that they destroyed records was used to show that they knew that they had done something wrong. Had the records been left alone, it would have been more difficult to establish intent.

E-mail messages are a relatively recent type of record that can be used in white-collar crime investigations. Two misconceptions about them exist. First, some assume that once e-mail is deleted it is gone forever. However, e-mail servers save deleted messages for set periods of time, and investigators have been able to access deleted messages to use as evidence in white-collar crime cases. Second, many people assume that their e-mail is private; however, most businesses have e-mail use policies that allow employers to access workers' e-mail without their consent. Also, for government workers who work in states with liberal open records laws, any of the workers' e-mail can be made public through freedom of information requests.

Undercover Investigations

Undercover investigations are also used in white-collar crime cases. On the surface, these investigations are no different from undercover criminal investigations in conventional criminal cases. However, as will be shown in the following examples, important differences exist between white-collar and conventional undercover investigations.

One basic difference is that **white-collar undercover investigations** are not typically begun unless there is already evidence of wrongdoing by the suspect or the corporation. Whereas many undercover drug investigations involve "reverse sting" activities where undercover officers pose as drug dealers and arrest whoever happens to try to purchase drugs, white-collar crime investigations are rarely conducted without already knowing who the specific target of the investigation is. In other words, typically, "there are no random spot checks" of white-collar employees (Payne & Berg, 1997, p. 226).

As part of an investigation beginning in 2013, the Department of Homeland Security created its own university—the University of Northern New Jersey (UNNJ). Advertised as a for-profit university serving a wide range of students, the university didn't offer any degrees. Instead, it was a fake university developed as part of an undercover sting designed to catch fraudulent college recruiters who were charging foreign nationals to gain admissions to universities so the fraudulent recruiters could illegally obtain student visas and work visas (Jackson, 2019). UNNJ had its own website with contact information for the admissions office, though the admissions officers were federal agents. Officials used social media to make the University of Northern New Jersey seem like any other university. Facebook posts were created using the name of a fictitious president and social media photos of "students" attending the university made the university seem even more real (Zambudio, 2016).

The investigation resulted in the arrest of 21 recruiters, brokers, and employees who were trying to gain admission for more than 1,000 foreign nationals. Announcing the charges in the investigation, U.S. Attorney Paul Fishman said, "'Pay to Stay' schemes not only damage our perception of legitimate student and foreign worker visa programs, they also pose a very real threat to national security" (USDOJ, 2016, April 5).

Criminologist Gary Marx (1982) has discussed several criticisms of undercover policing. While he focused on all types of undercover policing (e.g., undercover prostitution stings, drug stings), Marx used several examples of undercover white-collar crime investigations to frame his discussion. One criticism he levied against these investigations was that they deceive individuals and may coerce individuals into offending. He also noted the significant amount of stress police officers experience from undercover policing, and he argued that the independence given to law enforcement officers in these cases may be a breeding ground for corruption. In addition, overrelying on informers may give informers too much power and become problematic if informers take advantage of the undercover investigation. Marx also suggested that undercover work may promote poor police-community relationships.

One can envision how these criticisms have merit in undercover investigations involving street crimes and organized crime. The criticisms may not be as relevant when considering undercover investigations of white-collar crimes. Table 13.2 shows the similarities and differences between the two types of investigations. First, in terms of danger, there is very little risk for undercover agents in white-collar crime cases. Consider a case where an undercover officer goes to a pharmacist suspected of committing prescription fraud. There is virtually no danger in that assignment. Alternatively, for undercover investigations of street crimes, the investigations occur in dangerous areas and often target dangerous offenders.

TABLE 13.2 ■ Distinguishing Undercover Investigations of White-Collar Crime and Conventional Crime Cases		
	White-Collar Undercover Investigation	**Conventional Undercover Investigation**
Potential for danger	Minimal	High
Time to complete undercover investigation	Short period of time	Lengthy period of time
Centrality to the case	Supplemental evidence	Evidence central to case
Role playing	Some (as consumer)	Identity change (as criminal)
Stress potential	Unlikely	Likely

Based on the dynamics noted above, one can assume that the level of stress in the two types of cases varies. Undercover investigations of conventional crimes are dangerous and time consuming and involve situations where individuals have to pretend to be criminals. Certainly, one can accept Marx's premise that such activities would potentially stress undercover police officers. As well, these dynamics could potentially contribute to police corruption. For white-collar crime investigations, the fact that the investigations are short, in safe settings, and do not involve a great deal of role playing should reduce the amount of stress arising from these cases.

Another difference between the two types of undercover assignments has to do with the time element given to the undercover investigation. For many undercover investigations of street crimes or organized crime, undercover agents infiltrate the criminal subculture and spend significant amounts of time in the dangerous settings. For white-collar crime investigations, it is rare that an undercover agent would join the occupational subculture under investigation for an extended period of time.

Somewhat related, one can also distinguish the two types of investigation based on the role that the undercover work has in the broader investigation. For investigations of drug crimes or organized crime, the undercover work is central to the investigation. The centrality of the undercover work to the investigation is what justifies spending the extended amount of time on the case. For white-collar crime cases, the undercover investigation is typically a "supplemental component" to the investigation. This is not to diminish the importance of undercover work in these cases, as the cases may not be solved without the undercover work.

Another difference between the two types of investigation has to do with the nature of the role playing in white-collar and conventional undercover investigations. In undercover investigations of conventional crimes, the undercover agent must often act as if he or she is a criminal—a drug dealer, prostitute, thief, mobster, gang member, or some other identity relevant to the investigation. In white-collar crime investigations, the agent often does not have to take on the role of the criminal, but the agent may take on the role of a consumer. Consider a case in which a broker is suspected of stealing clients' funds. If an undercover investigation is initiated, the agent simply poses as someone interested in investing. Or if a doctor is being investigated for submitting fraudulent bills to insurance companies, then the investigator just has to act sick. Who among us has not acted sick at some point in our lives? Maybe some of us have acted sick to get out of work. For undercover investigations in health care fraud cases, undercover investigators act sick as part of their work.

Whistleblower Evidence

White-collar crime investigations often involve the collection of whistleblower evidence. **Whistleblowers** are individuals who notify authorities about wrongdoing in their organization. Two types of whistleblowers exist: internal whistleblowers and external whistleblowers (Vinten, 1994). **Internal whistleblowers** share information with officials within the organization where they work, often reporting the misconduct to the company's security program. **External whistleblowers** share the information with outside organizations such as law enforcement agencies or the media. Table 13.3 shows some whistleblowers whose stories eventually made it to Hollywood.

Working with whistleblowers can strengthen white-collar crime investigations significantly. One author team argued that such evidence "may be the best evidence for proving a case" (Botsko & Wells, 1994, p. 21). The same author team suggested that investigators must make sure that the emotional impact of participating in the investigation be minimized. One strategy they suggested for minimizing the emotional impact on whistleblowers was to not ask for too much information until the worker is at a place where he or she is comfortable providing the information. They wrote,

> Effective management of witnesses represents one of the most challenging responsibilities for white-collar crime investigators. To overcome such barriers as anger and fear and to collect and preserve the most accurate testimony possible from . . . whistleblowers, investigators should focus on the informer's emotional agenda. (Botsko & Wells, 1994, p. 21)

Research shows that whistleblowers decide to report their coworker's or organization's misconduct for several reasons (Latimer, 2002). Some workers report white-collar misconduct out of a sense of obligation or duty. Other workers report misconduct because they want to see the offender punished for the misconduct. Still other employees report misconduct so they will not get into trouble themselves. In some cases, whistleblowers are able to collect monetary awards, and these awards can be sizable. Some whistleblowers report misconduct because of the positive attention they get from participating in the investigation. These whistleblowers "have aspirations to become a hero" (Latimer, 2002, p. 23). Businesses might offer their employees funds for providing information about crimes fellow employees are committing. Federal agencies also have whistleblowing programs incentivizing witnesses to share information, though those less often result in financial payouts. For example, between August 2011 and September 2016, 14,000 whistleblowing complaints were filed with the SEC's whistleblowing program. Of those 14,000, just 34 resulted in payments to the whistleblowers (Baer, 2017).

TABLE 13.3 ■ Whistleblowers Who Made It to Hollywood			
Whistleblower	**Description**	**Name of Movie or Show**	**Actor Who Played Whistleblower**
W. Mark Felt	Felt was "Deep Throat," the individual who fed information about the Watergate scandal to reporters Bob Woodward and Carl Bernstein. He announced his role in Watergate three decades after the scandal.	*All the President's Men*	Hal Holbrook
Frank Serpico	Serpico told the *New York Times* about NYPD corruption and was subsequently suspiciously shot in the face during a drug bust. He also provided testimony in the Knapp Commission's investigation of corruption.	*Serpico*	Al Pacino
Karen Silkwood	Silkwood, a nuclear plant worker, was providing information about her factory's safety violations to a reporter. One night when she was delivering evidence to a coworker, she was suspiciously killed in a car accident. The evidence documents were not found in the wrecked car.	*Silkwood*	Meryl Streep
Linda Tripp	Tripp tape-recorded conversations she had with Monica Lewinsky about Lewinsky's sexual relations with President Clinton and provided the tapes to Independent Counsel Kenneth Starr.	*Saturday Night Live*	John Goodman
Sherron Watkins	Watkins sent a letter to Enron's CEO, Ken Lay, detailing Enron's misdeeds. She was named "2002 Person of the Year" by *Time* magazine, along with two other whistleblowers.	*Enron: The Smartest Guys in the Room*	Self (documentary)
Mark Whitacre	Whitacre was the FBI's highest level executive whistleblower in the early 1990s when he provided evidence about price fixing at Archer Daniels Midland (ADM). ADM settled the case for $100 million and alleged wrongdoing by Whitacre. An FBI investigation revealed that Whitacre had stolen $9 million himself. He served eight years in prison for his fraud.	*The Informant*	Matt Damon

Figure 13.5 shows the number of whistleblower tips made to the SEC between FY 2012 and FY 2019. First, note that up until 2019, there was a steady increase in the number of whistle-blower complaints filed. Second, the increase in reports should not be interpreted as directly caused by a proportional increase in misbehavior. Instead, the increase could be attributed to better publicity about the SEC whistleblower program. Third, note that this figure provides a limited view into whistleblower complaints filed with just one agency, and whistleblower complaints can be filed with several different agencies depending on which agency has jurisdiction over the behavior outlined in the complaint. Finally, for some agencies, including the SEC, the act of whistleblowing may have a lucrative benefit for the whistleblower. These benefits will be discussed in Chapter 14 in which lawsuits are discussed.

Technological Devices and White-Collar Crime Evidence

Various types of technological devices are used to search for evidence in white-collar crime cases. Several types of software, for example, are used to search for evidence of computer crimes against corporations. As well, cameras and tape recorders are sometimes used to substantiate wrongdoing. As an illustration, in one case, a senior financial analyst for WellCare—Sean Hellein—alerted authorities that his coworkers had defrauded Medicaid of approximately a half billion dollars. After alerting authorities about the misconduct, he was asked to wear "hidden microphones and miniature cameras disguised as buttons" (Hundley, 2010). He collected 1,000 hours of evidence that led the authorities to raid the company's headquarters.

Other forms of computer technology may also be used for some white-collar crime investigations. Some cyber policing strategies may rely on remote forensic software to detect offending and gather evidence (Abel, 2009). These strategies either (1) place software on a suspect's computer and monitor the suspect's activities or (2) place the software on a website and monitor who visits the website. Known as "police trojans," this type of software "require[s] the unwitting cooperation of the target" (p. 100). Internationally, companies are grappling with the question of whether law enforcement agencies should use remote forensic software tools "as a standard investigation method to combat cybercrime" (Abel, 2009, p. 99).

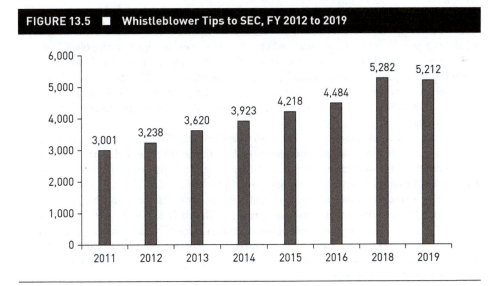

FIGURE 13.5 ■ Whistleblower Tips to SEC, FY 2012 to 2019

Source: U.S. Securities and Exchange Commission

Problems Addressing White-Collar Crime Through a Law Enforcement Response

Few criminal cases are actually simple to detect and investigate. White-collar crime cases are no exception. Problems that surface in criminal white-collar crime investigations include the following:

- Resource problems

- Relationship dynamics

- Time

- Complexity

- Establishing proof

- Perceptions of white-collar crime police work

Resource Problems

Resources are a problem inasmuch as white-collar crime police units are grossly under-resourced in comparison to police units focusing on conventional crimes. To be sure, police departments are underfunded in general, and many recent budget cuts have forced departments to eliminate various programs and services. It is likely much easier to reduce services addressing crimes like white-collar crime, which is often viewed as less serious than conventional crime. State and federal agencies have also experienced funding problems when it comes to responding to various types of white-collar crimes (Payne, 2006).

Resource problems are a little different for white-collar crime investigations than they are for conventional crime investigations. In particular, whereas most conventional offenders have limited resources that they can use to build their defense against the charges, white-collar offenders typically have significant resources that can be devoted to defending against the allegations. During investigations, corporations will often "lawyer up" as soon as the investigation begins (Williams, 2008, p. 322). Said one investigator, "This is one of the biggest things I've noticed in every interview we do. There's lawyers, upon lawyers, upon lawyers" (Williams, 2008, p. 322).

To be sure, many interviews with conventional offenders are conducted without defense attorneys present. This is less common in white-collar crime investigations. Williams (2008) highlights a process called *litigotiation,* where corporate lawyers engage with police in a way that makes it seem that they are cooperating through "interaction rituals." But they are simply protecting their client through "legal gamesmanship" (p. 322). Examples of litigotiation would include participating in interviews but stalling the case by making unnecessary requests of the police—requests that are not typically made in investigations of conventional criminal cases.

Varying amounts of resources will need to be assigned to different types of cases. Agencies must make decisions about the amount of resources they will devote to different cases. The SEC, the federal agency responsible for addressing securities fraud through civil actions, provides its enforcement division guidance in the Division of Enforcement's enforcement manual. In particular, home office associate directors and regional directors are asked to prioritize their top three cases and list their top 10 cases based on three criteria: "programmatic importance of enforcement action," "magnitude of potential violations," and "resources required to investigate potential violations" (Securities and Exchange Commission, Division of Enforcement, 2015, p. 9). Table 13.4 shows what is meant by each of these items.

TABLE 13.4 ■ Criteria Used to Decide Resource Allocation in Securities Fraud Investigations

Programmatic Importance Indicators	Indicators of Magnitude	Potential Indicators of Resources Required
• Whether the subject matter is an SEC priority • Whether the subject matter is a division priority • Whether an action would fulfill a programmatic goal of the SEC or the division • Whether an action would address a problematic industry practice • Whether the conduct undermines the fairness or liquidity of the U.S. securities markets • Whether an action would provide an opportunity for the SEC to address violative conduct targeted to a specific population or community that might not otherwise be familiar with the SEC or the protections afforded by the securities laws • Whether an action would present a good opportunity to work together with other civil and criminal agencies • Whether the conduct can be addressed by any other state or federal regulators • Whether an action would alert the investing public of a new type of securities fraud	• The egregiousness of the conduct • The length of time the conduct continued or whether it is ongoing • The number of violations • Whether recidivists were involved • Whether violations were repeated • The amount of harm or potential harm to victims • The amount of ill-gotten gains to the violators • Whether victims were specifically targeted based on personal or affinity group characteristics • For issuers or regulated entities, whether the conduct involved officers, directors, or senior management • Whether gatekeepers (such as accountants or attorneys) or securities industry professionals were involved	• The complexity of the potential violations • The approximate staff hours required over the course of the investigation • The number of staff assigned • The amount of travel required • The duration of the relevant conduct • The number of potential violators • The number and locations of potential witnesses • The number and location of relevant documents to be reviewed

Source: Securities and Exchange Commission, Division of Criminal Enforcement. (2015). In *Enforcement Manual.* Available from http://www.sec.gov/divisions/enforce/enforcementmanual.pdf

Relationship Dynamics

Relationship dynamics also present problems in white-collar crime investigations. Three types of relationships are relevant: (1) the victim-offender relationship, (2) the offender-witness relationship, and (3) the officer-offender relationship. First, in terms of the victim-offender relationship, recall that in many cases, white-collar crime victims are not aware of their victimization, perhaps partly because of the trust that the victim (consumer, client, coworker, etc.) places in the offender (Bucy, 1989). As a result, they are unable to report the victimization to the police and subsequently unable to participate as a witness in the investigation.

With regard to the offender-witness relationship, many of the witnesses that investigators want to interview will be in trusting relationships with the offender. These relationships might be work relationships or personal relationships. Either way, the relationship makes it more difficult for investigators to get accurate information from witnesses. For example, if the witness is a coworker or subordinate of the suspect, the witness has a level of trust in the suspect but may not trust the white-collar crime investigator (Payne, 2003a). As well, in certain professions, the occupational subculture is perceived as protecting members of that subculture in law enforcement investigations (Wilson, Lincoln, Chappell, & Fraser, 1986). When witnesses are interviewed, they often tell investigators that the suspects are "pillars of the community," making white-collar offenders, in the words of one investigator, "sympathetic defendants who do not look like criminals" (Payne, 2003a, p. 145). In other cases, witnesses might actually be colluding or conspiring with the suspect, thereby making it less likely that they will be cooperative witnesses (Payne, 2006). Alternatively, some witnesses might engage in the "blame game" by attributing wrongdoing—whether intentional or not—to others in workplace who, in reality, had little or nothing to do with the offenses. The blame is believed to stem from personality conflicts, past work-related problems, or other factors unrelated to the case (Gottschalk, 2017b).

The police officer-offender relationship may also present barriers in white-collar crime investigations. The relationship dynamics between officers and offenders are different in white-collar crime and conventional crime cases (see Table 13.5). First, one can note that class status differences between officers and white-collar offenders make these white-collar crime cases different from conventional crime cases. In white-collar crime cases, offenders typically come from a higher social class than most officers do. Alternatively, officers are in a higher social class than conventional offenders are in. This is potentially problematic when white-collar suspects try to use their class status to gain power over officers.

TABLE 13.5 ■ Relationship Dynamics Between Police Officers and White-Collar and Conventional Offenders

	White-Collar Offenders	Conventional Offenders
Class status	Have a higher class status than police officers	Have a lower class status than police officers
Education	Have either more or a different type of education than police officers	Tend to be less educated than police officers
Economic power	Have more economic power than police officers	Have less economic power than police officers
Political power	Have more political clout and political contacts than police officers	Have less political power than police officers
Familiarity with criminal justice	Very little prior contacts with police	Have longer criminal histories and more contacts with the police

Educational differences might also exist between officers and white-collar offenders. While more and more police officers are required to have college degrees, especially at the federal level, the vast majority of white-collar offenders will have higher educational levels than conventional offenders, and their educational expertise will be different from police officers' expertise. This can be problematic in that officers will need to be acquainted with the offender's occupational specialization in order to understand the nature and dynamics of the occupational misconduct. While those of us trained in criminology and criminal justice are well versed in our own fields, understanding the intricacies of careers in other fields is a difficult task.

White-collar offenders will have more political and economic power than police officers, while police officers have more economic and political power than conventional offenders. This becomes problematic when offenders use their expertise to try to call in favors from politicians, business leaders, and community leaders. In a case involving a 16-year-old kid from an innercity neighborhood, few outsiders might try to intervene on behalf of the kid. In a case involving a powerful white-collar offender, officers will sometimes need to take more precautions to ensure that the offender is not able to exert political power over the investigation. For example, they might wait longer to proceed with a white-collar case in order to have the strongest case possible.

One can point to the familiarity that police officers have with conventional offenders (as opposed to white-collar offenders) as another relationship barrier in these cases. Conventional offenders are typically more "familiar" with the criminal justice system, having longer arrest records and more contacts with law enforcement officers. Scholars have long talked about a courtroom workgroup to describe familiarity between actors in the courts. For offenders arrested many times, police officers and offenders have—in a very real sense—an informal relationship, albeit one that is based on formal control mechanisms. No such relationship exists between police officers and white-collar offenders, most of whom have had few prior contacts with the police. In the end, police officers lack familiarity with white-collar offenders. Ironically, the familiarity element might actually result in officers "liking" conventional offenders more than white-collar offenders. Said one white-collar crime investigator, "You cannot trust these white-collar criminals. They are not 'honest criminals' like traditional ones" (Alvesalo, 2003, p. 129).

Time

Time is another problem in white-collar crime investigations. Time becomes problematic in three ways. First, because white-collar crime victims often do not know they were victimized, a long period of time may pass between the time the crime was committed and the time the investigation begins. The longer the amount of time that elapses between the commission of the offense (whether a white-collar crime or conventional crime) and the time police become aware of the offense, the less likely that an arrest will occur in the case.

Second, time is problematic in that it can take an inordinate amount of time to collect all of the necessary records in white-collar crime cases (Payne, 2003a). While the collection of electronic evidence has made record collection more efficient, it still takes time to identify which records are needed and then to review all of the records. As well, writing up the results of the record review can be quite time consuming.

Third, some have argued that it takes longer to prepare for a white-collar crime interrogation than it takes to prepare for an interrogation of a conventional offender (Alvesalo, 2003). Alvesalo (2003) notes that interrogations of conventional offenders are usually not prepared ahead of time. Investigators, perhaps because they routinely complete such interrogations, are able to conduct the interrogations "by free narration" (p. 127). Describing the interrogation of white-collar offenders, he quotes one investigator who said:

> In the uniformed police . . . you never had to prepare for the . . . interrogation at all. You just went in there and asked, "What is going on?" and took the statements. In cases of

economic crime, you might write questions for a week and you have to do background work for a month and when you start to interrogate, you check the questions, and prepare yourself with all kinds of documents that you have to show the suspects . . . a totally different world. (p. 127)

As an analogy, think of a class you could attend, never study, and then ace the exams. This would be like interrogating conventional offenders. Alternatively, think of a class you have to work hard in, such as most of your criminal justice classes. This would be like interrogating white-collar offenders.

Complexity

Complexity is another problem in white-collar crime investigations. Three issues that make the cases particularly complex include (1) complex record searches, (2) extensive collaborations with partners, and (3) the lack of a systematic approach. In terms of complex record searches, the number of records collected in white-collar crime cases can be overwhelming to the investigations. It is estimated that the "average fraud case can entail fifty boxes of evidence" and 150,000 to 250,000 pages of information (Taylor, 2001, p. 22). Not only is sifting through all of those records time consuming, but a complex endeavor arises in efforts to take that information and narrow it down to evidence indicating that a crime has been committed.

The extensive collaborations with partners in white-collar crime cases can also make the investigations more complex than might be found in investigations of conventional crimes. Such collaboration is necessary in many white-collar crime investigations and can result in adding complexities to the investigation (Middlemiss & Gupta, 2007). For example, it may be difficult to determine which agencies should be involved in the investigation. As well, statutes may keep agencies partnering with one another from sharing relevant information (Payne, 2011). In addition, turf wars may erupt during the course of the investigation.

Also, participants in the partnership might have different goals—some might be obsessed with crime statistics, while others might be involved in the effort because they want a part of the funds recovered through the investigation. Also, bureaucratic inertia, which refers to situations where a large group of individuals is unable to move forward, may keep the partnership from attaining its goal (Middlemiss & Gupta, 2007). In effect, having to partner with other agencies can make white-collar crime investigations more complex.

The lack of systematic approaches has also contributed to complexity in some white-collar crime investigations. For example, some authors have contended that environmental crime investigations do not always follow systematic approaches (Van den Berg & Eshuis, 1996). Without a systematic approach, the investigatory process becomes more difficult than it needs to be. Remember the principle of parsimony discussed earlier in the text. This principle suggests that theorists must keep their explanations of white-collar crime as simple as possible. In a similar way, investigators must try to simplify the complexities of white-collar crime investigations. To do so, it has been argued that white-collar crime investigations need to be better planned, prioritized, and sensitive to group dynamics (Van den Berg & Eshuis, 1996).

Keep in mind that the police processing of white-collar crime cases varies across offense types. Some white-collar crime cases will be less complex and subsequently easier to investigate than other white-collar crime cases. FBI agent Daniel Bradley (2008) has suggested that records in real estate fraud cases are easier to review than those found in other white-collar crimes. According to Bradley,

PHOTO 13.2 White-collar crime investigations can involve complex record searches.

these false statements are clear and simple, provable through documentation and witness testimony, and therefore easily conveyed. For example, it is easy to compare a home value estimate from an appraisal form to the estimate actually listed on a mortgage document. (p. 3)

Establishing Proof

It is also difficult for investigators to gather evidence that prosecutors will be able to use to prove various aspects of the misconduct. In some white-collar crime cases, it is so difficult to establish intent that investigators might end up having to "devote their endeavors to less serious charges" (Wilson et al., 1986, p. 139). Consider Martha Stewart's case. She was accused of insider trading but ultimately convicted of perjury.

PHOTO 13.3 Traditional police work is seen as exciting. White-collar crime investigations are not held in the same regard. Rarely do you see kids playing "white-collar crime cops and robbers."

In a similar way, it is difficult to prove that specific suspects are responsible for the misconduct. This is particularly the case in corporate crimes where it is difficult to determine which employees participated in the offense. In investigations of conventional crimes, "the police ask 'Who did it?' In [white-collar] crime cases, they ask 'which one of the known suspects is responsible?'" (Alvesalo, 2003, p. 124). One criminal justice official commented, "as in any white-collar crime . . . defendants usually assert that they did not understand the complicated regulations, were bad record keepers, etc., but had no criminal intent. Absent a confession, that defense is difficult to overcome" (Payne, 2003a, p. 137).

Perceptions of White-Collar Crime Police Work

Another barrier in the response to white-collar crime is that police work in these cases is often perceived pejoratively, as if the activity is not real police work. On the one hand, such perceptions become problematic when funding for these activities is withheld or reduced based on perceptions that such police work is not "real" police work. On the other hand, given that even some police officers view white-collar crime police work as "not real police work" (see Alvesalo & Whyte, 2007), it may be difficult to recruit and retain seasoned criminal justice professionals in policing careers targeting white-collar offenders. This chapter's Streaming White-Collar Crime shows how one television show portrays white-collar crime police work.

STREAMING WHITE-COLLAR CRIME *White-Collar*

Plot	What You Can Learn	Discussion Questions
If you want to catch a white-collar criminal, you need to think like a white-collar criminal. That's the simple premise of *White-Collar*, a USA-Today series telling the story of FBI agent Peter Burke's efforts to enlist the help of the white-collar offender Neal Caffrey, who Burke spent much of his career trying to catch. Certainly, the two have trust issues they have to work out as they tackle crimes such as art theft, Wall Street corruption, judicial corruption, rare wine theft, and other crimes not typically conceptualized as white-collar crimes. In Caffrey's own words, "I'll admit I have done a lot of things I'm not proud of. Wait, that's not true . . . I'm proud of most things I do." The plot isn't farfetched. The FBI has reportedly called on former white-collar offenders including Frank Abagnale and Kevin Mitnick for consulting. Who said crime doesn't pay?	Former white-collar offenders sometimes become consultants for businesses. It's not as easy to catch a white-collar offender as Neal Caffrey makes it seem. In most cases, white-collar criminal justice professionals must work with other professionals to solve their cases.	What do you think of the saying "It takes a thief to catch a thief"? Would you hire a former white-collar criminal as a consultant? Why, or why not?

Photo by Kathleen Payne.

SUGGESTIONS FOR IMPROVING THE LAW ENFORCEMENT RESPONSE TO WHITE-COLLAR CRIME

A number of suggestions have been made for improving the law enforcement response to white-collar crime. For example, just as the media show celebrated white-collar offenders doing the "perp walk" to the police car, police department, or courthouse, some researchers have suggested that efforts should be undertaken to make sure that arrests are "publicized" to those in the workplace by arresting suspects when a lot of people are at work, as during shift changes (Payne & Gray, 2001). This same author team warns officers against assuming that labels given to white-collar crime are accurate descriptors of the behavior. For instance, some believe that "financial crimes" are not harmful, and this would, in turn, diminish the value that officers give to the work. Recognizing the seriousness of the offenses potentially increases the value that officers would place on law enforcement activities targeting white-collar crimes.

The search for a **"smoking gun"** has been suggested as a strategy for improving investigations in white-collar crime cases (Payne & Gray, 2001). In this context, the phrase *smoking gun* refers to indisputable evidence that substantiates that a crime has been committed. One contracted employee, for example, billed an employer for 800 consecutive days of work. Think about that. That's 27 straight months with no days off from work. Incidentally, this employee held a separate full-time job and took three vacations to New York, Aruba, and Mexico during the 27-month scam (Payne, 2003a). In another case, a professor blamed his students for what appeared to be an altered figure in his manuscript. He claimed the altered figure included correct data but that it appeared altered because his students messed with the initial calculations. The investigation concluded that the professor was lying. Accused of a second falsification, the professor attributed data he was using to a colleague who had given him the data at a conference. The investigation revealed that no such colleague existed and the professor didn't actually attend the conference (NSF OIG, 2019). Hence, a smoking gun was uncovered! Figure 13.6 shows some additional smoking gun cases.

Another recommendation for improving the police response to white-collar crime is related to the popular movie *Jerry Maguire*. Even if you have not seen the movie, you have probably heard the tag line by Rod Tidwell, played by Cuba Gooding, Jr., who said to Jerry, "Show me

FIGURE 13.6 ■ The Smoking Gun and White-Collar Crime

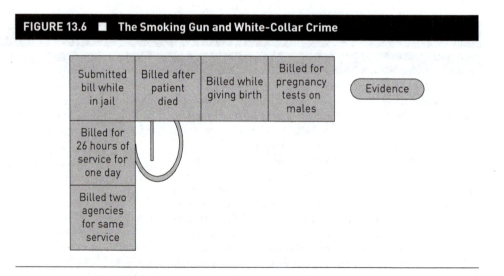

the money." The quote is among the most recognized movie lines. There's another quote that financial investigators recognize: "Follow the money" (Wells, 2003a, p. 84). Certainly, in many white-collar crime cases, money is the target. If investigators can find the money, then they find evidence that substantiates the crime. As Wells (2003b) wrote, "Money from any source—lawful or not—can be dispersed only four ways: It can be spent, saved, used to acquire assets, or to pay debts" (p. 76). Thus, investigators will review the suspects' assets (e.g., their possessions), liabilities, sources of funds, and expenditures.

Improved educational programs have also been hailed as strategies for helping law enforcement officers respond to white-collar crime. The need for these programs is supported by research showing that the qualities of investigators may impact the outcome of investigations (Gottschalk, 2017a). The underlying premise of these findings is startling—whether someone is caught and convicted of a white-collar crime depends not only on the offender's behavior but on the investigator's behavior as well. Since the early 2000s, efforts to improve professional responses to cases have expanded. These efforts now involve colleges and universities preparing current and future investigators to address white-collar crime. One example is the Internal Revenue Service Criminal Investigation's (IRS CI) Adrian Project. In this project, the IRS CI partners with a college and assigns a coach to work with students on an applied learning exercise. The students are given crime scene scenarios, including white-collar crime scenarios, and asked to investigate the offenses. The program has been found to improve students' detection skills, abilities to gather and organize data, abilities to use multiple investigative tools, and interviewing and communication skills (Brickner, Mahoney, & Moore, 2010). Higher education institutions have followed suit and developed academic programs providing graduates with similar skills (H. Richardson, 2010; Sowa, 2010; Wells, 2003b).

Following this same line of thinking, some have called for a more proactive educational response to white-collar crime that addresses the changing nature of societal systems. Said one official employed in a statistical financial analysis unit,

> The authorities find themselves in this position of running after the problems and their perpetrators—the robbers always keeping the advantage over the cops. With the advantage and with the ever-increasing innovations in technology that can be used for illicit ends, the risk grows that the criminal act cannot be [stopped]. (Nardo, 2004, p. 139)

Increasing technological awareness about white-collar crime should help improve the police response to white-collar crime. Just as technology has changed how police behave, it has also changed the behaviors of white-collar offenders. Adapting to new technologies will help law enforcement officials improve their responses to technology-driven crimes (Lord and Van Wingudu, 2019).

SELF-POLICING AND WHITE-COLLAR CRIME

Self-policing refers to efforts by companies and businesses to develop their own policing responses to white-collar crime. Businesses develop self-policing strategies for practical and economic reasons. Practically speaking, it is impossible for law enforcement agencies to police businesses on a daily basis, so businesses develop their own private policing systems. Economically, self-policing strategies help businesses protect their bottom lines by minimizing the economic costs of employee misconduct. Options available to businesses who identify crime as a result of self-policing strategies include (1) reporting the crime to the police, (2) filing civil charges, (3) negotiating a settlement with the offender, (4) sanctioning the offender with an internal reprimand, and (5) negotiating a nondisclosure agreement with the offender (Meerts, 2013). Types of self-policing efforts used by business to detect or prevent white-collar crime include loss prevention strategies, compliance programs, audits, and forensic accounting.

Loss Prevention Strategies

Loss prevention strategies are efforts that businesses use to keep employees from stealing from the business. Traub (1996) cites three types of loss prevention strategies. Category I strategies refer to efforts where businesses emphasize security. Security officials perform a number of different activities, including "surveillance, plain-clothes detective work, and undercover operations directed at criminal activity and other forms of misconduct" (p. 248). Some businesses have increased their reliance on security strategies to detect and prevent workplace crimes. Consider that the number of investigators hired in some accounting firms doubled in the wake of the Enron and WorldCom scandals in the early 2000s (Wells, 2003b).

Category II loss prevention strategies emphasize screening and education (Traub, 1996). During recruiting stages, workers are screened intensively in an effort to weed out those who have a likelihood of engaging in criminal acts on the job. Background checks and reference checks have long been used to screen out applicants that employers think might steal from the workplace. With the advent of technology, some employers now also conduct media and Internet searches to learn more about prospective employees. These searches can be quite enlightening. In one media search, the following information was uncovered:

> A candidate said he had been working in the family business for a few years, when in fact he had been in prison. A Kroll media search found out that the candidate had been in prison because he had shared a cell with mass murderer Fred West at some point and on being released, sold his story to a newspaper. (Huber, 2010, Labour Market Lies section, para. 3)

Facebook and similar social network sites have also been searched to determine the employability of job candidates. Criminal justice students should take note of this particular statement. In a conference presentation titled "What Were You Thinking? Criminal Justice Students and Their Social Networking Sites," a criminal justice professor and his graduate student discussed a research project where they reviewed public Facebook pages of criminal justice students at their university (J. Lee, 2010). The research team showed some of the pictures they found on students' Facebook pages. Many of the criminal justice majors included pictures of drunken celebrations and marijuana use. One that stood out showed two students in a bathroom, with one of them bent over the toilet. Even if the pictures were not of the students themselves, simply having these pictures on one's Facebook page might be enough to raise concern in future employers. (Note to readers—after you read this chapter, review your Facebook page to make sure it won't keep you unemployed in the future. Make sure you finish this chapter first, though.)

Category III strategies emphasize getting employees to share information about their coworkers' misconduct through efforts such as whistleblowing and anonymous hotlines (Traub, 1996). Anonymous hotlines have been found to be particularly effective "if accompanied by positive support from management" (Holtfreter, 2004, p. 89). What this means is that the leaders of the business must promote a culture that advances and supports ethical decision making in the workplace.

In conducting workplace investigations, it is imperative that information be secured and not shared with coworkers of suspects until necessary. Most workplace settings have tight-knit relationships among coworkers. Coworkers will share information—whether accurate or not—with one another. If information about an ongoing investigation becomes public, the internal investigation could be derailed.

The internal investigation process will follow stages similar to those followed in law enforcement investigations of white-collar crime (discussed previously). Some differences are worth noting. For example, if a business catches an employee engaging in misconduct, it may simply fire the employee and not refer the case to the authorities. This is often done to avoid negative publicity or simply to minimize the amount of time that would be spent in the criminal justice process.

Another difference has to do with the way interviews are conducted in self-policing and law enforcement investigations. Public law enforcement officers are held to a higher standard with regard to the rights of the individual they are interrogating. If, for example, a suspect "pleads the Fifth" and says that he or she will not answer specific questions in a criminal investigation, this cannot be held against that person at trial. If a suspect refuses to cooperate in an internal investigation, the person's employer can make decisions about the outcome of the investigation by inferring from the employee's refusal to answer questions (Schiff & Kramer, 2004).

Some also make a distinction between a "custodial interrogation" of arrested offenders and a **workplace interview** conducted in internal investigations. One expert advised,

> The interview is not a forum for cross-examination, but for information gathering. If cross-examination techniques are used, then often little is achieved. However, it is important for the investigator to use assistance language, "can you help me?" "can you be of assistance to me?" or "I do not understand some issues." (Coburn, 2006, p. 348)

The key distinction centers on a more inquisitorial approach found in internal investigations, as opposed to the adversarial approach used in criminal investigations.

Like criminal investigations, internal investigations might entail a significant number of records that need to be collected, analyzed, and secured. Coburn (2006) recommended that organizations develop policies for collecting and securing records. In particular, Coburn suggested the following:

- Have a written procedure for the collection of evidence;

- Document the collection of evidence, detailing time, place of origin, and circumstances of collection;

- Identify documents;

- Obtain relevant primary documents, i.e., contracts, invoices, share certificates, financial transaction documents, etc.;

- Obtain relevant secondary documents, e.g., entry documentation to buildings, telephone, facsimile and computer information;

- Verify primary and secondary documents; and

- Secure documents inside the organization (Coburn, 2006, p. 348).

Whereas a criminal investigation secures records in the law enforcement agency, self-policing efforts keep their records in-house. Whether those records become public depends on the seriousness of the offending and whether the business decides to report the case to the authorities.

Compliance Strategies

Compliance strategies are another form of self-policing. A **compliance program** is an "organizational system aimed at comprehensively detecting and preventing corporate criminality" (Goldsmith & King, 1997, p. 9). Such programs provide a mechanism for identifying and reporting misdeeds with a view toward keeping the misconduct from occurring in the first place. Strategies used in compliance programs include "audits, employee training, reporting mechanisms, and sanctions for illegal actions" (Goldsmith & King, 1997, p. 10).

Under the 1991 U.S. Sentencing Guidelines, corporations with strong compliance programs are eligible to receive lighter sanctions for misconduct. The sentencing guidelines indicate what is expected in compliance programs in order to be eligible for reduced sanctions. The guidelines state that organizations must have the following:

1. Established compliances standards and procedures

2. A specific high-level employee responsible for compliance

3. Not given decision authority to those who have a propensity to commit illegal activities

4. Implemented strategies to effectively communicate about the compliance program

5. Implemented procedures, policies, and practices to gain compliance

6. Consistently enforced compliance violations

7. Effectively responded to compliance violations and initiated steps to stop them from occurring again (U.S. Federal Sentencing Guidelines available from http://www.ethics. org/resource/federal-sentencing-guidelines)

Beyond allowing a lighter sanction if a corporation is found liable for corporate misconduct, compliance programs are valuable because they can potentially deter workplace transgressions. Scholars have offered suggestions for how to ensure that compliance programs effectively police workplace misconduct. Nestor (2004) argued that executives should "drive compliance from the top" (p. 348). He called for the development of a corporate code of ethics and mandated reporting by officials. If executives show they are serious about preventing corporate misconduct, Nestor suggested, the compliance program will serve as an effective self-policing strategy.

Others have viewed compliance programs as focusing on criminalization at the expense of compliance (Haugh, 2017). What this means is that officials become singularly focused on avoiding the criminal law at the expense of regulatory compliance. Such a lens allows corporate officials to engage in rationalizations and roll backs so long as they don't break the criminal law. Wrongful behaviors, including regulatory violations, are justified so long as they don't cross over into a legal definition of crime (Haugh, 2017).

Audits

Audits are included as a part of many organizations' compliance programs and can be seen as an effective self-policing strategy. In this context, audits are different from those discussed previously. Criminal investigation audits are conducted by law enforcement representatives for the purpose of searching for wrongdoing. **Self-policing audits** are done by the organization, and as a result, the organization has more control over the direction and timing of the audit.

Audits have been described as "a widely used organizational defense against fraud" (Holt-freter, 2004, p. 89). Audits are done as part of routine procedures, or they may be initiated out of a concern that fraud is occurring in the organization. Organizations will conduct either internal or external audits. **Internal audits** are conducted by the organization's accounting department, while **external audits** are conducted by consultants hired by the corporation (Holtfreter, 2004). Some red flags that surface from audits include the following:

- A lack of documentation for new projects

- Significant payments to new vendors

- Larger payments than usual

- Signs of managers systematically overriding internal controls (Heslop, 2007)

It is believed that, when fraud is discovered during a routine audit, the detection is typically "by chance" (Hemraj, 2002, p. 85). **Fraud audits**, or audits conducted for the purpose of exposing fraud, are more likely to reveal fraud. The objectives of a fraud audit include (1) identifying control mechanisms in a business, (2) identifying weaknesses in a business that place the business at risk for fraud, and (3) identifying those with access who have taken advantage of the weaknesses (Buckhoff, Higgins, & Sinclair, 2010). Some estimates suggest that nearly half of frauds against businesses are uncovered through audits (Peterson, 2004).

Audits are useful in helping companies identify parts of the company that are not profitable as well as potential areas of concern. In addition, audits help companies determine whether they are at risk of criminal and civil liability, and if conducted as part of a strong compliance program, audits allow companies more control over the direction of any subsequent criminal or civil investigation (Goldsmith & King, 1997).

In July 2002, the Sarbanes-Oxley Act (SOX) was passed in reaction to the scandals that were occurring at the time, including Enron's and WorldCom's crimes. Among other things, the act, known as SOX, developed standards for auditor independence in publicly traded companies and public accounting firms. The act states that an external auditor must meet these provisions:

- Cannot have been an employee of the company being audited in the prior year

- Must be approved by the company's audit committee

- Cannot offer additional services (such as bookkeeping) without the approval of the audit committee

- Cannot perform audits more than 5 years in a row for the same company

- Must communicate policies and changes to the audit committee

- Must publicly disclose fees (Nestor, 2004)

The SOX act included a number of other provisions relevant to the criminal and civil processing of corporate crimes. These other provisions will be discussed later in the text.

Forensic Accounting

Students are likely familiar with television shows like *CSI: Crime Scene Investigation,* where forensic scientists review crime scene evidence and solve the crime by the end of the show. Just as forensic scientists are able to piece together evidence to identify suspects, **forensic accountants** are able to review financial records and determine whether evidence indicates that a crime has been committed. Accordingly, forensic accounting is another self-policing strategy some businesses use to detect fraud.

When using forensic accountants, businesses will typically hire external consultants to perform the investigation. Just as a large private investigator business exists in the United States, an industry called "Forensic Accounting and Corporate Investigation" also exists (J. W. Williams, 2005). This industry has been described as "a diverse and loosely coupled network of private firms and professional groups providing investigative, advisory, and adjudicative service to clients embroiled in cases of economic and financial wrongdoing, whether as 'victims' or 'offenders'" (Williams, 2005, p. 188). Williams described three tiers in this industry: (1) specialized forensic accounting units in large accounting firms, (2) large forensic accounting firms devoted solely to corporate investigations, and (3) small private investigation agencies. When hired, forensic accountants can do investigative accounting, searching for evidence of fraud, economic loss calculations determining how much a company has lost to fraud or other events, and appraisals of the business to determine whether the company made or lost money as a result of misconduct (Rasmussen & Leauanae, 2004). For corporate offenders, forensic accounting firms offer services as expert witnesses, consulting about federal policies and laws, witness preparation, and a number of other services.

It is important to note that forensic accountants will also collect and scrutinize evidence other than financial records. They will review work schedules, read e-mail messages, interview workers and bosses, gather and review other available evidence, and develop a report detailing their conclusions about the presence of fraud in the business: (1) whether it is occurring in the business, (2) why it is occurring, and (3) who is possibly committing the fraud. A survey of 252 academics and forensic accountants found that the most necessary skills for forensic accountants included deductive reasoning, critical thinking, and the ability to serve as an expert witness (DiGabriele, 2008). The author of this study notes that an accounting education often focuses on a structured way to do accounting, but forensic accounting is different because the practitioners need to be able to improvise.

REGULATORY POLICING AND WHITE-COLLAR CRIME

Regulatory agencies are government agencies responsible for making sure that regulations are followed in industries and businesses across the United States. In this context, regulations are rules that guide workplace activities. Regulations "authorize as well as restrain behaviors" (Michalowski, 2020, p. 84). Note that the violation of a "rule" may not necessarily be treated as a violation of the criminal law, but these violations can be seen as white-collar crimes. To provide a framework for understanding regulatory policing, the following areas will be addressed:

- Conceptualizing regulatory policing

- Regulatory officials as police officers

- Regulatory policing styles

- Criticisms and concerns of regulatory policing

Conceptualizing Regulatory Policing

Different types of businesses are regulated by different regulatory agencies, depending on the different types of products or services the business provides. In reality, most businesses are regulated by multiple regulatory agencies. For example, restaurants and bars are regulated by (1) local and state agencies responsible for ensuring that food safety laws are not violated; (2) state alcohol control agencies to make sure that liquor laws are not violated; (3) occupational safety and health agencies to make sure businesses are not violating workers' rights or making them unsafe; and (4) local, state, and federal agencies charged with ensuring waste is disposed of correctly.

Regulatory agencies engage in policing activities in different ways that are tied to the specific agency's mission statement. Regulatory enforcement has been defined as "the consistent application of formal rules and sanctions to secure compliance with the enabling legislation and promulgated regulations" (Snider, 1990, p. 374). As Hazel Croall (1989) points out, regulatory officers "proceed very much like police" (p. 166). Others have added that regulators "are required to set in motion a process to identify . . . and punish those who have been irresponsible" (Jayasuriya & Sharp, 2006, p. 51).

Some have said that the financial crisis of the early 2000s actually served to "awaken the world to the role of the regulator in the fight against financial crimes" (Pusey, 2007, p. 300). Pusey (2007) draws attention to the changing nature of the regulator's role. The Obama administration increased regulatory efforts. Describing crackdowns on unsafe products and unsafe workplace settings, one reporter commented,

> The new regulators display a passion for rules and a belief that government must protect the public from dangers lurking at home and on the job—one more way the new White House is reworking the relationship between government and business. (Layton, 2009)

The more recent financial crises of the late 2000s also awakened some politicians to the need for additional regulation in the financial markets. After the economic collapse, which was compared to the Great Depression, the Dodd-Frank Wall Street Reform and Consumer Protection Act was passed in 2010. This act essentially overhauled the financial regulation system. Its stated purpose was

> [t]o promote the financial stability of the United States by improving accountability and transparency in the financial system, to end "too big to fail," to protect the American taxpayer by ending bailouts, to protect consumers from abusive financial services practices, and for other purposes.

The 848-page act was a piece of sweeping legislation aiming to prevent another situation where the economy would collapse as a result of poor decisions by financial institutions. Various federal agencies were called upon to create new strategies to regulate the financial industry. For example, after the passage of the act, the SEC created the following offices:

- Office of the Whistleblower
- Office of Credit Ratings
- Office of the Investor Advocate
- Office of Minority and Women Inclusion
- Office of Municipal Securities

The act also created the Consumer Financial Protection Bureau, which was developed as a strategy to prevent consumer fraud. The bureau is tasked to perform the following:

- Write rules, supervise companies, and enforce federal consumer financial protection laws
- Restrict unfair, deceptive, or abusive acts or practices
- Take consumer complaints
- Promote financial education
- Research consumer behavior
- Monitor financial markets for new risks to consumers
- Enforce laws that outlaw discrimination and other unfair treatment in consumer finance

Different offices were created in the Consumer Finance Protection Bureau to address the many different types of problems consumers in the United States confront. The offices focus on educating members of the public about ways to protect against consumer victimization; the offices also provide research and data that give insight into ongoing consumer complaint trends.

Regulatory Officials as Police Officers

In general, agencies receive information about violations through referrals, site inspections, news reports, and record reviews. In terms of referrals, regulatory agencies receive information about potential rule breaking from investors, consumers, anonymous tips, competitors, and other government agencies that uncover potential wrongdoing (Rutledge, 2006). Regulatory officials will review the referral by using traditional investigatory techniques, including interviewing witnesses, visiting the site of the alleged violation, reviewing records, and so on.

In addition to visiting business sites to follow up on complaints, regulatory officers will carry out routine site visits to conduct periodic reviews of businesses. Inspectors from local or state health departments, for example, will visit restaurants to ensure that the businesses are in compliance with food safety and health regulations. The inspectors assign the restaurant a score based on the inspection. In some places, the inspection reports are posted online. Inspectors can force a business to shut down until the violations are addressed. Consider a case in which an inspector temporarily closed a restaurant in south Florida for 17 violations uncovered as part of the inspection. Among other things, the inspection found "raw sewage in the back yard of the restaurant; more than 100 fresh rodent droppings in the kitchen; a live roach in the kitchen; ready-to-eat, potentially hazardous food prepared on site and held more than 24 hours and not properly date-marked" (Trischitta, 2011). In another case, a restaurant was shut down by inspectors who found employees butchering a deer in the kitchen when they visited the establishment to follow up on an anonymous tip ("Restaurant Closed Briefly," 2008).

As another example of site visits as part of regulatory policing of white-collar crime, the Centers for Medicare and Medicaid Services contracts with states to have state inspectors visit nursing homes receiving Medicare or Medicaid payments at least once a year and to conduct health and safety inspections. The inspectors conduct a thorough investigation assessing the degree to which the business is adhering to more than 150 different rules. Based on their findings, the team can fine the nursing homes, deny payments, and suspend the nursing home from participation in Medicare and Medicaid if it fails to address violations found by inspectors (Medicare.Gov, 2008).

Regulatory investigations sometimes stem from news reports demonstrating how a particular agency or industry is violating regulations. In July 2010, for example, the Department of Housing and Urban Development (HUD) initiated an investigation after a *New York Times* article titled "Need a Mortgage? Don't Get Pregnant," by reporter Tara Bernard (2010), showed that pregnant women and new moms were being denied loans because of their new babies. After the article appeared in print, HUD released a statement to the press that included the following comments:

A published report in the *New York Times* indicated that some mortgage lenders may be denying credit to borrowers because of a pregnancy or maternity leave. As a result, HUD's Office of Fair Housing Equal Opportunity is opening multiple investigations into the practices of lending institutions to determine if they are violating the Fair Housing Act.

"This report is profoundly disturbing and requires immediate action," said John Trasviña, HUD's Assistant Secretary for Fair Housing and Equal Opportunity, the office that will be directing these investigations. "Lenders must not carry out due diligence responsibilities in ways that have the practical effect of discriminating against recent or expectant mothers." (U.S. Department of Housing and Urban Development [HUD], 2010)

Regulatory agencies also learn about violations through record reviews. For businesses that receive payments from the government, regulatory officials review the bills submitted by the business to ensure the business is in compliance and to determine whether regulatory rules were violated. If officials detect errors in the claims, an additional examination is conducted to determine whether the error was intentional or accidental. For accidental errors, the funds are recovered from the business. For intentionally submitted false bills, the case is referred to another office for criminal and civil investigations. In securities fraud investigations, federal and "state regulators have authority to issue subpoenas for documents" (Rutledge, 2006, p. 340).

Regulatory Policing Styles

Generally speaking, two types of regulatory strategies exist—persuasion or cooperation strategies and retributive or punishment strategies (Frank, 1984; Snider, 1990). Persuasion strategies promote "education, negotiation, and cooperation" to get businesses and corporations to comply with regulations (Frank, 1984, p. 237). Retributive strategies emphasize finding violations and punishing offenders. An analogy to traffic enforcement helps distinguish between the two strategies. If your campus police develop strategies to educate and persuade students to obey traffic laws, this would be a persuasion strategy. If your campus police focus solely on catching traffic violators and giving them stiff fines, this would be a retributive strategy. Among regulatory agencies, some are more persuasion oriented, while others are more punishment oriented.

A question that often arises is whether regulatory officers are police officers. Using James Q. Wilson's typology of police officers, criminologist Nancy Frank (1984) shows how regulatory policing styles are similar to traditional law enforcement styles. First, some regulatory agencies follow a "service style" where the agencies serve the community through the provision of various services. According to Frank, administrators in these agencies see themselves as serving the government and not the public.

Second, some agencies follow a "watchman" style in their efforts to regulate corporate behavior—using discretion and staying out of the way, with officers who are described by Frank as possessing "only marginal competence" (Frank, 1984, p. 242). Consider the movie *Larry the Cable Guy: Health Inspector*, which one or two readers may have seen. In the movie, Larry the Cable Guy is portrayed as a health inspector letting businesses get away with all sorts of atrocities and enforcing laws only as a last resort. I won't give away the plot because it truly is worth watching to learn more about regulatory policing.

Third, "legalistic" agencies address regulatory violations more aggressively. Officers are more competent and more professional in such agencies, and the agencies "have formal guidelines instructing enforcement officers when to bring actions" (Frank, 1984, p. 245). These officers likely see their occupations as being oriented toward law enforcement and play by the book in their efforts to regulate businesses and corporations.

Fourth, the "free agent" style is similar to the legalistic style, but regulatory officers are given more leeway in deciding how to proceed with the case. Imagine Clint Eastwood's Dirty Harry character as a regulatory officer. Instead of a .44 magnum, he would be armed with a clipboard, rule book, and BlackBerry, but his efforts to root out corporate rule breaking would be similar to the way the fictional officer sought out criminals in the five movies about the detective's crime fighting.

As long as we are using a Dirty Harry analogy, in the 1983 Dirty Harry movie *Sudden Impact*, Detective Harry Callahan was pointing his gun at his nemesis when he said, "Go ahead, make my day"—a quote that has become part of our lexicon. Callahan was, in effect, communicating a very clear message to the offender—he wanted to shoot the suspect in the head. In a no-nonsense way, regulatory officers are expected to communicate messages to the businesses and organizations they regulate.

Researchers have suggested that how compliance messages are communicated to managers in the business or corporation may have an impact on how they respond to the regulatory activity (Makkai & Braithwaite, 1994). If the regulator's behaviors and messages are perceived as overly punitive, the business might continue to engage in rule breaking. Makkai and Braithwaite

(1994) call for a reintegrative shaming model to notify businesses about misconduct. They suggest that regulators do the following:

(a) communicate noncompliance in a way that is perceived as procedurally fair,
(b) communicate noncompliance in a way that does not communicate distrust,
(c) communicate noncompliance in a way that shows respect for professionalism,
(d) give praise to low self-efficacy actors when they fix one of the problems, and
(e) encourage disengagers to become reengaged. (p. 365)

In other words, the "Dirty Harry style of communicating" may not be the best way for regulators to communicate with corporations.

Criticisms and Concerns About Regulatory Policing

A number of different criticisms have been levied against regulatory policing, with most of these criticisms suggesting that the regulatory efforts do little to stop misconduct. In fact, some say that rather than stopping misconduct, such efforts may actually breed rule breaking. For example, one author team suggested that "much regulation . . . represents a facilitation, rather than diminishment, of environmental harm" (Halsey & White, 1998, p. 347). Others have blamed regulatory agencies for recent economic woes on the grounds that "light-handed" regulation allowed corporate misconduct to escalate to the point that markets collapsed and criminal prosecutions were inevitable (Tomasic, 2011).

Scholars have also argued that corporate power weakens the regulatory system. Snider (1990) suggested that "the entire agenda of regulation is the result of a struggle between the corporate sector opposing regulation and the much weaker forces supporting it" (p. 384). Another criticism that has been levied is that regulatory efforts are too lenient and corporate misconduct should be handled as violations of the criminal law, with more severe sanctions given to offenders.

While some have said the corporations, businesses, and offenders should be criminally punished rather than regulated, criminologist Susan Shapiro (1985) has argued that a clear sign that regulatory agencies have failed is the use of the criminal law to respond to corporate misconduct. From this perspective, if regulatory agencies were working, then companies would be abiding by corporate regulations, and there would be no need for the criminal law in these cases.

A more recent concern—and not necessarily a criticism of—regulatory efforts is the Trump administration's "dramatic destruction of regulatory agencies" (Snider, 2020, p. 86). Criminologists note the irony that the administration has "roll[ed] over the rights and protections historically afforded many other groups" while reducing the rules and regulations corporations must abide by (Wonders & Danner, 2020). White-collar crime experts have predicted that these deregulation efforts may lead to more regulatory violations (Friedrichs & Rothe, 2020; Haugh, 2016–2017).

Another concern centers around preparing regulators for their careers. Successful regulatory responses require a multidisciplinary and multiprofessional response (Braithwaite, 2020). As Braithwaite points out, regulators need a wide range of skills related to interviewing, law enforcement, business, legal studies, and so on. Regulators need to gain the trust of the businesses they are regulating while simultaneously being able to enforce regulations in a way that prevents rather than causes more problems. The most effective regulators develop cultures of compliance without damaging businesses in ways that harm the community. In many ways, regulators are expected to perform a balancing act. In the words of one author, "compliance interventions have to be crafted with a light touch or they will backfire" (Langevoort, 2017, p. 972).

THE GLOBAL POLICE AND WHITE-COLLAR CRIME

As noted throughout this book, white-collar offending occurs internationally. One author summed up this pattern stating, "with the globalization of the world economy, white-collar crime is increasingly transnational in nature" (Lardo, 2006, p. 867). Consequently, police agencies from across the world have been called upon to use law enforcement strategies to detect, respond to, and prevent white-collar crime. Initial problems that surface in global white-collar crime cases include the presence of "regulatory loopholes," which arise when multiple jurisdictions are involved in a fragmented global response system (Van Wingerde & Lord, 2020). A number of other issues arise in efforts to address international white-collar crimes, including the following:

- Countries vary in the types of records they maintain.

- Linguistic barriers make it difficult for officers to communicate with one another.

- Cultural barriers create situations where misconduct and offenders might be perceived differently.

- Gaining cooperation between agencies from different countries is difficult.

- Determining whether international enforcement policies are effective is an arduous task (Passas, 2004).

Barriers also arise when international companies do internal investigations within their own company. Different data protection laws between countries, for example, may limit a company's ability to transfer documents between countries (Dervan, 2011). In addition, the regulations governing how internal security officials can interview employees may vary across countries and make it more difficult to conduct these interviews in some cases (Dervan, 2011).

These barriers can be overcome, or at least minimized. For example, cooperation can be enhanced if officers are aware of cultural differences between countries (Larsson, 2006). Also, resource commitments by specific agencies involved in international partnerships would help to demonstrate that countries are committed to responding to white-collar crime (Berkman et al., 2008). Larsson (2006) suggested that international cooperation can be improved if officials do the following: (1) create networks where police officers can develop a "common language" (p. 463), (2) provide appropriate education and training to those involved in the international response to white-collar crime, (3) ensure that police agencies have the information they need to prevent crime, and (4) identify communication channels.

Summary

- White-collar crimes come to the attention of the police through several different avenues, and a number of different agencies are involved in the police response to white-collar crime.

- The notion of *police response* to white-collar crime describes different forms of policing, including criminal policing, private policing, and regulatory policing.

- Three types of agencies are involved in responding to white-collar crime. These include private agencies (or self-policing by corporations or businesses), formal criminal

- police agencies, and governmental regulatory agencies.

- A major portion of the police response to white-collar crime involves law enforcement strategies carried out by officials in the criminal justice system.

- White-collar crime investigations begin one of two ways—from referrals or as a part of a proactive policing initiative.

- Common strategies for gathering evidence in white-collar crime cases include (1) audits, (2) record reviews, (3) undercover strategies, (4) the use of whistleblowers, and (5) the use of technological devices.

- While not always sufficient by themselves, when combined with other forms of evidence-gathering strategies, audits can provide the evidence needed to substantiate wrongdoing.

- White-collar crime investigators will review an assortment of records in building their case. The number of records law enforcement investigators will need to review in these cases can be enormous.

- On the surface, undercover white-collar crime investigations are no different from undercover criminal investigations. However, important differences exist between white-collar and conventional undercover investigations.

- Compared to conventional undercover investigations, white-collar crime undercover investigations are less dangerous, less time consuming, involve lower degrees of role playing by officers, and are not as central to the case as undercover investigations in criminal cases.

- Whistleblowers are individuals who notify authorities about wrongdoing in their organization. Two types of whistleblowers exist: internal whistleblowers and external whistleblowers (Vinten, 1994).

- Various types of technological devices are used to search for evidence in white-collar crime cases.

- Problems that surface in criminal white-collar crime investigations include the following: resource problems, relationship dynamics, time, complexity, establishing proof, and perceptions of white-collar crime police work.

- Resources are a problem inasmuch as white-collar crime police units are grossly underresourced in comparison to police units focusing on conventional crimes.

- Three types of relationships present obstacles in white-collar crime investigations: (1) the victim-offender relationship, (2) the offender-witness relationship, and (3) the officer-offender relationship.

- Three issues that make white-collar crimes particularly complex are (1) complex record searches, (2) extensive collaborations with partners, and (3) the lack of a systematic approach.

- It is difficult for investigators to gather evidence that prosecutors will be able to use to prove various aspects of the misconduct.

- Police work in these cases is often perceived pejoratively, as if the activity is not real police work.

- A number of different suggestions have been made to improve the law enforcement response to white-collar crime, including searching for the "smoking gun," "following the money," and educating officials.

- Self-policing refers to efforts by companies and businesses to develop their own policing responses to white-collar crime.

- Types of self-policing efforts used by business to detect or prevent white-collar crime include loss prevention strategies, compliance programs, audits, and the use of forensic accountants.

- Loss prevention strategies are efforts that businesses use to keep employees from stealing from the business.

- A compliance program is an "organizational system aimed at comprehensively detecting and preventing corporate criminality" (Goldsmith & King, 1997, p. 9).

- Criminal investigation audits are conducted by law enforcement representatives for the purpose of searching for wrongdoing. Self-policing audits are done by the organization.

- Forensic accountants are able to review financial records to determine whether there is evidence indicating that a crime has been committed. Forensic accounting is another self-policing strategy some businesses use to detect fraud.

- Regulatory agencies are government agencies responsible for making sure that regulations are followed in industries and businesses across the United States.

- Different types of businesses are regulated by different regulatory agencies, depending on the different types of products or services the business provides.

- In general, agencies receive information about violations through referrals, site inspections, news reports, and record reviews.

- Two types of regulatory strategies exist: persuasion or cooperation strategies and retributive or punishment strategies (Frank, 1984; Snider, 1990).

- A number of different criticisms have been levied against regulatory policing, with most of these criticisms suggesting that the regulatory efforts do little to stop misconduct.

- Police agencies across the world have been called upon to use law enforcement strategies to detect, respond to, and prevent white-collar crime.

- Larsson (2006) suggested that international cooperation can be improved if officials do the following: (1) develop networks where police officers can create a "common language" (p. 463), (2) provide appropriate education and training, (3) ensure that police agencies have the information they need to prevent crime, and (4) identify communication channels.

Key Terms

Audits 380
Compliance program 395
External audit 396
External whistleblower 383
Forensic accountant 397
Fraud audits 397
Internal audits 396

Internal whistleblower 383
Loss prevention strategies 394
Proactive strategies 378
Reactive strategies 378
Record reviews 380
Regulatory agencies 398
Self-policing 393

Self-policing audits 396
Smoking gun 392
Whistleblower 383
White-collar undercover investigations 381
Workplace interview 395

Discussion Questions

1. How are white-collar crime investigations different from investigations of conventional crimes?

2. Review the police and regulatory agencies that respond to white-collar crimes. Which of those agencies would you want to work for? Explain.

3. What would you like most about being a white-collar crime investigator? What would you like the least?

4. Should businesses be required to report their employees to the police if they catch them stealing from the business? Explain.

5. Find a job advertisement related to a career policing white-collar crime. Would you apply for that job? Why, or why not?

6. Which types of evidence-gathering strategies do you think are the most effective for building white-collar crime cases?

7. Why is white-collar crime so difficult to address with law enforcement and regulatory efforts?

8. Select any business, and explain how misconduct is policed in that business.

9. How would you feel if you found out that one of your coworkers is an undercover investigator posing as an employee in your work setting? Explain.

JUDICIAL PROCEEDINGS AND WHITE-COLLAR CRIME

CHAPTER HIGHLIGHTS

- Types of Judicial Proceedings Responding to White-Collar Misconduct
- The Role of Judges in Addressing White-Collar Crime
- The Role of Prosecutors in Addressing White-Collar Crime
- The Role of Defense Attorneys in White-Collar Crime Cases
- Other Actors Involved in White-Collar Crime Judicial Proceedings
- Civil Lawsuits and White-Collar Crime
- Issues in White-Collar Crime Judicial Process

In what has since been called the "peephole lawsuit" by a *Washington Post* reporter, sports reporter Erin Andrews sued a Nashville hotel after a stalker, who convinced hotel staff to rent him a room next to Andrews, secretly filmed the reporter and posted nude photos of her online. The stalker, Michael David Barrett, plead guilty to criminal charges (which are not considered white-collar offending). The lawsuit also alleged wrongdoing by the hotel, which is considered white-collar misconduct. As a result of the lawsuit, the hotel and Barrett were ordered to pay $55 million in damages with Barrett expected to pay 51% of the penalty and the hotel the remaining 49% (SIWire, 2016). Such a split assigns fault suggesting the Barrett was "51 percent at fault," and the hotel was "49 percent at fault" (Keneally, 2016). Erin Andrews's case is just one of many that made its way through the courts. Consider a few excerpts from news reports and press releases describing different parts of the judicial process:

- Judge Alsup agreed with the prosecution that in white-collar cases such as these, deterrence is of upmost importance and a non-custodial sentence would be a "green light to every future brilliant engineer to steal trade secrets". He said that ++++++++ would begin his sentence once the coronavirus pandemic had peaked and also ordered

++++++++ to speak publicly about his crimes to deter other engineers from similar behavior" (E&T Editorial Staff, 2020).

- A former clerk of the Orange County Superior Court was sentenced today to 135 months in federal prison for orchestrating a scheme in which he was paid approximately $420,000 dollars in bribes to "fix" criminal cases and traffic offenses on terms favorable to hundreds of defendants without the knowledge of prosecutors or judges. +++++, of Anaheim, was sentenced this morning after pleading guilty in March to one count of conspiring to violate the federal Racketeer Influenced and Corrupt Organizations Act (RICO). +++++ sentenced by United States District Judge Josephine L. Staton, who said +++++ created, led and profited from the scheme. "This [criminal conduct] was not an aberration from his character—this was his character," the judge said. (USDOJ, 2017, September 22).

- Indianapolis-United States Attorney Josh J. Minkler announced today the sentencing of an Indianapolis man for his role in an elaborate scheme to defraud local business. ++++++, was sentenced to 48 months' imprisonment by U.S. District Judge Michael Reagan after being found guilty in a jury trial in September of this year. At trial, ++++++ was found guilty of two counts of wire fraud and two counts of money laundering. ++++++'s greed cost local businesses and the government nearly $600,000 in losses," said Minkler. "Let's call white collar crime, what it really is; stealing, and those who do will be held accountable for their actions." (USDOJ, 2017, December 20).

- Attorney General Kwame Raoul announced that a Chicago doctor pleaded guilty to Medicaid fraud for fraudulently billing the state for Medicaid services she never provided. +++++++++, of Chicago, pleaded guilty to felony vendor fraud and was sentenced to 24 months of probation and ordered to perform 30 hours of community service. . . . "I am committed to protecting the state's Medicaid funding for the thousands of residents and families who rely on the program for health care," Raoul said. "Defrauding the people of Illinois by misusing Medicaid resources will not be tolerated." (Illinois Attorney General, 2020, February 3).

The scrutiny that the "peephole lawsuit" received and the four other cases highlighted here demonstrate several important facts regarding the judicial response to white-collar crime. In particular, these cases show that white-collar crimes (1) are processed through several different judicial proceedings, (2) involve the efforts of many different actors in the judicial process, and (3) present numerous complexities to those involved in adjudicating the cases. To shed some light on the way the judicial system responds to white-collar crimes, in this chapter, attention is given to the following: types of judicial proceedings; the roles of judges, prosecutors, and defense attorneys; other actors involved in white-collar crime judicial proceedings; civil lawsuits; and issues in white-collar judicial proceedings. Addressing these areas will help students appreciate the complexities surrounding the judicial response to white-collar crime.

TYPES OF JUDICIAL PROCEEDINGS RESPONDING TO WHITE-COLLAR MISCONDUCT

White-collar misconduct cases are adjudicated in at least five different types of judicial or quasijudicial proceedings: (1) criminal proceedings, (2) civil proceedings, (3) administrative proceedings, (4) professional-disciplinary proceedings, and (5) workplace-disciplinary

FIGURE 14.1 ■ Types of Judicial Proceedings in White-Collar Misconduct Cases

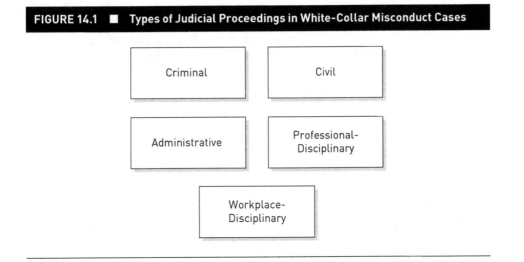

proceedings (see Figure 14.1). In **criminal proceedings**, criminal charges are filed against the defendant, and sanctions could include imprisonment, fines, probation, community service, and restitution. Because an individual's liberty is at stake (through incarceration), criminal proceedings offer offenders more protections than other proceedings, and the standard of proof is higher. The bulk of this chapter addresses criminal judicial proceedings as they relate to white-collar offenders.

In **civil proceedings**, an individual or government representative, referred to as a *plaintiff*, files civil charges against an individual or business. The charges focus on violations, allegedly committed by the defendant, which brought some sort of harm to the plaintiff. In some white-collar crime cases, the government will file motions in civil court that seek injunctive remedies. For instance, officials routinely ask civil courts to issue *cease and desist* orders, which tell a business or corporation to refrain from the activities under judicial review until the proceeding is completed. In civil proceedings, the standard of proof is less (e.g., plaintiffs must prove by a preponderance of evidence), and defendants are not afforded the same level of protection (e.g., while they may refuse to testify, the judge and jury are permitted to make inferences about such a refusal). Also, sanctions are primarily monetary in nature. More on civil proceedings will be provided below.

Administrative proceedings are different from criminal justice and civil proceedings. Technically, these proceedings are not designed to punish but are designed "to restrict . . . certain future actions" (M. A. Cohen, 1992, p. 1059). These proceedings are used more commonly for white-collar offenses than for conventional offenses. Many regulatory agencies use administrative proceedings to adjudicate cases brought to their attention. Depending on the laws that govern the regulatory agency, the types of decisions made in administrative proceedings could include the following:

- Issue civil fines

- Issue cease and desist orders to protect the health and safety of workers, consumers, citizens, and others

- Prevent specific individuals or groups from participating in corporate activities

- Prohibit the corporation from participating in specific types of government programs (Van Cleef, Silets, & Motz, 2004)

As an illustration, the Securities and Exchange Commission (SEC) will hold administrative proceedings before the Commission or an administrative law judge. The SEC has the authority to impose administrative sanctions, including cease and desist orders and monetary penalties. One issue that arises in the judicial processing of white-collar crime cases is that the boundaries between criminal, civil, and administrative proceedings "are often very fuzzy" (M. A. Cohen, 1992, p. 1060).

Professional-disciplinary proceedings are used to address different types of white-collar misconduct. Recall the discussion of the ways bar associations discipline lawyers in Chapter 5. These proceedings are administered through the state bar association, with the professional disciplinary association processing the case and deciding whether and how to sanction the attorney. Other professions have similar proceedings. For instance, medical professionals accused of misconduct could have their cases adjudicated by state medical boards, which are responsible for licensing different types of medical professionals. Other occupations that have professional boards reviewing their allegations of wrongdoing include but are not limited to social workers, counselors, barbers, teachers, and clergy.

Workplace-disciplinary proceedings are similar to the professional-disciplinary proceedings, except they are conducted entirely within the workplace where the misconduct was alleged. Cases heard in the workplace (quasijudicial hearings) often include labor violations and discrimination. The cases are typically handled through a company's equal opportunity office or human resources department. These cases may not necessarily be resolved in the workplace because the offended party might file a claim in civil or administrative court once the workplace proceedings are completed.

While white-collar misconduct cases are adjudicated in different ways, from a criminological perspective, the role of the criminal court is particularly important in understanding how white-collar crime cases are handled as crimes. In the following chapter, attention is given to various actors involved in criminally adjudicating white-collar offenses. This will be followed by a discussion of civil lawsuits and issues that arise in the judicial processing of white-collar offenders.

THE ROLE OF JUDGES IN ADDRESSING WHITE-COLLAR CRIME

Judges play an extremely important role in processing white-collar crime cases through the justice system. Among other things, it is their responsibility to ensure that the justice process unfolds in a way that is fair to the defendant and the state. Judges oversee cases from the time they are filed until they are resolved. They approve plea negotiations and oversee trials. They also sentence convicted offenders and even make recommendations about where incarcerated offenders will serve their sentences. Clearly, judges are afforded a great deal of power in the criminal justice system.

Unfortunately, few recent studies have examined the judicial role in white-collar crime cases, though a few classic studies create a foundation from which understanding about judges and white-collar crime can evolve. These earlier studies focused on how judges perceive white-collar offenders, offenses, and sanctions. With regard to studies on perceptions about offenders, one early study found that judges perceive public officials (e.g., politicians) as deserving of more severe sanctions than other offenders (Pollack & Smith, 1983).

Stanton Wheeler, Kenneth Mann, and Austin Sarat (1988) authored the seminal work *Sitting in Judgment: The Sentencing of White-Collar Criminals*, which was based on interviews with 51 federal judges who had significant involvement with hearing white-collar crime cases. Among other things, their research showed that judges varied in how they received information and used the information available to them. Their research also showed that the three most salient factors influencing judicial decision making in white-collar crime cases were (1) harm from the offense, (2) blameworthiness, and (3) consequences of the punishment.

In terms of harm, the more harm caused by the offense, the less favorably judges perceived white-collar offenders. In the words of the authors, for some judges, "if an offense is more serious, its perpetrator is therefore more culpable" (Wheeler et al., 1988, p. 54). Judges determined harm by considering how much was lost, the duration of the offending, whether there were identifiable victims and the types of victims, and whether trust violations occurred. In assessing blame, judges considered prior records, offender motive, the offender's life history, and evidence presented at the trial.

In terms of sentencing, the author team noted elsewhere that the judges perceived white-collar offenders as having a special sensitivity to imprisonment (Mann, Wheeler, & Sarat, 1980). They viewed this special sensitivity as providing a powerful general deterrent that would keep white-collar employees from engaging in future misconduct. As a result, the judges viewed publicity as an important ingredient in increasing the deterrent potential of jail. One judge indicated that "he had tried to make sure" that certain types of cases would receive publicity (p. 479). Others have also suggested that judicial sanctions, such as jail, have the ability to deter white-collar misconduct (Pollack & Smith, 1983).

Anecdotal evidence still surfaces suggesting judges are lenient on white-collar offenders. In one case, a judge justified a one-year probation sentence for a white-collar offender despite the sentencing guidelines recommending five years in prison. The judge stated,

> A prison term would end the current job that you have, with no guarantee that you would have this job or one like it when you got out of jail . . . I want you to keep your job, because I want you to have a good job to pay these victims back. (*United States v. Sample*)

The appellate court overturned the lenient probation sanction and remanded it back to the lower court for a new sentencing.

More will be written about sentencing of offenders in Chapter 15. At this point, attention can be given to factors contributing to judges' sentencing behaviors and judges' perceptions of criminal sanctions. With regard to the former, a study of U.S. federal antitrust sentences from the mid-1950s through the early 1980s showed that sentences appeared to be tied to judges' goals. For example, those seeking promotion to higher courts sentenced differently than those who did not aspire to a higher court (M. A. Cohen, 1992).

A number of researchers have drawn attention to the short sentences that white-collar offenders receive (Payne, 2003b). According to Mann and his colleagues (1980), judges justified these shorter sentences on three grounds. First, the judges did not want to do additional harm to the offender's family. Second, a shorter sentence was seen as providing offenders the opportunity to contribute back to the community. Third, with shorter sentences, offenders would be in better positions to pay victims back and make reparations for their misdeeds. The judges did not see fines as being useful for white-collar offenders.

Other researchers suggest that implicit racial biases may contribute to stiffer sentences for people of color. Such implicit biases are believed to surface among professionals throughout the justice system. Summarizing a body of research on the topic, one author concludes that "judges often favor whites over racial minorities, and wealthier defendants over the disadvantaged" (Ghandnoosh, 2014). White-collar defendants would be among those wealthier defendants.

Early legal scholars highlighted the difficulties that judges faced in sentencing corporate offenders. Orland (1980), for example, wrote, "Often judges find it difficult to condemn the acts of corporate executives which are undertaken not only to advance personal career goals, but also to maximize the profits of the corporation" (p. 511). He continued, "Many judges find it less difficult to punish criminal conduct undertaken at the expense of the corporation than conduct in which the corporation and its stakeholders are the ultimate beneficiaries of the criminal act" (p. 511). As will be shown in the following sections, corporations make better "victims" than "offenders."

Federal and state sentencing guidelines created in the mid-1980s gave judges less discretion in deciding how to punish white-collar offenders. Under these guidelines, judges refer to the guidelines to determine the sentence recommended for a specific offense. The sentence (time to be served) is typically offered as a range (e.g., 6 months to 1 year). Judges can depart from the recommended range, either increasing or decreasing the actual sentence given to the offender. In white-collar crime cases, upward departures usually result from significant monetary harm, emotional harm, offenses targeting vulnerable groups, and abuses of trust (J. W. Barnard, 2001). Judges don't always view the guidelines as helpful. One judge told a *Newsweek* reporter that the federal guidelines "are just too goddamn severe" (Goodman, 2014). The judge elaborated: "The arithmetic behind the sentencing calculations is all hocus-pocus—it's nonsensical, and I mean that sincerely. It gives the illusion of something meaningful with no real value underneath" (Goodman, 2014). Others have drawn attention to the growing severity of some of the sentences included in the guidelines. A fraud offense in 1987, would have resulted in a recommendation of 30 to 37 months in prison. By 2003, the same offense would have resulted in a recommendation of 151 to 188 months in prison (Bennett, Levinson, Hioki, 2017).

While federal judges had to follow the federal guidelines when they were first created, or justify why they departed from the guidelines, two court cases (*Booker v. Washington*; *Gall v. United States*) relaxed the mandatory nature of the guidelines to the point that the guidelines are now seen as recommendations rather than requirements. As one author team notes, "the combination of Booker and Gall swung the pendulum back toward individual discretion" (Bennett et al., 2017, p. 956). As an illustration of judges embracing this discretion, Bennett et al. (2017) note that while the recommended sanction for fraud increased by six months between 2004 and 2012, the average sentence given only increased by two months. The research team concluded, "while sentences became stiffer, judges have chosen not to keep up" (p. 960).

PHOTO 14.1 Judges oversee the criminal justice process. Regarding white-collar defendants, judges may hold the defendants to a higher set of expectations than conventional defendants.

Such a finding defies judges' stated commitments to give white-collar offenders harsher sentences to prevent future offending. Recall Chapter 12's discussion on deterrence theory: Judges frequently justify their sanctions by saying they want to "send a message" to others. After reviewing federal sentencing patterns in white-collar crime cases, Healy and McGrath (2019) conclude that such statements by public officials are mere political rhetoric that is "less about crime control . . . and more about making statements for public approval and electoral gain" (p. 1278).

Some experts point out that the federal guidelines for recommended sentences for white-collar offenders are still overly strict, and they have called for changes to make the recommended sentences closer to what judges are actually giving. One criticism of the guidelines is that the formula used to estimate financial loss in white-collar crime cases artificially inflates the estimated losses. Consequently, the guidelines recommend a stiffer sentence than perhaps should be given (Hewitt, 2016). When judges review cases and consider sentencing, they are able to more accurately identify actual losses in white-collar crime cases. Using their discretion, judges often give lower sentences in white-collar crime cases. Modifying the way losses are calculated would help to address this problem in the guidelines (Hewitt, 2016).

It is important to note that guidelines exist at the federal level for sentencing individuals and corporations. The guidelines, designed for informing sentences for corporations, are known as Organizational Guidelines. These guidelines are based on four principles:

- The corporation is responsible for addressing the harm it causes.

- The corporation that exists for criminal purposes will lose all of its assets in an effort to repay victims and society.

- The corporation that exists for legitimate reasons should be fined according to the seriousness of the offense.

- Corporations can be placed on probation, if necessary, for compliance. (Thompson & Yong, 2012)

THE ROLE OF PROSECUTORS IN ADDRESSING WHITE-COLLAR CRIME

Prosecutors have a central role in processing white-collar crime cases through the justice system. At the federal level, U.S. attorneys are the prosecutors responsible for prosecuting federal offenses. At the state and local level, prosecutors go by different names, including district attorney, commonwealth's attorney, solicitor, attorney general, and so on. In some jurisdictions, specific units devoted to white-collar crimes exist, while other jurisdictions rely on prosecutors who seem to have more expertise with white-collar crimes. Regardless of what they are called and their levels of expertise, these officials are responsible for making several important decisions about white-collar crime cases. Decisions prosecutors make include the following:

- Deciding whether to prosecute a white-collar crime case

- Deciding what to charge offenders with

- Deciding whether to accept plea bargains

- Deciding whether to charge corporations

- Deciding whether to defer prosecution

Each of these areas is addressed below.

Deciding Whether to Prosecute a White-Collar Crime Case

The prosecution of white-collar criminals is seen as necessary to demonstrate "moral outrage" for white-collar misconduct (M. A. Cohen, 1992). Obviously, not all white-collar crimes are prosecuted in the justice system (see Figure 14.2). Some crimes never come to the attention of authorities, others are detected but not investigated, and others are investigated but not prosecuted. So how do prosecutors decide which cases to prosecute? First, prosecutors must determine whether the case occurred in their jurisdiction. This used to be a relatively simple determination, but as technology has made it

PHOTO 14.2 The prosecutor is one of the most powerful officials in the criminal justice process.

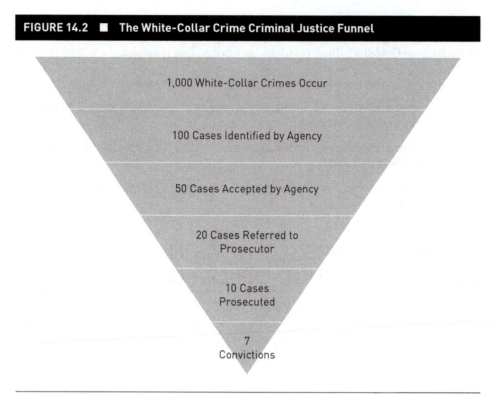

FIGURE 14.2 ■ The White-Collar Crime Criminal Justice Funnel

1,000 White-Collar Crimes Occur

100 Cases Identified by Agency

50 Cases Accepted by Agency

20 Cases Referred to Prosecutor

10 Cases Prosecuted

7 Convictions

Note: Numbers are hypothetical and meant to illustrate how few cases are prosecuted compared to the amount of white-collar crime.

possible for white-collar offenders to commit crimes against victims anywhere in the world, it has become more difficult for prosecutors to assign jurisdiction in many white-collar crime cases. For U.S. prosecutors to get involved, offenders must have some degree of contact with U.S. interests (which could include U.S. businesses or citizens (Foley, 2017). Prosecutors must also consider the legal issues surrounding the case; the amount of resources the prosecutor needs to devote to the case; the impact of prosecution on the community as a whole; the complexity of the evidence in the white-collar crime case; whether the prosecutor's office has the necessary skills; fairness; the potential for harming public or professional interests; and the strength of the defense by the defendant's attorneys (Artello & Albanese, 2019; Burns & Meitl, 2020).

Figure 14.3 shows the number of defendants in different types of white-collar crime cases filed by U.S. Attorneys in 2019. Health care, bank fraud/embezzlement, identity theft, and federal procurement fraud were the most common types of cases. Figure 14.4 shows the number of federal white-collar crime prosecutions between 1986 and 2019. As shown in the figure, the number of prosecutions dropped in recent years. It is important to note that the drop began in 2011 and has continued since then. In fact, there have been fewer white-collar crime prosecutions each year since 2016 than there were in 1986.

Table 14.1 shows how often different types of criminal cases were declined for prosecution at the federal level in 2019. On the surface, it appears that white-collar crime cases are declined more often than other cases. White-collar crime cases represented roughly one fifth of all declinations, but they are actually just a small fraction of all federal cases. Insufficient evidence is the most common reason cited for declining to prosecute white-collar crime cases at the federal level.

FIGURE 14.3 ■ **Federal White-Collar Crime Defendants in Cases Handled By U.S. Attorneys, Fiscal Year 2019 (ending September 30, 2019)**

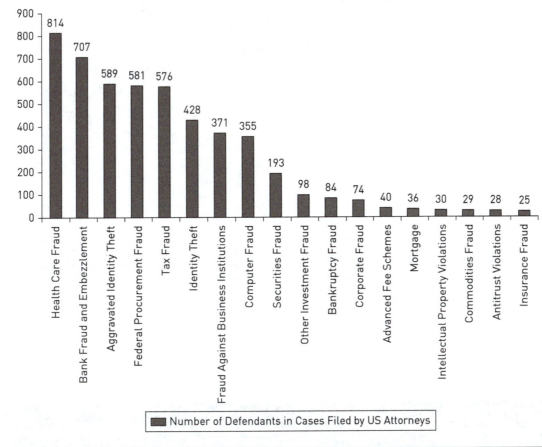

Number of Defendants in White-Collar Crime Cases Filed by US Attorneys

Source: U.S. Attorneys' Annual Statistical Report. (2020)

It is well accepted that the likelihood of winning a conviction drives prosecutorial decision making. This could explain the low number of white-collar crime prosecutions. As one legal scholar notes, these cases are "stacked against prosecutors" (Dayno, 2018, p. 322). Corporate crime prosecutions, in particular, have been called "rare events" (Diamantis & Laufer, 2019, p. 43). Former FBI director James Comey reportedly used the phrase "chickenshit club" to refer to "prosecutors who have never had an acquittal, or hung jury, because they do not want to jeopardize their positive record" (Carlson, 2018, p. 300).

It should not automatically be assumed that cases are declined out of some sort of intentional bias on the part of prosecutors toward lower class offenders. Three traditional explanations addressing why prosecutors choose not to prosecute include the organizational advantage argument, the alternative sentencing argument, and the system capacity argument (Tillman, Calavita, & Pontell, 1997). The **organizational advantage argument** suggests that "organizational structure may serve as a buffer between the white-collar offender and social control mechanisms" (Tillman et al., 1997, p. 55). The **alternative sanctions argument** points to the

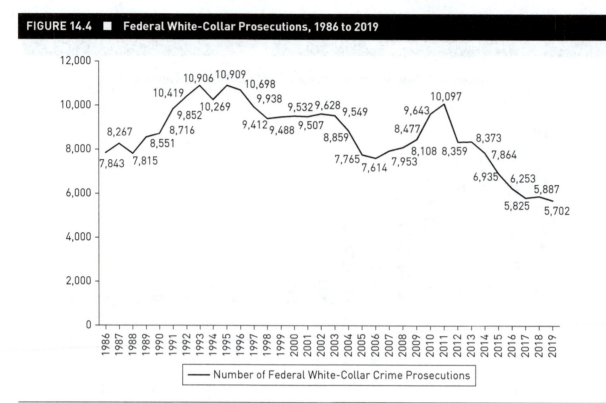

FIGURE 14.4 ■ Federal White-Collar Prosecutions, 1986 to 2019

Number of Federal White-Collar Crime Prosecutions

Source: U.S. Attorneys' Annual Statistical Report. (2020)

TABLE 14.1 ■ Reasons for Declination in Federal Cases, FY 2019

	Drugs	Official Corruption	Theft	Violent Crime	White-Collar Crime
Legally Barred	38	20	10	146	104
Insufficient Evidence	2290	400	328	4152	3272
Defendant Unavailable	62	4	18	128	106
Matter Referred to Another Jurisdiction	402	24	32	1309	316
Alternative to Federal Prosecution Appropriate	317	31	84	1192	251
Prioritization of Federal Resources and Interests	354	28	54	617	497
Totals	3463	507	526	7544	4546

Source: U.S. Department of Justice.

use of less costly civil and administrative procedures to respond to misconduct. The **system capacity argument** points to the difficulties officials face in responding to these crimes (Tillman et al., 1997).

Tillman and his research team (1997) examined how the criminal justice system responded to the savings and loan crisis to see which argument might best address the system's response to the fiasco. The researchers found limited support for the first two arguments and moderate support for the third argument—at least in some jurisdictions. They added a fourth possible explanation, for which they coined the term **damage control argument**. This orientation emphasizes the importance of "symbolic, high-visibility prosecutions in restoring public confidence" (p. 72).

Prosecutors face a number of other issues that may influence their decision-making process in white-collar crime cases. Issues include (1) that trials may be harder to win in white-collar crime cases, (2) the time to complete the cases is significant, (3) resource issues, (4) establishing intent, and (5) practical issues. With regard to trials, several features of the white-collar criminal trial mean that the cases may be harder for the prosecutor to win. The cases use complex evidence, the trials last a long time, and the defense attorneys are often among the most talented attorneys prosecutors will face. Brickey's (2006) review of the white-collar crime trials of the executives involved in the scandals that occurred in the early 2000s found that 18 defendants were convicted, 11 were acquitted, and 15 had their cases result in mistrials. By comparison, in conventional cases, trials almost always result in a victory for prosecutors.

The time to complete white-collar crime cases is also significant. These cases take far longer to complete than prosecutions of conventional crimes. Research shows that it can take twice as long to decide how to proceed with white-collar crimes as it takes to decide how to proceed with drug crimes and violent offenses (USGAO, 2003).

Resource issues potentially influence prosecutors' decisions about white-collar crime cases. In this context, *resources* refer to time, funds, staff, and materials needed to process the case through the justice system. Particularly at the local level, prosecutors lack the resources they need to address white-collar crimes. As a result, when prosecuted, the cases are more often handled by federal prosecutors (Benson, 1990). As illustrated previously, even at the federal level, many cases are not prosecuted.

Problems establishing intent may influence prosecutors' decisions to prosecute white-collar crime cases. As one author noted, "it is quite difficult to judge the motivation and behavior" of many white-collar offenders (Punch, 2000, p. 251). In fact, surveys from fraud prosecutors revealed that "the burden of the commonwealth/government to prove the mental state . . . beyond a reasonable doubt (knowledge and intent) . . . is the most difficult element of [white-collar] crime to establish" (Payne & Berg, 1997, p. 228).

Practical issues refer to an assortment of issues that commonly arise in the prosecution of most white-collar crime cases. For example, the cases typically require much more expertise to prosecute than conventional crimes might require (Jesilow, Pontell, & Geis, 1986). Also, prosecutors will often need technical assistance in these cases, and many have not been trained adequately in how to prosecute white-collar crimes (Payne, 2011). One topic for which prosecutors need specific training is deciding which charges to file against white-collar offenders. Also, a decline in resources to support these efforts is believed to have reduced the number of prosecutions. Pontell, Black, and Geis (2014) cite estimates that suggest white-collar crime prosecutions dropped 50% while George W. Bush was president and attribute these reductions to declines in FBI agents assigned to these cases after 9/11.

Deciding Charges

Prosecutors must decide what charges to file against white-collar criminals. These decisions follow rather lengthy investigations designed to inform prosecutors whether a charging decision is warranted. At the federal level, prosecutors have hundreds of possible statutes to choose from. In some instances, white-collar offenders are charged with violations of the **Racketeer Influenced and Corrupt Organizations (RICO) Act**. Because it is Title IX of the Organized Crime Control Act, many have assumed that RICO is limited to prosecutions of mobsters and other participants in organized crime ventures. However, as Beare (2002) notes, Robert Blakey who drafted the law, supported the use of controlling white-collar crime with the RICO act. In Blakey's words,

> there is nothing in RICO that says that if you act like a racketeer you
> will not be treated like a racketeer. Whatever the color of your shirt or your
> collar . . . people who run groups by extortion or violence or fraud ought to be
> called racketeers. (p. 225)

When considering the text of the RICO act, one can see how the act can be used in white-collar crime prosecutions. As one author team notes,

> Section 1962 of RICO prohibits "any person' from (i) using income derived from a
> pattern of racketeering activity, or from the collection of an unlawful debt, to acquire
> an interest in an enterprise affecting interstate commerce; (ii) acquiring or maintaining
> through a pattern of racketeering activity, or through collection of an unlawful debt, an
> interest in an enterprise affecting interstate commerce; (iii) conducting, or participating
> in the conduct of, the affairs of an enterprise affecting interstate commerce through a
> pattern of racketeering activity or through collection of an unlawful debt; or
> (iv) conspiring to participate in any of these activities. (Argust, Litvack, & Martin,
> 2010, p. 961)

Clearly, the breadth of this statute is such that many white-collar crime cases fall within the realm of RICO violations.

Other common charges against white-collar offenders at the federal level include violations of mail fraud statutes, the False Statements Act, the False Claims Act, and specific acts targeting specific forms of white-collar misconduct (Altschuler, Creekpaum, & Fang, 2008). **Mail fraud statutes** prohibit the use of the U.S. mail service to commit crimes. The **False Statements Act and False Claims Act** govern against the submission of fraudulent claims or bills for services. The False Claims Act was passed during the Civil War to guard against situations where individuals tried to defraud the government. It has gone through several changes since then, but it covers situations where individuals or businesses bill for goods that were not delivered or services that were not provided. Table 14.2 shows some specific laws targeting specific forms of white-collar misconduct. As shown in these statutes, the laws stipulate minimum and maximum sentences. Thus, the type of charge prosecutors file will have ramifications for the sentence convicted offenders receive.

It is important to recall that many white-collar crime cases are group offenses. As a result, prosecutors must decide not only what charges should be filed, but who the charges should be filed against (Hales, 2016). They have a range of options including charging no one, charging some offenders, and charging everyone. Charge type and number of defendants also influences decisions about plea bargaining.

Deciding About Plea Bargains

Prosecutors will also make decisions about **plea bargains** in deciding whether to allow a defendant to plead guilty in exchange for a reduced sentence or some other incentive. A common estimate is that 90% of offenders (white-collar and conventional) plead guilty (O'Hear, 2004). Consider that 90% of those involved in the corporate scandals of the early

TABLE 14.2 ■ U.S. Laws Governing Against White-Collar Crimes		
Law	**Type of Crime**	**Law Text**
§ 1344	Bank fraud	Whoever knowingly executes, or attempts to execute, a scheme or artifice—(1) to defraud a financial institution; or (2) to obtain any of the moneys, funds, credits, assets, securities, or other property owned by, or under the custody or control of, a financial institution, by means of false or fraudulent pretenses, representations, or promises; shall be fined not more than $1,000,000 or imprisoned not more than 30 years, or both.
§ 1347	Health care fraud	Whoever knowingly and willfully executes, or attempts to execute, a scheme or artifice—(1) to defraud any health care benefit program; or (2) to obtain, by means of false or fraudulent pretenses, representations, or promises, any of the money or property owned by, or under the custody or control of, any health care benefit program, in connection with the delivery of or payment for health care benefits, items, or services, shall be fined under this title or imprisoned not more than 10 years, or both. If the violation results in serious bodily injury (as defined in section 1365 of this title), such person shall be fined under this title or imprisoned not more than 20 years, or both; and if the violation results in death, such person shall be fined under this title, or imprisoned for any term of years or for life, or both.
§ 1348	Securities and commodities fraud	Whoever knowingly executes, or attempts to execute, a scheme or artifice—(1) to defraud any person in connection with any commodity for future delivery, or any option on a commodity for future delivery, or any security of an issuer with a class of securities registered under section 12 of the Securities Exchange Act of 1934 (15 U.S.C. 78l) or that is required to file reports under section 15(d) of the Securities Exchange Act of 1934 (15 U.S.C. 78o (d)); or (2) to obtain, by means of false or fraudulent pretenses, representations, or promises, any money or property in connection with the purchase or sale of any commodity for future delivery, or any option on a commodity for future delivery, or any security of an issuer with a class of securities registered under section 12 of the Securities Exchange Act of 1934 (15 U.S.C. 78l) or that is required to file reports under section 15(d) of the Securities Exchange Act of 1934 (15 U.S.C. 78o (d)); shall be fined under this title, or imprisoned not more than 25 years, or both.

Source: Reprinted From U.S. Code. (n.d.).

2000s (Adelphia, WorldCom, HeathSouth, Enron, etc.) entered guilty pleas (Brickey, 2006). After pleading, nearly all of them became cooperating witnesses "who assisted the government in developing the case against their peers" (Brickey, 2006, p. 403).

While similar proportions of white-collar and conventional offenders plead guilty, their reasons for pleading guilty might vary. For conventional offenders, a common reason is to avoid the costs of a trial that come along with paying the defense attorney higher fees for trial services. For white-collar offenders, many likely plead guilty in order to avoid the stigma and shame that would come along with a public trial. For both groups of offenders, a lighter sentence drives the decision to accept a plea bargain offered by prosecutors. Note that a lighter sentence does not necessarily mean that the defendant escapes a prison sentence. It may just mean that they get a shorter sentence. This chapter's White-Collar Crime in the News discusses a case involving the owner of a sleep clinic sentenced to three years in prison after scamming health benefit programs in a sleep study.

WHITE-COLLAR CRIME IN THE NEWS

SAN FERNANDO VALLEY WOMAN SENTENCED TO OVER 3 YEARS IN PRISON FOR RUNNING $11.5 MILLION SLEEP STUDY SCAM BILKING UPS AND COSTCO

The following is a press release from the Central District of California from March 5, 2020.

LOS ANGELES—The former owner of a Studio City medical clinic was sentenced today to 37 months in federal prison for causing more than $11.5 million in bills to be submitted to health care benefit programs for unnecessary—and sometimes nonexistent—sleep studies, primarily for employees of United Parcel Service, Inc., and Costco Wholesale Corp.

++++++++++, 52, of Valley Village, was sentenced by United States District Judge George H. Wu, who also ordered her to pay $2,747,071 in restitution.

++++++++++, who owned Atlas Diagnostic Services, Inc., pleaded guilty in November 2018 to one count of health care fraud.

From March 2014 until June 2016, ++++++++++ participated in a scheme to defraud health care benefit plans. ++++++++++ and others working at her direction recruited patients to participate in sleep study testing at Atlas by offering them cash. She also offered them additional cash if they brought in other sleep study participants, including their co-workers and relatives.

++++++++++ recruited patients, knowing that no doctor had prescribed sleep study testing for them and regardless of whether the testing was medically necessary or appropriate. ++++++++++ did not score or interpret the data from the testing or send it to anyone who could score or interpret it, which is necessary for diagnosis and treatment.

She submitted insurance claims for sleep study testing performed on the recruited patients, listing physicians that had never treated the patients. She also billed not only for the one night of sleep study testing that the patients had purportedly undergone—regardless of medical necessity—but also for an additional, consecutive night of sleep study testing that was never performed.

In total, ++++++++++ submitted more than $11.5 million in fraudulent insurance claims to health care benefit plans. She received approximately $3 million on those claims, of which $2,747,071 is still outstanding.

"[++++++++++'s] criminal activity victimized not only the plans, but also plan participants recruited into the scheme, as many of them have been required to pay back fraudulent insurance claims submitted using their names (on penalty of losing their health insurance)," prosecutors wrote in their sentencing memorandum.

A co-defendant, ++++++++++, of Torrance, pleaded guilty in November 2018 to one count of health care fraud and is serving a 30-month federal prison sentence in this case. ++++++++++ was a UPS driver who helped ++++++++++ recruit people to participate in the fraudulent sleep studies.

The United States Department of Labor-Employee Benefits Security Administration, the Department of Labor-Office of Inspector General, the FBI, and the Office of Personnel Management-Office of Inspector General investigated this matter.

This case was prosecuted by Assistant United States Attorney Kerry L. Quinn of the Major Frauds Section.

Reprinted from U.S. Department of Justice.

Source: https://www.justice.gov/usao-cdca/pr/san-fernando-valley-woman-sentenced-over-3-years-prison-running-115-million-sleep -study

Deciding Whether to Charge Corporations

Dating back as far as Sutherland (1941), some criminologists have claimed that prosecutors are reluctant to prosecute corporations or businesses. A common explanation for this refusal is that prosecutors are "persuaded by the argument that punishing a corporation in effect punishes innocent shareholders" (Plimton & Walsh, 2010, p. 331) and workers. Another explanation offered is that such prosecutions might harm the economic system. Former attorney general Eliot Spitzer chose the civil settlement route in response to securities fraud allegations against banks in 2003 in order to minimize the possibility of significant economic fallout (Tillman, 2013). Tillman explains why such a reason is problematic:

> The fact that prosecutors are often reluctant to pursue organizational defendants out of fear of the economic consequences suggests a situation in which, as Tillman and Indergaard (2005:263) have put it, America is being "held hostage" by corrupt corporations whose executives can operate with a sense of impunity knowing that they and their firms are not only too big to fail but also too big to prosecute and too big to jail. This situation also raises questions about the state's interests and goals in responding to financial crimes. (p. 32)

PHOTO 14.3 Being a part of the criminal justice process is embarrassing for white-collar defendants. Many will plead guilty to avoid the publicity.

In the face of this resistance to prosecuting corporations, one can point to three reasons justifying the prosecution of corporations. First, the harm from many corporate crimes is more severe than the harm from other crimes. Second, it is believed that corporate criminals are "just as morally culpable as traditional criminals" (Page, Savage, Stitt, & Umhoffer, 1999, p. 520). Third, corporate prosecutions send a message to other corporations that misconduct will not be tolerated.

Another reason corporations were not prosecuted was that it was not always clear when such a prosecution would be appropriate. To offer guidance to U.S. attorneys in determining when to prosecute corporations, the deputy attorney general sent a memo in November 2006 offering federal prosecutors guidance in making this determination. The factors McNulty (n.d.) addressed included offense characteristics, organizational characteristics, and the consequences of different types of reactions by the justice system. In terms of offense characteristics, the memo drew attention to the seriousness of the offense, the consequences of the offense, as well as the risk of harm from the offense. Attention was also given to whether the nature of the offense fit in with national priorities. Table 14.3 shows the types of questions prosecutors might now ask in determining whether to prosecute corporations.

In terms of organizational characteristics, McNulty (n.d.) urged prosecutors to consider the pervasiveness of wrongdoing in the corporation, with specific attention given to past misconduct by the business. Also, whether the corporation disclosed the misconduct in a timely manner was noted as a factor to consider along with whether the corporation had a strong compliance program. In addition, prosecutors were encouraged to consider the remedial actions taken by company officials to address the wrongdoing (e.g., replacing corporate leaders, disciplining workers, revising compliance policies, etc.).

In addition to addressing offense and corporate characteristics, attention was drawn to the consequences of the system's intervention. For example, if a prosecution would have a disproportionately adverse effect on those not responsible for the misconduct, prosecutors were encouraged by McNulty (n.d.) to take that into consideration. He also encouraged prosecutors to consider the adequacy of prosecution as well as "the adequacy of remedies such as civil or regulatory enforcement actions" (p. 4).

Despite these guidelines, or maybe because of them, corporations are still rarely prosecuted in the criminal justice system. According to one author, structural features of the criminal justice system assigning responsibility for handling these cases to regulatory agencies results in infrequent use of criminal laws to address corporate offenses (Slapper, 1993). This same author notes that corporate offenses are often framed as accidents, thereby allowing companies to hide behind this conceptual frame. Consider the British Petroleum (BP) oil disaster in the Gulf of Mexico in July 2010. The disaster was routinely portrayed as an "accident," implying that corporate wrongdoing did not occur.

TABLE 14.3 ■ Questions Prosecutors Ask When Deciding How to Address Corporate Crimes		
Was it a serious offense?	Yes	No
Was there a significant risk of harm to the public?	Yes	No
Was wrongdoing pervasive in the corporation?	Yes	No
Was corporate management complicit?	Yes	No
Does the corporation have a history of misconduct?	Yes	No
Was the corporation willing to cooperate?	Yes	No
Was the corporation's compliance program adequate?	Yes	No
Did the corporation voluntarily disclose wrongdoing?	Yes	No
Did the corporation take remedial actions including implementing an effective compliance program, replacing culpable management officials, disciplining wrongdoers, or paying restitution?	Yes	No
Were their collateral consequences on the shareholders, employees, or others not responsible?	Yes	No
Does it benefit victims to criminally prosecute?	Yes	No
Are other remedies such as civil or regulatory enforcement more appropriate?	Yes	No
Will there be a negative impact on the public from prosecuting criminally?	Yes	No

Source: Adapted from U.S. Department of Justice. (2020). Justice manual. Retrieved from https://www.justice.gov/jm/jm-9-28000-principles-federal-prosecution-business-organizations.

Local and state prosecutors also have authority to prosecute corporate crimes. Michael Benson and Frank Cullen (1998) described the most detailed study on how local prosecutors responded to corporate crime in *Combating Corporate Crime: Local Prosecutors at Work.* Among other things, they examined the impact of resources, the presence of alternative remedies, legal and technical difficulties, and political factors on local prosecutors' decisions to prosecute corporate crime. In terms of resources, attention was given to the lack of staff, funds, and time to prosecute corporate crime. With regard to alternative remedies, attention was given to deferring the cases to federal officials, relying on regulatory agencies, and filing civil suits against corporate criminals. Legal and technical difficulties considered included investigatory problems, proving intent, inappropriateness of criminal sanctions, and lack of expertise. Political factors included state of the local economy, the corporation's level of resources, and the prosecutor's career goals.

Part of their research efforts included a survey of district attorneys in California to determine how local prosecutors perceived corporate crime, how often they prosecuted these cases, and how community factors might contribute to decision making (see Benson, Cullen, & Maakestad, 1988). Their research found that "a significant majority of the district attorneys had prosecuted a variety of corporate crimes" (Benson et al., p. 505). The main barriers prosecutors confronted had to do with the limited resources available to respond to corporate misdeeds. They also found that rural prosecutors were more sensitive to prosecuting businesses that the community relied on, presumably because the rural prosecutors did not want to lose a business and harm the entire community. Elsewhere, Benson, Cullen, and Maakestad (1990) reported that half of the urban district attorneys said that corporate crime was "not serious", and only 11% of rural prosecutors said that the misconduct was serious or somewhat serious. Prosecutors described harm and blameworthiness as influencing their decisions to prosecute along with other factors such as multiple offenses, victim preference, and regulatory inaction at the federal level.

Scholars have noted other problems that arise when prosecuting corporations. For example, it is extremely difficult to identify the decision-making processes that led to the corporate misconduct (Punch, 2000). Take BP's, case, for example. What decisions were made by executives that contributed to the explosion in the Gulf of Mexico? Who made those decisions? Were those decisions made in good faith? Identifying this decision-making process is complex and sometimes impossible. In addition, laws are written and interpreted as applying to individuals and not organizations, resulting in atypical offenders in corporate crime prosecutions (Punch, 2000).

Although these obstacles exist, some corporate offenses are prosecuted in the criminal justice system. Geis and Dimento (1995) point to six principles of **corporate crime liability** that support the need to prosecute corporations criminally. These principles include the following:

- A corporation is the sum of the actors in the organization.

- It is ineffective to punish individuals for corporate misconduct.

- It is more shameful for a corporation to be prosecuted than it is for an individual.

- Corporations can change more than individuals.

- It is easier to prove intent in corporations than it is with individuals.

- The corporation has resources to pay fines.

Geis and Dimento (1995) stress that the principles are not empirically grounded and are potentially misguided and harmful (e.g., if executives continue their misconduct). They conclude,

> Punishing the corporation alone might well induce it to clean up its act, but such punishment, almost always a fine, could be regarded as not much more than an unfortunate consequence. . . . Punishing perpetrator and corporation together appears to offer the best deterrence, although it remains to be demonstrated that such punishment produces the kinds of results claimed for it. (p. 84)

When corporations are prosecuted, different legal standards apply to the prosecution. For example, business entities do not have the right to "plead the Fifth" (i.e., the Fifth Amendment of the U.S. Constitution offers protection against self-incrimination). This is an individual right, not an organizational right (Nakayama, 2007). Also, intent is determined somewhat differently in corporate crimes. For example, in corporate crime cases intent is (1) demonstrated through uncovering evidence of conspiracies, (2) inferred in a new corporation after two corporations merge, (3) applied if corporate officials actively try to conceal a felony, and (4) present if corporate officials actively ignore criminal activity (Plimton & Walsh, 2010).

Common defenses that corporations use are "rogue employee" defenses and due diligence defenses (Plimton & Walsh, 2010). The **rogue employee defense** argues that the corporate misconduct was the result of an individual employee and not the result of any corporate activities. To counter this defense, prosecutors must show that the employee was acting within the scope of employment, that the employee's actions were done to benefit the corporation, and that "the act and intent can be imputed to the organization" (Plimton & Walsh, 2010, p. 332).

Under the **due diligence defense**, the corporation contends that it did everything it could do, in good faith, to abide by the law. In determining whether the organization acted with due diligence, the court will consider seven factors. In particular, the organization must have met the following conditions:

- An established compliance program

- Assigned the responsibility for supervising the compliance program to a high-ranking employee

- Demonstrated that it did not give significant responsibility to an employee prone to misconduct

- Communicated compliance messages to employees

- Made a reasonable effort to meet compliance

- Enforced compliance standards when wrongdoing occurred

- Responded to wrongdoing and initiated measures to keep that misconduct from recurring (Goldsmith & King, 1997, p. 20)

Some have argued that prosecutors have become "unjustifiably heavy-handed" in corporate crime cases, "compelling corporations to cooperate in criminal investigations" (Bharara, 2007, p. 54). Strategies that have come under fire include situations where prosecutors (1) force companies to waive attorney-client privilege, (2) require corporations to fire employees, and (3) make unrealistic requests in exchange for leniency (Bharara, 2007). Bharara (2007) quotes several other legal scholars who used the following concepts to describe the notion of holding corporations criminally liable: "unprincipled, pointless, counterproductive, indiscriminate, incoherent, illogical, puzzling, and extreme" (p. 67).

Deciding Whether to Defer Prosecution

Another decision prosecutors will make is whether to enter into deferred prosecution agreements or nonprosecution agreements with corporations or businesses. Prosecutors have used pretrial diversion programs routinely over the last several decades for individual offenders. Their use for corporate offenders has been somewhat sparing until recently.

In a **deferred prosecution agreement (DPA)**, the prosecutor agrees not to prosecute the corporation if the corporation agrees to certain conditions to be completed over a probationary period. In a **nonprosecution agreement (NPA)**, the prosecutor indicates that the prosecution will not occur based on the corporation's agreement to certain conditions. A DPA is filed with the court, while an NPA is not (USGAO, 2009). Conditions that are imposed on corporations include the development of improved compliance programs, removal of certain personnel, fines, and a waiver of privileges (Spivack & Raman, 2008).

The number of DPAs and NPAs has increased over time. The agreements have become so frequent that some have suggested they have "become the standard means for concluding corporate crime prosecutions" (Spivack & Raman, 2008, p. 159). Deferrals are seen as advantageous because they save prosecutorial resources and protect "innocent" employees from experiencing collateral consequences that stem from corporate crime prosecutions (Spivack & Raman, 2008) Also, some policy makers believe that DPAs and NPAs prevent widespread economic damage to the global economy that might occur if corporations were punished too severely (Steinzor, 2017). They have been critiqued because it is not always clear that the agreements are used consistently (USGAO, 2009).

Figure 14.5 shows the number of pleas, DPAs, and NPAs between 2000 and 2019 included in the Corporate Prosecution Registry, a joint effort of law faculty at the University of Virginia and Duke University. As shown in the table, DPAs and NPAs are rare in comparison to pleas. The number of NPAs and DPAs has increased over time, perhaps offsetting the drop in prosecutions highlighted previously. The amount of restitution paid by companies in NPA and DPA cases, as compared to the amounts paid in corporate cases resolved through plea bargains, suggests that the deferrals are successful in generating larger dollar returns to victims and the government (see Table 14.4). In fact, DPAs, on average, resulted in restitution amounts roughly 19 times higher than the restitution amounts in cases resolved through pleas.

FIGURE 14.5 ■ Dispositions in Corporate Crime Cases in the Corporate Prosecution Registry

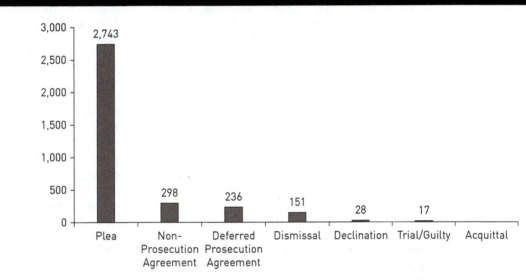

Source: Data compiled from the Corporate Prosecution Registry, a joint project of the Legal Data Lab at the University of Virginia School of Law and Duke University School of Law.

TABLE 14.4 ■ Impact of Disposition Strategy on Restitution Amounts

	Mean
Deferred Prosecution	$73.2 Million
Non-Prosecution Agreement	$20.4 Million
Plea	$3.6 Million

Compiled from Dunn, G. (2015). *2014 year-end update on corporate non-prosecution agreements (NPAs) and deferred prosecution agreements (DPAs).* Retrieved from http://www.gibsondunn.com/publications/Pages/2014-Year -End-Update-Corporate-Non-Prosecution-Agreements-and-Deferred-Prosecution-Agreements.aspx

Trac Reports. (2015). *Justice department data reveals 29 percent drop in criminal prosecutions of corporations.* Retrieved from http://trac.syr.edu/tracreports/crim/406

Historically, when agreements or concessions were offered to corporations in corporate prosecutions, very few corporate executives in those cases faced criminal charges (Henry, 2016; Steinzor, 2017). In a sense, then, such agreements insulated both the corporation and its executives from criminal adjudication. To address this dilemma, Deputy Attorney General Sally Yates published a memo in September 2015 outlining the requirement to hold corporate actors criminally accountable in order for corporations to receive any "cooperation credit" from the Department of Justice. Known as the Yates Memo (Yates, 2015), the directive stipulated the following steps be taken by federal prosecutors in promoting individual accountability in corporate crime cases:

> (1) in order to qualify for any cooperation credit, corporations must provide to the Department all relevant facts relating to the individuals responsible for the misconduct; (2) criminal and civil corporate investigations should focus on individuals from the inception of the investigation; (3) criminal and civil attorneys handling corporate investigations should be in routine communication with one another; (4) absent extraordinary circumstances or approved departmental policy, the Department will not release culpable individuals from civil or criminal liability when resolving a matter with a corporation; (5) Department attorneys should not resolve matters with a corporation without a clear plan to resolve related individual cases, and should memorialize any declinations as to individuals in such cases; and (6) civil attorneys should consistently focus on individuals as well as the company and evaluate whether to bring suit against an individual based on considerations beyond that individual's ability to pay.

In effect, the memo indicated that corporations had to share information about *all* involved employees in order to receive cooperation credit. The issuance of the memo did not occur in a vacuum. In fact, five prior deputy attorneys general had issued directives about how individual executives should be handled in corporate crime prosecutions (Mark, 2017). While the prior directives were unable to move the needle in prosecuting executives involved in corporate malfeasance, high hopes among those wanting corporate executives to be punished for the misdeeds surfaced after the content of the Yates Memo spread across those interested in the topic. Some scholars viewed the directive as opening the door to opportunities to better protect members of the public from wrongdoing. Among other things, the new shift in policy was believed to help address "perceptions of unfairness" surrounding apparent disparate treatment between corporate and traditional offenders (Steinzor, 2017). The hope that individuals had in promoting more prosecutions of executives did not pan out.

Indeed, individual prosecutions of corporate actors did not increase after the memo (Mark, 2017; Henry, 2016). The memo was "formally relaxed" under the Trump administration (Garrett, 2020, p. 105), and roughly three years after the Yates Memo, Deputy Attorney General Rod Rosenstein (2018) announced a revision of the directive and eliminated the DOJ's "all or nothing" approach to awarding credit to corporations facing corporate prosecutions. The shift still encouraged a focus on individual accountability, albeit with more discretion given to prosecutors about which individuals are most culpable.

After Rosenstein's directive, the new policy of limiting the focus to those individuals most culpable was codified in the Foreign Corrupt Practices Act Corporate Enforcement Policy where it is stipulated that cooperation credit for self-disclosures will be considered if the following conditions are met:

- The voluntary disclosure qualifies under U.S.S.G. § 8C2.5(g)(1) as occurring "prior to an imminent threat of disclosure or government investigation";

- the company discloses the conduct to the Department "within a reasonably prompt time after becoming aware of the offense," with the burden being on the company to demonstrate timeliness; and

- the company discloses *all relevant facts known to it at the time of the disclosure, including as to any individuals substantially involved* in or responsible for the misconduct at issue.

THE ROLE OF DEFENSE ATTORNEYS IN WHITE-COLLAR CRIME CASES

The defense attorney is responsible for defending the accused offender against the criminal charges. One legal scholar indicated that defense attorneys have four goals in defending white-collar defendants, depending on where the case is in the judicial process. These goals include (1) keeping the defendant from being indicted; (2) if indicted, keeping the defendant from being convicted; (3) if convicted, keeping the defendant from being imprisoned; and (4) if imprisoned, keeping the sentence shorter (Lawless, 1988). These goals demonstrate that the role of the defense attorney extends throughout the criminal justice process. Indeed, their work may begin very early in the criminal justice process (Gottschalk, 2014a).

Kenneth Mann (1985), author of *Defending White-Collar Crime: A Portrait of Attorneys at Work,* has provided the most descriptive overview of the defense attorney's role in white-collar crime cases. Conducting interviews with 44 defense attorneys experienced with defending white-collar offenders, Mann demonstrated how some attorneys have made a career out of white-collar crime defense work. Mann's research showed how attorneys worked to control the flow of information and to prepare white-collar offenders in how to act in the criminal justice process. A student from Norway found that lawyers "become more famous if [they] handle more white-collar crime cases" (Gottschalk, 2014b). This fame comes, in part, from the media attention the case receives. This chapter's Streaming White-Collar Crime discusses a docuseries focusing on how defense attorneys manipulate the media in the justice process.

STREAMING WHITE-COLLAR CRIME Trial By Media

Plot	What You Can Learn	Discussion Questions
With George Clooney as executive producer, *Trial by Media* is a six-part series focused on how media shapes public opinion in court cases as well as the way that justice professionals use the media to shape opinions about defendants and criminal cases. While not billed as a white-collar crime docuseries, four of the cases focus on the trials of individuals for behaviors related to their work. These include episodes on Rod Blagojevich's bribery trial and subsequent downfall as governor, HealthSouth founder Richard Scrushy's trial and subsequent conviction for multiple felonies, talk show host Jenny Jones's civil trial for failing to protect a talk show guest who was murdered after coming out about a homosexual crush on the show, and the trial of four New York city police officers for the shooting of Amadou Diallo. The focus of a fifth episode—the media's harmful treatment of rape victims—can also be seen as related to a form of organizational deviance.	Attorneys use the media to shape perceptions about defendants. The more money defendants have, the better representation they can afford. The media can shape the outcome of criminal trials.	Do you think it's fair that lawyers use the media to sway juries? Do you think the media portrays white-collar defendants differently than other defendants? Explain.

Several features of the white-collar criminal case make these cases different from traditional criminal cases for defense attorneys, leading some authors to suggest that defending white-collar criminals is an "art" (Copeland, 2014). Just as the complex record search creates problems for prosecutors and investigators, the sheer number of records can be difficult for defense attorneys to review (Leto, Pogrebin, & Stretesky, 2007). Also, the cases typically involve more witnesses than might be found in conventional crimes (Leto et al., 2007). In addition, defense attorneys will need to direct efforts toward dealing with the media more than they might in other cases (Preiser & Swisher, 1988). Somewhat related, defense attorneys will spend more time preparing the white-collar defendant for the emotional impact of the trial and for the attention the case will get from the media (Lawless, 1988). Note also that prosecutors will select only white-collar crime cases that are very strongly in their favor (Lawless, 1988).

Stereotypes about white-collar offenders can also make the cases a little more challenging for defense attorneys. For instance, one author team noted that the cases are harder for defense attorneys because juries are predisposed to assume that white-collar defendants are guilty (Preiser & \Swisher, 1988). Also, some defense attorneys perceive white-collar offenders as "defendants who are manipulative and [who] attempt to influence their defense team" (Leto et al., 2007, p. 106). In short, white-collar defense attorneys may have quite a task in front of them when they agree to defend white-collar defendants.

In-depth interviews of five federal public defenders by Jessica Leto and her colleagues (2007) found that defense attorneys used three strategies to manage their cases and their clients. First, the **process-oriented defense** strategy is guided primarily by a process that flows from one step to the next step (e.g., [1] read the indictment, [2] contact the defendant, [3] contact the prosecutor, [4] construct the defense). The attorneys "process" these cases the same way regardless of case or offender characteristics.

Second, the **discovery-oriented defense** is a more flexible defense strategy that is dictated by the characteristics of the charges, with no set formula used to respond to the cases. Attorneys using this strategy rely more on records and may not view the defendant (or the case) in a favorable light. The authors quote one attorney who—when asked about the first thing he did when assigned a white-collar crime case—responded, "Go tell [the chief] to kiss my ass for giving it to me. Then, I don't know beyond that" (Leto et al., 2007, p. 97).

Third, the **client-oriented defense** strategy involves situations where the client "direct[s] the way the attorney defends the case" (Leto et al., 2007, p. 100). In these situations, the client is given a little involvement in the beginning stages of the judicial proceedings and then more and more as the case progresses. The underlying assumption is that white-collar defendants have a great deal to offer in building and orchestrating their own defense strategies.

Leto and her research team (2007) note that strategies may change as the case proceeds. For example, sometimes a defense case may begin using process- or discovery-oriented strategies and then shift to a client-oriented defense case. They note that the attorneys in Mann's (1985) seminal research project tended to use "mistake of fact" defenses, but none of the attorneys in their research project used this defense. The strategy they used if the case made it to trial was to "find flaws in the government's case in order to cast doubt upon their client's guilt" (Leto et al., 2007, p. 104).

Part of the defense attorney's role will be devoted to information control where attorneys will limit the amount of information that the press and others have about the defendant (Gottschalk, 2014a). Because these cases receive more press attention than traditional criminal cases, attorneys will try to find a way to use their information control strategies to their advantage. These strategies "are normally kept hidden as a secrecy to other parties, including the client [because] success is often dependent upon the lack of awareness among other parties" (Gottschalk, 2014a, p. 62).

Mann (1985) suggested that defense attorneys will "portray the [white-collar] defendant as an innocent victim of circumstance" (p. 40). Benson (1989) argued that defense attorneys will paint a picture of the defendant as an upstanding member of the community who, through the publicity surrounding the case, has already been punished enough. To be sure, white-collar crime defense attorneys will use a variety of defenses that are tailored to the specific type of white-collar crime the defendant is charged with. Some of the common types of defenses used to defend white-collar defendants include the following:

1. The **good faith defense** is based on the argument that defendants lack knowledge and intent. They did not know the crime was being committed; therefore, they could not have formed the intent to commit the crime. The "ostrich instruction" means that this defense does not apply if defendants actively avoided finding out about the crime by simply ignoring behaviors they should have been monitoring (Fischer & Sheppard, 2008).

2. The **meeting competition defense** is raised in price discrimination cases to show that a business's price discriminations were done "in good faith to counter actions of a competitor" (Hill & Lezell, 2010, p. 257).

3. The **isolated occurrence defense** argues that the misconduct was a rare event done by a single employee and not part of any systematic criminal activity. This defense is "one of the most frequently litigated defenses in OSH Act citations" (Trumka, 2008, p. 348). The business must show that measures were implemented to stop similar incidents from occurring in the future.

4. The **lack of fraudulent intent defense** argues that the defendant did not intend to commit a criminal act (Heenan, Klarfeld, Roussis, & Walsh, 2010).

5. The **withdrawal from conspiracy defense** is used in offenses to argue that the defendant withdrew his or her involvement from the misconduct before the illegal actions occurred. The defendant must demonstrate active efforts to stop the conspiracy. Reporting the crime to authorities is seen as one strategy for demonstrating withdrawal from a conspiracy (Hill & Lezell, 2010).

6. The **reliance on the advice of counsel defense** is raised when defendants argue that their actions were carried out simply because they were following the advice of their attorneys. This is technically not a defense that would mitigate guilt, but this information may sway a jury to side with the defendant (Heenan et al., 2010).

7. The **ignorance defense** is raised to show that the defendant did not know that the criminal acts were occurring (Altschuler et al., 2008).

8. The **multiplicity of indictment defense** argues that the offender is being charged for one single offense on several different counts in the indictment. This defense suggests that the defendant is being tried twice and the defendant's double jeopardy rights are violated (Fischer & Sheppard, 2008).

Denial of criminal intent is among the most common denials offered by white-collar defendants (Benson, 1985a). In fact, one group of legal scholars wrote that "a typical defense . . . begins with a denial that the defendant carried out any violations with a criminal or fraudulent purpose" (Heenan et al., 2010, p. 1027). In addition to serving as a legal defense, such a denial allows white-collar offenders to shield themselves from the social stigma of a criminal label.

In cases where a corporation, business, or organization is the defendant, the company may rely on its internal general legal counsel for assistance and advice. In these situations, defendants sometimes raise the attorney-client privilege in an effort to keep information out of court (Yohay & Dodge, 1987). **Attorney-client privilege** has been described as "the oldest and most widely applied doctrine protecting confidential information" (Goldsmith & King, 1997, p. 24). There are restrictions regarding what type of information is protected under this privilege. Judges will occasionally use the "subject matter" test to see if the privilege applies. Under this test, five elements are necessary for the privilege to apply:

1. The communication must be made for the purpose of securing legal advice.

2. The employee making the communication must do so at the direction of a supervisor.

3. The direction must be given by the supervisor to obtain legal advice for the corporation.

4. The subject matter of the communication must be within the scope of the employee's corporate duties.

5. The communication may not be disseminated beyond those persons who need to know information (Goldsmith & King, 1997, p. 27).

Corporate attorneys often direct their efforts toward delaying the investigation and prosecution by filing motions and using an assortment of tactics to give them more time to build their own cases. One expert suggested that legal counsel should not see settling as a rational decision if a corporate executive is facing both criminal and civil charges (Zane, 2003).

One legal scholar argues that white-collar defense attorneys have done a poor job making a case for reducing sentences due to mitigating factors (Haugh, 2012). Drawing on the way that mitigating factors are used in death penalty cases to argue for life imprisonment rather than a sentence of capital punishment, Haugh (2012) offers the following suggestions to fellow defense attorneys:

- Defense attorneys should change their mindset about the weight that sentence guidelines have in determining the final sentence given to offenders.

- Defense attorneys should use a team approach to defend white-collar defendants so that the expertise of different attorneys is used to help make a case for a reduced sentence.

- Defense attorneys should begin thinking about mitigation factors early in the case.

- Defense attorneys should build trust with clients, using a mitigation specialist who will approach all involved in a warm and friendly manner.

- Defense attorneys should develop a mitigation defense tailored to the specific details of the case and the defendant.

- Defense attorneys should present the case for mitigation as strongly and passionately as possible.

- Defense attorneys should stay focused on the goal of mitigation.

Of course, prosecutors will not necessarily agree with these tactics, and they will engage in their own efforts to call for stiffer sentences for white-collar offenders.

OTHER ACTORS INVOLVED IN WHITE-COLLAR CRIME JUDICIAL PROCEEDINGS

When watching an episode of *Law & Order* or another television show depicting the trial process, viewers will always see other "actors" involved in the courts. These other actors include (1) jurors, (2) witnesses, (3) defendants, and (4) victims. While these actors are involved in all types of court proceedings, certain dynamics of white-collar crime cases mean that the roles of these participants are substantively different in white-collar versus traditional cases.

Jurors

In cases where trials are held before juries, jurors will determine guilt or innocence of accused offenders. In some places, juries may play a role in sentencing, and they may make recommendations about the amount of damages to be awarded in civil trials. Some have argued that juries are harsher than judges—in determining guilt and in meting out penalties (Levine, 1983).

Some researchers have hypothesized that offenders who do not have specific characteristics of what would be expected for different types of crimes will be judged by external or situational factors, meaning that jurors might be assessing offenders based on whether they look like the "typical offender" in a certain type of crime (Gordon, Michels, & Nelson, 1996). Gordon and his coauthors' (1996) mock juror study found that respondents sentenced white embezzlers to longer sentences than Black embezzlers, but Black burglars were given longer sentences than white burglars. The authors suggest that mock jurors "viewed a white defendant committing the white-collar crime as a more typical event than the black defendant committing the white-collar crime" (p. 159).

Such a finding is relevant to other forms of white-collar crime as well. In effect, jurors might be reluctant to see certain types of white-collar defendants as capable of engaging in wrongdoing (Jesilow, Pontell, & Geis, 1985). It may be difficult, for example, for jurors to accept that a trusted physician actually engaged in fraud. Fraud by some types of professionals is not a "typical event" among those professionals. Hence, jurors' perceptions are influenced by cognitive processes that define and assess defendants by preconceived notions.

Juries will occasionally "make mistakes" in white-collar crime cases—either failing to come to a unanimous agreement or engaging in behavior that allows defendants to appeal a conviction. In the Tyco case, for example, a mistrial was declared after a juror gave a thumbs-up sign to the defense table. In the first Enron trial, which lasted three months, a mistrial was declared after the jury was unable to come to an agreement on nearly 180 of the 202 charges filed against the executives (Brickey, 2006). The jury deliberated for only 4 days.

The complexity of white-collar crime cases sets them apart from many traditional criminal cases decided by jurors. Consider a robbery as opposed to a securities fraud case. In the robbery, the jury hears one type of evidence, and the evidence is typically easy to follow. In securities fraud cases, the jury will hear different types of evidence, which may not always be easy to follow. In some cases, the evidence—particularly environmental crime and corporate crime cases—might include material which is new to the jurors, or potentially even harmful to the public.

On the one hand, prosecutors will make efforts to simplify proceedings so all can understand the evidence. Using technology, for example, has been identified as a way for prosecutors to simplify complex white-collar crime topics (Jordanoska, 2017). On the other hand, defense attorneys may use the complexity of the cases to help demonstrate why the defendant should not be convicted. Brickey (2006) quotes a securities lawyer who said, "If you look at Bernie Ebbers, Adelphia, and Martha Stewart, the government has done an exceptional job when they keep it simple so juries understand" (p. 417).

The amount of time that jurors must devote to white-collar crime cases is also different from other types of cases. The time estimates for different types of white-collar crimes have been provided elsewhere. At this point it is important to suggest that *time* can influence juror decision making in that some jurors might vote certain ways out of a desire to end their involvement in the case.

Witnesses

Witnesses are also involved in white-collar crime trials. Generally speaking, types of witnesses include government witnesses, lay witnesses, cooperating witnesses, character witnesses, and expert witnesses. **Government witnesses** are police officers, investigators, auditors, and other officials who developed the case as part of the investigation process. These witnesses are trained in how to share information so that the evidence best reflects the government's interests. In terms of white-collar crimes, much of the testimony of government witnesses will be directed toward the records reviewed as part of the investigation.

Lay witnesses are individuals who have some relevant information to share about the white-collar crime case based on something they saw or experienced. Two issues arise in white-collar crime cases that limit the use of lay witnesses. First, white-collar crimes are not committed openly; few witnesses are available to describe the offense. Second, white-collar crime victims were often not aware of the victimization when it occurred and may, as a result, have little to offer at a trial.

Cooperating witnesses are witnesses who are cooperating with the prosecution as a result of some involvement they had in the case. In terms of white-collar crime cases, cooperating witnesses often include coworkers, subordinates of the defendant, supervisors, or informants who participated in the criminal investigation. Cooperating witnesses are sometimes offered a reduced sentence in exchange for their testimony.

Character witnesses are individuals who share information about the defendant that demonstrates, in theory, that it is not in the defendant's "character" to engage in wrongdoing. For white-collar crime trials, character witnesses are called upon to demonstrate that the defendant's work ethic, long history of contributions to the community, and good citizenship are not consistent with evidence that suggests wrongdoing. White-collar offenders, in particular, may have access to well-known and powerful character witnesses such as celebrities and politicians. There is debate surrounding the utility of such witnesses. After former Los Angeles Mayor Richard Riordan testified in the criminal case of an executive accused of fraud, one former prosecutor turned white-collar criminal defense attorney told a reporter, "High-profile character witnesses never concerned me. . . . While they are interesting to watch testify, they by definition don't know the facts of the case being prosecuted, and therefore the impact of their testimony is usually quite limited" (Pfiefer, 2010).

Expert witnesses are witnesses who share their professional insight and interpretation of the evidence used in the case. Typically hired for a fee, these witnesses are actually involved throughout the justice process (see Figure 14.6). At the pretrial phase, expert witnesses review evidence and provide advice about how the evidence can be used at trial. During the trial, the expert will testify and educate the jury about the evidence under review. After the trial, the expert will assist in filing appeals and helping to identify the grounds for appeal. Also, experts will be called upon to help white-collar offenders prepare for their punishment experience.

FIGURE 14.6 ■ Involvement of Expert Witness

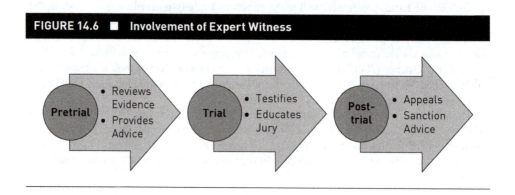

- Pretrial
  - Reviews Evidence
  - Provides Advice
- Trial
  - Testifies
  - Educates Jury
- Post-trial
  - Appeals
  - Sanction Advice

Perhaps the more important part of an expert witness's role involves his or her testimony in court. The individuals will discuss the strength of evidence for the side that hired them and will also address the limitations of the other side's evidence. In white-collar crime cases, they will communicate complex financial information or other industry-specific information in a way that jurors can understand.

Expert witnesses must exhibit a level of scientific expertise that is consistent with what would be expected in the expert's scientific area of study (Summerford, 2002). The judge determines whether someone is able to serve as an expert witness. In selecting experts for white-collar crime cases, one author team suggests that those hiring the expert consider the following: (1) the expert's academic training, (2) whether the expert is accredited by an accreditation body, (3) the expert's match to the specific type of case, (4) the expert's level of expertise, and (5) what the expert looks like (Rasmussen & Leauanae, 2004). This fifth factor might surprise readers. The authors use the phrase "beauty contest" in suggesting that "better looking" experts who have "charisma" will be better received by jurors.

One defense attorney team has noted that prosecutors will try to sneak expert testimony into white-collar crime cases by submitting written opinions from experts as part of nontestimonial documents (Frongillo, Simons, Essinger, & Knowles, 2014). This is done, they suggest, in order to get information before the judge or jury without allowing the defense to question the expert. They further suggest that defense attorneys should use the constitutional Confrontation Clause to try to keep the evidence out where warranted, or at least to allow the opportunity to cross-examine the expert. Specific steps they suggest include the following:

- Scrutinize the discovery documents to determine if the government intends to use a nontestifying expert

- Establish the purpose of the nontestifying expert option as testimony or litigation

- Establish that the information is being used to legally define the offense

Following these steps, they argue, will make it easier to keep expert testimony from being introduced without being cross-examined.

The Role of White-Collar Defendants

White-collar defendants play a role in judicial proceedings. Many scholars have pointed to the way that white-collar offenders deflect blame from themselves and onto others in an effort to portray themselves as honest professionals (Croall, 1993). This blame deflection is particularly evident during the judicial process when defendants blame the wrongdoing on administrative errors, coworker errors, unclear policies, or unfair regulations (Jesilow, Pontell, & Geis, 1986). Some white-collar defendants will describe their misdeeds as if they are analogous to what can be called a *Robin Hood defense* (e.g., their crimes help the poor). Here is how Paul Jesilow and his colleagues (1986) described efforts to shape perceptions about physicians accused of fraud: "Physicians are many times able to cast shady actions in a positive light. For example, providers who knowingly bill for unnecessary services can argue that the procedures were necessary for the health of the patient" (p. 17).

In most trials, white-collar defendants will not take the stand. The messages of denial and blame deflection are communicated through their attorneys. If white-collar defendants take the stand, then their efforts to lie and minimize would be frowned on by the judge (Mann, 1985). Consider Judge Marian Cedarbaum's comments to Martha Stewart at her sentencing hearing: "Lying to government agencies during the course of an investigation is a very serious matter, regardless of the outcome of the investigation" ("Martha Stewart Reads a Statement," 2004). Jurors also look unfavorably on white-collar defendants when they lie or blame others for their transgressions (Brickey, 2006).

For white-collar defendants, the trial experience will be different from the trial experience of many traditional offenders in four ways. First, in some cases, the corporation or business is on trial, not an individual offender. Second, many white-collar trials will have multiple defendants; one study showed that two thirds of the celebrated corporate fraud cases of the mid-2000s had more than one defendant (Brickey, 2006). Third, recall that many white-collar offenders have no criminal record, meaning that they have never been on trial before. Presumably, this could make the trial more stressful. Fourth, the longer length of white-collar crime trials can be particularly problematic for white-collar defendants (R. Wright, 2006). Depression, anxiety, and mental health problems have anecdotally been found among white-collar defendants. These problems can be attributed to the following: (1) Their lack of prior exposure to the trial process creates added stress, (2) they are used to being in control as leaders and executives but are not in control in court, (3) they have a great deal to lose if they are found guilty, and (4) a significant amount of shame or stigma is part of the trial process.

Where appropriate, defense attorneys may encourage defendants to take responsibility for their actions. This is done because accepting responsibility reduces the sentence that defendants receive if they are found guilty. In the words of one legal expert, "sentencers credit defendants who are contrite and demonstrate they would not commit future crimes" (Haugh, 2012, p. 51). This is borne out in research that shows that embezzlers who accepted responsibility for their sentences received sentences one month shorter on average than those offenders who did not accept responsibility (Madden, Hartley, Walker, & Miller, 2012). Accepting responsibility is also believed to reduce penalties given to corporations (Thompson & Yong, 2012).

While they typically will not take the stand, if convicted, white-collar offenders will go to great lengths to convince the judge why they should be punished leniently. For example, many white-collar offenders will send the judge a letter expressing remorse and begging for lenience. They will also call upon their family members and friends to write letters to the judge to appeal for a light sentence (Mann, 1985). In Martha Stewart's case, the judge received 1,500 letters from supporters who urged the judge to issue a light sentence to Stewart. One of the letters was from Stewart herself. Here is the letter Stewart sent her judge:

Dear Judge Cedarbaum:

We have never had the opportunity to speak one on one, you and I, despite the fact that I sat before you for five weeks. I am sorry that the legal system is such that even when a person's life is at stake—and for me that means my professional and personal life, not my physical being—the constraints prohibit conversation, communication, true understanding and complete disclosure of every aspect of the situation. I am not a lawyer, I am not skilled in legal processes, I am not even knowledgeable about many legal terms and legal procedures. I am still, after two and a half years of legal maneuverings and countless hours of preparation and trial time, abysmally confused and ill prepared for what is described to me as the next step in this process.

I am a 62 year old woman, a graduate of the excellent Nutley, New Jersey public school system and Barnard College. I have had an amazing professional life and several exciting careers, and I am grateful for that. I have a lovely family and a beautiful, upright, intelligent daughter (also a graduate of Barnard College), and I feel blessed and proud.

For more than a decade I have been building a wonderful company around a core of essential beliefs that are centered on home, family values and traditions, holidays, celebrations, weddings, children, gardening, collecting, home-making, teaching and learning. I have spent most of my professional life creating, writing, researching, and thinking on the highest possible level about quality of life, about giving, about providing, so that millions of people, from all economic strata, can enjoy beauty, good quality, well made products, and impeccably researched information about many hundreds of subjects which can lead to a better life and more rewarding family lifestyle.

I ask that in judging me you consider all the good that I have done, all the contributions I have made and the intense suffering that has accompanied every single moment of the past two and a half years. I seek the opportunity to continue serving my community in a positive manner, to attempt to repair the damage that has been done and to get on with what I have always considered was a good, worthwhile and exemplary life.

My heart goes out to you; my prayers are with you, and my hopes that my life will not be completely destroyed lie entirely in your hands.

Respectfully and most sincerely,
Martha Stewart

Source: Reprinted From Stewart, M. (2004 July 15). *Letter to judge Cedarbaum.* Retrieved from http://www.thesmokinggun.com/file/stewarts-letter-judge [End Box]

The Role of Victims in White-Collar Judicial Proceedings

Victims also have a role in white-collar judicial proceedings, though their role is limited. Criminologist Gilbert Geis (1975) has observed that the victim's role in the criminal justice process can be compared to the role that an expectant father has in the delivery room during the birth of his child. The father had a major role in the beginning of the pregnancy, but when the baby is being born, the father is tangential to the process. According to Geis, the victim has a similar role in the criminal justice process.

In white-collar crime proceedings at the federal level, historically, victims were not permitted to participate in the allocution process. **Allocution** refers to the part of the trial process where individuals are permitted to address the court prior to sentencing. Federal law reserved allocution for victims to those who had been victimized by violent crimes. This changed in 2004 with the passage of the **Crime Victims Rights Act**, which permitted victims of all types of federal offenses to participate in the allocution process.

The importance of victim allocution cannot be overstated. A sampling of the comments victims made in Bernard Madoff 's sentencing hearing include the following:

- "Last year, my mother died. Now I don't have my mother or my money."

- "Your sons despise you. . . . [You] are an evil lowlife."

- "For the first time in my life, I'm very, very frightened about my future."

- "I calculate again and again how long it is I can hold out." (R. Barnard, 2009)

Hearing victims' voices and seeing them in court reinforces that white-collar crimes are not victimless crimes.

It is certainly plausible that the voices could actually provide support for increasing offenders' sentences. Beyond the sentencing enhancement, participating in the process can be empowering and rehabilitative to victims (J. W. Barnard, 2002). Drawbacks include time and resources, identifying which victims should participate, how to deal with emotional outbursts, revictimization in the justice process, inarticulate victims, and emotional let downs for victims (J. W. Barnard, 2001).

In some cases, the victim may be a business or corporation. A question that has come up is the degree to which the business or corporation can contribute to the prosecutorial efforts in terms of financial support. In one case involving insurance fraud, an insurance company paid for some of the prosecutorial costs (see *People v. Eubanks*). The defendant appealed the case, and the California Supreme Court ruled that such activity has the potential to result in unfair treatment of the defendant and that the activity could lead to a conflict of interest. Courts do allow victims to provide assistance to the prosecution in some cases (e.g., they may hire a private investigator), though financial contributions are generally not permitted (Nahra, 1999).

CIVIL LAWSUITS AND WHITE-COLLAR CRIME

As noted previously, white-collar crime cases can be adjudicated in civil court through the use of lawsuits. Types of lawsuits can be categorized by the plaintiff-defendant relationship. The following types of lawsuits are relevant to white-collar crime:

- Individuals suing businesses

- Businesses suing businesses

- Government agencies suing individuals

- Government agencies suing businesses

- *Qui tam* lawsuits

- Class action suits

Within these types of lawsuits, different varieties of lawsuits exist. Two that are particularly relevant for white-collar crimes include tort lawsuits and contract lawsuits. A **tort lawsuit** involves "one party alleging injury, damage, or loss stemming from the negligent or intentional acts of another party" (T. H. Cohen, 2009, p. 1). **Contract lawsuits** "involve fraud, employment discrimination, tortious interference, or allegations of unfulfilled agreements between buyers and sellers [and] lenders and borrowers" (Farole, 2009, p. 1). These lawsuits can be filed in either state or federal court.

Figure 14.7 shows the types of civil court filings made in federal courts in June 2020. Note that the most common type of filing stemmed from victimization by a white-collar crime, namely "personal injury–product liability" cases. In fact, product liability suits were filed more often than the next nine types of lawsuits. "Personal injury–product liability" cases increased 3,591.6% when comparing June 2019 and June 2020 filings.

Table 14.5 shows the nature of the product liability cases filed in U.S. District Courts between 1990 and 2019. A few patterns are worth highlighting. First, the number of cases has increased dramatically since 1990. Second, 2010 was the year with the highest number of product liability cases filed. Third, 2010 was also the year that asbestos complaints peaked, with more than 40,000 asbestos cases filed that year.

Government agencies, particularly regulatory agencies, might also file civil lawsuits against individuals and businesses in an effort to stop white-collar offending, punish the individual or offender for the wrongdoing, and recover the economic costs arising from the misconduct. Recall the discussion in an earlier chapter of the billions of dollars that the Environmental Protection Agency recovered from environmental criminals. Most of these funds were recovered through civil enforcement actions.

In other cases, known as **qui tam lawsuits**, an individual can actually sue a corporation or company on behalf of the government. These lawsuits give private citizens the authority to take on the role of the government and sue corporations that have defrauded the government. Citizens who bring the charges can receive 25% to 30% of the damages received from the lawsuit. These are also known as *whistleblower lawsuits* in reference to the economic incentive given to whistleblowers to bring charges against a company (Payne, 2003a). Citizens must show that the

FIGURE 14.7 ■ Civil Court Filings in June 2020

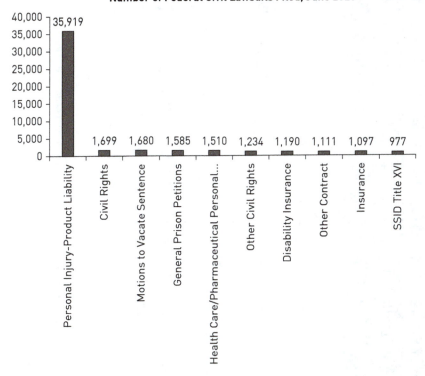

Number of Federal Civil Lawsuits Filed, June 2020

Source: https://trac.syr.edu/tracreports/bulletins/overall/monthlyjun20/cfil/

information they are using to file their suit did not come from public disclosures made by other parties. In other words, the citizen must be the "original source of the information" (Pacini, Qiu, & Sinason, 2007, p. 68). The goal of these lawsuits is to get either innocent or complicit individuals to bring forward information about wrongdoing (Baer, 2017).

As long as the lawsuits are filed in good faith, employees cannot be punished by their companies for filing the lawsuits. Employers, of course, do not see *qui tam* policies favorably. Beyond getting employees to report misconduct, the lawsuits "supplement the strained resources of government attorneys and investigators" (Pacini et al., 2007, p. 65). Figures 14.8 and 14.9 show the numbers of *qui tam* lawsuits filed by the U.S. Department of Justice's Civil Division between 2006 and 2016 as well as the amount of funds recovered in those lawsuits over the same time period. Note the relatively stable increase in *qui tam* suits over the timeframe and the significant dollar amount received in the lawsuits. Between 1988 and 2016, *qui tam* suits resulted in awards of more than $37.8 billion dollars. If citizens received 25% of the claims filed, this means that they received more than $9 billion from the lawsuits.

Class action lawsuits are used to address corporate wrongdoing. In these situations, a group of victims sues a business or corporation jointly for the harm caused by the corporation. Victims agree to be a part of the lawsuits with the understanding that any damages received would be split in a predetermined way. These lawsuits can be quite lucrative for attorneys and plaintiffs. A website even exists that publishes current class action suits—http://classactionworld.com/.

TABLE 14.5 ■ U.S. District Courts—Product Liability Cases Commenced, by Nature of Suit, During the 12-Month Periods Ending June 30, 1990, and September 30, 1995 Through 2019

Fiscal Year	Total	Contract Actions	Real Property	Property Damage	Airline	Marine	Personal Injury Motor Vehicle	Asbestos	Other
2019	57,632	455	526	494	188	19	405	267	55,278
2018	48,420	1,521	419	617	22	15	718	224	44,884
2017	36,733	237	308	474	31	17	395	351	34,920
2016	41,221	390	344	608	90	34	415	446	38,894
2015	46,167	279	342	3,782	63	9	404	1,982	39,306
2010	64,367	293	249	622	184	37	507	41,133	21,342
2005	30,295	224	103	431	79	46	531	1,243	27,638
2000	15,318	350	72	468	164	54	421	7,187	6,602
1995	28,226	249	64	366	155	53	566	6,916	19,857
1990[1]	19,428	361	65	323	196	330	575	13,687	3,891

[1]Twelve-month period ending June 30.

Sources: Personal injury/product liability data from Table C-11, Table S-7 (1990), and Table S-10 (1995, 2000, 2005), *Annual Report of the Director: Judicial Business of the United States Courts.*

FIGURE 14.8 ■ Number of Qui Tam Suits Filed, Civil Division, USDOJ, 2006–2016

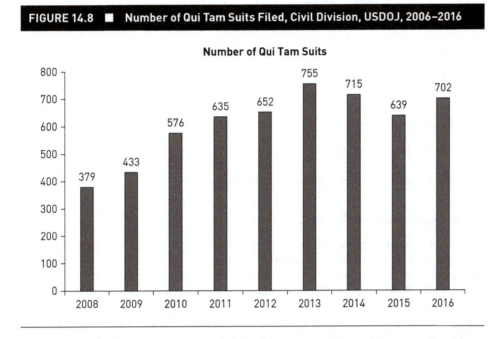

Number of Qui Tam Suits

FIGURE 14.9 ■ Amount Recovered in Qui Tam Suits, Civil Division, USDOJ, 2006–2016

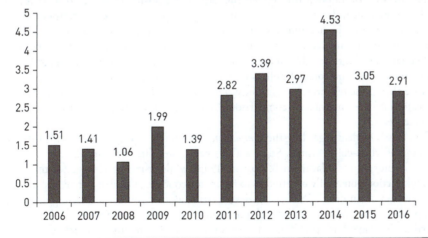

Amount Recovered in Qui Tam Suits (billions)

Source: https://www.justice.gov/opa/press-release/file/918361/download

ISSUES IN WHITE-COLLAR CRIME JUDICIAL PROCESS

A number of different issues arise concerning the judicial processing of white-collar offenders through the justice system. Some of these issues exist throughout the entire criminal justice system's processing of white-collar offenders, while others are unique to the judicial processing of white-collar offenders. These issues include the following:

- The need for networking
- Class bias
- The use of parallel proceedings
- Prosecutorial power
- The politics of prosecution

Each of these issues is discussed in the following sections.

Networking and the Judicial Process

As with the police response to white-collar crime, prosecutors must work with a number of different agencies in their efforts to battle white-collar misconduct. Unfortunately, interagency conflict and a lack of information sharing prohibit collaboration in some instances (Hammett & Epstein, 1993). Benson et al. (1990) commented that the "continued rarity of intergovernmental cooperation is troubling" (p. 371).

In effect, some prosecutors would likely pass on white-collar crime prosecutions simply to avoid the headache of collaboration. As an analogy, think of group projects in courses. Many students despise such projects and may even drop courses simply to avoid group projects. Prosecutors do the same thing in white-collar crime cases.

Class Bias

Class bias is also implicit throughout the judicial processing of white-collar crime cases. Such bias is evident in four ways: (1) the hiring of high-powered defense attorneys, (2) complacency of criminal justice officials adjudicating the cases, (3) the disparate treatment of corporations, and (4) inadequate laws. In terms of *hiring high-powered defense attorneys,* some white-collar defendants are able to assemble powerful defense teams that are paid hundreds of thousands, if not millions, of dollars to defend the white-collar defendant. These defense teams are able to use resources that far outweigh the types of resources prosecutors have available. Traditional defendants, by comparison, have few, if any, resources available to support their defense.

Class bias is evident regarding the *complacency* that some officials show toward the judicial processing of white-collar crimes. Some authors have noted that white-collar crimes are not a priority for prosecutors (Hammett & Epstein, 1993), while others have suggested that the failure to take action potentially contributes to future misconduct (Van den Berg & Eshuis, 1996). Consider the war on drugs. Prosecutors devote tremendous resources to battling drug crimes. These prosecutions tend to focus more on poor and minority suspects. So white-collar crimes are ignored while drug crimes are "attacked" in a warlike fashion. In terms of a lack of enforcement contributing to future misconduct, one can point to the way that drivers speed on certain highways because police officers never stop speeders on those highways. In Atlanta, Georgia, where I live, you have to go 20 miles an hour over the speed limit on some roads just to keep from being run over. The lack of traffic enforcement results in drivers speeding. The lack of white-collar crime prosecutions may contribute to future white-collar misconduct.

One can also recognize bias when considering the *disparate treatment of corporations.* Criminologist John Hagan drew attention to the dual role that corporations can have in the criminal justice system: (1) They can be victims of white-collar crime, or (2) they can be perpetrators of crime. Hagan (1982) wrote, "Corporate entities not only have successfully avoided large-scale prosecutions, they also have proven themselves effective in using criminal prosecutions to penalize those who offend them" (p. 994). Hagan suggested that prosecutors spend significant resources protecting corporations, but by comparison, fewer resources are devoted to prosecuting corporate entities. Hagan concluded that the criminal justice system "better serves corporate than individual interests" (p. 1016). Another scholar noted that businesses have a significant amount of "power" to get out of trouble (Punch, 2000, p. 273). Or, as suggested previously, they make great victims but lousy offenders.

Inadequate laws are another indicator of class bias in the judicial response to white-collar crimes. Conflict theorists have argued that laws are developed in a way that protects the powerful and weakens the poor and minority groups. This assumption will be discussed later. At this point, it is sufficient to point out that the consequences of inadequate laws are borne out in the judicial process. To be fair, it is important to note that efforts have been made to improve the laws to better address white-collar offending. For example, states have expanded their laws to make them apply to different types of white-collar crime. In New York, for example, a "scheme to defraud" statute was passed because it was recognized that the "false pretense larceny" statute was not sufficient for many white-collar crime cases (Clarey, 1978).

Still, problems remain that make traditional laws weak when processing white-collar crime cases. In one case, for example, a prosecutor charged contractors who tried to defraud an older woman with burglary. His rationale—the contractors committed the elements of "breaking" and "entering" into a home with "the intent to commit a crime." Incidentally, this prosecution was successful. More often than not, other prosecutors would have forgone charging the offenders because of the very real perception that the laws do not always cover the behavior of the white-collar offender.

The Use of Parallel Proceedings

Another issue that arises is the use of **parallel proceedings** in adjudicating a white-collar crime case. What this means is that a specific white-collar crime can be heard in more than one court simultaneously. There are different ways that proceedings might occur simultaneously. A criminal case could be processed with a civil or administrative proceeding, or a civil proceeding could be processed along with an administrative proceeding. Parallel proceedings are warranted under two circumstances: (1) Criminal proceedings may need to parallel civil or administrative hearings that address immediate needs to protect health and safety, and (2) simultaneous proceedings may be necessary to respond to cases that are especially serious (Nakayama, 2007).

Table 14.6 shows the advantages and disadvantages of using parallel proceedings in white-collar crime cases. Reasons criminal proceedings might be completed on their own include the following: (1) the ability to use evidence from the criminal proceeding in the civil case, (2) ensuring the civil case does not negatively impact the criminal case, (3) gaining an evidentiary advantage by not disclosing evidence too early, and (4) avoiding the surfacing of unnecessary issues. Reasons proceedings might occur simultaneously include (1) the need to address an immediate threat, (2) the threat of losing assets or bankruptcy, (3) the civil case was already underway when the criminal case began, and (4) the civil case fits within a national priority (Nakayama, 2007).

The use of parallel proceedings has been questioned on various grounds such as concerns about double jeopardy, excessive fines, and due process violations (McDade & O'Donnell, 1992). Despite these questions, the use of parallel proceedings remains a popular alternative. Note that the proceedings are expected to remain separate. For example, it is deemed unethical for authorities to "use the threat of a criminal enforcement to resolve a civil matter" (Nakayama, 2007, p. 8).

TABLE 14.6 ■ Pros and Cons of Parallel Proceedings Instead of Completing Criminal Proceedings First	
Pros of Parallel Proceedings	**Cons (Reasons Criminal Prosecution Should Be First)**
• Immediate threats to health and safety can be dealt with through injunction • Defendant's assets could "disappear" • Pending statute of limitations • Pending deadline for bankruptcy • Civil case is further along in justice process when criminal proceeding begins • Civil case directly relates to a national priority, and failing to address the case would jeopardize the national priority	• Criminal sanctions have potential to deter and punish offenders • Civil sanction could undermine criminal case and lessen penalty given to offender • Civil proceedings could expose ongoing investigation • Defendant could gain prosecutor's evidence prematurely • Officials from one proceeding may need to address unnecessary issues arising from other proceeding • Witnesses would be interviewed too frequently within short period of time

Source: Adapted from Environmental Protection Agency

Prosecutorial Power

Prosecutors enjoy considerable power in all criminal cases. Some have argued, however, that prosecutors have gained even more power in recent years in white-collar crime cases, especially in corporate crime prosecutions (Diamantis & Laufer, 2019). Legal scholar Ellen Podgor (2018) suggested that the lapse in federal prosecutions in the aftermath of the 2008 financial crisis was met with an overly aggressive response from federal prosecutors a few years later. These responses, she argues, include "shortcuts" prosecutors take in areas related to investigations (relying on corporations to investigate themselves), charges (stacking criminal charges), and plea bargains (allowing improper waivers). The consequences of the shortcuts, she argues, are that the behavior "undermines legitimacy and deterrence in the criminal justice process" (p. 93).

This power is exacerbated when considering the vagueness of the laws that prosecutors use when considering whether prosecutions are warranted. The irony of the vagueness is that prosecutions based on vague laws often result in acquittals or cases overturned on conviction. A popular example is the overturned conviction of Bob McDonnell, a former governor of Virginia who was convicted in 2014 for honest services fraud as a result of accepting gifts while engaging in "official acts" as governor. The defense alleged all along that the case was an abuse of prosecutorial power. After his conviction, McDonnell's lawyers appealed the case focusing on the vagueness of the law. While the U.S. District Court of the 4th Circuit upheld the conviction, the Supreme Court overturned the conviction and noted that the mere acceptance of gifts or convening of meetings does not constitute corruption (Kwok, 2019).

Politics and White-Collar Crime Prosecutions

Chapter 6 showed how white-collar crime occurs in the political system. In a similar way, the political system infiltrates into prosecution of white-collar and corporate crime cases. To be sure, the political system manifests itself in all types of criminal cases, but its role in white-collar crime cases is especially poignant. On the one hand, seasoned politicians often make their careers on being known as former prosecutors who were tough on white-collar and corporate offenders. Rudy Guliani, Eric Holder, Chris Christie, and Eliot Spitzer are just a few politicians who boasted about their tough response to white-collar crime in their efforts to seek higher political offices. On the other hand, political decisions influence the degree of priority given to prosecuting white-collar crime cases. Under the Trump administration, it has been argued that "changes in written policy, practices, and informal statements from the DOJ . . . have cumulatively softened the federal approach to corporate criminals" (Garrett, 2020, p. 109). Garrett (2020) points out the lower corporate crime penalties, a reduced focus on prosecuting individual executives, and less emphasis on corporate monitoring weakened the federal response to these cases.

A look at white-collar crime prosecution trends also shows a softer approach to white-collar offenses in general. TRAC Reports, a data clearinghouse service operating at Syracuse University, tracks data from various federal agencies and makes the data available in an easy to comprehend format. Data from TRAC Reports shows an enormous drop in white-collar crime prosecutions, with just 359 defendants charged in January 2020 by the U.S. Department of Justice, in comparison to more than 1,000 a month being charged in 2010 (Arends, 2020). TRAC Reports data show the 2020 data down 25% in comparison to 2015 data. A spokesperson from the DOJ questioned the accuracy of the TRAC Reports data (though the data is pulled directly from federal agencies) (Arends, 2020).

Summary

- White-collar misconduct cases are adjudicated in at least five different types of judicial or quasijudicial proceedings: (1) criminal proceedings, (2) civil proceedings, (3) administrative proceedings, (4) professional-disciplinary proceedings, and (5) workplace-disciplinary proceedings.

- Judges play an extremely important role in processing white-collar crime cases through the justice system.

- The three most salient factors influencing judicial decision making in white-collar crime cases are (1) harm from the offense, (2) blameworthiness, and (3) consequences of the punishment.

- At the federal level, U.S. attorneys are the prosecutors responsible for prosecuting federal offenses.

- The prosecution of white-collar criminals is seen as necessary in order to demonstrate "moral outrage" for white-collar misconduct (M. A. Cohen, 1992).

- Cohen (1992) argued that prosecutors will consider the following factors when deciding whether to prosecute white-collar offenders: the defendant's knowledge and intent, harm from the offense, whether misconduct continued after the regulatory agency initiated its investigation, amount of evidence, and how much the defendant benefited from the wrongdoing.

- Prosecutors face a number of other issues that may influence their decision-making process in white-collar crime cases, including (1) that trials may be harder to win in white-collar crime cases, (2) the time to complete the cases is significant, (3) resource issues, (4) establishing intent, and (5) practical issues.

- Dating back as far as Sutherland (1941), some criminologists have claimed that prosecutors are reluctant to prosecute corporations or businesses.

- The factors prosecutors are encouraged to address in deciding whether to prosecute corporations include offense characteristics, organizational characteristics, and the consequences of different types of reactions by the justice system.

- Common defenses that corporations use are "rogue employee" defenses and due diligence defenses (Plimton & Walsh, 2010).

- Another decision prosecutors will make is whether to enter into deferred prosecution agreements or nonprosecution agreements with corporations and businesses.

- The defense attorney is responsible for defending the accused offender against the criminal charges.

- Kenneth Mann (1985), author of *Defending White-Collar Crime: A Portrait of Attorneys at Work*, has provided the most descriptive overview of the defense attorney's role in white-collar crime cases.

- In-depth interviews of five federal public defenders by Jessica Leto and her colleagues (2007) found that defense attorneys used three strategies to manage their cases and their clients: *process-oriented, discovery-oriented, and client-oriented strategies.*

- Denial of criminal intent is among the most common denials offered by white-collar defendants.

- Other actors in the court include (1) jurors, (2) witnesses, (3) defendants, and (4) victims.

- Jurors might be reluctant to see certain types of white-collar defendants as capable of engaging in wrongdoing (Jesilow et al., 1986).

- Types of witnesses include government witnesses, lay witnesses, cooperating witnesses, character witnesses, and expert witnesses.

- Many scholars have pointed to the way that white-collar offenders will deflect blame from themselves and onto others in an effort to portray themselves as honest professionals (Croall, 1993).

- The 2004 Crime Victims Rights Act permitted victims of all types of federal offenses to participate in the allocution process.

- Two types of lawsuits that are particularly relevant for white-collar crimes are tort lawsuits and contract lawsuits.

- In *qui tam* lawsuits, an individual can actually sue a corporation or company on behalf of the government.

- Issues arising in the adjudication of white-collar crime cases include the need for networking, class bias, and the use of parallel proceedings.

Key Terms

Discussion Questions

1. Identify three reasons why corporate crime cases should not be prosecuted criminally.

2. Do you think class bias exists in prosecuting white-collar crimes? Explain.

3. What are the advantages and disadvantages of prosecuting corporations?

4. How are civil proceedings different from criminal justice proceedings? How are different types of judicial proceedings punitive?

5. Would you want to defend white-collar offenders as a defense attorney? Why, or why not?

6. Go to Classactionworld.com. Review five cases. How are those cases like white-collar crimes? How are they different?

7. If you were called for jury duty, would it matter to you whether the type of case was a white-collar crime case or a conventional case? Explain.

8. How is prosecuting white-collar offenders similar to group projects your professors give you in your college courses?

9. What factors influence prosecutorial decision making?

10. Find two white-collar crime court cases described in a news report. Describe themes from this chapter that relate to the cases.

15

THE CORRECTIONS SUBSYSTEM AND WHITE-COLLAR CRIME

CHAPTER HIGHLIGHTS

- Sentencing Dynamics and White-Collar Offenders
- The Prison Experience for White-Collar Offenders
- The Probation and Parole Experience for White-Collar Offenders
- Monetary Fines and White-Collar Offenders
- Alternative Sanctions and White-Collar Offenders
- Punishing Corporations for White-Collar Crimes
- Reasons for Punishing White-Collar Offenders

A college president spent two years in prison after being convicted for bilking the state out of thousands of dollars for personal expenses. In addition to stealing from his higher education institution, he reportedly enlisted his son to apply for a student loan to pay for tuition that was already covered. The president showed great remorse after being released, even telling community college colleagues about his fall from grace at a national conference he probably used to attend as a respected academic leader. He was able to provide insight into the prison experience: "I was told I'd end up in a country-club prison. . . . I ended up in maximum security." He explained that because of his PhD, "They all thought I was a medical doctor, so they started to come to me with every ailment. . . . After a while, I gave in. I'd tell them to take two aspirins and if it persists, go see the nurse" (Heyboer, 2016).

This college president, like many other white-collar criminals, was sent to prison for his misdeeds. In another case, an oncologist ruined the lives of hundreds of patients by telling them they had cancer when they didn't and administering unnecessary and harmful cancer treatments. The oncologist also stole more than $17 million from insurers. The 55-year-old doctor was sentenced to 45 years in prison, essentially a life sentence. Still, some of his victims were outraged at the sentence. The sentence, in their view, did not demonstrate the severity of the offense, even though it ensured that the doctor would never be free again. In the words of the daughters of one the overtreated victims who lived the end of her life being exposed to harmful medical treatment, "Of course, everybody would want to see life. . . . No matter what happens, nobody wins in this situation. There will never be justice" (R. Allen, 2015). Among other things, what this case shows is that the sentencing of white-collar offenders is complex and necessary in order for ideals of justice to be met. Whether justice is met through sentencing depends on one's perspective and experiences.

These two cases are provided as illustrations of white-collar offenders being sentenced to prison. A few other examples show how white-collar offenders experience the prison sanction. Consider the following excerpts of news articles describing how three white-collar offenders characterize prison:

- In her first television interview since being released from federal prison, *Real Housewives of New Jersey* star Teresa Giudice said she experienced horrible living conditions while incarcerated and described it like "living in hell." "I mean there was mold in the bathrooms. There was not running water constantly. The showers were freezing cold . . . I mean, the living conditions were really horrible. Like, horrible," she said in an exclusive interview with *ABC News'* Amy Robach that aired Tuesday on "*Good Morning America.* "There were some nights that we didn't even have heat. . . . It was—it was hell." (Singh and Conway, 2016)

- For Blagojevich, a man who rose to political heights [as Governor of Illinois] from modest roots (he is the son of a Serbian-born steelworker and a CTA ticket clerk), prison has been a humbling experience, full of little indignities. As at most correctional facilities, inmates are assigned menial jobs, such as washing dishes, mopping floors, and scrubbing toilets. At the low-security facility, Blagojevich did a three-month stint in the kitchen, one of the toughest tasks, but primarily worked in the law library and taught classes on the Civil War and World War II. His current job as an orderly at the camp pays $8.40 a month. "My jurisdiction was once all of the State of Illinois. Now I've got two hallways to clean," he says. "I feel like I was a very good governor, and now I feel like I'm doing a pretty good job on those floors." (Berstein, 2017)

  It's like if you got on an airplane and landed in Mongolia, and you don't speak the language, you don't know the culture, you have no money in your pocket, and somehow you have to still navigate your way from the airport to wherever you gotta go. (how an incarcerated lawyer described prison to Cantrell, 2018)

It is important to note that white-collar offenders, like other offenders, can be sentenced to punishments other than prison. In addition, to fully address how punishment is meted out against this group of offenders, in this chapter, attention is given to sentencing dynamics, prison, probation and parole, fines, alternative sanctions, the punishing of corporations, and reasons for punishing white-collar offenders. By addressing these areas, readers will gain insight into the dynamics guiding the sanctioning of white-collar offenders and an appreciation of the underlying factors that contribute to the punishment experience for white-collar offenders.

SENTENCING DYNAMICS AND WHITE-COLLAR OFFENDERS

To some, the sentencing of offenders is the most important part of the justice process in that it is through sanctioning offenders that goals of the justice system can be addressed and equal treatment of offenders can be promoted. Indeed, the ideals of justice are borne out through the application of just and fair punishments that are tied to the nature of the offense rather than to the class or status of the offender. The ability of the justice system to actually achieve "blind justice" can be assessed through an examination of the sentencing dynamics surrounding white-collar offenses. These dynamics can be understood through a consideration of sentencing practices, sentencing policies, and sentencing patterns.

Sentencing Practices and White-Collar Offenders

Research on the sentencing of white-collar offenders has provided mixed messages about issues related to the dispositions given to this group of offenders. The conventional assumption has been that white-collar offenders are sentenced more leniently than other offenders. Some studies on specific types of white-collar offenders have uncovered evidence of leniency. For example, a study of offenders convicted of Medicaid fraud in California found that this type of white-collar offenders received more lenient sentences than comparable conventional offenders (Tillman & Pontell, 1992). Tillman and Pontell (1992) cite three factors that contribute to the leniency afforded white-collar offenders. First, white-collar offenders have a "status shield" as a result of their occupational prestige, and this prestige is seen as protecting them from the stiff sentences given to street offenders. Second, white-collar offenders are able to hire better attorneys than conventional offenders. Third, the complexity of white-collar crime cases potentially creates enough doubt that more lenient sanctions are justified by criminal justice officials. Incidentally, the authors' own research found that when civil and administrative sanctions were added to the "total sentence," sanctions were more equitable.

Wheeler and his colleagues' (Wheeler, Weisburd, & Bode, 1982) interviews with judges found that the judges considered how the white-collar offender experienced the criminal justice process, and some viewed participation in the process as a punishment in and of itself for white-collar offenders. The judges also reported considering the sanctions imposed on white-collar offenders by civil, administrative, and professional proceedings. In addition, the age of the offender, his or her health, and the impact that the sentence might have on family members were considered by judges.

Interestingly, while the judges reported considering extralegal variables in sentencing white-collar offenders, some studies have found that white-collar offenders actually receive longer sentences than comparable conventional offenders—they are sentenced more severely than people think. One study, for example, found that after Watergate, white-collar offenders "were more likely to be sentenced to prison, but for shorter periods of time than less educated persons convicted of common crimes" (Hagan & Palloni, 1986, p. 603). Examining presentence investigation of 1,094 crimes occurring in seven federal districts between 1976 and 1978, Wheeler, Weisburd, and Bode (1982) found that white-collar offenders were more likely to go to prison and to be sentenced for longer periods of time than comparable conventional offenders were.

Another study showed that the type of sanction given to offenders was not tied to their status, but it was tied to the occupation in which the white-collar defendant worked (Hagan & Parker, 1985). Based on this perspective, Hagan and Parker (1985) suggested "that the substitution of class for status measures is crucial" (p. 312). In essence, the structure of certain occupations (which are related to the class of occupations) provides different opportunities for offenders, as well as different types of remedies from the criminal justice system.

Examining the influence of class position, Benson (1989) reviewed the sanctions given to 174 white-collar offenders sentenced in the 1970s. He found that informal social control sanctions were influenced by class position, but class position did not influence formal social control responses. Focusing on how loss of a job impacted sentencing, he found that losing one's job did not influence the sentence given in the justice process. Managers and employers (as white-collar offenders) were less likely to lose their jobs than nonmanagers and employees. He also found that public officials and professionals were "more vulnerable to informal sanctioning than employers and managers," leading Benson to conclude "the advantage of certain class positions seems to be more pronounced outside rather than inside the legal system" (p. 475).

Using the same data that they used in their 1982 study but adding a social class variable, Weisburd, Waring, and Wheeler (1990) found that class and occupational status were "complementary not competing indicators" (p. 237). They found that offenders "with high class positions receive the most severe prison sanction" (p. 237). In a subsequent study, Weisburd, Wheeler, Waring, and Bode (1991) found that most offenders convicted of offenses labeled white-collar offenses are not actually upper class offenders but middle-class white-collar offenders.

Researchers have identified factors other than class and status that seemed to influence the sentencing of white-collar offenders. One study showed that the judicial district where the white-collar case was tried influenced sentencing outcomes at the federal level (Hagan, Nagal, & Albonetti, 1980). Another study found that the combination of sanctions available to punish different types of white-collar offenders influenced the type of sentence given to them (Waldfogel, 1995). Research by Albonetti found that the sanctioning of white-collar offenders was tied to the complexity of the cases and to pleading guilty (Albonetti, 1999). In terms of guilty pleas, she noted that "pleas vary in their worth to prosecuting attorneys" (p. 321). In other words, in exchange for some guilty pleas, prosecuting attorneys are willing to offer a more greatly reduced sentence. For example, a complex case that could be difficult to prove might receive a greater sentence reduction in exchange for a plea as opposed to a "smoking gun" case where the case should be easy to prove.

Sentencing Policies and White-Collar Offenders

The Sentencing Reform Act was passed in 1984 as part of the Comprehensive Crime Control Act. One aim of the act was "to remedy individualized disparity in federal criminal sentences and to equalize sentences for 'street criminals' and 'whitecollar offenders'" (Ryan-Boyle, Simon, & Yebler, 1991, p. 739). The **U.S. Sentencing Commission** was created as part of the act; it has the responsibility of developing strategies to promote fairer sentencing at the federal level through the development of sentencing guidelines. As initially envisioned, judges were expected to sentence offenders within a certain range based on the recommendation found in the guidelines. Judges could decrease or increase sanctions through departures if circumstances warranted. For white-collar offenders, the guidelines promoted imprisonment because incarceration was seen "as the most effective deterrent for white-collar offenders" (Ryan-Boyle et al., 1991, p. 756). As a result, the guidelines "increased both the probability of imprisonment and the length of the sentence for most white-collar offenses" (M. A. Cohen, 1992, p. 1100). Note that researchers question whether the threat of incarceration truly deters white-collar offenders (Bagaric, Du Plessis, & Silver, 2016).

As noted in Chapter 14, when first created, the federal guidelines were seen as mandatory in nature, with judges required to provide a justification for departing from the guidelines. After the U.S. Supreme Court reviewed the guidelines in *Booker v. Washington,* the guidelines were revised to be advisory in nature, thus, theoretically giving judges back the discretion that had been taken away when the guidelines were first created.

For some white-collar crimes, sentences at the federal level became even stiffer with the passage of the Sarbanes-Oxley Act in 2002. Passed in reaction to the corporate scandals that had just occurred, the act called for a number of restrictive strategies to prevent white-collar crime.

In terms of penalties, the act doubled prison sentences from up to 10 years to up to 20 years for managers who falsified financial statements. In addition to stricter penalties, the act called for improved ethics training, improved corporate governance strategies, and better understanding of internal control efforts (Canada, Kuhn, & Sutton, 2008). The act has been described as "the most comprehensive economic regulation since the New Deal" (Vakkur, McAfee, & Kipperman, 2010, p. 18).

Surveys of 43 corporate executives and 130 graduate students in accounting found that the threat of jail time that is prescribed in the Sarbanes-Oxley Act has limited effectiveness in deterring financial statement fraud (Ugrin & Odom, 2010). The authors found that changing from one to 10 years' incarceration had a deterrent effect but changing from 10 to 20 years did not. Respondents indicated they would be no more deterred by a 20-year sentence than they would by a 10-year prison sentence. While research shows that the sanctions would not deter criminal behavior, research also shows that corporate risk taking declined after the act was passed; however, the decrease is possibly attributed to other types of regulations, including internal controls and increased board oversight (A. Dey, 2010).

Sentencing Patterns

Table 15.1 shows the types of penalties given for different types of offenses at the federal level between October 1, 2018 and September 20, 2019. As shown in the figure, variation exists among white-collar offenders and between white-collar and conventional offenders. Among specific types of white-collar offenders, the following patterns are shown:

- Three fourths of embezzlers and fraud offenders were sentenced prison.

- Just one fourth of environmental offenders were sentenced to prison, and nearly two thirds were given probation.

- Three fourths of bribery/corruption cases resulted in a prison sentence.

Offenses with the highest incarceration rates included kidnapping (100%), murder (99.7), robbery (98.6%), arson (97%), and drug trafficking (96.3%).

TABLE 15.1 ■ Number of Prison and Probation Sanctions in White-Collar Crime Convictions		
	Prison n (%)	**Probation** n (%)
Antitrust	17 (85.0)	3 (15.0)
Arson	65 (97.0)	2 (3.0)
Assault	654 (87.4)	89 (11.9)
Bribery/Corruption	235 (73.0)	82 (25.5)
Drug Trafficking	18,731 (96.3)	716 (3.7)
Environmental	44 (25.6)	109 (63.4)
Firearms	8,380 (94.3)	474 (5.7)
Food and Drug	13 (27.1)	35 (72.9)

	Prison n (%)	Probation n (%)
Forgery/Counterfeiting/Copyright	212 (77.4)	62 (22.6)
Fraud/Theft/Embezzlement	4,576 (74.1)	1,529 (24.7)
Kidnapping	93 (100.0)	0(0.0)
Murder	345 (99.7)	(.3)
Robbery	1,740 (98.6)	25 (1.4)
Sexual Abuse	1,135 (99.4)	7 (.6)
Tax	342 (64.3)	187 (35.2)

Source: U.S. Sentencing Commission

In reviewing the table, it becomes obvious that, with the exception of bribery, a higher percentage of conventional offenders get prison sentences than any of the white-collar offense types. On the surface, this may seem to suggest that white-collar offenders are less likely to be sentenced to prison than conventional offenders. However, these estimates do not control for past criminal histories or other factors that might influence sentencing decisions.

Table 15.2 shows the average lengths of sentences for various offense types during the same time frame. Note that white-collar offenders tend to receive shorter prison sentences than other offenders. Some will say that the shorter sentences are justified, while others point to the sentences as evidence of a biased justice process.

| TABLE 15.2 ■ Length of Federal Sentences Imposed, by Offense, October 1, 2018–September 30, 2019 |

4th Quarter 2019 Preliminary Cumulative Data (October 1, 2018, through September 30, 2019)

Tupe of Crime	Mean Months	Median Months	N
TOTAL	42	18	75,056
Administration of Justice	12	8	684
Antitrust	6	4	20
Arson	76	60	67
Assault	64	36	748
Bribery/Corruption	22	12	322
Burglary/Trepass	16	14	62
Child Pornography	103	84	1,347
Commercialized Vice	23	19	88

(Continued)

TABLE 15.2 ■ (Continued)

Tupe of Crime	Mean Months	Median Months	N
Drug Possession	2	0	515
Drug Trafficking	77	60	19,449
Environmental	3	0	172
Extortion/Recketeering	31	26	178
Firearms	50	39	8,380
Food and Drug	9	0	48
Forgery/Counter/Copyright	15	12	274
Fraud/Theft/Embezzlement	21	12	6,178
Immigration	9	6	29,015
Individual Rights	30	3	66
Kidnapping	169	120	93
Manslaughter	70	60	74
Money Laundering	61	33	1,151
Murder	260	240	346
National Defense	41	24	191
Obscentity/Other Sex Offenses	20	18	386
Prison Offenses	11	8	588
Robbery	109	92	1,765
Sexual Abuse	205	180	1,142
Stalking/Harassing	29	24	218
Tax	16	12	532
Other	3	0	957

Source: US Sentencing Commission

Some have argued that the sentencing of white-collar offenders has gotten a little out of control, with some sentences seemingly far too severe. Noting that the sentences are the result of the development of sentencing guidelines, Podgor (2007) writes,

In an attempt to achieve a neutral sentencing methodology, one that is class-blind, a system has evolved in the U.S. that fails to recognize unique qualities of white-collar offenders, fails to balance consideration of both the acts and the actors, and subjects offenders to draconian sentences that for some cases exceed their life expectancy. (p. 734)

Jonathan Simon, a law professor at the University of California, Berkeley, compared the severe prison sentences given to white-collar offenders to the types of sentences given to drug offenders, stating that "both represent increasingly irrational levels of punishment" (L. Moyer, 2009a).

Prison sentences for some first-time white-collar offenders "can exceed the sentences seen for violent street crimes, such as murder and rape" (Podgor, 2007, p. 733). Podgor contrasts white-collar sentencing with so-called three strikes laws. In the three strikes policies, the primary emphasis is on the actor. If the actor commits three offenses, a strict penalty results. In white-collar sentencing practices, attention is on the action of committing a white-collar offense. If an offender commits one white-collar offense, a stricter penalty results. According to one author team, these long sentences for white-collar offenders do not exist in other countries, such as Norway and Germany (Gottschalk & Glase, 2013).

Some have suggested that the apparent disparate sentencing resulting in long sentences for white-collar offenders might simply reflect the fact that the vast majority of white-collar offenders are kept out of the justice system in the first place. Gerber (1994) commented, "The apparent harshness of sentencing of white-collar offenders proves to be the result of a diversion of less serious offenders from the criminal court" (p. 164). For those white-collar crime cases that make their way into the justice system, by the time the offenders get to the judge, the government often has substantial evidence showing that the white-collar offenders have done something remarkably harmful (Wheeler et al., 1982). In other words, white-collar offenders do not go to court unless they have done something "really bad." Even in these cases, some believe that it does not make sense to spend large amounts of taxpayer dollars to punish white-collar offenders who could be punished in ways that don't simultaneously hurt the public (Bagaric et al., 2016).

The white-collar offender with the longest prison sentence on record is Shalmon Weiss. Weiss, whose misdeeds resulted in the collapse of National Heritage Life Insurance, was sentenced in 2000 by a Florida judge to 845 years in prison. According to the Bureau of Prisons, Weiss is scheduled to be released on November 23, 2754 (L. Moyer, 2009b). Chances are he will not live until his release date.

Other studies have suggested that there is very little evidence that white-collar offenders are sentenced more severely than other offenders. A study comparing auto thieves and embezzlers sentenced in U.S. district courts in 1993 found that auto thieves were four times more likely than embezzlers to go prison, and their average prison sentence was five months longer (Madden, Hartley, Walker, & Miller, 2012). Another study of white-collar offenders sentenced in Florida between 1994 and 2004 found that white-collar offenders tended to receive more lenient sentences than burglars and thieves (Van Slyke & Bales, 2012). In this same study, among white-collar offenders, some received stiffer sentences than others, suggesting differential treatment among white-collar offenders (not between white-collar offenders and street offenders). Comparing those convicted of Medicaid provider fraud to those convicted of public assistance fraud (a low status white-collar crime), the researchers found that the odds of imprisonment were 98.7% lower for the upper class providers.

It is plausible that sanctioning is not determined solely by type of offense. A study of sentencing in six judicial circuits in Florida found that "female street offenders sentenced by male judges received the most lenient sentences—not female white-collar offenders sentenced by male judges" (Van Slyke & Bales, 2013, p. 188). The authors of this study posit that while white-collar offenders might try to use their status to protect themselves, judges might be more likely to show mercy to disadvantaged offenders.

Studies continue to focus on sentencing in white-collar crime cases and provide insight into the way that systemic and political changes have influenced sentencing. Research by Van Slyke and Bales (2013) found that white-collar offenders' likelihood of going to prison increased 30% after the Enron scandals. A sentencing study of offenders convicted of the same crimes in Wheeler's study found that those convicted of white-collar offenses were more likely "to be eligible for a prison sentence compared to other prison sentences" and "at greater risk of incarceration compared to others offenses" (Galvin & Simpson, 2019, p. 393). However, the same study found that white-collar offenders did not receive longer prison sentences, leading the authors to conclude that status-liability applies to the likelihood of being sentenced to prison but not to the length of the prison sentence.

Summing up the sentencing research on white-collar offenders, one author has identified two types of sentencing studies: (1) advantage-focused studies comparing upper class and lower class offenders and (2) time-oriented studies that examine how sanctions have changed over time. One limitation Simpson (2013) identifies with the advantage studies is that they ignore other types of penalties, such as civil and administrative sanctions. Many white-collar offenders are punished; they are just punished differently. Whether this is fair is a philosophical and theoretical question.

THE PRISON EXPERIENCE FOR WHITE-COLLAR OFFENDERS

While a handful of studies have considered sentencing issues related to white-collar offenders, very few studies have focused on the experience of white-collar offenders in prison. Part of this lack of research has to do with the relatively few white-collar inmates in prison at any given time in the United States. It is extremely difficult to gain access to these inmates, and even if access is granted to a prison, it is even more unlikely that white-collar inmates would agree to participate in a study while incarcerated. Some researchers have done an excellent job locating and interviewing white-collar inmates after they have been released (Benson & Cullen, 1988). Others have relied on anecdotal accounts and media reports to generate understanding about how white-collar offenders experience prison (Payne, 2003b). From these efforts, one can point to five dynamics of the white-collar prison experience: (1) depression, (2) danger, (3) deprivations, (4) deviance, and (5) doldrums (see Payne, 2003b, for a thorough discussion of each of these dynamics). It is important to stress that the experience of incarceration for conventional offenders might be described through a discussion of similar dynamics. However, these characteristics and their consequences likely vary between the two types of offenders. After discussing these dynamics, attention will be given to the way that white-collar offenders adjust to prison.

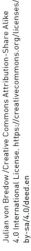

Julian von Bredow /Creative Commons Attribution–Share Alike 4.0 International License. https://creativecommons.org/licenses/by-sa/4.0/deed.en

PHOTO 15.1 White-collar inmates will wear the same uniform as other inmates. They will lose their identity as a white-collar employee and gain a new identity as an inmate.

Depression and the White-Collar Offender

For some white-collar offenders, it is likely that various degrees of depression will be experienced, particularly in the initial stages of incarceration. While all inmates likely experience different forms of depression, the sources of depression for white-collar offenders manifest themselves differently. Their sources of depression include (1) stressful changes coming from one's first exposure to prison life, (2) loss of job, (3) loss of status, (4) isolation, and (5) sentencing dynamics (Payne, 2003b). This chapter's Streaming White-Collar Crime describes an award-winning Netflix hit that showed just how depressing prison can be.

With regard to *stressful changes* as a source of depression, white-collar offenders who have never been to prison experience an enormous amount of anxiety that exists both before their incarceration and in the early stages of the incarceration. As Michael Benson and Frank Cullen (1988) point out, "For the first-time offender, the stress created by the prospect of going to prison

STREAMING WHITE-COLLAR CRIME   *Orange Is the New Black*: **Have Orange Collars Replaced White-Collars?**

Plot	What You Can Learn	Discussion Questions
Created by Jenji Kohan, and based on the hit memoir by Piper Kerman, *Orange Is the New Black* won accolades for its portrayal of the stark reality of prison life for female offenders, most of whom entered the criminal lifestyle either through victimization experiences or as not-so-innocent partners to more powerful criminal husbands or loved ones. In complete transparency, the story is not about a white-collar criminal. After all, Piper was convicted of a drug crime. However, her upper-class standing allows viewers to see what prison is like through the lens of the elite class. Showing how the class power she held outside of prison is meaningless in an institution meant to dehumanize and punish, Piper's experiences parallel those who would truly be characterized as white-collar criminals.	Prison is difficult for all inmates, including white-collar inmates. Inmates from privileged backgrounds are able to get used to being incarcerated, though they may use different coping strategies. Most inmates in prison come from lower social strata, meaning white-collar inmates will be in the minority.	How might prison be different for white-collar inmates? How concerned should we be with whether white-collar inmates experience prison as punitive? Explain.

probably exceeds any other that the person may have experienced" (p. 209). Another expert told a reporter that for white-collar offenders, "prison is equivalent to shock therapy, suddenly exposing [white-collar] offenders to people and circumstances they never would have imagined" ("Is Martha Stewart Truly a Changed Woman?," 2005). Prison administrators have been encouraged to watch for signs of depression in an effort to prevent possible suicide attempts among white-collar offenders. For those who experience stress in their initial stages of incarceration, as time passes, they will better adjust to the incarceration experience (Benson & Cullen, 1988).

Another source of depression for white-collar offenders is the *loss of their jobs*. Although their crimes were often committed against their employers and as part of their jobs, individuals define themselves by their careers. For convicted white-collar inmates, their loss of a career identity can be particularly problematic. They go from having a respectable job title to having an inmate number. Former California Republican Randy "Duke" Cunningham went from being a member of the U.S. House of Representatives to inmate 94405-198 after being sentenced to prison for accepting bribes from military contractors. Some inmates will have prison jobs to replace their former white-collar jobs. Not surprisingly, the pay is not so good in prison. White-collar inmates will go from making hundreds of thousands, if not millions, of dollars to making 12 cents an hour "for scrubbing floors and toilets" (S. Green, 2007). In the end, these changes in career identities can potentially be a source of depression, at least initially in the incarceration experience.

Somewhat related, *loss of status* can be another potential source of depression for white-collar inmates. These are individuals who go from being in charge in their occupations and businesses to individuals who are ordered around by prison officials and intimidated by fellow inmates. In other words, they go from being at the top of the social and occupational hierarchy outside

PHOTO 15.2 White-collar inmates typically have little in common with other incarcerated offenders. They are usually older, have different life histories, have had little exposure to violence, and have not led the traditional criminal lifestyle.

of prison to the bottom of the social hierarchy inside of prison. Benson's (1990) interviews with white-collar offenders found that inmates experience what he referred to as *status degradation* as a result of their conviction. He notes that white-collar inmates even lose "control over the presentation of self" (p. 522).

Isolation is another potential source of depression for white-collar inmates. Because so few white-collar offenders are in prison at any given time, it may be difficult for them to find peers with whom they can interact in prison. Much of their time may be spent alone until they find ways to communicate with fellow inmates. For example, Bernie Madoff reportedly doled out financial advice to fellow inmates who sought it and spent his time with a fellow white-collar inmate and an organized crime boss (Searcey & Efrati, 2011).

Interestingly, *sentencing dynamics* can be a source of depression in white-collar inmates. Recall from above that white-collar inmates receive shorter sentences than conventional inmates. What makes this particularly ironic is that depression and adjustment problems are more prone to occur in the first 6 months or so of incarceration (Payne, 2003b). After that initial introduction to incarceration, inmates are able to adjust to the incarceration experience (Benson & Cullen, 1988). By the time white-collar inmates are released from prison, many have, in effect, likely become accustomed to the incarceration experience.

Danger and the White-Collar Offender

Another dynamic surrounding the incarceration experience of white-collar offenders centers on their concerns about being injured. Four themes arise regarding danger and white-collar offenders: (1) celebrity bashing, (2) prison placement, (3) prison culture and socialization, and (4) exaggerated concerns (Payne, 2003b). With regard to **celebrity bashing**, some celebrity offenders are attacked by inmates seeking fame and notoriety. John Geoghan, a Catholic priest well known for sexually abusing more than 130 children over his career, was beaten and strangled to death by inmate Joseph Druce in August 2003. Bernie Madoff was allegedly beaten up in prison and treated for broken ribs and multiple bruises in the first year of his incarceration. While receiving widespread media attention, the story was never confirmed by prison officials or Madoff, which is not surprising given that reporting victimization would potentially place Madoff at risk for subsequent victimization.

In terms of prison placement, some prisons and jails are more dangerous than others for white-collar offenders. Between sentencing and admissions, offenders are often held in a detention center that may include all types of offenders. White-collar offenders, particularly those who might be targeted for an attack, might be placed in solitary confinement for their protection (L. Moyer, 2009b). Also, while many white-collar offenders are sentenced to minimum-security prisons, where the risk of violence is much lower, with the growing trend of longer prison sentences for white-collar offenders, some are being sent to higher-security-level prisons, which are more dangerous (J. O'Donnell, 2004).

Prison culture and socialization are relevant to the danger faced by white-collar inmates in that this offender group is not typically aware of the prison culture, nor have these offenders been socialized in how to behave in prison. The prison subculture includes offenders who have been exposed to, and have histories of, a great deal of violence in their lives. This is most likely not the case for white-collar offenders. One reporter quoted a prison consultant to white-collar offenders who said, "These guys have never been in a fight in their lives—they don't know what violence is, and now they're entering a world where anything can happen" (R. Schapiro, 2009). Describing the importance of prison socialization, another prison consultant advised that white-collar offenders do not know prison rules, such as that "changing the television channel can start a fight" (O'Donnell & Willing, 2003).

Though danger exists, from a scientific perspective, one can note that the concerns about danger are somewhat exaggerated. Violence is relatively infrequent in minimum security prisons, where most white-collar offenders are housed. As well, the rate of prison assaults against inmates is much lower today than in the past (Bureau of Justice Statistics, 2011). In some ways, the fear of harm is likely more inhibiting and significant than the actual experience of harm for white-collar offenders. With time, they adjust to the prison environment, and anxiety decreases (Benson & Cullen, 1988). Here is how one incarcerated white-collar offender described this process to an interviewer: "The inmates see me as someone they can talk to because . . . I've worked with the general public. . . . I expected to be ridiculed because I've been to school. And I expected to be bullied, but I haven't been" (Dhami, 2007, p. 68).

Deprivations and the White-Collar Offender

Prison deprives inmates of liberties, rights, freedom, and lifestyles to which they were previously accustomed. For white-collar inmates accustomed to certain lifestyles, the experience of deprivation might be particularly problematic. Something as basic as food consumption will be very different for white-collar inmates. One reporter team said that the food at one low-security prison was so bad that inmates "prefer microwaved groundhogs captured in the prison yard" (O'Donnell & Willing, 2003). A law professor told a reporter the following about a white-collar offender who was preparing for a prison stint: "His meal choices will not be what he's used to. . . . His diet will be prison food, which probably makes military or college dorm food look good" (S. Green, 2007). As the son of a cafeteria worker, I won't disparage cafeteria food. But the point is worth reiterating—those not accustomed to this environment will experience it differently from those who have been in similar situations in the past. The loss of identity, in particular, may be most vivid for white-collar offenders during their initial entry to prison (Hunter, 2019).

Of course, it is not just bad food that is a deprivation for white-collar offenders. The enormous status deprivation—or degradation, as Benson (1990) calls it—is particularly salient for white-collar offenders. This degradation can be experienced as a punishment in and of itself. Trying to use this perspective as an argument for a more lenient sentence, Tom DeLay's attorney pointed out in DeLay's sentencing hearing that DeLay "has fallen from the third most powerful position in this country to a man who is unemployed and unemployable" (P. Meyer, 2011).

For some offenders, the deprivations may be more significant than the danger they are concerned about in prison. Consider the following comments from former New York Chief Judge Sol Wachtler about his 13-month stay in prison as told to an interviewer:

> Believe it or not, the worst moment was not when I was stabbed and put in solitary confinement—although if you put splints under my fingernails and told me to tell you what happened in solitary, I couldn't, because the human mind locks these unpleasant thoughts out. No, the worst moment was when I was flown from one prison to another, with my wrists shackled together and a waist chain on, and I had to walk across the airport tarmac with everyone staring at me. And then the two sets of guards from the different prisons argued as to whom the chains belonged to. ("Judge Not," 1997, p. 2)

The judge was used to being above (and in control of) correctional officers. Upon his imprisonment, they were in control of him. This chapter's White-Collar Crime in the News shows the press release of a similar case involving a judge.

WHITE-COLLAR CRIME IN THE NEWS
FORMER BUCKS COUNTY JUDGE SENTENCED TO 6 ½ YEARS IN PRISON FOR PUBLIC CORRUPTION

The following is a press release from the Eastern District of Pennsylvania from June 10, 2019.

PHILADELPHIA—U.S. Attorney William M. McSwain announced that John Waltman, 61, of Trevose, Pennsylvania was sentenced to 78 months' incarceration by Judge Gene E. K. Pratter. In January 2019, the defendant pleaded guilty to conspiracy to commit money laundering and Hobbs Act Extortion Under Color of Official Right.

From 2011 to December 2016, Waltman served as a Magisterial District Judge in Bucks County, Pennsylvania. Together with his co-defendants who will both be sentenced later this week, Bernard Rafferty and Robert Hoopes, Waltman participated in a scheme to extort bribes and kickbacks from Bucks County businessmen. They also conspired to launder money for individuals they believed were engaged in narcotics trafficking and health care fraud.

For example, in November 2016, Waltman, Hoopes, and Rafferty accepted a bribe of $1,000, as well as the promise of other fees, in exchange for Waltman, Hoopes, and Rafferty to use their positions as public officials to "fix" a traffic case before Waltman in Bucks County Magisterial District Court.

In addition, from June 2015 to November 2016, Waltman, Hoopes, and Rafferty conspired to launder funds represented to be proceeds from health care fraud, illegal drug trafficking, and bank fraud. From June 2016 to August 2016, Waltman, Hoopes, and Rafferty laundered $400,000 in cash, represented to be proceeds from health care fraud and illegal drug trafficking, and took money laundering fees totaling $80,000 in cash.

"The laws of the land apply to everyone—especially to public officials who hold office to serve the public good," said U.S. Attorney McSwain. "When public servants choose to flout the rule of law, they disgrace themselves and the offices they hold. Every public official should be on notice after today's sentence: federal law enforcement is watching and we will hold you accountable if you make the wrong choices."

"A crooked judge trading on his position of trust is beyond disheartening," said Michael T. Harpster, Special Agent in Charge of the FBI's Philadelphia Division. "It's offensive. At every level, the justice system must operate in a fair and impartial manner. This is exactly the sort of case that deepens the public's distrust of elected officials and government, which is why the FBI takes public corruption so seriously."

"It is unacceptable for anyone, let alone an elected public official, to engage in such conduct," said IRS-Criminal Investigation Special Agent in Charge Guy Ficco. "John Waltman betrayed the public's trust when he accepted bribes in exchange for official acts. The sentence he received shows that there is no tolerance for such criminal behavior."

"Today's sentencing reflects Homeland Security Investigations' commitment to, and focus on, the investigation of financial crimes," said Marlon V. Miller, Special Agent in Charge of HSI Philadelphia. "By using his official position for his personal gain, Mr. Waltman violated the trust placed in him by the public. HSI and our law enforcement partners will continue to vigorously investigate those who conspire to knowingly launder illicit funds derived from criminal activities."

Reprinted from U.S. Department of Justice

Source: https://www.justice.gov/usao-edpa/pr/former-bucks-county-judge-sentenced-6-years-prison-public-corruption

Prison Deviance and the White-Collar Offender

As many sociologists have noted, any time you have a group of individuals together, someone in that group will engage in some form of deviance. With a group of convicted offenders together, it seems safe to suggest that some will engage in deviant acts while incarcerated. Many offenders have long histories of rule breaking. They are not going to decide to "behave" simply because they are behind bars. Three types of violations are relevant with regard to white-collar inmates: rule violations, deviant use of the justice process, and jailstripe crimes (Payne, 2003b). In this context, the phrase *rule violations* simply refers to situations where inmates break prison rules. Sometimes, the rule violations seem relatively minor. Martha Stewart, for example, supposedly made more ceramic figures per month than prison rules allowed. She made 12 figures in five months but should have made only one per month (Waller, 2007). Other times, the rule violations might be more significant. For example, Washington, DC Mayor Marion Barry, allegedly received oral sex from a prostitute in a crowded visiting room while he was incarcerated ("Ex-Mayor in 'Jail-Sex' Row," 1992, p. 3).

Deviant misuse of the justice process refers to situations where offenders misuse the justice process in a way that gains them some sort of advantage. Filing unnecessary or unwarranted appeals, misuse of furloughs, and unnecessary participation in treatment programs are examples. Unnecessary participation in treatment programs is believed to be particularly problematic with white-collar offenders. While some believe that it is easier for white-collar offenders to be paroled than conventional offenders (e.g., one prosecutor said, "they present much better than a guy with scars and tattoos and a nickname like 'snake'" ["White-Collar Crime Rising," 2003]), others have said that the nature of programming at the federal level makes it more difficult for white-collar offenders to have time taken off their sentences.

In particular, offenders receive time off of their sentences if they participate in a certain number of hours of treatment programs. The problem that arises is that white-collar inmates are often not in need of the types of treatment programs that are available. To take advantage of the opportunity to have their sanctions reduced, some white-collar offenders have allegedly "faked" their way into treatment programs. In his presentence report, for example, Sam Waksal (the former ImClone Systems Inc. CEO caught up in Martha Stewart's scandal) told the probation officer that he was a social drinker and that he consumed about five glasses of wine a week. By the time his sentencing hearing came around—about three months later—Waksal's attorney told the judge that Waksal had "recently developed a dependence on alcohol and would benefit from treatment for his newly acquired addiction" (Falkenberg, 2008). Waksal is not alone in this category. Prison consultants report telling white-collar offenders how to get into the best treatment programs in order to be released earlier (Falkenberg, 2008). Federal authorities have caught on to this manipulative behavior. In separate cases, prison coaches and consultants in Connecticut, New York, and Michigan were charged for coaching future inmates to fake drug abuse problems in order to serve less time (Collins, 2019).

The phrase **jailstripe crimes** refers to criminal acts that offenders commit while incarcerated. In one case, for example, an offender who had been convicted of fraud and was serving his sentence in a minimum-security prison orchestrated an identity theft scheme from inside prison that netted him $250,000 ("Inmate Ran Identity Theft Ring," 2011). An investigation by the Department of Justice's Office of Inspector General found that inmates routinely used prison telephones to commit criminal acts. Their investigation found that U.S. attorneys had prosecuted 117 cases where offenders used prison phones to commit crime (U.S. Office of Inspector General, 1999). Of those 117, 25 were financial fraud cases. In one case uncovered in the investigation, an inmate used a prison telephone to run a "fraudulent employment match service" (p. 3). Consumers who contracted with the employment service would have been paying the inmate for services that he never provided. In another case, an inmate stole more than $100,000 from a trucking company (U.S. Office of Inspector General, 1999).

Doldrums

Another aspect of the white-collar inmates' experiences in prison can be characterized as "the doldrums." After becoming acquainted with the incarceration experience, white-collar inmates report being very bored with it. One former white-collar inmate told Benson and Cullen (1988): "It was kind of an unexperience. It was not nearly as frightening as I thought it would be" (p. 209). Perhaps that is because white-collar offenders expected the experience to be much worse than it actually was, and it turned out not to be as bad as feared, that boredom and monotony "have been cited as the worst part of the white-collar inmate's incarceration experiences" (Payne, 2003b, p. 105).

Adjusting to Prison Life

The previous discussion is not meant to make it seem as if prison is too punitive for white-collar offenders or that white-collar offenders should be treated differently than conventional offenders. Instead, the intent was to call attention to the fact that the "incarceration experience" varies between conventional and white-collar offenders. One area where the experience is also different has to do with the tendency among members of the public to assume that white-collar offenders are not being "punished enough" during their prison stay. The moniker "Club Fed" is used to describe the supposed club-like atmosphere surrounding the prisons where white-collar inmates are often incarcerated. There are no bars, no fences, and no prison cells. Often, no structural barriers separate these prisons from the rest of society. Hence, it must not be that bad to be sentenced to Club Fed.

Club Fed is a myth. Being incarcerated can be a difficult process for any offender. Offenders have limited rights, they have no autonomy, they are away from their family members, there is nothing to do, and they have concerns about their safety. Describing the punitive nature of prisons for white-collar offenders, one author commented,

> But the grim reality of prison life for today's whitecollar criminal—the utter absence of privacy, the body-cavity strip searches, standing in line 90 minutes, much of it outdoors in any weather, to get unspeakable food—is definitely worse than they or the public expect. (Colvin, 2004)

For white-collar offenders, the most significant part of the prison experience is their initial adjustment period. With this in mind, recall that judges justified shorter prison sentences (or no prison sentence) for white-collar offenders based on their "special sensitivity to incarceration" (Mann, Wheeler, & Sarat, 1980). Though it may be the case that the initial stages of incarceration are particularly difficult for white-collar offenders, some scholars have argued that white-collar offenders have the personalities, skills, and resources to adjust effectively to the stresses of prison life. Benson and Cullen (1988) interviewed 13 white-collar offenders incarcerated in four different correctional institutions. Their research showed that while offenders initially found incarceration to be quite stressful (probably the most stressful event they had ever faced), offenders were able to "eventually adjust to prison life" (p. 209). The authors note that some offenders found the experience "interesting in a sociological sense" (p. 209). They also found that many of the offenders denied their criminal status as a coping strategy. In addition, Benson and Cullen noted that white-collar inmates searched for ways to increase their social status (compared to fellow inmates) while incarcerated. In doing so, they "reject the prison subculture" (p. 213). Another study offered a similar conclusion, finding that white-collar inmates fare as well in prison as other inmates and have characteristics that "may mitigate the negative effects of imprisonment" (Stadler, Benson, & Cullen, 2011, p. 18).

In another study, researchers used data from a national sample of inmates (n = 1,978) to test the special sensitivity and resilience hypotheses. The study found no support for the notion that white-collar criminals have a special sensitivity for incarceration; the study found some support for the resilience perspective with high risk status offenders demonstrating less risk for experiencing hopelessness while incarcerated (Logan, Morgan, Benson, & Cullen, 2019). The authors point out that certain qualities such as the ability to control one's feelings, avoid conflict, and develop prosocial contacts with staff help white-collar inmates adjust to prison. Former Enron CFO Andrew Fastow—who spent five years in prison for his role in the energy company's misdeeds—implicitly described his ability to adapt, telling an interviewer, "the inmates in prison camp were easier to get along with than Enron executives" (Primeaux, 2016).

THE PROBATION AND PAROLE EXPERIENCE FOR WHITE-COLLAR OFFENDERS

As shown previously, many white-collar offenders are sentenced to probation, and some are placed on parole after their incarceration in states where parole still exists. These are **community-based sanctions**. Community-based alternatives are popular for all types of offenders—conventional and white-collar alike. There is a misperception that these sanctions are not punitive, when, in fact, offenders tend to define certain types of probation as especially punitive. While all types of offenders are subject to these sentencing alternatives, the way the sanctions are experienced varies between types of offenders.

One of the first studies on the probation experience of white-collar offenders was done by Michael Benson (1985b). He interviewed 22 federal probation officers and 30 white-collar probationers and found that for white-collar offenders, the probation experience could be characterized as "going through the motions" (p. 429). He also found that the types of interactions between probation officers and white-collar offenders often allowed the offenders to continue to deny their criminal status. The officers interviewed did not believe that white-collar probationers would get in trouble while on probation, and one agency viewed control as "unnecessary in the case of white-collar offenders" (p. 431). Said one probation officer, "They don't need supervision. Some of it is just chit chat" (p. 431). Other probation officers highlighted the need to help offenders get accustomed to the fact that they had been convicted and "to adjust psychologically to the stigmatization effects of conviction" (p. 432).

Focusing on their status, Benson (1985b) highlights one flaw that community supervision has for white-collar probationers. In particular, he notes that probation officers spend most of their time supervising offenders from a lower class than the officer's social class. In fact, one can argue that officers are trained both formally and informally how to supervise lower class offenders. Conversely, officers are not always adequately prepared "to supervise their social equals or betters" (p. 435).

In a more recent study, Karen Mason (2007) interviewed 35 white-collar probationers to examine how shifts in penology have impacted their probation experiences. Her results highlighted the differences between white-collar offenders' probation experiences as compared to the experiences of other offenders. Among other things, she noted that the "workaday world of these offenders does not easily accommodate the demands of supervision, monitoring, and surveillance that are central to probation" (p. 28). The offenders described what they perceived as a bureaucratic model of probation that failed to offer offenders any sort of services or guidance. Referring to the loss of occupational status common among white-collar offenders, Mason noted that assisting white-collar offenders with reintegrative efforts "is no longer a priority in community supervision under the new penology" (p. 29).

Similar to Benson's research, Mason (2007) uncovered dynamics showing that white-collar offenders used aspects of the sanction to reject a criminal identity. In particular, she found that the probationers experienced the bureaucratic nature of probation (e.g., filling out forms or turning in records) in a way that allowed them to continue to deny their criminal status. They played by the rules in an effort to maintain "their own feelings of superiority and self-worth" (p. 30). Though maintaining a noncriminal identity, the white-collar probationers experienced a loss of autonomy, stigma, stress from the loss of autonomy, anxiety, shame for what they did to their families, and status degradation.

The notion of status degradation is particularly relevant with white-collar probationers. A power inversion occurs whereby probation officers gain a higher level of control over white-collar offenders (who are in an equal if not higher social status than probation officers). These aspects can be somewhat difficult to adjust to for white-collar offenders. Said one defense attorney about his client's probation sentence: "For someone who's not used to that, it's a real humiliation" (Sayre, 2011). Some have warned that community corrections officers might exert extra power over white-collar offenders in order to make up for the difference in social statuses between white-collar probationers and officers. Minkes (1990) wrote,

> There is a temptation to gloat at the discomfiture of the rich and leave them to their fate. After all, poor people are sent to prison every day for property offenses of far less value; how much more should the rich be punished. However, this argument must not be turned on its head. . . . Probation officers should be considering recommendations for probation, community service, compensation orders, and fines . . . and using formal and informal contacts with sentencers to press home the comparisons of seriousness. (p. 130)

In other words, probation officers have an important role in ensuring that white-collar offenders are punished fairly.

MONETARY FINES AND WHITE-COLLAR OFFENDERS

White-collar offenders are punished through the use of different types of monetary penalties. **Monetary penalties** include criminal fines, restitution, civil settlements, and compensatory and punitive damages awarded in civil trials. **Criminal fines** are monetary penalties awarded by the judge after an offender has been convicted of a crime. The fine is collected by the state (or federal) government, and funds are allocated accordingly in the jurisdiction where the case was heard. Fines are not designed to go directly back to victims.

Some legal scholars have advocated that fines be the primary sanction given to white-collar offenders and that imprisonment is an inappropriate, ineffective, and costly alternative. Richard Posner (1979–1980) called for large fines to deter wrongdoing. He argued that a large fine would have deterrent power equal to imprisonment. He wrote,

> In a social cost benefit analysis of the choice between fining and imprisoning white-collar criminals, the cost side of the analysis favors fining because . . . the cost of collecting a fine from one who can pay it . . . is lower than the cost of imprisonment. (p. 410)

From his perspective, such a practice was not unfair or biased toward the poor because he viewed a large fine as just and to be as punitive as incarceration.

Research shows that judges do not see fines as having a significant impact on offending (Mann et al., 1980). In the judges' views, by the time offenders were convicted, many were either already bankrupt or too affluent to actually feel the effects of fines. Providing judges guidance on when to issue fines, the federal guidelines state "that a court must impose a fine in all cases, except where the defendant establishes that he is unable to pay and is not likely to become able to pay any fine" (Schanzenbach & Yaeger, 2006, p. 764). The amount of the fine is tied to the nature of the offense and the recommendations in the guidelines. In fraud cases, consideration is given to the economic harm experienced by the victim and the gain experienced by the offender, while in antitrust cases—where it may be virtually impossible to identify economic costs and offender gains—consideration is given to the impact that the offending had on the economy (Ryan-Boyle et al., 1991).

A theoretical perspective known as optimal penalty theory predicts that fines will be used "to the maximum extent possible before they are supplemented with imprisonment" (Waldfogel, 1995, p. 107). The basis for the assumption is that fines are "costless" and prison is costly. Others, however, have noted that fines probably have little deterrent value, particularly "for high-stakes crime with low detection rates" (Diamantis & Laufer, 2019). Also, the wide range of fines has been critiqued. On the one hand, it has been noted elsewhere in this text that large fines are simply seen as a cost of doing business for some organizations, meaning that the companies don't experience the sanction as punitive. On the other hand, some critics of large fines point out that they are unfair to investors who had nothing to do with corporate wrongdoing (Masters, 2020).

A study by Waldfogel (an economist; 1995) examined penalties given to 7,502 fraud offenders convicted at the federal level in 1984. He found that prison sentences were tied to harm from offenses, and fines were tied to the offender's ability to pay the penalty. In line with optimal penalty theory, his research found that those who were given higher fines were sentenced to prison for shorter periods of time. A study of 22,508 federal white-collar offenders sentenced under the sentencing guidelines between 1991 and 2001 found similar results: Paying fines reduced the amount of prison time for white-collar offenders (Schanzenbach & Yaeger, 2006). Such a finding is potentially problematic because it means that lower class individuals are being awarded longer prison sentences because of their inability to pay a fine.

Restitution is a monetary penalty that orders an offender to pay victims back for their suffering. In terms of white-collar crime, victims could be those individuals directly harmed by white-collar misconduct, the employer victimized by the offense, or a government agency that was either victimized or had to devote a great deal of resources to address the wrongdoing. The aim of restitution is to make victims "whole" through payments (Ryan-Boyle et al., 1991). Not surprisingly, those who receive restitution as a penalty are not as likely to be sent to prison (Van Slyke & Bales, 2012). One expert has called for "voluntary retribution" as a punitive strategy that would allow victims to be paid back and offenders to be held accountable (Faichney, 2014). The same expert believes that restitution would "mean more" if the offender chose to give it rather than being ordered to give it. Here is how he described his proposal:

> Voluntary restitution may remedy the harm caused by white-collar crime at the place where its effects have been most directly felt. In addition to improving victims' economic well-being, voluntary restitution may also be morally significant. An affirmative compensatory act by the offender may demonstrate acceptance of responsibility and restore social trust and goodwill, especially if the offender must work arduously to provide it. While a court may (and in many circumstances, must) order restitution, it can only do so after an adjudication of guilt. Ordering restitution at sentencing does not require the offender to accept any responsibility for his crime and does not discourage financial gamesmanship by offenders. (Faichney, 2014, p. 429)

Civil courts can order defendants found liable to pay several different types of monetary penalties. Monetary penalties awarded in civil court are called "damages." Compensatory damages and punitive damages are particularly relevant to white-collar crime cases. **Compensatory damages** are awards made to plaintiffs (victims) that the defendants are ordered to pay in order to compensate victims for their victimization experience. **Punitive damages** are "awarded when the defendant's conduct is determined to have been so 'willful, malicious, or fraudulent' that it exceeds the legal criteria for mere or gross negligence" (T. H. Cohen, 2005, p. 1). Awarded by juries, in theory punitive damages are designed to punish and deter (T. H. Cohen, 2005; Stevens & Payne, 1999).

A number of issues arise regarding the use of punitive damages. For example, large punitive damage awards against a company may inadvertently punish innocent workers who lose their jobs or consumers who pay higher prices as the punished business continues to seek profits. Also, the question of whether large damages can be seen as cruel and unusual punishment has surfaced, with the U.S. Supreme Court deciding that such damages are not violations of the Eighth Amendment. However, it is expected that the damages "bear a reasonable relationship to the actual harm they are intended to punish" (Stevens & Payne, 1999, p. 198).

One can question the practice of justifying punitive damages on deterrent ideals. The sanction of punitive damages does not meet the tenets of classical deterrence theory, which suggests that sanctions must be swift, certain, and severe enough to outweigh offender gain without being too severe. The penalties are not applied quickly, especially given the lengthy judicial process and the fact that many defendants will tie the case up in a drawn-out appeals process. The size of the damages is random and uncertain, with little evidence that any sort of constant factors contribute to jury awards. Also, the size of some punitive damages often far exceeds what might be called for from a classical deterrence theory perspective (Stevens & Payne, 1999). Note that judges have the authority to reduce punitive damage penalties and that many judges exercise this right in cases involving large punitive damages.

Sometimes these financial penalties are negotiated as a way for white-collar and corporate offenders to avoid admitting guilt. These situations do not always meet the ideals of retribution. Here is an example from one criminologist illustrating this theme:

> In April 2013, news sources reported an agreement among federal agencies and some of the largest banks in the United States designed to compensate the millions of Americans who *"allegedly"* were targeted in wrongful foreclosures during the housing crisis. *I use the term allegedly because these types of settlements typically place no guilt on the offending parties and no admission of criminal conduct.* Bank of America, JPMorgan, Chase, Wells Fargo, and Citigroup, for example, agreed to pay $9.3 billion in cash and in reductions of mortgage balances. A total of $3.6 billion will go directly to borrowers who lost their homes or faced foreclosure. The 4.2 million victims will receive payments ranging from $300 to $125,000 as compensation. (Dodge 2013, p. 28; italics added)

ALTERNATIVE SANCTIONS AND WHITE-COLLAR OFFENDERS

Several types of alternative sanctions, both formal and informal, are used to punish offenders. In some ways, the application of these sanctions to white-collar offenders is comparable to the way the sanctions are applied to conventional offenders. For example, because certain types of white-collar offenders are more likely to reoffend, some experts have called for the use of risk assessment instruments (similar to those used for conventional offenders) to guide supervision (Harbinson, Benson, & Latessa, 2019). In other ways, these sanctions vary. The way these sanctions are used for white-collar offenders is at least partly distinct from how the sanctions are used for conventional offenders. In this context, alternative sanctions include (1) house arrest, (2) community service, (3) shaming, and (4) loss of a job.

House Arrest and White-Collar Offenders

Under **house arrest**, offenders are told that they must be at home either all of the time or when they are not at work, the doctor's office, or a religious service. Probation and parole officers use various strategies to make sure that offenders are at home. House arrest is used as (1) a pretrial strategy to keep offenders out of jail before trial, (2) a sanction imposed as part of the offender's probation experience, or (3) as a condition of release after an offender has been incarcerated in jail or prison.

With regard to white-collar crime, a perception exists that suggests it is better to be on house arrest in a white-collar offender's home than it is to be on house arrest in a conventional offender's home. Before Madoff was sentenced, he was placed on house arrest. Comments such as "Madoff has been under house arrest in his $7 million Manhattan penthouse" demonstrate the frustration that people seem to have with putting affluent individuals on house arrest (Neumeister & Hays, 2009). It is important to bear in mind that Madoff, at that point, had not yet been sentenced, and that punishment is a relative experience (Payne & Gainey, 1998). What one offender "feels" as punitive will be different from what another offender might "feel" as punitive. Where the punishment (or controlling actions of the justice system) occurs may actually have very little to do with the punitiveness of house arrest. Having said that, I'll go ahead and contradict myself—if I were to be placed on house arrest, I'd prefer to be in a penthouse than one of my old college apartments. Either way, though, the experience of house arrest would be controlling and punitive for me.

House arrest has been lauded as an appropriate sanction for some types of white-collar offenders for five reasons (see Rackmill, 1992). First, it is a cost-effective sanction in that there are no incarceration costs. Second, the sanction allows offenders to find (or maintain) employment, which will help the offender pay the victim back. Third, given that most white-collar offenders are nonviolent, there is little risk that they would physically harm anyone while on house arrest. Fourth, the house arrest sanction minimizes the trauma that the family might endure from the criminal justice process. To be sure, a number of different types of offenders—conventional and white-collar alike—are good candidates for house arrest sanctions. Finally, for inmates with health problems, serving their time on house arrest allows them to maintain appropriate health care, and the cost of the health care is paid by the offender rather than the government. Some defense attorneys highlight the health needs of older white-collar inmates in an effort to convince judges to select the alternative sanction (Daugherty, 2017).

House arrest with electronic monitoring is a variation of the house arrest alternative. In these situations, offenders wear an ankle monitor, and the probation or parole officer monitors the offender's whereabouts through the use of satellite technology. Many will recall how Martha Stewart was placed on house arrest with electronic monitoring after her brief stay in prison. As with house arrest in general, some assume that even the addition of electronic monitoring results in the sanction being lenient as compared to other sanctions. It is interesting to note, however, that studies show that certain types of individuals with exposure to the justice process actually prefer prison to electronic monitoring (May & Wood, 2005; Payne & Gainey, 1998). Offenders cite the degree of control that community corrections officers have over their lives as being particularly problematic for them. In other words, house arrest with electronic monitoring is a punitive experience (again, whether one lives in a penthouse or the trailer where I once lived).

Randy Gainey and I, in 1998, interviewed offenders on house arrest with electronic monitoring to shed some light on this punitive experience. We were able to identify how the sanction might apply similarly and differently to white-collar and conventional offenders. In particular, using Gresham Sykes' (1958) pains of imprisonment as a guide, we highlighted how offenders on electronic monitoring experienced the types of "pains" that offenders in prison experienced and how they experienced additional pains that are unique to the electronic monitoring experience (see Table 15.3).

As an illustration of how the electronic-monitoring experience can be punitive for white-collar offenders, consider the following deprivations experienced by incarcerated and electronically monitored offenders:

- *Deprivation of autonomy:* Just as inmates lose control over their lives, so white-collar offenders on house arrest with electronic monitoring are forced to give up their freedom and abide by controls and restrictions that are placed on them by the court and reviewed by probation officers. White-collar offenders are virtually always used to being in control of their lives and the lives of others. Having someone else control them, especially someone from a lower social status, could be difficult for some offenders.

TABLE 15.3 ■ The Pains of Electronic Monitoring for White-Collar Offenders		
Pain	**What It Means**	**White-Collar Offender Experience**
Deprivation of autonomy	Electronically monitored offenders lose their freedom and have very little control over decisions about movement.	White-collar offenders would be permitted to leave home only for work, medical reasons, probation officer visits, and so on.
Deprivation of goods/ services	Electronically monitored offenders are not permitted to engage in activities outside of the home that others take for granted.	White-collar offenders would lose their social activity and would not be permitted to shop, eat out, or do other things without approval.
Deprivation of liberty	Electronically monitored offenders lose many of their rights, with some losing their right to vote.	White-collar offenders would experience these same losses.
Deprivation of heterosexual relations	Electronically monitored offenders do not lose their ability to have relations with others, but these relations are certainly influenced by the sanction.	Because of the loss of status experienced by the offender, partners may also lose status, thereby potentially influencing the relationship.
Monetary costs	Electronically monitored offenders usually have to pay to be on the sanction.	White-collar offenders would experience the same losses as conventional offenders here, though relatively speaking this may be more of a cost for conventional offenders.
Family effects	The family members of electronically monitored offenders must change their actions when someone in their home is monitored.	The loss of status would be experienced by the entire family, and some may actually lose their home as well as other taken-for-granted comforts.
Watching-others effects	Electronically monitored offenders see others engaging in activities that they would like to be doing.	White-collar offenders would experience the same losses.
Bracelet effects	Electronically monitored offenders often complain about having to wear the bracelet.	Offenders who are working would find the most discomfort with the bracelet, especially if it was noticeable.

Source: Payne, B. (2003b). *Incarcerating white-collar offenders: The prison experience and beyond.* Springfield, IL: Charles C Thomas.

- *Deprivation of goods and services:* Just as inmates have reduced access to goods and services, so white-collar offenders on house arrest with electronic monitoring will have limited access to the kinds of goods and services they are accustomed to. This could represent a major shift in an offender's lifestyle, which would be experienced as punitive.

- *Deprivation of liberty:* Convicted felons lose many rights (e.g., in various states—the right to own a gun, to vote). For white-collar offenders involved in the political process, losing the right to participate in that process can be especially difficult.

- *Deprivation of heterosexual relations:* Whereas inmates do not have the same kinds of heterosexual relationships while they are incarcerated, monitored offenders also have their intimate relationships disrupted while on house arrest with electronic monitoring. In a very real sense, the nonmonitored family members have more social power than monitored offenders because they are able to maintain a social lifestyle. For white-collar offenders accustomed to an active social life, the fact that their social lives are put on hold while family members continue engaging in social activities can be problematic.

- *Monetary costs:* These affect all offenders because they are required to pay for the costs of the monitoring experience. For white-collar offenders, however, paying for the electronic monitoring sanction may be less difficult.

- *Family effects:* Families of white-collar offenders can face a reduced quality of life, a lower social status, and a reduction in the types of materials and goods they are used to. With electronic monitoring, the stigma of wearing the ankle bracelet may also affect the family. In addition, these effects are experienced by white-collar offenders when the family loses its lifestyle, status, or other material goods as a result of the conviction. Also, the monitored offender will rarely have time alone in his or her own residence.

- *Watching-others effects:* Monitored offenders have to watch others do things they are unable to participate in because of the restrictive probation conditions.

- *Bracelet effects:* This refers to instances when the monitor is felt as an invasive or stigmatizing tool attached to the body as a reminder of one's misdeeds. This can be particularly difficult for women in the workplace if they are unable to conceal the monitor (Payne, 2003b).

It is important to note that the *pains of electronic monitoring* typology was developed by focusing on all types of offenders, most of which are conventional offenders. Additional research on the experience of white-collar offenders on house arrest with electronic monitoring is needed.

Community Service

Community service involves situations where offenders are told to perform a certain number of hours or days of community service. In some cases, judges will order white-collar offenders to complete a specific type of community service, while in others, the offender might be ordered simply to perform some general service activities. Given the skills that white-collar offenders have, many are in positions to offer their specific skills for the good of the community. Consider the following examples:

- As part of her sanction for the Operation Varsity Blues case, actress Felicity Huffman did "community service at the Teen Project, a local rehab center for girls who have lived on the streets and who are trying to earn their GEDs" (Fernandez, 2019).

- A tenured law professor convicted of tax fraud was sentenced to "200 hours of community service with legal aid organizations" (Robert, 2020).

- A former Ohio mayor was "required to perform 30 days of community service with the Mahoning County Sheriff's Office" (Richland Source, 2020).

- Educators involved in a cheating scandal with Atlanta Public Schools were sentenced to community service "at Atlanta's jail teaching inmates, some of whom are the victims of the problems in Atlanta's school system" (Lowry, 2015).

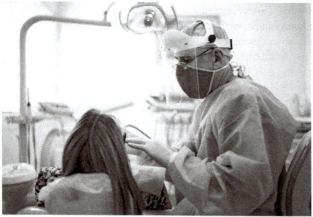

PHOTO 15.3 Sentencing white-collar inmates with community service makes great sense when their skills are used to serve the public. Sentencing a dentist to give free dental work would be an example of an appropriate use of the community service sanction.

Community service has numerous advantages. The sanction holds offenders accountable for their misdeeds, helps reintegrate offenders back into the community, and benefits the community through the offenders' contributions. Despite these advantages, the sanction appears to be rarely applied. A study of home health care providers convicted of white-collar offending, for example, found that less than a third were sentenced to community service (Payne & Gray, 2001).

In one of the few studies exploring community service among convicted white-collar offenders, researchers found that female health care professionals convicted for health care crimes were more likely to be given community service sanctions than male health care professionals convicted of relatively similar offenses (Supernor, 2017). Focusing on 100 health care offenders given community service and 100 health care offenders who were not given the sanction, the research found that 56% of women received community service in comparison to 39% of men. In addition, women were given shorter community service sanctions than men. Possible explanations Supernor (2017) cites for the differences include the possibility that judges see community service as more lenient and use the sanction to protect female offenders. Supernor also cites that judges could be behaving in a patriarchal manner and controlling women by putting them to work so to speak.

Corporations can also be sentenced to community services. When this occurs, corporations typically give funds to a charitable organization, though in rare cases executives might be ordered to perform specific volunteer activities (Homer & Higgins, 2020). Research by Homer and Higgins (2020) shows that community service is more likely to be given to corporations if they have higher fines, suggesting that the sanction is reserved in cases where those companies are more blameworthy. The underutilization of community service for corporations mirrors the underutilization of the sanction for all white-collar offenders.

Shaming

Shaming is another alternative sanction strategy used to punish white-collar offenders. Shaming strategies are used for all types of offenders, but they may be particularly effective for white-collar offenders given the higher amount of stigma and shame that accompany the conviction of white-collar offenders (Benson, 1990). Countless examples of these shaming sanctions could be provided. As an illustration, consider a case where a judge ordered a former state official convicted of corruption to write a letter of apology and have it published in at least six outlets. Just a few days after the sentence was imposed, the following letter was published across the state:

Dear New Mexicans,

I cannot begin to express how deeply sorry I am for my transgressions and the damage I caused to the public's trust in public officials. I only hope the people of the state of New Mexico will move forward and someday forgive my actions which were not borne out of greed but rather a result of very tragic personal circumstances which led to some very poor decisions on my part. I have not made excuses for my actions. I have simply tried to explain the circumstances which led to my transgressions. I only hope the people of this great state find it within themselves to forgive me. (Duran, 2015)

Shaming can also be used as a strategy to punish corporations for wrongdoing. In fact, many federal and state agencies announce their sanctions and maintain a public database of offenders and do so out of shaming ideals. As well, judges may order companies to engage in behavior designed to shame the company. One company, for example, had to run the following advertisement:

We Apologize for Polluting

The Environment General Wood Preserving Company recently pled guilty in federal court to illegally disposing of hazardous waste in 1985 at its plant in Leland, North Carolina. As a result of that crime, General Wood Preserving was fined $150,000, and was ordered to publish the following advertisement:

We are sorry for what we did, and we hope that our experience will be a lesson to others that environmental laws must be respected.

Board of Directors General Wood Preserving Co., Inc. (Kostelnik, 2012, p. 150)

The idea of shaming white-collar offenders as a sanction has been gaining popularity over the years. Said one legal scholar, "Some of legal academia's brightest stars have jumped on the shame train, arguing that modern versions of the dunce cap, rather than shackles, best fit the 'white collar' criminal" (Owens, 2000, p. 1047). Shaming by itself can be counterproductive. Scholars have called for what is called **reintegrative shaming**, a process characterized by a shaming sanction followed by efforts to reengage offenders in the community.

John Braithwaite (1989) and Michael Benson (1990) have been the leading criminologists calling for the use of reintegrative shaming for white-collar offenders. Braithwaite notes that overly punitive and stigmatizing responses to white-collar misconduct can be counterproductive and result in offenders becoming disengaged from the community. Building on Braithwaite's ideas, Benson notes that **disintegrative shaming** embarrasses offenders, causes anger, and potentially leads to additional harm. Alternatively, reintegrative shaming focuses on the bad act and communicates messages of disapproval, which are followed by efforts to reintegrate the offender back into the community.

One author team identified several reasons that reintegrative shaming strategies should be effective for white-collar offenders. These reasons included the following:

- White-collar offenders want to minimize the harm done to their family members, and reintegrative shaming strategies provide an opportunity to do this.

- Others possibly steer clear of white-collar misconduct because they do not want to be embarrassed.

- Those who have a higher attachment to their jobs, families, and society should be less likely to want to be shamed.

- Reintegration affirms individuals, while disintegration breaks them down (Ivancevich, Konopaske, & Gilbert, 2008).

For white-collar offenders, reintegrative shaming is effective inasmuch as offenders take responsibility for their actions. In other words, reintegrative shaming will be more powerful if offenders "respect the shamer" (Ivancevich et al., 2008). What this means is that if the offender has no respect for those doing the shaming, there is little likelihood that the shaming will have deterrent qualities. Or to put it more bluntly, if you don't care what someone thinks about you, their efforts to shame you will not keep you from behaving a certain way. Also, according to one author, "shaming sanctions are most viable when used in conjunction with alternative sanctions so that courts can impose sanction bundles of costs commensurate with the level of offense committed by an offender" (Kostelnik, 2012, p. 141).

Related to shaming but justified on deterrence ideals, Utah is the first state, and the only state to date, to create a white-collar crime registry that publicly identifies certain types of white-collar offenders convicted in Utah. The registry is meant to provide individuals protections against being victims of "affinity" crimes where offenders might target victims to get them to participate or invest in fraudulent schemes (Dye & Mano, 2016). The registry isn't technically designed to shame, though the collateral consequences of other types of offender registries suggest that such a consequence is likely.

The website quotes Utah Attorney General Sean D. Reyes saying,

> This registry has been a goal of mine for years and will further equip citizens to protect themselves from financial fraud by making information much more accessible in this digital age. A simple search could curtail a fraudulent investment and save an entire nest egg. (Utah, n.d.)

Offenders included in the registry are those who have been convicted in a Utah State court since 2006 for a second degree felony involving securities fraud, theft by deception, unlawful dealing of property by fiduciary, insurance fraud, mortgage fraud, communications fraud, or money laundering. Offenders convicted in federal court are not included (Utah, n.d.).

Critics of the white-collar crime registry point to the long-term shame that offenders will experience from their use. Said one critic, "But the real problem with public registries is that they're inhumane, turning every crime into a life sentence. In branding people with a permanent public mark of shame, registries punish the convicted long after they have served their time" (Robinson, 2015). The one empirical benefit of the registry is that researchers have used the publicly available data to explore various dimensions of white-collar crime (Dearden & Gottschalk, 2020).

Loss of Job

Loss of job is another sanction that can be imposed on white-collar offenders. For many individuals, this potential loss is likely enough to keep workers from engaging in misconduct. Once caught, not only do offenders lose their current jobs, but they are also often ordered out of their careers for various amounts of time. Martha Stewart, for example, was not able to serve as a CEO of a publicly traded company (including her own) from the time of her conviction until 2011. When Ivan Boesky was convicted of his securities crimes, he was barred from working in the securities industry for the remainder of his life (K. Adams, 2009). Boesky was not alone. A study of 2,206 individuals charged with financial misrepresentation in enforcement actions by the Securities Exchange Commission (SEC) and Department of Justice (DOJ) found that 93% of the individuals had lost their jobs by the time the enforcement action was completed (Karpoff, Lee, & Martin, 2008). When other professionals such as lawyers, doctors, educators, and so on are caught committing crime on the job, they too face the likelihood of losing their jobs.

At some point, white-collar offenders who lost their jobs and have completed their criminal justice sanction will seek new employment. A study by Kent Kerley and Heith Copes (2004) found that, for the most part, white-collar offenders "are better able to rebound following contact with the criminal justice system" (p. 65). In particular, they found that white-collar offenders were better able to find new jobs than conventional offenders were. The caveat they uncovered in their research was that white-collar offenders with more arrests and a later onset of offending found it just as difficult as conventional offenders to find a stable job.

White-collar offenders may be able to adjust to postprison life better than conventional offenders. However, because of the potential problems that arise when seeking employment after a white-collar crime conviction, some former white-collar offenders are self-employed. Among others, these self-employment options include becoming prison consultants, crime consultants, YouTube personalities, and writers. Prison consultants provide future inmates with guidance on adjusting to prison. Serving time in federal prison is not a requirement to serve as a prison consultant, but former inmates have insight and advice that many future inmates would be more prone to believe given these consultants' first-hand experiences. Combine that first-hand experience with innovation and hard work ethics, and former white-collar inmates can create lucrative careers in the prison consulting industry. One of the earliest prison consulting businesses was a 900 number individuals could call (Timko, 1995). Since then, the white-collar prison consulting industry has expanded considerably. In 2012, one reporter identified more than three dozen prison consulting groups; their names included "Executive Prison Coaching," "The Real Prison Consultant," and "The Prison Doctor."

Today, these consultants help future inmates adjust to the thought of going to prison. One white-collar offender was so afraid of going to prison that he had his 17-year-old son shoot him in the leg the day before his sentencing hearing so he could delay his incarceration (Zarrell, 2018). Rather than asking their kids to shoot them, many others call on consultants for advice and comfort. The consultants are hired to tell the future inmates "how to negotiate the perils of the U.S. penal system" (C. Kelly, 2009, p. 1). Said C. Kelly (2009), "They teach you how to behave, they teach unwritten rules, most important, they teach how to survive" (p. 1). As noted previously, they also teach white-collar inmates how to get into the "best" treatment programs to earn early release.

Steven Oberfest, CEO of Prison Coach, charges $200 an hour to prepare offenders for prison. He uses his past experience as an inmate as the source of his information (R. Schapiro, 2009). Oberfest, who calls himself an "inmate adaptation specialist," told an interviewer, "I can prepare you to go into hell" (K. Johnson, 2009, p. 1A). To capture this white-collar market (pun intended), one consultant even "changed his company name from American Prison Consultants to Wall Street Prison Consultants" (K. Johnson, 2009, p. 1A).

Some former white-collar inmates become crime consultants and provide insight and advice to companies and criminal justice agencies about white-collar offending. Described as a "poacher turned gamekeeper role," these white-collar offenders use their white-collar crime skills to help authorities catch other white-collar criminals (Hunter, 2019). Kevin Mitnick is among the most famous former offenders who was able to develop a lucrative business telling others how to avoid crime. His website (mitnicksecurity.com) includes the following promotional material:

> The World's Most Famous Hacker is on Your Side. Behind the scenes of the most secure organizations in the world, Kevin Mitnick and his global ghost team are there to provide an extraordinary advantage in the battle for real information security. Through testing, training, and awe-inspiring presentations, the Mitnick Security team can help your organization make cyber threats vanish.

A few former white-collar inmates have turned to YouTube as part of their consulting careers. Justin Paperny runs a business called whitecollaradvice.com and has consulted for businesses, government agencies, and future white-collar inmates. He has also created a YouTube channel where he provides a wide range of information in videos he develops. With titles such as "Six Bad Habits I Quit in Federal Prison," "9 Smart Things White-Collar Defendants Do," and "7 Uncomfortable Truths About Federal Prison," the videos have been viewed thousands of times. Viewers provide favorable feedback. Here is an example of a comment made by a viewer in response to the "7 Uncomfortable Truths" video": "What Justin says is so true. I just got out of a FPC and had to endure the two month process of being furloughed before it occurred. Unfortunately there is no sense of urgency in the BOP."

Michael Santos has also published several informative videos and is one of Paperny's business partners. Paperny and Santos work with other former white-collar inmates in their educational, advocacy, and consultant roles.

Former white-collar inmates have also turned to writing as part of their self-employment efforts. Topics commonly addressed by the former inmates include prison reform advocacy, how to survive prison, and autobiographical accounts of their experiences. Among the more popular autobiographical accounts is Jordan Belfort's *The Wolf of Wall Street*, which went on to be a Hollywood hit starring Leonardo DiCaprio.

PUNISHING CORPORATIONS FOR WHITE-COLLAR CRIME

Corporations can be punished both formally and informally for misconduct. If they are convicted (in criminal court), found liable (in civil court), or determined responsible (in administrative or regulatory proceedings), various types of sentencing alternatives arise. Criminal penalties include fines, restitution, probation, and disbarment, and civil penalties, including compensatory and punitive damages, can be applied. In administrative proceedings, a corporate offender can be given civil fines and required to pay restitution. Corporations can also experience "marketplace sanctions," such as loss of investor confidence (M. A. Cohen, 1992). It is also important to note that when corporations are sanctioned, individuals leading the corporation are also sanctioned as individual offenders.

With regard to criminal sanctions, the *U.S. Sentencing Guidelines* includes an Organizational Guidelines section that provides judges guidance in determining how to sentence corporations. The guidelines specify three sanctions: probation, fines, and restitution. The Organizational Guidelines were implemented in November 1991 and included recommended sanctions that were stricter than the types of sanctions applied earlier. For example, fine amounts recommended in the Organizational Guidelines were 5 to 10 times higher in the guidelines than the fines that had traditionally been applied in corporate misconduct cases (M. A. Cohen, 1992). The guidelines have been critiqued for appearing to arbitrarily stipulate sanctions relative to organizational characteristics (e.g., size of the company, number of employees; see Rackmill, 1992). It is an interesting philosophical question: If two companies commit the exact same offense, should one of them be punished more severely because it is larger and wealthier? (A similar question can be asked about individual white-collar offenders.)

Fining Corporate Offenders

The use of fines to punish corporations has been a hotly debated issue among criminologists and economists. As suggested above, some economists apply concepts of cost-benefit analysis in determining the relevance of fines to control corporate misconduct. Some criminologists, on the other hand, view fines as less than useful, to put it nicely. Snider (1990) suggested that "fines for large organizations typically represent a fraction of the profits made in one hour of operation" (p. 380). Another scholar noted that fines are simply a "cost of doing business" and that ultimately fines hurt stockholders and corporations (Orland, 1980). To put it bluntly, it's cheaper for some organizations to break the law than it is to abide by the law (Werle, 2019).

Cohen (1989) has considered how corporate fines compare to the harm committed by the corporation. Focusing on 288 non-antitrust corporate offenders prosecuted between 1984 and 1987, he found that monetary sanctions "seldom exceed—and often are much less than—total harm" (M. A. Cohen, 1989, p. 618). To quantify the difference, he suggested that "a firm convicted of causing $1.00 in harm might pay a criminal fine of $.76 in addition to any other sanctions such as criminal restitution or civil penalties" (p. 658).

While Cohen's study was done before the Organizational Guidelines were in effect, criminological studies since then also question the effectiveness of fines for corporations. A review of 405 cases where organizations were sentenced through 1996 found that organizational offenders were able to avoid paying fines "by convincing a U.S. District Court that they have no money" (Green & Bodapati, 1999, p. 556). The authors noted a particularly interesting irony: Organizations might commit crimes because of a lack of money. Then, they can argue that the "lack of money motive" can be used to avoid sanctioning the organization. They also call for organizational sales (where the business is sold) or forced dissolution (which is an organizational death penalty) in these cases. Judges are unwilling to make these decisions out of concern for workers, investors, and consumers (Orland, 1980).

More recently, Nicole Piquero and Jason Davis (2004) reviewed sanctions imposed on organizations after the guidelines were developed to see whether certain factors impacted the penalty given to corporations. They found that although legal factors consistent with the guidelines impacted sentencing to a degree, two extralegal variables influenced organizational sentencing: (1) economic solvency and (2) closely held organizations. These two factors influenced the amount of the fine, "but did not significantly impact the placement of the fine within the guideline range" (p. 652).

Probation and Corporate Offenders

Corporations can be sentenced to a term of probation. The first use of **organizational probation** occurred in 1971 in *U.S. v. Atlantic Richfield, Co.,* when Judge James B. Parsons, Jr., sentenced ARCO (the Atlantic Richfield Company) to probation and "ordered it to develop an oil response plan" (Lofquist, 1993, p. 160). Lofquist notes that by the eighties, one fifth of all corporate offenders convicted at the federal level were given a probation sentence. The use of organizational probation was not formalized until the development of the Organizational Guidelines in 1991. The federal sentencing guidelines specify that corporations cannot be sentenced to more than five years of probation.

Corporations can be required to meet certain conditions while on probation. Probation conditions must be tied to the characteristic of the organization and the offense (Plimton & Walsh, 2010). Probation conditions are, as a result, tied to type of industry. For instance, judges have ordered bakeries convicted of wrongdoing to provide food for the underprivileged (M. Levin, 1984). One condition sometimes used is that companies are told to apologize publicly, in various media sources, for their misconduct (M. A. Cohen, 1992). Table 15.4shows the factors that drive organizational probation decisions and the types of conditions that organizations can be ordered to abide by as part of their probation.

Issues Surrounding Corporate Sanctions

Two issues surface when considering how to sanction organizations. These include (1) determining appropriate sanctions to reduce recidivism and (2) avoiding harm to innocent parties. With regard to recidivism, one basis for punishing companies is to keep them from committing future acts of misconduct. Research shows that recidivism by corporations is tied more to the nature of the industry as opposed to the type of intervention (e.g., criminal justice, civil, or administrative) (Simpson & Koper, 1992). However, the authors found that for those corporations with past guilty verdicts, stiffer penalties (measured by changing from a misdemeanor to a felony) reduced subsequent recidivism.

In terms of punishing innocent parties, some sentences (corporate manslaughter and penalties for violations of safety laws) are potentially too strict and harmful to innocent employees

TABLE 15.4 ■ Dynamics Surrounding Corporate Probation

The Court Shall Order a Term of Probation	Mandatory Conditions of the Probation	Discretionary Conditions
• If necessary to ensure satisfaction of other sanctions; • If an organization of 50 or more employees lacks an effective program to prevent and detect law violations; • If the organization or high-level personnel participating in the offense have been convicted of a similar offense in the past five years; • If necessary to ensure that changes are made within the organization to reduce the likelihood of future criminal conduct; • If the sentence does not include a fine; or • If necessary to accomplish one of the four purposes of sentencing.	• Commission of no further crimes • Payment of a fine or restitution, or performance of community service; and • Any other conditions reasonably related to the instant offense and imposing no unnecessary deprivations of liberty or property.	• Publicity paid for by the defendant in media specified by the court detailing the crime, conviction, sentence, and remedial steps taken; • Development by the defendant, with court approval, of an effective program to prevent and detect future law violations; • Notification of employees and shareholders of the offense and of the details of the compliance program; • Periodic reports to the court regarding progress in implementing the compliance program, occurrence of new offenses, or investigations involving the defendant; and • Periodic examinations of facilities and records, and interviews of employees by the court or a special probation officer to monitor compliance.

Source: Lofquist, W. (1993). Organizational probation and the U.S. sentencing commission. *Annals of the American Academy of Political and Social Science, 525,* 157–169.

or shareholders (Stevens & Payne, 1999). As noted before, a desire to avoid harming individuals leads some judges to give relatively lenient sentences in some corporate misconduct cases. When corporations become so large that communities and large segments of the population rely on them, it becomes increasingly difficult to administer a sanction that doesn't ultimately harm the public. As one legal scholar notes, "some corporations have become so large of systematically important that when they violate the law, the government cannot credibly threaten 'efficient' criminal sanctions" (Werle, 2019, p. 1366). The phrase "too big to jail" is used to describe these situations.

REASONS FOR PUNISHING WHITE-COLLAR OFFENDERS

Criminologists have described several reasons that society punishes criminals. These reasons include (1) retribution, (2) specific deterrence, (3) general deterrence, (4) rehabilitation, and (5) just deserts, and (6) incapacitation, which refers to removing dangerous offenders from the street to protect society from harm. With the exception of the sixth reason, all of the reasons easily demonstrate reasons that white-collar criminals are punished.

Retribution and White-Collar Offenders

As a philosophy of punishment, **retribution** means that offenders should be punished to meet societal demands. Philosophers have long noted that formal punishment satisfies public demands. Another way to say it is that punishment of wrongdoers makes some people "happy." This may be especially the case for victims of white-collar crimes. When Bernie Madoff was being led away in handcuffs after being sentenced, one of his victims was heard saying, "What a sweet sight. What a sweet sight" (Healy & Mandell, 2009). Some members of the media could not help gloating over Madoff 's plight. In a way that hinted at pleasure, one team of reporters said about Madoff the day after he was sentenced,

> the swanky East 64th Street duplex where Madoff spent the previous night must have felt like a distant memory as he looked around his Spartan cell. Instead of having his loving wife, Ruth, for company, Madoff is sharing a roof with . . . rapists, murderers, even thieves like him. (Zambito, Martinez, & Siemaszko, 2009)

Madoff is not the only white-collar offender members of society want punished. A survey of 1,512 respondents from across the United States found that more than three fourths of the respondents supported longer prison sentences for white-collar offenders (Unnever, Benson, & Cullen, 2008, p. 177). Podgor (2007) wrote that "Wealth, education, and prestige are often cited as reasons for giving white-collar offenders a harsher punishment" (p. 750). As an illustration, one U.S. attorney commented that white-collar criminals "should be treated more harshly because you're talking about people who have gotten every opportunity that you can give them . . . the drug dealers have had no opportunities" (O'Donnell & Willing, 2003). It seems that some members of the public may be less forgiving of white-collar offenders.

Specific Deterrence and White-Collar Offenders

Specific deterrence ideals suggest that punishment should occur in order to stop the punished offender (in this context, either a white-collar offender or a corporation) from engaging in future wrongdoing. Deterrence theory has been addressed elsewhere in this text. At this point, it is sufficient to suggest that some believe that sanctions proportional to the harm committed by the offender will keep individuals and corporations from engaging in future misconduct (Spurgeon & Fagan, 1981). Note that some research has called into question the deterrent ability of imprisonment for individual offenders (Weisburd, Waring, & Chayet, 1995), while others have found that sanctions might deter corporations from future misconduct (Simpson & Koper, 1992).

General Deterrence and White-Collar Offenders

General deterrence ideals suggest that offenders should be punished in order to keep other potential offenders from engaging in misconduct. As noted earlier, judges often justify their stern responses to white-collar offenders on general deterrence ideals (Mann et al., 1980). There is a perception that fines and probation do not have general deterrent power for white-collar offenders. One government official with the Environmental Crime Division of the Department of Justice has been quoted saying, "incarceration is the cost of business that you can't pass on to the consumer" (Stuart, 1995, p. 255). The underlying assumption is that fines are passed on to consumers, and as a result, it will not keep offenders from engaging in white-collar misconduct.

In line with general deterrence ideals, educators have used incarcerated white-collar offenders to teach future white-collar professionals how to avoid white-collar offending. Castleberry (2007), a marketing professor, takes his students on prison field trips as part of his efforts to teach business ethics and to make sure that students understand the laws governing workplace behavior. He argues that the visits show students that laws apply to them, that there are consequences for bad workplace decisions, and that criminal workplace decisions sometimes result from "seemingly insignificant acts." He also argues that visits will help students understand what prison life is like for the white-collar offender and that from this, it is assumed that students would be less prone to engage in workplace misconduct.

Rehabilitation and White-Collar Offenders

Rehabilitation, as a philosophy of punishment, suggests that offenders are brought into the justice process so that the government can play a role in treating whatever issues offenders have that may have contributed to their wrongdoing. White-collar offenders might receive individual-level counseling from probation and parole officers to help them deal with their status degradation and to regain employment (Payne, 2003b). In general, though, treatment programs tend to be designed more for drug and violent offenders. If individuals with a white-collar status find themselves in a treatment program, it is more apt to result from a commission of a drug offense.

Just Deserts and White-Collar Offenders

Just deserts as a punishment orientation suggests that offenders should be punished for one primary reason: because they deserve it. Braithwaite (1982) highlights the difficulties that arise in applying this philosophy to white-collar offenders:

- How do you identify who is responsible?

- Do you punish the individual or the organization?

- If punishing both, how much punishment is appropriate, and how would it be divided?

- How do you keep individuals (consumers and workers) from being punished? (p. 525)

Braithwaite (1982) suggests that the negative consequences arising from overly strict responses to white-collar offending support the selective enforcement of white-collar crimes. He quotes the justice theorem: "Where desert is greatest, punishment will be the least" (p. 755).

Braithwaite (1982) draws attention to the debate about whether white-collar offenders should be punished more severely so that they are punished the same as conventional offenders. In doing so, he calls for a utilitarian approach to balance the scales of justice. His perspective is quite simple: Rather than punishing white-collar offenders more severely, why not punish conventional offenders less and white-collar offenders only slightly more so that both groups are punished similarly?

Experts recognize that effective punishments balance ideals of retribution, just deserts, deterrence, and rehabilitation. Benson (1985b) calls for short sentences of white-collar offenders that are split between a short prison sentence and a short probation sentence. Such an approach would have deterrent, retributive, and rehabilitative qualities. As well, it would be more cost-effective than other remedies.

Summary

- White-collar offenders are subject to a wide range of sentencing alternatives, including prison, probation, restitution, fines, and various alternative sanctions. Organizations—as well as individuals—can be sanctioned in white-collar crime cases.

- Research on the sentencing of white-collar offenders has provided mixed messages about issues related to the disposition of white-collar offenders.

- Wheeler and his colleagues' (1982) interviews with judges found that the judges considered how the white-collar offender experienced the criminal justice process; some judges viewed participation in the process as a punishment in and of itself for white-collar offenders.

- The Sentencing Reform Act was passed in 1984 as part of the Comprehensive Crime Control Act. One aim of the act was "to remedy individualized disparity in federal criminal sentences and to equalize sentences for 'street criminals' and 'white-collar offenders'" (Ryan-Boyle et al., 1991, p. 739).

- Some have argued that the sentencing of white-collar offenders has gotten a little out of control, with some sentences seeming far too severe.

- Some have suggested that the apparently disparate sentencing resulting in long sentences for white-collar offenders might simply reflect the fact that the vast majority of white-collar offenders are kept out of the justice system in the first place.

- Very few studies have focused on the experience of white-collar offenders in prison. One can point to five dynamics of the white-collar prison experience: (1) depression, (2) danger, (3) deprivations, (4) deviance, (5) doldrums.

- For white-collar offenders, the sources of depression include (1) stressful changes coming from one's first exposure to prison life, (2) loss of job, (3) loss of status, (4) isolation, and (5) sentencing dynamics (Payne, 2003b).

- Four themes arise regarding danger and white-collar offenders: (1) celebrity bashing, (2) prison placement, (3) prison culture and socialization, and (4) exaggerated concerns.

- For white-collar inmates accustomed to certain lifestyles, the experience of deprivation might be particularly problematic.

- Three types of inmate violations are relevant with regard to white-collar inmates: rule violations, deviant use of the justice process, and jailstripe crimes (Payne, 2003b).

- After becoming acquainted with the incarceration experience, white-collar inmates report being very bored with prison.

- Benson (1985b) found that for white-collar offenders, the probation experience could be characterized as "going through the motions" (p. 429).

- Monetary penalties include criminal fines, restitution, civil settlements, and the compensatory and punitive damages awarded in civil trials.

- Alternative sanctions given to white-collar offenders include (1) house arrest, (2) community service, (3) shaming, and (4) loss of a job.

- Utah is the first state, and so far the only state, to create a white-collar crime registry.

- With regard to white-collar crime, a perception exists that it is better to be on house arrest in a white-collar offender's home than it is to be on house arrest in a conventional offender's home.

- Community service holds offenders accountable for their misdeeds and helps to reintegrate offenders back into the community, and the community benefits from the offenders' contributions.

- Shaming strategies are used for all types of offenders, but they may be particularly effective for white-collar offenders given the higher amount of stigma and shame that accompanies the conviction of white-collar offenders (Benson, 1990).

- A study of 2,206 individuals charged with financial misrepresentation in enforcement actions by the SEC and DOJ found that 93% of the individuals had lost their jobs by the time the enforcement action was completed (Karpoff et al., 2008).

- Corporations can be punished both formally and informally for misconduct. Depending on whether convicted (in criminal court), found liable (in civil court), or determined responsible (in administrative or regulatory proceedings), various types of sentencing alternatives are available.

- Two issues surface when considering how to sanction organizations: (1) determining appropriate sanctions to reduce recidivism and (2) avoiding harm to innocent parties.

- Reasons for punishing white-collar offenders include (1) retribution, (2) specific deterrence, (3) general deterrence, (4) rehabilitation, and (5) just deserts.

Key Terms

Discussion Questions

1. A blue-collar and a white-collar offender commit the same crime. The blue-collar offender is sentenced to prison for one year. Should the white-collar offender be given the same sentence?

2. A blue-collar and a white-collar offender both steal from their job. Each of them stole the same amount. The blue-collar offender is fined $500.00. Should the white-collar offender

receive the same fine? Would it be unfair to punish the white-collar offender more because of the offender's higher income? Should the offender be given a lower prison sentence in exchange for the higher fine? Explain.

3. How is incarceration different for white-collar offenders as compared to conventional offenders?

4. What do you think of research that shows that white-collar offenders are more likely than conventional offenders to be sentenced to prison? What are some possible reasons for this finding?

5. Visit Utah's white-collar crime registry. What are the strengths and weaknesses of the registry? Should other states follow suit?

6. How could punishing an organization hurt employers and customers?

7. Describe the different ways that organizations are punished. Do you think businesses should ever be forced to close as a result of misconduct? Explain.

8. Which types of alternative sanctions might be most appropriate for white-collar offenders? Explain.

9. Why do we punish white-collar offenders?

GLOSSARY

Academic dishonesty: intellectual theft

Academic sexual relationships: intimate relationships between individuals who have academic connections

Administrative proceedings: proceedings that are not designed to punish but are designed to control certain future actions

Advance-fee fraud: occurs when financial consultants or other individuals charge fees in advance of helping homeowners address their financial problems

Airbag fraud: when mechanics fraudulently repair airbags and charge customers for repair

Allocution: refers to the part of the trial process where individuals are permitted to address the court prior to sentencing

Alternative sanctions argument: suggests the use of less costly civil and administrative procedures to respond to misconduct

Animal fighting: instances when individuals organize fights between animals

Annuities fraud: when insurance agents misrepresent the types of returns that their clients would get from investing in annuities

Antitrust laws: designed to promote and protect competition among businesses and corporations

Apolitical white-collar crime: situations where politicians get into trouble for doing things that are outside the scope of politics but are violations of the public trust

Appeal to higher loyalties: a neutralization where offenders justify their wrongdoing by suggesting that the misbehavior was done for the good of a larger group

Applied general systems theory: where society is considered to be composed of a number of different types of systems that operate independently and in conjunction with other systems

Appraisal fraud: occurs when appraisers misrepresent the actual value of a home

Archival research: studies that use some form of record (or archive) as a database in the study

Attorney-client privilege: a doctrine that protects confidential information shared by a defendant with attorney

Audits: conducted to identify fraud by financial-fraud or forensic accountants

Auto insurance fraud: when mechanics dupe the insurance company into paying for unnecessary or nonexistent repairs

Automotive sales fraud: a variety of actions, including turning an odometer back, selling unsafe cars, and selling stolen cars

Auto repair fraud: billing for services not provided, unnecessary repairs, airbag fraud, and insurance fraud

Awareness strategies: increasing awareness among employees about various issues related to employee theft

Bait and switch practices: instances when customers are lured into a store with the promise of a sale item that does not exist or is not available in an appropriate amount

Benghazi attacks: a major scandal that involved allegations that the deaths of four Americans could be attributed to decisions made by the state department

Bid rigging: occurs when competitors conspire to set specific bids for goods or services they would supply in response to a request for bids; it is also known as collusion

Bid rotation: occurs when competitors take turns submitting the lowest bid on a series of bids

Bid suppression: refers to instances where competitors agree not to submit a bid for a particular job on the understanding that a specific competitor will likely be selected for that job

Billing for nonexistent prescriptions: when pharmacists bill for prescriptions that do not exist

Billing for services not provided: when auto mechanics bill customers for services not provided

Biological theory: explanations of crime that consider the physiological or genetic contributions toward crime

Boundary maintenance: individuals learn the rules of the workplace when some individuals are caught breaking those rules

Breadth of victimization: when one single corporate offense could harm thousands, perhaps millions, of individuals

Broker embezzlement: when brokers take money that is supposed to be in an investment account and use it for their own personal use

Broker fraud: when stockbrokers fail to meet their legal obligations to investors

Bucketing: when "A floor trader will take a position opposite that of a customer's position, either directly or by using another floor trader, again in collusion." (Schlegel, 1993, p. 63)

Builder bailout scheme: occurs when builders offer buyers "excessive incentives" but hide those offers from the mortgage company to make it appear that the property is worth more than it is actually worth

Campaign finance laws: place restrictions on the way political campaigns are financed, with specific attention given to contributions and expenditures

Case records: official records that are housed in an agency that has formal social control duties

Case studies: entails researchers selecting a particular crime, criminal, event, or other phenomena and studying features surrounding the causes and consequences of those phenomena

Celebrity bashing: refers to instances where celebrity offenders are attacked by inmates seeking fame and notoriety

Censure: when officials may withdraw support or withhold information

Character witnesses: individuals who share information about the defendant that demonstrates that it is not like the defendant's character to engage in wrongdoing

Chunking: occurs when investors buy several properties without telling the bank about the properties other than the one the bank is financing

Churning: excessive selling of the same property for the purpose of generating fees and commissions

Civil justice system: the system of justice where individuals seek recourse for offenses by way of a civil lawsuit

Civil proceedings: occur when an individual or government representative, referred to as a plaintiff, files civil charges against an individual or business

Class action lawsuits: used to address corporate wrongdoing; it refers to situations in which a group of victims jointly sue a business or corporation for the harm caused by the corporation

Class bias: refers to bias implicit throughout the entire judicial processing of white-collar cases that includes the hiring of high powered defense attorneys, the complacency of criminal justice officials adjudicating the cases, the disparate treatment of corporations, and inadequate laws that all work to protect the powerful and weaken the minority

Client-oriented defense: occurs when the client is the one directing how the attorney is defending the case

Collective embezzlement: occurs when a crime is committed by the organization against the organization

Commodities: raw materials such as natural gas, oil, gold, agricultural products, and other tangible products sold in bulk form

Commodities fraud: the "fraudulent sale of commodities investments" (Federal Bureau of Investigation [FBI], 2009)

Community-based sanctions: refer to instances where offenders are sentenced to probation or parole after their incarceration

Community integration: situation in which groups of individuals who otherwise would not have become acquainted with one another come together in their response to white-collar crime

Community service: refers to situations where offenders are told to perform a certain number of hours or days of service for the community

Compensatory damages: awards made to plaintiffs that the defendants are ordered to pay in order to compensate victims for their victimization experience

Complementary bidding: occurs when competitors submit bids with artificially high estimates or specific demands that cannot be met so that a specific competitor with a lower price or without the demands is awarded a contract

Compliance program: "organizational system aimed at comprehensively detecting and preventing corporate criminality" (Goldsmith & King, 1997, p. 9)

Comprehensive Environmental Response Compensation and Liability Act: also known as the Superfund Act, it was passed in 1980 to fund the cleanup of earlier environmental damage

Computer crime (cybercrime): a range of computer-related behaviors that are criminally illegal or otherwise harmful

Conceptual ambiguity: vaguely and loosely defined terms

Condemnation of condemners: a neutralization where offenders blame the criminal justice and social control systems for their misdeeds

Conflict theorists: focus on the way that those with power exert influence in order to use the law to their advantage as an instrument of power

Conformists: individuals who accept the goals and means proscribed by society

Conspiracy appraisal fraud: occurs when appraisers work with other offenders as part of broader mortgage schemes

Contract lawsuits: refer to allegations between buyers and sellers and/or lenders and borrowers that involve fraud, employment discrimination, tortious interference, or allegations of unfulfilled agreements

Control theory: suggests that individuals' bonds to society keep them from engaging in criminal behavior

Cooperating witnesses: refers to witnesses who are cooperating with the prosecution as a result of some involvement they had in the case

Co-pay waivers: when providers waive the patient's co-pay but still bill the insurance company

Copyright violations of computer software: occur when users use software for purposes beyond what was intended under the copyright agreement described on the software

Corporate crime: illegal behavior that is committed by employees of a corporation to benefit the corporation, company, or business

Corporate crime liability: occurs when a corporation is held liable and criminally prosecuted

Corporate system: businesses and corporations that carry out business activity as part of our capitalist society

Corruption: the use of political power or influence in exchange for illegal personal gain

Counterfeiting software crimes: when individuals make counterfeit copies of particular software programs

Coupon stuffing: when retail employees steal coupons and use them later

Crackers: individuals who crack into computer systems "with [the intent] to sabotage and cause chaos to [the] corporation" (Wiggins, 2002, p. 20)

Credits for nonexistent returns: when employees give credit for returns to collaborators

Crime Victims Rights Act: permits victims of all types of federal offenses to participate in the allocution process

Crimes by big-game operators: instances when individuals running hunting businesses illegally harm animals as part of their business

Criminal fines: monetary penalty awarded by the judge after an offender has been convicted of a crime

Criminal justice system: the system of justice that handles violations of the criminal law

Criminaloid concept: engaging in harmful acts behind a mask of respectability

Criminal proceedings: occur when criminal charges are filed against the defendant; sanctions could include imprisonment, fines, probation, community service, and restitution

Critical infrastructure: refers to public services provided that society needs on a daily basis, including water, electricity, banking, and so on

Damage control argument: orientation that emphasizes the importance restoring the public's confidence by means of public prosecutions

Deceptive sales: illicit sales practices that are driven by corporate policies and directives

Deferred prosecution agreement (DPA): refers to instances where the prosecutor agrees not to prosecute the corporation if the corporation agrees to certain conditions to be completed over a probationary period

Defiance: when officials block any efforts toward change

Definitions socially constructed by businesses: behaviors defined by a particular company or business as improper

Deflated appraisal fraud: occurs when appraisers underestimate the value of the home in order to force the seller to lower the home's price

Delivery of a controlled substance: when the pharmacist wrongfully provides a controlled substance to a customer

Denial of responsibility: refers to situations where offenders neutralize their behaviors by suggesting that they are not responsible for their misconduct

Denial of victim: refers to situations where offenders convince themselves that victims deserve the harm they experience

Determinism: behavior is caused or influenced by preceding events or factors

Deterrence theory: based on the assumption that punishment can stop individuals from offending if it is certain, swift, and severe

Deviant misuse of the justice process: refers to situations where offenders misuse the justice process in a way that gains them some sort of advantage

Differential association theory: assumes individuals learn to commit crime from their peers through a process in which they learn how to commit crimes, why to commit those crimes, and why laws restricting those crimes are inappropriate

Discovery-oriented defense: a particular defense strategy dictated by the characteristics of the charges, with no set formula used to respond to the cases

Disintegrative shaming: focuses on the bad act and embarrasses offenders, causes anger, and potentially leads to additional harm

Double billing: when two or more parties are billed for the same procedure or service

Due diligence defense: argues that the corporation did everything it could do, in good faith, to abide by the law

Economic system: the system that drives our economy

Educational system: where white-collar careers typically develop because this system provides opportunities to increase the understanding of white-collar crime

Elder abuse: "any criminal, physical, or emotional harm or unethical taking advantage that negatively affects the physical, financial, or general well-being of an elderly person" (Payne, Berg, & Byars, 1999, p. 81)

Elder financial abuse: when workers steal money or property from older persons in their care

Elder neglect: when workers fail to provide the appropriate level of care required by the patient

Elder physical abuse: instances where workers hit, slap, kick, or otherwise physically harm an older person for whom they are being paid to provide care

Elder sexual abuse: when workers have inappropriate and harmful sexual contact with older persons in their care

Election law violations: situations where political officials violate rules guiding the way that elections are supposed to be conducted

Electronic and software piracy: the theft of copyright protected electronic information, including software, electronic programs, and electronic files such as movies and music

Embezzlement: when employees steal money from an account to which they have access

Emotional consequences: experiences such as stress, violation of trust, and damage of public morale that victims of white-collar crime and all members of society are exposed to

Empirical ambiguity: refers to confusion regarding ways to measure white-collar crime in research studies

Enemy civilian social system crimes: crimes against residents of countries in which the U.S. military is fighting

Entertainment services system: settings where customers consume or purchase various forms of services designed at least partially for entertainment or pleasure

Environmental defenders: refers to individuals trying to protect the environment through protests and other environmental advocacy strategies

Environmental Protection Agency (EPA): enforces criminal and civil laws as an agency aiming to protect public health and deter future misconduct as well as to facilitate fund generation and cost savings

Environmental racism: a term used to describe the heightened risk of victimization for minorities

Environmental state crime: refers to criminal or deviant behaviors by a governmental representative(s) that result in individuals and/or the environment being harmed by pollutants and chemicals

Equity skimming: occurs when investors persuade financially distressed homeowners to use their home equity to "hire" the investor to buy the home, or part of the home, from the homeowner and rent it back to the homeowner

Experimental group: the group that receives the independent variable (or the treatment)

Experiments: studies in which researchers examine how the presence of one variable produces an outcome

Expert witnesses: witnesses who share their professional insight and interpretation of the evidence used in a case

Exploitation: refers to situations where businesses take advantage of their workers

External audits: refers to audits conducted by consultants hired by the corporation

External whistleblowers: term for individuals who share damaging information regarding their employer with outside organizations such as law enforcement agencies or the media

Extra-occupational crimes: crimes committed against the American civilian social system

Faculty double billing: when professors bill multiple sources for the same effort of work or reimbursement

Faculty embezzlement: when faculty members or college or university staffers steal funds from an account to which they have access

Failure to report: when workers in the health care field fail to report suspected cases of abuse

False advertising: occurs when businesses make inaccurate statements about their products or services in order to facilitate the sale of those items or services

False Statements Act and False Claims Act: govern against the submission of fraudulent claims or bills for services; these acts guard against situations where individuals try to defraud the government

Falsifying account information: when agents or brokers change account information without the client's knowledge

Falsifying records: when providers change medical forms in an effort to be reimbursed from the insurance provider

Faulty credit enhancements: occurs when builders engage in measures that make it appear as if buyers have better credit than they actually have

Fear mongering: when officials create fear to "overshadow" real issues

Federal consent decrees: judicially approved legal agreements requiring local police departments to implement reforms in order to improve law enforcement operations

Federal Water Pollution Control Act: requires companies to self-disclose to the EPA instances when they have discharged potentially harmful substances into navigable waters

Field research: strategies where researchers enter a particular setting to gather data through their observations

Flipping: occurs when scammers buy and resell properties with inflated prices

Foreign exchange fraud: when brokers or other officials persuade "victims to invest in the foreign currency exchange market" (FBI, 2009) through illegitimate and fraudulent practices

Foreign friendly civilian crimes: crimes committed against citizens of another country

Forensic accountants: review financial records and work schedules, read e-mail messages, interview workers and bosses, gather and review other available evidence, and develop a report detailing their conclusions about the presence of fraud in a business

Fraud: efforts to steal money from individuals through deceit

Fraud audits: identify control mechanisms and weaknesses in a business that place the business at risk for fraud and identify those with access who have taken advantage of the weaknesses

Fraudulent loan origination: scams where professionals help buyers qualify for loans for which the buyers are not actually qualified

Front running: when "a broker takes advantage of the special knowledge about a pending custom order and trades on his or her own account before executing that order" (Schlegel, 1993, p. 63)

Futures contracts: "agreement[s] to buy or sell a given unit of a commodity at some future date" (Schlegel, 1993, p. 60)

Futures trading fraud: fraud occurring in the trading of futures contracts and options on the futures trading market

Ganging: situations where providers bill for multiple family members, though they treat only one of them

Gender harassment: sexist remarks and behavior

General deterrence: suggests that offenders should be punished in order to keep other potential offenders from engaging in misconduct

General strain theory: a sociopsychological approach to explaining how crime is an adaptation to stress and frustration

Generic drug substitution: when pharmacists give the customer a generic drug but bill the insurance company for the more expensive brand-name drug

Ghostwriting: situations where professors or researchers have their work written by someone else, but only the professor's name appears on the work

Good faith defense: argues that the defendant lacked knowledge and intent and therefore did not know the crime was being committed

Government definitions: illegal acts characterized by deceit, concealment, or violation of trust that are not dependent on the application or threat of physical force or violence; individuals and organizations commit these acts to obtain money, property, or services or to secure personal or business advantage

Government witnesses: the category of witnesses that includes police officers, investigators, auditors, and other officials who developed a case as part of the investigation process

Grades for sex: where professors use the power of grading to solicit sexual favors from students

Group boycotts: situations where competitors agree not to do business with specific customers or clients

Harmful consumer products: goods that enter the marketplace that cause significant harm to consumers

Harmful treatment of animals: instances when individuals harm animals

Harmful treatment of consumers: refers to situations where businesses either intentionally or unintentionally put consumers who are using their services at risk of harm

Health Insurance Portability Act of 1996: made health care fraud a federal offense, with penalties ranging from 10 years to life in prison

High-yield investment schemes: promise investors low risk or even no risk investment strategies when in fact the funds are not actually invested

Home health care: where the provision of health care services occurs at the patient's home

Home improvement scams: occur when agents or investors conceal problems with homes that should be disclosed to potential buyers

Home repair fraud: when contractors and repair persons rip off individuals for various types of repairs or repairs not made

Horizontal price fixing: involves instances where competing businesses conspire to charge prices at a similar level

House arrest: refers to instances where offenders are told that they must be at home either all of the time or when they are not at work, the doctor's office, or a religious service

Housing discrimination: discriminating against individuals in making decisions about rental or sales properties

Ignorance defense: refers to situations where the defendant argues that he or she did not know that the criminal acts were occurring

Illegal dumping: refers to situations where employees or businesses dump products they no longer need in sites that are not recognized as legal dump sites

Illegal emissions: refers to situations where companies or businesses illegally allow pollutants to enter the environment

Illegal fishing: instances when individuals violate local, state, or federal regulations while fishing

Illegal gratuities: cases in which officials receive something that they were not supposed to receive

Illegally buying prescriptions: when a pharmacist buys prescriptions from patients and then bills the insurance company without filling the prescription

Importation strategies: strategy used that focuses on hiring employees unlikely to steal

Individual economic losses: the losses that individual victims or businesses experience due to white-collar crimes

Inflated appraisals: instances when there is an intentional overestimation of the value of a home in order to allow the home to be sold at an inflated price

Innovators: accept the goal of financial success but replace legitimate means with illegitimate means

Insider trading: when individuals share or steal information that is "material in nature" (Leap, 2007) for future investments

Inspector general: position given the duty of investigating allegations of wrongdoing within governmental units

Institutional anomie: occurs because society promotes values related to financial success but fails to promote values that are consistent with using legitimate means to attain financial success

Internal audits: audits conducted by the organization's accounting department

Internal strategies: policies and practices performed within the retail setting in an effort to prevent employee theft

Internal whistleblowers: individuals who share information with officials within the organization where the employee works, often reporting the misconduct to the company's security program

International environmental crimes: environmental offenses that cross borders of at least two different countries or occur in internationally protected areas

Internet crimes: a range of offenses committed through the use of the Internet

Internet piracy: stealing software, music, videos, or other copyright protected material through the Internet

Inter-occupational crimes: phrase Bryant (1979) uses to describe situations where members of the military criminally victimize the enemy

Intra-occupational crimes: phrase Bryant (1979) uses to describe instances where military officials commit criminal acts against the American military system

Investment fraud: when investments made by consumers are managed or influenced fraudulently by stockbrokers or other officials in the economic system

Iran-Contra affair: occurred in the mid-1980s when U.S. political officials authorized the sale of weapons to Iran as a part of covert efforts to trade arms for hostages

Isolated occurrence defense: argues that the misconduct was a rare event done by a single employee and not part of any systematic criminal activity

Jailstripe crimes: a term for criminal acts that offenders commit while incarcerated

Just deserts: a punishment orientation that suggests that offenders should be punished for one primary reason, because they deserve it

Kickbacks: when providers direct patients to other providers in exchange for a pecuniary response from the other provider

Knowing endangerment: refers to situations where individuals or businesses intentionally mishandle hazardous wastes or pollutants that pose risks to their workers or to community members

Labeling theory: focuses on the way that individuals develop criminal labels; it suggests that the act of labeling individuals can result in behaviors consistent with those labels

Lack of fraudulent intent defense: argues that the defendant did not intend to commit a criminal act

Lay witnesses: individuals who have some relevant information to share about the white-collar crime case based on something they saw or experienced

Learning theory: body of theories that suggest that criminal behavior is learned

Liar loans: situations where investors lie about loans they have or are trying to get

Life course theory: uses a social psychological orientation to identify how events early in one's life course shape experiences later in one's life

Loss prevention strategies: efforts that businesses use to keep employees from stealing from the business

Mail fraud statutes: prohibit the use of the U.S. mail service to commit crimes

Market allocation: when competitors agree to divide markets according to territories, products, goods, or some other service

Market manipulation: situations where executives or other officials do things to artificially inflate trading volume and subsequently affect the price of the commodity or security

Media reports: news articles, press reports, and television depictions of white-collar crimes to help demonstrate what kind of information members of the public receive about white-collar crime and to uncover possible patterns guiding white-collar offenses that may not be studied through other means

Medicaid: a state-level health care program that serves the poor

Medical malpractice: situations where health care providers "accidentally" injure patients while delivering health care

Medical snowballing: when providers bill for several related services, though only one service was provided

Medicare: a federally funded program that serves the elderly population

Medication errors: when health care providers deliver or prescribe the wrong medications to patients

Meeting competition defense: argues that a business's price discriminations were done in good faith in order to stop undesirable actions of a competitor

Mislabeling of drugs: when pharmacists label drugs incorrectly in an effort to hide that they did not provide the prescription drug to the patient

Misrepresentation: deliberately misinforming the customer about the coverage of an insurance policy

Misrepresenting services: occurs when providers describe the service differently on medical forms in an effort to gain payment for the services

Monetary penalties: include criminal fines, restitution, civil settlements, and compensatory and punitive damages awarded in civil trials

Mortgage fraud: when a real estate or bank representative intentionally provides false information to a financial institution in order to secure a loan

Mueller investigation: special prosecutor investigation into allegations that the Trump campaign conspired with Russia to alter the 2016 election

Multiplicity of indictment defense: argues that the offender is being charged for one single offense on several different counts in the indictment

Natural law: behaviors or activities that are defined as wrong because they violate the ethical principles of a particular culture, subculture, or group

Neutralization theory: assumes juveniles understand right from wrong and that before delinquents commit delinquent acts, they neutralize or rationalize their behavior as appropriate

Noble cause corruption: situations where officers engage in corruption in order to assure what they see as justice

Nonprosecution agreement (NPA): refers to instances where the prosecutor indicates that the prosecution will not occur, based on the corporation's agreement to certain conditions

Objectivity: researchers must be value-free in doing their research

Occupational crime: phrase used by Clinard and Quinney (1973) to describe crimes committed in any type of legal occupation

Occupational system: the system where the bulk of professionals are found

Organizational advantage argument: the explanation for why prosecutors choose not to prosecute that suggests that "organizational structure may serve as a buffer between the white-collar offender and social control mechanisms" (Tillman et al., 1997, p. 55)

Organizational culture strategies: strategies for promoting a sense of organizational culture that inhibits theft

Organizational justice: explanations that consider the way that organizational features might lead to corruption

Organizational misconduct: refers to instances where laws, rules, or administrative regulations are violated by an individual or group of individuals in an organization that, in its organizational role, acts or fails to act in ways that further the attainment of organizational goals

Organizational probation: refers to cases where corporations can be sentenced to a term of probation

Overcharging: when employees charge customers more than they should

Overcharging patients: refers to situations where providers charge patients more than regulations permit

Overordering supplies: when employees order more supplies than are needed and keep the supplies that were not needed

Overtreatment: providing more auto repairs than are actually needed in order to charge more

Pacification: a form of elder physical abuse where a worker overmedicates an elder

Parallel proceedings: instances where a specific white-collar crime is heard in more than one court simultaneously

Parsimony: researchers and scientists should keep their levels of explanation as simple as possible

Pecuniary-based offenses: misbehaviors that are ultimately done for the economic gain that comes along with the commission of the offenses

Personal liability: measures that have been identified as strategies to combat police misconduct

Phantom treatment: when providers bill Medicare, Medicaid, or other insurance agencies for services they never provided

Phishing: distribution of a large number of e-mails in an effort to scam someone

Physical harm: injuries victims experience that cause negative physical consequences

Pingponging: when patients are unnecessarily referred to other providers, or "bounced around" to various medical providers

Plausible deniability: when officials conceal actions to make behavior seem appropriate

Plea bargains: a stage of adjudication where the prosecutors decide whether to allow a defendant to plead guilty in exchange for a reduced sentence or some other incentive

Police brutality: the misuse of force on the part of law enforcement officers

Police corruption: when police officers violate the trust they have been given and abuse their law enforcement authority

Police sexual misconduct: "Any behavior by a police officer, whereby an officer takes advantage of his or her unique position in law enforcement to misuse his or her authority and power to commit a sexually violent act or to initiate or respond to some sexually motivated cure for the purpose of personal gratification" (Maher, 2003, p. 355)

Political extortion and bribery: political officials use their power to shape outcomes of various processes

Political system: defines laws and regulations describing all forms of crime

Ponzi schemes: those that scam investors by paying them from future investors' payments into the offender's scheme

Prearranged trading: when "brokers, or brokers and local brokers, first agree on a price and then act out the trade as a piece of fiction in the pit, thereby excluding other potential bidders from the offering" (Schlegel, 1993, p. 63)

Prescription fraud: schemes where pharmacists work with drug addicts to carry out an offense

Presentence reports: reports developed by probation officers that include a wealth of information about offenders, their life histories, their criminal careers, and the sentence they receive

Price discrimination: refers to practices where different prices are charged simply to restrict competition between competitors

Price fixing: occurs when competitors agree on a price at which goods or services should be sold

Price gouging: refers to situations where businesses conspire to set artificially high prices on goods and services

Proactive strategies: refer to situations where the police develop criminal cases in an active way

Process-oriented defense: this refers to instances when the attorneys process these cases the same way, independent of case or offender characteristics

Professional-disciplinary proceedings: proceedings that are administered through the state bar association where professional boards review allegations of wrongdoing

Promissory note fraud: when agents get clients to invest in promissory notes that are scams

Provision of unnecessary services: when health care providers perform and bill for tests or procedures that are not needed

Punitive damages: awarded when the defendant's conduct exceeds the legal criteria for mere or gross negligence

Qualifications fraud: refers to situations where professionals lie about a buyer's qualifications in order to secure a mortgage and allow the buyer to purchase the home

Quasi-experimental designs: studies that mimic experimental methods but lack certain elements of the classical experimental design

Questionable Doctors: a report and database published by the nonprofit group Public Citizen, which collects data on physicians involved in misconduct

Qui tam **lawsuits:** situations where an individual sues a corporation or company on behalf of the government

Racketeer Influenced and Corrupt Organizations (RICO) Act: found in Title IX of the Organized Crime Control Act; it targets criminal groups by legislating against extortion, violence, and fraud

Ransomware: type of virus that freezes a computer's operations and asks the owner to pay a ransom

Rational choice theory: considers the limits of human rationality while still considering humans as rational; it suggests that offenders will consider the benefits of offending and weigh those benefits against possible negative consequences that arise from misconduct

Reactive strategies: situations where the police respond to reports of criminal incidents

Real estate agent and/or investor fraud: a variety of scams committed by agents and investors, including home improvement scams, fraudulent loan origination, chunking, liar loans, and churning

Rebels: workers who reject the goals and means of society and replace the societal-prescribed goals and means with their own goals and means

Record reviews: occur when white-collar crime investigators review an assortment of records such as financial records, banking records, sales records, e-mail correspondence, phone records, property deeds, loan applications, and any other records that are relevant to the case under investigation

Recreational path: when pharmacists initially begin using illegal street drugs and then expand their drug use to include prescription drugs once they enter pharmacy training

Redirection: when officials feign interest but change the subject

Regulatory agencies: governmental agencies responsible for making sure that regulations are followed in industries and businesses across the United States; these exist to make sure that businesses and their workers are abiding by laws and regulations

Regulatory system: consists of local, state, and federal agencies charged with regulating various businesses

Rehabilitation: a philosophy of punishment that suggests that offenders are brought into the justice process so that the government can play a role in treating whatever issues the offenders have that may have contributed to their wrongdoing

Reintegrative shaming: focuses on the bad act and communicates messages of disapproval that are followed by efforts to reintegrate the offender back into the community

Relativism: where all things are related

Reliance on the advice of counsel defense: legal defense where defendants argue that their attorneys advised them to perform the action in question

Religious system: the collection of religious organization and institutions

Religious system deception: situations where church leaders lie to their congregants in an effort to promote an appearance of "holier than thou"

Relying on self-righteousness: when official minimize allegations

Resale fraud: refers to instances where used items are sold as new

Research definitions: when researchers define white-collar crime through studying and gathering data that allow them to reliably and validly measure the behavior

Research misconduct: a range of behaviors that center on researchers engaging in various forms of wrongdoing during the course of their research

Restitution: a monetary penalty that offenders are ordered to pay to victims for their suffering

Retail system: setting where consumers purchase various types of products

Retaliation: when corporate or business officials target advocates exposing the wrongdoing

Retreatist: a white-collar worker who accepts neither the goals of society nor the means to attain those goals

Retribution: a philosophy of punishment that suggests offenders should be punished to satisfy societal demands

Reverse mortgage fraud: situations where fraudulent activities occur as part of the reverse mortgage transaction

Ritualist: white-collar worker who does not accept the goals of society but goes through the motions of engaging in the means prescribed by society

Robinson-Patman Act: makes price discrimination illegal if it is done to lessen competition

Rogue employee defense: argues that corporate misconduct was the result of an individual employee and not the result of any corporate activities

Rolling over: persuading the customer to cancel an old insurance policy and replace it with a more expensive, "better" policy

Routine activities theory: assumes that crime occurs because of the presence of motivated offenders, the absence of capable guardians, and the availability of suitable targets that all exist at the same time and place

Sales-directed crimes: occur against consumers when agents or brokers steal from consumers by using fraudulent sales tactics

Sales/service system: businesses that sell basic goods and services to customers

Scapegoating: refers to excuses where offenders blame others for their wrongdoing

Seductive behavior: inappropriate sexual advance

Self-control theory: assumes all types of crime are caused by the presence of low self-control

Self-policing: refers to efforts by companies and businesses to develop their own policing responses to white-collar crime

Self-policing audits: refers to audits either done as part of routine procedures or that may be initiated out of concern that fraud is occurring in the organization

Sexual abuse: hands-on offenses where the offender inappropriately touches victims, hands-off offenses such as voyeurism and exhibitionism, and/or harmful genital practices where genital contact is made between the offender and the victim

Sexual bribery: offering rewards for sex

Sexual coercion: threatening punishment to get sex

Sexual contact with students: instances where professors have some form of direct contact of a sexual nature with students in their classes or under their supervision

Sexual harassment: a range of behaviors where employees perform sexually inappropriate actions against their colleagues or consumers

Sexualized behavior: goes beyond comments and includes actual activities of a sexual nature committed by the offending party

Sexualized comments: when individuals make comments to others that are of a sexual nature

Shaming: an alternative sanction strategy that promotes shaming and stigmatization

Sherman Antitrust Act: in general, an act that makes it illegal for competitors to engage in activities that restrict competition

Shortchanging: when employees do not give customers all of their change and pocket the difference

Short counting: when pharmacists dispense fewer pills than prescribed but bill the insurance company as if they had dispensed all of the pills

Short sale fraud: lending institutions allow homes to be sold for amounts that are lower than what the homeowner owed on the home's mortgage

Situational crime prevention: refers to strategies that alter features of a specific environment in an effort to prevent offending

Skepticism: the concept that social scientists must question and requestion their findings

Sliding: when agents include insurance coverage that was not requested by the customer

Smoking gun: indisputable evidence that substantiates that a crime has been committed

Social change: occurs because those who survive white-collar crime victimization become stronger

Social disorganization theory: suggests that a neighborhood's crime rate is shaped by the ability of its members to agree on and work toward a common goal, such as crime control

Social harm: workplace behaviors that might not be illegal or deviant but might actually create forms of harm for various individuals

Social services system: the numerous agencies involved in providing services to members of the public

Social system: a setting where individuals have various needs fulfilled and learn how to do certain things, as well as why to do those things

Societal economic losses: the total amount of losses incurred by society from white-collar crime

Software crimes: situations that arise when computer software is central to the offense

Specific deterrence: suggests that punishment should occur in order to stop the punished offender from engaging in future wrongdoing

Stacking: persuading persons to buy more insurance policies than are needed

Staff-on-inmate sexual victimization: sexual misconduct or sexual harassment perpetrated against an inmate by staff

Staff sexual harassment: repeated verbal comments or gestures of a sexual nature to an inmate by staff

Staff sexual misconduct: any consensual or nonconsensual behavior or act of a sexual nature directed toward an inmate by staff, including romantic relationships

State-corporate crime: crimes and misconduct committed by employees of government agencies

State crime: situations where governments, or their representatives, commit crime on behalf of the government

Strain theory: traces the source of strain to interactions between the social and economic structures; it assumes strain is caused by the failure to achieve economically valued goals

Straw buyer fraud: individuals who do not plan on living in or even owning a house purchase it and then deed over the home to the person who will live there

Subcontracting: when competitors hire one another on subcontracts after the winning bid has been selected

Substitute providers: employees who perform medical services though they are not authorized to do so

Sunshine laws: embrace transparency and call for publicizing public information

Sweetheart deals: when employees give friends and family members unauthorized discounts

Switching: when a salesperson switches the customer's policy so that the coverage and the premiums are different from what the victim was told

System capacity argument: explanation for why prosecutors do not prosecute that points to the difficulties officials face in responding to these crimes

Systems theory: assumes all systems are interrelated and focuses on the interconnections between various societal systems and the way that various systems influence white-collar wrongdoing

Technological strategies: the use of various forms of technology to prevent employee theft in retail settings

Technological system: societal system that includes structures and agencies involved in developing and promoting technology

Telemedicine: refers to the provision of health services through the telephone, computer, or other telephonic or digital mediums

Textbook fraud: when faculty members sell complimentary textbooks that they received from publishers to book dealers who resell the books

Theft crimes against consumers: occur when workers or employers steal directly from clients or customers

Theft of credit card information: when employees steal a customer's credit card information

Theft of goods: when employees steal the items the retail setting is trying to sell

Theft of money from the cash register: when employees take money out of the register

Theft of production supplies and raw materials: when employees steal items used to produce goods for retail settings

Theft of software: when workers steal computer software that their company owns and use it for their own purposes

Therapeutic self-medicators: pharmacists whose involvement in drug use typically focused on specific therapeutic goals

Tort lawsuit: refers to situations where someone claims loss, injury, or damage from the negligence or intent of another

Trump University: a real estate program that promised participants more than the program delivered

Unauthorized access: when individuals break into various computer databases to which they do not have legitimate access

Unbundling: when providers bill separately for tests and procedures that are supposed to be billed as a single procedure

Undertreatment: providing fewer services than should be provided in auto repairs

Unfair labor practices: corporate violations where workers are subjected to unethical treatment by their bosses and corporate leaders

Unnecessary auto repairs: when mechanics perform repairs that were not necessary and bill the customer for those services

Upcoding: situations where providers bill for services that are more expensive than the services that were actually provided

U.S. Sentencing Commission: the entity responsible for developing strategies for promoting fairer sentencing at the federal level through the development of sentencing guidelines

Vertical price fixing: refers to situations where parties from different levels of the production and distribution chain agree to set prices

Viatical settlement fraud: when insurance agents conceal information on viatical settlement policies, allowing individuals to invest in other people's life insurance policies

Victimization surveys: surveys that sample residents and estimate the extent of victimization from the survey findings

Violations of civil law: behaviors that violate rules governed by civil law

Violations of criminal law: white-collar crimes defined as criminally illegal behaviors committed by upper-class individuals during the course of their occupation

Violations of regulatory law: workplace misdeeds that might not violate criminal or civil laws but that violate a particular occupation's laws

Violations of trust: when white-collar offenders use their positions of trust to promote misconduct

Virus: type of computer program or software that is designed to harm a computer system

Voter fraud: see election law violations

Voter identification laws: laws adopted to curb election offenses

Warning light syndrome: outbreaks of white-collar crime that could potentially send a message to individuals, businesses, or communities that something is wrong in a particular workplace system

Whistleblowers: individuals who notify authorities about wrongdoing in their organization

White-collar crime: any violations of criminal, civil, or regulatory law—or deviant, harmful, or unethical actions—committed during the course of employment in various occupational systems

White-collar crime victims: individuals, businesses, nongovernmental institutions, or the "government as a buyer, giver, and protector-gatekeeper" (Edelhertz, 1983, p. 117)

White-collar cybercrime: describes situations when cybercrimes are committed at work by employees or employers

White-collar environmental crimes: situations where individuals or businesses illegally pollute or destroy the environment as part of an occupational activity

White-collar gangs: a gang is "a self-formed association of peers, bound together by mutual interests, with identifiable leadership, well-developed lines of authority, and other organizational features, who act in concert to achieve a specific purpose or purposes which generally include the conduct of illegal activity and control over a particular territory, facility, or type of enterprise" (Miller, 1975, p. 121); the phrase *white-collar gang* suggests that white-collar workers often commit their crimes in groups

White-collar undercover investigations: typically occur when white-collar crime investigators already have evidence of wrongdoing by the suspect or the corporation

Windshield appraisal fraud: occurs when appraisers fail to even go into the home to determine its value; the home's value is determined by appraisers looking through the windshield of their automobile

Withdrawal from conspiracy defense: used in antitrust offenses to argue that the defendant withdrew his or her involvement from the misconduct before the illegal actions occurred

Workplace deviance: broader definition of white-collar crime that includes all of those workplace acts that violate the norms or standards of the workplace, regardless of whether they are formally defined as illegal

Workplace interview: conducted in internal investigations to gather information about any wrongdoing

Workplace-disciplinary proceedings: allegations of wrongdoing reviewed through a company's equal opportunity office or human resources department

Worm: virus that spreads through computer networks

REFERENCES

5News Web Staff. (2020). *Arkansas professor arrested for wire fraud, accused of having ties with Chinese government.* Retrieved from https://www.5newsonline.com/article/news/local/ua-professor-chinese-government/527-86c471d0-f69e-4138-8786-a348c29b38df. Accessed September 13, 2020.

21-year-old jailed for posing as doctor says he still wants to be one. (2018, August 31). *Inside Edition.* Retrieved from https://www.youtube.com/watch?v=iN0n6ZaWq0o

Abel, W. (2009). Agents, trojans and tags: The next generation of investigators. *International Review of Law, Computers & Technology, 23*(1-2), 99–108.

Abrami, A. (2020). *UVM Medical Center doctor arrested on multiple counts of voyeurism.* Retrieved from https://www.burlington-freepress.com/story/news/2020/04/18/uvm-medical-center-doctor-arrested-multiple-voyeurism-charges/5158650002/.

Abramo, G., D'Angelo, C. A., & Murgia, G. (2013). Gender differences in research collaboration. *Journal of Infometrics, 3,* 811–822.

AbuDagga, A., Carome, M., & Wolfe, S. M. (2019). Time to end physician sexual abuse of patients: Calling the U.S. medical community to action. *Journal of General Internal Medicine, 34*(7), 1330–1333.

AbuDagga, A., Wolfe, S. M., Carome, M., & Oshel, R. E. (2016). Cross-sectional analysis of the 1039 U.S. physicians reported to the National Practitioner Data Bank for sexual misconduct, 2003–2013. *PLoS One, 11*(2), e0147800.

Accused dentist claims breast rubs appropriate. (2007, October 16). *MSNBC.com.* Retrieved from http://www.msnbc.msn.com/id/21325760/wid/11915773?GT1=10514

Ackerman, J. (2001, January 16). Massachusetts regulators take action against two securities dealers. *The Boston Globe.* Retrieved from http://www.boston.com/news/special/archives/

Ackman, D. (2001). Tire trouble. *Forbes.com.* Retrieved from http://www.forbes.com/2001/06/20/tireindex.html

Adam, A. J. (2008, July 15). Fidelity investments life insurance—Fraud big time variable annuities—The gimmick—Targeting the seniors. *U.S. Securities and Exchange Commission.* Retrieved from http://www.sec.gov/comments/s7-14-08/s71408-306.htm

Adams, B., & Guyette, J. E. (2009, March). Dummy proof. *Automotive Body Repair News, 48*(3), p. 56.

Adams, K. (2009, July 2). Notorious white collar criminals: Where are they now? *Financial Edge.* Retrieved from http://financialedge.investopedia.com/financial-edge/0709/Notorious-White-Collar-Criminals-Where-Are-They-Now.aspx

Adams, M. (2010, May 8). Is Gulf oil rig disaster far worse than we're being told? *NaturalNews.com.* Retrieved from http://www.naturalnews.com/028749_Gulf_of_Mexico_oil_spill.html

Aeilts, T. (2005, January). Defending against cybercrime and terrorism: A new role for universities. *FBI Law Enforcement Bulletin, 74*(1), 14–20.

Agar, J. (2020). Michigan medical marijuana seller gets prison: 'Federal law has not changed,' judge says. *MLive.* Retrieved from https://www.mlive.com/news/grand-rapids/2020/01/michigan-medical-marijuana-seller-gets-prison-federal-law-has-not-changed-judge-says.html

Agnew, R. (1985). A revised strain theory of delinquency. *Social Forces, 64,* 151–167.

Agnew, R. (1992). Foundation for a general strain theory of crime and delinquency. *Criminology, 30,* 47–88.

Albanese, J. S. (1984). Corporate criminology: Explaining deviance of business and political organizations. *Journal of Criminal Justice, 12,* 11–19.

Albanese, J. S. (2018). Illegal gambling businesses & organized crime: An analysis of federal convictions. *Trends in Organized Crime, 21*(3), 262–277.

Albanese, J. S., & Artello, K. (2019). Behavior of corruption: An empirical typology of public corruption by objective & method. *Actual Problems of Economics and Law.,* 1215.

Albanese, J. S., Artello, K., & Nguyen, L. T. (2019). Distinguishing corruption in law and practice: Empirically separating conviction charges from underlying behaviors. *Public Integrity, 21*(1), 22–37.

Albonetti, C. A. (1999). The avoidance of punishment: A legal-bureaucratic model of suspended sentencing in federal white-collar cases prior to federal sentencing guidelines. *Social Forces, 78*(1), 303–329.

Albright, M. (2007, December 8). Retail thieves these days are often technically savvy and organized. *McClatchy-Tribune Business News*.

Allen, K. G. (2015, June). Retailers estimate shoplifting, incidents of fraud cost $44 billion in 2014. *National Retail Federation*. Washington D.C.: National Retail Foundation.

Allen, R. (2015, July 10). Cancer doc patients say 45 years in prison is not enough. *Detroit Free Press*. Retrieved from http://www.freep.com/story/news/local/michigan/oakland/2015/07/10/fatasentence-handed-down/29952245/

Alschuler, A. W. (1972). Courtroom misconduct by prosecutors and trial judges. *Texas Law Review, 50*(4), 629–667.

Altschuler, M., Creekpaum, J. K., & Fang, J. (2008). Health care fraud. *American Criminal Law Review, 45*(2), 607–664.

Aluede, O., Omoregie, E. O., & Osa-Edoh, G. I. (2006). Academic dishonesty as a contemporary problem in higher education: How academic advisers can help. *Reading Improvement, 43*(2), 97–106.

Alvesalo, A. (2003). Economic crime investigators at work. *Policing and Society, 13*(2), 115–138.

Alvesalo, A., & Whyte, D. (2007). Eyes wide shut: The police investigation of safety crimes. *Crime, Law, and Social Change, 48*, 57–72.

American Greed. (2019). *Fyre Festival disaster: How to avoid fraud when booking your vacation*. Retrieved from https://www.cnbc.com/2019/08/16/fyre-festival-disaster-how-to-avoid-fraud-when-booking-your-vacation.html.

Anderman, E. M., Cupp, P. K., & Lane, D. (2010). Impulsivity and academic cheating. *Journal of Experimental Education, 78*, 135–150.

Anderson, C. (2010, January 2). '09, the year of the Ponzi scam; schemes that collapsed quadrupled this year; investors lost $16.5 B., not counting Madoff case. *Newsday*, p. A27.

Anderson, C. (2018). *One person, no vote: How voter suppression is destroying our democracy*. New York, NY: Bloomsbury.

Anderson, G., Hussey, P., Frogner, B., & Waters, H. (2005). Health spending in the United States and the rest of the industrialized world. *Health Affairs, 24*, 903–914.

Anderson, J. (2015, December 21). Employee theft is popular but not inevitable. *Portland Tribune*. Retrieved from http://www.pamplinmedia.com/pt/239-business/286186-161176-employeetheft-is-popular-but-not-inevitable

Anderson, J. C. (2010, June 18). *Arizona mortgage-fraud prosecutions*. Retrieved from http://www.azcentral.com/12news/news/articles/2010/06/18/20100618arizona-mortgage-fraud-indictments.html

Anderson, K. (2010, September 10). More harsh criticism of EPA at D.C. forum. *Brownfield AG News for America*. Retrieved from http://brownfieldagnews.com/index.php?s=More+harsh+criticism+of+EPA+at+ D.C.+forum

Anderson, K. (2013). Consumer fraud in the United States, 2011. The third FTC survey. Retrieved from https://www.ftc.gov/sites/default/files/documents/reports/consumer-fraud-united-states-2011-third-ftc-survey/130419fraudsurvey_0.pdf

Anderson, T. (2007, October). Retail workers don't plan thefts. *Security Management, 51*(10), p. 38.

Andone, D. (2020). A dentist was filmed extracting a tooth while on a hoverboard. He was found guilty on 46 counts. *CNN.com*. Retrieved from https://www.cnn.com/2020/01/19/us/alaska-dentist-hoverboard-convicted-trnd/index.html.

Andsager, J., Bailey, J. L., & Nagy, J. (1997). Sexual advances as manifestations of power in graduate programs. *Journalism & Mass Communication Educator, 52*(2), 33–42.

Angel, J., & McCabe, D. M. (2009). The ethics of speculation. *Journal of Business Ethics, 90*, 277–286.

Anonymous. (1991). Sexual harassment: A female counseling student's experience. *Journal of Counseling & Development, 69*(2), 502–506.

Appelbaum, B., Hilzenrath, D., & Paley, A. R. (2008, December 13). "All just one big lie"; Bernard Madoff was a Wall Street whiz with a golden reputation. Investors, including Jewish charities, entrusted him with billions. It's gone. *The Washington Post* (Suburban ed.), p. D01.

Arends, B. (2020). 'It's disturbing.' U.S. Justice Department white-collar criminal prosecutions fall to their lowest level on record, study says. *MarketWatch*.

Argust, C. P., Litvack, D. E., & Martin, B. W. (2010). Racketeer influenced and corrupt organizations. *American Criminal Law Review, 47*(2), 961–1013.

Armstrong, T. A., & Boutwell, B. B. (2012). Low resting heart rate and rational choice: Integrating biological correlates of crime in criminological theories. *Journal of Criminal Justice, 40*, 31–39.

Armsworth, M. (1989). Therapy for incest survivors. *Child Abuse and Neglect, 13*, 549–562.

Arnold, B. L., & Hagan, J. (1992). Careers of misconduct: The structure of prosecuted professional deviance among lawyers. *American Sociological Review, 57*(6), 771–780.

Artello, K., & Albanese, J. S. (2019). Rising to the surface: The detection of public corruption. *Criminology, Criminal Justice, Law & Society, 21*, 1.

Artello, K., & Albanese, J. (2020). Rising to the surface. *Criminology, Criminal Justice, Law, and Society, 21*(1). Available online at https://ccjls.scholasticahq.com/article/12471 -rising-to-the-surface-the-detection-of-public-corruption

Associated Press. (2017, January 9). Penn State pays out nearly $250M for role in child sex abuse scandal. *New York Post.* Retrieved from https://nypost.com/2017/01/09/penn -state-pays-out-nearly-250m-for-role-in-child-sex-abuse -scandal/.

Associated Press (2019). *New wave of sexual abuse lawsuits could cost Catholic Church over 4 billion.* Retrieved from https://www.marketwatch.com/story/new-wave-of-sexual -abuse-lawsuits-could-cost-catholic-church-over-4-billion -2019-12-02

Associated Press. (2020, April 30). *Ala. inmates sue COs after being beaten while cuffed.* Retrieved from https://www .corrections1.com/lawsuit/articles/ala-inmates-sue-cos -after-being-beaten-while-cuffed-mxJQfQ5jLYBgGIwL/.

Associated Press. (2020, May 12). *Fmr. SF building commission president charged with bank fraud after allegedly stealing $478K.* Retrieved from https://sanfrancisco.cbslocal .com/2020/05/12/fmr-sf-building-commission-president -charged-bank-fraud-after-allegedly-stealing-478k/.

Attorney General Holder announces civil lawsuit regarding Deepwater Horizon oil spill. (2010, December 15). *Justice News.* Retrieved from www.justice.gov/iso/opa/ag/ speeches/2010/agspeech-101215.html

Auciello, J. (2020). Superstorm Sandy contractor gets three-year prison term for scamming 19 homeowners. *Whyy.* Retrieved from https://whyy.org/articles/superstorm-sandy-contractor -gets-3-year-prison-term-for-scamming-19-homeowners

Austin, Z., Simpson, S., & Reynen, E. (2005). "The fault lies not in our students, but in ourselves": Academic honesty and moral development in health professions education—Results of a pilot study in Canadian pharmacy. *Teaching in Higher Education, 10*(2), 143–156.

Aycock, E. B., & Hutton, M. F. (2010). Election law violators. *American Criminal Law Review, 47,* 363–400.

Azari, S. (2020). *Unprecedented: A simple guide to the crimes of the Trump campaign and presidency.* Lincoln: University of Nebraska Press.

Baer, M. H. (2017). Reconceptualizing the whistleblower's dilemma. *U.C. Davis Law Review, 50*(5), 2215–2280.

Bagaric, M., Du Plessis, J., & Silver, J. (2016). Halting the senseless civil war against white-collar offenders: The conduct undermined the integrity of the markets and other fallacies. *Michigan State Law Review, 2016*(4), 1019–1090.

Baldston, K. (1979). Hooker Chemical's nightmarish pollution record. *Business and Society Review, 30,* 25.

Balestra, M. (2018). Telehealth and legal implications for nurse practitioners. *The Journal for Nurse Practitioners, 14*(1), 33–39.

Ballor, C. (2017). Dallas doctor who performed questionable surgeries gets life in prison. *Dallas News.* Retrieved from https://www.dallasnews.com/news/courts/2017/02/20/ dallas-doctor-who-performed-questionable-surgeries -gets-life-in-prison

Bancroft, K. X. (2013). Regulating information security in the government contracting industry: Will the rising tide lift all the boats? *American University Law Review, 62,* 1145–1202.

Banerjee, N., & Goodstein, L. (2006, November 5). Church board dismisses pastor for "sexually immoral conduct." *The New York Times.* Retrieved from http://www.nytimes .com/2006/11/05/us/05haggard.html?scp=1&sq=Church%20 board%20dismisses%20pastor%20for%20%E2% 80%98sexually%20immoral%20conduct&st=cse

Bangert, D. (2019). Purdue prof, wife plead guilty in $1.3M scheme, pocketing federal research money. *Journal & Courier.* Retrieved from https://www.jconline.com/story/ news/2019/10/19/purdue-prof-wife-plead-guilty-1-3-m -scheme-pocketing-federal-research-money/4035498002

Banta, M. (2019, August 7). Former MSU Dean William Strampel sentenced to one year in jail. *Lansing State Journal.* Retrieved from https://www.lansingstatejournal.com/story/news/ local/2019/08/07/former-msu-dean-william-strampel -sentenced-larry-nassar-michigan-state/1933906001

Banta, M. (2020). Judge dismisses charges against former MSU President Lou Anna Simon *Lansing State Journal.* Retrieved from https://www.lansingstatejournal.com/ story/news/local/2020/05/13/michigan-state-university -msu-president-lou-anna-simon-charges-dismissed-larry -nassar/5183378002

Barboza, D., & Lohr, S. (2007, July 25). F.B.I. and Chinese seize $500 million of counterfeit software. *The New York Times.* Retrieved from http://www.nytimes.com/2007/07/25/ business/worldbusiness/25soft.html

Barker, T. (2002). Ethical police behavior. In K. Lersch (Ed.), *Policing and misconduct* (pp. 1–25). Upper Saddle River, NJ: Prentice Hall.

Barker, T., & Roebuck, J. (1973). *Empirical typology of police corruption—A study in organizational deviance.* Springfield, IL: Charles C Thomas.

Barnard, J. W. (2001). Allocution for victims of economic crimes. *Notre Dame Law Review, 77*(1), 39–70.

Barnard, J. W. (2002). The SEC's suspension and bar powers in perspective. *Tulane Law Review*, (76), 1253–1273.

Barnard, R. (2009, July 2). Madoff case: Act gives fraud victims a voice. *Richmond Times-Dispatch*. Retrieved from http://www2.timesdispatch.com/search/?source=all&query=%22madoff+case%3A+act+gives+fraud+victim s+a+voice%22

Barnes, W., & Kozar, J. M. (2008). The exploitation of pregnant workers in apparel production. *Journal of Fashion Marketing and Management*, 12, 285–293.

Barnett, C. (n. d.). *The measurement of white-collar crime using uniform crime reporting (UCR) data*. Federal Bureau of Investigation, U.S. Department of Justice. Retrieved from http://www.fbi.gov/about-us/cjis/ucr/nibrs/nibrs_wcc.pdf

Barnett, H. (1999). The land ethic and environmental crime. *Criminal Justice Policy Review*, 10(2), 161–191.

Barnett, H. C. (1981). Corporate capitalism, corporate crime. *Crime and Delinquency*, 27(1), 4–23.

Barnett, H. C. (1993). Crimes against the environment: Superfund enforcement at last. *Annals of the American Academy of Political and Social Science*, 525, 119–133.

Barrett, S., & White, R. (2017). Disrupting environmental crime at the local level: An operational perspective. *Palgrave Communications*, 3(1), 1–8.

Barrows, C. W., & Powers, T. (2009). *Introduction to management in the hospitality industry* (9th ed.). Hoboken, NJ: Wiley.

Bartlett, T. (2019). The criminologist accused of cooking the books. *Chronicle of Higher Education*. Retrieved from https://www.chronicle.com/article/the-criminologist-accused-of-cooking-the-books

Bartz, D., & Stempel, J. (2020). U.S. states accuse 26 drugmakers of generic drug price fixing in sweeping lawsuit. *Reuters*. Retrieved from https://www.reuters.com/article/us-usa-drugs-antitrust-lawsuit/u-s-states-accuse-26-drugmakers-of-generic-drug-price-fixing-in-sweeping-lawsuit-idUSKBN23H2TR.

Bashshur, R., Doarn, C. R., Frenk, J. M., Kvedar, J. C., & Woolliscroft, J. O. (2020, May). Telemedicine and the COVID-19 pandemic, lessons for the future. *Telemedicine and e-Health*, 26(5), 571–573.

Batabyal, G., & Chowdhury, A. (2015). Curbing corruption, financial development and income inequality. *Progress in Development Studies*, 15(1), 49–72.

Bartolacci, M. R., LeBlanc, L. J., & Podhradsky, A. (2014). Personal denial of service (PDOS) attacks: A discussion and exploration of a new category of cybercrime. *Journal of Digital Forensics, Security and Law*, 9(1), 19–36.

Bashshur, R. L. (1995). Telemedicine effects: cost, quality, and access. *Journal of Medical Systems*, 19(2), 81–91.

Basken, P. (2009, September 10). Medical "ghostwriting" is still a common practice, study shows. *Chronicle of Higher Education*. Retrieved from http://chronicle.com/article/Medical-Ghostwriting-Is-a/48347/

Bassnett, S. (2006, September 29). Hands off my bottom, mister! *The Times Higher Education Supplement*. Retrieved from http://www.timeshighereducation.co.uk/story.asp?storyCode=205661&sectioncode=26

Baumer, E. P., Ranson, J. W. A., Arnio, A. N., Fulmer, A., & De Zilwa, S. (2017). Illuminating a dark side of the American dream: Assessing the prevalence and predictors of mortgage fraud across U.S. counties. *American Journal of Sociology*, 123(2), 549–603. https://doi-org.proxy.lib.odu.edu/10.1086/692719

Baumgartel, S. (2016). Privileging professional insider trading. *Georgia Law Review*, 51(1), 71–120.

Beare, M. (2002). Organized corporate criminality: Tobacco smuggling between Canada and the US. *Crime, Law, and Social Change*, 37, 225–243.

Beaver, W. (2012). Fraud in for-profit higher education. *Social Science and Public Policy*, 49, 274–278.

Beck, D. G. (1981). The Federal Water Pollution Control Act's self-reporting requirement and the privilege against self-incrimination: Civil or criminal proceeding and penalties? *United States v. Ward. Brigham Young University Law Review*, (4), 983–991.

Beck, E. (1979). The Love Canal tragedy. *EPA Journal*. Retrieved from http://www.epa.gov/aboutepa/history/topics/lovecanal/01.html

Beck, A., Kerschbamer, R., Qui, J., & Sutter, M. (2013). Car mechanics in the lab: Investigating the behavior of real experts on experimental markets for credence goods. *Working Papers in Economics and Statistics*, 2014(02).

Beck, A., Kerschbamer, R., Qiu, J., & Sutter, M. (2014). Car mechanics in the lab––Investigating the behavior of real experts on experimental markets for credence goods. *Journal of Economic Behavior & Organization*, 108, 166–173.

Behrmann, N. (2005, September 19). Collapse of U.S. fund exposes global debt scam: Bayou seen caught in fraudsters' trap while trying to recoup losses. *The Business Times Singapore*. Retrieved from http://www.aussiestockforums.com/forums/archive/index.php/t-1993.html

Belser, A. (2008, January 1). Be careful with thieving workers. *Pittsburgh Post-Gazette*. Retrieved from http://www.postgazette.com/pg/08021/850539-28.stm

Bennett, M. W., Levinson, J. D., & Hioki, K. (2017). Judging federal white-collar fraud sentencing: An empirical study revealing the need for further reform. *Iowa Law Review*, *102*(3), 939–1000.

Bennett, W. F. (2007). Real estate scam emerges. *North County Times*. Retrieved from http://www.nctimes.com/news/local/article_897f29dd-0903-53af-bbfc-7029267ac1d3.html

Bensinger, K., & Vartabedian, R. (2009, October 25). New details in crash that prompted Toyota recall. *Los Angeles Times*.

Benson, M. L. (1985a). Denying the guilty mind: Accounting for involvement in a white-collar crime. *Criminology*, *23*(4), 583–607.

Benson, M. L. (1985b). White collar offenders under community supervision. *Justice Quarterly*, *2*(3), 429–436.

Benson, M. L. (1989). The influence of class position on the formal and informal sanctioning of white-collar offenders. *Sociological Quarterly*, *30*(3), 465–479.

Benson, M. L. (1990). Emotions and adjudication: Status degradation among white-collar criminals. *Justice Quarterly*, *73*(3), 515–528.

Benson, M. L. (2016). Developmental perspectives on white-collar criminality. In S. R. Van Slyke, M. L. Benson, & F. T. Cullen (Eds.), *The Oxford handbook of white-collar crime* (pp. 253–274). New York, NY: Oxford University Press.

Benson, M. L., & Chio, H. L. (2020). Who commits occupational crimes? In M. Rorie (Ed.), *The handbook of white-collar crime* (pp. 95–112). New York, NY: John Wiley & Sons.

Benson, M. L., & Cullen, F. T. (1988). The special sensitivity of white-collar offenders to prison: A critique and research agenda. *Journal of Criminal Justice, 16*, 207–215.

Benson, M. L., & Cullen, F. T. (1998). *Combating corporate crime: Local prosecutors at work*. Boston, MA: Northeastern University Press.

Benson, M. L., & Cullen, F. T. (2018). White-collar crime, self-deception, and subterranean values. in delinquency and drift revisited: The criminology of David Matza and beyond. In T. G. Blomberg, F. T. Cullen, C. Carlsson, and C. L. Jonson (Eds.), *Advances in criminological theory* (vol. 21, pp. 99–124). New York, NY: Routledge

Benson, M. L., Cullen, F. T., & Maakestad, W. J. (1988). *Local prosecutors and white-collar crime: Final report*. Washington, DC: U.S. Department of Justice, National Institute of Justice.

Benson, M. L., Cullen, F. T., & Maakestad, W. J. (1990). Local prosecutors and corporate crime. *Crime and Delinquency*, *36*(3), 356–372.

Benson, M. L., & Kerley, K. (2001). Life course theory and white-collar crime. In H. Pontell & D. Shichor (Eds.), *Contemporary issues in criminology and criminal justice: Essays in honor of Gilbert Geis* (pp. 121–136). Upper Saddle River, NJ: Prentice Hall.

Benson, M. L., & Moore, E. (1992). Are white-collar and common offenders the same? An empirical and theoretical critique of a recently proposed general theory of crime. *Journal of Research in Crime and Delinquency*, *29*, 251–272.

Benson, M. L., Van Slyke, S. R., & Cullen, F. T. (2016). Core themes in the study of white-collar crime. In S. R. Van Slyke, M. L. Benson, & F. T. Cullen (Eds.), *The Oxford handbook of white-collar crime* (pp. 1–21). New York, NY: Oxford University Press.

Ben-Yehuda, N., & Oliver-Lumerman, A. (2017). *Fraud and misconduct in research: Detection, investigation, and organizational response*. Ann Arbor: University of Michigan Press.

Berdejo, C. (2017). Small investments, big losses: The states' role in protecting local investors from securities fraud. *Washington Law Review, 92*(2), 567–630.

Berg, B. L. (2009). *Qualitative research methods for the social sciences* (7th ed.). Boston, MA: Allyn & Bacon.

Berkman, S., Boswell, N. Z., Bruner, F. H., Gough, M., McCormick, J. T., Egens, P. . . . Zimmerman, S. (2008). The fight against corruption: International organizations at a crossroads. *Journal of Financial Crime, 15*(2), 124.

Bernard, T. S. (2010, July 19). Need a mortgage? Don't get pregnant. *The New York Times*. Retrieved November 20, 2015, from http://www.nytimes.com/2010/07/20/your-money/mortgages/20 mortgage.html

Bernat, I., & Whyte, D. (2020). State-corporate crimes. In M. Rorie (Ed.), *The handbook of white-collar crime* (pp. 127–138). New York, NY: John Wiley & Sons.

Bernate, F. P., & Godlove, N. (2012). Understanding 21st century cybercrime for the 'common' victim: Frances P. Benat and Nicholas Godlove argue that it is time to extend the principles of universal justice to the typical types of cyber-offenses. *Criminal Justice Matters, 89*(1), 4–5.

Berstein, D. (2017). His life in prison. *Chicago Magazine*. Retrieved from https://www.chicagomag.com/Chicago-Magazine/October-2017/Blago-His-Life-in-Prison

Bertrand, D. (2003, August 14). Auto fixer in scam jam: 6 at shop busted in insure fraud. *New York Daily News*, (Suburban section), p. 1.

Bharara, P. (2007). Cry uncle and their employees cry foul: Rethinking prosecutorial pressure on corporate defendants. *American Criminal Law Review*, 44(1), 53–114.

Bierstedt, R. (1970). *The social order* (3rd ed.). Bombay, India: Tata McGraw-Hill.

Bies, K. J. (2017). Let the sunshine in: Illuminating the powerful role police unions play in shielding officer misconduct. *Stanford Law & Policy Review*, 28(1), 109–[vi].

Bilimoria, D. (1995). Corporate control, crime, and compensation: An empirical examination. *Human Relations*, 48(8), 891–908.

Bisson, D. (2015, September 1). The Ashley Madison hack-A timeline (updated: 9/10/15). *Tripwire Inc*. Retrieved from http://www.tripwire.com/state-of-security/security-data-protection/cyber-security/the-ashley-madison-hack-atimeline

Bittle, S. (2020). In the land of corporate impunity: Corporate killing law in the United States. *Journal of White Collar and Corporate Crime, 1*(2), 131–139.

Black, A. (2005, October 7). Unnecessary surgery exposed! Why 60% of all surgeries are medically unjustified and how surgeons exploit patients to generate profits. *Health*. Retrieved from http://www.naturalnews.com/012291.html

Blake, A. (2020). State IG Linick transcript casts doubt on Pompeo claim about not knowing of probe. *The Washington Post*. Retrieved from https://www.washingtonpost.com/politics/2020/06/10/new-transcript-raises-huge-questions-about-mike-pompeos-denial-that-he-retaliated-against-fired-inspector-general/

Bloch, K. E. (2019). Harnessing virtual reality to prevent prosecutorial misconduct. *Georgetown Journal of Legal Ethics, 32*(1), 1–56.

Bloomquist, L. (2006, December 21). Workers walk off jobs at Days Inn. *Knight Ridder/Tribune Business News*, p. 1.

Blumenstyk, G. (2012, May 29). Attorneys general urge congress to close military 'loophole' at for-profit colleges. *The Chronicle of Higher Education*. Retrieved from http://chronicle.com/article/Attorneys-General-Urge/132030/

Boesky, I. (n.d.). A golden opportunity, white-collar crime, Michael Milken, the junk bond king, the symbol of greed. *Law.com* Retrieved from http://law.jrank.org/pages/12165/Boesky-Ivan.html

Bohm, R. M., & Vogel, B. L. (2011). *A primer on crime and delinquency theory* (3rd ed.). Belmont, CA: Wadsworth.

Böhm, M. L. (2020). Criminal business relationships between commodity regions and industrialized countries: The hard road from raw material to new technology. *Journal of White Collar and Corporate Crime, 1*(1), 34–49.

Bolton, F. (2013). Cybersecurity and emergency management: Encryption and the inability to communicate. *Homeland Security and Emergency Management, 10*(1), 1–7.

Booker v Washington, 543 U.S. 220, (2005).

Bossler, A., & Holt, T. (2011). Malware victimization: A routine activities framework. *Cyber criminology: Exploring internet crimes and criminal behavior, 317*.

Botsko, C. A., & Wells, R. C. (1994). Government whistleblowers: Crime's hidden victims. *FBI Law Enforcement Bulletin, 63*(7), 17–21.

Bowe, B., Xie, Y., Yan, Y., & Al-Aly, Z. (2019). Burden of cause-specific mortality associated with PM2. 5 air pollution in the United States. *JAMA network open, 2*(11), e1915834–e1915834.

Bradley, D. (2008). Real estate fraud. *FBI Law Enforcement Bulletin, 77*(9), 1–4. Retrieved from https://leb.fbi.gov/2008-pdfs/leb-september-2008

Brainard, J. (2008, August 29). Scientists who cheated had mentors who failed to supervise them. *Chronicle of Higher Education*. Retrieved from http://chronicle.com/article/Scientists-Who-Cheated-Had/1112

Braithwaite, J. (1982). Challenging just deserts: Punishing white-collar criminals. *Journal of Criminal Law and Criminology, 73*(2), 723–763.

Braithwaite, J. (1989). *Crime, shame, and reintegration*. New York, NY: Cambridge University Press.

Braithwaite, J. (1991). Poverty, power, white-collar crime and the paradoxes of criminological theory. *Australian and New Zealand Journal of Criminology, 24*(1), 40–48.

Braithwaite, J. (1993). The nursing home industry. In M. H. Tonry & A. J. Reiss (Eds.). *Beyond the law: Crime in complex organizations* (pp. 11–54). Chicago, IL: University of Chicago Press.

Braithwaite, J. (2020). Regulatory mix, collective efficacy, and crimes of the powerful. *Journal of White Collar and Corporate Crime, 1*(1), 62–71.

Brasner, S. (2010, April 23). In brief: Florida agent hit with fraud charge. *Wall Street Journal Abstracts*, p. 3.

Brawley, O. (2009). Prostate cancer screening: Is this a teachable moment? *Journal of the National Cancer Institute, 101*, 19, 1295–1297.

Bredemeier, K. (2002, May 16). Memo warned of Enron's Calif. strategy: West Coast senators complain about market manipulation during power crisis. *The Washington Post*, p. A04.

Brickey, K. F. (2006). In Enron's wake: Corporate executives on trial. *Journal of Criminal Law and Criminology, 96*(2), 397–433.

Briquelet, K. (2020). Televangelist Jim Bakker fights to keep selling Covid-19 cure from God. *Daily Beast*. Retrieved from https://www.thedailybeast.com/televangelist-jim-bakker-fights-to-keep-selling-sham-covid-19-cure-from-god

Brenner, S. W. (2006). Cybercrime jurisdiction. *Crime, Law and Social Change, 46*, 189–206.

Brenner, S. W. (2007). "At light speed": Attribution and response to cybercrime/terrorism/warfare. *The Journal of Criminal Law & Criminology, 97*(2), 379–475.

Breuninger, K. (2020). Here are the charges Trump's ex-lawyer Michael Cohen admitted to in federal court. *CNBC*. Retrieved from https://www.cnbc.com/2018/08/21/here-are-the-charges-michael-cohen-admitted-to-in-federal-court.html

Brickner, D. B., Mahoney, L. S., & Moore, S. J. (2010). Providing an applied-learning exercise in teaching fraud detection: A case of academic partnering with IRS criminal investigation. *Issues in Accounting Education, 25*(4), 695–719.

Brinkley, J. (1994, January 23). The nation: The coverup that worked: A look back. *The New York Times*. Retrieved from http://www.nytimes.com/1994/01/23/weekinreview/thenation-the-cover-up-that-worked-a-look-back.html?scp=1&sq=The%20nation:%20The%20cover-up%20that%20worked:%20A%20look%20back&st=cse

Brockman J. (2018). The research challenges of exposing physicians' sexual misconduct in Canada. *Critical Criminology, 26*(4), 527–544. doi:10.1007/s10612-018-9418-7

Broggi, J. J. (2014). Building on executive order 13,363 to encourage information sharing for cybersecurity purposes. *Harvard Journal of Law & Public Policy, 37*(2), 653–676.

Brooks, G., Button, M., & Gee, J. (2012). The scale of health-care fraud: A global evaluation. *Security Journal, 25*(1), 76–87.

Brown, E. (2004, December 12). Can for-profit schools pass an ethics test? *The New York Times*. Retrieved from http://query.nytimes.com/gst/fullpage.html?res=9907 E3D81131F931A25751C1A9629C8B63&page wanted=all

Brown, W. (1995, December 9). It's getting tougher. *Thrifty Herald*, p. 21.

Brownlee, M. (2015, October 20). Audit finds more the $230,000 in misspent money in Neola. *The Daily Nonpareil*. Retrieved from http://www.nonpareilonline.com/news/local/auditfinds-more-than-in-misspent-money-in-neola/article_0a006b5c-7739-11e5-bfc2-7355134f2cae.html

Bryant, C. (1979). *Khaki-collar crime*. New York, NY: Free Press.

Buckhoff, T., Higgins, L., & Sinclair, D. (2010). A fraud audit: Do you need one? *Journal of Applied Business Research, 26*(5), 29–34.

Bucy, P. H. (1989). Fraud by fright: White collar crime by health care providers. *North Carolina Law Review, 67*, 855–937.

Buell, M., & McCampbell, S. W. (2003). Preventing staff misconduct in the community correction setting. *Corrections Today, 65*(1), 90–91.

Buell, S. W. (2018). The responsibility gap in corporate crime. *Criminal Law & Philosophy, 12*(3), 471–491. Retrieved from https://doi-org.proxy.lib.odu.edu/10.1007/s11572-017-9434-9

Buettner, R., Craig, S., & McEntire, M. (2017). Trump's taxes show chronic losses and years of income tax avoidance. *The New York Times*. Retrieved from https://www.nytimes.com/interactive/2020/09/27/us/donald-trump-taxes.html

Burdeau, C. (2010, December 2). Judge: Deal to fix homes with Chinese drywall going well. *Business Week*. Retrieved from http://www.businessweek.com/ap/financialnews/D9JS1TIG0.htm

Bureau of Justice Statistics. (2011). *State and federal prisoners and prison facilities*. Washington, DC: U.S. Department of Justice.

Bureau of Justice Statistics. (n.d.). Terms and definitions—Prison Rape Elimination Act. Retrieved from https://www.bjs.gov/index.cfm?ty=tdtp&tid=20

Burke, A. S. (2010). I got the shotgun: Reflections on the wire, prosecutors, and Omar Little. *Ohio State Journal of Criminal Law, 8*, 447.

Burns, A. (2020). Former Emory professor pleads guilty to not reporting income from China on tax returns. *Atlanta Journal Constitution*. Retrieved from https://www.ajc.com/news/crime--law/former-emory-professor-convicted-not-reporting-income-from-china-tax-returns/jNJWUhh8kClisAkmuC3ETM

Burns, J. (2017). Breach of faith: lack of policy for responding to data breaches and what the government should do about it. *Florida Law Review, 69*(3), 959–988.

Burns, K., & Millhiser, I. (2020). Sen. Richard Burr and the coronavirus insider trading scandal, explained. *Vox*. Retrieved from https://www.vox.com/policy-and-politics/2020/5/14/21258560/senator-richard-burr-coronavirus-insider-trading-scandal-explained

Burns, R. G., & Lynch, M. J. (2004). *Environmental crime: A sourcebook*. New York, NY: LFB Scholarly.

Burns, R. G., & Meitl, M. B. (2020). Prosecution, defense, and sentencing of white-collar crime. In M. Rorie (Ed.), *The handbook of white-collar crime* (pp. 279–296). New York, NY: John Wiley & Sons.

Burns, R. G., & Orrick, L. (2002). Assessing newspaper coverage of corporate violence: The dance hall fire in Goteborg, Sweden. *Critical Criminology*, *11*, 137–150.

Burnstein, J. (2008a, November 19). Man arrested in Delray Beach on remodeling fraud charges; he's already awaiting trial in Broward: Awaiting trial in Broward, he's arrested in Delray Beach over 4 jobs never completed. *Sun Sentinel*, p. 6.

Burnstein, J. (2008b, November 18). Oakland Park man arrested again on construction-related theft charges. *Sun Sentinel*, p. 7.

Burton, D., Erdman, E., Hamilton, G., & Muse, K. (1999). *Women in prison: Sexual misconduct by correctional staff)* (GAO/GGD-99-104. Washington, DC: U.S. Government Accounting Office.

Butt, I. H., Tatlah, I. A., Rehman, A., & Azam, A. (2019). In-class time theft in higher education classrooms: An exploratory study. *Pakistan Journal of Social Sciences (PJSS)*, *39*(1).

Button, M., Shepherd, D., & Blackbourn, D. (2018). "The higher you fly, the further you fall": white-collar criminals, "special sensitivity" and the impact of conviction in the United Kingdom. *Victims & Offenders*, *13*(5), 628–650.

Byars, K., & Payne, B. (2000). Medical students' and doctors' perceptions about medicaid: A content analysis. *Journal of health and human services administration*, 65–82.

Calavita, K., & Pontell, H. N. (1991). Other people's money revisited: Collective embezzlement in the savings and loan and insurance industries. *Social Problems*, *38*, 94–112.

Calavita, K., Pontell, H. N., & Tillman, R. H. (1997). *Big money crime: Fraud and politics in the savings and loan crisis*. Berkeley: University of California Press.

Campbell, J. (2009). Mother of all swindles. *Sunday Herald Sun*, p. 70.

Canada, J., Kuhn, J. R., & Sutton, S. G. (2008). Accidentally in the public interest: The perfect storm that yielded the Sarbanes-Oxley Act. *Critical Perspectives in Accounting*, *7*, 987–1003.

Candeub, A. (2013). Transparency in the administrative state. *Houston Law Review*, *51*(2), 385–416.

Cano-Urbina, J., Clapp, C. M., & Willardsen, K. (2019). The effects of the BP Deepwater Horizon oil spill on housing markets. *Journal of Housing Economics*, *43*, 131–156.

Cantrell, A. (2018). Surviving prison as a wall street convict. *Institutional Investor*. Retrieved from https://www.institutionalinvestor.com/article/b18b7g0qjk5pwb/Surviving-Prison-as-a-Wall-Street-Convict

Capitol Forum. (2019). Twenty states without any dedicated criminal enforcement staff for environmental crimes. Retrieved from https://prospect.org/environment/epa-twenty-states-lack-dedicated-criminal-enforcement

Carden, A. (2008). Beliefs, bias, and regime uncertainty after Hurricane Katrina. *International Journal of Social Economics*, *35*(7), 531–545.

Cardinal, C. (2010). Podium politics and the Olympics. *The Vancouver Observer*. Retrieved from http://www.vancouverobserver.com/olympics/2010/01/19/podiumpolitics-and-olympics

Carey, C., & Webb, J. K. (2017). Ponzi schemes and the roles of trust creation and maintenance. *Journal of Financial Crime*, *24*(4), 589–600. https://doi-org.proxy.lib.odu.edu/10.1108/JFC-06-2016-0042

Carlson, E. T. (2018). The (not-so) brave new world of international criminal enforcement: The intricacies of multi-jurisdictional white-collar investigations. *Brooklyn Law Review*, *84*(1), 299–[ii].

Carlson, S. M. (2020). The US student loan debt crisis: State crime or state-produced harm? *Journal of White Collar and Corporate Crime*, *1*(2), 140–152.

Carrera, J. (2018). Pot-sniffing dog helps curb employee theft at local marijuana dispensary. *8newsnow.com*. Retrieved from https://www.8newsnow.com/news/pot-sniffing-dog-helps-curb-employee-theft-at-local-marijuana-dispensary

Carter, D., L., & Katz, A., J. (1996). Computer crime: An emerging challenge for law enforcement. *FBI Law Enforcement Bulletin*, *65*(12), 1.

Carter, T. S. (1999). Ascent of the corporate model in environmental-organized crime. *Crime, Law and Social Change*, *31*(1), 1–30.

Carucci, D., Overhuls, D., & Soares, N. (2011). Computer crimes. *American Criminal Law Review*, *48*, 375–419.

Casten, J. A., & Payne, B. K. (2008). The influence of perceptions of social disorder and victimization on business owners' decisions to use guardianship strategies. *Journal of Criminal Justice*, *36*(5), 396–402.

Castleberry, S. B. (2007). Prison field trips: Can whitecollar criminals positively affect the ethical and legal behavior of marketing and MBA students? *Journal of Marketing Research*, *29*(5), 5–17.

Cauley, L. (2007, August 6). Rigas tells his side of the Adelphia story; on his way to prison, former cable mogul describes the scandal from his point of view. *USA Today*, p. 1B.

Cavazos-Rehg, P. A., Krauss, M. J., Cahn, E., Lee, K. E., Ferguson, E., Rajbhandari, B., . . . & Bierut, L. J. (2019). Marijuana promotion online: An investigation of dispensary practices. *Prevention Science, 20*(2), 280–290.

Cavender, G., & Miller, K. W. (2013). Corporate crime as trouble: Reporting on the corporate scandals of 2002. *Deviant Behavior, 36,* 916–931.

Center County Gazette. (2019, July 25). 'We were about ready to give up.' Baby's looking to future after former manager sentenced for theft from restaurant. *Statecollege.com.* Retrieved from https://www.statecollege.com/we-were -about-ready-to-give-up-babys-looking-to-future-after -former-manager-sentenced-for-theft-from-restaurant/

Centers for Disease Control (CDC). (2009). *Centers for disease Control and Prevention investigation update: Outbreak of* Salmonella typhimurium *infections.* Retrieved from http://www .cdc.gov/salmonella/typhimurium/update.html

Chabinsky, S. (2013, November 5). Top five reasons to report computer intrusions to law enforcement. *Security,* 92. Retrieved from http://www.securitymagazine.com/articles/84898 -top-5-reasons-to-report-computerintrusions-to-law -enforcement

Chabinsky, S. (2015, April 1). The top 10 cybersecurity myths, part I. *Security,* 46. Retrieved from http:// www.securitymagazine.com/articles/86207-the-top-10 -cybersecuritymyths-part-1

Chabinsky, S. (2015, May 1). The top 10 cybersecurity myths, part II. *Security,* 26. Retrieved from http://www.securitymagazine .com/articles/86326-the-top-10-cybersecuritymyths-part-2

Chan, M. (2016). Florida teen accused of posing as doctor also (sort of) fooled his family. *Time.* Retrieved from https://time .com/4229405/florida-doctor-teenager-love-robinson

Chan, T. Y., Chen, Y., Pierce, L., & Snow, D. (2020). The influence of peers in worker misconduct: Evidence from restaurant theft. *Manufacturing & Service Operations Management.*

Chang, L. Y. C. (2013). Formal and informal modalities for policing cybercrime across the Taiwan Strait. *Policing & Society, 23*(2), 540–555.

Chappell, B. (2020). Acclaimed Harvard scientist is arrested, accused of lying about ties to China. *NPR.* Retrieved from https:// www.npr.org/2020/01/28/800442646/acclaimed-harvard -scientist-is-arrested-accused-of-lying-about-ties-to-china

Chavez, N. (2019). Congressional report says multiple institutions could have stopped Larry Nassar. CNN.com. Retrieved from https://www.cnn.com/2019/07/31/us/larry-nassar-senate -report/index.html

Cheit, R. E., & Davis, Z. R. (2010). Magazine coverage of child sexual abuse. *Journal of Child Abuse, 19*(1), 99–117.

Chien, E., & Kleiner, B. H. (1999). Sex discrimination in hiring. *Equal Opportunities International, 18*(5/6), 32–36.

Chinese goods scare prods regulators. (2007). *Oxford Analytica Daily Briefing Service.* Retrieved from http://www.oxan .com/display.aspx? ItemID=DB137125

Chittum, M. (2003, December 20). USDA to investigate Natural Bridge Zoo bears. *Roanoke Times and World News.* Retrieved from http://www.highbeam.com/doc/1P2-12671138.html

Cicchini, M. D. (2018). Combating prosecutorial misconduct in closing arguments. *Oklahoma Law Review, 70*(4), 887–942.

Cicchini, M. D. (2019). Combating judicial misconduct: Stoic approach. *Buffalo Law Review, 67*(5), 1259–1328.

Citizens Police Data Project. (2020). Retrieved from https:// data.cpdp.co/data/LdR59g/citizens-police-data-project.

Clarey, R. L. (1978). Prosecution of consumer fraud—New York's new approach. *Criminal Law Bulletin, 14*(3), 197–202.

Clarke, R. V., & Cornish, D. B. (1985). Modeling offenders' decisions. In M. Tonry & N. Morris (Eds.), *Crime and justice* (vol. 6, pp. 147–185). Chicago, IL: University of Chicago Press.

Clayton, C. (2010). Lincoln calls hearing on EPA impact on farmers. *Progressive Farmer.* Retrieved from http://www .dtnprogressive farmer.com/dtnag/view/ag/printablePage.do ?ID=BLOG_PRINTABLE_PAGE&bypassCache=true&pageLayo ut=v4&blogHandle=policy&blogEntryId=8a82c0bc2a8c873001 2b351b985a0825&articleTitle=Lincoln+Calls+Hearing+on+EP A+Impact+on+Farmers&editionName=DTNAgFreeSiteOnline

Clinard, M., & Quinney, R. (1973). *Criminal behavior systems: A typology* (2nd ed.). New York, NY: Holt, Rinehart & Winston.

Clinard, M. B., & Yeager, P. C. (1980). *Corporate crime.* New York, NY: Free Press.

CNN.Com. (2020). *Transcripts.* Retrieved from http:// transcripts.cnn.com/TRANSCRIPTS/2008/16/sotu.01.html

CNN.Com. (2021). *Controversial police encounters fast facts.* Retrieved from https://www.cnn.com/2015/04/05/us/ controversial-police-encounters-fast-facts/index.html

Coburn, N. F. (2006). Corporate investigations. *Journal of Financial Crime, 13*(3), 348–368.

Coffee, J. C. (1980). Corporate crime and punishment: A non-Chicago view of the economics of criminal sanctions. *American Criminal Law Review, 17*(4), 419–476.

Coffey, L. T. (2000, January 23). Beware of door-to-door scams. *St. Petersburg Times,* p. 3H.

Cohen, J. (2019). University of Illinois at Chicago missed warning signs of research going awry, letters show. *Chicago Sun Times*. Retrieved from https://chicago.suntimes.com/2019/3/20/18467517/records-uic-missed-warning-signs-on-child-psychiatrist-s-research-going-awry

Cohen, L. E., & Felson, M. (1979). Social change and crime rate trends: A routine activities approach. *American Sociological Review, 44*, 588–608.

Cohen, M. A. (1989). Corporate crime and punishment: A study of social harm and sentencing practice in the federal courts, 1987–1987. *American Criminal Law Review, 26*(3), 605–660.

Cohen, M. A. (1992). Environmental crime and punishment: Legal/economic theory and empirical evidence on enforcement of federal environmental statutes. *Journal of Criminal Law and Criminology, 82*(4), 1054–1108.

Cohen, M. A. (2016). The costs of white-collar crime. In S. R. Van Slyke, M. L. Benson, & F. T. Cullen (Eds.), *The Oxford handbook of white-collar crime* (pp. 78–98). New York, NY: Oxford University Press.

Cohen, M. A. (2020). Punishing corporations. In M. Rorie (Ed.), *Handbook of White-collar Crime* (pp. 314–333). New York, NY: John Wiley & Sons.

Cohen, T. H. (2005). *Punitive damage awards in large counties, 2001*. Washington, DC: Bureau of Justice Statistics.

Cohen, T. H. (2009). Tort bench and jury trials in state courts, 2005. *U.S. Department of Justice*. Retrieved from http://bjs.ojp.usdoj.gov/content/pub/pdf/tbjtsc05.pdf

Cohen, T. H., & Hughes, K. A. (2007). *Bureau of Justice Statistics special report: Medical malpractice insurance claims in seven states, 2000–2004*. Retrieved from http://bjs.ojp.usdoj.gov/content/pub/pdf/mmicss04.pdf

Cole, C., Maroney, P., McCullough, K., & Powell, L. (2015). Automobile insurance vehicle repair practices: Politics, economics, and consumer interests. *Risk Management and Insurance Review, 18*(1), 101–128.

Coleman, J. (1982). *The asymmetric society*. Syracuse, NY: Syracuse University Press.

Coleman, J. (1994). *The criminal elite: The sociology of white-collar crime*. New York, NY: St. Martin's.

Coleman, J. (2020). McEnany: 'No one seemed to care' when Obama fired holdover IGs. *The Hill*. Retrieved from https://thehill.com/homenews/administration/498492-mcenany-no-one-seemed-to-care-when-obama-fired-inspectors-general/

Coleman, J. W. (1987). Toward an integrated theory of white-collar crime. *American Journal of Sociology, 93*(2), 406–439.

Collier, J. (2016). From the outside in: law and economics perspective on insider trading cases involving cybercrime. *Journal of High Technology Law, 17*(1), 141–176.

Collin, B. C. (2001). *The future of cyberterrorism: Where the physical and virtual worlds converge*. 11th Annual International Symposium on Criminal Justice Issues. Retrieved from http://afgen.com/terrorism1.html

Collins, D. (2019). Show up drunk: Indictments spotlight prison rehab scams. *APNews*. Retrieved from https://apnews.com/article/1f6521be263f4c5f855a179e2039dab7.

Collins, J. D., Saintano, V. A., & Khey, D. N. (2011). Organizational data breaches 2005–2010: Applying SCP to the healthcare and education sectors. *International Journal of Cyber Criminology, 5*(1), 794–810.

Collman, A. (2014). Sociology professor promised me an 'A' in exchange for sex, claims student. *DailyMail.com*. Retrieved from https://www.dailymail.co.uk/news/article-2769569/We-just-cover-webcam-pull-blinds-University-Delaware-sociology-professor-promised-student-A-exchange-oral-sex.html

Colvin, G. (2004, July 26). White-collar crooks have no idea what they're in for. *Fortune Magazine*. Retrieved from http://money.cnn.com/magazines/fortune/fortune_archive/2004/07/26/377147/index.htm

Commission on Judicial Qualifications. (2019). *Kansas courts*. Retrieved from https://www.kscourts.org/KSCourts/media/KsCourts/Appellate%20Clerk/Commission_on_Judicial_Qualifications/2018-Annual-Report.pdf6589

Comte, F. (2006). Environmental crime and the police in Europe: A panorama and possible paths for future action. *European Environmental Law Review, 15*(7), 190–231.

Condon, S. (2010, May 3). How much does BP owe for Gulf oil spill? *Political hotsheet*. Columbia Broadcasting System (CBS) News. Retrieved from http://www.cbsnews.com/8301-503544_162-20004034-503544.html

Congressman resigns over affair with female aide; "I have sinned." (2010, May 10). *National Post*. Retrieved from http://www.nationalpost.com/news/world/story.html?id=3045823

Conley, J. (2007, October 18). Natural Bridge Zoo faces penalties. *Roanoke Times and World News*. Retrieved from http://www.roanoke.com/news/roanoke/wb/136282

Cooper, A. (2009, October 30). Obama rules over false U.S. ads in the Wild West. *Campaign*, p. 19.

Cooper, J. A. (2012). Noble cause corruption as a consequence of role conflict in the police organization. *Policing & Society, 22*(2), 169–184.

Copeland, K. (2014). Teaching the art of defending white collar criminal case. *Ohio State Journal of Criminal Law, 11*(2), 763–766.

Copes, H., & Vieraitis, L. M. (2009). Understanding identity theft: Offenders' accounts of their lives and crimes. *Criminal Justice Review, 33*, 329–349.

Cordis, A. S., & Milyo, J. (2016). Measuring public corruption in the United States: Evidence from administrative records of federal prosecutions. *Public Integrity, 18*(2), 127–148.

Cosgrove-Mather, B. (January 7, 2003). New era for white-collar criminals. *CBS News*. Retrieved from http://www .cbsnews.com/news/new-era-for-white-collar-criminals/

County of Los Angeles Department of Consumer Affairs. (2010). *False advertising*. Retrieved from http://dca.lacounty .gov/tsFalse Advertising.htm

Coursen, D. F. (2020). A just EPA budget for environmental justice. *The Hill*. Retrieved from https://thehill.com/ opinion/energy-environment/513525-a-just-epa-budget-for -environmental-justice

Court, E. (2017). Valeant gets a new name to shed its scandals, but will it work? *MarketWatch*. Retrieved from https:// www.marketwatch.com/story/valeant-will-get-a-new -name-again-hoping-to-shed-its-scandals-2018-05-08

Coustasse, A., Frame, M., & Mukherjee, A. (2018). Is Upcoding Anesthesia Time the Tip of the Iceberg in Insurance Fraud? *JAMA network open, 1*(7), e184302-e184302.

Coutts, H. (2009). Enrollment abuse allegations plague University of Phoenix [Electronic version]. *The Nation*. Retrieved from http://www.thenation.com/article/enrollment-abuse -allegations-plague-university-phoenix

Cox, L. (2010). The "July effect": Worst month for fatal errors, study says. *American Broadcasting Company (ABC) World News.Com*. Retrieved from http://abcnews.go.com/WN/Well nessNews/july-month-fatal-hospital-errorsstudy-finds/ story?id=10819652

Coyle, P. (1995). Bench stress. *American Bar Association Journal, 81*, 60–63.

Craig, J. M. (2019). "Extending situational action theory to white-collar crime." *Deviant Behavior, 40*(2), 171–186.

Craig, J. M., & Piquero, N. L. (2017). Sensational offending: An application of sensation seeking to white-collar and conventional crimes. *Crime & Delinquency, 63*(11), 1363–1382.

Cramm, P. D. (2009, May 26). The perils of prosecutorial misconduct. *FindLaw*. Retrieved from http://knowledgebase .findlaw.com/kb/2009/May/1208577_1.html

Crandal, J. (2019). Cybersecurity and offshore oil: The next big threat. *ONE J: Oil and Gas, Natural Resources, and Energy Journal, 4*(6), 703–736.

Crawford, K. (June 21, 2005). For Kozlowski, future looks especially grim. *CNN Money*. Retrieved from http://money .cnn.com/2005/06/21/news/newsmakers/prisons_state/

Cressey, D. R. (1953). *Other people's money: A study in the social psychology of embezzlement*. Glencoe, IL: Free Press.

Creswell, J. (2007, May 21). Mortgage fraud is up, but not in their backyards. *The New York Times*. Retrieved from http://www.nytimes.com/2007/05/21/business/21fraud .html?scp=1&sq=Mortgage%20fraud%20is%20up,%20 but%20not%20in%20their%20backyards.%20&st=csehttp:// www.nytimes.com

Croall, H. (1989). Who is the white-collar criminal? *British Journal of Criminology, 29*(2), 157–174.

Croall, H. (1993). Business offenders in the criminal justice process. *Crime, Law and Social Change, 20*(4), 359–372.

Croall, H. (2016). What is known and what should be known about white-collar crime victimization. In S. R. Van Slyke, M. L. Benson, & F. T. Cullen (Eds.), *The Oxford handbook of white-collar crime* (59–77). New York, NY: Oxford University Press.

Crofts, P. (2003). White collar punters: Stealing from the boss to gamble. *Current Issues in Criminal Justice, 15*(1), 40–52.

Crumb, D. J., & Jennings, K. (1998, February). Incidents of patient abuse in health care facilities are becoming more and more commonplace. *Dispute Resolution Journal*, 37–43.

Cullen, F. T., Chouhy, C., & Jonson, C. L. (2020). Public opinion about white-collar crime. In M. Rorie (Ed.), *The handbook of white-collar crime* (pp. 209–228). New York, NY: John Wiley & Sons.

Cullen, F. T., Clark, G. A., Mathers, R. A., & Cullen, J. B. (1983). Public support for punishing white-collar crime: Blaming the victim revisited? *Journal of Criminal Justice, 11*, 481–493.

Cullen, F. T., Link, B. J., & Polanzi, C. W. (1982). The seriousness of crime revisited: Have attitudes toward white-collar crime changed? *Criminology, 20*(1), 83–102.

Cullen, F. T., Maakestad, W. J., & Cavender, G. (1987). *Corporate crime under attack: The Ford Pinto case and beyond*. Cincinnati, OH: Anderson.

Culpepper, D., & Block, W. (2008). Price gouging in the Katrina aftermath: Free markets at work. *International Journal of Social Economics*, *35*(7), 512–520.

Curry, P. (2007). *Common forms of mortgage fraud*. Retrieved from http://www.bankrate.com/brm/news/real-estate/remini guide07/mortgage-fraud-most-common-a1.asp

Dabney, D. (1995). Neutralization and deviance in the workplace: Theft of supplies and medicines by hospital nurses. *Deviant Behavior*, *16*(4), 313–331.

Dabney, D. (2001). Onset of illegal use of mind-altering or potentially addictive prescription drugs among pharmacists. *Journal of American Pharmaceutical Association*, *41*, 392–400.

Dabney, D., & Hollinger, R. C. (1999). Illicit prescription drug use among pharmacists: Evidence of a paradox of familiarity. *Work and Occupations*, *26*(1), 77–106.

Dabney, D., & Hollinger, R. C. (2002). Drugged druggists: The convergence of two criminal career trajectories. *Justice Quarterly*, *19*(1), 181–213.

Daly, H. L. (2000). Telemedicine: The invisible legal barriers to the health care of the future. *Annals of Health Law*, *9*, 73.

Daly, K. (1989). Gender and varieties of white-collar crime. *Criminology*, *27*(4), 769–794.

Danner, M. J. E. (1998). Three strikes and it's *women* who are out: The hidden consequences for women of criminal justice reforms. In S. L. Miller (Ed.), *Crime control and women: Feminist implications of criminal justice policy* (pp. 1–14). Thousand Oaks, CA: Sage.

Daugherty, S. (2017). Judge spares Ronnie Boone Sr. jail time in bank fraud, bribery case in light of high blood pressure. *Virginian Pilot*. Retrieved from https://www.pilotonline.com/news/crime/article_877d2e48-d0a9-5266-865d-bc42e1fd613e.html,

Davenport, C., & Lipton, E. (2016). Trump picks Scott Pruitt, climate change denialist, to lead E.P.A. *New York Times*. Retrieved from https://www.nytimes.com/2016/12/07/us/politics/scott-pruitt-epa-trump.html

Davies, J., & Ollus, N. (2019). Labour exploitation as corporate crime and harm: outsourcing responsibility in food production and cleaning services supply chains. *Crime, Law & Social Change*, *72*(1), 87–106. https://doi-org.proxy.lib.odu.edu/10.1007/s10611-019-09841-w

Davies, K. R. (2003, December). Broken trust: Employee stealing. *Dealernews*, *39*(12), p. 22.

Davila, M., Marquart, J. W., & Mullings, J. L. (2005). Beyond mother nature: Contractor fraud in the wake of natural disasters. *Deviant Behavior*, *26*(3), 271–293.

Davis, J. B. (2003, August). Cybercrime fighters: Companies have more legal weapons to defend against attacks on their computer systems. *ABA Journal*, 37–42.

Dayno, Z. M. (2018). Private citizens policing corporate behavior: Using qui tam model to catch financial fraud. *Vermont Law Review*, *43*(2), 307–350.

Dearden, T., & Gottschalk, P. (2020). Gender and white-collar crime: Convenience in target selection. *Deviant Behavior*, 1–9.

Debusmann, B., Jr. (2010, June 24). Madoff aide's arcade games, off-road vehicles up for auction. *Reuters*. Retrieved from http://www.reuters.com/article/2010/06/25/us-madoff-auction-idUS-TRE6500CJ20100625

Delgado, C. F., Ullery, M. A., Jordan, M., Duclos, C., Rajagopalan, S., & Scott, K. (2018). Lead exposure and developmental disabilities in preschool-aged children. *Journal of Public Health Management and Practice*, *24*(2), e10–e17.

Denney, A. S., Kerley, K. R., & Gross, N. G. (2018). Child sexual abuse in Protestant Christian congregations: A descriptive analysis of offense and offender characteristics. *Religions*, *9*(1), 27.

Denzin, N. K. (1983). A note on emotionality, self, and interaction. *American Journal of Sociology*, *89*(2), 402–409.

Derri, D. K., & Popoola, G. (2017). The challenge of globalization and transnational environmental crime. *Journal of Law, Policy and Globalization*, *65*, 80–89.

Dernbach, B. (2020). Not just Roger Stone: A shockingly long list of Trump's controversial pardons and commutations. *Mother Jones*. Retrieved from https://www.motherjones.com/politics/2020/07/trump-roger-stone-pardon-commutation

Dervan, L. (2011). Information warfare and civilian populations: How the law of war addresses a fear of the unknown. *Goettingen Journal of International Law*, *3*(1), 373–396.

De Vries, C. E., & Solaz, H. (2017). The electoral consequences of corruption. *Annual Review of Political Science*, *20*, 391–408.

Dey, A. (2010). The chilling effect of Sarbanes-Oxley. *Journal of Accounting and Economics*, *49*, 53–57.

Dey, I. (2009, June 28). The final curtain falls for Madoff: US prosecutors demand 150 years in jail for the $65Bn fraudster. *The Sunday Times* (1st ed.), p. 10.

Dhami, M. K. (2007). White-collar prisoners' perceptions of audience reaction. *Deviant Behavior, 28*(1), 57–77.

Diamantis, M. E., & Laufer, W. S. (2019). Prosecution and punishment of corporate criminality. *Annual Review of Law and Social Science, 15*, 453–472.

Diamond, J., Watkins, E., & Summers, J. (2018). EPA chief Scott Pruitt resigns amid scandals, citing 'unrelenting attacks'. *CNN.com*. Retrieved from https://www.cnn.com/2018/07/05/politics/scott-pruitt-epa-resigns/index.html

Diehl, S., & Batsford, M. (2019). Auto industry compliance: Will the tone at the top go tone deaf in the wake of deregulation. *Wayne State University Journal of Business Law, 2*, 1–11.

DiGabriele, J. A. (2008). An empirical investigation of the relevant skills of forensic accountants. *Journal of Education for Business, 83*(6), 331–338.

Dilanian, K. (2018, September 7). Papadopoulos sentenced to 14 days in jail for lying to FBI in Mueller probe. *NBC News*. Retrieved from https://www.nbcnews.com/news/all/papadopoulos-sentenced-14-days-jail-lying-fbi-mueller-probe-n907266

Dincer, O., & Johnston, M. (2016). Political culture and corruption issues in state politics: A new measure of corruption issues and a test of relationships to political culture. *Publius: The Journal of Federalism, 47*(1), 131–148.

Disaster in the Gulf: 107 days and counting. (2010, August 4). *FoxNews.com*. Retrieved from http://www.foxnews.com/politics/2010/05/28/disaster-gulf-days-counting

Ditkowsky, M. (2019). # UsToo: The disparate impact of and ineffective response of sexual harassment of low-wage workers. *UCLA Women's Law Journal, 26*, 69.

Dobovsek, B., & Slak, B. (2015). Old horizons on organised-white collar crime: Critical remarks about the current definition, development and perceptions of organized and white-collar crime. *Journal of Financial Crime, 22*(3), 305–317.

Doctor "threatened to withhold drugs from patient if she refused to have sex." (2009, August 24). *Telegraph*. Retrieved from www.telegraph.co.uk

Dodd, V. (2020). Oxford professor arrested on suspicion of ancient papyrus theft. *The Guardian*. Retrieved from https://www.theguardian.com/uk-news/2020/apr/16/oxford-professor-arrested-ancient-papyrus-bible-theft-dirk-obbink

Dodge, M. (2013). The importance of integrating victimology in white-collar crime: A targeted comment on Barak's analysis in theft of a nation. *Western Criminology Review, 14*(2), 27–30.

Dodge, M. (2016). Gender constructions. In S. R. Van Slyke, M. L. Benson, & F. T. Cullen (Eds.), *The Oxford handbook of white-collar crime* (pp. 200–216). New York, NY: Oxford University Press.

Dodge, M. (2020). Who commits corporate crime? In M. Rorie (Ed.), *Handbook of White-Collar Crime* (pp. 113–126). New York, NY: John Wiley & Sons.

Dodge, M., Bosick, S. J., & Van Antwerp, V. (2013). Do men and women perceive white-collar crime and street crime differently? Exploring gender differences in the perception of motives, seriousness, and punishment. *Journal of Contemporary Criminal Justice, 29*(3), 399–415.

Donnelly, E. A., & Salvatore, N. J. (2019). Emerging patterns in federal responses to police misconduct: review of pattern or practice agreements over time. *Criminology, Criminal Justice, Law & Society, 20*(3), 23–45.

Donato, L. (2009). An introduction to how criminal profiling could be used as a support for computer hacking investigations. *Journal of Digital Forensic Practice, 2*, 183–195.

Donohue, K. (2004). *Statement of Kenneth Donohue, Inspector General Department of Housing and Urban Development. Statement before the House of Representatives Subcommittee on Housing and Community Opportunity Committee on Financial Services*. Retrieved from www.hud.gov/offices/oig/data/DonohueTestify10-7.doc

Donsanto, C. C., & Simmons, N. (2007). *Federal prosecutions of elected officials* (7th ed.). Washington, DC: U.S. Department of Justice.

doodlebug. (2009, August 4). Joel Tenenbaum fined $675,000 for illegally downloading music [Web log post]. *SodaHead Opinions*. Retrieved from http://www.sodahead.com/living/joel-tenenbaum-fined-675k-for-illegally-downloading-music-does-the-punishment-fit-thecrime/question-538253/

Dorn, N., Van Daele, S., & Vander Beken, T. (2007). Reducing vulnerabilities to crime of the European waste management industry: The research base and the prospects for policy. *European Journal of Crime, Criminal Law, and Criminal Justice, 15*(1), 23–36.

Doughman, A. (2010, May 21). Judge says UW can fire assistant research professor. *The Seattle Times*. Retrieved from http://seattletimes.nwsource.com/html/localnews/2011924401_aprikyan22m.html

Doyle, C. (2014). Cybercrime: An overview of the federal computer fraud and abuse statute and related federal criminal laws. *Journal of Current Issues in Crime, Law and Law Enforcement, 5*(2), 69–162.

Duran, D. (2015, December 17). Hoping for forgiveness for transgressions. *Clovis News Journal*. Retrieved from http://www.cnjonline.com/2015/12/17/letter-to-the-editor-dec-18

Dye, C., & Mano, R. (2016). Utah's white collar crime registry. *ACFE Fraud Basics*. Retrieved from https://www.acfe.com/article.aspx?id=4294994113.

E&T Editorial Staff. (2020). Former Waymo and Uber engineer jailed for trade secret theft. *Engineering and Technology*. Available online at https://eandt.theiet.org/content/articles/2020/08/former-waymo-and-uber-engineer-jailed-for-trade-secret-theft

Edelhertz, H. (1983). White-collar and professional crime: The challenge for the 1980s. *American Behavioral Scientist*, *27*, 109–128.

Edwards, M. A. (2020). The concept and federal crime of mortgage fraud. *American Criminal Law Review, 57*(1), 57–108.

Egan, M. (2016). 5,300 Wells Fargo employees fired over 2 million phony accounts. *CNN Business*. Retrieved from https://money.cnn.com/2016/09/08/investing/wells-fargo-created-phony-accounts-bank-fees/index.html.

Egan. P. (2020, May 26). Whitmer says husband's boat dock request was bad joke: 'I wasn't laughing either.' *Detroit Free Press*. Retrieved from https://www.freep.com/story/news/local/michigan/2020/05/26/whitmer-husband-boat-launch-marc-mallory/5259644002/

Efrati, A. (2009, May 7). Madoff relatives got millions, court filing says; disgraced financier's long-time secretary says she believes he isn't cooperating with investigators in order to protect others. *Wall Street Journal*, p. B11.

Eidelson, J., & Soper, S. (2016, March 7). *How Amazon shames warehouse workers for alleged theft*. Retrieved from http://www.bloomberg.com/news/articles/2016-03-07/amazon-s-story- time-is-kind-of-a-bummer

Eisler, P., & Hansen, B. (2013, June 19). Doctors perform thousands of unnecessary surgeries. *USA Today*. Retrieved from https://www.usatoday.com/story/news/nation/2013/06/18/unnecessary-surgery-usa-today-investigation/2435009/

Elis, L. A., & Simpson, S. S. (1995). Informal sanction threats and corporate crime: Additive versus multiplicative models. *Journal of Research in Crime & Delinquency, 32*(4), 399.

Ellis, B., & Hicken, M. (2017). Sick, dying, and raped in America's nursing homes. *CNN.com*. https://www.cnn.com/interactive/2017/02/health/nursing-home-sex-abuse-investigation/

Enste, D. H., & Heldman, C. (2018). The consequences of corruption. In B. Ward (Ed.), *Handbook on the Geographies of Corruption* (106–119). Cheltenham, UK: Edward Elgar.

Epstein, J. (2011, February 10). Tom Delay lawyers seek a retrial. *Politico*. Retrieved from http://www.politico.com/news/stories/0211/49224.html

Ericson, R., & Doyle, A. (2006). The institutionalization of deceptive sales in life insurance. *British Journal of Criminology, 46*, 993–1010.

Ermann, M. D., & Lundman, R. (1978). *Corporate and governmental deviance: Problems of organizational behavior in contemporary society*. New York, NY: Oxford University Press.

Ermann, M. D., & Lundman, R. (2002). *Corporate and governmental deviance* (6th ed.). New York, NY: Oxford University Press.

Escalares, M., Calcagno, P. T., & Shughart, W. (2012). Corruption and voter participation: Evidence from the U.S. states. *Public Finance Review*. https://doi.org/10.1177%2F1091142112446846

Etters, K. (2020). Former Trulieve employee accused of stealing marijuana, selling it; more arrests possible. *Tallahassee Democrat*. Retrieved from https://www.tallahassee.com/story/news/2020/02/21/former-trulieve-employee-accused-stealing-marijuana-and-selling-illegally/4831031002

Euben, D., & Lee, B. (2005, February 22). *Faculty misconduct and discipline*. Paper presented at the National Conference on Law and Higher Education, Stetson University College of Law. Retrieved from http://www.aaup.org/AAUP/programs/legal/topics/misconduct–discp.htm

Evans, R. D., & Porche, D. A. (2005). The nature and frequency of Medicare/Medicaid fraud and neutralization techniques among speech, occupational, and physical therapists. *Deviant Behavior, 26*, 253–270.

Evans, S. S., & Scott, J. E. (1984). Effects of item order on the perceived seriousness of crime: A reexamination. *Journal of Research in Crime & Delinquency, 21*, 139–151.

Ex-mayor in "jail-sex" row. (1992, January 6). *Daily Telegraph*, p. 3.

Ex-pastor testifies in embezzlement trial. (2010, September 2). *Wolfe Bank News and Shoes (WBNS)-10TV*. Retrieved from http://www.10tv.com/live/content/local/stories/2010/09/02/story-columbus-ex-pastortestifies-embezzlement-trial.html?sid=102

Ex U.S. mortgage executive charged with huge fraud. (2010, June 16–17). *Reuters*. Retrieved from http://in.mobile.reuters.com/article/businessNews/idUSN1614313320100616

Faichney, D. (2014). Comments: Autocorrect? A proposal to encourage voluntary restitution through white-collar sentencing calculus. *The Journal of Law & Criminology, 104*(2), 389–430.

Fair, L. (2019). $191 million FTC settlement with University of Phoenix addresses deceptive employment claims. *Federal Trade Commission Blog*. Retrieved from https://www.ftc.gov/news-events/blogs/business-blog/2019/12/191-million-ftc-settlement-university-phoenix-addresses.

Falkenberg, K. (2008, December 22). Time off for bad behavior: White-collar offenders can get a year off their terms for doing rehab. *Forbes*. Retrieved from http://www.forbes.com/2008/12/20/prison-crime-waksal-biz-beltway-cz_kf_1222prison.html

Famighetti, C., Keith, D., & Pérez, M. (2017). *Noncitizen voting: The missing millions*. New York: Brennan Center for Justice at New York University School of Law.

Fannie Mae. (2007). *Mortgage fraud overview*. Retrieved, from www.efanniemae.com/utility/legal/pdf/mtgfraudoverview.pdf

Faragher, J. (2007, December 4). Shut out. *Personnel Today*, 22–23.

Faria, R. (2018). *Research misconduct as white-collar crime: A criminological approach*. New York, NY: Springer.

Farole, D. J. (2009). *Contract bench and jury trials in state courts, 2005*. Washington, DC: Bureau of Justice Statistics. Retrieved from http://www.bjs.gov/content/pub/pdf/cbajtsc05.pdf.

Fasanello, D., Umans, L., & White, T. (2011). Financial institutions fraud. *The American Criminal Law Review, 48*(2), 697–748.

Fatal crash spurs review of Toyota floor mats. (2009, September 15). *Associated Press*. Retrieved from at http://beta2.tbo.com/business/breaking-news-business/2009/sep/15/fatalcrash-spurs-review-toyota-floor-mats-ar-74585/

Fattah, E. A., & Sacco, V. F. (1989). Offences the elderly commit and their explanations. In *Crime and victimization of the elderly* (pp. 34–68). New York, NY: Springer.

FDA: Georgia plant knowingly sold peanut butter tainted with salmonella. (2009). *NYDailyNews.com*. Retrieved from http://articles.nydailynews.com/2009-02-06/news/17916106_1_private-lab-tests-peanut-butter-usda

Fearn, H. (2008, May 22). Sex and the university. *The Times Higher Education Supplement*. Retrieved from http://www.timeshighereducation.co.uk/story.asp?sectioncode=26&storycode=40193 5&c=1.

Federal Bureau of Investigation (FBI). (2005). *Mortgage fraud operation "quick flip."* [Press release]. Retrieved, from http://www.fbi.gov/pressrel/pressrel05/quickflip121405.htm

Federal Bureau of Investigation (FBI). (2009). *2008 financial crimes report*. Retrieved from http://www.fbi.gov/stats-services/publications/fcs_report2008

Federal Bureau of Investigation (FBI). (2010a). *2009 financial crimes report*. Retrieved from http://www.fbi.gov/stats-services/publications/financial-crimes-report-2009

Federal Bureau of Investigation (2010b). *Internet crime complaints on the rise*. Retrieved from http://www.fbi.gov/news/stories/2010/march/ic3_031710

Federal Bureau of Investigation. (2018). *2018 crime in the United States*. Retrieved from https://ucr.fbi.gov/crime-in-the-u.s/2018/crime-in-the-u.s.-2018/tables/table-23

Federal Bureau of Investigation. (2019, April 9). *Billion-Dollar Medicare fraud bust: FBI announces results of Operation Brace Yourself*. Retrieved from https://www.fbi.gov/news/stories/billion-dollar-medicare-fraud-bust-040919

Federal Bureau of Investigation. (2020). *What we investigate: White-collar crime*. Retrieved from https://www.fbi.gov/investigate/white-collar-crime

Federal Deposit Insurance Corporation (FDIC). (2007). *Staying alert to mortgage fraud*. Retrieved from http://www.fdic.gov/regulations/examinations/supervisory/insights/sisum07/article02_staying-alert.html

Federal Trade Commission (FTC). (2001). Advertising FAQs: A guide for small businesses. Retrieved from http://business.ftc.gov/documents/bus35-advertising-faqs-guide-small business.pdf

Federal Trade Commission (FTC). (2010). *Price discrimination among buyers: Robinson-Patman violations*. Retrieved from http://www.ftc.gov/bc/antitrust/price_discrimination.shtm

Federal Trade Commission. (2020, March 4). *Marketers of pain relief device settle FTC false advertising complaint*. Retrieved from https://www.ftc.gov/news-events/press-releases/2020/03/marketers-pain-relief-device-settle-ftc-false-advertising

Federal Trade Commission. (2020, March 19). *Health Center, Inc. settles FTC allegations that it targeted older consumers with deceptive claims for health and wellness products*. Retrieved from https://www.ftc.gov/news-events/press-releases/2020/03/health-center-inc-settles-ftc-allegations-it-targeted-older

Federal Trade Commission. (2020, May 13). *Operators of business coaching scheme will pay at least $1.2 million to settle FTC charges they deceived consumers starting new Internet-based businesses*. Retrieved from https://www.ftc.gov/news-events/press-releases/2020/05/operators-business-coaching-scheme-will-pay-least-12-million

Federal Trade Commission. (2020, June 25). *FTC puts an end to deceptive advertising of light therapy device*. Retrieved from https://www.ftc.gov/news-events/press-releases/2020/06/ftc-puts-end-deceptive-advertising-light-therapy-device

Federal Trade Commission. (2020, July 27). *In final court summary, FTC reports Volkswagen repaid more than $9.5 billion to car buyers who were deceived by "Clean Diesel" ad campaign.* Retrieved from https://www.ftc.gov/news-events/press-releases/2020/07/final-court-summary-ftc-reports-volkswagen-repaid-more-than-9-billion

Federal Trade Commission (FTC). (n.d.). *Guide to antitrust laws.* Retrieved from http://www.ftc.gov/bc/antitrust/factsheets/antitrustlawsguide.pdf

Feiden, D. (2010). Trump U. hit by complaints from those who paid up to 30G, and say they got very little in return. *New York Daily News.* Retrieved from https://www.nydailynews.com/news/trump-u-hit-complaints-paid-30g-return-article-1.446342

Feiner, L., & Rodriguez, S. (2019). FTC slaps Facebook with record $5 billion fine, orders privacy oversight. *CNBC.com.* Retrieved from https://www.cnbc.com/2019/07/24/facebook-to-pay-5-billion-for-privacy-lapses-ftc-announces.html

Feldman, S. (2009, April 30). Dangerous liaisons. *The Times Higher Education Supplement.* Retrieved from http://www.timeshigher education.co.uk/story.asp?storyCode=406375&sectioncode=26

Fernandez, A. (2019, December 2). Felicity Huffman is all smiles after doing community service following Thanksgiving. *People.* Retrieved from https://people.com/movies/felicity-huffman-leaves-community-service-after-thanksgiving

Financial Crimes Enforcement Network (FinCEN). (2009). *Mortgage loan fraud connections with other financial crime.* Retrieved from http://www.fincen.gov/news_room/rp/files/mortgage_fraud.pdf

Financial Crimes Enforcement Network (FinCEN). (2010a, April 27). *FINCEN warns lenders to guard against home equity conversion mortgage fraud schemes.* Retrieved from http://www.fincen.gov/news_room/nr/pdf/20100427.pdf

Financial Crimes Enforcement Network (FinCEN). (2010b, December 14). *Mortgage fraud suspicious activity reports rise 7 percent.* Retrieved from http://www.fincen.gov/news_room/nr/pdf/20101214.pdf

Financial Crimes Enforcement Network (FinCEN). (2020). *SAR Stats.* Retrieved from https://www.fincen.gov/reports/sar-stats

Finkel, E. (2014, July). Law firms' own employees are among the major cyberthreats to be protected against. *ABA Journal.* Retrieved from http://www.abajournal.com/magazine/article/law_firms_own_employees_are_among_the_major_cyberthreats_they_must_protect_

Fischer, A., & Sheppard, J. (2008). Financial institutions fraud. *American Criminal Law Review, 45,* 531–559.

Fisher, A. (2015, January 26). U.S. retail workers are no. 1 . . . in employee theft. *Fortune.* Retrieved from http://fortune.com/2015/01/26/us-retail-worker-theft/

Fisse, B. (1991). Introduction: Corporate and whitecollar crime. *Current Issues in Criminal Justice, 3*(1), 7–8.

Fitzgerald, J. D., & Cox, S. M. (1994). *Research methods in criminal justice.* Belmont, CA: Cengage.

Fitzgerald, L. F. (1990). Sexual harassment: The measurement of a construct. In M. Paludi (Ed.), *Ivory power: Sexual harassment on campus* (pp. 21–44). New York, NY: State University of New York Press.

Flitter, E. (2020). The price of Wells Fargo's fake account scandal grows by $3 billion. *New York Times.* Retrieved from https://www.nytimes.com/2020/02/21/business/wells-fargo-settlement.html#:~:text=Wells%20Fargo%20has%20agreed%20to,to%20meet%20impossible%20sales%20goals

Florida OKs emergency adjusters, brings in fraud strike teams for Sally recovery. (2020, September 23). *Insurance Journal.* Retrieved from https://www.insurancejournal.com/news/southeast/2020/09/23/583761.htm

Foley, K. (2017). Worldwide reliance: Is it enough: The importance of personal jurisdiction and push for minimum contacts in prosecuting foreign defendants for financial crime. *DePaul Law Review, 67*(1), 139–168.

Foli, K. J., Reddick, B., Zhang, L., & Edwards, N. (2019). Substance use in registered nurses: Where legal, medical, and personal collide. *Journal of Nursing Regulation, 10*(2), 45–54.

Foo, L. J. (1994). The vulnerable and exploitable immigrant workforce and the need for strengthening worker protective legislation. *Yale Law Journal, 103*(8), 2179–2212.

Forti, G., & Visconti, A. (2020). From economic crime to corporate violence: The multifaceted harms of corporate crime. In M. Rorie (Ed.), *The handbook of white-collar crime* (pp. 64–80). New York, NY: John Wiley & Sons.

Fox, M. F. (1994). Scientific misconduct and editorial and peer review processes. *Journal of Higher Education, 65*(3), 298–309.

Francis, A., & Ryder, N. (2020). Preventing and intervening in white collar crimes: The role of regulatory agencies. In M. Rorie (Ed.), *The handbook of white-collar crime* (pp. 262–278). New York, NY: John Wiley & Sons.

Frank, N. (1984). Policing corporate crime: A typology of enforcement styles. *Justice Quarterly, 1*(2), 235–251.

Frank, N. (1993). Maiming and killing: Occupational health crimes. *Annals of Political and Social Science, 525,* 107–118.

Frank, N. K., & Lynch, M. J. (1992). *Corporate crime, corporate violence: A primer.* Albany, NY: Harrow and Heston.

Frankel, T. (2006). *Trust and honesty: America's business culture at a crossroad.* New York, NY: Oxford University Press.

Frankel, T. (2018). Insider trading. *SMU Law Review, 71*(3), 783–798.

Frankel, T. (2020). Product recalls under Trump fall to lowest level in about 16 years. *Columbia Daily Herald.* Retrieved from https://www.columbiadailyherald.com/news/20200113/product-recalls-under-trump-fall-to-lowest-level-in-about-16-years

Frean, A., & Lea, R. (2010, February 3). Toyota recall: Last words from a family killed as Lexus crashed. *The Times.* Retrieved from http://www.timesonline.co.uk/tol/news/world/us_and_americas/article7012913.ece

Friedman, J. (2019). Cal Poly professor convicted of peeping up colleague's skirt. *Coastalnews.com.* Retrieved from https://calcoastnews.com/2019/09/cal-poly-professor-convicted-of-peeping-up-colleagues-skirt

Friedman, M. (2009, September 28). Retailers report "shrinkage" of inventory on the rise. *Arkansas Business, 26*(39), 17.

Friedrichs, D. (2004). Enron et al.: Paradigmatic white collar crime cases for the new century. *Critical Criminology, 12,* 113–132.

Friedrichs, D. O. (2002). Occupational crime, occupational deviance, and workplace crime: Sorting out the difference. *Criminology and Criminal Justice, 2,* 243–256.

Friedrichs, D. O. (2019). White collar crime: Definitional debates and the case for a typological approach. In M. Rorie (Ed.), *The handbook of white-collar crime* (pp. 16–31). New York, NY: John Wiley & Sons.

Friedrichs, D. O., & Rothe, D. L. (2020). Regulatory rollback and white-collar crime in the era of Trump: The challenges of perspective. *Journal of White Collar and Corporate Crime, 1*(2), 95–102.

Frongillo, T. C., Simons, C. K., Essinger, J., & Knowles, M. (2014). The reinvigorated confrontation clause: A new basis to challenge the admission of evidence from nontestifying forensic experts in white collar prosecutions. *Defense Counsel Journal, 18*(1), 11–31.

Fugitive phony doctor nabbed. (October 12, 2004). *Reuters.* Retrieved from http://www.sysopt.com/forum/showthread.php? t=171184

Furnell, S. (2008). End-user security culture: A lesson that will never be learnt? *Computer Fraud & Security, 4,* 6–9.

Futty, J. (2010, July 16). Man sentenced for illegal tire dumping. *Columbus Dispatch.* Retrieved from http://www.dispatch.com/live/content/local_news/stories/2010/07/16/tire_dumping.html

Fyfe, J. J., & Kane, R. (2005). *Bad cops: A study of career-ending misconduct among New York City police officers.* Rockville, MD: National Institute of Justice.

Galbraith, J. K. (2005). Introduction: Control fraud and economic criminology [Editorial]. *Journal of Socioeconomics, 34,* 731–733.

Galvin, M. A., Loughran, T. A., Simpson, S. S., & Cohen, M. A. (2018). Victim compensation policy and white-collar crime: Public preferences in a national willingness-to-pay survey. *Criminology & Public Policy, 17*(3), 553–594.

Gall v. United States, 552 U.S. 38 (2007).

Galvin, M. A., & Simpson, S. S. (2019). In M. Rorie (Ed.), Prosecuting and sentencing white-collar crime in U.S. federal courts: Revisiting the Yale findings. *The handbook of white-collar crime* (pp. 381–397). New York, NY: John Wiley & Sons.

Gandel, S. (2020). Moderna CEO and other execs made millions on vaccine announcement. *CBS News.* Retrieved from https://www.cbsnews.com/news/moderna-ceo-executives-made-millions-on-vaccine-announcement

Garoupa, N. (2005). The economics of business crime: Theory and public policy. *Security Journal, 18*(1), 24–41.

Garrett, B. L. (2020). Declining corporate prosecutions. *American Criminal Law Review, 57*(1), 109–156.

Garrett, R. (2010, April). Digital defense begins at home: Protecting the Internet's digital borders begins with protecting local citizens from cyber harm. *Law Enforcement Technology,* 16–22.

Gauthier, D. K. (2001). Professional lapses: Occupational deviance and neutralization techniques in veterinary medical practice. *Deviant Behavior, 22*(6), 467–490.

Geis, G. (1975). Victims of crimes of violence and the criminal justice system. In D. Chappell & J. Monahan (Eds.), *Violence and criminal justice.* Lexington, MA: Lexington Books.

Geis, G. (1978). White-collar crime. *Crime and Delinquency, 24,* 89–90.

Geis, G. (2000). On the absence of self-control as the basis for a general theory of crime: A critique. *Theoretical Criminology, 4,* 35–53.

Geis, G., & Dimento, J. (1995). Should we prosecute corporations and/or individuals? In F. Pearce & L. Snider (Eds.),

Corporate crime: Contemporary debates (pp. 72–90). Toronto, Ontario, Canada: University of Toronto Press.

Geis, G., Jesilow, P., Pontell, H., & O'Brien, M. (1985). Fraud and abuse of government medical programs by psychiatrists. *American Journal of Psychiatry, 142*, 231–234.

Geisler, S. (2020). Landlords or slumlords? *The New Englander eNewspaper*. Retrieved from https://www.the-new-englander.com/2020/02/05/landlords-or-slumlords

Gerber, J. (1994). "Club Fed" in Japan? Incarceration experiences of Japanese embezzlers. *International Journal of Offender Therapy and Comparative Criminology, 38*(2), 163–174.

Gerber, J., Jensen, E. L., & Fritsch, E. J. (1996). Politics and white collar crime: Explaining government intervention in the savings and loan scandal. *Critical Criminology, 7*(2), 59–73.

Gershman, B. (1999). Judicial misconduct during jury deliberations. In L. Stolzenberg & S. J. D'Alessio (Eds.), *Criminal courts for the 21st century* (pp. 291–314). Upper Saddle River, NJ: Prentice Hall.

Gershman, B. L. (1982). Abscam, the judiciary, and the ethics of entrapment. *Yale Law Journal, 91*(8), 1565–1591.

Ghandnoosh, N. (2014). Race and punishment: Racial perceptions of crime and support for punitive policies. *The Sentencing Project*. Retrieved from https://www.sentencingproject.org/publications/race-and-punishment-racial-perceptions-of-crime-and-support-for-punitive-policies/#B.%20The%20Racial%20Gap%20in%20Punitiveness

Ghiselli, R., & Ismail, J. A. (1998). Employee theft and efficacy of certain control procedures in commercial food service operations. *Journal of Hospitality & Tourism Research, 22*, 174–187.

Gibbs, C. (2012). Corporate citizenship and corporate environmental performance. *Crime, Law and Social Change, 57*, 345–372.

Gibbs, C., & Pugh, D. (2017). An ounce of prevention: Opportunity structures for white-collar crime in environmental markets. *Crime, Law & Social Change, 67*(2), 133–151. https://doi-org.proxy.lib.odu.edu/10.1007/s10611-016-9667-x

Gibson Dunn. (2015). *2014 year-end update on corporate non-prosecution agreements (NPAs) and deferred prosecution agreements (DPAs)*. Retrieved from http://www.gibsondunn.com/publications/Pages/2014-Year-End-Update-Corporate-Non-Prosecution-Agreements-and-Deferred-Prosecution-Agreements.aspx

Gibson, K. (2000). Excuses, excuses: Moral slippage in the workplace. *Business Horizons, 43*, 65–85.

Gilbert, D., & Kent, S. (2015, July 2). Spill claims: Settlement of all federal and state claims brings total costs to nearly $54 billion. *The Wall Street Journal*. Retrieved from http://www.wsj.com/articles/bp-agrees-to-pay-18-7-billion-to-settle-deepwater-horizon-oilspill-claims-1435842739

Gill, M. (2011). Fraud and recessions: Views from fraudsters and fraud managers. *International Journal of Law, Crime and Justice, 39*, 204–214.

Givens, A. D., & Busch, N. E. (2013). Investigating federal approaches to post-cyber incident mitigation. *Homeland Security & Emergency Management, 10*(1), 1–28.

Glasberg, D. S., & Skidmore, D. (1998a). The dialectics of white-collar crime: The anatomy of the savings and loan crisis and the case of Silverado Banking, Savings and Loan Association. *American Journal of Economics and Sociology, 57*(4), 423–449.

Glasberg, D. S., & Skidmore, D. L. (1998b). The role of the state in the criminogenesis of corporate crime: A case study of the savings and loan crisis. *Social Science Quarterly, 79*(1), 110–128.

Glazer, M. (1983, December). Ten whistleblowers and how they fared. *Hastings Center Report, 13*(6), 33–41.

Glink, I. (2009). *Mortgage fraud v. 2009*. Retrieved from http://moneywatch.bnet.com/saving-money/blog/home-equity/mortgagefraud-v2009/715/

Global Witness. (2017). *Global Witness annual report 2017*. Retrieved from https://www.globalwitness.org/en/about-us/annual-reviews/

Global Witness. (2019). *Annual report 2019: Protecting people and planet*. Retrieved from https://www.globalwitness.org/en/about-us/annual-report-2019-protecting-people-and-planet/

Glor, J. (2010, January 29). Toyota recall costing the automaker dearly. *Columbia Broadcasting System (CBS) News*. Retrieved from http://www.cbsnews.com/stories/2010/01/29/business/main6153710.shtml

Glovin, D. (2009a, March 17). Madoff property is subject to forfeiture, U.S. says. *The Globe and Mail*, p. B13.

Glovin, D. (2009b, April 4). Mum's the word; Madoff 's secret say nothing about methods. *The Gazette*, p. C4.

Goel, R. K., & Nelson, M. A. (2011). Government fragmentation versus fiscal decentralization ad corruption. *Public Choice, 148*, 471–490.

Gogolin, G. (2011). The chasm between law enforcement and digital crime. *Journal of Current Issues in Crime, Law and Law Enforcement, 4*(4), 469–478.

Goh, E., & Kong, S. (2018). Theft in the hotel workplace: Exploring frontline employees' perceptions towards hotel employee theft. *Tourism and Hospitality Research, 18*(4), 442–455.

Gold, M. (2019, May 14). Anthony Weiner released from prison after serving 18 months for sexting teenager. *The New York Times*. Retrieved from https://www.nytimes.com/2019/05/14/nyregion/anthony-weiner-prison-release.html

Goldman, B. M., Gutek, B. A., Stein, J. H., & Lewis, K. (2006). Employment discrimination in organizations: Antecedents and consequences. *Journal of Management, 32*, 786–830.

Goldman, Z. K., & McCoy, D. (2016). Deterring financially motivated cybercrime. *Journal of National Security Law and Policy, 8*(3), 595–620.

Goldsmith, J., & Gluck, M. (2020, July 11). Trump's aberrant pardons and commutations. *Lawfare*. Retrieved from https://www.lawfareblog.com/trumps-aberrant-pardons-and-commutations

Goldsmith, M., & King, C. W. (1997). Policing corporate crime: The dilemma of internal compliance programs. *Vanderbilt Law Review, 50*(1), 1–47.

Goodboy, A. K., & Myers, S. A. (2015). Revisiting instructor misbehaviors: A revised typology and development of a measure. *Communication Education, 64*(2), 133–153.

Goodchild, J. (2008, December 1). Criminology professor Hollinger on forthcoming results from the National Retail Security Survey and trends in retail shrinkage. *CSO Online*. Retrieved from http://www.csoonline.com/article/461365/richard-hollinger-on-shoplifting-and-retail-shrink

Goodman, L. M. (2014, June 26). Nonsensical sentences for white collar criminals. *Newsweek*. Retrieved from http://www.news week.com/2014/07/04/nonsensical-sentenceswhite-collar-criminals-256104.html

Gore, M. L., Braszak, P., Brown, J., Cassey, P., Duffy, R., Fisher, J., . . . & White, R. (2019). Transnational environmental crime threatens sustainable development. *Nature Sustainability, 2*(9), 784–786.

Gordon, A. M. (2014). Rational choice and moral decision making in research. *Ethics & Behavior, 24*(3), 175–194.

Gordon, R. A., Michels, J. L., & Nelson, C. L. (1996). Majority group perceptions of criminal behavior: The accuracy of race-related crime stereotypes. *Journal of Applied Social Psychology, 26*, 148–159.

Gottfredson, M. R., & Hirschi, T. (1990). *A general theory of crime*. Stanford, CA: Stanford University Press.

Gottschalk, P. (2014a). *Financial crime and knowledge workers: An empirical study of defense lawyers and white-collar criminals*. New York, NY: Palgrave Macmillan.

Gottschalk, P. (2014b). White-collar crime defense knowledge: Predictors of lawyer fame. *Journal of Information & Knowledge Management, 13*(1), 1–9.

Gottschalk, P. (2017a). Entrepreneurs in white-collar crime: A convenience perspective. *International Journal of Entrepreneurial Knowledge, 5*(2), 47–55.

Gottschalk, P. (2017b). How to assess work by fraud examiners: Evaluation criteria for private internal investigations. *Pakistan Journal of Criminology, 9*(1), 1.

Gottschalk, P. (2020). From crime convenience to punishment inconvenience: The case of detected white-collar offenders. *Deviant Behavior*, 1–11.

Gottschalk, P., & Glase, L. (2013). Corporate crime does pay! The relationship between financial crime and imprisonment in white-collar crime. *International Letters of Social and Humanistic Sciences, 5*, 63–78.

Grabosky, P., & Gant, F. (2000). *Improving environmental performance, preventing environmental crime*. Canberra, Australia: Australian Institute of Criminology.

Grady, T. (2003, December). Repairers balk at study citing 42 percent fraud rate. *Automotive Body Repair News, 42*(12), p. 1.

Grande, G., Ljungman, P., Eneroth, K., Bellander, T., & Rizzuto, D. (2020). Long-term exposure to air pollution and the risk of dementia: The role of cardiovascular disease (1839). *Neurology, 94*(15 Supplement). Retrieved from https://n.neurology.org/content/94/15_Supplement/1839.abstract

Grantin, L. (2020). Fultondale doctor pleads guilty to health care fraud. *WVTM13*. Retrieved from https://www.wvtm13.com/article/fultondale-doctor-demopolis-pharmacist-pleads-guilty-to-healthcare-fraud/32376842#

Grasmick, H. G., Tittle, C. R., Bursik, R. J., Jr., & Arneklev, B. J. (1993). Testing the core empirical implications of Gottfredson and Hirschi's general theory of crime. *Journal of Research in Crime & Delinquency, 30*, 5–29.

Graves, J. T., Acquisti, A., & Anderson, R. (2019). Perception versus punishment in cybercrime. *Journal of Criminal Law and Criminology, 109*(2), 313–364.

Gray, C. (2004). The line between legal error and judicial misconduct: Balancing judicial independence and accountability. *Hofstra Final, 32*, 1245–1269.

Gray, D., Citron, D. K., & Rinehart, L. C. (2013). Fighting cybercrime after *United States v. Jones*. *The Journal of Criminal Law & Criminology, 103*(3), 745–801.

Great White band manager faces relatives. (2006, May 9). *FoxNews.com*. Retrieved from http://www.foxnews.com/story/0, 2933,194658,00.html.

Green, A. (2019). Fred Meyer loss prevention manager gets prison for stealing $230,000. *OregonLive*. Retrieved from https://www.oregonlive.com/news/2019/04/fred-meyer-loss-prevention-officer-gets-4-years-in-prison-for-stealing-230000-on-surveillance-video.html

Green, G., & Bodapati, M. (1999). The "deterrence trap" in the federal fining of organizations: A research note. *Criminal Justice Policy Review, 10*(4), 547–559.

Green, G. S. (1990). *Occupational crime*. Chicago, IL: Nelson-Hall.

Green, G. S. (1993). White-collar crime and the study of embezzlement. *Annals of the American Academy of Political and Social Science, 525*, 95–106.

Green, S. (2007, December 11). Washing toilets for 12 cents an hour; Florida jail won't be Disney World. *Toronto Sun*, p. 4.

Greife, M. J., & Maume, M. O. (2020a). Stealing like artists: Using court records to conduct quantitative research on corporate environmental crimes. *Journal of Contemporary Criminal Justice, 36*(3), 451–469.

Greife, M. J., & Maume, M. O. (2020b). Do companies pay the price for environmental crimes? Consequences of criminal penalties on corporate offenders. *Crime, Law and Social Change, 73*(3), 337–356.

Greife, M., Stretesky, P. B., Shelley, T. O. C., & Pogrebin, M. (2017). Corporate environmental crime and environmental justice. *Criminal Justice Policy Review, 28*(4), 327–346.

Griffin, O., & Spillane, J. (2016). Confounding the process: Forgotten actors and factors in the state-corporate crime paradigm. *Crime, Law & Social Change, 66*(4), 421–437. https://doi-org.proxy.lib.odu.edu/10.1007/s10611-016-9634-6

Guastaferro, W. (2013). Crime, the media, and constructions of reality: Using HBO'S the wire as a frame of reference. *College Student Journal, 47*(2), 264–270.

Gubler, Z. J. (2020). Insider trading as fraud. *North Carolina Law Review, 98*(3), 533–594.

Gunter, W. D. (2009). Internet scallywags: A comparative analysis of multiple forms and measurements of digital piracy. *Western Criminology Review, 10*(1), 15–28.

Hackett, E. J. (1993). A new perspective on scientific medicine. *Academic Medicine, 68*(9, Suppl.), S72–S76.

Hagan, J. (1982). The corporate advantage: A study of the involvement of corporate and individual victims in a criminal justice system. *Social Forces, 60*(4), 993–1022.

Hagan, J., Nagel, I., & Albonetti, C. (1980). The differential sentencing of white-collar offenders in ten federal district courts. *American Sociological Review, 48*, 802–820.

Hagan, J., & Palloni, A. (1986). Club Fed and the sentencing of white-collar offenders before and after Watergate. *Criminology, 24*(4), 603–621.

Hagan, J., & Parker, P. (1985). White-collar crime and punishment: The class structure and legal sanctioning of securities violations. *American Sociological Association, 50*(3), 302–316.

Hagedorn, G., Kalmus, P., Mann, M., Vicca, S., Van Den Berge, J., van Ypersele, J-P., . . . Hayhoey, K. (2019).Concerns of young protesters are justified. *Science*. Retrieved from https://science.sciencemag.org/content/364/6436/139.2?__cf_chl_jschl_tk__=e3175e77a246179c06c342b7e6acbda6c6a06028-1616708219-0-ASxyGNLG80b5Cdz3tLNTIzn1mt71o6VgqdUFvhO1FiEmyaoy_bZkEEByOJ8NXzlIRBUdpkcbEhZm5ZzACfN7RmvDgUojPHLqGSdCc3ay8zrH7163zeg8VCGCHLclyO

Haiken, M. (2011, May 18). Annuities may not be a good choice for your parents. *Your Guide to Better Living*. Retrieved from http://www.betterliving.com/finance/2011/05/beware-annuities-may-not-be-a-good-choice-for-your-agingparents

Haines, F. (2014, February). Corporate fraud as misplaced confidence: Exploring ambiguity in the accuracy of accounts and the materiality of money. *Theoretical Criminology, 18*, 20–37.

Hajnal, Z., Lajevardi, N., & Nielson, L. (2017). Voter identification laws and the suppression of minority votes. *The Journal of Politics, 79*(2), 363–379.

Hale, C. (2002). Cybercrime: Facts & figures concerning this global dilemma. *Crime and Justice International, 18*(65), 5–26.

Hales, C. S. (2016). Fraud takes village: Charging considerations after seven connected mortgage fraud trials. *United States Attorneys' Bulletin, 64*(4), 53–58.

Hall, J., & Brajer, V. (2008). *Benefits of meeting federal clean air standards in the South Coast and San Joaquin Valley Air Basins*. Fullerton: California State University. Retrieved from http://business.fullerton.edu/centers/iees/reports/Benefits%20of%20Meeting%20Clean%20Air%20Standards.pdf

Hall, P. (2015, November 20). Lehigh university professor and wife convicted of cheating NASA. *The Morning Call*. Retrieved, from http://www.mcall.com/news/breaking/mc-lehigh professor-nasa-fraud-verdict-20151120-story.html

Halsey, M. (1997). The wood for the paper. *Australian and New Zealand Journal of Criminology, 30*, 121–148.

Halsey, M. (2004). Against "green" criminology. *British Journal of Criminology, 44*(6), 833–853.

Halsey, M., & White, R. (1998). Crime, ecophilosophy, and environmental harm. *Theoretical Criminology, 2*(3), 345–371.

Hamermesh, D. (2009, November 6). *Charity won't contain this secondary market.* Retrieved from http://www.freakonomics.com/2009/11/06/charity-wont-contain-this-secondary-market/

Hamm, M. S. (2007). "High crimes and misdemeanors": George W. Bush and the sins of Abu Ghraib. *Crime, Media, & Culture, 3*(3), 259–284.

Hammett, T. M., & Epstein, J. (1993). *Local prosecution of environmental crime (Technical Report).* Washington DC: National Institute of Justice.

Hanna, J., & Allen, K. (2019). *A nurse is charged with impregnating woman in vegetative state.* Retrieved from https://www.cnn.com/2019/01/23/health/arizona-woman-birth-vegetative-state

Hansard, S. (2007, June 18). Judges cracking down on securities fraud; States report more convictions, longer sentences. *Investment News.* Retrieved from http://www.investmentnews.com/article/20070618/FREE/70614017

Harbinson, E., Benson, M. L., & Latessa, E. J. (2019). Assessing risk among white-collar offenders under federal supervision in the community. *Criminal Justice and Behavior, 46*(2), 261–279.

Harker, T. C. (2018). Faithful execution: The persistent myth of widespread prosecutorial misconduct. *Tennessee Law Review, 85*(3), 847–iv.

Harknett, R. J., & Stever, J. A. (2009). The cybersecurity triad: Government, private sector partners, and the engaged cybersecurity citizen. *Journal of Homeland Security and Emergency Management, 6*(1), 1–14.

Harris, A. (1989, October 25). Jim Bakker gets 45-year sentence; Televangelist fined $500,000; Eligible for parole in 10 years. *The Washington Post.* Retrieved from http://www.highbeam.com/doc/1P2-1219165.html

Harris, D., & Benson, M. (1996). Nursing home theft: An overlooked form of elder abuse. In R. Cibik, R. Edwards, G. C. Graber, & F. H. Marsh (Eds.), *Advances in bioethics* (Vol. 1, pp. 171–188). Greenwich, CT: JAI Press.

Harris, D. K., & Benson, M. L. (1999). Theft in nursing homes: An overlooked form of elder abuse. *Journal of Elder Abuse & Neglect, 11*(3), 73–90.

Harris, G. (2009, March 10). Doctors' pain studies were fabricated, hospital says. *The New York Times.* Retrieved from http://www.nytimes.com/2009/03/11/health/research/11pain.html?_r=2&adxnnl=1&ref=us&adxnnlx=1312053446-quDa4FtMaqjedJ592V8caA

Harris, L. C., & He, H. (2019). Retail employee pilferage: A study of moral disengagement. *Journal of Business Research, 99*, 57–68.

Hasegawa, I. (2010). Film interview: Zac Efron and Claire Danes. *Buzzine.* Retrieved October 6, 2010, from http://www.buzzinefilm.com/interviews/film-zac-efron-claire-danes-01062010

Haugh, T. (2012). Can the CEO learn from the condemned? The application of capital mitigation strategies to white collar cases. *American University Law Review, 62*(1), 1–58.

Haugh, T. (2016-2017). Cadillac compliance breakdown. *Stanford Law Review Online, 69*, 198–208.

Haugh, T. (2017). Exactly wrong: Why the Trump Administration's stated policies will increase corporate crime. *Federal Sentencing Reporter, 29*(2–3), 91–92.

Hay, K. (2010, October 19). Asbestos disposal draws fine: Waste illegally put in dumpster. *Albuquerque Journal.* Retrieved from http://www.abqjournal.com/biz/192154380471biz10-19-10.htm

Hayman, G., & Brack, D. (2002). *International environmental crime: The nature and control of environmental black markets: Workshop report.* London, UK: Royal Institute of International Affairs, Sustainable Development Programme.

Hays, K. (2006, May 16). Lay, Skilling, used 'hocus pocus' to hide fraud, prosecutor tells jury. *The New York Times.* Retrieved from https://news.google.com/newspapers?nid=1665&dat=20060516&id=tXU0AAAAIBAJ&sjid=YCUEAAAAIBAJ&pg=4395,3364258&hl=en

Hazard, G. (1991). The future of legal ethics. *Yale Law Journal, 100*, 1239–1250.

Headworth, S., & Hagan, J. L. (2016). White-collar crimes of the financial crisis. In S. R. Van Slyke, M. L. Benson, & F. T. Cullen (Eds.), *The Oxford handbook of white-collar crime* (pp. 275–293). New York, NY: Oxford University Press.

Healy, B. (2009a, February 12). Madoff's wife pulled $15.5m from account withdrawals in weeks before husband's arrest. *The Boston Globe* (3rd ed.), p. A1.

Healy, B. (2009b, June 23). Broker aided Madoff, US says; Jaffe's profits called fraudulent; SEC seeks return of investigator money. *The Boston Globe*, p. 1.

Healy, B., & Mandell, H. (2009, March 13). An apologetic Madoff goes to jail; Admits to massive Ponzi scheme, awaits many-years sentence. *The Boston Globe*, p. A1.

Healy, B., & Syre, S. (2008, December 13). Boston donors bilked out of millions—Trader accused of $50 billion con game—One nonprofit closes; others may suffer. *The Boston Globe*, p. A1.

Healy, D., & McGrath, J. (2019). Simple rhetoric and complex punitiveness: Federal criminal justice responses to white-collar criminality. *Justice Quarterly*, *36*(7), 1258–1283.

Heenan, P. T., Klarfeld, J. L., Roussis, M. A., & Walsh, J. K. (2010). Securities fraud. *American Criminal Law Review*, *47*(2), 1015–1087.

Heil, K. A. (2019). The fuzz(y) lines of consent: Police sexual misconduct with detainees. *South Carolina Law Review*, *70*(4), 941–976.

Held, A. (2018). Michigan State University reaches $500 million settlement with Nassar abuse victims. *National Public Radio*. Retrieved from https://www.npr.org/sections/thetwo-way/2018/05/16/611624047/michigan-state-university-reaches-500-million-settlement-with-nassar-abuse-victi

Heller, K., (2019). Trump campaign held a Halloween witch hunt party. *Washington Post*. https://www.washingtonpost.com/lifestyle/style/the-trump-campaign-held-a-halloween-witch-hunt-party-and-tortured-a-metaphor-to-death/2019/10/31/25bcd214-fb7d-11e9-ac8c-8eced29ca6ef_story.html

Hemraj, M. B. (2002). The detection of financial irregularities in the U.S. corporations. *Journal of Financial Crime*, *10*(1), 85–90.

Henning, P. J. (2010, March 25). When legal bills become a cause for dispute. *The New York Times*. Retrieved from http://dealbook.blogs.nytimes.com/2010/02/01/when-legalbills-become-an-item-of-dispute

Henry, P. C. (2016). Individual accountability for corporate crimes after the yates memo: Deferred prosecution agreements & criminal justice reform. *American University Business Law Review*, *6*(1), 153–[vii].

Herbeck, D. (2019). Does Catholic Church have a bigger child sex abuse problem than other religions? *Buffalo News*. Retrieved from https://buffalonews.com/2019/08/16/does-catholic-church-have-bigger-child-sex-abuse-proble/

Herman, K., Sunshine, P., Fisher, M., Zwolenik, J., & Herz, J. (1994). Investigating misconduct in science. *Journal of Higher Education*, *65*, 384–400.

Hernandez, J. C. (2010, April 2). U.S. urges homeowners to remove Chinese drywall. *The New York Times*. Retrieved from http://www.nytimes.com/2010/04/03/business/03drywall.html

Heslop, G. (2007). Fraud at the top. *Internal Auditor*, *64*(2), 87–89.

Hewitt, J. (2016). Fifty shades of gray: Sentencing trends in major white-collar cases. *Yale Law Journal*, *125*(4), 1018–1071.

Heyboer, K. (2016). NJ college president details 2 years of hell in prison. *NJ.com*. Retrieved from https://www.nj.com/education/2016/04/nj_college_president_details_2_years_of_hell_in_pr.html

Heydon, J. (2019). Greening the concept of state crime. *State Crime Journal*, *8*(1), 39–58.

Higgins, G. E. (2006). Gender differences in software piracy: The mediating roles of self-control theory and social learning theory. *Journal of Economic Crime*, *4*(1), 1–22.

Higgins, G. E., Fell, B. D., & Wilson, A. L. (2006). Digital piracy: Assessing the contributions of an integrated self-control theory and social learning theory using structural equation modeling. *Criminal Justice Studies*, *19*(1), 3–22.

Hill, T. J., & Lezell, S. B. (2010). Antitrust violations. *American Criminal Law Review*, *47*(2), 245–285.

Hinduja, S. (2001). Correlates of Internet software piracy. *Journal of Contemporary Criminal Justice*, *17*, 369–382.

Hinduja, S., & Kooi, B. (2013). Curtailing cyber and information security vulnerabilities through situational crime prevention. *Security Journal*, *26*(4), 383–401.

Hippensteele, S. K., Adams, A. K., & Chesney, M. L. (1992). Sexual harassment in academia: Students' reactions to unprofessional behavior. *Journal of Criminal Justice Education*, *3*(2), 315–330.

Hirschi, T. (1969). *Causes of delinquency*. Berkeley, CA: University of California Press.

Hirschi, T., & Gottfredson, M. (1987). Causes of whitecollar crime. *Criminology*, *25*(4), 949–972.

Hiscox. (2018). *2018 Hiscox embezzlement study: An insider's view of employee theft*. New York, NY: Author. Retrieved from https://www.hiscox.com/documents/2018-Hiscox-Embezzlement-Study.pdf

Hochstetler, A., & Mackey, W. (2016). The pool of potential white-collar criminals. In S. R. Van Slyke, M. L. Benson, & F. T. Cullen (Eds.), *The Oxford handbook of white-collar crime* (pp. 149–167). New York, NY: Oxford University Press.

Hoffman, L. J., Burley, D., & Toregas, C. (2011, Nov. 11). Thinking across stovepipes: Using a holistic development strategy to build the cyber security workforce. *The George Washington University Cyber Security Policy and Research Institute*. Report GW-CSPRI-2011-8. Retrieved from http://static1.squarespace.com/static/53b2efd7e4b0018990a073c4/t/553e79b7e4b0c962703678cc/1430157751568/stovepipes_gw_cspri_report_2011_8.pdf

Hohn, D. A., Muftic, L. R., & Wolf, K. (2006). Swashbuckling students: An exploratory study of Internet policy. *Security Journal*, *19*, 110–127.

Hollinger, R. C., & Lanza-Kaduce, L. (1988). The process of criminalization: The case of computer crime laws. *Criminology*, *26*(1), 101–126.

Hollinger, R. C., Slora, K. B., & Terris, W. (1992). Deviance in the fast-food restaurant: Correlates of employee theft, altruism, and counterproductivity. *Deviant Behavior*, *13*(2), 155–184.

Holt, T. J. (2018). Regulating cybercrime through law enforcement and industry mechanisms. *The ANNALS of the American Academy of Political and Social Science*, *679*(1), 140–157.

Holt, T. J., & Bossler, A. M. (2008). Examining the applicability of lifestyle-routine activities theory for cybercrime victimization. *Deviant Behavior*, *30*, 1–25.

Holt, T. J., & Bossler, A. M. (2012). Police perceptions of computer crimes in two southeastern cities: An examination from the viewpoint of patrol officers. *American Journal of Criminal Justice*, *37*, 396–412.

Holt, T. J., & Bossler, A. M. (2013). Examining the relationship between routine activities and malware infection indicators. *Journal of Contemporary Criminal Justice*, *29*(4), 420–436.

Holt, T. J., Bossler, A. M., & May, D. C. (2012). Low self-control, deviant peer associations, and juvenile cyberdeviance. *American Journal of Criminal Justice*, *37*, 378–395.

Holt, T. J., & Lampke, E. (2010). Exploring stolen data markets online: Products and market force. *Criminal Justice Studies*, *23*(1), 33–50.

Holtfreter, K. (2004). Fraud in U.S. organisations: An examination of control mechanisms. *Journal of Financial Crime*, *12*(1), 88–95.

Holtfreter, K. (2005). Is occupational fraud "typical" white collar crime? A comparison of individual and organizational characteristics. *Journal of Criminal Justice*, *33*, 353–365.

Holtfreter, K., Reisig, M. D., & Pratt, T. C. (2008). Low self-control, routine activities, and fraud victimization. *Criminology*, *46*(1), 189–220.

Holtfreter, K., Van Slyke, S., Bratton, J., & Gertz, M. (2008). Public perceptions of white-collar crime and punishment. *Journal of Criminal Justice*, *36*, 50–60.

Holtz, D. (2009, March 21). Confections disappear, employee nabbed. *McClatchy-Tribune Business News*. Retrieved from ABI.

Homer, E. M., & Higgins, G. E. (2020). Community service sentencing for corporations. *Criminal Justice Policy Review*, 0887403420903379.

Howe, L. K. (1977). *Pink collar workers*. New York, NY: Avon.

Huber, N. (2010, August 6). Taking the risk out of hiring. *Caterer & Hotelkeeper*, *200*, 40. Retrieved from https://www.thecaterer.com/articles/334609/staff-screening-taking-therisk-out-of-hiring

Huckabee, C. (2009, March 15). *Professor whose article was retracted resigns from Harvard Medical School*. Chronicle of Higher Education. Retrieved from http://chronicle.com/article/Professor-Whose-Article-Was/42521

Huey, L., & Rosenberg, R. S. (2004). Watching the web: Thoughts on expanding police surveillance opportunities under the cyber-crime convention. *Canadian Journal of Criminology and Criminal Justice*, *46*(5), 597–606.

Huff, R., Desilets, C., & Kane, J. (2010). *The national public survey on white collar crime*. Fairmont, WV: National White Collar Crime Center. Retrieved from http://www.fraudaid.com/library/2010-national-publicsurvey-on-white-collar-crime.pdf

Hundley, K. (2010, June 29). Whistle-blower case details allegations of massive fraud at WellCare. *Tampa Bay Times*. Retrieved from http://www.tampabay.com/news/business/whistle-blower-case-details-allegations-of-massivefraud-at-wellcare/1105487

Hunt, D. E., & Topalli, V. (2019). To control or be controlled: Predicting types of offending in a corporate environment using control-balance theory. *Journal of Quantitative Criminology*, *35*(3), 435–464.

Hunter, B. (2019). The correctional experiences of white-collar offenders. In M. Rorie (Ed.), *The handbook of white-collar crime* (pp. 297–313). New York, NY: John Wiley & Sons.

Hunter, R. D. (1999). Officer opinions on police misconduct. *Journal of Contemporary Criminal Justice*, *15*, 155–170.

Hurricane Harvey contractor who stole $180K from victims gets 10-year sentence. (2020, February 18). *abc7 Eyewitness News*. Retrieved from https://abc7chicago.com/hurricane-harvey-benjamin-wood-contractors-contractor-accused-of-fraud/5943021/

Hytrek, N. (2019, November 5). Sioux City hotel worker sentenced to probation for credit card. *Sioux City Journal*. Retrieved from https://siouxcityjournal.com/news/

local/crime-and-courts/sioux-city-hotel-worker-sentenced
-to-probation-for-credit-card-scheme/article_fce91351
-84a8-5399-97ce-222961555a72.html

Illinois Attorney General (2020). *Raoul: Chicago woman pleads guilty to defrauding state out of approximately $100,000 in Medicaid funding.* Retrieved from https://illinoisattorney general.gov/pressroom/2020_02/20200203.html

Illinois Environmental Protection Agency. (2010). *Open dumps.* Retrieved http://www.epa.state.il.us/land/illegal-dumping/open-dumps.html

Inmate ran identity theft ring from inside prison: Judge sentences him to 14.5 more years behind bars. (2011, January 22). *Consumer Affairs.* Retrieved from http://www.consumer affairs.com/news04/2011/01/inmate-ran-identity-theft -ringfrom-inside-prison.html

Institute for College Access and Success. (2015, July 25). *Q&A on the for-profit college "90-10 rule."* Retrieved from http:// ticas.org/sites/default/files/pub_files/90-10_qa_0.pdf

Insurance agent accused of scam. (2007, September 19). *St. Petersburg Times*, p. 1.

Insurers' recent success a milestone in a year of Chinese drywall litigation. (2010). *Insurance Journal.* Retrieved from http://www.insurancejournal.com/news/southcentral/ 2010/12/23/115924.htm

Interlandi, J. (2006, October 22). An unwelcome discovery. *New York Times.* Retrieved from http://www .nytimes.com/2006/10/22/magazine/22sciencefraud.html ?pagewanted=1

Internal Revenue Service (IRS). (2010). *Examples of mortgage and real estate fraud investigations—Fiscal year 2010.* Retrieved from http://www.irs.gov/compliance/enforcement/ article/0,,id=230291,00.html

Internal Revenue Service. (2020, March 10). *Former Rapid City priest convicted on 65 counts in theft, wire fraud and money laundering scheme.* Retrieved from https://www.irs .gov/compliance/criminal-investigation/former-rapid-city -priest-convicted-on-65-counts-in-theft-wire-fraud-and -money-laundering-scheme

Internet Crime Complaint Center. (2020). *2019 annual report.* Retrieved from https://www.ic3.gov/Media/PDF/AnnualReport/ 2019_IC3Report.pdf

Internet Crime Complaint Center. (2021). *2020 annual report.* Retrieved from https://www.ic3.gov/Media/PDF/Annual Report/2020_IC3Report.pdf

Inuwa, I., Kah, M. M., & Ononiwu, C. G. (2019). Understanding how the traditional and information technology anti-corruption strategies intertwine to curb public sector corruption: A systematic literature review. *In PACIS* (p. 15).

Ionescu, L. (2013a). Perceptions of corrupt in emerging economics. *Economics, Management and Financial Markets, 8*(1), 365–395.

Ionescu, L. (2013b). The role of technology in combating corruption. *Economics, Management and Financial Markets, 8*(3), 126–131.

Iqbal, F., Binalleeh, H., Fung, B. C. M., & Debbabi, M. (2010). Mining writeprints from anonymous e-mails for forensic investigation. *Digital Investigation, 7*, 56–64.

Is Martha Stewart truly a changed woman? (2005, March 7). *MSNBC.com.* Retrieved from http://www.msnbc.msn.com/ id/7112803/ns/business-us_business

Isely, P. J., Isely, P., Freiburger, J., & McMackin, R. (2008). In their own voices: A qualitative study of men abused as children by Catholic clergy. *Journal of Child Sexual Abuse, 17*(3/4), 201–215.

Ivancevich, J., Konopaske, R., & Gilbert, J. (2008). Formally shaming white-collar criminals. *Business Horizons, 51*, 401–410.

Iyer, R., & Eastman, J. K. (2006). Academic dishonesty: Are business students different from other college students? *Journal of Education for Business, 82*(2), 101–110.

Jackson, L. (2019). Online, the U. of Farmington looked real. Behind the scenes, it was a federal sting operation. *Chronicle.* Retrieved from https://www.chronicle.com/article/online -the-u-of-farmington-looked-real-behind-the-scenes-it -was-a-federal-sting-operation/

Jacobsen, R. A., Jr., Seat, K. L., Shugarman, K. D., & Gildea, A. J. (1991). *International Financial Law Review: Supplement, 57* (United States). Retrieved from ABI/INFORM Global database (Document ID No. 1385266).

Jacobson, S. (2009, September 7). Ex-pastor delivers apology: Haggard, omits details of sex scandal in tour of churches with wife. *Dallas Morning News.* Retrieved from http:// nl.newsbank.com/nl-search/we/Archives?p_product= DM&p_theme=dm&p_action=search&p_maxdocs=200 &s_ hidethis=no&s_dispstring=ex-pastor%20 and%20haggard& p_field_advanced-0=&p_text_advanced-0=(ex-pastor%20 and%20haggard)&xcal_numdocs=20&p_perpage=10&p_sort= YMD_date:D&xcal_useweights=no

Jagsi, R. (2018). Sexual harassment in medicine—# MeToo. *N Engl J Med, 378*(3), 209–211.

Janowski, E. (2020). Timeline: Trump impeachment inquiry. *NBCNews.com*. Retrieved from https://www.nbcnews.com/politics/trump-impeachment-inquiry/timeline-trump-impeachment-inquiry-n1066691

Jansen, J., & Leukfeldt, R. (2018). Coping with cybercrime victimization: An exploratory study into impact and change. *Journal of Qualitative Criminal Justice and Criminology, 6*(2), 205–228.

Jarcho, N., & Shechter, N. (2012). Public corruption. *Criminal Law Review, 49*, 1107–1156.

Jarrell, M. L. (2007). *Environmental crime and the media: News coverage of petroleum refining industry violations*. New York, NY: LFB Scholarly.

Jarrett, L, & Reston, M. (2018, August 22). Rep. Duncan Hunter and his wife indicted in use of campaign funds for personal expenses. *CNN Politics*. Retrieved from https://www.cnn.com/2018/08/21/politics/duncan-hunter-campaign-charges/index.html

Jayasuriya, D., & Sharp, C. (2006). Auditors in a changing regulatory environment. *Journal of Financial Crime, 13*(1), 51–55.

Jefferson, J. (1997, October). Deleting cyberbooks. *ABA Journal*, 68–74.

Jenkins, A., & Braithwaite, J. (1993). Profits, pressure and corporate lawbreaking. *Crime, Law and Social Change, 20*, 221–232.

Jenkins, C. (2008, October 6). State kicks off task force to protect seniors from fraud. *Tampa Bay Times*. Retrieved from http://www.tam pabay.com/news/politics/state/state-kicks -offtask-force-to-protect-seniors-from-fraud/841696

Jesilow, P. (2012). Is Sweden doomed to repeat U.S. errors? Fraud in Sweden's health care system. *International Criminal Justice Review, 22*(1), 24–42.

Jesilow, P., Geis, G., & O'Brien, M. J. (1985). "Is my battery any good?" A field test of fraud in the auto repair business. *Journal of Crime and Justice, 8*, 1–20.

Jesilow, P., Geis, G., & O'Brien, M. J. (1986). Experimental evidence that publicity has no effect in suppressing auto repair fraud. *Sociology and Social Research, 70*(3), 222–223.

Jesilow, P., Pontell, H. N., & Geis, G. (1985). Medical criminals: Physicians and white-collar offenses. *Justice Quarterly, 2*, 149–166.

Jesilow, P., Pontell, H. N., & Geis, G. (1986). Physician immunity from prosecution and punishment for medical program fraud. In G. Newman & W. B. Groves (Eds.), *Punishment and privilege* (pp. 7–22). Albany, NY: Harrow and Heston.

Jessie, L., & Tarleton, M. (2014). *2012 census of governments: Employment summary report*. Washington, DC: U.S. Census Bureau. Retrieved from http://www2.census.gov/govs/apes/2012_summary_report. pdf.

Jetha, K. (2013). *Cybercrime and punishment: An analysis of the deontological and utilitarian functions of punishments in the information age*. ASFSL Conference on Digital Forensics, Security and Law, 15–20.

Jin, D., Kim, K., & DiPietro, R. B. (2020). Workplace incivility in restaurants: Who's the real victim? Employee deviance and customer reciprocity. *International Journal of Hospitality Management, 86*, 102459.

Johnsen, D., & Marcus, A. (2017). Pension forfeiture and police misconduct. *Journal of Law, Economics & Policy, 14*(1), 1–34.

Johnson, C. (2005, July 14). Ebbers gets 25 year sentence for role in WorldCom fraud. *The Washington Post*. Retrieved from http://www.washingtonpost.com/wp-dyn/content/article/2005/07/13/AR2005071300516.html

Johnson, C. (2006, May 26). Enron trial update. *The Washington Post*. Retrieved from http://www.washingtonpost.com/wp-dyn/content/discussion/2006/05/24/DI2006052400684.html

Johnson, C. (2019, November 16). Stents and bypass surgery are no more effective than drugs for stable heart disease, highly anticipated trial results show. *The Washington Post*. Retrieved from https://www.washingtonpost.com/health/2019/11/16/embargoed-drugs-are-effective-invasive-procedures-patients-with-stable-heart-disease-major-trial-finds/

Johnson, H. (2010, May 31). And off to jail they go: Disney duo nabbed by SEC. *Investment News*, p. 50.

Johnson, K. (2009, July 15). White-collar cons ask the pros: The tab for prison prep: Up to $20K. *USA Today*, p. 1A.

Johnstone, P. (1999). Serious white collar fraud: Historical and contemporary perspectives. *Crime, Law and Social Change, 30*, 107–130.

Jordan, S. R. (2014). Research integrity, image, manipulation, and anonymizing photographs in visual social science research. *International Journal of Social Research Methodology, 17*(4), 441–458.

Jordanoska, A. (2017). Case management in complex fraud trials: Actors and strategies in achieving procedural efficiency. *International Journal of Law in Context, 13*(3), 336–355.

Jordanoska, A. (2018). The social ecology of white-collar crime: Applying situational action theory to white-collar offending. *Deviant Behavior*, *39*(11), 1427–1449.

Jordanoska, A., & Schoultz, I. (2020). The "discovery" of white-collar crime: The legacy of Edwin Sutherland. In M. Rorie (Ed.), *The handbook of white-collar crime* (pp. 1–15). New York, NY: John Wiley & Sons.

Jou, S., Hebenton, B., & Chang, L. (2016). Cultural variation. In S. R. Van Slyke, M. L. Benson, & F. T. Cullen (Eds.), *The Oxford handbook of white-collar crime*, 345–366. New York, NY: Oxford University Press.

Judge not: Fall from honor. How Sol Watchler went from esteemed chief judge of New York to shamed prison inmate. (1997, July 1). *Psychology Today*, p. 30. Retrieved from https://www.psychologytoday.com/articles/199707/judge-not

Judicial Conduct Commission. (2011). Types of judicial misconduct. Retrieved from http://courts.ky.gov/NR/rdonlyres/DA400052–42DB-4129–89EF-8BE5554928B9/0/P12Judicial-ConductCommission Brochure711.pdf

Kadzielski, M. A., & Kim, J. Y. (2014, July). Telemedicine: Many opportunities, many legal issues, many risks. *AHLA Connections*. Retrieved from http://www.pepperlaw.com/resource/178/2412.

Kamps, J., & Kleinberg, B. (2018). To the moon: Defining and detecting cryptocurrency pump-and-dumps. *Crime Science*, *7*(1), 1. https://doi-org.proxy.lib.odu.edu/10.1186/s40163-018-0093-5

Kane, J., & Wall, A. D. (2006). *The 2005 National Public Survey on White Collar Crime*. Fairmont, WV: National White Collar Crime Center.

Kane, P., & Cillizza, C. (2009, June 17). Sen. Ensign acknowledges an extramarital affair. *The Washington Post*. Retrieved from http://www.washingtonpost.com/wp-dyn/content/article/2009/06/16/AR2009061602746.html

Kane, R. J. (2002). Social ecology of police misconduct. *Criminology*, *40*(4), 867–896.

Kanyam, D. A., Kostandini, G., & Ferreira, S. (2017). The mobile phone revolution: have mobile phones and the internet reduced corruption in Sub-Saharan Africa? *World Development*, *99*, 271–284.

Karpoff, J. M., Lee, D. S., & Martin, J. S. (2008). The consequences to managers for financial misrepresentation. *Journal of Financial Economics*, *88*(2), 193–215.

Kasm, S., & Alexander, A. (2018). State crime and digital resistance: Introduction. *State Crime Journal*, *7*(1), 4–7.

Kaufman, J. (1988, March 7). The fall of Jimmy Swaggart [Electronic version]. *People*, *29*(9). Retrieved from http://www.people.com/people/archive/article/0,,20098413,00.html

Kawalec, A. (2013, April 15). As cited in J. Griffin: *Keeping up with the hackers*. Retrieved from http://www.securityinfowatch.com/blog/10915705/keeping-up-with-the-hackers

Kawalec, A. (2014, August). How do you steal $60 million in 60 seconds. *BVEX*. Retrieved from http://businessvalueexchange.com/blog/2014/04/07/steal-60-million-60-seconds

Keane, A. G., & Kitamura, M. (2009, November 25). Toyota's recalls test promise to make "better cars" (update 1). *Bloomberg News*. Retrieved from http://www.bloomberg.com/apps/news?pid=news archive&sid=ayG_dQWAhApO

Kearney, P., Plax, T. G., Hays, E. R., & Ivey, M. J. (1991). College teacher misbehaviors: What students don't like about what teachers say and do. *Communication quarterly*, *39*(4), 309–324.

Keenan, C. E., Brown, G. C., Pontell, H. N., & Geis, G. (1985). Medical students' attitudes on physician fraud and abuse in the Medicare and Medicaid programs. *Academic Medicine*, *60*(3), 167–173.

Kelley, F. (2005). The sweating system. *American Journal of Public Health*, *95*, 49–52.

Kelley, M. L., & Parsons, B. (2000). Sexual harassment in the 1990s: A university-wide survey of female faculty, administration, staff, and students. *Journal of Higher Education*, *71*(5), 548–568.

Kelly, C. (2009, August 29). Going to the big house? Let us plan your stay: A growing U.S. industry coaches criminals on how to prepare for, and survive, life behind bars. *Toronto Star*, p. IN01.

Kelly, C., & Jones, S. (2020, January 18). Former Rep. Chris Collins, the first member of Congress to endorse Trump, sentenced to 26 months in prison in insider trading case. *CNN Politics*. Retrieved from https://www.cnn.com/2020/01/17/politics/collins-sentencing/index.html

Kelly, J., & Nichols, M. (2019). Police misconduct: Discipline records for thousands of cops uncovered. *USAToday.com*. Retrieved from https://www.usatoday.com/in-depth/news/investigations/2019/04/24/usa-today-revealing-misconduct-records-police-cops/3223984002/

Keneally, M. (2016). Erin Andrews awarded $55 million in lawsuit. *ABCNews.Com*. Retrieved from https://abcnews.go.com/US/erin-andrews-jury-set-deliberate-75-million-lawsuit/story?id=37460110.

Kennedy, B. (2019). Do California dispensary owners deserve jail for looping? *Leafly*. Available online at https://www.leafly.com/news/industry/do-colorado -dispensary-owners-deserve-jail-for-looping.

Kennedy, J. P. (2016). Employee theft. In S. R. Van Slyke, M. L. Benson, & F. T. Cullen (Eds.), *The Oxford handbook of white-collar crime* (pp. 409–434). New York, NY: Oxford University Press.

Kennedy, J. P., & Benson, M. L. (2016). Emotional reactions to employee theft and the managerial dilemmas small business owners face. *Criminal Justice Review (Sage Publications)*, *41*(3), 257–277. https://doi-org.proxy.lib.odu .edu/10.1177/0734016816638899

Kerbs, J. J., & Jolley, J. M. (2007). The joy of violence: What about violence is fun in middle-school? *American Journal of Criminal Justice*, *32*(1), 12–29.

Kerley, K. R., & Copes, H. (2004). The effects of criminal justice contact on employment stability for whitecollar and street-level offenders. *International Journal of Offender Therapy and Comparative Criminology*, *48*, 65–84.

Kim, S. (2020). Trump associates who have been sent to prison or faced criminal charges. *abc NEWS*. Retrieved from https://abcnews.go.com/Politics/trump-associates -prison-faced-criminal-charges/story?id=68358219

Kimball, P. (2005). *Syndi-Court justice: Judge Judy and exploitation of arbitration*. Retrieved from http://www.americanbar .org/content/dam/aba/migrated/dispute/essay/syndicourt justice.authcheckdam.pdf

"Kingpin of commodities fraud" gets 17 1/2 years: Florida telemarketer even offered clients high interest loans to buy his non-existent products. (2006, June 23). *Edmonton Journal*, p. E2.

Kinnaird, B. A. (2007). Exploring liability profiles: A proximate cause analysis of police misconduct: Part II. *International Journal of Police Science and Management*, *9*(3), 201–213.

Kintisch, E. (2006, June 28). Poehlman sentenced to 1 year of prison. *ScienceNow*. Retrieved from http://news.scienence. org/science now/2006/06/28-01.html

Klenowski, P. M. (2012). "Learning the good with the bad": Are occupational white-collar offenders taught how to neutralize their crimes? *Criminal Justice Review*, *37*(4), 461–477.

Klenowski, P. M., Copes, H., & Mullins, C. W. (2011). Gender, identity, and accounts: How white collar offenders do gender when making sense of their crimes. *Justice Quarterly*, *28*(1), 46–69.

Klenowski, P. M., & Dodson, K. D. (2016). *Who commits white-collar crime, and what do we know about them* (pp. 101–26). Oxford: Oxford University Press.

Klieger, S. B., Gutman, A., Allen, L., Pacula, R. L., Ibrahim, J. K., & Burris, S. (2017). Mapping medical marijuana: state laws regulating patients, product safety, supply chains and dispensaries, 2017. *Addiction*, *112*(12), 2206–2216.

Knickmeyer, E. (2019). EPA enforcement drops sharply in Trump's 2nd year in office. *APNews.com*. Retrieved from https://apnews.com/9d10456338af48dc918cbaa24ea6a4ce

Knight, J. (1995, November 17). The misuse of mandatory counseling. *Chronicle of Higher Education*, p. B1.

Knopp, J., Jr. (1966). Branding and the Robinson-Patman Act. *Journal of Business*, *39*(1), 24.

Knottnerus, J. D., Ulsperger, J. S., Cummins, S., & Osteen, E. (2006). Exposing Enron: Media representations of ritualized deviance in corporate culture. *Crime, Media & Culture*, *2*, 177–195.

Knox, N. (1997, September 7). Broker fraud sanctions hit a record high. *Chicago Sun-Times*, p. 56.

Knox, N. (2000, June 2). Task force scours for note fraud: 4,600 investors fell victim to promissory note scam. *USA Today*, p. 1B.

Kolker, R. (2009, September). The Madoff exfiles. *New York Magazine*. New York, NY: New York Media LLC.

Konigsmark, A. R. (2006, October 24). Crooked builders hit storm victims. *USA Today*, p. 3A.

Kopperud, S. (2010, September 24). Senate ag panel spanks EPA. *Brownfield Ag News*. Retrieved from http://brown fieldagnews.com/2010/09/24/senate-ag-panel-spanks-epa

Korolishin, J. (2003, September). Store employees remain largest source of shrink. *Stores*, *85*(9), p. LP24.

Kostelnik, J. (2012). Sentencing white-collar criminals: When is shaming viable? *Global Crime*, *13*(3), 141–159.

Kowalski, M. A., Mei, X., Turner, J. R., Stohr, M. K., & Hemmens, C. (2020). An analysis of statutes criminalizing correctional officer sexual misconduct with inmates. *The Prison Journal*, *100*(1), 126–148.

Krafcik, M. (2020). Kalamazoo doctor pleads guilds to Medicare fraud reusing rectal devices on patients. *WVMT.com*. Retrieved from https://wwmt.com/news/local/kalamazoo -area-doctor-pleads-guilty-to-medicare-fraud-re-using -rectal-devices-on-patients

Kramer, R. C. (1984). Is corporate crime serious crime? Criminal justice and corporate crime control. *Journal of Contemporary Criminal Justice, 2*, 7–10.

Kramer, R. C. (2013). Carbon in the atmosphere and power in America: Climate change as state corporate crime. *Journal of Crime and Justice, 36*(2), 153–170.

Kramer, R. C. (2020). Rolling back climate regulation: Trump's assault on the planet. *Journal of White Collar and Corporate Crime, 1*(2), 123–130.

Kramer, R. C., Michalowski, R. J., & Kauzlarich, D. (2002). The origins and development of the concept and theory of state corporate crime. *Crime and Delinquency, 48*(2), 263–282.

Kreag, J. (2019). Disclosing prosecutorial misconduct. *Vanderbilt Law Review, 72*(1), 297–352.

Kreidler, J. (2020). Williams-Sonoma: Made in the U.S.A.? Available online at https://www.consumer.ftc.gov/blog/2020/04/williams-sonoma-made-usa

Kreps, D. (2010, January 8). Settlements near for victims of 2003 Great White night club fire. *Rolling Stone*. Retrieved from http://www.rollingstone.com/music/news/settlements-near-for-victims-of-2003-great-white-nightclub-fire-20100108

Kresevich, M. (2007, February). Using culture to cure theft. *Security Management, 51*(2), p. 46.

Kurkjian, S., Ebbert, S., Ebbert, T., & Farragher, T. (2003, June 9). Series of errors sealed crowd's fate. *The Boston Globe*. Retrieved from http://www.boston.com/news/packages/nightclub_fire/Series_of_errors_sealed_crowd_s_fate+.shtml

Kwok, D. (2019). Is vagueness choking the white-collar statute. *Georgia Law Review, 53*(2), 495–548.

La France, M., Boblick, J., Dimitriadis, J., Fox, C., Lanuti, J., Villalba, D., & Wisser, L. (2018). Securities fraud. *American Criminal Law Review, 55*(4 Annual Survey of White Collar Crime), 1677–1772.

Langevoort, D. C. (2017). Cultures of compliance. *American Criminal Law Review, 54*(4 Annual Survey of White Collar Crime), 933–978.

Langton, L., & Piquero, N. L. (2007). Can general strain theory explain white-collar crime? A preliminary investigation of the relationship between strain and select white-collar offenses. *Journal of Criminal Justice, 35*(1), 1–15.

Lardo, A. E. (2006). Comment: The 2003 extradition treaty between the United States and United Kingdom: Towards a solution to transnational white-collar crime prosecution. *Emory International Crime Review, 20*, 867–903.

Larsson, P. (2006). International police co-operation: A Norwegian perspective. *Journal of Financial Crime, 13*(4), 456–466.

Lasley, J. R. (1988). Toward a control theory of whitecollar offending. *Journal of Quantitative Criminology, 4*(4), 347–362.

Latimer, P. (2002). Reporting suspicions of money laundering and "whistleblowing": The legal and other implications for intermediaries and their advisers. *Journal of Financial Crime, 10*(1), 23–29.

Lauchs, M., Keast, R., & Yousefpour, N. (2011). Corrupt police networks: Uncovering hidden relationship patterns, functions and roles. *Policing & Society, 21*(1), 110–127.

Lawless, J. F. (1988). The white-collar defendant: High visibility, high stakes. *Trial, 24*(9), 42–48.

Layman, E., McCampbell, S., & Moss, A. (2000). Sexual misconduct in corrections. *American Jails, 14*(5), 23–35.

Layton, L. (2009, October 13). Under Obama, regulatory agencies step up enforcement. *The Washington Post*. Retrieved from http://www.washingtonpost.com/wp-dyn/content/article/2009/10/12/AR2009101202554.html

Leap, T. L. (2007). *Dishonest dollars: The dynamics of white-collar crime*. Ithaca, NY: Industrial and Labor Relations (ILR) Press.

LeClair, J., Abraham, S., & Shih, S. (2013). An interdisciplinary approach to educating an effective cyber security workforce. *InfoSecCD, 13*, 71.

Lederman, D. (2009, September 11). The game of ghost writing. *Inside Higher Ed*. Retrieved from http://www.insidehighered.com/news/2009/09/11/ghostwrite

Lee, D. E. (2009). Cheating in the classroom: Beyond policing. *Clearing House, 82*(4), 171–174.

Lee, H., Lim, H., Moore, D. D., & Kim, J. (2013). How police organizational structure correlates with frontline officers' attitudes toward corruption: A multilevel model. *Police Practice and Research, 14*(5), 386–401.

Lee, J. (2010, November 12). *What were you thinking? Criminal justice students and their social networking sites*. Paper presented at a meeting of the Georgia Political Science Associations, Savannah, GA.

Lee, M. S. (1998). *United States v. Nippon Paper Industries Co.*: Extending the criminal provisions of the Sherman Act to foreign conduct producing a substantial intended effect in the United States. *Wake Forest Law Review, 33*(1), 189–217.

Lee, M. T., & Ermann, M. D. (1999). Pinto "madness" as a flawed landmark narrative. *Social Problems, 46*, 30–47.

Leegin Creative Leather Products, Inc. v. PSKS, Inc., 127 S.Ct. 2705 (2007).

Leighton, P. (2013). Corporate crime and the corporate agenda for crime control: Disappearing awareness of corporate crime and increasing abuses of power. *Western Criminology Review, 14*(2), 38–51

Leighton P. (2016). Mass salmonella poisoning by the Peanut Corporation of America: State-Corporate crime involving food safety. *Critical Criminology, 24*(1):75–91. doi:10.1007/s10612-015-9284-5.

Leon, K., & Ken, I. (2017). Food fraud and the Partnership for a "Healthier" America: A case study in state-corporate crime. *Critical Criminology, 25*(3), 393–410. https://doi-org.proxy.lib.odu.edu/10.1007/s10612-017-9363-x

Leon, K. S., & Ken, I. (2019). Legitimized fraud and the state-corporate criminology of food—A spectrum-based theory. *Crime, Law & Social Change, 71*(1), 25–46. https://doi-org.proxy.lib.odu.edu/10.1007/s10611-018-9787-6

Lerner, C. S. (2018). The trial of Joseph Dotterweich: The origins of the "responsible corporate officer" doctrine. *Criminal Law & Philosophy, 12*(3), pp. 493–512, 2018. DOI 10.1007/s11572-017-9439-4.

Leto, J. L., Pogrebin, M. R., & Stretesky, P. B. (2007). Defending the indigent white-collar criminal: Federal public defender defense strategies for post-indictment representation. *Journal of Crime and Justice, 30*(2), 79–113.

Levi, M. (2006). Media construction of financial whitecollar crimes. *British Journal of Criminology, 46*(6), 1037–1057.

Levi, S. D. (2014, February). Cybersecurity: Amid increasing attacks and government controversy, a framework to reduce risk emerges. *Financial Fraud Law Report. 6*(2), 165–171.

Levin, B. (2019). Report: trump happily employing undocumented workers while ICE rounds them up. *Vanity Fair.* Retrieved from https://www.vanityfair.com/news/2019/08/trump-organization-undocumented-workers

Levin, M. (1984). Corporate probation conditions. *Fordham Law Review, 52*, 637–662.

Levine, J. P. (1983). Using jury verdict forecasts in criminal defense strategy. *Judicature, 66*(10), 448.

Lim, H. A. (2002). Women doctors and crime: A review of California physician sanctioning data 1990–1994. *Justice Professional, 15*(2), 149–167.

Lin, T. (2017). The new market manipulation. *Emory Law Journal, 66*(6), 1253–1314.

Litton, R. (1998). Fraud and the insurance industry: Why don't they do something about it, then? *International Journal of Risk and Crime Prevention, 3*(3), 193–205.

Loane, S. (2000, December). White-collar criminals suffer a bad case of jailhouse blues. *Sydney Morning Herald.* Retrieved from http://www.sheilas.com.au/sheilas-articles/2000/12/11/whitecollar-criminals-suffer-a-bad-case-of-jailhouse-blues

Locker, J. P., & Godfrey, B. (2006). Ontological boundaries and temporal watersheds in the development of white-collar crime. *British Journal of Criminology, 46*, 976–992.

Lofquist, W. S. (1993). Organizational probation and the U.S. sentencing commission. *Annals of the American Academy of Political and Social Science, 525*, 157–169.

Logan, M. W., Morgan, M. A., Benson, M. L., & Cullen, F. T. (2019). Coping with imprisonment: Testing the special sensitivity hypothesis for white-collar offenders. *Justice Quarterly, 36*(2), 225–254.

Lokanan, M. E. (2019). A fraud investigation plan for a false accounting and theft case. *Journal of Financial Crime, 26*(4), 1216–1228. https://doi-org.proxy.lib.odu.edu/10.1108/JFC-09-2017-0086

Lokken, F., & Mullins, C. (2014). *Trends in eLearning Tracking the impact of eLearning at community colleges.* Washington, DC: Instructional Technology Council.

Londoño, E. (2007, August 19). Gaithersburg man admits to equity-skimming scam. *The Washington Post.* Retrieved from http://www.washingtonpost.com/wp-dyn/content/article/2007/08/18/AR2007081801136.html?nav=emailpage

Longshore, D., & Turner, S. (1998). Self-control and criminal opportunity: Cross-sectional test of the general theory of crime. *Criminal Justice and Behavior, 25*(1), 81–98.

Lopez, G. (2020). The rise in murders, explained. *Vox.* Retrieved from https://www.vox.com/2020/8/3/21334149/murders-crime-shootings-protests-riots-trump-biden

Lord, N., Spencer, J., Albanese, J., & Elizondo, C. F. (2017). In pursuit of food system integrity: The situational prevention of food fraud enterprise. *European Journal on Criminal Policy and Research, 23*(4), 483–501.

Lord, N., & van Wingerde, K. (2019). In M. Rorie (Ed.), Preventing and intervening in white-collar crimes: The role of law enforcement. *The handbook of white-collar crime* (pp. 246–261). New York, NY: John Wiley & Sons.

Lowry, D. (2015). All but one in Atlanta cheating scandal to serve time. *USA Today.* Retrieved from https://www.usatoday.com/story/news/nation/2015/04/14/atlanta-educators-sentenced/25759985

Lowry, D. S. (2018). Redpilling: A professional reflects on white racial privilege and drug policy in American health care. *Journal of Ethnicity in Substance Abuse, 17*(1), 50–63.

Lu, D. W., Lall, M. D., Mitzman, J., Heron, S., Pierce, A., Hartman, N. D., . . . & Strout, T. D. (2020). # MeToo in EM: A multicenter survey of academic emergency medicine faculty on their experiences with gender discrimination and sexual harassment. *Western Journal of Emergency Medicine, 21*(2), 252.

Lugosi, P. (2019). Deviance, deviant behaviour and hospitality management: Sources, forms and drivers. *Tourism Management, 74*, 81–98.

Lusk, L. (2017). The myth of millions: Voter fraud and the Trump Administration's impact on voter-ID litigation in the first 100 Days. *University of Illinois Law Review Online, 1*(6).

Lusthaus, J. (2012, May). Trust in the world of cybercrime. *Global Crime, 13*(2), 71–94.

Lyman, F. (2003a). Anger builds over EPA's 9/11 report. *Msnbc.com*. Retrieved http://www.msnbc.msn.com/id/3076626/ns/health-your_environment/t/anger-builds-over-epas-report/

Lyman, F. (2003b). *Messages in the dust: What are the lessons of the environmental health response to the terrorist attacks of September 11?* National Environmental Health Association. Retrieved from http://www.neha.org/pdf/messages_in_the_dust.pdf

Lynch, M. J. (2013). The extraordinary relevance of Barak's *Theft of a Nation. Western Criminology Review, 13*(2): 52–60.

Lynch, M. J. (2020). Green criminology and environmental crime: criminology that matters in the age of global ecological collapse. *Journal of White Collar and Corporate Crime, 1*(1), 50–61.

Lynch, M. J., Stretesky, P., & Hammond, P. (2000). Media coverage of chemical crimes, Hillsborough County, Florida, 1987–97. *British Journal of Criminology, 40*, 112–126.

Lynn, S. (2020). Top 5 cannabis security services for marijuana dispensaries. *Indicaonline*. Retrieved from https://indicaonline.com/blog/cannabis-security-services-marijuana-dispensaries

Madden, S., Hartley, R. D., Walker, J. T., & Miller, J. M. (2012). Sympathy for the devil: An exploration of federal judicial discretion in the processing of white-collar offenders. *American Journal of Criminal Justice, 37*, 4–18.

Madden, S., Walker, K. T., & Miller, M. J. (2008). Does size really matter? A reexamination of Sheldon's somatypes and criminal behavior. *The Social Science Journal, 45*, 330–344.

Madensen, T. D. (2016). Opportunities for white-collar crime. In S. Van Slyke, M. L. Benson, & Francis T. Cullen (Eds.), *The Oxford handbook of white-collar crime* (pp. 382–408). New York, NY: Oxford University Press.

Madoff's victims. (2009). *Wall Street Journal*. Retrieved from http://s.wsj.net/public/resources/documents/st_madoff_victims_20081215.html

Maher, T. M. (2003). Police sexual misconduct: Officers' perceptions of its extent and causality. *Criminal Justice Review, 28*(2), 355–381.

Maimon, D., Alper, M., Sobesto, B., & Cukier, M. (2014). Restrictive deterrent effects of a warning system banner in an attacked computer system. *Criminology, 52*(1), 33–59.

Maimon, D., Kamerdze, A., Cukier, M., & Sobesto, B. (2013). Daily trends and origin of computer-focused crimes against a large university computer network. *British Journal of Criminology, 53*, 319–343.

Makkai, T., & Braithwaite, J. (1991). Criminological theories and regulatory compliance. *Criminology, 29*(2), 191–217.

Makkai, T., & Braithwaite, J. (1994). Reintegrative shaming and compliance with regulatory standards. *Criminology, 32*(3), 361–385.

Malos, S. (2007). Appearance-based sex discrimination and stereotyping in the workplace: Whose conduct should we regulate? *Employment Responses Rights, 19*, 95–111.

Mann, K. (1985). *Defending white-collar crime: A portrait of attorneys at work*. New Haven, CT: Yale University Press.

Mann, K., Wheeler, S., & Sarat, A. (1980). Sentencing the white-collar offender. *American Criminal Law Review, 17*, 479–500.

Mannheim, H. (1949). Sutherland, Edwin, H.: Whitecollar crime. *Annals of the American Academy of Political and Social Science, 266*, 243–244.

Manos, J., & Chase, D. (Writers), & Coulter, A. (Director). (1999). College [Television series episode]. In D. Chase (Producer), *The Sopranos*. New York, NY: Silvercup Studios.

Mansfield-Devine, S. (2009, March). Google hacking 101. *Network Security*, 4–6.

Marion, N., & Hill, J. B. (2018). Presidential rhetoric as crime control theater: The case of cybercrime. *Criminology, Criminal Justice, Law & Society, 19*(2), [i]-v.

Mark, G. (2017). The Yates memorandum. *UCDL Rev., 51*, 1589.

Mars, G. (1983). *Cheats at work: An anthropology of workplace crime*. London, UK: Allen and Unwin.

Martha Stewart reads a statement outside Manhattan federal court Friday after she was sentenced to five months in prison. (2004, July 17). *Associated Press*.

Retrieved from http://nl.newsbank.com/nl-search/we/Archives?p_product=APAB&p_theme=apab&p_action=search&p_maxdocs=200&s_dispstring=martha%20stewart%20statement&p_field_advanced-0=&p_text_advanced-0=%28%22martha%20stewart%20statement%22%29&xcal_numdocs=20&p_perpage=10&p_sort=YMD_date:D&xcal_useweights=no

Martin, N., & Rice, J. (2011). Cybercrime: Understanding and addressing the concerns of stakeholders. *Computers & Security, 30,* 803–814.

Martin, R., Mutchnick, R., & Austin, W. T. (1990). *Pioneers in criminological thought.* New York, NY: Macmillan.

Martin, S. (2007). A rule of reason for vertical price fixing. *The Metropolitan Corporate Counsel.* Retrieved from http://www.metrocorpcounsel.com/current.php?artType=view&artMonth=June&artYear=2011&EntryNo=7284

Martin, S. L., Coyne-Beasley, T., Hoehn, M., Mathew, M., Runyan, C. W., Orton, S., & Royster, L-A. (2009). Primary prevention of violence against women: Training needs of violence practitioners. *Violence Against Women, 15*(1), 44–56.

Martin, V. (2004). Detection and prevention of mortgage loan fraud. *Risk Management Association (RMA) Journal.* Retrieved from http://find articles.com/p/articles/mi_m0ITW/is_1_87/ai_n14897572/

Martinelli, T. J. (2007). Minimizing risk by defining off duty police misconduct. *Police Chief, 74*(6), 40–45.

Marx, G. T. (1982). Who really gets stung? Some issues raised by the new police undercover work. *Crime & Delinquency, 28*(2), 165–200.

Maryland contractor fined $1.2 million for asbestos violations. (2010, June 7). *Mesothelioma News.* Retrieved from http://www.meso theliomanews.com/2010/06/07/maryland contractor-fined/

Mason, K. A. (2007). Punishment and paperwork: Whitecollar offenders under community supervision. *American Journal of Criminal Justice, 31*(2), 23–36.

Mason, K. A., & Benson, M. L. (1996). The effect of social support on fraud victims' reporting behavior: A research note. *Justice Quarterly, 13*(3), 511–524.

Mass, A. (1986). U.S. prosecution of state and local officials for political corruption: Is the bureaucracy out of control in a high-stakes operation involving the constitutional system? *Publius: Journal of Federalism, 17*(3), 195–230.

Masters, B. (2020). Make the punishment fit the white-collar crime. *Financial Times.* Retrieved from https://www.ft.com/content/4794f918-40f9-11ea-a047-eae9bd51ceba,

Masters, B. A. (2005, July 15). Are executives' sentences too harsh? Debate is rising about deterrence of corporate crime. *Houston Chronicle,* T2. Retrieved from http://www.chron.com/business/article/Are-executives-sentences-too harsh-1926161.php

Matza, D. (1964). *Delinquency and drift.* New York, NY: Wiley.

May, D. C., & Wood, P. B. (2005). What influences offenders' willingness to serve alternative sanctions? *Prison Journal, 85*(2), 145.

Mazur, L., Helak, D., Van Demark, D., & Stauffer, R. (2020). Avoiding confusion over state licensing laws as CMS further loosens telemedicine restrictions. *Of Digital Interest.* Retrieved from https://www.ofdigitalinterest.com/2020/04/avoiding-confusion-over-state-licensing-laws-as-cms-further-loosens-telemedicine-restrictions

Mazur, T. (2001, April 16). Culture beats internal theft. *DSN Retailing Today, 40*(8), p. 14.

McCarthy, B. J. (1981). *Exploratory study of corruption in corrections.* Unpublished doctoral dissertation, Florida State University.

McConnaughey, J., & Kunzelman, M. (2015, December 2). Manslaughter charges dropped for BP supervisors in oil spill. *Providence Journal.* Retrieved http://www.providence journal.com/article/ZZ/20151202/NEWS/312029907

McCoy, K. (2009, June 30). Appeal of Madoff 's 150-year sentence wouldn't matter. *USA Today.* Retrieved from http://abc news. go.com/Business/story?id=7973772&page=1

McCready, B., & Tinley, J. (2009, December 16). Alleged embezzler in FBI custody. *New Haven Register.* Retrieved from http://www.nhregis ter.com/articles/2009/12/16/news/milford/al— embezzle_1216.txt

McDade, R. J., & O'Donnell, K. (1992). Parallel civil and criminal proceedings. *American Criminal Law Review, 29*(2), 697–738.

McDowell, M. G. (2013). 'Becoming a waste land where nothing can survive': Resisting state-corporate environmental crime in a 'forgotten' place. *Contemporary Justice Review, 16*(4), 394–411.

McGettrick, A. (2013, August 30). Toward curricular guidelines for cybersecurity: Report of on a workshop on cybersecurity education and training. *Association for Computing Machinery.* Retrieved from https://www.acm.org/edu cation/TowardCurricularGuidelinesCybersec.pdf

McGurrin, D., Jarrell, M., Jahn, A., & Cochrane, B. (2013). White collar crime representation in the criminological literature revisited, 2001–2010. *Western Criminology Review, 14*(2), 3–19.

McGurrin, D., & Kappeler, V. E. (2002). Media accounts of police sexual violence: Rotten apples or state supported violence? In K. M. Lersch (Ed.), *Policing and misconduct* (pp. 121–142). Upper Saddle River, NJ: Prentice Hall.

McKinney, L., Roberts, T., & Shefman, P. (2013). Perspectives and experiences of financial aid counselors on community college students who borrow. *Journal of Student Financial Aid*, *43*(1), 3–17.

McLaughlin, E. (2019). Michigan State president resigns after he claimed Nassar victims were 'enjoying' spotlight. *CNN .com*. Retrieved from https://www.cnn.com/2019/01/16/us/michigan-state-president-nassar-victims/index.html

Mclaughlin, T. (2010, April 15). BRIEF: Destin man gets 5 years for fraud: Owen collected $2.2 million for Oasis futures business. *Northwest Florida Daily New*, p. B1.

McMullan, J. L., & Perrier, D. C. (2007). Controlling cyber-crime and gambling: Problems and paradoxes in the mediation of law and criminal organization. *Police Practice & Research*, *8*(5), 431–444.

McNamara, M. (2006, May 23). FTC head opposes anti-gouging law: Says regulation would be hard to enforce and could cause fuel shortages. *Columbia Broadcasting System (CBS) News*. Retrieved from http://www.cbsnews.com/stories/2006/05/22/business/main 1639514.shtml

McNeill, B. (2010, May 28). UV fights inquiry by Cuccinelli. *Charlottesville Daily Progress*. Retrieved from http://www2 .dailyprogress.com/cdp/news/local/education/article/uva_fights_inquiry_by_cuccinelli/56663

McNerney, M., & Papadopoulos, E. (2013). Hacker's delight: Law firm risk and liability in the cyber age. *American University Law Review*, *62*, 1243–1269.

McNulty, P. (n.d.). *Principles of federal prosecution of business organizations*. Washington, DC: U.S. Department of Justice, Office of Deputy Attorney General.

McReynolds, A., & Stewart, C. (2020). Let's put the vote-by-mail 'fraud' myth to rest. *The Hill*. Retrieved from https://thehill.com/opinion/campaign/494189-lets-put-the-vote-by-mail-fraud-myth-to-rest

McShane, L. (2009, July 31). Hoboken mayor Peter Cammarano resigns after arrest in sweeping corruption probe. *NY Daily News*. Retrieved from http://www.nydailynews.com/news/ny_crime/2009/07/31/2009-07-31_hoboken_mayor_peter_cammarano_resigns_after_arrest_in_sweeping_corruption_probe.html

MeddlingatEPA?Activistspointtosurvey.(2008,April23).*Wapedia, Mobile Encyclopedia*. Retrieved from http://wapedia.mobi/en/United_States_Environmental_Protection_Agency?t=9

Medicare.Gov. (2008). *Nursing homes: About nursing home inspections*. Retrieved July 29, 2011 from http://www .medicare.gov/nursing/aboutinspections.asp?PrinterFriendly=true

Meerts, C. (2013). Corporate security–Private justice? (Un)settling employer-employee troubles. *Security Journal*, *26*(3), 264–279.

Meier, K. J., & Holbrook, T. M. (1992). "I seen my opportunities and I took 'em": Political corruption in the American states. *Journal of Politics*, *54*(1), 135–155.

Meiners, A. (2020). *Ten years later, BP oil spill continues to harm wildlife—especially dolphins*. National Geographic. Retrieved from https://www.nationalgeographic.com/animals/article/how-is-wildlife-doing-now--ten-years-after-the-deepwater-horizon

Melenyzer, L. (1999). Double jeopardy protection from civil sanctions after *Hudson v. United States*. *Journal of Criminal Law and Criminology*, *89*(3), 1007.

Mell, P., Kent, K., & Nusbaum, J. (2005, November). Guide to malware incident prevention and handling: Recommendations of the national institute of standards and technology. *National Institutes of Standards and Technology*, Special Publication 800–83. Retrieved from http://csrc.nist.gov/publications/nistpubs/800-83/SP800-83.pdf

Mendez, F. (2014). Can corruption foster regulatory compliance? *Public Choice*, *158*, 189–207.

Merton, R. K. (1938). Social structure and anomie. *American Sociological Review*, *3*, 672–682.

Messner, S., & Rosenfeld, R. (2007). *Crime and the American dream* (4th ed.). Belmont, CA: Wadsworth.

Mettler, L. (2019). Popeyes launches chicken sandwich at restaurant that ripped them off. Retrieved from https://www .today.com/food/popeyes-launches-chicken-sandwich-restaurant-ripped-them-t160417.

Meyer, C. (2015, June). High stakes games: Cybersecurity awareness training. *Security*, 35–36.

Meyer, P. (2011, January 11). Tom DeLay is sentenced to three years. *Los Angeles Times*. Retrieved from http://articles .latimes.com/2011/jan/11/nation/la-na-tom-delay-20110111

Meyers, T. J. (2017). Examining the network components of a Medicare fraud scheme: the Mirzoyan-Terdjanian organization. *Crime, Law and Social Change*, *68*(1-2), 251–279.

Mian, A., & Sufi, A. (2015). *House of debt: How they (and you) caused the great recession, and how we can prevent it from happening again*. Chicago, IL: University of Chicago Press.

Michalowski, R. (2020). The necropolitics of regulation. *Journal of White-Collar and Corporate Crime, 1*(2), 83–85.

Michel, C. (2016). Violent street crime versus harmful white-collar crime: A comparison of perceived seriousness and punitiveness. *Critical Criminology, 24*(1), 127–143.

Michel, C., Cochran, J. K., & Heide, K. M. (2016). Public knowledge about white-collar crime: An exploratory study. *Crime, law and social change, 65*(1-2), 67–91.

Microsoft. (2010). *What is counterfeiting?* Retrieved from http://www.microsoft.com/resources/howtotell/en/counterfeit.mspx

Middlemiss, A. D., & Gupta, N. (2007). US interagency law enforcement cooperation since September 11, 2001: Improvements and results. *Journal of Financial Crime, 14*(2), 138–149.

Milian, J. (2020). Boca doctor accused of nearly $900,000 in medical insurance fraud. *Palm Beach Post.* Retrieved from https://www.palmbeachpost.com/news/20200311/boca-doctor-accused-of-nearly-900000-in-medical-insurance-fraud.

Miller, W. (1975). *Violence by youth gangs and youth groups as a crime problem in major American cities* (Final Report). Washington, DC: U.S. Department of Justice, Office of Justice Programs, Office of Juvenile Justice and Delinquency Prevention.

Miller, G. (1993). White-collar criminals share one trait—Greed. *Corrections Today, 55*(3), 22–24.

Minkel, W. (2002). Sniffing out the cheaters. *School Library Journal, 48*(6), 25.

Minkes, J. (1990). Crimes of the rich. *Probation Journal, 37,* 127–130.

Minnaar, A. (2008). 'You've received a greeting e-card from . . .' The changing face of cybercrime e-mail spam scams. *Acta Criminologica CRIMSA Conference Special Edition 2,* 92–116.

Minnaar, A. (2013). Editorial: Information security, cybercrime, cyberterrorism and the exploration of cybersecurity vulnerabilities. *Southern African Journal of Criminology, 26*(2), 1–4.

Minor, W. W. (1981). Techniques of neutralization: A reconceptualization and empirical examination. *Journal of Research in Crime and Delinquency, 18*(2), 295–318.

Mishra, B. K., & Prasad, A. (2006). Minimizing retail shrinkage due to employee theft. *International Journal of Retail and Distribution Management, 34*(11), p. 817.

Mohr, H., Pritchard, J., & Lush, T. (2010, June 9). BP spill response plans severely flawed. *MSNBC. com.* Retrieved from http://www.msnbc.msn.com/id/37599810

Mon, W. (2002). Causal factors of corporate crime in Taiwan: Qualitative and quantitative findings. *International Journal of Offender Therapy and Comparative Criminology, 46*(2), 183–205.

Montano, E. (2001, June 21–22). *Technologies of electronic crime.* Paper presented at the 4th National Outlook Symposium on Crime, Canberra, Australia.

Montell, G. (2009). President of University of Texas-Pan American, accused of plagiarism, will retire. *Chronicle of Higher Education.* Retrieved from http://chronicle.com/blogs/onhiring/president-of-u-of-texas-pan-american-accused-of-plagiarism-will-retire/826

Montgomery, W. D., Baron, R. A., & Weisskopf, M. K. (2007). Potential effects of proposed price gouging legislation on the cost and severity of gasoline supply interruptions. *Journal of Competition Law & Economics, 3*(3), 357–397.

Moore, E., & Mills, M. (1990). The neglected victims and unexamined costs of white-collar crime. *Crime and Delinquency, 36,* 408–418.

Morgan, T. (1995). Sanctions and remedies for attorney misconduct. *Southern Illinois University Law Journal, 19,* 343–370.

Moritz, J. (2020). Judicial conduct draws attention; Arkansas case leads officials to take part in U.N. events. *Arkansas Online.* Retrieved from https://www.arkansasonline.com/news/2020/mar/16/judicial-conduct-draws-attention-202003-1

Morris, J. (1999). Big hairy pile of whoa! Heroin, Pinochet, ABBA—Oh my! from http://www.gettingit.com/article/261

Morris, J. (2010). America's asbestos age. *The Center for Public Integrity.* Retrieved from http://www.publicintegrity.org/investigations/asbestos/articles/entry/2184/

Morris, R. G., & Blackburn, A. G. (2009). Cracking the code: An empirical exploration of social learning theory and computer crime. *Journal of Crime and Justice, 32*(1), 1–34.

Morris, R. G., & El Sayed, S. (2013). The development of self-reported white-collar offending. *Journal of Contemporary Criminal Justice, 29*(3), 369–384.

Morrison, J., & Morrison, T. (2001). Psychiatrist disciplined by state medical board. *American Journal of Psychiatry, 158*(3), 474–478.

Moyer, L. (2009a, March 12). Bernie behind bars. *Forbes. com.* Retrieved http://www.forbes.com/2009/03/12/madoff-white-collarcrime-fraud-business-wall-street-prisons.html

Moyer, L. (2009b, June 29). A history of long prison sentences. *Forbes.com.* Retrieved from http://www.cbc.ca/money/story/2009/06/25/f-forbes-madoff-prison-sentences.html

Moyer, W. (2010, December 18). Love Canal—A city built on a toxic dump. *Ezine Articles.* Retrieved from http://ezinearticles.com/?Love-Canal—A-City-Built-On-A-Toxic-Dump&id=5578148

Mrcela, M., & Vuletic, I. (2018). Healthcare, privacy, big data and cybercrime: Which one is the weakest link?. *Annals of Health Law, 27*(2), 257–[viii].

Mueller, G. (1996). An essay on environmental criminality. In S. Edwards, T. Edwards, & C. Fields (Eds.), *Environmental crime and criminality* (pp. 1–34). New York, NY: Garland.

Mullen, F. (1999, January 25). Six steps to stopping internal theft. *Discount Store News, 38*(2), p. 12.

Mullins, C., & Rothe, D. (2007). The forgotten ones. *Critical Criminology, 15,* 135–158.

Munroe, T. (1992, July 22). Senate panel hears about fraud, deception in auto-repair industry. *Washington Times,* p. C3.

Nader, R. (2013, March 22). Getting tough on devastating corporate crime. *Huff Post Business.* Retrieved from http://www.huffingtonpost.com/ralph-nader/corporate-crime_b_2934600.html

Nahra, K. J. (1999, October). Handling the double-edged sword: Insurers and the fight against health care fraud. *Health Law, 12,* 12–17.

Nakashima, E. (2020, April 7). Trump removes inspector general who was to oversee $2 trillion stimulus spending. *The Washington Post.* Retrieved from https://www.washingtonpost.com/national-security/trump-removes-inspector-general-who-was-to-oversee-2-trillion-stimulus-spending/2020/04/07/2f0c6cb8-78ea-11ea-9bee-c5bf9d2e3288_story.html

Nakayama, G. (2007, September 34). *Transmittal of final OECA parallel proceedings policy.* Washington, DC: Office of Enforcement and Compliance Assurance, Environmental Protection Agency. Retrieved from http://www2.epa.gov/sites/production/files/documents/parallel-proceedings-policy-09-24-07.pdf

Nammour, M. (2009, November 1). Two former hotel guards jailed for stealing guests' belongings. *McClatchy-Tribune Business News.* Retrieved from ABI/INFORM Complete database (Document ID No. 1890524941).

Nardo, M. (2004). Mapping the trails of financial crime. *Journal of Financial Crime, 12*(2), 139–143.

Nash, R., Bouchard, M., & Malm, A. (2017). Social networks as predictors of the harm suffered by victims of a large-scale ponzi scheme. *Canadian Journal of Criminology & Criminal Justice, 59*(1), 26–62. https://doi-org.proxy.lib.odu.edu/10.3138/cjccj.2014.E16

Nath, L., & Lovaglia, M. (2008). Cheating on multiple choice exams: Monitoring, assessment, and an optional assignment. *College Teaching, 57*(1), 3–8.

National Association of Medicaid Fraud Control Units. (1991, March). *Medicaid fraud report March 1991.*

National Association of Medicaid Fraud Control Units. (2014, November/December). *Medicaid fraud report November/December.* Retrieved from http://www.namfcu.net/resources/medicaid-fraud-reports-newsletters/2014-publications/14NovDec.pdf

National Center on Elder Abuse. (2008). *Major types of elder abuse.* Retrieved http://www.ncea.aoa.gov/NCEAroot/Main_Site/FAQ/Basics/Types_Of_Abuse.aspx

National Health Care Anti-Fraud Association. (2010). *The problem of health care fraud.* Retrieved from http://www.nhcaa.org/resources/health-care-anti-fraud-resources/thechallenge-of-health-care-fraud.aspx

National Health Care Anti-Fraud Association. (2020). The challenge of health care fraud. Retrieved from https://www.nhcaa.org/tools-insights/about-health-care-fraud/the-challenge-of-health-care-fraud

National Highway Traffic Safety Administration. (2002, April). Preliminary report: The incidence rate of odometer fraud. *U.S. Department of Transportation.* Retrieved from http://www.nhtsa.gov/cars/rules/regrev/evaluate/809441.html

National Oceanic and Atmospheric Administration. (2010). *New federal rule allows NOAA to deny port entry to illegal fishing vessels* [Press release]. Retrieved from http://www.noaanews.noaa.gov/stories2010/20101013_fishing.html

National Registry of Exonerations. (2020). Retrieved from http://www.law.umich.edu/special/exoneration/Pages/about.aspx.

National Safety Council. (2020). *Consumer product injuries, 2019.* Retrieved from https://injuryfacts.nsc.org/home-and-community/safety-topics/consumer-product-injuries

National Science Foundation (NSF). (2015). *Women, minorities and people with disabilities in science and engineering.* Retrieved from http://www.nsf.gov/statistics/2015/nsf15311

National Science Foundation. (2019a). *Semiannual report to Congress.* Retrieved from https://www.nsf.gov/oig/_pdf/NSF_OIG_SAR_60.pdf

National Science Foundation. (2019b). *Semiannual report to Congress.* Retrieved from https://www.nsf.gov/oig/_pdf/NSF_OIG_SAR_61.pdf

National Science Foundation. (2020). *Semiannual report to Congress.* Retrieved from https://www.nsf.gov/oig/_pdf/NSF_OIG_SAR_62.pdf

National Science Foundation, Office of Inspector General (NSF, OIG). (2019). *Semiannual report to Congress.* Retrieved from https://www.nsf.gov/nsb/publications/2019/NSF-OIG-SAR-05312019.pdf

National White Collar Crime Center (NW3C). (2009). *Welcome.* Retrieved July 30, 2011, from http://www.nw3c.org/

Naylor, B. (2020). Impeachment timeline: From early calls to a full House vote. *NPR.org.* Retrieved from https://www.npr.org/2019/12/17/788397365/impeachment-timeline-from-early-calls-to-a-full-house-vote

Neimark, B. (2019). Address the roots of environmental crime. *Science, 364*(6436), 138–138.

Nelson, J. (2010, February 5). Supervisor Blane spent $50,000 to hire white-collar criminal lawyer. *Daily Bulletin.* Retrieved from http://inlandpolitics.com/blog/2010/02/06/dailybulletin-supervisor-biane-spent-50000-to-hire-whitecollar-criminal-lawyer/

Nelson, L. (2016). Trump University, explained. *Vox.* Retrieved from https://www.vox.com/2015/7/29/9067429/trump-university

Nestor, S. (2004). The impact of changing corporate governance norms on economic crime. *Journal of Financial Crime, 11*(4), 347–352.

Neuhauser, A. (2019). 100,000 Americans die from air pollution, study finds. *US News.* Retrieved from https://www.usnews.com/news/national-news/articles/2019-04-08/100-000-americans-die-from-air-pollution-study-finds

Neumeister, L., & Hays, T. (2009). Madoff to plead guilty to eleven counts. *HuffingtonPost.com.* Retrieved from http://www.huffingtonpost.com/2009/03/10/bernard-madoff-expected-t_n_173424.html

Nguyen, T. H., & Pontell, H. N. (2011). Fraud and inequality in the subprime mortgage crisis. In M. Deflem (ed.), *Economic crisis and crime: Sociology of crime, law and deviance* (vol. 16, pp. tk–tk). Cambridge, MA: Emerald Group.

Ninemsn staff. (2010, January 18). Doctor convicted over lemon juice antiseptic. *Ninemsn.* Retrieved from http://news.ninemsn.com.au/world/1001073/doctor-convicted-over-lemonjuice-antiseptic

Nobles, M. R. (2019). Environmental crime and contemporary criminology: Making a difference. *American Journal of Criminal Justice, 44*(4), 656–669.

Nolasco, C. A. R. I., Vaughn, M. S., & del Carmen, R. V. (2013). Revisiting the choice model of Ponzi and pyramid schemes: Analysis of case law. *Crime, Law and Social Change, 60,* 375–400.

Noto, A. (2018). *Judge awards Fyre Festival attendees $5 million in lawsuit.* Retrieved from https://www.bizjournals.com/newyork/news/2018/07/05/judge-awards-fyre-festival-attendees-5-million-in.html. September 16, 2020.

Obeidallah, (2020, May 1). *Trump's Twitter defense of Flynn shows he can sympathize — just not with coronavirus victims.* Retrieved from https://www.nbcnews.com/think/opinion/trump-s-twitter-defense-flynn-shows-he-can-sympathize-just-ncna1197186

O'Colmain, S. (2014, May/June). Skip class and collect cash: Student financial aid fraud schemes. *Fraud Magazine.* Retrieved from http://www.fraud-magazine.com/article.aspx?id=4294982419

O'Connor, B. (2017). Here's your Rx to avoid medical identity theft. *Experian.com.* Retrieved from https://www.experian.com/blogs/ask-experian/heres-your-rx-to-avoid-medical-identity-theft

O'Connor, T. (1991, November). *Workplace violence in the fast food domain.* Paper presented at the annual meetings of the American Society of Criminology, Baltimore, MD.

O'Donnell, J. (2004, March 18). State time or federal prison? *USA Today.* Retrieved from http://www.usatoday.com/money/companies/2004-03-18-statetime_x.htm

O'Donnell, J., & Willing, R. (2003, May 11). Prison time gets harder for white-collar crooks. *USA Today.* Retrieved from http://www.usatoday.com/money/companies/management/2003-05-11-bighouse_x.htm

O'Hear, M. M. (2004). Sentencing the green-collar offender: Punishment, culpability, and environmental crime. *Journal of Criminal Law and Criminology, 95*(1), 133–276.

O'Sullivan, S. (2011, February 3). Delaware crime: Wilmington pastor charged with embezzlement. *News Journal.* Retrieved March 10, 2011, from http://www.delawareonline.com/article/20110203/NEWS01/102030351/Delaware-crime-Wilmington-pastor-charged-embezzlement

Occupational Safety and Health Administration (OSHA). (2006). *All about OSHA.* Retrieved July 29, 2011 from http://www.osha.gov/Publications/3302-06N-2006-English.html

Occupational Safety and Health Administration (OSHA). (2010a). *OSHA frequently asked questions.* Retrieved December 17, 2010 from http://osha.gov/osha_faqs.html

Occupational Safety and Health Administration (OSHA). (2010b). *The whistleblower protection program.* Retrieved December 17, 2010 from http://www.whistleblowers.gov/index.html

Occupational Safety and Health Administration. (2011a). *About OSHA*. Retrieved December 23, 2011 from http://www.osha.gov/about.html

Occupational Safety and Health Administration. (2011b). *OSHA we can help*. Retrieved December 23, 2011 from http://www.osha.gov/workers.html

Occupational Safety & Health Administration (OSHA), United States Department of Labor. (2015). *Employer rights and responsibilities following an OSHA inspection*. Retrieved from https://www.osha.gov/Publications/osha3000.pdf.

Occupational Safety and Health Administration. (2019). *2018 enforcement summary*. Retrieved from https://www.osha.gov/enforcement/2018-enforcement-summary

Office of Attorney General Maura Healey. (2020). *AG Healey announces criminal charges against superintendent and former medical director of Holyoke Soldiers' Home for their roles in deadly COVID-19 outbreak*. Retrieved from https://www.mass.gov/news/ag-healey-announces-criminal-charges-against-superintendent-and-former-medical-director-of

Office of Inspector General. (2020). *Inspector General Act*. Retrieved from https://oig.federalreserve.gov/inspector-general-act.htm

Office of New York State Attorney General. (2010). Cuomo announces charges against former UB researcher for hiring actors to testify during misconduct hearing and attempting to siphon $4 million in taxpayer funds. *Office of the Attorney General Media Center*. Retrieved from http://www.ag.ny.gov/media_center/2010/feb/feb16a_10.html

Office of Research Integrity. (2010). *About ORI*. Rockville, MD: U.S. Dept. of Health & Human Services. Retrieved from http://ori.hhs.gov/about

Office of Research Integrity. (n.d.). *Case summary: Kim, Shin-Hee*. Retrieved from https://ori.hhs.gov/content/case-summary-kim-shin-hee

Office of the Governor Rick Perry. (2010). *Statement by Gov. Rick Perry on EPA's efforts to take over Texas' air permitting program* [Press release]. Retrieved from http://governor.state.tx.us/news/press-release/14677

Office of Attorney General, Commonwealth of Pennsylvania. (2018). Pennsylvania Diocese Victims' Report. *Report I of the 40th Statewide Investigation by the Grand Jury*. Available online at https://www.attorneygeneral.gov/report/

Oleson, J. C. (2018). Access denied: Studying up in the criminological encounter. *Criminological Encounters*, *1*, 45–56.

Oliphant, B. J., & Oliphant, G. C. (2001). Using a behavior-based method to identify and reduce employee theft. *International Journal of Retail and Distribution Management*, *29*(10), 442–451.

Olivarez-Giles, N. (2010, January 26). Owner of 22 Midas auto shops settles fraud claims. *Los Angeles Times, Business*, Part B, p. 7.

Orebaugh, A., Kinser, J., & Allnut, J. (2016). Cyber profiling. *Journal of Cybersecurity and Information Systems*. Retrieved from https://www.csiac.org/wp-content/uploads/2016/02/CSIAC_Journal_V2N2.pdf

Orland, L. (1980). Reflections on corporate crime: Law in search of theory and scholarship. *American Criminal Law Review*, *17*, 501–520.

Ormseth, M. (2020). L.A. *father whose tip exposed Singer's college admissions scandal gets one year in prison*. Retrieved from https://www.latimes.com/california/story/2020-08-12/college-admissions-scandal-morrie-tobin-sentenced

Osei, Z. (2019). Duke to pay $112.5 million to settle scientific-misconduct lawsuit. *Chronicle of Higher Education*. Retrieved from https://www.chronicle.com/article/duke-to-pay-112-5-million-to-settle-scientific-misconduct-lawsuit

Ouziel, L. M. (2018). The regulatory challenge of public corruption. *Journal of Criminal Law & Criminology*, *108*(3), 639–652.

Owens, J. B. (2000, June). Have we no shame? Thoughts on shaming, "white-collar" criminals, and the Federal Sentencing Guidelines. *American University Law Review*, *49*, 1047–1058.

Pacini, C., Qiu, L. H., & Sinason, D. (2007). Qui tam actions: Fighting fraud against the government. *Journal of Financial Crime*, *14*(1), 64–78.

Page, R., Savage, A., Stitt, K., & Umhoffer, R. (1999). Environmental crimes. *American Criminal Law Review*, *36*(3), 515–592.

Palladin Security. (n.d.). *Cannabis security dogs*. Retrieved September 12, 2020 from https://paladink9.com/cannabis-security-dogs

Palloto, B. (2019). Former Baby's Burgers and Shakes manager sentenced for stealing from business. *Centredaily.com*. Retrieved from https://www.centredaily.com/news/local/crime/article232678422.html#storylink=cpy

Pao, T., Tzeng, L. Y., & Wang, K. C. (2014). "Typhoons and opportunistic fraud": Claim patterns of automobile theft insurance in Taiwan. *Journal of Risk and Insurance*, *81*(1), 91–112.

Parker, W. (2009). *A gynecologist's second opinion*. New York, NY: Penguin.

Partlow, J., & Fahrenthold, D. (2019). 'If you're a good worker, papers don't matter': How a Trump construction crew has relied on immigrants without legal status. *WashingtonPost.com*. Retrieved from https://www.washingtonpost.com/politics/if-youre-a-good-worker-papers-dont-matter-how-a-trump-construction-crew-has-relied-on-immigrants-without-legal-status/2019/08/09/cf59014a-b3ab-11e9-8e94-71a35969e4d8_story.html

Passas, N. (2001). False accounts: Why do company statements often offer a true and a fair view of virtual reality? *European Journal on Criminal Policy and Research, 9*(2), 117–135.

Passas, N. (2004). Law enforcement challenges in Hawala-related investigations. *Journal of Financial Crime, 12*(2), 112–119.

Passas, N. (2005). Lawful but awful: "Legal corporate crimes." *Journal of Socio-Economics, 34,* 771–786.

Pathal, P. (2016). International environmental crime: Growing concern of international environmental governance. *US-China Law Review, 13*(5), 382–398.

Patten, D. (2019). Motivations, opportunities, and controls of environmental crime: An empirical test of Kramer and Michalowski's integrated theoretical model of state-corporate crime. *Crime, Law & Social Change, 72*(2), 195–210. https://doi-org.proxy.lib.odu.edu/10.1007/s10611-019-09811-2

Paul, T. (2006). Five reverse home mortgage scams to watch out for. *Ezine Articles.* Retrieved from http://ezinearticles.com/?five-Home-Mortgage-Scams-to-Watch-Out-For&id=273604

Payne, B. K. (1995). Medicaid fraud. *Criminal Justice Policy Review, 7,* 61–74.

Payne, B. K. (2003a). *Crime in the home health care field.* Springfield, IL: Charles C Thomas.

Payne, B. K. (2003b). *Incarcerating white-collar offenders: The prison experience and beyond.* Springfield, IL: Charles C Thomas.

Payne, B. K. (2005). *Crime and elder abuse: An integrated perspective* (2nd ed.). Springfield, IL: Charles C Thomas.

Payne, B. K. (2006). Problems controlling fraud and abuse in the home health care field: Voices of fraud control unit directors. *Journal of Financial Crime, 13*(1), 77–92.

Payne, B. K. (2010). Understanding elder sexual abuse and criminal justice system's response: Comparisons to elder physical abuse. *Justice Quarterly, 27*(2), 206–224.

Payne, B. K. (2011). *Crime and elder abuse: An integrated perspective* (3rd ed.). Springfield, IL: Charles C Thomas.

Payne, B. K. (2013). Elder physical abuse and failure to report cases: Similarities and differences in case type and the justice system's response. *Crime and Delinquency 59*(5), 697–717.

Payne, B. K. (2015). Expanding the boundaries of criminal justice: Emphasizing the "s" in the criminal justice sciences through interdisciplinary efforts. *Justice Quarterly, 33*(1), 1–20.

Payne, B. K. (2018). White-collar cybercrime: White-collar crime, cybercrime, or both. *Criminology, Criminal Justice, Law & Society, 19*(3), 16–32.

Payne, B. K., & Berg, B. L. (1997). Looking for fraud in all the wrong places. *The Police Journal: A Quarterly Review for the Police of the World, 70,* 220–230.

Payne, B. K., & Berg, B. L. (1999). Perceptions of nursing home workers, police chiefs, and college students regarding crime against the elderly. *American Journal of Criminal Justice, 24,* 139–149.

Payne, B. K., Berg, B. L., & Byars, K. (1999). A qualitative examination of the similarities and differences of elder abuse definitions among four groups: Nursing home directors, nursing home employees, police chiefs and students. *Journal of Elder Abuse & Neglect, 10*(3/4), 63–86.

Payne, B. K., & Burke-Fletcher, L. B. (2005). Elder abuse in nursing homes: Prevention and resolution strategies and barriers. *Journal of Criminal Justice, 33*(2), 119–125.

Payne, B. K., & Cikovic, R. (1995). An empirical examination of the characteristics, consequences, and causes of elder abuse in nursing homes. *Journal of Elder Abuse & Neglect, 7*(4), 61–74.

Payne, B. K., & Dabney, D. (1997). Prescription fraud: Characteristics, causes, and consequences. *Journal of Drug Issues, 27*(4), 807–820.

Payne, B. K., & Gainey, R. (1998). A qualitative assessment of the pains experienced on electronic monitoring. *International Journal of Offender Therapy and Comparative Criminology, 42,* 149–63.

Payne, B. K., & Gainey, R. (2006). The criminal justice response to elder abuse in nursing homes: A routine activities perspective. *Western Criminology Review, 7*(3), 67–81.

Payne, B. K., & Gainey, R. (2009). *Family violence and criminal justice.* Cincinnati, OH: Anderson.

Payne, B. K., & Gray, C. (2001). Fraud by home health care workers and the criminal justice response. *Criminal Justice Review, 26,* 209–232.

Payne, B. K., & Stevens, E. D. (1999). An examination of recent professional sanctions imposed on Alabama lawyers. *Justice Professional, 12,* 17–43.

Payne, B. K., & Strasser, S. M. (2012). Financial exploitation of older persons in adult care settings: Comparisons to physical abuse and the justice system's response. *Journal of Elder Abuse & Neglect, 24*(3), 231–250.

Payne, B. K., Time, V., & Raper, S. (2005). Regulating legal misconduct in the Commonwealth of Virginia: The gender influence. *Women and Criminal Justice, 15*(3), 81–95.

Pendlebury, R. (2010, June 18). Special investigation: Why is BP taking all the blame? *Daily Mail*. Retrieved from http://www.dailymail.co.uk/news/article-1287226/GULF-OIL-SPILL-Whys-BP-taking-blame.html

Penn State Scandal, Fast Facts. (2020, May 13). *CNN*. Retrieved from https://www.cnn.com/2013/10/28/us/penn-state-scandal-fast-facts/index.html

Penzenstadler, N., & Page, S. (2016). Exclusive: Trump's 3,500 lawsuits unprecedented for a presidential nominee. *USA Today*. Retrieved from https://www.usatoday.com/story/news/politics/elections/2016/06/01/donald-trump-lawsuits-legal-battles/84995854

People v. Eubanks, 927 F.2d 310 (Cal. 1996).

Perlin, M. L. (2016). Merchants and thieves, hungry for power: Prosecutorial misconduct and passive judicial complicity in death penalty trials of defendants with mental disabilities. *Washington and Lee Law Review, 73*(3), 1501–1548.

Permanent Subcommittee on Investigations. (2019, November 18). *Carper, Portman bipartisan report reveals lack of federal response to China's talent recruitment plans*. Retrieved from https://www.hsgac.senate.gov/subcommittees/investigations/media/carper-portman-bipartisan-report-reveals-lack-of-federal-response-to-chinas-talent-recruitment-plans

Perri, F. S., & Brody, R. G. (2011). The dark triad: Organized crime, terror, and fraud. *Journal of Money Laundering Control, 14*(1), 44–59.

Petchenik, M. (2020). *Hotel workers charged with stealing 40th anniversary ring from guest's room*. Available online at https://www.wsbtv.com/news/local/north-fulton-county/hotel-worker-charged-with-stealing-40th-anniversary-ring-guests-room/VCTUYOVMPFBHNBW6ZN7GVR66JQ/

Petcu, B. (2018). Fake news and financial markets: 21st century twist on market manipulation. *American University Business Law Review, 7*(2), 297–326.

Peterson, B. K. (2004). Education as a new approach to fighting financial crime in USA. *Journal of Financial Crime, 11*(3), 262–267.

Petras, G., Loehrke, J., Padilla, R., Zarracina, J., & Borreson, J. (2021, February 9). Timeline: How the storming of the U.S. Capitol unfolded on Jan. 6. *USA Today*. Retrieved from https://www.usatoday.com/in-depth/news/2021/01/06/dc-protests-capitol-riot-trump-supporters-electoral-college-stolen-election/6568305002/

Petress, K. C. (2003). Academic dishonesty: A plague on our profession. *Education, 123*(3), 624–627.

Pfiefer, W. (2010, April 12). Bruce Karatz bring in star witness. *Los Angeles Times*. Retrieved from http://articles.latimes.com/2010/apr/02/business/la-fi-karatz2-2010apr02

Pfleeger, S. L., Sasse, M. A., & Furnham, A. (2014). From weakest link to security hero: Transforming staff security behavior. *Homeland Security & Emergency Management, 11*(4), 489–510.

Philippsohn, S. (2001). Trends in cybercrime—An overview of current financial crimes on the internet. *Computers & Security, 20*(1), 53–69.

Pickett, J. T. (2020). The Stewart retractions: A quantitative and qualitative analysis. *Econ Journal Watch, 17*(1), 152.

Pilger, R. C. (Ed). (2017). Federal prosecution of election offenses (8th ed.). Retrieved from https://www.justice.gov/criminal/file/1029066/download

Pillemer, K., & Moore, D. (1990). Highlights from a study of abuse of patients in nursing homes. *Journal of Elder Abuse & Neglect, 2*, 5–29.

Pino, N. W., & Smith, W. L. (2003). College students and academic dishonesty. *College Student Journal, 37*(4), 490–500.

Piquero, N. L. (2012). The only thing we have to fear is fear itself: Investigating the relationship between fear of falling and white-collar crime. *Crime & Delinquency, 58*(3), 362–379.

Piquero, N. L., & Benson, M. L. (2004). White-collar crime and criminal careers: Specifying a trajectory of punctuated situational offending. *Journal of Contemporary Criminal Justice, 20*(2), 148–165.

Piquero, N. L., Carmichael, S., & Piquero, A. R. (2008). Research note: Assessing the perceived seriousness of white-collar and street crime. *Crime and Delinquency, 54*, 291–312.

Piquero, N. L., & Davis, J. (2004). Extralegal factors and the sentencing of organizational defendants: An examination of the federal sentencing guidelines. *Journal of Criminal Justice, 32*(6), 643–654.

Piquero, N. L., Exum, M. L., & Simpson, S. S. (2005). Integrating the desire-for-control and rational choice in a corporate crime context. *Justice Quarterly, 22*(2), 252–280.

Piquero, N. L., Ling, S., Raine, A., & Piquero, A. R. (2019). Heart rate fails to predict white collar crime. *American Journal of Criminal Justice*, 1–14.

Piquero, N. L., & Piquero, A. R. (2016). White-collar criminal participation and the life course. In S. R. Van Slyke,

M. L. Benson, & F. T. Cullen (Eds.), *The Oxford handbook of white-collar crime* (p. 238–252). New York, NY: Oxford University Press.

Piquero, A. R., Piquero, N., Terry, K. J., Youstin, T., & Nobles, M. (2008). Uncollaring the criminal: Understanding criminal careers of criminal clerics. *Criminal Justice and Behavior, 35*, 583–599.

Piquero, N. L., Piquero, A. R., & Weisburd, D. (2016). Long-term effects of social and personal capital on offending trajectories in a sample of white-collar offenders. *Crime & Delinquency, 62*(11), 1510–1527.

Piquero, N. L., Schoepfer, A., & Langton, L. (2010). Completely out of control or the desire to be in complete control? How low self-control and the desire for control relate to corporate offending. *Crime & Delinquency, 56*(4), 627–647.

Piquero, N. L., Tibbetts, S. G., & Blankenship, M. B. (2005). Examining the role of differential association and techniques of neutralization in explaining corporate crime. *Deviant Behavior, 26*, 159–188.

Piquero, N. L., Vieraitis, L. M., Piquero, A. R., Tibbetts, S. G., & Blankenship, M. (2013). The interplay of gender and ethics in corporate offending decision making. *Journal of Contemporary Criminal Justice, 29*(3), 385–398.

Pirrong, C. (2010). Energy market manipulation: Definition, diagnosis, and deterrence. *Energy Law Journal, 31*(1), 1–20.

Plimton, E. A., & Walsh, D. (2010). Corporate criminal liability. *American Criminal Law Review, 47*, 331–343.

Plushnick-Masti, R. (2010, December 30). Rick Perry, Texas continue to wage battle against EPA as fight over regulations grows fierce. *Huffington Post*. Retrieved http://www.huffingtonpost.com/2010/12/30/rick-perry-texas-epa_n_802643.html

Podgor, E. S. (2007). The challenge of white collar sentencing. *Journal of Criminal Law and Criminology, 97*(3), 731–759.

Podgor, E. (2018). White collar shortcuts. *University of Illinois Law Review,3*, 925–968

Polantz, K. (2019, December 17). Rick Gates, former Trump campaign aide who testified to Mueller, sentenced to 45 days in jail. *CNN Politics*. Retrieved from https://www.cnn.com/2019/12/17/politics/rick-gates-sentencing/index.html

Policastro, C., & Payne, B. P. (2013). An examination of deviance and deviants in the durable medical equipment (DME) field: Characteristics, consequences, and responses to fraud. Deviant Behavior, 34(3), 191–207.

Pollack, H., & Smith, A. B. (1983). White-collar v. street crime sentencing disparity: How judges see the problem. *Judicature, 67*(4), 175–182.

Pollock, J. (2004). *Ethics in crime and justice* (4th ed.). Belmont, CA: Wadsworth.

Ponemon Institute. (2015, May). *2015 cost of data breach study: Global analysis*. Traverse City, MI: Poneman Institute LLC.

Ponemon Institute. (2015, October). *2015 cost of cyber-crime study: Global*. Traverse City, MI: Poneman Institute LLC.

Pontell, H. N. (2005). White-collar crime or just risky business? The role of fraud in major financial debacles. *Crime, Law and Social Change, 42*, 309–324.

Pontell, H. N. (2016). Theoretical, empirical, and policy implications of alternative definitions of "white-collar crime." In S. R. Van Slyke, M. L. Benson, & F. T. Cullen (Eds.), *The Oxford handbook of white-collar crime* (pp. 39–58). New York, NY: Oxford University Press.

Pontell, H. N., Black, W. K., & Geis, G. (2014). Too big to fail powerful to jail? On the absence of criminal prosecutors after the 2008 financial meltdown. *Crime, Law and Social Change, 61*, 1–13.

Pontell, H. N., & Geis, G. (2014). The trajectory of white-collar crime following the great economic meltdown. *Journal of Contemporary Criminal Justice, 30*(1), 70–82.

Pontell, H. N., Jesilow, P., & Geis, G. (1982). Policing physicians: Practitioner fraud and abuse in a government medical program. *Social Problems, 30*(1), 117–125.

Pontell, H. N., Jesilow, P., & Geis, G. (1984). Practitioner fraud and abuse in medical benefit programs. *Law and Policy, 6*, 405–424.

A Ponzi nation. (2009, December 29). *New Zealand Herald*. Retrieved from http://www.nzinvestors.com/business-news/15831-ponzi-nation.html

Posner, R. (1979–1980). Optimal sentences for whitecollar criminals. *American Criminal Law Review, 17*, 409–440.

Powell, S. M. (2010, December 5). Perry taking his rebellion national: States' rights crusade will begin with EPA battle. *[Houston] Chron.com*. Retrieved from http://www.chron.com/disp/story.mpl/metropolitan/7324941

Power, L. G. (2009). University students' perceptions of plagiarism. *Journal of Higher Education, 80*(6), 643–662.

Pratt, M. K. (2001, November 23). Retailers take steps to combat employee-theft epidemic. *Boston Business Journal, 21*(42), 37.

Preiser, S. E., & Swisher, C. C., III. (1988). Representing the white-collar defendant: How to avoid the trap. *Trial, 24*(10), 72–78.

Price Waterhouse v. Hopkins, 490 U.S. 228 (1989).

Primeaux, E. (2016, March/April). Number manipulator describes Enron's descent. *Fraud Magazine*. Retrieved from https://www.acfe.com/article.aspx?id=4294991880

PR Newswire. (2007, August 9). *Profnet wire: Government & law: Safety of imported products*. Retrieved from http://www.smart brief.com/news/aaaa/industryPR-detail.jsp?id=24DF678E-43D9-453F-AD14-D0EFFF2F9015

Pulkkinen, L. (2010, May 25). State: UW doctor traded addict drugs for sex. *KATU-TV*. Retrieved from http://www.katu.com/news/94853414.html

Punch, M. (2000). Suite violence: Why managers murder and corporations kill. *Crime, Law and Social Change*, 33, 243–280.

Punch, M. (2008). The organization did it: Individuals, corporations, and crime. In J. Minkes & L. Minkes (Eds.), *Corporate and white-collar crime* (pp. 102–121). Thousand Oaks, CA: Sage.

Punch, M. (2009). *Police corruption: Deviance, accountability, and reform in policing*. Portland, OR: Willan.

Pusey, I. (2007). The role of the regulator in combating financial crimes: A Caribbean perspective. *Journal of Financial Crime*, 14(3), 299–319.

Queisser, S., Sutton, S., & Fultz, V. (2015, July). *Two loan disbursements + midterm grades = increase in student success*. Paper presented at the NASSAA national conference, New Orleans, LA.

Quinney, R. (1974). *The social reality of crime*. Boston, MA: Little, Brown.

Rackmill, S. J. (1992). Understanding and sanctioning the white collar offender. *Federal Probation*, 56(2), 26–34.

Rader, N. (2008). *Criminal brain: Understanding biological theories of crime*. New York: NYU Press.

Rael, Z. (2019). Employees at metro medical marijuana dispensary accused of selling to people without cards. *Koco News 5*. Retrieved from https://www.koco.com/article/employees-at-metro-medical-marijuana-dispensary-accused-of-selling-to-people-without-cards/29628665

Raine, A., Laufer, W. S., Yang, Y., Narr, K. L., Thompson, P., & Toga, A. W. (2012). Increased executive functioning, attention, and cortical thickness in whitecollar criminals. *Human Brain Mapping*, 33, 2,932–2,940.

Rakovski, C. C., & Levy, E. S. (2007). Academic dishonesty: Perceptions of business students. *College Student Journal*, 41(2), 466–481.

Rakowski, J. J. (2004). Does the consumer have an obligation to cooperate with price discrimination? *Business Ethics Quarterly*, 14(2), 263–274.

Raloff, J. (2010, June 2). July: When not to go to the hospital. *Science News*. Retrieved from http://www.sciencenews.org/view/generic/id/59865

Ramsey-Klawsnik, H. (1999, June). *Elder sexual abuse: Workshop handouts*. Presented at a workshop of the Virginia Coalition for the Prevention of Elder Abuse, June, Virginia Beach, Virginia.

Randall, D. (2010, May 9). Million gallons of oil a day gush into Gulf of Mexico. *The Independent*. Retrieved from http://www.independent.co.uk/news/world/americas/milliongallons-of-oil-a-day-gush-into-gulf-of-mexico.1969472.html

Ranson, J. W. A., Arnio, A. N., & Baumer, E. P. (2019). Extending research on neighborhoods and crime: An examination of mortgage fraud across Chicago census tracts. *Journal of Quantitative Criminology*, 35(3), 465–491. https://doi-org.proxy.lib.odu.edu/10.1007/s10940-018-9392-y

Rao, A., & Wang, E. (2015). *Demand for "healthy" products: False claims in advertising*. Retrieved from http://ssrn.com/abstract=2559980

Rasmussen, D. G., & Leauanae, J. L. (2004). Expert witness qualifications and selection. *Journal of Financial Crime*, 12(2), 165–171.

Rashbaum, W. K., & Weiser, B. (2020, August 3). DA is investigating Trump and his company over fraud, filing suggests. *New York Times*. Retrieved from https://www.nytimes.com/2020/08/03/nyregion/donald-trump-taxes-cyrus-vance.html

Rataj, T. (2001). Cybercrime causes chaos. *Law and Order*, 49(5), 43–46.

Raval, V., & Raval, V. (2019). Differentiating risk factors of Ponzi from non-Ponzi frauds. *Journal of Financial Crime*, 26(4), 993–1005. https://doi-org.proxy.lib.odu.edu/10.1108/JFC-07-2018-0075

Re, G. (2020). Dems hammering Trump overlook Obama administration's record of firing inspectors general. *Fox News*. Retrieved from https://www.foxnews.com/politics/obama-admins-record-of-firing-inspectors-general

Reardon, S. (2015, July 1). US vaccine researcher sentenced to prison for fraud. *International Weekly Research Journal of Science*. Retrieved from http://www.nature.com/news/usvaccine-researcher-sentenced-to-prison-forfraud-1.17660

Record number of shoplifters and dishonest employees apprehended by US retailers according to 20th Annual Theft

Survey by Jack L. Hayes International. (2008, October 1). *Business Wire*. Retrieved from http://www.businesswire .com/news/home/20090901005013/en/Shoplifters-Dishonest -Employees-Apprehended-Record-Numbers-Retailers

Restaurant admits to serving Popeye's chicken as its own. (2017, October 20). *Youtube.com*. Retrieved from https://www .youtube.com/watch?v=0l30m0DlvX8.

Reed, G. E., & Yeager, P. C. (1996). Organizational offending and neoclassical criminology: Challenging the reach of a general theory of crime. *Criminology*, *34*(3), 357–382.

Reed, M. A., & Scott, E. D. (2013, July/August). Five cyber-security mistakes companies make that could result in their prosecution. *Financial Fraud Law Report*, 615–623.

Rege-Patwardhan, A. (2009). Cybercrimes against criti-cal infrastructures: A study of online criminal organization techniques. *Criminal Justice Studies*, *22*(3), 261–271.

Reilly, M., Lott, B., & Gallogly, S. (1986). Sexual harassment of university students. *Sex Roles*, *15*, 333–358.

Reilly, S. (2016, June 9). USA TODAY exclusive: Hundreds allege Donald Trump doesn't pay his bills. *USA Today*. Retrieved from https://www.usatoday.com/story/news/ politics/elections/2016/06/09/donald-trump-unpaid-bills -republican-president-laswuits/85297274/

Reinhart, M. (2019). Fraud and misconduct in research: Detection, investigation, and organizational response. *Amer-ican Journal of Sociology*, *124*(5), 1598–1600. https://doi-org .proxy.lib.odu.edu/10.1086/701692

Reiss, A. J., & Biderman, A. D. (1980). *Data sources on white-collar law-breaking*. Rockford, MD: National Institute of Justice.

Rejesus, R. M., Little, B. B., & Lovell, A. C. (2004). Using data mining to detect crop insurance fraud: Is there a role for social scientists? *Journal of Financial Crime*, *12*(1), 24–32.

Restaurant closed briefly after dead deer found in kitchen. (2008, October 27). *USA Today*. Retrieved from www.usatoday .com/news/2008-10-27-2714710309_x.htm

Rhoten, D., & Pfirman, S. (2007). Women in interdisciplinary science: Exploring preferences and consequences. *Research Policy*, *36*, 56–75.

Richardson, H. (2010). WVU tackles white-collar crime in forensic accounting program. *State Journal*, *26*(27), 10.

Richburg, K. B. (2009, July 24). Rabbis, politicians snared in FBI sting: Corruption probe brings 44 arrests in N.J. and N.Y. *The Washington Post*. Retrieved from http://www .washingtonpost.com/wp-dyn/content/article/2009/07/23/ AR2009072301449.html

Richer, A. (2020). Top Harvard professor arrested, charged with lying about income to feds. *NBCBoston.Com*. Retrieved from https://www.nbcboston.com/news/local/ harvard-professor-charged-federally-with-lying-about -income/2068591

Richland Source. (2020). Former Youngstown mayor pleads guilty to felonies. *Richland Source*. Retrieved from https:// www.richlandsource.com/news/former-youngstown -mayor-pleads-guilty-to-felonies/article_bd7c97c4-67ac -11ea-adaa-3f529af19ea4.html

Riggins, A. (2020). Chula Vista police arrest four during raid of unlicensed dispensary. *San Diego Tribune*. Retrieved from https://www.sandiegouniontribune.com/news/ public-safety/story/2020-04-27/chula-vista-police-raid -cannabis-dispensary

Riggs, A. (2007, August 20). Beware of post-storm home repair scams. *Knight Ridder/Tribune Business News*. Retrieved from ABI/INFORM Complete database (Document ID No. 1322672341).

Ristovic, S. (2018). Environmental crime prevention through the work of community policing. *International Journal of Economics and Law*, *8*, 75–86.

Ritchie, D. (2014, July). Security talk: Why customized cyber-security training is essential. *Security*, 50.

Robert, A. (2020). Tenured law professor who lied to IRS will return to teaching. *ABA Journal*. Retrieved from https://www .abajournal.com/news/article/tenured-law-professor-who -lied-to-irs-will-return-to-teaching

Roberts, C. (2007). Rarer than rabies: The legacy of Michael Nifong. *RenewAmerica.com*. Retrieved from http://www .renewamerica.com/columns/roberts/070725

Robertson, G. (2017). Mysterious symptoms and medical marijuana: Patients are looking for answers. *Globe and Mail*. Retrieved from https://www.theglobeandmail.com/cannabis/ article-mysterious-symptoms-and-medical-marijuana -patients-are-looking-for

Robie, C., Kidwell, R., & King, J. (2003). The ethics of profes-sorial book selling. *Journal of Business Ethics*, *47*, 61–76.

Robin, G. D. (1974). White-collar crime and employee theft. *Crime and Delinquency*, *20*, 251–262.

Robinson, C. (2019). Alabama sheriff charged with defrauding church in jail food fund scheme. *AL.com*. Retrieved from https://www.al.com/news/tuscaloosa/2019/06/alabama-sheriff-charged-with-defrauding-church-in-jail-food-fund-scheme.html

Robinson, M. (2015). Utah's new registry for white collar criminals is inhumane. *The New Republic*. Retrieved from https://newrepublic.com/article/121291/utah-white-collar-crime-registry-useless-and-inhumane.

Robinson, M., & Murphy, D. (2009). *Greed is good: Maximization and elite deviance in America*. Lanham, MD: Rowman & Littlefield.

Robinson, M. B. (2004). *Why crime? An integrated systems theory of antisocial behavior*. Upper Saddle River, NJ: Pearson/Prentice Hall.

Rogers, D. (2002). Eye of the storm: Cybercrime poses a threat to national security, but is the threat overblown or underestimated? *Law Enforcement Technology*, *29*(11), 60–62, 64–65.

Rorie, M. (2020). Preface. In M. Rorie (Ed.), *The handbook of white-collar crime* (pp. xviii–xxiii). New York, NY: John Wiley & Sons.

Rosenbaum, E. (2019). Colorado passes $1 billion in marijuana state revenue. *CNBC.COM*. Retrieved from https://www.cnbc.com/2019/06/12/colorado-passes-1-billion-in-marijuana-state-revenue.html

Rosenbaum, P. (2009, April). Loss prevention. *AFP Exchange*, *29*(3), 40.

Rosenmerkel, S. P. (2001). Wrongfulness and harmfulness as components of seriousness of white-collar offenses. *Journal of Contemporary Criminal Justice*, *17*, 308–327.

Rosenstein, R. (2018). Deputy Attorney General Rod J. *Rosenstein delivers remarks at the American Conference Institute's 35th International Conference on the Foreign Corrupt Practices Act*. Retrieved from https://www.justice.gov/opa/speech/deputy-attorney-general-rod-j-rosenstein-delivers-remarks-american-conference-institute-0

Rosner, H. (2019). The Popeye's chicken sandwich is here to save America. *New Yorker.com*. Retrieved from https://www.newyorker.com/culture/annals-of-gastronomy/the-popeyes-chicken-sandwich-is-here-to-save-america

Rosoff, S. M. (1989). Physicians as criminal defendants. *Law and Human Behavior*, *13*(2), 231–236.

Ross, E. A. (1907). *Sin and society: An analysis of latter day iniquity*. Boston, MA: Houghton Mifflin.

Ross, J., & Rothe, D. (2008). Ironies of controlling state crime. *International Journal of Law, Crime, and Justice*, *36*, 196–210.

Rossetti, S. J. (1995). Impact of child abuse on attitudes toward God and the Catholic Church. *Child Abuse & Neglect*, *19*(12), 13.

Rothe, D. (2009). Beyond the law: The Reagan administration and Nicaragua. *Critical Criminology*, *17*(1), 39–67.

Rothe, D., & Friedrichs, D. (2006). The state of the criminology of crimes by the state. *Social Justice*, *33*, 147–161.

Rothe, D., Muzzatti, S., & Mullins, C. (2006). Crime on the high seas. *Critical Criminology*, *14*, 159–180.

Rothe, D., & Ross, J. (2008). The marginalization of state crime in introductory textbooks on criminology. *Critical Sociology*, *34*, 741–752.

Rothe, D. L. (2020). Moving beyond abstract typologies? Overview of state and state-corporate crime. *Journal of White Collar and Corporate Crime*, *1*(1), 7–15.

Rothe, D. L., & Medley, C. (2020). Beyond state and state-corporate crime typologies: The symbiotic nature, harm, and victimization of crimes of the powerful and their continuation. In M. Rorie (Ed.), *The handbook of white-collar crime* (pp. 81–94). New York, NY: John Wiley & Sons.

Rowbottom, J. (2016). Corruption, transparency, and reputation: The role of publicity in regulating political donations. *Cambridge Law Journal*, *75*(2), 398–425.

Rowe, E. A. (2016). Rats, traps, and trade secrets. *Boston College Law Review*, *57*(2), 381–426.

Ruankaew, T. (2019). Employee theft among college students in the workforce. *International Business Research*, *12*(4), 40–49.

Rudra, A. (2010). What is title insurance & how you can use it to protect your home. *Daily Markets*. Retrieved from http://www.dailymarkets.com/contributor/2010/03/28/what-is-title-insurance-how-you-can-use-it-to-protectyour-home

Ruggiero, V. (2007). It's the economy, stupid! Classifying power crimes. *International Journal of the Sociology of Law*, *35*, 163–177.

Ruiz, M. (2010). Where is Bernie Madoff still a hero? *America Online (AOL) News*. Retrieved from http://www.aolnews.com/2010/06/06/where-is-bernie-madoff-still-a-hero-prison

Rutledge, G. P. (2006). Disclosure and sharing of sensitive information: A US securities regulatory perspective. *Journal of Financial Crime*, *13*(3), 339–347.

Ryan-Boyle, C., Simon, J., & Yebler, J. (1991). Sentencing of organizations. *American Criminal Law Review, 29*, 743–770.

Saba, C. (2019). Employment law violations. *American Criminal Law Review, 56*(3 Annual Survey of White Collar Crime), 759–806.

Sage (n.d.). *Journal description: Journal of White Collar and Corporate Crime: SAGE Journals Sagepub.com.* Retrieved from https://journals.sagepub.com/description/wcc#:~:text= The%20journal%20is%20aimed%20at,social%20intervention %20and%20policy%20change. Accessed Feb. 28, 2021.

Sambides, N., Jr. (2009, June 24). Police charge contractor with Lincoln paving scam. *McClatchy-Tribune Business News.* Retrieved from ABI/INFORM Complete database (Document ID No. 1758884291).

Sarna, S. F. (2012). Advertising on the Internet: An opportunity for abuse? *Journal of Civil Rights and Economic Development, 11*(3), 683–689.

Savage, C. (2020). Michael Atkinson, fired by Trump, urges whistle-blowers 'to bravely speak up.' *The New York Times.* Retrieved from https://www.nytimes.com/2020/04/06/us/ politics/michael-atkinson-inspector-general-fired.html

Savage, C., & Baker, P. (2020). Trump ousts coronavirus spending watchdog Glenn Fine. *The New York Times.* Retrieved from https://www.nytimes.com/2020/04/07/us/ politics/trump-coronavirus-watchdog-glenn-fine.html

Sayre, K. (2011, January 13). Developer who pleaded guilty to harboring stolen antiques gets 3 years probation. *Al. com.* Retrieved from http://blog.al.com/live/2011/01/matt_ walker_sentenced_to_three.html

Scannell, K. (2007, May 7). Insider trading: It's back with a vengeance. *Wall Street Journal*, p. B1.

Schanzenbach, M., & Yaeger, M. L. (2006). Prison time, fines, and federal white collar criminals: The anatomy of a racial disparity. *Journal of Criminal Law and Criminology, 96*(2), 757–793.

Schapiro, R. (2009, July 19). Shanks for the advice: White-collarcrookslearnjailsurvivalfromex-con.*NewYorkDailyNews.* Retrieved from http://www.nydailynews.com/news/money/ shanks-advice-white-collar-crooks-learn-jailsurvival -ex-con-article-1.400539

Schell-Busey, N., Simpson, S. S., Rorie, M., & Alper, M. (2016). What works? A systematic review of corporate crime deterrence. *Criminology & Public Policy, 15*(2), 387–416.

Schiff, M. B., & Kramer, L. C. (2004). Conducting internal investigations of employee theft and other misconduct. *The Brief, 33*(3), 62–64.

Schlegel, K. (1993). Crime in the pits. *Annals of the American Academy of Political and Social Science, 525*, 59–70.

Schmidt, P. (2003, September 19). Reports allege misconduct at UConn. *Chronicle of Higher Education, 50*(4), A26.

Schneider, H. S. (2012). Agency problems and reputation in expert services: Evidence from auto repair. *The Journal of Industrial Economics, 60*(3), 406–433.

Schoenfeld, H. (2005). Violated trust: Conceptualizing prosecutorial misconduct. *Journal of Contemporary Criminal Justice, 21*(3), 250–271.

Schoepfer, A., Carmichael, S., & Piquero, N. L. (2007). Do perceptions of punishment vary between white-collar and street crime? *Journal of Criminal Justice, 35*, 151–163.

Schoepfer, A., & Piquero, N. L. (2006). Exploring white-collar crime and the American dream: A partial test of institutional anomie theory. *Journal of Criminal Justice, 34*(3), 227–235.

Schoepfer, A., Piquero, N. L., & Langton, L. (2014). Low self-control versus the desire-for-control: An empirical test of white-collar crime and conventional crime. *Deviant Behavior, 35*, 197–214.

Schrager, L. S., & Short, J. F. (1978). Toward a sociology of organizational crime. *Social Problems, 25*, 407–419.

Schram, S. (2013). Acupuncture, medical necessity, and automobile insurance fraud. *American Acupuncturist, 62*, 33–38.

Schroyer, J. (2015). For marijuana companies, biggest security concern comes from the inside. *Marijuana Business Daily.* Retrieved from https://mjbizdaily.com/for-marijuana -companies-biggest-security-concern-comes-from-the-inside/

Schudson, M. (2004). Notes on scandal and the Watergate legacy. *American Behavioral Scientist, 47*(9), 1231–1238.

Schwemberger, J., Mosby, J., Doa, M., Jacobs, D., Ashley, P., Brody, D., . . . Homa, D. (2005). Blood lead levels: United States, 1999–2002. *Mortality Weekly Report, 54*(20), 513–516.

Sci Tech Blog. (2009, August 5). *Student arrested for "modding" Xbox consoles* [Web log post]. Retrieved January 4, 2016 from http://scitech. blogs.cnn.com/2009/08/05/student -arrested-formodding-xbox-consoles

Scott, M. B., & Lyman, S. (1968). Accounts. *American Sociological Review, 33*, 46–62.

Scullin, S. (2014, April). Big crime, big borders and the bitcoin. *Law Enforcement Technology*, 8–11.

Searcey, D. (2010, October 20). BP claims process moves forward, but not without grumbling. *Wall Street Journal.* Retrieved from http://blogs.wsj.com/law/2010/10/20/

bp-claimsprocess-moves-forward-but-not-without-grumbling

Searcey, D., & Efrati, A. (2011, March 18). Madoff beaten in prison: Ponzi schemer was assaulted by another inmate in December; Officials deny incident. *Wall Street Journal.* Retrieved from http://online.wsj.com/article/SB1000 142405 274870474340457512803114342 4928.html

Securities and Exchange Commission (SEC). (2009). Ponzi schemes—Frequently asked questions [Press release]. Retrieved from http://www.sec.gov/answers/ponzi.htm# PonziVsPyramid

Securities and Exchange Commission (SEC). (2010). *Investigation of the failure of the SEC to uncover Bernard Madoff's Ponzi scheme.* Washington, DC: SEC Office of Investigations. Retrieved from http://www.sec.gov/news/studies/2009/oig -509.pdf

Securities and Exchange Commission, Division of Enforcement. (2015, June 15). *Enforcement manual.* Retrieved from http://www.sec.gov/divisions/enforce/enforcement manual.pdf

Securities and Exchange Commission (2020). *Division of Enforcement 2019 annual report.* Retrieved from https://www .sec.gov/reports

Seibel, J. (2009, June 11). Warrant accuses auto repair shop of fraud. *Journal Sentinel, Inc.* Retrieved from http://www .jsonline.com/news/waukesha/47881922.html

Shalby, C. (2019). UCLA professor faces 219 years in prison for conspiring to send U.S. *missile chips to China.* Retrieved from https://www.latimes.com/local/lanow/la-me-ucla -professor-military-china-20190711-story.html

Shapiro, S. (1985). The road not taken: The elusive path to criminal prosecution for white-collar offenders. *Law and Society Review, 12,* 179–218.

Shapiro, S. P. (1990). Collaring the crime, not the criminal: Reconsidering the concept of white-collar crime. *American Sociological Review, 55*(3), 346–365.

Shea, D. J. (2008). Effects of sexual abuse by Catholic priests on adults victimized as children. *Sexual Addiction and Compulsivity, 15*(3), 250–268.

Sheets, C. (2018). Etowah sheriff pockets $750k in jail food funds, buys $740k beach house. *AL.com.* Retrieved from https://www.al.com/news/birmingham/2018/03/etowah_ sheriff_pocketed_over_7.html

Sherman, N. I. (2005, January 12). Yale professor ousted for misconduct. *Harvard Crimson.* Retrieved from http://www.thecrimson.com/article/2005/1/12/yale -professor-ousted-for-misconduct-following/?print=1

Shichor, D. (1989). Corporate deviance and corporate victimization: A review and some elaborations. *International Review of Victimology, 1*(1), 67–88.

Shover, C. L., Vest, N. A., Chen, D., Stueber, A., Falasinnu, T. O., Hah, J. M., . . . & Humphreys, K. (2020). Association of state policies allowing medical cannabis for opioid use disorder with dispensary marketing for this indication. *JAMA Network Open, 3*(7), pp.e2010001-e2010001.

Shover, N., Fox, G., & Mills, M. (1994). Long term consequences of victimization by white-collar crime. *Justice Quarterly, 11,* 75–98.

Shover, N., & Routhe, A. (2005). Environmental crime. *Crime and Justice, 32,* 321–371.

Shuler, D. (2010). Connie Francis and Dionne Warrick: Two divas in Vegas. Retrieved from http://www.examiner.com/ arts-in-newyork/connie-francis-and-dionne-warwick -twodivas-las-vegas.

Siebecker, M. R. (2017). Political insider trading. *Fordham Law Review, 85*(6), 2717–2768.

Siemaszko, C. (2019). Michigan State fined $4.5M by feds for 'complete failure' in protecting students from Larry Nassar. Retrieved from https://www.nbcnews.com/news/us -news/feds-hit-michigan-state-hit-record-4-5-million -fine-n1050096

Silverman, H., & Almasy, S. (2020, January 18). Former Drexel professor arrested and accused of spending $185,000 in grant money on strippers, sports bars and iTunes. *CNN.* Retrieved from https://www.cnn.com/2020/01/18/us/drexel -former-professor-grant-money-strippers-trnd/index.html

Simon, D. R. (2000). Corporate environmental crimes and social inequality: New directions for environmental justice research. *American Behavioral Scientist, 43*(4), 633–645.

Simon, D. R. (2006). *Elite deviance* (8th ed.). New York, NY: Random House.

Simpson, S. S. (2013). White-collar crime: A review of recent developments and promising directions for future research. *Annual Review of Sociology, 39,* 309–331.

Simpson, S. S. (2019). Reimagining Sutherland 80 years after white-collar crime. *Criminology 57,* 189–207.

Simpson, S. S., Gibbs, C., Rorie, M., Slocum, L. A., Cohen, M. A., & Vandenbergh, M. (2013). An empirical assessment of corporate environmental crime-control strategies. *Journal of Criminal Law and Criminology, 103*(1), 231–278.

Simpson, S. S., & Koper, C. S. (1992). Deterring corporate crime. *Criminology, 30*(3), 347–375.

Simpson, S. S., & Koper, C. S. (1997). The changing of the guard: Top management characteristics, organizational strain, and antitrust offending. *Journal of Quantitative Criminology, 13*(4), 373–404.

Simpson, S. S., & Piquero, N. L. (2002). Low self-control, organizational theory, and corporate crime. *Law & Society Review, 36*(3), 509–547.

Simpson, S. S., & Rorie, M. (2016). Economic fluctuations and crises. In S. R. Van Slyke, M. L. Benson, & F. T. Cullen (Eds.), *The Oxford handbook of white-collar crime* (pp. 326–344). New York, NY: Oxford University Press.

Simpson, S. S., & Yeager, P. C. (2015). *Building a comprehensive white-collar violations data system, final technical report.* Retrieved from https://www.ncjrs.gov/pdffiles1/bjs/grants/248667.pdf

Sims, R. L. (1993). The relationship between academic dishonesty and unethical business practices. *Journal of Education for Business, 68*(4), 207–211.

Singer, S. I. (2016). Adolescent precursors of white-collar crime. In S. R. Van Slyke, M. L. Benson, & F. T. Cullen (Eds.), *The Oxford handbook of white-collar crime* (217–237). New York, NY: Oxford University Press.

Singh, N., & Conway, K. (2016). 'Real Housewives' star Teresa Giudice says prison was like 'living in Hell'. *ABC News.* Retrieved from https://abcnews.go.com/Entertainment/exclusive-real-housewives-star-teresa-giudice-prison-living/story?id=36798513

Singletary, M. (2000, June 7). Promissory scams leave many broke. *The Washington Post*, p. H01. Retrieved from http://articles.sun-sentinel.com/2000-06-12/news/0006090663_1_conartists-promissory-notes-investors.

Sinrod, E. J., & Reilly, W. P. (2000). Cyber-crimes: A practical approach to the application of federal computer crime laws. *Santa Clara Computer and High Technology Law Journal, 16*, 177–196. [E-version, pp. 1–55: http://www.sinrodlaw.com/cybercrime.doc]

Sipes, D. D. (1988). Legal and ethical perspectives of selling complimentary copies of the college textbook. *Journal of Law and Education, 17*(3), 355–373.

Sisak, M. (2019, December 18). *New York fraud charges against Paul Manafort dropped over double jeopardy concern.* Retrieved from https://www.chicagotribune.com/nation-world/ct-nw-paul-manafort-fraud-case-dropped-20191218-gz6itq6ugrborf7etek762ygkm-story.html

SIWire. (2016). Erin Andrews awarded $55 million in Marriott lawsuit. *Sports Illustrated Online.* Retrieved from https://www.si.com/more-sports/2016/03/07/erin-andrew-marriott-video-lawsuit-decision-55-million

Skinner, L., Giles, M. K., Griffith, S. E., Sonntag, M. E., Berry, K. K., & Beck, R. (1995). Academic sexual intimacy violations: Ethicality and occurrence reports from undergraduates. *Journal of Sex Research, 32*(2), 131–143.

Skinner, W. F., & Fream, A. M. (1997). A social learning theory analysis of computer crime among college students. *Journal of Research in Crime and Delinquency, 34*(4), 495–518.

Skylar, V. (2012). Cyber security of safety-critical infrastructure: A case study for nuclear facilities. *Information & Security: An International Journal, 28*(1), 98–107.

Slapper, G. (1993). Corporate manslaughter: An examination of the determinants of prosecutorial policy. *Social and Legal Studies, 2*, 423–443.

Smietana, B. (2005). New interfaith report focuses on pastors who steal from unsuspecting congregations. *Religion News Service.* Retrieved from http://www.adventistreview.org/2005-1508/story5.html

Smith, A., & Horowitz, J. (2017). Martin Shkreli trial goes to jury. *abc57.* Retrieved from https://www.abc57.com/news/martin-shkreli-fraud-trial-goes-to-the-jury.

Smith, B. V., & Yarussi, J. M. (2007). *Breaking the code of silence: Correctional officers' handbook on identifying and addressing sexual misconduct with offenders.* Washington, DC: National Institute of Corrections.

Smith, C. (2011, February 16). Heiress to testify in Edwards inquiry. *Pittsburgh Tribune-Review.* Retrieved from http://www.pittsburghlive.com/x/pittsburghtrib/news/pittsburgh/s_723051.html

Smith, G. S. (2015). Management models for international cybercrime. *Journal of Financial Crime, 22*(1), 104–125.

Smith, R. (1997, December). Some used car dealers may be dishonest. *Credit Management*, p. 16.

Smith, R. (2006). Research misconduct: The poisoning of the well. *Royal Society of Medicine, 99*, 232–237.

Smith, T. R. (2004). Low self-control, staged opportunity, and subsequent fraudulent behavior. *Criminal Justice and Behavior, 31*(5), 542–563.

Snider, L. (1990). Cooperative models and corporate crime: Panacea or cop-out? *Crime and Delinquency, 36*(3), 373–390.

Snider, L. (2020). Beyond Trump: Neoliberal capitalism and the abolition of corporate crime. *Journal of White Collar and Corporate Crime, 1*(2), 86–94.

Snyder, E. A. (1989). New insights into the decline of antitrust enforcement. *Contemporary Policy Issues, 7*(4), 1–18.

Snyder, E. A. (1990). The effect of higher criminal penalties on antitrust enforcement. *Journal of Law and Economics, 33*(2), 439–462.

SoCal restaurant 'proudly' serves Popeyes chicken as their own. (2017, October 18). *Youtube.com*. Retrieved from https://www.youtube.com/watch?v=z5tzwup4KjU

Sokol, C. (2020). Banned University of Idaho professor arrested on drug, burglary charges. *The Spokesman-Review*. Retrieved from https://www.spokesman.com/stories/2019/sep/25/banned-ui-professor-arrested-on-drug-burglary-char

Solomon, C. M. (1992, July). Keeping hate out of the workplace. *Personnel Journal, 71*(7), 30–36.

Soltes, E. (2019). The frequency of corporate misconduct: public enforcement versus private reality. *Journal of Financial Crime, 26*(4), 923–937. https://doi-org.proxy.lib.odu.edu/10.1108/JFC-10-2018-0107

Sorensen, P. T. (2009). The failure of *Sprint v. Mendelsohn* and what courts should do now. *Labor Law Journal, 60*, 185–195.

Sorkin, M. (2008). Watchdog group blasts agency over child safety. *St. Louis Post-Dispatch*. Retrieved from http://business.highbeam.com/435553/article-1G1-174735507/watchdoggroup-blasts-agency-over-child-safety

Souryal, S. S. (2009). Deterring corruption by prison personnel: A principle-based perspective. *Prison Journal, 89*(1), 21–45.

Sowa, T. (2010, March 20). GU joins police to fight fraud: Accountant teams help solve small-scale crime. *Spokesman Review*. Retrieved from http://www.spokesman.com/stories/2010/mar/20/gu-joins-police-^=to-fight-fraud/

Spahr, L. L., & Alison, L. J. (2004). US savings and loan fraud: Implications for general and criminal culture theories of crime. *Crime, Law and Social Change, 41*, 95–106.

Spalek, B. (2001, October). White-collar crime victims and the issue of trust. *British Society of Criminology, Vol.* 4 [Papers from the British Society of Criminology Conference, Leicester, July 2000]. Abstract retrieved from http://www.britsoccrim.org/volume4/003.pdf

Speer, D. L. (2000). Redefining borders: The challenges of cybercrime. *Crime, Law and Social Change, 34*(3), 259–273.

Spivack, P., & Raman, S. (2008). Regulating the "new regulators": Current trends in deferred prosecution agreements. *American Criminal Law Review, 45*(2), 159–193.

Spurgeon, W. A., & Fagan, T. P. (1981). Criminal liability for life-endangering corporate conduct. *Journal of Criminal Law and Criminology, 72*(2), 400.

Sramcik, T. (2004, January 1). San Diego shop chain latest to be accused of fraud. *Automotive Body Repair News (ABRN)*, p. 16. Retrieved from http://www.search-autoparts.com/search autoparts/Industry+News/San-Diegoshop-chain-latest-to-be-accused-of-fraud/ArticleStandard/Article/detail/88775

St. Louis Police Department. (2006). *Home repair fraud*. Retrieved July 29, 2011 from http://ww5.stlouisco.com/police/PDFDIR/Brochures/Repair_Fraud.pdf

Stadler, W. A., & Benson, M. L. (2012). Revisiting the guilty mind: The neutralization of white-collar crime. *Criminal Justice Review, 37*(4), 494–511.

Stadler, W. A., Benson, M. L., & Cullen, F. T. (2011). Revisiting the special sensitivity hypothesis: The prison experience of white-collar inmates. *Justice Quarterly, 30*(6), 1–25.

Stahel, P. F., VanderHeiden, T. F., & Kim, F. J. (2017). Why do surgeons continue to perform unnecessary surgery?. *Patient Safety in Surgery, 1*(2). Retrieved from https://pssjournal.biomedcentral.com/articles/10.1186/s13037-016-0117-6.

Stanko, E. A. (1992). Intimidating education: Sexual harassment in criminology. *Journal of Criminal Justice Education, 3*(2), 331–340.

Stannard, C. I. (1973). Old folks and dirty work: The social conditions for patient abuse in a nursing home. *Social Problems, 20*, 329–342.

State of California Commission on Judicial Performance. (2010). *2009 Annual Report*. Retrieved from http://cjp.ca.gov/res/docs/Annual_Reports/2009_Annual_Report(1).pdf

Steen, R. G. (2010). Retractions in the scientific literature: Do authors deliberately commit research fraud? *Journal of Medical Ethics*, 1–5.

Steen, R. G. (2011). Misinformation in the medical literature: What role do error and fraud play? *Journal of Medical Ethics, 37*, 498–503.

Steffensmeier, D. J., Schwartz, J., & Roche, M. (2013). Gender and twenty-first-century corporate crime: Female involvement and the gender gap in Enron-era corporate frauds. *American Sociological Review, 78*(3), 448–476.

Steinzor, R. (2017). White-collar reset: The DOJ's Yates memo and its potential to protect health, safety, and the environment. *Wake Forest Journal of Law & Policy, 7*(1), 39–86.

Stempel, J., & Plumb, C. (2008, December 13). Billions "gone to money heaven": Friends, high-profile firms among those who invested with alleged fraudster Bernie Madoff. *Toronto Star*, p. B04.

Stenzel, P. L. (2011). Resource Conservation and Recovery Act. In *Encyclopedia of Business* (2nd ed.). Retrieved from http://www.referenceforbusiness.com/encyclopedia/Res -Sec/Resource-Conservation-and-Recovery-Act.html

Stephenson-Burton, A. (1995). Public images of white collar crime. In D. Kidd-Hewitt & R. Osborne (Eds.), *Crime and the media: The post-modern spectacle*. London, UK: Pluto.

Stern, S., & Lemmens, T. (2011). Legal remedies for medical ghostwriting: Imposing fraud liability on guest authors of ghostwritten articles. *Policy Forum, 8*(1), 1–5.

Stevens, E., & Payne, B. K. (1999). Applying deterrence theory in the context of corporate wrongdoing: Limitations on punitive damages. *Journal of Criminal Justice, 27*(3), 195–207.

Stewart, M. (2004, June 15). *Letter to judge Cedarbaum*. Retrieved from http://www.thesmokinggun.com/file/ stewarts-letter-judge

Stinson, P. M. (2009). *Police crime: A newsmaking criminology study of sworn law enforcement officers arrested, 2005–2007*. Unpublished doctoral dissertation, Indiana University of Pennsylvania.

Stinson, P. M. (2015). Police crime: The criminal behavior of sworn law enforcement officers. *Sociology Compass, 9*(1), 1–13.

Stinson, P. M. (2020). *Criminology explains police violence* (Vol. 1). Berkeley: University of California Press.

Stinson Sr., P. M., Brewer, Jr., S. L., Mathna, B. E., Liederbach, J., & Englebrecht, C. M. (2015). Police sexual misconduct: Arrested officers and their victims. *Victims & Offenders, 10*(2), 117–151.

Stinson, Sr., P. M., & Liederbach, J. (2013). Fox in the henhouse: A study of police officers arrested for crimes associated with domestic and/or family violence. *Criminal Justice Policy Review, 24*(5), 601–625.

Stinson, P. M., Liederbach, J., Lab, S. P., & Brewer, S. L., Jr. (2016). Police integrity lost: A study of law enforcement officers arrested. *Criminal Justice Faculty Publications, 63*. Retrieved from https://scholarworks.bgsu.edu/ crim_just_pub/63

Stinson, P. M., Todak, N. E., & Dodge, M. (2015). An exploration of crime by policewomen. *Police practice and research, 16*(1), 79–93.

Stockler, A. (2020). What is the STOCK Act? Senators Richard Burr, Kelly Loeffler accused of insider trading as calls mount for investigations. *Newsweek*. Retrieved from https://www.news week.com/stock-act-richard-burr-kelly-loeffler-1493497

Strom, P., & Strom, R. (2007). Cheating in middle school and high school. *Educational Forum, 71*(2), 104–116.

Stuart, D. (1995). Punishing corporate criminals with restraint. *Criminal Law Forum, 6*(2), 219–256.

Suffolk County New York. (2019). 'Operation Pay Dirt' Dirt Broker Sentenced to Prison. Retrieved from https://suffolkcountyny .gov/da/News-and-Public-Information/Press-Releases/ operation-pay-dirt-dirt-broker-sentenced-to-prison

Sullivan, C., & Hull, H. (2019). Preserving life and health by preventing fraud in healthcare. *Journal of Business and Behavioral Sciences, 31*(1), 48–58.

Šumah, Š. (2018). Corruption, causes and consequences. *Trade and Global Market*. IntechOpen.

Summerford, R. Q. (2002, July–August). Expert witnessing. *The White Paper: Topical Issues on White-Collar Crime (A bimonthly publication from the Association of Certified Fraud Examiners)*. Retrieved from http://www.forensic strategic.com/ Articles/Expert%20Witnessing%20 The%20Changing%20 Landscape.pdf

Suneson, G., & Harrington, J. (2020). What products were among those marketed with the most outrageous claims of all time? *USA Today*. Retrieved from https://www.usatoday .com/story/money/2020/06/09/39-most-outrageous-false -product-claims-of-all-time/111913486

Supernor, H. (2017). Community service and white-collar offenders. *Journal of Financial Crime, 24*(1), 148–156. https:// doi-org.proxy.lib.odu.edu/10.1108/JFC-04-2016-0023

Sutherland, E. H. (1934). *Principles of criminology* (2nd ed.). Philadelphia, PA: J. B. Lippincott.

Sutherland, E. H. (1940). White-collar criminality. *American Sociological Review, 5*, 1–12.

Sutherland, E. H. (1941). Crime and business. *Annals of the American Academy of Political and Social Science, 217*, 112–118.

Sutherland, E. H. (1949). *White collar crime*. Austin, TX: Holt, Rinehart & Winston.

Sutter, J. D. (2010, August 9). Gulf oil spill is stopped, but true story of damage will be long in coming, scientists say. *Cleveland.com*. Retrieved from http://www.cleveland.com/science/ index. ssf/2010/08/gulf_oil_spill_is_stopped_but.html

Sykes, G. (1958). *A society of captives*. Princeton, NJ: Princeton University Press.

Sykes, G., & Matza, D. (1957). Techniques of neutralization. *American Sociological Review, 22*, 664–670.

Tabachnik, S. (2019). Owners of Sweet Leaf dispensary chain sentenced to a year in prison for illegal marijuana distribution. *Denver Post*. Retrieved from https://www.denverpost.com/2019/01/25/sweet-leaf-marijuana-owners

Takahashi, K., Landrigan, P. J., & Ramazzini, C. (2016). The global health dimensions of asbestos and asbestos-related diseases. *Annals of Global Health*, *82*(1), 209–213.

Tappan, P. D. (1947). Who is the criminal? *American Sociological Review*, *12*, 96–102.

Tappan, P. W. (1960). *Crime, justice, and correction*. New York, NY: McGraw-Hill.

Taub, S. (2006, December 20). Four former Enterasys execs convicted. *CFO.com*. Retrieved from http://www.cfo.com/article.cfm/84 66560/c_8465548?f=todayinfinance_next

Taylor, M. (2001). Fraud control central. *Modern Healthcare*, *31*(19), 22–23.

Taylor, R. B., & Eidson, J. L. (2012). "The Wire," William Julius Wilson, and the three Sobotkas: Conceptually integrating "Season 2: The Port" into a macro-level undergraduate communities and crime course. *Journal of Criminal Justice Education*, *23*(3), 257–282.

Tenpas, K. (2020). And then there were ten: With 85% turnover across President Trump's A Team, who remains? *brookings.edu*. Retrieved from https://www.brookings.edu/blog/fixgov/2020/04/13/and-then-there-were-ten-with-85-turnover-across-president-trumps-a-team-who-remains/

Tergesen, A. (2009, August 27). Mortgage fraud: A classic crime's latest twist: As "reverse" loans grow more popular, scams put older adults at risk. *Wall Street Journal Online*. Retrieved from http://online.wsj.com/article/SB100014240 52970204044204574362641338197748.html

Terry, M. (2009). Medical identity theft and telemedicine security. *Telemedicine and e-Health*, *15*(10), 928–933.

Tews, M. J., & Stafford, K. (2019). The relationship between tattoos and employee workplace deviance. *Journal of Hospitality & Tourism Research*, *43*(7), 1025–1043.

"'There's no brakes . . . hold on and pray': Last words of man before he and his family died in Toyota Lexus crash." (2010, February 3). *Daily Mail*. Retrieved from http://www.dailymail.co.uk/news/article-1248177/Toyota-recall-Lastwords-father-family-died-Lexus-crash.html.

Thomas, O. (2010, May 19). Facebook CEO's latest woe: Accusations of securities fraud. *VentureBeat*. Retrieved from http://venturebeat.com/2010/05/19/facebook-connectu-securitiesfraud

Thomsen, L. C. (2006). *Testimony concerning insider trading before the Senate Judiciary Committee, December 5*. Washington, DC: U.S. Securities and Exchange Commission. Retrieved from http://www.sec.gov/news/testimony/2006/ts120506lct.pdf

Thomson, R., Espin, J., & Samuels-Jones, T. (2020). Green crime havens: A spatial cluster analysis of environmental crime. *Social Science Quarterly*, *101*(2), 503–513.

Thompson, B., & Yong, A. (2012). Corporate criminal liability. *American Criminal Law Review*, *49*, 489–522.

Thrall, R., III. (2003). "Study" a fraud. *Automotive Body Repair News*, *42*(12), 6.

Three men plead guilty to Hurricane Michael repair scam. (2020, February 28). *Panama City News Herald*. Retrieved from https://www.newsherald.com/news/20200228/three-men-plead-guilty-to-hurricane-michael-repair-scam

Tillman, R. (2013). Too big to jail. *Western Criminology Review*, *14*(2), 31–37.

Tillman, R., Calavita, K., & Pontell, H. (1997). Criminalizing white-collar misconduct: Determinants of prosecution in savings and loan fraud cases. *Crime Law and Social Change*, *26*(1), 53–76.

Tillman, R., & Pontell, H. (1992). Is justice "collar blind"? Punishing Medicaid provider fraud. *Criminology*, *30*(4), 547–574.

Tillman, R., & Pontell, H. (1995). Organizations and fraud in the savings and loan industry. *Social Forces*, *73*(4), 1439–1463.

Times Staff Report. (2017). Ex-SCSU professor convicted, sentenced to jail time. *South Carolina Times*. Retrieved from https://www.sctimes.com/story/news/local/2017/08/25/ex-scsu-professor-convicted-sentenced-jail-time/601334001

Timko, S. (1995, April 21). Fallen Angel. *USA Today*, p, 1A.

Tomasic, R. (2011). The financial crisis and the haphazard pursuit of financial crime. *Journal of Financial Crime*, *18*(1), 7–31.

Tombs, S. (2008). Corporations and health safety. In J. Minkes & L. Minkes (Eds.), *Corporate and whitecollar crime* (pp. 18–38). Thousand Oaks, CA: Sage.

Tombs, S., & Whyte, D. (2020). The shifting imaginaries of corporate crime. *Journal of White Collar and Corporate Crime*, *1*(1), 16–23.

Tomlinson, E. C., & Pozzuto, A. (2016). Criminal decision making in organizational contexts. In S. R. Van Slyke,

M. L. Benson, & F. T. Cullen (Eds.), *The Oxford handbook of white-collar crime* (pp.367–381). New York, NY: Oxford University Press.

Trac Reports. (2015). *Justice department data reveals 29 percent drop in criminal prosecutions of corporations.* Retrieved from http://trac.syr.edu/tracreports/crim/406/

Trahan, A., Marquart, J. W., & Mullings, J. (2005). Fraud and the American dream: Toward an understanding of fraud victimization. *Deviant Behavior, 26*(6), 601–620.

Traub, S. H. (1996). Battling employee crime: A review of corporate strategies and programs. *Crime and Delinquency, 42*(2), 244–256.

Triplett, R. (1993). The conflict perspective, symbolic interactionism and the status characteristics hypothesis. *Justice Quarterly, 10*, 541–558.

Trischitta, L. (2011, March 8). Three south Florida restaurants briefly closed by state inspectors. *Sun Sentinel.* Retrieved from http://articles.sun-sentinel.com/keyword/inspector/recent/2

Tromadore, C. E. (2016). Police officer sexual misconduct: An urgent call to action in context disproportionately threatening women of color. *Harvard Journal on Racial & Ethnic Justice, 32*, 153–188.

Trumka, R. (2008). Employment-related crimes. *American Criminal Law Review, 45*(2), 341–380.

Tu, Y. (2019). *Toy-related deaths and injuries calendar year 2018.* Bethesda, MD: U.S. Consumer Product Safety Commission.

Ugrin, J. C., & Odom, M. D. (2010). Exploring Sarbanes-Oxley's effect on attitude: Perceptions of norms, and intentions to commit financial statement fraud from a general deterrence perspective. *Journal of Accounting and Public Policy, 29*(5), 439–458.

Ulrich, L. (2000). *Music on the Internet: Is there an upside to downloading?* Hearing before the Committee on the Judiciary, United States Senate, July 11, 2000. Retrieved from http://www.gpo.gov/fdsys/pkg/CHRG-106shrg74728/html/CHRG-106shrg74728.htm

Union of Concerned Scientists (UCS). (2008, April). *Interference at the EPA: Science and politics at the U.S. Environmental Protection Agency.* Retrieved from https://www.ucsusa.org/sites/default/files/legacy/assets/documents/scientific_integrity/interference-at-the-epa.pdf

United Nations. (2019). *Stressing air pollution kills 7 million people annually, Secretary-General urges governments to build green economy, in message for World Environment Day.* Retrieved from https://www.un.org/press/en/2019/sgsm19607.doc.htm

United Nations Office on Drugs and Crime. (2020). *COVID-19-related trafficking of medical products as a threat to public health.* Research. Retrieved from https://www.unodc.org/documents/data-and-analysis/covid/COVID-19_research_brief_trafficking_medical_products.pdf

United States, 552 U.S. 38 (2007)

United States v. Booker, 543 U.S. 220 (2005)

United States v. Sample, 17-2086 (10th Cir. 2018)

University of Colorado Investigative Committee Report. (2006). *Report of the Investigative Committee on the standing committee on research misconduct at the University of Colorado at Boulder concerning allegations of academic misconduct against Professor Ward Churchill.* Retrieved from http://www.colorado.edu/news/reports/churchill/download/WardChurchillReport.pdf

University of Phoenix parent guilty of fraud. (2008, January 16). *Associated Press.* Retrieved from http://www.azcentral.com/business/articles/0116biz-apollogroupsuit16-ON.html

Ungar, M. (2017). Prosecuting environmental crime: Latin America's policy innovation. *Latin American Policy, 8*(1), 63–92.

Unnever, J. D., Benson, M. L., & Cullen, F. T. (2008). Public support for getting tough on corporate crime: Racial and political divides. *Journal of Research in Crime and Delinquency, 45*(2), 163–190.

U.S. Attorney's Annual Statistical Report. (2020). Washington D.C.: U.S. Department of Justice. Available online at https://www.justice.gov/usao/resources/annual-statistical-reports

U.S. Bureau of Labor Statistics. (2020). *Injuries, illnesses, and fatalities.* Retrieved from https://www.bls.gov/iif/news.htm

U.S. Code. (n.d.). Available online at https://uscode.house.gov/

U. S. Conference of Catholic Bishops. (2004). *The nature and scope of the problem of sexual abuse of minors by Catholic priests and deacons in the United States 1950–2002: A research study conducted by the John Jay College of Criminal Justice.* Washington, DC: Author. Retrieved from http://www.usccb.org/issues-and-action/child-andyouth-protection/upload/The-Nature-and-Scope-of-Sexual-Abuse-of-Minors-by-Catholic-Priests-and-Deacons-in-the-United-States-1950-2002.pdf

U.S. Consumer Product Safety Commission (USCPSC). (2010a). *Imported drywall and health: A guide for health care professionals.* Retrieved from http://www.atsdr.cdc.gov/drywall/docs/Drywall_for_Healthcare_Providers.pdf

U.S. Consumer Product Safety Commission (USCPSC). (2010b). *Investigation of imported drywall: Status update, September 2010.* Retrieved from http://www.cpsc.gov/info/drywall/sep2010 status.pdf

U.S. Consumer Product Safety Commission (USCPSC). (2010c). *2010 performance and accountability report*. Retrieved from http://www.sec.gov/about/secpar2010.shtml

U.S. Consumer Product Safety Commission (USCPSC). (n.d.). *CPSC has completed its investigation into problem drywall. Learn how to identify problem drywall and to fix the problem.* Retrieved from https://www.cpsc.gov/Safety-Education/Safety-Education-Centers/Drywall-Information-Center

U. S. Consumer Product Safety Commission. (2019). *Toy-related deaths and injuries calendar year 2018*. Retrieved from https://www.cpsc.gov/s3fs-public/Toy_Related_Deaths_and_Injuries_Calendar_Year_2018.pdf?WM0sDY9UaFK2Mpz0xpBoqmqPvoUdbzDN

U. S. Department of Education. (2014, November 14). *Federal Student Aid Annual report FY 2014*. Retrieved from https://www2.ed.gov/about/reports/annual/2014report/fsareport.pdf

U.S. Department of Education. (2019). Secretary DeVos levies largest-ever Clery fine against Michigan State University, requires major corrective action following systemic failure to address sexual abuse. Retrieved from https://www.ed.gov/news/press-releases/secretary-devos-levies-largest-ever-clery-fine-against-michigan-state-university-requires-major-corrective-action-following-systemic-failure-address-sexual-abuse

U.S. Department of Health and Human Services. (2010). *Office of Inspector General semiannual report to Congress*. Washington, DC: Health and Human Services.

U.S. Department of Health and Human Services, & Department of Justice. (2020). *Health care fraud and abuse control program annual report for Fiscal Year 2019*. Retrieved from https://oig.hhs.gov/publications/docs/hcfac/FY2019-hcfac.pdf

U.S. Department of Housing and Urban Development. (2010, November 10). *HUD to investigate mortgage lenders who discriminate* [Press release]. Retrieved from http://portal.hud.gov/hudportal/HUD?src=/press/press_releases_media_advisories/2010/HUDNo.10-158

U.S. Department of Justice (USDOJ). (1994). *Environmental justice strategy*. Washington, DC: U.S. Department of Justice.

U. S. Department of Justice (USDOJ). (2015, November 16). *For-profit college company to pay $95.5 million to settle claims of illegal recruiting, consumer fraud and other violations.* Retrieved from http://www.justice.gov/opa/pr/profitcollege-company-pay-955-million-settle-claimsillegal-recruiting-consumer-fraud-and

U.S. Department of Justice. (2016, April 5). *21 defendants charged with fraudulently enabling hundreds of foreign nationals to remain in the United States through fake 'pay to stay' New Jersey College*. Retrieved from https://www.justice.gov/usao-nj/pr/21-defendants-charged-fraudulently-enabling-hundreds-foreign-nationals-remain-united.

U.S. Department of Justice. (2017, January 11). *Volkswagen AG agrees to plead guilty and pay $4.3 billion in criminal and civil penalties; Six Volkswagen executives and employees are indicted in connection with conspiracy to cheat U.S. emissions tests*. Retrieved from https://www.justice.gov/opa/pr/volkswagen-ag-agrees-plead-guilty-and-pay-43-billion-criminal-and-civil-penalties-six

U.S. Department of Justice. (2017, September 22). *Former clerk in Orange County Superior Court sentenced to over 11 years in federal prison for racketeering offense stemming from bribery scheme to 'fix' criminal cases and traffic charges*. Retrieved from https://www.justice.gov/usao-cdca/pr/former-clerk-orange-county-superior-court-sentenced-over-11-years-federal-prison

U.S. Department of Justice. (2017, December 14). *I.T. specialist arrested for allegedly hacking into servers of north suburban company where he formerly worked as contractor*. Retrieved from https://www.justice.gov/usao-ndil/pr/it-specialist-arrested-allegedly-hacking-servers-north-suburban-company-where-he

U.S. Department of Justice. (2017, December 20). *Indianapolis businessman sentenced to four years in federal prison*. Retrieved from https://www.justice.gov/usao-sdin/pr/indianapolis-businessman-sentenced-four-years-federal-prison

U.S. Department of Justice. (2018, September 28). *New Jersey attorney admits role in multimillion-dollar mortgage fraud scheme*. Retrieved from https://www.justice.gov/usao-nj/pr/new-jersey-attorney-admits-role-multimillion-dollar-mortgage-fraud-scheme

U.S. Department of Justice. (2018, October 11). *William Mcfarland sentenced to 6 years in prison in Manhattan federal court for engaging in multiple fraudulent schemes and making false statements to a federal law enforcement agent*. Retrieved from https://www.justice.gov/usao-sdny/pr/william-mcfarland-sentenced-6-years-prison-manhattan-federal-court-engaging-multiple

U.S. Department of Justice. (2018, November 29). *Suffield man involved in stock "pump and dump" scheme is sentenced*. Retrieved from https://www.justice.gov/usao-ct/pr/suffield-man-involved-stock-pump-and-dump-scheme-sentenced

U.S. Department of Justice. (2018, December 3). *Political operative convicted of federal campaign finance crimes in two congressional campaigns and of obstructing investigation by federal election commission*. Retrieved from https://www.justice.gov/opa/pr/political-operative-convicted-federal-campaign-finance-crimes-two-congressional-campaigns-and

U.S. Department of Justice. (2019, March). *Report on the investigation into Russian interference in the2016 presidential election* (vol. 1). Retrieved from https://www.justice.gov/archives/sco/file/1373816/download

U.S. Department of Justice. (2019, April 9a). *Federal indictments & law enforcement actions in one of the largest health care fraud schemes involving telemedicine and durable medical equipment marketing executives results in charges against 24 individuals responsible for over $1.2 billion in losses.* Retrieved from https://www.justice.gov/opa/pr/federal-indictments-and-law-enforcement-actions-one-largest-health-care-fraud-schemes.

U.S. Department of Justice. (2019, April 9b). *Former Philadelphia police officer sentenced to prison for fraud and ordered to forfeit over $653,000 in ill-gotten gains.* Retrieved from https://www.justice.gov/usao-edpa/pr/former-philadelphia-police-officer-sentenced-prison-fraud-and-ordered-forfeit-over

U.S. Department of Justice. (2019, May 3). *CEO of medical equipment company sentenced to 40 months for Medicare fraud.* Retrieved from https://www.justice.gov/usao-sdga/pr/ceo-medical-equipment-company-sentenced-40-months-medicare-fraud. Accessed September 13, 2020.

U.S. Department of Justice. (2019, June 27). *Former Equifax employee sentenced for insider trading.* Retrieved from https://www.justice.gov/usao-ndga/pr/former-equifax-employee-sentenced-insider-trading

U.S. Department of Justice. (2019, July 24). *Former Candidate for U.S. House of Representatives sentenced after conviction for fraud and campaign finance violation.* Retrieved from https://www.justice.gov/opa/pr/former-candidate-us-house-representatives-sentenced-after-conviction-fraud-and-campaign

U.S. Department of Justice. (2019, August 31). *University of Kansas researcher indicted for fraud for failing to disclose conflict of interest with Chinese university.* Retrieved from https://www.justice.gov/opa/pr/university-kansas-researcher-indicted-fraud-failing-disclose-conflict-interest-chinese

U.S. Department of Justice. (2019, September 30). *Founder of Delta Homes and former employees sentenced for mortgage fraud scheme.* Retrieved from https://www.justice.gov/usao-edca/pr/founder-delta-homes-and-former-employees-sentenced-mortgage-fraud-scheme

U.S. Department of Justice. (2019, November 6). *South Carolina man sentenced to 10 years in prison for forcing man with intellectual disability to work at restaurant.* Retrieved from https://www.justice.gov/opa/pr/south-carolina-man-sentenced-10-years-prison-forcing-man-intellectual-disability-work

U.S. Department of Justice. (2019, December 19). *San Diego woman sentenced to nearly six years in federal prison for ponzi scheme run via sham commercial real estate investments.* Retrieved from https://www.justice.gov/usao-cdca/pr/san-diego-woman-sentenced-nearly-six-years-federal-prison-ponzi-scheme-run-sham

U.S. Department of Justice (2020, February 27). *Researcher at university arrested for wire fraud and making false statements about affiliation with a Chinese university.* Retrieved from https://www.justice.gov/opa/pr/researcher-university-arrested-wire-fraud-and-making-false-statements-about-affiliation

U.S. Department of Justice. (2020, March 10). *Former West Virginia university professor pleads guilty to fraud that enabled him to participate in the people's republic of china's "thousand talents plan."* Retrieved from https://www.justice.gov/opa/pr/former-west-virginia-university-professor-pleads-guilty-fraud-enabled-him-participate-people

U.S. Department of Justice. (2020, March 25). *Southland man arrested on federal charges alleging fraudulent investment scheme featuring bogus claims of COVID-19 cure.* Retrieved from https://www.justice.gov/usao-cdca/pr/southland-man-arrested-federal-charges-alleging-fraudulent-investment-scheme-featuring

U.S. Department of Justice. (2020, April 9). *Darknet vendor arrested on distribution and money laundering charges.* Retrieved from https://www.justice.gov/usao-edva/pr/darknet-vendor-arrested-distribution-and-money-laundering-charges

U.S. Department of Justice. (2020, April 28). *North Dakota man sentenced for wildlife violations involving bald eagle deaths.* Retrieved from https://www.justice.gov/usao-sd/pr/north-dakota-man-sentenced-wildlife-violations-involving-bald-eagle-deaths

U.S Department of Justice. (2020a, May 11). *University of Arkansas professor arrested for wire fraud.* Retrieved from https://www.justice.gov/opa/pr/university-arkansas-professor-arrested-wire-fraud

U.S Department of Justice. (2020b, May 11). *Former Emory University professor and Chinese "thousand talents" participant convicted and sentenced for filing a false tax return.* Retrieved from https://www.justice.gov/opa/pr/former-emory-university-professor-and-chinese-thousand-talents-participant-convicted-and

U.S. Department of Justice. (2020, May 15). *Former Fulton County tannery owner ordered to pay restitution for cleanup of hazardous waste.* Retrieved from https://www.justice.gov/usao-ndny/pr/former-fulton-county-tannery-owner-ordered-pay-restitution-clean-hazardous-waste

U.S. Department of Justice. (2020, May 28). *IT manager sentenced for hacking into and sabotaging his former employer's* computer network. Retrieved from https://www.justice.gov/usao-ndga/pr/it-manager-sentenced-hacking-and-sabotaging-his-former-employer-s-computer-network.

U.S. Department of Justice. (2020, June 1). *Professor of International Studies pleads guilty to money laundering*. Retrieved from https://www.justice.gov/usao-sdny/pr/professor-international-studies-pleads-guilty-money-laundering

U.S. Department of Justice. (2020, June 2). *Man admits to "spoof" email fraud scheme and more*. Retrieved from https://www.justice.gov/usao-sdtx/pr/man-admits-spoof-email-fraud-scheme-and-more

U.S. Department of Justice. (2020, June 19). *Doctor sentenced to prison for illegal distribution of Adderall*. Retrieved from https://www.justice.gov/usao-edva/pr/doctor-sentenced-prison-illegal-distribution-adderall-oxycodone

U.S. Department of Justice. (2020, June 24). *British man sentenced to 70 months in prison for fraud scheme that victimized hundreds of thousands of U.S. consumers*. Retrieved from https://www.justice.gov/opa/pr/british-man-sentenced-70-months-prison-fraud-scheme-victimized-hundreds-thousands-us

U.S. Department of Justice. (2020, June 25). *Novartis Hellas S.A.C.I. and Alcon Pte Ltd agree to pay over $233 million combined to resolve criminal FCPA cases*. Retrieved from https://www.justice.gov/opa/pr/novartis-hellas-saci-and-alcon-pte-ltd-agree-pay-over-233-million-combined-resolve-criminal

U.S. Department of Justice. (2020, June 26). *Russian national sentenced to prison for operating websites devoted to fraud and malicious cyber activities*. Retrieved from https://www.justice.gov/opa/pr/russian-national-sentenced-prison-operating-websites-devoted-fraud-and-malicious-cyber

U.S. Department of Justice Fraud Section. (2020). *2019 Year in Review*. Retrieved from https://www.justice.gov/criminal-fraud/file/1245236/download

U.S. Department of Justice Public Integrity Section. (2019). *Report to Congress on the Activities and Operations of the Public Integrity Section for 2018*. Retrieved from https://www.justice.gov/criminal/file/1216921/download

U.S. Department of Justice (USDOJ). (n.d.a). *Anti-Trust Enforcement and the Consumer*. Retrieved November 27, 2015, from http://www.justice.gov/sites/default/files/atr/legacy/2015/03/06/anti trust-enfor-consumer.pdf

U.S. Department of Justice (USDOJ). (n.d.b). *Price fixing, bid rigging, and market allocation schemes: What they are and what to look for*. Retrieved November 27, 2015, from http://www.justice.gov/atr/price-fixingbid-rigging-and-market-allocation-schemes.

U.S. Department of Justice, Environment and Natural Resources Division. (2010). *Summary of litigation*. Retrieved from https://www.justice.gov/sites/default/files/enrd/legacy/2015/04/13/ENRD_FY2009_Accomplishments_Report_Text_Only_508.pdf

U.S. Environmental Protection Agency (EPA). (1992). *The guardian: Origins of the EPA*. Retrieved from http://epa.gov/aboutepa/history/publications/print/origins.html

U.S. Environmental Protection Agency (EPA). (1998). *Illegal dumping prevention guidebook: U.S. EPA Region 5, Waste, Pesticides, and Toxics Division*. Chicago, IL: Region.

U.S. Environmental Protection Agency (EPA). (2010a). *About the Office of Research and Development*. Retrieved July 30, 2011, from http://www.epa.gov/aboutepa/ord.html

U.S. Environmental Protection Agency (EPA). (2010b, December 2). *Beazer Homes USA, Inc. settlement* [Press release]. Retrieved from http://www.epa.gov/compliance/resources/cases/civil/cwa/beazer.html

U.S. Environmental Protection Agency (EPA). (2010c). *Environmental justice*. Retrieved December 17, 2010, from http://www.epa.gov/compliance/environmentaljustice/basics/index.html

U.S. Environmental Protection Agency (EPA). (2010d). *Laws that we administer*. Retrieved on December 17, 2010, from http://www.epa.gov/lawsregs/laws/index.html

U.S. Environmental Protection Agency (EPA). (2010e). *What is an environmental crime?* Retrieved on December 17, 2010, from http://www.epa.gov/compliance/criminal/investigations/environmentalcrime.html

U.S Environmental Protection Agency (EPA). (2019a). *EPA announces 2019 annual environmental enforcement results*. Retried from http://www.epa.gov/newsreleases/epa-announces-2019-annual-environmental-enforcement-results

U.S Environmental Protection Agency (EPA). (2019b). *EPA FY 2020 budget proposal released*. Retrieved from https://www.epa.gov/newsreleases/epa-fy-2020-budget-proposal-released

U. S. Environmental Protection Agency (EPA). (2020, January 30). *Kohler Co. Clean Air Act settlement information sheet*. Retrieved from https://www.epa.gov/enforcement/kohler-co-clean-air-act-settlement-information-sheet

U. S. Environmental Protection Agency (EPA). (2020, February 27). *Dyno Nobel Inc. Missouri information sheet*. Retrieved from https://www.epa.gov/enforcement/dyno-nobel-inc-missouri-information-sheet

U. S. Environmental Protection Agency (EPA). (2021). *EPA announces FY 2020 enforcement and compliance achievements*.

Retrieved from https://www.epa.gov/newsreleases/epa-announces-fy-2020-enforcement-and-compliance-achievements

U.S. Environmental Protection Agency. (n.d.). *Richard Dorenkamp*. Retrieved from https://www.epa.gov/sites/production/files/2020-03/documents/richard_dorenkamp_final.pdf.

U.S. Government Accountability Office (USGAO). (2003). *Medicaid: A program highly vulnerable to fraud*. Washington, DC: Government Printing Office.

U.S. Government Accountability Office (USGAO). (2009). *Corporate crime: DOJ has taken steps to better track its use of deferred and non-prosecution agreements, but should evaluate effectiveness*. Washington DC: Government Printing Office.

U.S. Government Accountability Office (USGAO). (2010). *For-profit colleges: Undercover testing finds colleges encouraged fraud and engaged in deceptive and questionable marketing practices*. Retrieved from http://www.gao.gov/products/GAO-10-948T

U.S. Office of Inspector General (USOIG). (1999). *Criminal calls: A review of the Bureau of Prisons' management of inmate telephone privileges* [Report]. Retrieved from http://www.justice.gov/oig/special/9908/index.htm

U.S. Office of Inspector General (USOIG). (2008). *An investigation of allegations of politicized hiring and other improper personnel actions in the Civil Rights Division*. Washington, DC: U.S. Department of Justice.

U.S. Senate Olympics Investigation. (2019). *The courage of survivors: A call to action*. Retrieved from https://www.moran.senate.gov/public/_cache/files/c/2/c232725e-b717-4ec8-913e-845ffe0837e6/FCC5DFDE2005A2EACF5A9A25FF76D538.2019.07.30-the-courage-of-survivors--a-call-to-action-olympics-investigation-report-final.pdf

Utah (n.d.). White-collar crime offender registry. Retrieved September 14, 2020 from http://www.utfraud.com/Registry Lists

Vaitlin, P. (2019). How employers must deal with the source of the greatest threat to their business survival. *Tampa Bay Business Journal*. Retrieved from https://www.bizjournals.com/tampabay/news/2019/06/24/how-employers-must-deal-with-the-source-of-the.html

Vakkur, N., McAfee, R., & Kipperman, F. (2010). The unintended effects of the Sarbanes-Oxley Act of 2002. *Research in Accounting Regulation*, *22*, 18–20.

Valeri, L. (1998). The information warriors. *Journal of Financial Crime*, *6*(1), 52–53.

Van Cleef, C. R., Silets, H. M., & Motz, P. (2004). Does the punishment fit the crime? *Journal of Financial Crime*, *12*(1), 56–65.

Van den Berg, E. A. I. M., & Eshuis, R. J. (1996). *Major investigations of environmental crimes*. Arnheim, Netherlands: Gouda Quint.

van der Wagen, W., & Pieters, W. (2015). From cybercrime to cyborg crime: Botnets as hybrid criminal actor-networks. *British Journal Criminology*, *55*, 578–595.

Van Gigch, J. P. (1978). *Applied general systems theory* (2nd edition). New York, NY: Harpercollins.

van Rijnsoever, F. J., & Hessels, L. K. (2011). Factors associated with disciplinary and interdisciplinary research collaboration. *Research Policy*, *40*(3), 551–562.

Van Slyke, S., & Bales, W. D. (2012). A contemporary study of the decision to incarcerate white-collar and street property offenders. *Punishment & Society*, *14*(2), 217–246.

Van Slyke, S., & Bales, W. D. (2013). Gender dynamics in the sentencing of white-collar offenders. *Criminal Justice Studies*, *26*(2), 168–196.

van Wingerde, K., & Lord, N. (2020). The elusiveness of white-collar and corporate crime in a globalized economy. In M. Rorie (Ed.), *The handbook of white-collar crime* (pp. 469–483). New York, NY: John Wiley & Sons.

Van Wyk, J. A., Benson, M. L., & Harris, D. K. (2000). A test of strain and self-control theories: Occupational crime in nursing homes. *Journal of Crime and Justice*, *23*(2), 27–44.

Varian, B. (2000, February 3). Former insurance agent guilty of fraud. *St. Petersburg Times*, p. 1.

Vars, F. E. (2017). Prosecutorial misconduct: The best defense is good defense. *Washington and Lee Law Review Online*, *73*, 481–486.

Vaughan, D. (1992). The macro-micro connection in white-collar crime theory. In K. Schlegel & D. Weisburd (Eds.), *White-collar crime reconsidered* (pp. 124–145). Boston, MA: Northeastern University Press.

Vaughan, D. (2001). Sensational cases, flawed theories. In H. N. Pontell & D. Shichor (Eds.), *Contemporary issues in crime and criminal justice: Essays in honor of Gilbert Geis* (pp. 45–66). Upper Saddle River, NJ: Prentice Hall.

Vaughan, D., & Carlo, G. (1975). The appliance repairman: A study of victim responsiveness and fraud. *Journal of Research in Crime and Delinquency*, *12*, 153–161.

Verges, J. (2020). University of Minnesota law professor sentenced in $4 million fraud case. *Duluth News Tribune*.

Retrieved from https://www.duluthnewstribune.com/news/crime-and-courts/4879224-University-of-Minnesota-law-professor-sentenced-in-4-million-fraud-case

Verstein, E. (2014). The law as violence: Essay: Violent white-collar crime. *Wake Forest Law Review*, *49*, 873–887

Viano, E. C. (2006). Cybercrime: A new frontier for criminology. *International Annals of Criminology*, *44*(1/2), 11–22.

Vieraitis, L. M., Piquero, N. L., Piquero, A. R., Tibbetts, S. G., & Blankenship, M. (2012). Do women and men differ in their neutralizations of corporate crime? *Criminal Justice Review*, *37*(4), 478–493.

Vinograd, S. (2020, May 16). *Trump's dangerous assault on government watchdogs*. Retrieved from https://www.cnn.com/2020/05/16/opinions/inspector-general-steve-linick-fired-vinograd/index.html

Vinten, G. (1994). Asset protection through whistleblowing. *Journal of Asset Protection and Financial Crime*, *2*(2), 121–131.

Vito, G. F., Wolfe, S., Higgins, G. E., & Walsh, W. F. (2011). Police integrity: Rankings of scenarios on the Klockars scale by "management cops." *Criminal Justice Review*, *36*(2), 152–164.

Vogell, H. (2019, October 16). Never-before-seen Trump tax documents show major inconsistencies. *Propublica*. Retrieved from https://www.propublica.org/article/trump-inc-podcast-never-before-seen-trump-tax-documents-show-major-inconsistencies

Vollaard, B. (2017). Temporal displacement of environmental crime: Evidence from marine oil pollution. *Journal of Environmental Economics and Management*, *82*, 168–180.

Vuletic, I. (2018). Data-driven healthcare and cybercrime: Threat we are not aware of. *Asia Pacific Journal of Health Law & Ethics*, *11*(2), 16–32.

Wahl, A. (2009, November 23). Toy safety still a crapshoot. *Canadian Business*, *82*(20), 16.

Waldfogel, J. (1995). Are fines and prison terms used efficiently? Evidence on federal fraud offenders. *Journal of Law and Economics*, *38*(1), 107–139.

Walker, J. (2010, May 19). Academics fight Cuccinelli's call for climate-change records. *The Virginian-Pilot*. Retrieved from http://hamptonroads.com/2010/academics-fight-cuccinellis-call-climatechangerecords

Walker, N., & Holtfreter, K. (2015). Applying criminological theory to academic fraud. *Journal of Financial Crime*, *22*(1), 48–62. https://doi-org.proxy.lib.odu.edu/10.1108/JFC-12-2013-0071

Walker, S., & Alpert, G. P. (2002). Early warning systems as risk management for police. In K. M. Lersch (Ed.), *Policing and misconduct* (pp. 219–230). Upper Saddle River, NJ: Prentice Hall.

Wall, D. S. (2007). Policing cybercrimes: Situating the public police in networks of security within cyberspace. *Police Practice and Research*, *8*(2), 183–205.

Wall, D. S. (2008). Cybercrime, media and insecurity: The shaping of public perceptions of cybercrime. *International Review of Law Computers & Technology*, *22*(1–2), 45–63.

Wall, D. S. (2013). Policing identity crimes. *Policing and Society: An International Journal of Research and Policy*, *23*(4), 437–460.

Wallack, T. (2013, March 18). Attorneys generals to Congress: Don't let for-profit colleges use federal grants and loans for advertising: States seek limits on US funds. *boston.com*. Retrieved from http://www.boston.com/business/news/2013/03/17/attorney-generals-congressdon-let-for-profit-colleges-use-federal-grantsand-loans-for-advertising/lMzPoQYWOjKHlCepMMffOL/story.html

Waller, M. (2007, December 29). Even in prison Martha Stewart could not resist breaking the rules. *The Times* (London). Retrieved from http://business.timesonline.co.uk/tol/business/columnists/article3105406.ece

Wall-Parker, A. (2020). Measuring white collar crime. In M. Rorie (Ed.), *The handbook of white-collar crime* (pp. 32–44). New York, NY: John Wiley & Sons.

Walsh, A. (2002). *Biosocial criminology: Introduction and integration*. Cincinnati, OH: Anderson.

Walters, R. (2007). Food crime, regulation, and the biotech harvest. *European Journal of Criminology*, *4*(2), 217–235.

Wang, T. A., & Wang, T. (2012). *The politics of voter suppression*. Ithaca, NY: Cornell University Press.

Ward, K. C., Thompson, A. J., Iannacchione, B. M., & Evans, M. K. (2019). Crime, laws, and legalization: Perceptions of Colorado Marijuana dispensary owners and managers. *Criminal Justice Policy Review*, *30*(1), 28–51.

Washington, E. (2006). The impact of banking and fringe banking regulation on the number of unbanked Americans. *Journal of Human Resources*, *41*(1), 106–137.

Washington State Liquor Control Board. (n.d.). Frequently asked questions about marijuana advertising. Retrieved September 12, 2020 from https://lcb.wa.gov/mj2015/faq_i502_advertising

Watkins, E., & Foran, C. (2018). EPA chief Scott Pruitt's long list of controversies. *CNN.com*. Retrieved from https://www.cnn.com/2018/04/06/politics/scott-pruitt-controversies-list/index.html

Watt, R. (2012). University students' propensity towards white-collar versus street crime. *Studies by Undergraduate Researchers at Guelph, 5*(2), 5–12.

Wear, D., Aultman, J. M., & Borges, N. J. (2007). Retheorizing sexual harassment in medical education: Women students' perceptions at five U.S. medical schools. *Teaching and Learning in Medicine, 19*(1), 20–29.

Weaver, J. (2020). South Florida pharmacists charged in $87 million fraud case linked to former UF player. *Miami Herald.* Retrieved from https://www.miamiherald.com/news/local/article242651426.html

Webb, T., & Pilkington, E. (2010, June 20). Gulf oil spill: BP accused of lying to Congress. *The Guardian*. Retrieved from http://www.guardian.co.uk/environment/2010/jun/20/gulf-oil-spill-bp-lying

Weber, J., Kurke, L. B., & Pentico, D. W. (2003). Why do employees steal? Assessing differences in ethical and unethical employee behavior using ethical work climates. *Business & Society, 42*, 359–380.

Weisburd, D., Chayet, E. F., & Waring, E. (1990). White-collar crime and criminal careers: Some preliminary findings. *Crime and Delinquency, 36*, 342–355.

Weisburd, D., Waring, E., & Chayet, E. (1995). Specific deterrence in a sample of offenders convicted of white-collar crimes. *Criminology, 33*, 587–607.

Weisburd, D., Waring, E., & Wheeler, S. (1990). Class, status, and the punishment of white-collar criminals. *Law and Social Inquiry, 15*(2), 223–243.

Weisburd, D., Wheeler, S., Waring, E., & Bode, N. (1991). *Crimes of the middle class: White-collar offenders in the federal courts.* New Haven, CT: Yale University Press.

Welch, H. (2008, February 5). Avoiding scams: 20,700 Americans fall for these investment schemes every year. *Jacksonville.Com*, Retrieved from http://jacksonville.com/tu-online/stories/020508/bus_243662551.shtml

Welch, M. (2009). Fragmented power and state-corporate killings: A critique of Blackwater in Iraq. *Crime, Law and Social Change, 51*, 351–364.

Wells, C. (2014, April 2). Morgan state university professor convicted of fraud scheme. *The Baltimore Sun*. Retrieved from http://articles.baltimoresun.com/2014-04-02/news/bs-md-morgan-professor-convicted-20140402_1_mor

gan-state-university-infrastructure-engineeringresearch-manoj-kumar-jha

Wells, J. T. (2003a). Follow the greenback road. *Journal of Accountancy, 196*(5), 84–87.

Wells, J. T. (2003b). The fraud examiners. *Journal of Accountancy, 196*(4), 76–79.

Wells, J. T. (2010). Ponzis and pyramids. *CPA Journal, 80*(2), 6–10.

Werle, N. (2019). Prosecuting corporate crime when firms are too big to jail: Investigation, deterrence, and judicial review. *Yale Law Journal, 128*(5), 1366–1438.

Wheeler, S., Mann, K., & Sarat, A. (1988). *Sitting in judgment: The sentencing of white-collar criminals*. New Haven, CT: Yale University Press.

Wheeler, S., Weisburd, D., & Bode, N. (1982). Sentencing the white collar offender: Rhetoric and reality. *American Sociological Review, 47*(5), 641–659.

Wheeler, S., Weisburd, D., & Bode, N. (1988). *Nature and sanctioning of white collar crime, 1976–1978*. Rockville, MD: National Institute of Justice.

Wheeler, S., Weisburd, D., & Bode, N. (2000). *Nature and sanctioning of white collar crime, 1976– 1978: Federal judicial districts*. Ann Arbor, MI: Inter-university Consortium of Political and social Research.

Wheeler, S., Weisburd, D., Waring, E., & Bode, N. (1988). White-collar crimes and criminals. *American Criminal Law Review, 25*, 331–358.

White, J. B., Power, S., & Aeppel, T. (2001, June 20). Agency to comment on Ford tire safety, while inquiry into Explorer is considered. *Wall Street Journal*, p. A.3.

White, M. D., & Kane, R. J. (2013). Pathways to career ending police misconduct: An examination of patterns, timing, and organizational responses to officer malfeasance in the NYPD. *Criminal Justice and Behavior, 40*(11), 1301–1325.

White, M. D., & Terry, K. J. (2008). Child sexual abuse in the Catholic Church: Revisiting the rotten apples explanation. *Criminal Justice and Behavior, 35*(5), 658–678.

White, R. (2008). Depleted uranium, state crime, and the politics of knowing. *Theoretical Criminology, 12*(1), 31–54.

White, R. (2017). Reparative justice, environmental crime and penalties for the powerful. *Crime, Law and Social Change, 67*(2), 117–132.

White-collar crime rising. (2003, December 23). *Desert News*. Retrieved from http://findarticles.com/p/articles/mi_qn4188/is_20031223/ai_n11419131/?tag=rbxcra.2.a.11

The White House. (2013). *Executive Order—Improving Critical Infrastructure Cybersecurity*. Retrieved from https://obama whitehouse.archives.gov/the-press-office/2013/02/12/executive -order-improving-critical-infrastructure-cybersecurity

Whyte, D. (2016). It's common sense, stupid! Corporate crime and techniques of neutralization in the automobile industry. *Crime, Law & Social Change, 66*(2), 165–181. https://doi-org .proxy.lib.odu.edu/10.1007/s10611-016-9616-8

Wiggins, L. M. (2002). Corporate computer crime: Collaborative power in numbers. *Federal Probation, 66*(3), 19–29.

Wiggins, O. (2009, June 12). Insurance agent accused of defrauding seniors of $280,000. *The Washington Post*, p. B02.

Wilkins, L. (1965). *Social deviance*. Englewood Cliffs, NJ: Prentice Hall.

Williams, F. P., & McShane, M. D. (2008). *Criminological theory* (5th ed.). Upper Saddle River, NJ: Prentice Hall.

Williams, J. W. (2005). Governability matters: The private policing of economic crime and the challenge of democratic governance. *Policing and Society: An International Journal of Research and Policy, 15*(2), 187–211.

Williams, J. W. (2008). Out of place and out of line: Positioning the police in the regulation of financial markets. *Law and Policy, 30*(3), 306–355.

Williams, M., Evangelopoulos, D., Katsouyanni, K., & Walton, H. (2019). *Personalising the health impacts of air pollution: Summary for decision makers*. Retrieved from http:// www.erg.kcl.ac.uk/research/home/projects/personalised- health-impacts.html

Williams, M. L., Levi, M., Burnap, P., & Gundur, R. V. (2019). Under the corporate radar: Examining insider business cybercrime victimization through an application of routine activities theory. *Deviant Behavior, 40*(9), 1119–1131.

Williamson, C., Amann, N., Athans, L., Bansal, V., & Zahedi, P. (2019). Election law violations. *American Criminal Law Review, 56*(3 Annual Survey of White Collar Crime), 711–758.

Wilson, P. R., Lincoln, R., Chappell, D., & Fraser, S. (1986). Physician fraud and abuse in Canada: A preliminary examination. *Criminology, 28*, 129–143.

Wislar, J., Flanagin, A., Fontanarosa, P., & DeAngelis, C. D. (2010). Prevalence of honorary and ghost authorship in six general medical journals. *Peer Review Congress 2009*. Retrieved from http://www.ama-assn.org/public/peer/abstracts-0910.pdf

Wolfe, S. E., & Piquero, A. R. (2011). Organizational justice and police misconduct. *Criminal Justice and Behavior, 38*(4), 332–353.

Wonders, N. A., & Danner, M. J. (2020). Regulatory rollbacks and deepening social inequalities. *Journal of White Collar and Corporate Crime, 1*(2), 103–112.

Worcester, B. A. (1998, July 6). Summer staffs open to scrutiny. *Hotel and Motel Management, 213*(12), 7.

World Health Organization. (2015). *WHO estimates of the global burden of foodborne diseases*. Retrieved from https://apps.who .int/iris/bitstream/handle/10665/199350/9789241565165_ eng.pdf;jsessionid=66662D3B2A648489317CA100070597AA ?sequence=1

World Health Organization. (2018). *The global health observatory*. Retrieved from https://www.who.int/data/gho/data/ indicators/indicator-details/GHO/ambient-and-household-air -pollution-attributable-death-rate-(per-100-000-population -age-standardized)

World Health Organization. (n.d.). *Mortality and burden of disease from ambient air pollution*. Retrieved from https://www .who.int/gho/phe/outdoor_air_pollution/burden/en

Wright, D. E, Titus, S. L., & Cornelison, J. B. (2008). Mentoring and research misconduct: An analysis of research mentoring in closed ORI cases. *Science and Engineering Ethics, 14*(3), 323–336.

Wright, J. P., Tibbetts, S. G., & Daigle, L. E. (2008). *Criminals in the making: Criminality across the life course*. Thousand Oaks, CA: Sage.

Wright, R. (2006). Why (some) fraud prosecutions fail. *Journal of Financial Crime, 13*(2), 177–182.

Yablon, C. M. (2019). The lawyer as accomplice: Cannabis, uber, airbnb, and the ethics of advising disruptive businesses. *Minnesota Law Review, 104*(1), 309–384.

Yagiello, J. (2019). Marijuana security: Top tips for cannapreneurs. *HempStaff*. Retrieved from https://www.hempstaff .com/marijuana-security-tips

Yakovlev, P., & Sobel, R. (2010). Occupational safety and profit maximization: Friends or foes. *Journal of Socio-Economics, 39*, 429–435.

Yar, M. (2006). *Cybercrime and society*. Thousand Oaks, CA: Sage.

Yates, S. (2015). *Yates memo*. U.S. Department of Justice. Retrieved from https://www.justice.gov/archives/dag/ file/769036/download

Yeager, P. (1986). Analyzing corporate offenses. In J. E. Post (Ed.), *Research on corporate social performance and policy*. Greenwich, CT: JAI Press.

Yeager, P. C. (2016). The elusive deterrence of corporate crime. *Criminology & Public Policy*, *15*(2), 439–451. https://doi-org.proxy.lib.odu.edu/10.1111/1745-9133.12201

Yohay, S. C., & Dodge, G. E. (1987). Criminal prosecutions for occupational injuries: An issue of growing concern. *Employee Relations Law Journal*, *13*(2), 197–223.

Yoskowitz, A. (2007, April 5). *2/3 of students don't care about illegal downloading says survey.* Oulu, Finland: AfterDawn.com. Retrieved from http://www.afterdawn.com/news/article.cfm/2007/04/06/2_3_of_students_don_t_care_about_illegal_downloading_says_survey

Young, J. R. (2008). Judge rules plagiarism-detection tool falls under "fair use." *Chronicle of Higher Education*, *54*(30), A13.

Yu, O., & Zhang, L. (2006). Does acceptance of corporate wrongdoing begin on the "training ground" of professional managers? *Journal of Criminal Justice*, *34*, 185–194.

Zahneis, M. (2018). This professor made up a job offer from another university. *Chronicle of Higher Education*. Retrieved from https://www.chronicle.com/article/this-professor-made-up-a-job-offer-from-another-university-now-he-faces-a-criminal-charge

Zambito, T., Martinez, J., & Siemaszko, C. (2009, June 29). Bye, bye Bernie: Ponzi king Madoff sentenced to 150 years. *New York Daily News*. Retrieved from http://articles.nydailynews.com/2009-06-29/news/17924560_1_ruth-madoff-irasorkin-bernie-madoff

Zamudio, F. (2016). Inside the elaborate web presence of the government's fake university. *Chronicle*. Retrieved from https://www.chronicle.com/article/inside-the-elaborate-web-presence-of-the-governments-fake-university/

Zane, P. C. (2003). The price fixer's dilemma: Applying game theory to the decision of whether to plead guilty to antitrust crimes. *Antitrust Bulletin*, *48*(1), 1–31.

Zarrell, M. (2018). White-collar convict makes son shoot him in legs to delay prison. *New York Daily News*. Retrieved from https://www.nydailynews.com/news/crime/white-collar-convict-son-shoot-legs-delay-prison-article-1.3848660.

Zernike, K. (2003, September 20). Students shall not download. Yeah, sure. *The New York Times*. Retrieved from http://www.nytimes.com/2003/09/20/technology/20COLL.html

Zhang, B. (2016). The benefits and risks of telemedicine. *Risk Management*, *63*(6), 14.

Zhang, Z. (2011). Cyberwarfare implications for critical infrastructure sectors. *The Homeland Security Review*, *5*(3), 281–295.

Zheng, Y., Huang, X., Graham, L., Redman, T., & Hu, S. (2020). Deterrence effects: The role of authoritarian leadership in controlling employee workplace deviance. *Management and Organization Review*, *16*(2), 377–404.

Zohny, H., Douglas, T., & Savulescu, J. (2019). Biomarkers for the rich and dangerous: why we ought to extend bioprediction and bioprevention to white-collar crime. *Criminal Law and Philosophy*, *13*(3), 479–497.

Zuckoff, M. (2005). *Ponzi's scheme.* New York, NY: Random House.

Zwolinski, M. (2008). The ethics of price gouging. *Business Ethics Quarterly*, *18*(3), 347–378.

INDEX